Refugee and Immigrant Resource Directory

1990-1991

Alan Edward Schorr

THE DENALI PRESS

Denali, a Tanaina Indian word meaning "the great one," is the native name for Mount McKinley. Mount McKinley, at 20,320 feet, the highest mountain on the North American continent, is located in Denali National Park. The lowlands surrounding this majestic mountain provide a diverse wildlife habitat for a variety of animals including grizzly bears, wolves, caribou and moose.

Copyright © 1990 by The Denali Press
Designed and typeset by Janos Sturm

Published by The Denali Press
Post Office Box 021535
Juneau, Alaska USA 99802-1535
(907) 586-6014

For information on obtaining mailing labels please contact Marketing Director.

Library of Congress Cataloging-in-Publication Data

Schorr, Alan Edward.
　　　Refugee and immigrant resource directory, 1990-1991 / Alan Edward Schorr.
　　　　　p.　cm.
　　　Includes bibliographical references.
　　　ISBN 0-938737-19-8 : $37.50
　　　1. Refugees—Services for—United States—Directories.
　　　2. Immigrants—Services for—United States—Directories
　　　HV640.4.U54S365　1989
　　　362.8'4'002573—dc20
　　　　　　　　　　　　　　　　　　　　　　　89-37157
　　　　　　　　　　　　　　　　　　　　　　　CIP

∞ The paper in this book complies with the Permanent Standard issued by the National Standards Organization.

Our role as a beacon of freedom in a darkening world is too precious a part of our tradition, too central to our strength as a free people, to allow it to weaken even in the hardest times. If we ever determine that the Statue of Liberty has become obsolete, we may find that we have become obsolete also.

Victor Palmieri
former United States Coordinator
for Refugee Affairs

Fear

Today the ghetto knows a different fear,
Close in its grip, Death wields an icy scythe.
An evil sickness spreads a terror in its wake,
The victims of its shadow weep and writhe.

Today a father's heartbeat tells his fright
And mothers bend their heads into their hands.
Now children choke and die with typhus here,
A bitter tax is taken from their bands.

My heart still beats inside my breast
While friends depart for other worlds.
Perhaps it's better—who can say?—
Than watching this, to die today?

No, no, my God, we want to live!
Not watch our numbers melt away.
We want to have a better world,
We want to work—we must not die!

Eva Picková
Born 1929, Nymburk, Czechoslovakia
Exterminated 1943, Auschwitz, Poland

[Quoted with permission from *Children's Drawings and Poems Terezín 1942-1944*, Schocken Books, 1978]

Table of Contents

Foreword by The Honorable Stephen J. Solarz _____ 11

Foreword by Hans Thoolen _____ 13

Preface _____ 15

User's Guide _____ 19

Directory of Organizations   23

Alabama	25	Montana	114
Alaska	26	Nebraska	115
Arizona	26	Nevada	116
Arkansas	29	New Hampshire	117
California	29	New Jersey	117
Colorado	54	New Mexico	121
Connecticut	56	New York	122
Delaware	58	North Carolina	138
District of Columbia	59	North Dakota	140
Florida	69	Ohio	140
Georgia	75	Oklahoma	144
Hawaii	78	Oregon	146
Idaho	79	Pennsylvania	148
Illinois	80	Rhode Island	153
Indiana	87	South Carolina	155
Iowa	89	South Dakota	155
Kansas	90	Tennessee	156
Kentucky	91	Texas	158
Louisiana	92	Utah	167
Maine	94	Vermont	168
Maryland	95	Virginia	169
Massachusetts	97	Washington	172
Michigan	102	West Virginia	176
Minnesota	107	Wisconsin	177
Mississippi	111	Wyoming	180
Missouri	112		

Appendices

Appendix A   United States Immigration and Refugee Policy: Entering the
1990's. Essay prepared by the Refugee Policy Group.   183

Appendix B Directories   201

  Immigration and Naturalization Service   203
  Office of the Immigration Judge   205
  United Nations High Commissioner for Refugees   206

Appendix C Documents   207

  Glossary   209
  U.S. Visa Symbols   217
  Chronology of U.S. Immigration Policy   220
  IRCA Key Dates   221
  1988 Chronology of U.S. Refugee and
   Asylum Programs and Policies   222
  Joint Statement of the Interfaith Delegation to
   South Texas (1989)   225
  Jewish Covenant of Sanctuary (1989)   226
  Statement on Principles for Legal
   Immigration Policy (1988)   227
  Statement by Ghassan Arnaout (1989)   228
  City of Refuge Resolution, Takoma Park, MD (1985) 230

Appendix D Statistical Data   235

Indices

Index I Organizational Names   263

Index II Contact Persons   275

Index III Services   283

  Advocacy   285   Legal   308
  Community Education/   Library & Information 312
  Political Organizing   291   Religion   314
  Cultural   295   Research   317
  Economic   299   Sanctuary   319
  Education   303   Scholarships   320
  Health   306   Social Services   321

Index IV Clientele   329

Africa	329	Oceania	332
Asia (excluding SE Asia)	329	South America	332
Central America/		Southeast Asia	332
Caribbean/Mexico	329	USSR	333
Europe	331	World	333
Middle East	332		

Index V Religious Affiliation   341

Baptist	341	Lutheran	344
Brethren	341	Mennonite	344
Buddhist	341	Methodist	344
Catholic	341	Presbyterian	344
Church of Christ	343	Quaker	344
Disciples of Christ	343	Seventh Day Adventist	345
Episcopal	343	Unitarian	345
Jewish	343	Ecumenical	345

Index VI Board of Immigration Appeals   347

Suggestion, Correction and Addition Form

Foreword

The Honorable Stephen J. Solarz
United States House of Representatives

America is preeminently a nation of immigrants and refugees. Indeed, the very first Americans were both immigrants and refugees, seeking in the New World relief from the political oppression and economic deprivation of the Old.

Today the United States is not, as we once believed, a melting pot. Rather it is a remarkable mosaic of many races, creeds, and ethnic backgrounds. Look around any city in this great nation. You will see not a single uniform mixture emanating from some steaming cauldron, but a collection of vibrant and vital communities, each with a distinct and distinctive culture that has left its imprint and enriches us all. Indeed, we are not just a mosaic but a kaleidoscope, a changing canvas of many colors and cultures, the emblem of a dynamic and free society.

Few questions go more to the heart and character of our country than our attitude toward immigrants and refugees. Yet some will tell us that we cannot maintain the open door to the homeless and the helpless. Some will tell us that our own economic difficulties preclude a magnanimous response to the plight of the wretched souls tossed up on our shores by the tempests of a troubled world.

It can, of course, fairly be asked why, amidst all the competing demands for our resources and our compassion, we should concern ourselves with the fate and future of the homeless, the huddled masses yearning to be free, the wretched refuse of other lands. The answer can be stated very simply: Because we are Americans. Because, in this land of opportunity, in this home of the Statue of Liberty, to turn our backs would constitute a denial and a rejection of our Americanism.

Were we to prove unwilling to extend a helping hand to the victims of oppression, we would render hypocritical our professions of faith in human rights and human dignity. Were we to deny those in need of assistance our compassion and our concern, we would surrender to the most parochial, the most petty, and the most pernicious elements in our society.

The real measure of a nation is not just the count of its population, the size of its cities, the magnitude of its economy, or the might of its military. The true measure of a nation is what it believes, what it values, what it stands for. And above all else, America has stood for openness, optimism, and opportunity.

When the ultimate history of our age is written, it may well be said that the refugee is the archetypical figure of the twentieth century. Our century has almost certainly seen more refugees than any previous century in the troubled history of mankind. Indeed, the twentieth century has probably generated more refugees than all other centuries of recorded history combined.

In all corners of the globe, innocent men, women, and children have found themselves fleeing from the ravages of war, disease, famine and oppression—our century's Four Horsemen of the Apocalypse. Sadly, these deadly riders represent not just a scourge of the past, but an affliction of the present. Today there are well over eleven million refugees in the world, including almost four million in Africa and over seven million in South Asia and the Near East.

As the fortuitous inhabitants of a land of plenty, Americans have a special obligation not to forget those who, for entirely accidental reasons, have been less fortunate than themselves in place of birth or residence. We have a responsibility to speak out for the right of people to leave their native land—unharried, without fear of discrimination or persecution. And we have a comparable obligation to welcome these people in our own land—to extend to them the same tolerance and generosity that earlier Americans granted our forebears.

We must guard against backslidding, against complacency, against "compassion fatigue." Why? Because America must remain the beacon of hope it has always been. Because America must remain a citadel of freedom and democracy amidst a world of war and woe. And most of all, because America must remain a refuge for the oppressed and the dispossessed.

Foreword

Hans Thoolen
Chief
Centre for Documentation on Refugees
United Nations High Commissioner for Refugees

In general one could say that growing interest in the refugee problems and the problems of refugees coincides with rapid developments in information technology. UNHCR is aware of these trends and is in the process of strengthening its own information-handling capacity for the benefit of its only constituency: the world's refugees. In addition to publishing several periodicals such as the monthly *Refugees* and the quarterly *Refugee Abstracts*, UNHCR is establishing bibliographic, legal and other databases, introducing electronic mail and—in close cooperation with non-governmental organizations—is developing an International Refugee Documentation Network. The key element in all these efforts is to provide better and quicker access to information needed by the refugees and the community of refugee workers.

Refugees often find themselves in the most abject of circumstances. Even when they are fortunate enough to find a place for permanent settlement in an economically advanced society, they face many obstacles which the average citizen does not have to overcome. They usually have problems in communication as the language and culture are strange to them. Their need for appropriate social, economic, educational and legal services is well-known and over the years has led to a tremendously rich institutional response in the United States. This response ranges from Government services at the federal and state level to voluntary agencies and minority self-help organizations.

However, this vast gamut of potential support has to be accessible to those who need it most, the refugees and immigrants themselves, and their first-line assistants, individual helpers and community-based groups. The *Refugee and Immigrant Resource Directory 1990-1991* is a most important tool in providing access to information which, in turn, will provide access to available services.

One of the slogans which UNHCR uses to describe the ultimate aim of its activities, is "helping the refugees so that they may help themselves". *RIRD* is very much an expression of this approach by providing those who need assistance in adjusting to a new life with access to the many organizations and agencies which could help.

Preface

When published in March, 1987 the *Directory of Services for Refugees and Immigrants (DISERI)* immediately established itself as the first comprehensive guide to resources for the refugee and immigrant community in the United States. It was very well received by refugees and immigrants, service providers and library and information science professionals. *Refugee and Immigrant Resource Directory 1990-1991 (RIRD 1990-1991)*, which supersedes *DISERI*, is a greatly expanded version of *DISERI*. Numerous suggestions from readers worldwide resulted in the inclusion of extensive appendices which contain a variety of information hitherto unavailable in any single source. Hence, *RIRD 1990-1991* not only includes detailed data about organizational resources for refugees and immigrants but also chronologies, important policy statements and numerous statistical tables. The book has been totally redesigned. In addition, to better prepare the reader the Refugee Policy Group was commissioned to prepare an essay which provides an excellent overview of United States refugee and immigration policy. Readers are encouraged to forward suggestions for future editions. Plans are to revise *RIRD* on a biennial basis with the next edition scheduled for publication in 1992.

Refugee and Immigrant Resource Directory 1990-1991 is clearly the single most comprehensive guide available and includes extensive information on 958 local, regional and national (and a few international) organizations, associations, research centers, academic programs, foundations, museums, government agencies and other groups in the United States that offer services or provide information/policy analysis about refugees and immigrants. These groups provide one or more of the following services: advocacy; community education and/or political organizing; cultural; economic; educational; health; legal; library and information; religious; research; sanctuary; scholarships; and social services. This main section is arranged by state (including the District of Columbia) and city followed by the entry for the organization. Access to this data is through a series of six indices and forty sub-indices.

Organizations have been excluded if they are principally political-action/solidarity groups concerned, for example, with the Latin American policy of the United States. Also omitted are migrant/farmworker organizations that may include limited immigration services as a part of their overall program. A list of these organizations can be found in *Hispanic Resource Directory* (The Denali Press, December, 1988).

RIRD 1990-1991 includes a specially commissioned essay by the Refugee Policy Group. RPG is the leading independent center of policy analysis and research on domestic and international refugee issues. Their staff have taken a complex subject and presented in a straightforward manner a review and analysis of United States refugee and immigration policy as we enter the last decade of this century.

Appendix B includes listings of offices of the Immigration & Naturalization Service, Office of the Immigration Judge, and the UN High Commissioner for Refugees. Appendix C contains contemporary documents, such as a sample sanctuary covenant, as well as a glossary of terms and chronologies. Appendix D includes 26 tables and charts on current and historical trends in immigration and refugee admissions to the United States, as well as selected data on the world refugee situation.

A refugee is defined as an individual who would be persecuted or has a well-founded fear of persecution in their country of nationality on account of race, religion, nationality, membership in a particular social group, or political opinion. An immigrant is defined as an individual who has been granted permission to enter and establish residence in the United States. Generally, immigrants are those who leave their home country voluntarily, as oppossed to refugees who are forced to leave their homeland.

Throughout American history individuals have emigrated to the United States to escape persecution, tyranny and repression. This nation was founded as a sanctuary and that sentiment was engraved on the Statue of Liberty. Emma Lazarus's famous lines represent the highest ideals of the Open Door of American Immigration:

...Give me your tired, your poor,
Your huddled masses yearning to breathe free,
The wretched refuse of your teeming shore,
Send these, the homeless, tempest-tost, to me:
I lift my lamp beside the Golden Door.

Though *Refugee and Immigrant Resource Directory 1990-1991* provides information about groups serving both refugees and immigrants, the emphasis is clearly on those which assist refugees. Whether a survivor of the Holocaust, the Central American death squads, pirates of South Asia or a recent Polish immigrant, the foreign born have a unique set of needs. Over the years a variety of groups have risen to meet the challenge of serving this population.

RIRD 1990-1991 includes a directory of organizational resources for refugees and immigrants as well as related directories, documentary material, and statistical data about this group. It is designed to assist refugees and immigrants, service providers, researchers and scholars, government officials, library and information professionals and others interested in this population. As with all directories, the material may already be dated: some groups will have relocated, staff changes will have taken place, new organizations will be created and some groups will cease operations. I encourage individuals to use the form at the back of this book to report changes, errors and omissions. It is anticipated that this book will be published in even numbered years.

There are over fourteen million refugees throughout the world requiring protection and assistance. As a refugee worker noted:

It is the refugee who reveals to us the defective society in which we live. He is a kind of mirror through whose suffering we can see the injustices, the oppression and maltreatment of the powerless by the powerful.

They have little control over their lives and require humanitarian aid from the developed countries working with developing nations. What is needed is moral leadership in the highest places to support a generous refugee, asylee and immigration policy that offers sanctuary to the persecuted and displaced. It is a struggle that cuts across borders, races and religions. The image of boats being turned away from a safe haven force one to remember a half century ago when the *Saint Louis* returned to Europe after the United States and other nations refused permission for the Jewish passengers to disembark. There was no sanctuary then, only the horrors of the death camps. We are all boat people—whether in 1990 in Asian or Florida waters, or when our ancestors travelled in steerage to a new life in America.

U.S. refugee policy must be flexible to adapt to changing circumstances. Perhaps the clearest example is the dramatic change in Soviet emigration policy. Applications at the U.S. Embassy in Moscow have soared from a rate of about 1,500 per month in FY 1988 to some 4,000 per month as of Summer, 1989. One response has been the Presidential Determination on Refugee Admissions of April 5, 1989 to increase the refugee admissions ceilings from 94,000 to 112,500. Also under discussion in Congress are several bills that address admission ceilings and the question of eligibility of Soviet applicants.

President Reagan referred to America as "still a beacon, still a magnet for those who must have freedom." Unfortunately, as the *New York Times* noted, "…Mr. Reagan's policy failed to match his rhetoric. It's George Bush's turn to relight the beacon." * Raising admission ceilings and working with Congress on ways to provide humanitarian assistance is a step in the right direction.

I would like to thank the hundreds of individuals who completed questionnaires and corresponded or spoke with me about their organizations. A special word of appreciation to Congressman Stephen J. Solarz, a leading national advocate for refugees and human rights, and Hans Thoolen, an international leader in refugee documentation.

* *New York Times*, January 13, 1989, Editorial Page.

Between January and July 1989 questionnaires were mailed to organizations and agencies throughout the United States concerned with refugees and immigrants. Names were located through a variety of sources, including the *Directory of Services for Refugees and Immigrants* as well as numerous state and local directories, telephone books, newsletters, journals, computer databases, etc. In order to be included in *RIRD 1990-1991* respondents must provide services primarily to refugees and immigrants or make available substantial information/data about refugees and immigrants. Information contained in *RIRD 1990-1991* was gathered from the questionnaires, printed materials supplied by the organizations, by telephonic interview, and in a very few cases from secondary sources.

Arrangement of the Book

The main section of *RIRD 1990-1991* contains 958 entries arranged alphabetically by state (including the District of Columbia) and city and then by name of group. Individual entries list the following information about each group.

> Name, address, telephone and FAX number
> Contact person and title
> Services offered
> Year established
> Number of staff
> Budget
> Board of Immigration Appeals status
> Religious affiliation
> Clientele
> Narrative
> Publications

Services   The specific services and/or activities offered by these groups are coded in the entries as follows:

AD   advocacy role in supporting equal opportunity and fair and equitable treatment.

CE   community education and/or political organizing. This includes: lobbying; consciousness raising activities; community lectures, workshops, seminars, etc. These activities are designed to change policies and attitudes and increase public awareness of issues.

CU   cultural activities, including music, dance, art, theatre, museum services, etc. Programs preserve/share cultural values.

EC   jobs programs, job counseling, economic development activities, etc.

ED   educational, academic and general training programs.

HE   health services (medical, dental, etc.).

LE	legal services, including court representation, legal advice and paralegal assistance.
LI	operate library/media/information center, often open to the public with prior arrangement.
RE	religious activities.
RS	research services, i.e., gather, analyze and make available information about refugees and immigrants.
SA	either actively provide sanctuary for refugees (principally Central American), provide assistance to sanctuary groups or refer individuals to sanctuary groups.
SC	scholarships and other forms of financial assistance.
SS	social services is a broad category which includes emergency services, casework management, substance abuse programs, counseling, housing assistance, orientation/acculturation, information & referral, placement & resettlement, etc.
BIA Status	BIA recognition indicates that the group can officially represent aliens before the Immigration and Naturalization Service and the U.S. Board of Immigration Appeals.
Clientele	This data is aranged by nine geographic regions as well as an entry for "World." A maximum of three regions are listed. "World" indicates group serves clientele from all parts of the world. However, this may be qualified by up to two additional geographic regions, from where, for example, a significant number of their clientele migrated.
Narrative	Respondents were requested to provide a brief overview of their programs, services, goals, etc. Often this information was supplemented by printed materials and telephonic interviews. The narrative reflects the views of the organization.
Publications	With few exceptions only serial titles (newsletters, annual reports, monographic series, etc.) are listed. Use of upper case indicates exact title of publication.

Appendices

Appendix A United States Immigration and Refugee Policy: Entering the 1990's. Essay prepared by the Refugee Policy Group.

Appendix B Directories

Contains three directories for the Immigration and Naturalization Service, Office of the Immigration Judge, and UN High Commissioner for Refugees.

Appendix C Documents

Contains ten documents (see Table of Contents), including contemporary speeches, chronologies, glossary, etc.

Appendix D Statistical Data

Contains 25 tables and charts (see page 235) on immigrants, refugees and asyless admitted to the U.S. and world refugee situation.

Indices Access to data in the main section of *RIRD 1990* is through a series of six indices.

Index I Organizational names–alphabetical arrangement of entries

Index II Contact persons–alphabetical arrangement of all group contacts

Index III Services–contains thirteen sub-indices for each of the services listed above

Index IV Clientele–contains ten sub-indices for geographic regions listed in the Table of Contents

Index V Religious affiliation–contains seventeen sub-indices for religious groups listed in the Table of Contents

Index VI Board of Immigration Appeals–indicates if recognized by BIA

Directory of
Organizations

1   *Auburn*
Conscientious Alliance for Peace

517 Moores Hill Road
Auburn, AL 36830
Judy Cumbee, Refugee Coordinator
(205) 826-3378

Services Offered: AD, CE, RE, SS.
Established: 1980. **Clientele**: Central
America/Caribbean. Provide food to refugees seeking
sanctuary in the United States and Canada.

2   *Mobile*
Cambodian Association of Mobile

Box 160812
Mobile, AL 36616
Sanh Suon, President
(205) 957-2096

Services Offered: CU, EC, ED, HE, SS.
Established: 1981. **Staff**: 3. **Budget**: $46,000.
BIA. **Religious Affiliation**: Ecumenical.
Clientele: Southeast Asia. Engaged in preserving
and promoting the cultural heritage of its members by
sponsoring such activities as the Cambodian New
Year, wedding ceremonies, etc. Also has a history of
self-help social services by providing assistance for
resettlement of newly arrived refugee families and
miscellaneous economic and social services to the
Cambodian Community of Mobile.

3   *Mobile*
Catholic Social Services. Refugee Program

211 South Catherine Street, Suite 2
Mobile, AL 36604
Michelle Johnson Prockup, Director
(205) 471-1305

Services Offered: CU, CE, EC, ED, HE, LI, SS.
Established: 1975. **Staff**: 17. **Budget**:
$385,000. **Religious Affiliation**: Catholic.
Clientele: World, Southeast Asia, Europe. The
Refugee Resettlement Program provides: job assistance, orientation and placement; assistance in finding
housing, clothing and furniture; orientation for sponsors, volunteers and refugees about cultural differences; reunification assistance for separated families;
social service referrals; counseling; interpretation and
translation; and referrals for citizenship, visas, status
adjustment, and information concerning documents
and related matters. Amerasian resettlement site.
Publications: BULLETIN (monthly, free); TIN

VIET (quarterly, free); Annual Report.

4   *Montgomery*
Alabama Baptist State Convention

Box 11870
Montgomery, AL 36198
Earl Potts, Executive Secretary
(205) 288-2460

Services Offered: RE, SS. **Staff**: 101. **Budget**:
$25,125,000. **Religious Affiliation**: Baptist.
Clientele: World. Coordinates refugee resettlement
work among Baptist churches in Alabama.
Publications: ALABAMA BAPTIST (weekly);
Annual report.

5   *Montgomery*
Alabama Department of Human Resources. Refugee Resettlement Program

Folsom Administrative Building
Montgomery, AL 36130
Joel Sanders, Coordinator
(205) 261-2920

Services Offered: SS. **Clientele**: World. Agency
does not provide direct services. However, work with
contractors in Alabama and federal government to enhance services offered to refugees.

6   *Anchorage*

Catholic Social Services

225 Cordova Street, Building B
Anchorage, AK 99501
Leonore Ortiz, Resettlement Director
(907) 277-2554

Services Offered: AD, CU, RE, SS. **Staff**: 1.
Religious Affiliation: Catholic. **Clientele**:
World. Refugee resettlement activities coordinated
through U.S. Catholic Conference Migration &
Refugee Services.

7   *Phoenix*

Arizona Center for Immigrants

214 East Willeta
Phoenix, AZ 85004
Susan Rascon, Director
(602) 253-3657

Services Offered: AD, CE, LE, SS. **Clientele**:
World, Central America/Caribbean. Legal advice and
representation in immigration and asylum actions.
Also provides community outreach and limited social
services.

8   *Phoenix*

Arizona Department of Economic Security. Refugee Resettlement Program

Box 6123
Phoenix, AZ 85005
Tri H. Tran, Coordinator
(602) 229-2743

Services Offered: AD, CU, EC, ED, HE, SS.
Established: 1977. **Staff**: 18. **Budget**:
$1,200,000. **Clientele**: World. State coordinating
body for refugee resettlement in the State of Arizona.

9   *Phoenix*

Catholic Social Service of Phoenix

1825 West Northern Avenue
Phoenix, AZ 85021
Helen Shea, Executive Director
(602) 997-6105

Services Offered: AD, ED, SS. **Established**:
1933. **Staff**: 59. **Budget**: $1,500,000. **BIA**.
Religious Affiliation: Catholic. **Clientele**:
World, Southeast Asia, Central America/Caribbean.
Refugee resettlement program is coordinated through
US Catholic Conference Migration & Refugee
Services. Offers social services, foster care, immigra-
tion counseling, etc.

10   *Phoenix*

Central American Refugee Project

6802 South 24th Street
Phoenix, AZ 85040
Juan Rascon, Contact
(602) 253-3657

Services Offered: AD, CE, LE, SS.
Established: 1981. **BIA**. **Clientele**: Central

America/Caribbean. Legal services to refugees and asylees from Central America, in Phoenix and at the Florence Detention Center. Social services include: housing, food, education, medical and dental referrals. Speakers for church and community groups.

---

11 *Phoenix*
Friendly House

802 South First Avenue
Phoenix, AZ 85030
Eugene Brassard, President
(602) 257-1870

Services Offered: CU, ED, LE, SS.
Established: 1920. **Staff**: 40. **Budget**: $2,200,000. **BIA**. **Clientele**: Central America/Caribbean. Since 1920 the group's objective has been to eliminate illiteracy among immigrants. Dedicated to the betterment of immigrants who reside in South Phoenix. A lawyer, Certified Immigration Specialists and several experienced specialists provide professional counseling, guidance and assistance with all aspects of the legal process. Assistance ranges from document translation and preparation to legal representation. In addition, offers a full array of social services designed for the newcomer. **Publications**: FRIENDLY HOUSE NEWS (quarterly).

---

12 *Phoenix*
Jewish Family & Children's Service

2033 North Seventh Street
Phoenix, AZ 85006
Carol Seidberg, President
(602) 257-1904

Services Offered: AD, RE, SS. **Religious Affiliation**: Jewish. **Clientele**: World. Provides counseling, financial assistance and advocacy for newly arrived immigrants and refugees.

---

13 *Phoenix*
Lutheran Social Ministry of the Southwest. Refugee Program

805 East Camelback Road
Phoenix, AZ 85014
Hilda Nguon, Caseworker
(602) 266-9007

Services Offered: AD, CU, RE, SS.
Established: 1975. **Religious Affiliation**: Lutheran. **Clientele**: World. Work with Lutheran churches to sponsor, resettle and reunify refugee fami-

lies.

---

14 *Phoenix*
Tolstoy Foundation

1429 North First Street
Phoenix, AZ 85004
David Lockey, Director
(602) 252-2943

Services Offered: AD, CU, CE, EC, LI, SS.
Established: 1984. **Staff**: 8. **BIA**. **Clientele**: World. Variety of programs designed to assist integration of new arrivals in the community. Refugee resettlement agency.

---

15 *Phoenix*
Valley Religious Task Force on Central America

37 East Indian School Road
Phoenix, AZ 85012
James A. Oines, Chair
(602) 265-9800

Services Offered: AD, CU, CE, EC, ED, HE, LE, LI, RE, SA, SS. **Established**: 1981. **Staff**: 6. **Budget**: $95,000. **Religious Affiliation**: Ecumenical. **Clientele**: Central America/Caribbean. Serves Central American refugees in their social, spiritual, emotional and legal needs. Works for change in policies toward Central America. **Publications**: VALLEY RELIGIOUS TASK FORCE NEWSLETTER (monthly); Annual Report.

---

16 *Tucson*
Catholic Social Services. Migration & Refugee Services

3200 North Los Altos
Tucson, AZ 85705
Ronald G. Olson, Administrator
(602) 623-0344

Services Offered: SS. **Established**: 1978.
Staff: 12. **Budget**: $450,000. **Religious Affiliation**: Catholic. **Clientele**: World. Reception, placement and social adjustment services for refugees from all parts of the world. Foster home placement and supervision for minor Vietnamese children who enter the United States unaccompanied by an adult relative.

---

17 *Tucson*

Jewish Family Service

2424 East Broadway, Suite 100
Tucson, AZ 85719
Fern Marmis, Executive Director
(602) 792-3641

Services Offered: AD, CU, RE, SS. **BIA.**
Religious Affiliation: Jewish. **Clientele:**
USSR, World. Refugee resettlement program coordinated with Hebrew Immigrant Aid Society.

18 *Tucson*

San Juan Bautista Lutheran Church. Sanctuary Committee

1130 East Bilby
Tucson, AZ 85706
(602) 294-2772

Services Offered: AD, CE, SA. **Religious Affiliation:** Lutheran. **Clientele:** Central America/Caribbean. Advocacy, community outreach and sanctuary for refugees fleeing Central America.

19 *Tucson*

Southern Arizona Legal Aid

160 East Alameda
Tucson, AZ 85702
Nancy Trease, Director
(602) 623-9461

Services Offered: AD, CE, LE, LI.
Established: 1968. **Staff:** 2. **Clientele:** World, Central America/Caribbean. Immigration representation provided to indigent clients. Legal advice, representation and referral. **Publications:**
IMMIGRATION PROJECT NEWSLETTER (free).

20 *Tucson*

TECHO Central American Education Center

1748 South Seventh Avenue
Tucson, AZ 85713
(602) 792-1925

Services Offered: AD, CU, ED, CE, LI.
Clientele: Central America/Caribbean, South America. Services designed to assist the transition of the Central and South American refugee. Educational programs, cultural programs and community outreach projects.

21 *Tucson*

Temple Emanu-El. Sanctuary Committee

225 North Country Club
Tucson, AZ 85716
Rabbi Joseph Weizenbaum, Coordinator
(602) 327-4501

Services Offered: AD, CE, SA. **Religious Affiliation:** Jewish. **Clientele:** Central America/Caribbean. Advocacy and sanctuary for refugees fleeing persecution and terror in Salvador and Guatemala.

22 *Tucson*

Tucson Ecumenical Council. Central America Task Force

Box 43243
Tucson, AZ 85733
Ken Kennon, Director
(602) 628-7525

Services Offered: AD, CE, ED, LE, RE, SA, SS.
Established: 1981. **Religious Affiliation:** Ecumenical. **Clientele:** Central America/Caribbean. Goal is the establishment of sanctuary in the United States for Central American refugees. Services range from legal assistance and representation to emergency help with housing, food, clothing, pastoral support, etc.

23 *Tucson*

Tucson Ecumenical Council. Legal Assistance Program

Box 3007
Tucson, AZ 85702
Carol Brown, Director
(602) 623-5739

Services Offered: AD, LE, LI. **Established:** 1985. **Staff:** 4. **Budget:** $112,000. **BIA.**
Religious Affiliation: Ecumenical. **Clientele:** Central America/Caribbean. TECLA provides legal representation to Central American refugees. Represent refugees in all areas before the INS, especially in matters of political asylum. Services available to refugees detained in Southern Arizona.
Publications: Annual Report.

24 *Fort Smith*
Refugee Resettlement Office

501 South Twentieth Street
Fort Smith, AR 72901
Betty Morris, Director
(501) 782-1491

Services Offered: CU, EC, ED, LI, SS.
Established: 1975. **Staff**: 6. **Clientele**:
Southeast Asia, Central America/Caribbean. Main
thrust is the resettlement of Indochinese and Cuban
refugees. Services include acculturation, language
training, and employment skills and placement.
Publications: XAY DUNG (monthly newsletter,
free).

25 *Little Rock*
Arkansas Department of Human Services. Refugee Resettlement Program

Box 1437
Little Rock, AR 72203
Walt Patterson, Director
(501) 682-8263

Services Offered: EC. **Established**: 1980.
Staff: 3. **Budget**: $327,126. **Clientele**: World.
RRP operates with federal grants from the U.S.
Office of Refugee Resettlement. The state agency coordinates federal monies and contractors who provide
specific social services. The refugee cash assistance
and refugee medical assistance programs are provided
by agency personnel in county offices. Goal is to assist with successful economic and cultural integration
of new arrivals.

26 *Little Rock*
Refugee Resettlement Program

Box 2620
Little Rock, AR 72204
(501) 372-1244

Services Offered: CE, EC, ED, HE, SS.
Established: 1985. **Staff**: 2. **Budget**: $32,000.
Religious Affiliation: Baptist. **Clientele**:
World. Refugee resettlement services include: translation and interpretation; assistance with document
preparation; job orientation and placement; home
management; counseling; etc.

27 *Anaheim*
Anaheim Independencia Center

10841 Garza Avenue
Anaheim, CA 92804
Alice Lopez-Perez, Contact
(714) 826-9070

Services Offered: AD, EC, ED, LE, HE, SS.
Clientele: Central America/Caribbean. Advocacy
and social service support for immigrants and
refugees. Legal advice and referrals.

28 *Arcata*
Humboldt Congregations for Sanctuary

634 14th
Arcata, CA 95221
Gretchen Ferrin, Coordinator
(707) 822-4433

Services Offered: SA. **Religious Affiliation**:
Ecumenical. **Clientele**: Central America/Caribbean.
Sanctuary covenant amongst congregations in
Northern California.

29 *Bakersfield*
Catholic Social Services. Immigration Services

310 Baker Street
Bakersfield, CA 93305
Joseph Espitia, Director
(805) 325-7751

Services Offered: AD, CU, ED, LE, SS.
Religious Affiliation: Catholic. **Clientele**:
World. Immigration advice, counsel and representa-
tion in immigration-related matters.

30 *Bayside*
Humboldt Unitarian-Universalist Fellowship

Old Arcata Road at Bayside Cutoff
Bayside, CA 95524
Howard Stauffer, President
(707) 822-3793

Services Offered: RE, SA. **Religious
Affiliation**: Unitarian. **Clientele**: Central
America/Caribbean. Church sanctuary for political
refugees from Central America. **Publications**:
FELLOWSHIP NEWS (monthly, free).

31   *Bell Gardens*

Human Services Association

5856 Ludell Street
Bell Gardens, CA 90201
Barbara Hernandez, Supervisor
(213) 773-3911

Services Offered: AD, CU, CE, ED, LE, RS, SS.
Clientele: Central America/Caribbean, South
America. Broad range of services to immigrants and
refugees including advocacy, extensive legal referral
network.

---

32   *Berkeley*

City of Berkeley. Public Sanctuary

2425 College Avenue
Berkeley, CA 94704
Gus Schultz, Coordinator
(415) 843-6230

Services Offered: SA. **Clientele:** Central
America/Caribbean. The City of Berkeley is a declared
public sanctuary for Central American refugees.

---

33   *Berkeley*

East Bay Sanctuary Covenant

2320 Dana Street
Berkeley, CA 94704
Irene Litherland, Coordinator
(415) 540-5296

Services Offered: AD, CE, ED, HE, LE, LI, SA,
SS. **Established:** 1982. **Staff:** 2. **Budget:**
$72,000. **Religious Affiliation:** Ecumenical.
Clientele: Central America/Caribbean. EBSC is 29
congregations of the East Bay that have publicly declared sanctuary - protection, support, and advocacy -
to refugees from El Salvador and Guatemala. Provide
direct services as well as outreach, library resources,
etc. Help is offered out of concern for the welfare of
the refugees, regardless of their official immigrant status. The covenant is undertaken as an act of conscience and moral imperative. **Publications:**
EXODUS (monthly newsletter, $5).

---

34   *Berkeley*

South and Meso-American Indian Information Center

Box 7550
Berkeley, CA 94707
Nilo Cayuqeo, Coordinator

(415) 834-4263

Services Offered: AD, CU, CE, ED, LI, RS, SA.
Established: 1983. **Staff:** 3. **Clientele:** Central
America/Caribbean, South America. Assist Indian
refugees and Indians in South and Central America
communicate directly with each other and work toward building unity and the successful struggle for
survival and self-determination. **Publications:**
SAIIC NEWSLETTER (quarterly, $8); monographs.

---

35   *Colton*

Catholic Charities. Refugee Resettlement Program

1427 North LaCadena Drive
Colton, CA 92324
Brigitte Helmer, Director
(714) 370-1488

Services Offered: AD, EC, ED, LE, RE, SS.
Religious Affiliation: Catholic. **Clientele:**
World. Resettlement and immigration services avail-
able to refugees.

---

36   *Compton*

Community Legal Services

401 East Compton Boulevard
Compton, CA 90221
Rita Canales, Attorney
(213) 638-6194

Services Offered: LE. BIA. **Clientele:** Central
America/Caribbean, World. Legal assistance for indigent individuals in immigration-related matters.

---

37   *Davis*

City of Davis. Office of the Mayor

605 Sunset Court
Davis, CA 95616
(916) 756-6904

Services Offered: SA. **Clientele:** Central
America/Caribbean. Davis is a declared public sanctuary for refugees fleeing from Central America.

---

38   *Davis*

Plenty USA

Box 2306
Davis, CA 95617
Peter Schweitzer, Executive Director
(916) 753-0731

Services Offered: SS. **Established:** 1974. **Staff:** 4. **Religious Affiliation:** Ecumenical. **Clientele:** Central America/Caribbean. Supports Central American refugees (principally from Guatemala) by providing limited direct assistance in the United States as well as coordinating indigenous cooperative marketing efforts. **Publications:** PLENTY BULLETIN (quarterly); Annual Report.

---

39   *Davis*

University of California. School of Law. Immigration Law Clinic

University of California
Davis, CA 95616
James F. Smith, Director
(916) 752-6942

Services Offered: LE. **Established:** 1981. **Staff:** 5. **Budget:** $125,000. **BIA. Clientele:** World, Central America/Caribbean. Represents low-income clients in political asylum, deportation and legalization cases. Second and third year law students work with clients under the supervision of the clinic's director.

---

40   *East Palo Alto*

Comite de Refugiados Salvadorenos

Box 1565
East Palo Alto, CA 94301

Services Offered: AD, CE, CU, LE. **Clientele:** Central America/Caribbean.

---

41   *East Palo Alto*

Immigrant Legal Resource Center

1395 Bay Road
East Palo Alto, CA 94303
(415) 853-1600

Services Offered: CE, LE, LI, SA. **Established:** 1979. **Staff:** 7. **BIA. Clientele:** World, Central America/Caribbean. Legal support and community education and organizing of behalf of refugees and immigrants. **Publications:** List of Publications.

---

42   *El Centro*

El Centro Asylum Project

107 South Fifth Street, Suite 218

El Centro, CA 92243
Dave Rabin, Managing Attorney
(619) 353-2920

Services Offered: AD, CE, EC, LE, RE, SS. **Established:** 1987. **Budget:** $50,000. **BIA. Clientele:** Central America/Caribbean. Program provides legal representation for Central American refugees detained by the INS at the El Centro facility. Also offer direct social services to clients upon release from detention. **Publications:** Annual Report.

---

43   *Fresno*

California Southern Baptist Convention. Refugee Resettlement Program

678 East Shaw Avenue
Fresno, CA 93710
Mark Yeast, Director
(209) 229-9533

Services Offered: AD, CU, EC, RE, SS. **Established:** 1975. **Staff:** 2. **Religious Affiliation:** Baptist. **Clientele:** World, Southeast Asia, Central America/Caribbean. Statewide sponsorship development amongst congregations of the Southern Baptist Convention as well as social services to assist the new arrivals.

---

44   *Fresno*

Catholic Charities. Resettlement Program

3510 East Ventura Avenue
Fresno, CA 93702
Tam Nguyen, Supervisor
(209) 237-0851

Services Offered: AD, CU, EC, ED, RE, SS. **BIA. Religious Affiliation:** Catholic. **Clientele:** World. Resettlement and immigration services for immigrants and refugees.

---

45   *Fresno*

El Concilio. Immigration Project

2814 Mariposa
Fresno, CA 93721
Lily Torres, Coordinator
(209) 485-0679

Services Offered: AD, CU, CE, EC, ED, LE, SS. **Clientele:** Central America/Caribbean. El Concilio provides a wide range of services for the Hispanic community. This project concentrates on services for immigrants and refugees.

---

46   *Fresno*

Fresno Ecumenical Resettlement Project

1343 East Barstow
Fresno, CA 93710
Knar Guekguezian
(209) 225-1826

Services Offered: AD, CU, EC, SS. **Religious Affiliation**: Ecumenical. **Clientele**: World, USSR, Southeast Asia. Church World Service affiliate provides refugee resettlement and sponsorship services.

---

47   *Fresno*

Hmong American Human Rights Committee

2333 North Price Avenue
Fresno, CA 93703
Dang Vang, Chair
(209) 264-4080

Services Offered: AD, LE. **Staff**: 9. **Clientele**: Southeast Asia. Support and advocacy for the rights of Hmong in the U.S.

---

48   *Fresno*

Hmong Council

4670 East Butler Avenue
Fresno, CA 93702
Phen Vue, Executive Director
(209) 4561-1220

Services Offered: AD, CU, EC, ED, HE, LE, SS. **Established**: 1982. **Staff**: 4. **Budget**: $120,000. **Clientele**: Southeast Asia. Combination of services designed to assist integration of Hmong into the Fresno community.

---

49   *Fresno*

International Rescue Committee

1220 North Abby, Suite D
Fresno, CA 93703
Chu Ning Yang, Director
(209) 486-0640

Services Offered: AD, SS. **BIA**. **Clientele**: World. Voluntary agency that helps refugees escape from religious, racial and political oppression. Operates refugee resettlement programs throughout the United States.

---

50   *Fresno*

Nationalities Service of Central California

1118 North Fulton
Fresno, CA 93729
(209) 292-8757

Services Offered: AD, CU, ED, LI, SS. **Established**: 1983. **BIA**. **Clientele**: Southeast Asia, World. Resettlement services, immigration counseling and social services available to all foreign born and refugees.

---

51   *Garden Grove*

Jewish Family Service

Box 3120
Garden Grove, CA 92642
Jay Masserman, President
(714) 537-4980

Services Offered: AD, CU, EC, RE, SS. **Established**: 1975. **Religious Affiliation**: Jewish. **Clientele**: World. Refugee resettlement activities are coordinated through the Hebrew Immigrant Aid Society. Services range from orientation and acculturation to counseling and limited emergency services.

---

52   *Garden Grove*

St. Anselm's Immigrant & Refugee Community Center

13091 Galway Street
Garden Grove, CA 92644
Marianne Blank, Executive Director
(714) 537-0608

Services Offered: AD, CU, CE, EC, ED, RE, SS. **Established**: 1976. **Staff**: 20. **Budget**: $600,000. **BIA**. **Religious Affiliation**: Ecumenical. **Clientele**: World. Extensive services offered to refugees and immigrants: resettlement; family reunification; language training; job orientation, training and placement; social adjustment; and general immigration assistance. Ecumenical religious funding.

---

53   *Garden Grove*

Vietnamese Service Center

Box 814
Garden Grove, CA 92642
Duc X. Nguyen, Director
(714) 539-6530

Services Offered: AD, CU, SS. **Established**:
1978. **Clientele**: Southeast Asia. Orientation and
acculturation services, translation and interpretation
and counseling available to Indochinese refugees.

---

54   *Garden Grove*

World Relief

12852 Palm Street, Suite 205
Garden Grove, CA 92640
Roberto Chavez, Resettlement Coordinator
(714) 530-0930

Services Offered: AD, CU, EC, SS.
Established: 1980. **BIA**. **Clientele**: World,
Southeast Asia. Immigration, refugee resettlement
and placement services available.

---

55   *Hawthorne*

All Culture Friendship Center
Refugee & Immigration Services

4754 West 120th Street
Hawthorne, CA 90250
Sharon R. Kellman, Executive Director
(213) 675-0391

Services Offered: AD, EC, ED, RE, SS.
Established: 1975. **Staff**: 12. **Budget**: $165,000.
Religious Affiliation: Ecumenical. **Clientele**:
World. Seeks to ameliorate the tumultuos experience
of the refugee/immigrant seeking stability and understanding in the midst of radical transition. Services
include sponsorship assistance, documentation, newcomer orientation, multi-lingual counseling, social
services referrals, classes in English, employment
orientation and referrals, translation and interpretation,
and advocacy. In 1987 ACFC resettled 1,448
refugees.

---

56   *Hayward*

Federation of Vietnamese & Allied Veterans

27763 Orlando Avenue
Hayward, CA 94545
Jack Nhuan N. Tran, Chair
(415) 785-9575

Services Offered: CU, ED, SS. **Established**:
1979. **Staff**: 74. **Clientele**: Southeast Asia, Asia.
Represents some 60 Vietnamese military and veterans
organizations. Goals are to provide mutual assistance
and sponsorship for Vietnamese seeking to flee from
Vietnam. **Publications**: REPUBLICAN FIGHTER
(quarterly).

---

57   *Long Beach*

Cambodian Association of America

602 Pacific Avenue
Long Beach, CA 90802
Nil Hul, Executive Director
(213) 432-5849

Services Offered: CU, EC, SS. **Established**:
1975. **Staff**: 10. **Budget**: $400,000. **Clientele**:
Southeast Asia. Cambodian self-help group whose
goals are the successful economic, political and social
integration of Cambodian refugees within the United
States. **Publications**: Newsletter.

---

58   *Long Beach*

Cambodian Business Association

602 Pacific Avenue
Long Beach, CA 90802
Vora Kanthoul, President
(714) 836-0463

Services Offered: AD, CU, CE, EC.
Established: 1984. **Staff**: 1. **Budget**: $20,000.
Clientele: Southeast Asia. Programs designed to
increase business opportunities for Cambodian
refugees.

---

59   *Long Beach*

Khemara Buddhikarma - The Cambodian Buddhist Monastery

2100 West Willos Street
Long Beach, CA 90810
Rev. Kong Chhean, Executive Director
(213) 595-0566

Services Offered: CU, RE. **Established**: 1982.
Staff: 8. **Religious Affiliation**: Ecumenical.
Clientele: Southeast Asia, World. Maintain and
foster Cambodian arts, culture and tradition and provide education and a forum for community issues.

---

60   *Long Beach*

Temple Israel. Sanctuary Committee

3538 East Third Street
Long Beach, CA 90803
Rabbi Sheldon Marder, Coordinator
(213) 434-0996

Services Offered: AD, CE, SA. **Religious Affiliation:** Jewish. **Clientele:** Central America/Caribbean. Advocacy and sanctuary for refugees fleeing Salvador and Guatemala.

---

61 *Long Beach*

Unitarian Universalist Church

5450 Atherton Avenue
Long Beach, CA 90815
Michael O'Kelly, Minister

Services Offered: SA. **Religious Affiliation:** Unitarian. **Clientele:** Central America/Caribbean. Declared public sanctuary for Central American refugees.

---

62 *Long Beach*

United Cambodian Community

1432 Atlantic Avenue
Long Beach, CA 90813
Than Pok, Executive Director
(213) 599-2210

Services Offered: AD, CU, CE, EC, ED, HE, SS. **Established:** 1978. **Staff:** 60. **Budget:** $2,500,000. **Clientele:** Southeast Asia, World. Large organization with offices throughout Southern California offers a variety of services to Cambodians and others from Southeast Asia as well as refugees from throughout the world. The Amnesty Project alone served over 500 individuals in 1988. **Publications:** Newsletter.

---

63 *Los Altos*

Afghan Refugee Fund

Box 176
Los Altos, CA 94023
Robert Ornstein, President
(415) 948-9436

Services Offered: AD, SS. **Established:** 1983. **Clientele:** Asia. Provide assistance to Afghan refugees throughout world.

---

64 *Los Angeles*

AFL/CIO Immigration Project

515 Shatto Place, Room 200
Los Angeles, CA 90020
Andres Bustamante, Director
(213) 381-2170

Services Offered: AD, CE, ED, LE. **Clientele:** Central America/Caribbean, World. Advocacy, educational and legal services for immigrants and refugees.

---

65 *Los Angeles*

All Culture Friendship Center Refugee & Immigration Services

5250 Santa Monica Boulevard
Los Angeles, CA 90029
(213) 667-0489

Services Offered: AD, EC, ED, RE, SS. **Established:** 1984. **Religious Affiliation:** Ecumenical. **Clientele:** World. Provides basic educational, economic and social services to refugees from throughout the world. Affiliated with Church World Service.

---

66 *Los Angeles*

Amnesty International

3407 West Sixth Street, Suite 704
Los Angeles, CA 90005
Mahtb Rezvani, Administrator
(213) 388-1237

Services Offered: AD, CE, LI, RS. **Established:** 1961. **Clientele:** World. Provides documentation on human rights abuses in specific countries for asylum lawyers. AI is a world-wide movement working for the release of all prisoners of conscience, fair and prompt trials for political prisoners and an end to torture and executions.

---

67 *Los Angeles*

Asian Pacific American Legal Center of Southern California

1010 South Flower Street, Suite 302
Los Angeles, CA 90015
Stewart Kwoh, Executive Director
(213) 748-2022   Fax: (213) 748-0679

Services Offered: LE. **Established:** 1983. **Staff:** 15. **Budget:** $300,000. **BIA. Clientele:** Asia, World. Offers multilingual legal, education and civil rights work on behalf of the one million Asian

Pacific Americans in Southern California. Services range from offering over 100 legal education seminars and training sessions to the Immigration Project which oversees protection of employment rights of immigrants and refugees. **Publications:** Newsletter (free).

68   *Los Angeles*

Catholic Charities. Immigration & Refugee Division

1400 West Ninth Street
Los Angeles, CA 90015
Elizabeth Kirsnis, Associate Director
(213) 251-3400

Services Offered: AD, CU, CE ED, LE, LI, RS, SS. **Established:** 1971. **Staff:** 24. **Budget:** $692,497. **Religious Affiliation:** Catholic. **Clientele:** World. Broad range of services offered to undocumented persons, newly legalized immigrants, and refugees within the Archdiocese of Los Angeles. This includes family reunification programs, immigration counseling, vocational assistance, general advocacy, etc.

69   *Los Angeles*

Central American Refugee Center

660 South Bonnie Brae
Los Angeles, CA 90057
Angella Castillo, Executive Director
(213) 483-6868

Services Offered: AD, CU, EC, LE, SS. **Established:** 1983. **Staff:** 7. **Budget:** $300,000. **Clientele:** Central America/Caribbean. Advocacy and support of Central American refugees in Los Angeles. Services include employment and legal assistance as well as social services. **Publications:** Newsletter; Annual Report.

70   *Los Angeles*

Chinatown Service Center

600 North Broadway, Suite A
Los Angeles, CA 90012
Irene K. Chu, Executive Director
(213) 680-9955

Services Offered: CU, EC CE, EC, HE, SS. **Established:** 1971. **Staff:** 52. **Budget:** $1,000,000. **Clientele:** Asia, Southeast Asia, World. CSC is a community based, non-profit organization that serves primarily people of Asian descent throughout the greater Los Angeles area. The mission

is to offer quality social services to the community: to people of low income and especially the growing population of recently arrived immigrants and refugees - in the areas of employment, cultural adjustment and basic human care. Programs enhance and integrate newcomers into the social and economic mainstream of Los Angeles. **Publications:** CSC NEWSLETTER (free).

71   *Los Angeles*

Clinica Msr. Oscar A. Romero

2675 West Olympic Boulevard
Los Angeles, CA 90006
Ana Zeledon Friendly, Administrator
(213) 389-0288

Services Offered: CU, CE, EC, ED, HE, SS. **Established:** 1983. **Staff:** 10. **Budget:** $250,000. **Religious Affiliation:** Ecumenical. **Clientele:** Central America/Caribbean. Variety of economic, cultural, educational and basic social services available to refugees from Central America. **Publications:** Newsletter.

72   *Los Angeles*

Downtown Legalization Project

1010 South Flower Street, Suite 404
Los Angeles, CA 90015
Frank Acosta, Director
(213) 747-4097

Services Offered: AD, CU, CE, ED, LE, RS. **Established:** 1987. **Staff:** 10. **Budget:** $300,000. **Religious Affiliation:** Methodist. **Clientele:** World, Southeast Asia, Central America/Caribbean. Mission is to help all immigrants become full and active members of society. Provides legal services in 10 languages, community outreach and education, and advocacy (anti-discrimination monitoring, impact litigation, public policy, etc.).

73   *Los Angeles*

El Rescate

2565 West Olympic Boulevard
Los Angeles, CA 90006
Lauren McMahan, Executive Director
(213) 387-3284   Fax: (213) 387-9189

Services Offered: AD, CU, LE, LI, RS, SS. **Established:** 1981. **Staff:** 14. **Budget:** $591,000. **Clientele:** Central America/Caribbean. Legal and social services center offers humanitarian aid and hope for the over 500,000 Central American refugees in the

Los Angeles area. Services and programs: food and clothing distribution; job placement and housing; medical referrals; and language training. Legal staff secures the release of refugees from INS detention and works to prevent their involuntary deportation by seeking political asylum. A project of the Southern California Ecumenical Council. **Publications:** Newsletter (irregular); CHRONOLOGY OF HUMAN RIGHTS VIOLATIONS; Annual Report.

74   *Los Angeles*
Immigrants' Rights Office

1636 West 8th Street
Los Angeles, CA   90017
Michael J. Ortiz, Directing Attorney
(213) 487-6551

Services Offered: AD, LE, LI. **Established:** 1984. **Staff:** 7. **BIA. Clientele:** Central America/Caribbean. Serves the needs of the immigrant community in deportation proceedings. Main focus of representation is toward Mexican nationals and Central American refugees.

75   *Los Angeles*
Immigration Project

2111 Brooklyn Avenue
Los Angeles, CA   90033
Antonio Rodriguez, Contact
(213) 260-7121

Services Offered: AD, ED, LE, SS. **BIA. Clientele:** Central America/Caribbean. Advocacy, educational programs and legal advice and representation for immigrants, refugees and asylees.

76   *Los Angeles*
International Institute of Los Angeles. Immigrant & Refugee Services Division

435 South Boyle Avenue
Los Angeles, CA   90033
Silvia Gonzalez, Director
(213) 264-6210

Services Offered: AD, EC, LE, SS. **Established:** 1914. **Staff:** 20. **BIA. Clientele:** World. Services to immigrants include application for family reunion; adjustment of status; visa processes; political asylum; labor certification and citizenship assistance. In conjunction with immigration services, a variety of social services such as information & referral, counseling and other social services related to

cultural adjustment and family conflict are provided. IRSD staff provides a full range of refugee resettlement services which include sponsorship, airport reception, cultural orientation, information & referral and counseling. In addition, assistance in obtaining employment is provided through classes in job preparedness and the efforts of job developers. 12,000 clients served annually.

77   *Los Angeles*
International Ladies Garment Workers Union. Immigration Project

675 South Park View Street
Los Angeles, CA   90057
Beatrice Nava, Director
(213) 380-5498

Services Offered: AD, CE, ED, LE. **Clientele:** World. Services available to ILGWU families.

78   *Los Angeles*
International Rescue Committee

1833 West Eighth Street, Suite 201
Los Angeles, CA   90057
Bruce Whipple, Coordinator
(213) 413-2200

Services Offered: AD, RS, SS. **BIA. Clientele:** World. Established in the 1930's this is one of the leading refugee resettlement agencies in the United States.

79   *Los Angeles*
Jewish Family Service. Refugee Services

6380 Wilshire Boulevard
Los Angeles, CA   90048
Sima Furman, Refugee Coordinator
(213) 651-5573   Fax: (213) 651-5649

Services Offered: AD, CU, EC, ED, RE, SS. **Staff:** 3. **Religious Affiliation:** Jewish. **Clientele:** World, USSR. Refugee resettlement services coordinated through Hebrew Immigrant Aid Society.

80   *Los Angeles*
Los Angeles County Bar Association. Immigration Legal Assistance Project

300 North Los Angeles Street, Room 4349
Los Angeles, CA 90012
Mary Mucha, Director
(213) 485-1872

Services Offered: LE. **Established**: 1975.
Staff: 4. **Clientele**: World. Provides legal assistance and representation to low income persons in need of immigration help. Counseling for U.S. citizens, prospective immigrants, all categories of non-immigrants, and visa seekers, as well as those seeking naturalization, refugees and relatives of refugees.

---

81   *Los Angeles*

Lutheran Social Services. Immigration & Refugee Service

1345 South Burlington Avenue
Los Angeles, CA 90006
Kathleen Howe, Director
(213) 385-2191

Services Offered: AD, CU, LE, SS.
Established: 1975. **BIA. Religious
Affiliation**: Lutheran. **Clientele**: World. Lutheran Immigration & Refugee Service ministers to refugees, asylum seekers, undocumented persons and immigrants. Helps refugees resettle in the United States by mobilizing sponsors and serving as an advocate for the protection and humane treatment of uprooted people. Also provide educational and technical assistance in immigration matters. Operates the Immigration Counseling and Advocacy Project.
Publications: MAKING HELP HAPPEN (newsletter); Annual Report.

---

82   *Los Angeles*

National Center For Immigrants' Rights

1636 West Eighth Street, Suite 215
Los Angeles, CA 90017
Charles Wheeler, Directing Attorney
(213) 487-2531

Services Offered: LE, RS, SS. **Established**:
1979. **Staff**: 9. **BIA. Clientele**: World. National support center funded by the Legal Services Corporation and affiliated with the Legal Aid Foundation of Los Angeles. NCIR provides legal assistance to other legal service programs, client organizations and pro bono attorneys throughout the United States in the area of immigration and naturalization law. One major duty is to respond to specific requests for legal research, advice and practical guidance on individual cases. In addition, NCIR conducts training seminars on various aspects of immigration law; distributes recent case decisions, updates and information in this area of law to organizations; and refers aliens in need of representation to the appropriate volunteer organizations. A final important function of NCIR is the undertaking of impact litigation to protect and vindicate the rights of immigrants.
Publications: Newsletter (monthly, $10); DIRECTORY.

---

83   *Los Angeles*

One Stop Immigration & Educational Center

3600 Whittier Boulevard
Los Angeles, CA 90023
Jose Gutierrez, Director
(213) 268-8472

Services Offered: LE, RE, RS. **Established**:
1972. **BIA. Clientele**: World. Basic immigration services provided in East Los Angeles.

---

84   *Los Angeles*

Presbyterian Synod of Southern California and Hawaii. Immigration & Resettlement Program

1501 Wilshire Boulevard
Los Angeles, CA 90017
Donald Smith, Director
(213) 483-3840

Services Offered: AD, CU, LI, RE, RS, SS.
Established: 1980. **Staff**: 2. **Budget**: $5,000.
Religious Affiliation: Presbyterian. **Clientele**:
World. Advocacy for refugees includes sponsorship amongst religious congregations and resource sharing. Affiliated with Church World Service.

---

85   *Los Angeles*

Sarrlano Chirino Amaya Central American Refugee Committee

2675 West Olympic Boulevard
Los Angeles, CA 90006
Sara Martinez, Director
(213) 387-7730

Services Offered: AD, CU, CE, LI, RS, SS.
Established: 1981. **Clientele**: Central America/Caribbean. Voluntary organization that provides services to Central American refugees and immigrants as well as general outreach activities to the community at large.

---

86 *Los Angeles*
Southern California Interfaith Task Force on Central America. Sanctuary Committee

1010 South Flower Street
Los Angeles, CA 90015
Mary Brent Wehrli, Executive Director
(213) 746-8375

Services Offered: AD, CU, CE, ED, SA, RE. Established: 1982. Staff: 1. Budget: $50,000. Religious Affiliation: Ecumenical. Clientele: Central America/Caribbean. Work with congregations to support sanctuary for Central American refugees as well as general community outreach programs on current affairs in Central America and the relationship to the increasing numbers of refugees and asylees in California. Publications: Newsletter (monthly).

87 *Merced*
Catholic Social Services. Resettlement Program

504 West 13th Street
Merced, CA 95340
Ramiro Coronado, Director
(209) 383-5220

Services Offered: AD, EC, CU, ED, RE, SS. Religious Affiliation: Catholic. Clientele: World, Central America/Caribbean. Resettlement and immigration services coordinated with US Catholic Conference, Migration & Refugee Services.

88 *Merced*
Lao Family Community

855 West 15th Street
Merced, CA 95340
Houa Yang, Executive Director
(209) 384-7384

Services Offered: AD, CU, CE, ED, HE, LE, SS. Established: 1983. Staff: 6. Budget: $100,000. Clientele: Southeast Asia. Provide emergency assistance as follows: housing; medical care; law enforcement; public assistance; citizenship; family crisis; cultural advocacy; referrals; aculturation; educational programs; and referrals and coordination with other social welfare agencies.

89 *Modesto*
Lao Family Community

142 North Ninth Street, Suite 10
Modesto, CA 95350
Chou Yang, Counselor
(209) 572-1244

Services Offered: EC, SS. Established: 1979. Staff: 11. Budget: $280,516. Clientele: Southeast Asia. Goal is to assist refugees to overcome the barriers to employment and self-sufficiency. Services: language training; assessment; counseling; transportation; child care reimbursement; and service referrals.

90 *Montclair*
Refugee Resettlement Committee

9315 Mills Avenue, Suite 3
Montclair, CA 91763
Carmen Myers, Coordinator
(714) 626-0138

Services Offered: AD, CU, ED, CE, LE, SS. Clientele: Central America/Caribbean, World. Broad based resettlement services include advocacy for rights of refugees, legal assistance and social services to adjust to life in the U.S.

91 *Moreno Valley*
Lao Family Community

22700 Alessandro Boulevard
Moreno Valley, CA 92388
Lee Hai, Director
(714) 653-1179

Services Offered: CU, EC, SS. Established: 1985. Staff: 13. Budget: $300,000. BIA. Clientele: Southeast Asia, World. Support services primarily for Laotians and Southeast Asians. Includes cultural programs, some vocational and language training, and emergency services.

92 *Norwalk*
Community Legal Services

11550 Rosecrans
Norwalk, CA 90650
Graciela Zavala, Coordinator
(213) 864-9935

Services Offered: AD, CE, ED, LE. BIA. Clientele: World. Educational outreach, advocacy and legal services offered to low income immigrants and refugees.

93   *Oakland*

Asian Immigrant Womens Advocates

310 Eighth Street, Suite 205
Oakland, CA 94607

Services Offered: AD, CE, LE. **Clientele**: Asia, Southeast Asia.

94   *Oakland*

Catholic Charities. Immigration Project

1232 33rd Avenue
Oakland, CA 94601
Raquel Aguirre, Director
(415) 261-1538

Services Offered: LE. **Established**: 1982.
Staff: 3. **Religious Affiliation**: Catholic.
Clientele: World, Central America/Caribbean.
Legal assistance for immigrants and refugees within the Diocese of Oakland. Coordinated with US Catholic Conference Migration & Refugee Services.

95   *Oakland*

Committee to Defend Immigrant & Refugee Rights

Box 28102
Oakland, CA 94604

Services Offered: AD, CE, ED, LE. **Clientele**: World.

96   *Oakland*

Datacenter

464 19th Street
Oakland, CA 94612
Fred Goff, President
(415) 835-4692

Services Offered: LI, RS. **Established**: 1977.
Staff: 10. **Budget**: $300,000. **Clientele**: World.
Non-profit library and resource center offering research service and documentation retrieval. Provides the Political Asylum and Deportation Suspension Legal Brief Service which provides carefully selected documentation for use on immigration law cases. Public interest information resource center specializing in public policy issues. **Publications**: List of Publications and Services.

97   *Oakland*

Filipinos for Affirmative Action

310 Eighth Street
Oakland, CA 94607
Lillian Galedo, Executive Director
(415) 465-9876

Services Offered: AD, CU, EC, CE, RS, SS.
Established: 1973. **Staff**: 5. **Clientele**: Asia.
Formerly Filipino Immigrant Services. Assist immigrants with adjustment to life in the United States - immigration counseling; employment counseling and job referral; general information and referral; community organizing; and advocacy for the rights of Filipinos. **Publications**: Newsletter (quarterly); Annual Report.

98   *Oakland*

International Institute of the East Bay

297 Lee Street
Oakland, CA 94610
Zoe Borkowski, Executive Director
(415) 451-2846

Services Offered: AD, CU, CE, EC, ED, HE, LE, SS. **Established**: 1935. **Staff**: 27. **Budget**: $700,000. **BIA**. **Clientele**: World. Provides social and legal services for the foreign born, including immigration counseling, problem solving, counseling concerning resources and responsibilities; community organization, advocacy and support services. Resource for community at large about nationality communities, immigration problems, adjustment and policies affecting the lives of refugees and immigrants. **Publications**: OPPORTUNITY (quarterly newsletter); RESOURCE LIST (semi-annual, $7.50); Annual Report.

99   *Oakland*

Jewish Family Service

3245 Sheffield Avenue
Oakland, CA 94602
San Sanfran, Administrator
(415) 532-6314

Services Offered: AD, RE, SS. **Religious Affiliation**: Jewish. **Clientele**: World. Refugee resettlement program provides assistance (counseling, emergency assistance, orientation, etc.) to immigrants and refugees. Work coordinated through Hebrew

Immigrant Aid Society.

---

100   *Oakland*

Lao Family Community

534 22nd Street
Oakland, CA 94612
Chaosarn S. Chao, Executive Director
(415) 451-6878

Services Offered: AD, CU, CE, EC, LE, SC.
Established: 1980. **Staff:** 27. **Budget:** $450,000.
Clientele: Southeast Asia, World. Services for
Southeast Asian refugees include cultural preservation, educational leadership, employment training,
and general social services. **Publications:** Annual
Report.

---

101   *Oakland*

National Network for Immigrant & Refugee Rights

310 Eighth Street, Suite 307
Oakland, CA 94607
Bill Tamayo, Chair
(415) 465-1984

Services Offered: AD, CE, LI, RS.
Established: 1986. **Staff:** 2. **Budget:** $100,000.
Clientele: World. NNIRR was organized to bring
together the various groups and individuals who favor
full rights for all immigrants, in order to advocate and
organize for a long term government committment to
immigrant and refugee rights, to expose and educate
the communities and general public about the various
abuses against immigrants, and to take up the concrete defense of immigrant & refugee rights. The
Network provides a clearinghouse for its affiliates,
develops resources, communications, and necessary
coordination of activities. **Publications:**
NETWORK NEWS (monthly); List of Publications.

---

102   *Oakland*

Temple Sinai. Sanctuary Committee

2808 Summit
Oakland, CA 94609
(415) 451-3263

Services Offered: SA. **Religious Affiliation:**
Jewish. **Clientele:** Central America/Caribbean.
Provide sanctuary to political refugees from Central
America.

---

103   *Pacific Grove*

Monterey County Sanctuary

Box 898
Pacific Grove, CA 93950
Heidi Hall, Legal Services Coordinator
(408) 372-4440

Services Offered: AD, CU, CE, EC, ED, LE,
SA, SS. **Established:** 1985. **Staff:** 2. **Budget:**
$35,000. **Religious Affiliation:** Ecumenical.
Clientele: Central America/Caribbean. Ecumenical,
community-based organization designed to build
bridges of understanding and assistance between the
refugee community and the North American community. Support services: job referral and assistance; legal counsel, assistance and representation; emergency
aid; educational and vocational training.
Publications: ALIANZA (monthly newsletter).

---

104   *Pacoima*

San Juan Macias Immigrant Center

13616 Van Nuys Boulevard
Pacoima, CA 91331
Mike Garcia, Director
(818) 896-1156

Services Offered: LE, RE, SS. **Established:**
1978. **BIA.** **Clientele:** Central America/Caribbean.
Legal advice, assistance and representation for immigrants and refugees as well as limited social services.

---

105   *Pacoima*

Valley Immigrants Rights Center

13327 Van Nuys Boulevard
Pacoima, CA 91331
(818) 890-2406

Services Offered: AD, CE, LE. **Established:**
1985. **BIA.** **Clientele:** World, Central
America/Caribbean. Legal assistance and representation in immigration and related-matters to low income individuals.

---

106   *Palm Springs*

Catholic Charities. Immigration Services

934 Vella Road
Palm Springs, CA 92264
David Greene, Director
(619) 327-1579

Services Offered: AD, CE, LE, SS. **Religious
Affiliation:** Catholic. **Clientele:** Central

America/Caribbean, World. Advocacy, limited social services and legal advice and counseling for the foreign born.

---

107 *Palo Alto*
Palo Alto Friends Meeting

957 Colorado
Palo Alto, CA 94303
Lincoln Moses, Clerk

Services Offered: AD, CE, SA, SS. **Budget**: $600. **Religious Affiliation**: Quaker. **Clientele**: Central America/Caribbean, Southeast Asia. Continuing aid to refugees given sanctuary or helped after the Vietnam War. Assist new arrivals through South Bay Sanctuary Covenant.

---

108 *Pasadena*
American Friends Service Committee. Immigration Program

980 North Fair Oaks Avenue
Pasadena, CA 91103
Tony Henry, Executive Secretary
(818) 791-1978

Services Offered: AD, CE, LI. **Staff**: 4. **Religious Affiliation**: Quaker. **Clientele**: World, Central America/Caribbean, Oceania. Provide information about current immigration law; monitor INS and Border Patrol abuses; and work in coalition on issues with immigrants and refugees. **Publications**: SPOTLIGHT (newsletter, 3X/year).

---

109 *Porterville*
O.L.A. Raza

Box 190
Porterville, CA 93257
Roberto De la Rosa, Executive Director
(209) 784-1702

Services Offered: AD, CE, LE, SC, SS. **Established**: 1976. **Clientele**: Central America/Caribbean, World. Legal representation for all refugees and immigrants as well as basic social services, advocacy, and community support programs.

---

110 *Redwood City*
Comite en Defensa de los Immigrantes

412 Stabaugh Street
Redwood City, CA 94063
Guadalupe Beruman, Contact

Services Offered: AD, CU, CE, LE, SS. **Clientele**: Central America/Caribbean. Advocacy and support for immigrants (and refugees).

---

111 *Riverside*
Inland Counties Legal Services

1860 Chicago Avenue, Building I-3
Riverside, CA 92507
Irene C. Morales, Executive Director
(714) 784-1020

Services Offered: LE. **Established**: 1958. **Staff**: 60. **Budget**: $2,400,000. **BIA**. **Clientele**: World, Central America/Caribbean. Legal representation in selected immigration matters and proceedings. Affiliated with the National Center for Immigrant Rights.

---

112 *Sacramento*
Asian Legal Services Outreach

1903 14th Street
Sacramento, CA 95814
Susana Wong, Executive Director
(916) 447-7971

Services Offered: AD, CU, CE, LE, SS. **Established**: 1974. **Staff**: 4. **BIA**. **Clientele**: Southeast Asia. Non-profit organization provides counseling and legal representation to low-income residents, including immigration, asylum, change of status, etc. **Publications**: CURRENTS (quarterly newsletter, free).

---

113 *Sacramento*
Asian Resources

2251 Florid Road, Station E
Sacramento, CA 95822
May O. Lee, Executive Director
(916) 424-8960

Services Offered: EC, ED, SS. **Established**: 1980. **Staff**: 10. **Budget**: $500,000. **Clientele**: Southeast Asia, Asia. Non-profit organization involved in and committed to providing employment and training services to immigrants and refugees.

---

114 *Sacramento*

California Department of Social Services. Office of Refugee Services

744 P Street
Sacramento, CA 95814
Walter Barnes, Chief
(916) 324-1576

Services Offered: AD, EC, ED, HE, SS.
Clientele: World. Statewide coordination of federal, state and private resources for effective refugee resettlement including cash and medical assistance, support services and such other activities as necessary.

---

115   Sacramento

Catholic Social Service. Refugee Resettlement Project

5890 Newman Court
Sacramento, CA 95819
Cau Lao, Director
(916) 452-1445

Services Offered: SS. Established: 1975. Staff: 9. Budget: $160,000. Religious Affiliation: Catholic. Clientele: World. Refugee Resettlement Project provides the following services/programs: orientation; arrival and placement; financial assistance; counseling and referrals; and coordination and help with social security, school registration, medical, housing, interpretation, etc.

---

116   Sacramento

City of Sacramento. Office of the Mayor

City Hall, Room 205
Sacramento, CA 95814
(916) 449-5426

Services Offered: SA. Clientele: Central America/Caribbean. Sacramento is a declared public sanctuary for refugees fleeing Central America.

---

117   Sacramento

Indochinese Assistance Center

5625 24th Street
Sacramento, CA 95822
Jan S. Hunt, Director
(916) 421-1036

Services Offered: CE, SS. Staff: 8. Budget: $155,599. Religious Affiliation: Presbyterian. Clientele: Southeast Asia. Community outreach

and social services (mental health, counseling, substance abuse, etc.) available to Indochinese refugees in Greater Sacramento.

---

118   Sacramento

International Rescue Committee

2020 29th Street, Suite 103
Sacramento, CA 95817
By Khang, Director
(916) 739-0122

Services Offered: AD, LI, SS. BIA. Clientele: World. Operates extensive refugee resettlement network throughout the United States and maintains offices abroad to assist refugees fleeing persecution.

---

119   Sacramento

Lao Family Community

5840 Franklin Boulevard
Sacramento, CA 95824
Yia B. Yang, Director
(916) 424-0864

Services Offered: AD, CU, CE, ED, SS. Established: 1981. Staff: 7. Budget: $160,000. Religious Affiliation: Ecumenical. Clientele: World, Southeast Asia. Advocacy and support programs designed to encourage economic self-sufficiency as quickly as possible.

---

120   Sacramento

Legal Services of Northern California

515 12th Street
Sacramento, CA 95814
Victor M. Geminiani, Director
(916) 444-6760

Services Offered: AD, CE, LE. Staff: 60. Clientele: World. Legal counseling and/or representation available to low-income immigrants. Publications: Newsletter; Annual Report.

---

121   Sacramento

Sandigan California

7300 Franklin Boulevard, Suite 103
Sacramento, CA 95823
Leni Locson, Executive Director
(916) 429-0565

Services Offered: AD, CU, ED, SS. Established: 1986. Staff: 7. Budget: $95,500.

Clientele: Southeast Asia, Central America/Caribbean. Following services offered to immigrants and refugees: advocacy and cultural support; educational and civic classes; social services; and recreational activities. **Publications:** Newsletter (free); Annual Report.

---

122   *Sacramento*

Unitarian Society of Sacramento. Sanctuary Committee

2425 Sierra Boulevard
Sacramento, CA 95825
Rev. Eileen Karpeles
(916) 483-9283

Services Offered: SA. **Religious Affiliation:** Unitarian. **Clientele:** Central America/Caribbean. Declared sanctuary for refugees fleeing Central America.

---

123   *San Diego*

Access

6970 Linda Vista Road
San Diego, CA 92111
Robert Peer, Executive Director
(619) 560-0871

Services Offered: AD, EC, SS. **Established:** 1968. **Staff:** 14. **Budget:** $450,000. **BIA. Clientele:** World. Vocational training, orientation and job placement as well as social services for immigrants and refugees.

---

124   *San Diego*

Boat People SOS

6870 Linda Vista Road
San Diego, CA 92111
Nguyen Huu Xuong, Chair
(619) 571-3957

Services Offered: AD, CE, RS. **Established:** 1980. **Staff:** 1. **Clientele:** Southeast Asia. Advocacy, public relations and research on behalf of the Vietnamese boat people and information about the pirates and others that have attacked the vessels, and killed and kidnapped refugees. **Publications:** NEWS BULLETIN.

---

125   *San Diego*

Catholic Community Services. Resettlement & Immigration Services

4643 Mission Gorge Place
San Diego, CA 92120
Gwen W. Plank, Director
(619) 287-9454

Services Offered: AD, LE, RE, SS. **Established:** 1975. **BIA. Religious Affiliation:** Catholic. **Clientele:** World. General resettlement social services as well as immigration counseling.

---

126   *San Diego*

Impact

1789 National Avenue
San Diego, CA 92113
Ernesto Azhocar, Director
(619) 239-3881

Services Offered: AD, LE. **Established:** 1973. **Staff:** 3. **BIA. Clientele:** Central America/Caribbean, World. Services focus on advocacy for rights of refugees and immigrants with particular emphasis on immigration counseling including representation in deportation and political asylum proceedings.

---

127   *San Diego*

International Rescue Committee

3869 42nd Street
San Diego, CA 92105
Cindy Jensen, Director
(619) 584-8283

Services Offered: AD, RS, SS. **Established:** 1985. **BIA. Clientele:** World. One of the oldest refugee resettlement agencies in the United States. Assists refugees from throughout the world resettle in the United States.

---

128   *San Diego*

Jewish Family Service. Resettlement Program

3355 Fourth Avenue
San Diego, CA 92103
Jill Borg Spitzer, Executive Director
(619) 291-0473

Services Offered: AD, EC, ED, HE, LE, RE, SS. **Established:** 1918. **Staff:** 6. **Budget:** $300,000.

Religious Affiliation: Jewish. **Clientele**: USSR, Middle East. Provides and coordinates assistance to refugees to help them become established in San Diego. **Publications**: FAMILY FOCUS (quarterly newsletter, free).

---

129   *San Diego*

Legal Aid Society. Alien Rights Unit

110 South Euclid Avenue
San Diego, CA 92114
Sana Loue, Directing Attorney
(619) 262-5557

Services Offered: LE. **BIA**. **Clientele**: Central America/Caribbean. Legal advice and representation for low income individuals in deportation proceedings, asylum, naturalization, etc.

---

130   *San Diego*

Refugee Assistance Program

5202 Orange Avenue
San Diego, CA 92115
Do Thien, Coordinator
(619) 286-4335

Services Offered: AD, CE, ED, LE. **BIA**. **Religious Affiliation**: Church of Christ. **Clientele**: Central America/Caribbean. Legal advice, counseling and referral; community outreach and educational programs. Affiliated with METRO.

---

131   *San Fernando*

Immigration Services of Santa Rosa

606 Chatsworth Drive
San Fernando, CA 91340
Eduardo R. Palacios, Executive Director
(818) 361-4341

Services Offered: CE, LE, SS. **Established**: 1970. **Staff**: 6. **Budget**: $500,000. **BIA**. **Clientele**: Central America/Caribbean, South America. Provides legal and social services to refugees and political asylees. Offer citizenship classes and limited language training.

---

132   *San Francisco*

Amnesty International USA

655 Sutter, Suite 402
San Francisco, CA 94102
Nicholas J. Rizza, Refugee Coordinator
(415) 776-2473   Fax: (415) 441-2641

Services Offered: LE, LI, RS. **Established**: 1985. **Staff**: 2. **Clientele**: World. Provide information and at times letters of support to asylees and attorneys. Participate in appeals of selected political asylum cases, when issues on appeal relate to organizations mandate. Provide documentation on general human rights conditions in a particular country and other documents relevant to political asylum claims. **Publications**: Annual Report.

---

133   *San Francisco*

Buddhist Council for Refugee Rescue and Resettlement

800 Sacramento Street
San Francisco, CA 94108
Douglas Powers, Deputy Director
(415) 421-6117

Services Offered: EC, ED, SS. **Established**: 1981. **Staff**: 17. **Religious Affiliation**: Buddhist. **Clientele**: Southeast Asia, Asia. Provides education, employment and general social services as part of the program to resettle refugees from Asia. **Publications**: BUDDHIST COUNCIL NEWS (irregular).

---

134   *San Francisco*

Catholic Charities. Immigration Program

2940 16th Street, Room 206
San Francisco, CA 94103
Mary Lou Goeke, Executive Director
(415) 861-8306

Services Offered: AD, CE, EC, LE, LI, RE, SA, SS. **Established**: 1982. **Staff**: 9. **Budget**: $403,000. **BIA**. **Religious Affiliation**: Catholic. **Clientele**: World, Central America/Caribbean. The Immigration Program provides legal representation before the INS, food, shelter, clothing and social service advocacy to immigrants and refugees. Also, community organizing and education around the plight of the refugees from Central America. **Publications**: Newsletter (quarterly, free).

---

135   *San Francisco*

Chinese Newcomer Service Center

777 Stockton Street
San Francisco, CA 94108
Po S. Wong, Executive Director
(415) 421-0943

Services Offered: AD, CU, EC, CE, SS.
Established: 1969. **Staff**: 13. **Budget**: $300,000.
Clientele: Asia. Goal is to assist monolingual Chinese-speaking residents, both oldtimers and newcomers to the Bay Area, in their adjustment process to become contributing and participating members of American society. Acculturation and orientation programs to reduce initial adjustment difficulties of immigrants and refugee newcomers. Services: information & referral; adjustment counseling; translation & interpretation; emergency service; acculturation service; mental health education and counseling; job preparation, referral and placement; community information; media outreach program; and interstate service. **Publications**: Newsletter; Annual Report.

---

136 *San Francisco*

Coalition for Immigrant and Refugee Rights & Services

2111 Mission Street
San Francisco, CA 94110
Emily Goldfarb, Executive Director
(415) 626-2360

Services Offered: AD, CU, CE, EC, ED, HE, LE, LI, SS. **Established**: 1986. **Staff**: 5. **Budget**: $200,000. **Clientele**: World. Following services and programs offered: operate Immigrant Assistance Hotline (554-2444) for information & referral on all immigration related matters; provide client advocacy at INS offices; paralegal assistance for immigration/refugee/asylum, etc. issues; produce literature for clients and other professionals in the field; and provide immigration seminars for service providers. **Publications**: DIGNIDAD (quarterly, free).

---

137 *San Francisco*

Father Moriarty Asylum Program

2940 Sixteenth Street, Suite 206
San Francisco, CA 94103
Jane Fischberg, Executive Director
(415) 861-8306

Services Offered: AD, CE, LE, RE, LI, SS.
Religious Affiliation: Catholic. **Clientele**: Central America/Caribbean. Advocacy, outreach, legal and social services for asylees from El Salvador and Guatemala.

---

138 *San Francisco*

Good Samaritan Community Center

1292 Portrero Avenue
San Francisco, CA 94110
Rev. Will Wauters, Executive Director
(415) 824-3500

Services Offered: AD, CU, EC, HE, CE, LE, LI, SS. **Established**: 1980. **Staff**: 8. **Budget**: $240,000. **Religious Affiliation**: Episcopal. **Clientele**: Central America/Caribbean, World. Services and programs designed to meet the needs primarily of Central American refugees in the Episcopal Mission. Include: social and health care; legal representation in asylum cases; job development and educational programs; counseling; and a variety of cultural and advocacy programs. **Publications**: Newsletter (semi-annual).

---

139 *San Francisco*

Immigrant Assistance Line

1435 Market Street
San Francisco, CA 94105
Hilda Jones, Contact
(415) 554-2444

Services Offered: AD, CE, LE. **Clientele**: Central America/Caribbean, Southeast Asia, World. Advocacy, information, outreach, advice and referrals for those seeking immigration assistance.

---

140 *San Francisco*

Immigrant Legal Resource Center

536 Mission Street
San Francisco, CA 94105
Mark Silverman, Directing Attorney
(415) 442-7294

Services Offered: LE, LI, RS. **BIA**. **Clientele**: World. Provide back-up support to attorneys engaged in immigration activities. Produces publications designed to assist lawyers in asylum, deportation, etc. proceedings.

---

141 *San Francisco*

International Institute of San Francisco

2209 Van Ness Avenue
San Francisco, CA 94109
Don Eiten, Executive Director
(415) 673-1720

Services Offered: AD, CU, CE, EC, ED, HE, LE, SS. **Established**: 1918. **Staff**: 46. **Budget**: $1,100,000. **BIA**. **Clientele**: World, Southeast

Asia, Central America/Caribbean. Broad based services to all immigrants and refugees. However, through June 30, 1989 vast majority of immigration and refugee resettlement cases involved Asian and Hispanic clients. In addition, assisted 75 torture survivors (25 Asian, 50 Hispanic). **Publications:** Annual Report.

---

142   *San Francisco*

International Rescue Committee

1367 Folsom Street
San Francisco, CA 94103
Don Climent, Director
(415) 863-3777

Services Offered: AD, LE, SS. **Established:** 1975. **BIA. Clientele:** World. IRC San Francisco office is primarily concerned with resettlement activities, family reunification and immigration assistance to those lawfully admitted to the United States with refugee status.

---

143   *San Francisco*

Japanese Newcomer Service

1840 Sutter, Suite 201
San Francisco, CA 94115
Yoshiko Kitawaki, Director
(415) 922-2033

Services Offered: AD, CU, EC, ED, LI, RS, SS. **Established:** 1974. **BIA. Clientele:** Asia. Following services and programs designed to meet the needs of the immigrant population in the Japanese community: vocational counseling; social services; educational programs; workshops and forums; recreational activities; and indirect activities and services.

---

144   *San Francisco*

Jewish Family & Children Services

1600 Scott Street
San Francisco, CA 94115
Anita Friedman, Director
(415) 567-8860

Services Offered: AD, CU, RE, LI, SS. **Religious Affiliation:** Jewish. **Clientele:** World, Europe, USSR. Provides pre-migration and immigration counseling, core resettlement and follow-up services to refugees and immigrants in the Bay Area. Activities coordinated with Hebrew Immigrant Aid Society.

---

145   *San Francisco*

Jewish Vocational & Career Counseling Service

870 Market Street
San Francisco, CA 94102
Jane Field, Emigre Services
(415) 391-3595

Services Offered: EC, SS. **Established:** 1973. **Religious Affiliation:** Jewish. **Clientele:** World. Employment and counseling services (orientation, training, placement, counseling, etc.) designed to make the newly arrived individual as self-sufficient as possible in as short a period of time as possible.

---

146   *San Francisco*

Lutheran Social Services of Northern California

1101 O'Farrell Street
San Francisco, CA 94109
Rev. Carl H. Pihl, Consultant
(415) 474-8400

Services Offered: AD, SS. **Established:** 1966. **Staff:** 4. **BIA. Religious Affiliation:** Lutheran. **Clientele:** World. Provide core resettlement services through Lutheran Immigration & Refugee Service as well as immigration counseling and related social services. **Publications:** VENTURES (quarterly newsletter, free).

---

147   *San Francisco*

Mission Community Legal Defense

2940 Sixteenth Street, Suite 301
San Francisco, CA 94103
Alfredo Rodriguez, Director
(415) 552-3910

Services Offered: LE, LI, RS. **Established:** 1973. **Staff:** 11. **Budget:** $320,000. **BIA. Clientele:** Central America/Caribbean, World. Legal assistance and representation for immigrants, both documented and undocumented. This includes citizenship classes and counseling on INS rules and regulations.

---

148   *San Francisco*

Refugee Employment Assistance Project

1049 Market Street

San Francisco, CA 94103
Nancy Betts, Director
(415) 558-7090

Services Offered: EC, SS. **Established:** 1976.
Clientele: World. Employment counseling, orientation, training and placement services to refugees in the Bay Area.

---

149   *San Francisco*

Rosenberg Foundation

210 Post Street
San Francisco, CA 94108
Kirke Wilson, Executive Director
(415) 421-6105

Services Offered: RS. **Budget:** $1,100,000.
Clientele: Central America/Caribbean. Provide funding for research on policy issues in the field of immigration with emphasis on migration from Mexico. **Publications:** Application guidelines.

---

150   *San Francisco*

San Francisco Lawyers' Committee. Immigrant & Refugee Rights Project

301 Mission Street
San Francisco, CA 94105
Robert Rubin, Managing Attorney
(415) 543-9444

Services Offered: AD, LE, RS. **Established:** 1981. **Staff:** 7. **Clientele:** World, Southeast Asia, Central America/Caribbean. Administrative, legislative and legal advocacy on behalf of immigrants and refugees in the following areas: health care, education, employment, and public benefits. **Publications:** Newsletter; Annual Report.

---

151   *San Francisco*

San Francisco Lawyers' Committee. Political Asylum Program

301 Mission Street
San Francisco, CA 94105
Sara Campos, Coordinator
(415) 543-9444

Services Offered: LE, LI. **Established:** 1983.
Staff: 2. **Clientele:** Central America/Caribbean. Program coordinates pro bono representation of Salvadorans and Guatemalans seeking political asylum. Volunteer attorney, assisted by volunteer interpreter and a consulting attorney expert in asylum and immigration law, take individual asylum cases from

application stage through U.S. Court of Appeals.

---

152   *San Francisco*

Sanctuary Covenant of San Francisco

376 Missouri Street
San Francisco, CA 94118
Sr. Kathleen Healy, Chair
(415) 285-5272

Services Offered: AD, CE, RE, SA, SS.
Established: 1985. **Staff:** 1. **Religious Affiliation:** Ecumenical. **Clientele:** Central America/Caribbean. To support, protect and provide assistance to refugees from El Salvador and Guatemala. **Publications:** Newsletter.

---

153   *San Francisco*

St. Teresa's Church. Sanctuary Committee

390 Missouri
San Francisco, CA 94107
Sr. Kathleen Healy, Coordinator
(415) 285-5272

Services Offered: SA. **Religious Affiliation:** Catholic. **Clientele:** Central America/Caribbean. Provide sanctuary for asylees fleeing Central America.

---

154   *San Francisco*

U.S. Catholic Conference. Migration & Refugee Services. Regional Immigration Office

582 Market Street, Room 318
San Francisco, CA 94104
James Hoffman, Director
(415) 362-8677

Services Offered: AD, LE, SS. **Staff:** 6. **BIA.**
Religious Affiliation: Catholic. **Clientele:** World, Southeast Asia, Central America/Caribbean. Regional office responsible for the northwestern United States.

---

155   *San Francisco*

U.S. Department of Health & Human Services. Family Support Administration. Office of Refugee Resettlement

50 UN Plaza Mall, MS 351

San Francisco, CA 94102
Rick Spear, Contact
(415) 556-8582

Services Offered: Clientele: World. ORR regional office responsible for coordination of assistance (cash & medical, social services, etc.) to refugees.

---

156   *San Francisco*

United Methodist Church. Refugee Concerns Committee

Box 467
San Francisco, CA 94101
Lucia Ann McSpadden, Coordinator
(415) 474-3101

Services Offered: AD, CU, EC, LI, RE, SC, SS. **Established:** 1979. **Staff:** 2. **Budget:** $82,000. **Religious Affiliation:** Methodist. **Clientele:** World. Refugee resettlement with assisting Protestant congregations and/or relatives. Advocacy for refugees; education as to the needs of refugees; refugee sponsorship; referrals for health and legal assistance; and oversight of related church committees. Affiliated with Church World Service and the United Methodist Committee on Relief. **Publications:** Newsletter (irregular).

---

157   *San Francisco*

World Relief

220 Golden Gate Avenue
San Francisco, CA 94102
Ron Curtain, Director
(415) 775-5151   Fax: (415) 775-9691

Services Offered: ED, SS. **Established:** 1980. **Staff:** 25. **Budget:** $1,100,000. **BIA. Religious Affiliation:** Ecumenical. **Clientele:** World. Primarily involved in two programs: refugee resettlement and related immigration assistance including educational programs and application processing. **Publications:** PARTNERSHIP UPDATE (bimonthly newsletter, free).

---

158   *San Gabriel*

International Institute of Los Angeles. Refugee Relocation & Placement Program

164 West Valley Boulevard
San Gabriel, CA 91776
Thongsy Chen, Director

(818) 307-1084

Services Offered: AD, CU, CE, EC, SS. **Staff:** 8. **BIA. Clientele:** World. Promotes integration into American society of individuals in cultural transition, assisting them in becoming economically and socially self-sufficient. Program provides refugee relocation and placement services to refugees legally admitted to the United States. Agency sponsorship assures them of housing, health care, access to education, and employment and orientation services.

---

159   *San Jose*

Adult and Child Guidance Center. Indochinese Mental Health Project

950 West Julian Street
San Jose, CA 95126
Bart Charlow, Executive Director
(408) 292-9353

Services Offered: AD, CU, ED, SS. **Staff:** 40. **Clientele:** Southeast Asia, Asia. The Indochinese Mental Health Project was implemented in response to the critical needs of Indochinese residents who were experiencing extreme difficulty in adjusting to American life, including a multiplicity of personal problems requiring specialized assessment, education and supportive guidance and counseling. Since inception, the project has provided over 5700 units of service to more than 1,000 individuals. The project is designed to assist individuals and families overcome cultural and emotional barriers to self-sufficiency. The project provides services in 6 major Indochinese languages. **Publications:** ADVOCATE (newsletter).

---

160   *San Jose*

Aid To Refugee Children Without Parents

1239 Shadowfax Drive
San Jose, CA 95121
Huu D. Nguyen, Executive Director
(408) 226-7031

Services Offered: AD, CU, SS. **Established:** 1988. **Staff:** 6. **Clientele:** Southeast Asia. Provides the following assistance to refugee children without parents or guardians: educational materials; funds for recreational and sports activities; funds for traditional celebrations; emergency assistance and welfare; and recruitment of sponsors in order to place unaccompanied refugee minors. Predominant group served are Southeast Asians. **Publications:** NEWSLETTER (quarterly, free); Annual report.

161   *San Jose*

Catholic Charities. Immigration Counseling Center

1456 Monterey Highway
San Jose, CA 95110
Maria Picetti, Director
(408) 293-5374

Services Offered: AD, LE, RE, LI, SS.
Established: 1979. **Staff**: 10. **BIA. Religious
Affiliation**: Catholic. **Clientele**: Central
America/Caribbean, World. Direct casework and
counseling provides immigration assistance and social
service support to immigrants and refugees.

---

162   *San Jose*

International Rescue Committee

90 East Gish Road
San Jose, CA 95102
Dang Thi Lieu, Director
(408) 298-7273

Services Offered: CU, LE, SS. **Established**:
1979. **Clientele**: World. Extensive refugee resettlement services throughout the world.

---

163   *San Jose*

Santa Clara County Health Department. Refugee Health Services Program

976 Lenzen Avenue
San Jose, CA 95126
James Powell, Program Manager
(408) 299-6970

Services Offered: AD, ED, HE, SS.
Established: 1980. **Staff**: 25. **Budget**: $750,000.
Clientele: World. All refugees eligible for a variety
of preventative health care services. Services offered:
health assessment; examination; various tests and
immunizations; health counseling and education;
community outreach; and referral services. Operates
the Cambodian Family Planning Project.

---

164   *Santa Ana*

American Immigrant Foundation

Box 1213
Santa Ana, CA 92702
Dorothy Edwards, Executive Director
(714) 834-9348

Services Offered: AD, CE, ED, LE, LI.
Clientele: World, Central America/Caribbean,
Southeast Asia. Offers advocacy, community educa-
tion and legal services for immigrants and refugees.

---

165   *Santa Ana*

Cambodian Family

1111 East Wakeham Avenue, Suite E
Santa Ana, CA 92705
Rifka Hirsch, Executive Director
(714) 542-2907

Services Offered: AD, CU, EC, ED.
Established: 1981. **Clientele**: Southeast Asia.
The Cambodian Family is a grass roots organization,
arising out of the Cambodian community in response
to its own needs. Helped refugees learn English, find
jobs, solve their problems and preserve their culture.
Services range from vocational counseling to the
Khmer Culture Club.

---

166   *Santa Ana*

Catholic Charities. Resettlement Services

1506 Brookhollow, Suite 112
Santa Ana, CA 92705
Thus Tran, Coordinator
(714) 662-7500

Services Offered: AD, CU, EC, RE, SS.
Religious Affiliation: Catholic. **Clientele**:
World, Southeast Asia, Central America/Caribbean.
Coordination of refugee resettlement services and
immigration services. Affiliated with US Catholic
Conference Migration & Refugee Services.

---

167   *Santa Ana*

Community Law Center

317 East Santa Ana Boulevard
Santa Ana, CA 92701
Sr. Annette Debs, Coordinator
(71$) 547-5884

Services Offered: CE, LE. **Clientele**: Central
America/Caribbean. Legal representation for low income refugees and immigrants, from advice to representation in deportation, asylum, labor certification,
etc.

---

168   *Santa Ana*

International Rescue Committee

1801 West 17th Street
Santa Ana, CA 92706
Alicia Cooper, Director
(714) 953-6912

Services Offered: CU, LE, LI, SS. **Clientele:** World. Extensive services for refugees offered through this office as well as coordination with other IRC offices throughout the world.

Dedicated to the monitoring, protection and advocacy of immigrant rights in Orange County through its member agencies, representing community, educational, legal, labor and religious organizations. Formed with the specific goal of assuring equitable implementation of the new immigration law. Offers the following resources and services: information clearinghouse; outreach activities; and advocacy and lobbying efforts.

---

169   *Santa Ana*

Lao Family Community

1140 South Bristol Street
Santa Ana, CA 92704
Cheu Thao, Executive Director
(714) 556-9520

Services Offered: CU, EC, ED, SS. **Established:** 1977. **Staff:** 20. **Budget:** $900,000. **Clientele:** Southeast Asia, World. Following services and programs offered to refugees: language training; vocational training and employment services; and community and cultural outreach projects. National headquarters for a system of Lao support groups throughout the United States. **Publications:** LAO FAMILY NEWSLETTER (monthly, free).

---

170   *Santa Ana*

National Association for Vietnamese American Education

1405 French Street
Santa Ana, CA 92701
Khamchong Luangpraseut, President
(714) 558-5729

Services Offered: CU, ED, SS. **Established:** 1979. **Clientele:** Southeast Asia. Advocacy and action group that seeks better education, quality social services, professional opportunities and constructive roles for all Indochinese Americans **Publications:** THE CHANNEL (quarterly).

---

171   *Santa Ana*

Orange County Coalition for Immigrant Rights

1300 South Grand
Santa Ana, CA 97205
Fr. Jaime Soto, Chair
(714) 567-7470

Services Offered: AD, CE, RS, SS. **Established:** 1987. **Staff:** 2. **Clientele:** Southeast Asia, Central America/Caribbean.

---

172   *Santa Ana*

Orange County Community Consortium

430 South Standard Avenue
Santa Ana, CA 92701
Mary Ann Salamida, Executive Director
(714) 835-3097

Services Offered: AD, CU, CE, EC, ED, HE, RS, SS. **Established:** 1986. **Staff:** 5. **Budget:** $150,000. **Religious Affiliation:** Ecumenical. **Clientele:** Central America/Caribbean, Southeast Asia. Coalition of public and private health, education and social service providers concerned about conditions among refugees and immigrants, principally individuals from Mexico, Central America and Southeast Asia.

---

173   *Santa Ana*

Vietnamese Community of Orange County

3701 West McFadden Avenue, Suite M
Santa Ana, CA 92704
Tuong Nguyen, Executive Director
(714) 775-2637

Services Offered: CU, EC, ED, SS. **Established:** 1978. **Staff:** 20. **Budget:** $500,000. **Clientele:** Southeast Asia. Cultural, economic and social services for Indochinese refugees in Orange County. **Publications:** CONG DONG NEWSLETTER (monthly, free).

---

174   *Santa Clara*

Catholic Charities. Immigration & Refugee Programs

100 North Winchester Boulevard
Santa Clara, CA 95050
James M. Purcell, Executive Director
(408) 249-2541

Services Offered: EC, ED, SS. **Staff:** 120.
Budget: $5,000,000. **BIA. Religious
Affiliation:** Catholic. **Clientele:** World.
Immigration Counseling Center: assists persons with
immigration visa petitions, political asylum applications, suspension and witholding of deportation, citizenship, legalization, etc. The Refugee Programs
Office handles the sponsorship and resettlement of
refugees from throughout the world (approximately
1,200 annually) plus related services such as job
placement, adjustment to permanent resident status,
etc. Also operates a day care program for elderly
refugees. **Publications:** CHARITIES IN ACTION
(newsletter); Annual report.

---

175   *Santa Cruz*

Central Coast Sanctuary

Box 3132
Santa Cruz, CA 95063
Laura Martinez-Chavez, Director
(408) 426-4467

Services Offered: SA. **Religious Affiliation:**
Ecumenical. **Clientele:** Central America/Caribbean.
Public sanctuary for refugees fleeing Central America.

---

176   *Santa Monica*

Westside Legal Services

612 Colorado Avenue, Suite 107
Santa Monica, CA 90401
Elena Popp, Executive Director
(213) 396-5456

Services Offered: LE. **Established:** 1981.
Staff: 8. **Budget:** $275,000. **Clientele:** World.
Immigration legal assistance and representation to
low income individuals requiring help with immigration matters: amnesty, denial & appeals, registration
and advice & referrals.

---

177   *Santa Rosa*

Catholic Immigration & Resettlement Office

Box 4900
Santa Rosa, CA 95402
Herb Castillo, Director
(707) 578-6000

Services Offered: AD, CE, LE, SS.
Established: 1981. **Staff:** 5. **Budget:** $100,000.
BIA. Religious Affiliation: Catholic.
Clientele: World, Southeast Asia, Central

America/Caribbean. Offers the following services:
visa petition processing; naturalization petitions; adjustment of status; all matters relating to legalization;
stays of deportation; language classes; education and
outreach related to immigration law and the rights of
the undocumented; and assistance with housing, job
problems and general social services and referrals.

---

178   *Santa Rosa*

Intercultural Action Center

Box 4566
Santa Rosa, CA 95402
Pam Teague, Program Coordinator
(707) 542-3773

Services Offered: AD, CU, CE, LE, SS.
Established: 1980. **Staff:** 2. **Budget:** $45,000.
BIA. Clientele: World. IAC assists refugees in becoming self-sufficient so that they may become productive citizens while maintaining their cultural identity. Also identifies, coordinates and integrates community resources for the benefit of the refugees.
Maintains central intake unit, employment counseling and language training. Affiliated with the
International Institute of San Francisco.
Publications: NEW FACES (bimonthly newsletter, free).

---

179   *Seaside*

Catholic Social Services. Refugee Resettlement Program

Box 6
Seaside, CA 93955
Mary Ekise Robertson, Supervisor
(408) 394-4656

Services Offered: AD, CU, ED, SS. **Religious
Affiliation:** Catholic. **Clientele:** World,
Southeast Asia, Central America/Caribbean.
Resettlement and immigrant services for refugees in-
cludes advocacy and social services.

---

180   *Sepulveda*

Sepulveda Unitarian Universalist Society

9550 Haskell Avenue
Sepulveda, CA 91343
Rev. Charlotte Shavvers, Minister
(818) 894-9251

Services Offered: AD, CU, CE, RE, SA. **Staff:**
3. **Religious Affiliation:** Unitarian. **Clientele:**
World. Church is designated sanctuary church for

refugees fleeing persecution. **Publications:** Newsletter.

---

181 *Stockton*

Asia Pacific Concerns Committee

Box 1259
Stockton, CA 95201
Raj Rama Ya, Program Associate
(209) 465-4265

Services Offered: AD, CU, CE, ED, HE, LI, RS. **Established:** 1985. **Staff:** 2. **Budget:** $40,000. **Clientele:** Southeast Asia, Asia. APCC consists of the northern California residents who are immigrants from the Asian-Pacific region and individuals/organizations that work on Asia Pacific issues. Objectives are to to exchange views on issues (social, political and economic) affecting their daily lives. An area of concern is immigration, citizenship, refugee status, amnesty, etc.

---

182 *Stockton*

Catholic Charities. Refugee Resettlement Office

634 East Main Street
Stockton, CA 95202
Kham Baccam, Director
(209) 467-7014

Services Offered: AD, CU, CE, ED, LE, RE, SS. **Established:** 1975. **Staff:** 5. **Budget:** $144,500. **Religious Affiliation:** Catholic. **Clientele:** World. Refugee resettlement services and immigration assistance. Services: general legal and social services; employment counseling and asistance; provide sponsorships; translation and interpretation; and referrals.

---

183 *Stockton*

First Unitarian Church

2737 Pacific Avenue
Stockton, CA 95204
Rev. Robert Edward Green
(209) 466-7743

Services Offered: AD, CE, RE, SA. **Staff:** 2. **Budget:** $60,000. **Religious Affiliation:** Unitarian. **Clientele:** World, Southeast Asia, Central America/Caribbean. Sanctuary to refugees fleeing persecution. Support services and assistance to refugees. **Publications:** Newsletter (weekly); Annual Report and Directory.

---

184 *Stockton*

Holy Cross Mission

115 East Miner
Stockton, CA 95202
Rev. Justo Andres, Coordinator
(209) 941-0216

Services Offered: AD, CU, ED, LE, RE, SS. **Religious Affiliation:** Episcopal. **Clientele:** Central America/Caribbean, Southeast Asia, World. Broad based advocacy, outreach, educational, legal and social services for refugees and immigrants.

---

185 *Stockton*

International Rescue Committee

4910 Claremont Avenue
Stockton, CA 95207
Mary Waltermire, Director
(209) 473-2923

Services Offered: AD, LI, SS. **BIA. Clientele:** World. American voluntary agency devoted to helping refugees escape from religious, racial and political persecution. Operates large resettlement program throughout the United States.

---

186 *Stockton*

Lao Khmu Association

425 North California Street
Stockton, CA 95202
Boon H. Khoonsrivong, Executive Director
(209) 463-3410

Services Offered: AD, CE, SS. **Established:** 1985. **Staff:** 11. **Budget:** $200,000. **Religious Affiliation:** Presbyterian. **Clientele:** Southeast Asia. Support, advocacy and social services for Laotians and other refugees from Southeast Asia.

---

187 *Stockton*

World Relief

4212 North Pershing
Stockton, CA 95207
Joy Dorman, Supervisor
(209) 952-1414

Services Offered: AD, SS. **Established:** 1985. **Staff:** 3. **BIA. Clientele:** World. Family reunification and resettlement services offered to refugees from throughout the world.

---

188 — Sunnyvale

Sunyvale Community Services

810 West McKinley Avenue
Sunnyvale, CA 94086
Janet Gundrum, Executive Director
(408) 738-4321

Services Offered: SS. **Established**: 1970.
Staff: 12. **Budget**: $500,000. **Clientele**: World,
Southeast Asia, Central America/Caribbean.
Following services offered to refugees and immigrants: emergency assistance; escorted transportation and case management for seniors; social adjustment services; home care assistance; and interpretation and translation services. Special emphasis on Spanish, Vietnamese and Chinese-speaking individuals.
Publications: Directory.

189 — Sylmar

Immigration Service of Santa Rosa

Box 4377
Sylmar, CA 91342
Eduardo Palacios, Director
(818) 361-4341

Services Offered: AD, LE, RS, SS. **BIA**.
Clientele: Central America/Caribbean. Legal and related immigration counseling for refugees and the undocumented.

190 — Union City

Afghan Center

6 Union Square, Suite G
Union City, CA 94587
Zalmy Popal
(415) 487-5540

Services Offered: AD, CU, RE, SS. **Religious Affiliation**: Church of Christ. **Clientele**: Asia.
Church World Service affiliate provides refugee resettlement program for Afghan refugees.

191 — Van Nuys

International Institute of Los Angeles

14646 Sherman Way
Van Nuys, CA 91405
Milagros Mercado, Director
(818) 780-1155

Services Offered: AD, CU, CE, EC, ED, SS.
Established: 1914. **BIA**. **Clientele**: World.
Promotes the integration into society of individuals

in cultural transition, assisting them in becoming economically and socially self-sufficient participants into their new homeland. Serves immigrants, refugees, and asylees from throughout the world.

192 — Van Nuys

Tolstoy Foundation

14553 Delano Street, Suite 211
Van Nuys, CA 91411
Michael Popov, Director
(818) 782-0420

Services Offered: ED, SS. **Established**: 1975.
Staff: 4. **Clientele**: World. Services for the foreign born includes a refugee resettlement programs.

193 — Visalia

O.L.A. Immigration Rights Center

115 West Main
Visalia, CA 93291
Teresa de la Rosa, Director
(209) 627-6291

Services Offered: AD, CU, CE, LE. **Clientele**:
Central America/Caribbean. Advocacy, community outreach services and legal advice and representation in immigration matters.

194 — Watsonville

Immigration Project

406 Main Street, Suite 217
Watsonville, CA 95076
Jane Yokoyama, Contact
(408) 724-5667

Services Offered: AD, CE, LE, SS. **Clientele**:
Central America/Caribbean, World. Provides assistance to immigrants, including advocacy, social services, legal counseling and referral.

195 — Watsonville

People's Immigration Service

6 Alexander Street
Watsonville, CA 95076
Amy Locks, Coordinator
(408) 425-5852

Services Offered: AD, CE, LE. **Established**:
1982. **Clientele**: Central America/Caribbean.
Advocacy and community outreach and legal advice

and referrals on all immigration-related matters.

---

196   *West Hollywood*
City of West Hollywood. City Council

8611 Santa Monica Boulevard
West Hollywood, CA 90069
(213) 398-1331

Services Offered: AD, CE, SA. **Clientele:**
Central America/Caribbean. City of West Hollywood
is a declared public sanctuary for those fleeing persecution in Central America.

---

197   *Alamosa*
Christian Community Services

Box 984
Alamosa, CO 81101
Donna Peichel, Guatemalan Advocate
(719) 589-6464

Services Offered: AD, CU, CE, ED, HE, LE, SS.
Established: 1985. **Staff:** 1. **Budget:** $4,000.
Religious Affiliation: Ecumenical. **Clientele:**
Central America/Caribbean. Services provided for
refugees and immigrants in the San Luis Valley in
Southern Colorado. **Publications:** MESSENGER
(newsletter).

---

198   *Aurora*
Vietnamese American Cultural Alliance of Colorado

986 South Ventura Way
Aurora, CO 80017
Henry Tuoc Pham, President
(303) 368-0657

Services Offered: CU, CE, ED, LI, RS, SS.
Established: 1980. **Staff:** 4. **Clientele:** World,
Southeast Asia. Support services for Vietnamese
refugees in Colorado. **Publications:** Newsletter;
monographs.

---

199   *Denver*
Catholic Immigration and Refugee Services

3417 West 38th Avenue
Denver, CO 80211
Barbara Carr, Coordinator
(303) 458-0222

Services Offered: LE, SS. **Established:** 1974.
Staff: 10. **BIA. Religious Affiliation:**
Catholic. **Clientele:** World. Goal of the immigration program is to provide legal assistance for family
reunification and obtaining asylum for those residing
in the service area. Services: visa processing, adjustment of status, court representation and political asylum; community education; and translation. The goal
of the resettlement program is to assist refugees to
achieve self-sufficiency in the shortest time possible.
Offers: pre-arrival sponsorship, orientation and travel
coordination; and initial and post-3 month assistance
(orientation, registrations, interpretation, etc.).
Publications: Annual Report.

---

200   *Denver*
Central American Refugee Project

1400 Lafayette
Denver, CO 80218
Cheryl Martinez, Coordinator
(303) 832-4329

Services Offered: AD, CE, LE, SS.
Established: 1982. **Clientele**: Central
America/Caribbean. Provide pro bono legal aid and
social service assistance for Central Americans seeking political asylum in the United States and Canada.

201   *Denver*
Colorado Refugee and Immigrant Services Program

190 East Ninth Avenue, Room 390
Denver, CO 80203
Laurel Bagan, State Refugee Coordinator
(303) 863-8211

Services Offered: EC, ED, HE, SS.
Established: 1980. **Staff**: 18. **Budget**:
$3,358,000. **Clientele**: World, Southeast Asia.
CRISP provides cash assistance, medical assistance
and self-sufficiency services to refugees residing in
Colorado. In addition to administration and refugee
services coordination, CRISP provides refugee services directly and through purchase of service contracts. Funding is from the federal Office of Refugee
Resettlement. Approximately 1,000 refugees were resettled in FY 1987. **Publications**: GRAPEVINE
(bimonthly newsletter, free); Annual Report.

202   *Denver*
Ecumenical Refugee Services

190 East Ninth Street, Suite 420
Denver, CO 80203
Patricia Vorwerk, Director
(303) 425-1179

Services Offered: AD, CU, ED, EC, LE, RE, SS.
Established: 1979. **Religious Affiliation**:
Ecumenical. **Clientele**: World. Broad range of services for refugees in Colorado, from advocacy to social services to help with new life and make refugee
self-sufficient in as short a time as possible.

203   *Denver*
Jewish Family and Children's Service

300 South Dahlia
Denver, CO 80222

Jerry Grossfeld, Executive Director
(303) 321-3115

Services Offered: AD, CU, SS. **Religious
Affiliation**: Jewish. **Clientele**: World.
Resettlement services for refugees, includes orienta-
tion, acculturation, counseling, etc.

204   *Denver*
Lutheran Refugee Resettlement

3245 West 31st Avenue
Denver, CO 80211
Ruth Dieck, Director
(303) 433-3301

Services Offered: AD, CU, CE, ED, LE, RE, SS.
Established: 1975. **Religious Affiliation**:
Lutheran. **Clientele**: World. Seek and assist sponsors for refugees within congregations and through
coordination with Lutheran Immigration & Refugee
Services. Services range from legal representation and
immigration counseling to case management and material assistance.

205   *Denver*
U.S. Department of Health & Human Services. Family Support Administration. Office of Refugee Resettlement

1961 Stout Street
Denver, CO 80294
Vo Van Ha, Coordinator
(303) 844-6130

Services Offered: **Established**: 1982.
Clientele: World. Federal regional office from the
U.S. Office of Refugee Resettlement. Administers six
state refugee programs.

206   *Englewood*
Ukrainian Research Foundation

6931 South Yosemite Street
Englewood, CO 80112
Bodhan S. Wynar, President
(303) 770-1220

Services Offered: CU, CE, LI, RS.
Established: 1975. **Clientele**: USSR. Scholarly
group concerned with preserving Ukrainian heritage in
the United States and provides information about
Ukrainian affairs, especially efforts to secure human
rights. **Publications**: Monographs.

207 *Pueblo*

Catholic Social Service. Resettlement Program

302 Jefferson
Pueblo, CO 81004
Shirley Knafelc, Contact
(303) 544-4215

Services Offered: AD, CU, ED, LE, SS.
Established: 1942. **Religious Affiliation:**
Catholic. **Clientele:** World. Refugee Resettlement
Program assists new arrivals adapt to life in Denver
and provide social services and counseling to help
with transition.

208 *Bridgeport*

Episcopal Social Service

1067 Park Avenue
Bridgeport, CT 06604
James Grant, Executive Director
(203) 366-4356

Services Offered: CU, RS, SS. **Established:**
1982. **Staff:** 3. **Religious Affiliation:**
Episcopal. **Clientele:** World. Refugee and immigrant assistance services and programs include: resettlement; social services; case management; cultutal
orientation and training; and information and referral.
Publications: Newsletter.

209 *Bridgeport*

International Institute of Connecticut

670 Clinton Avenue
Bridgeport, CT 06605
Myra M. Oliver, Executive Director
(203) 336-0141

Services Offered: AD, CU, EC, ED, LE, SS.
Established: 1918. **BIA. Clientele:** World.
Established over 70 years ago to assist immigrants
and their families, and to promote cross cultural understanding and cooperation in the community.
Services and programs include: refugee resettlement;
immigration counseling and referral; job orientation
and training; cultural orientation; interpretation and
translation; cultural activities; and social services to
meet the needs of the foreign born.

210 *Bridgeport*

Jewish Family Service. Resettlement Services

2370 Park Avenue
Bridgeport, CT 06604
Harvey Paris, Executive Director
(203) 366-5438

Services Offered: AD, SS. **Established:** 1922.
Religious Affiliation: Jewish. **Clientele:**
World. Refugee resettlement services are coordinated
through the Hebrew Immigrant Aid Society.

211 *Hartford*

Catholic Charities. Migration and Refugee Services

125 Market Street
Hartford, CT 06103

Sr. Dorothy Strelchun, Director
(203) 548-0059

Services Offered: AD, ED, RE, SS.
Established: 1975. **Staff**: 12. **Budget**: $450,000.
BIA. **Religious Affiliation**: Catholic.
Clientele: World. Offers resettlement services to refugees including reception and placement, case management, and employment services. Immigration component deals with all types of immigration matters. **Publications**: Annual Report.

212   Hartford
Connecticut Department of Human Resources. State Refugee Coordinator

1049 Asylum Avenue
Hartford, CT 06115
Elliot Ginsberg, Coordinator
(203) 566-4329

Services Offered: AD, EC, ED, HE, SS.
Clientele: World. Statewide coordination of federal, state and private resources for effective refugee resettlement including cash and medical assistance, support services and such other activities as necessary.

213   Hartford
International Institute of Connecticut

25 Charter Oak Avenue
Hartford, CT 06106
Robert Money, Director
(203) 278-1987

Services Offered: AD, CU, CE, EC, ED, LE, LI, SS. **BIA**. **Clientele**: World. Extensive services, from advocacy to legal representation in deportation hearings. Programs and services designed to assist the foreign born become culturally, socially and economically self-sufficient.

214   Hartford
Vietnamese Catholic Community in Connecticut

494 New Britain Avenue
Hartford, CT 06106
Rev. Peter D. Young, Board Chair
(203) 246-4856

Services Offered: AD, CU, ED, RE, SS.
Established: 1981. **Staff**: 9. **Budget**: $10,000.
Religious Affiliation: Catholic. **Clientele**: Southeast Asia. Offers a wide variety of services to

the Vietnamese Community through the Catholic Church. **Publications**: TIN MUNG (quarterly newsletter, free); Annual Report.

215   Stamford
Jewish Family Service

Box 3038
Stamford, CT 06905
Benjamin Greenspan, Executive Director
(203) 322-6938

Services Offered: AD, CU, EC, LE, RE, SS.
Established: 1975. **Staff**: 5. **Budget**: $150,000.
Religious Affiliation: Jewish. **Clientele**: Europe, Asia. JFS Refugee Resettlement Program works closely with the Hebrew Immigrant Aid Society to welcome and integrate newcomers into the community. Services are offered to all religious groups. Volunteers, under professional supervision, provide most of the services for the emigres, including finding housing, preparing for employment and making friendships with Americans. **Publications**: JFS REPORTER (quarterly newsletter).

216   West Hartford
Greater Hartford Jewish Federation

333 Bloomfield Avenue
West Hartford, CT 06117
Don Cooper, Executive Director
(203) 232-4483

Services Offered: CU, CE, RE, RS, SS.
Religious Affiliation: Jewish. **Clientele**: World. Assists refugees and immigrants in the Jewish community.

217   West Hartford
Khmer Health Advocates

8 Lowell Road
West Hartford, CT 06119
Mary Scully, Executive Director
(203) 233-0313

Services Offered: AD, HE, LI, RS, SS.
Established: 1982. **Staff**: 5. **Budget**: $100,000.
Clientele: Southeast Asia. KHA is a non-profit Cambodian Mutual Assistance Society which is committed to the health of the Cambodian family in America. Provides several essential services to the 2,000 Cambodians in Connecticut: cross-cultural mental health; cultural awareness; integration of Western medical practice and traditional Khmer medicine; and family reunification. Operates the

Cambodian Family Reunification Project which is designed to provide assistance to relatives in the camps at the Thailand-Cambodian border. **Publications:** KHMER-AMERICAN HEALTH (quarterly newsletter, $10).

---

218 *Westport*

Unitarian Church. Sanctuary Committee

10 Lyons Plain Road
Westport, CT 06880
Rev. Frank Hall, Contact
(203) 227-7205

Services Offered: AD, CE, SA. **Religious Affiliation:** Unitarian. **Clientele:** Central America/Caribbean. Advocacy, outreach and sanctuary for Salvadoran and Guatemalan refugees.

---

219 *New Castle*

Delaware Department of Health & Social Services. Division of Economic Services.

Box 906, CP Building
New Castle, DE 19720
Thomas P. Eichler, Refugee Coordinator
(302) 421-6153

Services Offered: AD, EC, ED, HE, SS. **Clientele:** World. Responsible for statewide coordination of federal, state and private resources for effective refugee resettlement including cash and medical assistance, support services and other activities.

---

220 *Wilmington*

Catholic Charities. Refugee Resettlement Program

100 North Philadelphia Pike
Wilmington, DE 19809
Richard V. Pryor, Executive Director
(302) 573-3140

Services Offered: AD, CU, RE, SS. **Religious Affiliation:** Catholic. **Clientele:** Southeast Asia, World. Refugee resettlement program is coordinated through US Catholic Conference Migration & Refugee Services. Activities range from sponsorship development to counseling and other social acculturation services.

---

221 *Wilmington*

Delaware Department of Justice. Service for Foreign Born

820 North French Street, 7th Floor
Wilmington, DE 19801
Gladys C. Johnson, Director
(302) 571-3047

Services Offered: AD, LI. **Established:** 1927. **Staff:** 2. **BIA. Clientele:** World. Provides information, assistance and counseling on matters relating to immigration and citizenship, though agency does not act as legal counsel and does not engage in the practice of law. **Publications:** Annual Report.

222 *Washington*

Adventist Community Services

6840 Eastern Avenue NW
Washington, DC 20012
Monte Sahlin, Coordinator
(202) 722-6450   Fax: (202) 722-6990

Services Offered: AD, RE, SS. **Staff**: 2.
Budget: $95,000. **Religious Affiliation**:
Seventh Day Adventist. **Clientele**: World.
Responsible for the placing of Adventist refugees
through local sponsorships. **Publications**: A.C.S.
NEWSLETTER (quarterly, free).

223 *Washington*

American Arab Anti-Discrimination Committee

1731 Connecticut Avenue
Washington, DC 20008
Al Mokhiber, Contact
(202) 244-2990

Services Offered: AD, CU, CE, EC, ED, LE, LI,
RS, SS. **Clientele**: Middle East. Advocacy organization for the rights of Arab-Americans. In addition to
educational and community outreach programs offers
legal advice and representation in immigration-related
proceedings.

224 *Washington*

American Immigration Lawyers Association

1000 16th Street NW, Suite 604
Washington, DC 20036
Warren Leiden, Executive Director
(202) 331-0046

Services Offered: LE. **Established**: 1946.
Staff: 9. **BIA**. Professional association, affiliated
with the American Bar Association, concerned with
immigration, asylum and nationality law. Holds seminars and issues publications relating to immigration
and nationality law. **Publications**: AILA
MONTHLY MAILINGS ($295); AILA
IMMIGRATION JOURNAL (quarterly, $20);
Directory of Members; List of Publications.

225 *Washington*

American Public Welfare Association. Task Force on Immigration Reform

810 First Street NE
Washington, DC 20002
Eliza May, Project Manager
(202) 682-0100

Services Offered: AD. **Established**: 1987.
Staff: 42. **Clientele**: World. **Publications**:
NEWS (quarterly); PUBLIC WELFARE
DIRECTORY ($20).

226 *Washington*

American Red Cross. International Services

17th and D Streets NW
Washington, DC 20006
Richard Schubert, President
(202) 737-8300

Services Offered: SS. **Established**: 1881.
Clientele: World. Assists with family reunification
through identification and location of separated
refugee families. Contacts should be made through
local Red Cross chapter. **Publications**: RED
CROSS NEWS (quarterly, free); Annual Report.

227 *Washington*

Americans For Immigration Control

717 Second Street NE
Washington, DC 20002
Palmer A. Stacy, President
(202) 543-3719

Services Offered: CE, RS. **Established**: 1982.
Staff: 3. **Budget**: $385,000. **Clientele**: World.
Political organizing and research relating to a more effective implementation of existing immigration laws,
especially limiting immigration and enforcing employer sanctions. **Publications**: IMMIGRATION
WATCH (newsletter).

228 *Washington*

Armenian Assembly of America

122 C Street NW, Suite 350
Washington, DC 20001
Ross Vartian, Executive Director
(202) 393-3434   Fax: (212) 638-4904

Services Offered: AD, CU, CE, SS. **Clientele**:
USSR. Advocates for a humane and appropriate response to the plight of Armenian refugees, providing
direct assistance as well as public education and
community outreach.

229 *Washington*

Casa de la Esperanza

Box 43719
Washington, DC 20010
(202) 667-5444

Services Offered: AD, CU, CE, EC, ED, LE, SS.
Established: 1984. **Staff:** 3. **Budget:** $70,000.
Religious Affiliation: Ecumenical. **Clientele:**
Central America/Caribbean. Provide social services to
assist Central American refugees as well as ecumeni-
cal and community outreach programs.
Publications: PUERTA ABIERTA (newsletter).

230 *Washington*

Catholic Charities. Refugee Service Center

1501 Columbia Road NW
Washington, DC 20009
Ywyet Dang, Director
(202) 667-9006

Services Offered: AD, CU, RE, SS.
Established: 1981. **Staff:** 3. **Religious
Affiliation:** Catholic. **Clientele:** World. General
social services for refugees in the Metropolitan area.

231 *Washington*

Center for Applied Linguistics. Refugee Service Center

1118 22nd Street NW
Washington, DC 20037
Allene Grognet, Director
(202) 429-9292   Fax: (202) 659-5641

Services Offered: ED, LI, RS. **Established:**
1980. **Staff:** 5. **Clientele:** Southeast Asia, Europe.
Provides technical and material support to the
Department of State-funded Overseas Refugee
Training Program. Provide linkage between overseas
training program and domestic service providers in
U.S. resettlement communities. **Publications:** IN
AMERICA: PERSPECTIVES ON REFUGEE
RESETTLEMENT (bi-monthly).

232 *Washington*

Center for Immigration Studies

1775 T Street NW
Washington, DC 20009
David Simcox, Director
(202) 328-7228

Services Offered: CE, LI, RS. **Established:**
1985. **Staff:** 5. **Budget:** $110,000. **Clientele:**
World. Nonprofit research and educational institution
concerned with socio-political and economic implications of U.S. immigration policy. Advocate for effective enforcement of immigration laws (and employer
sanctions) and providing reliable data for decision-
makers.

233 *Washington*

Central American Refugee Center

3112 Mt. Pleasant Street NW
Washington, DC 20010
Sylvia Rosales, Director
(202) 328-9799

Services Offered: AD, CE, CU, LE, HE, RE, LI,
SS. **Established:** 1981. **Staff:** 15. **Budget:**
$$425,000. **BIA. Clientele:** Central
America/Caribbean. System of emergency services
available to refugees from Central America. Includes
legal and health services, information & referral and
general social services. Community educational
outreach regarding abuses of American policy in
Central America. Social service referrals.
Publications: CARECEN NEWS (bimonthly).

234 *Washington*

Commission for the Study of International Migration and Cooperative Economic Development

1111 18th Street NW, Suite 800
Washington, DC 20036
Diego C. Asencio, Chairman
(202) 254-4954   Fax: (202) 254-4965

Services Offered: RS. **Established:** 1987.
Staff: 3. **Clientele:** Mexico, Central
America/Caribbean, South America. The
Commission was created by the Immigration Reform
and Control Act of 1986 and the 12 Commissioners
were appointed by the Congress. Charge: in consulta-
tion with the governments of Mexico and other send-
ing countries in the Western Hemisphere to examine
the conditions which contribute to unauthorized mi-
gration to the U.S. Charged with reporting to the
President and Congress by July 1990 on mutually
beneficial, reciprocal trade and investment programs
to alleviate such conditions. The mandate represents
the first official inquiry by the U.S. into the linkages
between undocumented migration and the level of
economic development of countries from which sig-
nificant numbers of people emigrate. **Publications:**

NEWSLETTER (quarterly, free).

235   *Washington*

District of Columbia Department of Human Services. Office of Refugee Resettlement

1660 L Street NW
Washington, DC 20036
Hiram Ruiz, Acting Director
(202) 673-3420

Services Offered: AD, EC, ED, HE, SS. **Clientele**: World. Coordination of federal, district and private resources for effective refugee resettlement.

236   *Washington*

Ethiopian Community Center

2607 24th Street NW, Suite 3
Washington, DC 20008
Lissane Negussie, Executive Director
(202) 328-3102

Services Offered: AD, CU, CE, EC, SS. **Established**: 1980. **Staff**: 5. **Budget**: $150,000. **Clientele**: Africa. The objectives of ECC is to provide resettlement to Ethiopian refugees and immigrants who resettle in the Washington metropolitan area. Major programs are: acculturation counseling, job placement, immigration counseling, information and referral, transportation, translation and interpretation, and community outreach and advocacy. **Publications**: ECC NEWS (quarterly, free); Annual Report.

237   *Washington*

Federation for American Immigration Reform

1666 Connecticut Avenue NW, Suite 400
Washington, DC 20009
Dan Stein, Executive Director
(202) 328-7004   Fax: (202) 387-3447

Services Offered: CE, LI, RS. **Established**: 1979. **Staff**: 15. Supports tightening of American immigration laws and the enforcement of laws against undocumented individuals in the U.S. Monitors and reports on immigration laws and policies. Works to establish a single combined ceiling for immigrants and refugees. **Publications**: FAIR NEWSLETTER; FAIR IMMIGRATION REPORT.

238   *Washington*

General Conference of Seventh-Day Adventists. Refugee Affairs Office

6840 Eastern Avenue NW
Washington, DC 20012
Rosemary Entz, Refugee Coordinator
(202) 722-6146

Services Offered: SS. **Religious Affiliation**: Seventh Day Adventist. **Clientele**: World. Sponsorship and resettlement services for refugees. **Publications**: Newsletter.

239   *Washington*

George Washington University. National Law Center. Immigration Clinic

720 20th Street NW
Washington, DC 20052
Paul Grussendorf, Supervisory Attorney
(202) 994-7463

Services Offered: AD, LE. **Established**: 1980. **Staff**: 11. **BIA**. **Clientele**: World. Primarily representation in deportation and exclusion hearing, and filings of certain visa applications.

240   *Washington*

Guatemala Human Rights Commission/USA

1359 Monroe Street NE
Washington, DC 20017
Alice Zachmann, Coordinator
(202) 529-6599

Services Offered: AD, ED, LI, RS. **Established**: 1982. **Staff**: 2. **Budget**: $50,000. **Clientele**: Central America/Caribbean. Through its considerable library of documented violations of human rights and reports on conditions in Guatemala, the Commission aids professional advocates in search of legal documentation for political asylum claims. It also provides information for publications, researchers, international and national organizations, and refugee support groups in the United States and abroad. **Publications**: INFORMATION BULLETIN (bi-monthly, $10); QUARTERLY REPORT ON HUMAN RIGHTS ABUSES ($8/issue); HUMAN RIGHTS ALERT (irregular); monographs.

241   *Washington*

Indochina Resource Action Center

1628 16th Street, 3rd Floor
Washington, DC 20009
Le Xuan Khoa, President
(202) 667-4690   Fax: (202) 667-6449

Services Offered: AD, CU, CE, LE, LI, SS.
Established: 1979. **Staff:** 8. **Budget:** $$350,000.
Clientele: Southeast Asia. IRAC's mission is to
assist the Indochinese in the United States in their
transition from dependent refugees to a responsible
and productive Asian-American minority. For this
purpose, IRAC has committed itself to serve as a
voice and a resource to all Indochinese ethnic groups
in the U.S. Addresses the long term development of
the Indochinese community in America. IRAC's pro-
jects reflect its continuing development objectives.
These include: education; economic development; cit-
izenship education; leadership development; resource
development; preservation of ethnic heritage; and co-
operation with established community development
agencies, including other ethnic and minority groups.
Publications: THE BRIDGE (quarterly newsletter,
$15); INDOCHINESE BUSINESS DIRECTORY
(annual).

242   *Washington*

International Catholic Migration Commission

1319 F Street NW, Suite 820
Washington, DC 20004

Services Offered: AD, CE, SS. **Religious
Affiliation:** Catholic. **Clientele:** World. Links
Catholic assistance agencies in both first asylum and
refugee resettlement countries, providing logistical
and financial assistance for their emigration process-
ing activities. Administers U.S. component of
Orderly Departure Program.

243   *Washington*

International Rescue Committee

1825 Connecticut Avenue NW, Suite 219
Washington, DC 20009
Ray Evans, Contact
(202) 667-7714

Services Offered: AD, SS. **Clientele:** World.
One of the leading nonsectarian refugee resettlement
agencies in the United States. Offices throughout the
world.

244   *Washington*

Jesuit Refugee Service

1424 16th Street NW
Washington, DC 20036
Rev. Simon Smith, National Coordinator
(202) 462-5200

Services Offered: AD, CE, RE, RS.
Established: 1983. **Budget:** $$12,000.
Religious Affiliation: Catholic. **Clientele:**
World. Advocacy of refugee issues and direct assis-
tance in applying for refugee status in the United
States. **Publications:** MUSTARD SEED (bi-
monthly newsletter).

245   *Washington*

Lutheran Immigration & Refugee Services

5121 Colorado Avenue NW
Washington, DC 20011
Ruth McLean, Director
(202) 829-7640

Services Offered: AD, CU, CE, RE, SS.
Established: 1975. **Religious Affiliation:**
Lutheran. **Clientele:** World. Coordinates and facili-
tates work of local congregations to sponsor refugees.
Refugee resettlement and family reunification programs provide support mechanisms (immigration
counseling, social services, I&R, etc.) for refugees
and immigrants.

246   *Washington*

Mennonite Immigration and Refugee Services

110 Maryland Avenue SE, Suite 502
Washington, DC 20002
Carlos Neuschwander, Director
(202) 546-8115

Services Offered: AD, CU, CE, LE, SA, SS.
Established: 1978. **Staff:** 1. **Budget:** $35,000.
BIA. Religious Affiliation: Mennonite.
Clientele: Central America/Caribbean, Asia, World.
Provides counseling to immigrants from all over the
work regarding immigration and refugee matters.
Publications: MENNONITE IMMIGRATION
AND REFUGEE NEWSLETTER (quarterly, free);
Annual Report.

247   *Washington*

National Immigration, Refugee, and Citizenship Forum

227 Massachusetts Avenue NE
Washington, DC 20002
Dale Frederick Swartz, President
(202) 544-0004

Services Offered: AD, CE, LI, RS. **Clientele:** World. National non-profit, educational organization with a broad multi-institutional and multi-ethnic membership. Mission is to establish positive working relationships among the diverse communities represented by its membership, and to promote the pro-immigrant, pro-refugee philosophy. By creating and preserving a national atmosphere conducive to and supportive of the migration and full integration of newcomers into our society, helps assure that its diverse membership can best carry out their respective missions.

248   *Washington*

Organization of Chinese Americans

2025 Eye Street NW, Suite 926
Washington, DC 20024
Melinda Yee, Executive Director
(202) 223-5000

Services Offered: ED, HE, LE. **Established:** 1974. **Clientele:** Asia. OCA is a national, non-profit, bipartisan organization of concerned Chinese Americans. Committed to: promoting the active participation of Chinese Americans in civic affairs at all levels; securing justice, equal treatment and equal opportunities for Chinese Americans; eliminating ignorance and bigotry; promoting cultural heritage; and fostering positive images of Chinese and Asian Americans. Sponsor of the Asian Immigration Coalition Forum. **Publications:** IMAGE (newsletter).

250   *Washington*

Refugee Voices

713 Monroe Street NE
Washington, DC 20017
Rev. Frank Moan, Director
(202) 832-0020

Services Offered: AD, CE, RS. **Clientele:** World. Public education organization that, through various media, attempts to inform Americans of the plight of refugees settled in the United States and those in camps throughout the world.

251   *Washington*

Refugee Women in Development

810 First Street NE
Washington, DC 20002
Sima Wali, Executive Director
(202) 628-9600

Services Offered: AD, EC, RS, SS. **Established:** 1981. **Staff:** 3. **Clientele:** World. Only national program for Third World Women who have sought asylum in the United States as refugees. Primary goal is to support the economic self-help efforts of refugee women. Extensive legal and social services. **Publications:** QUILTING BEE (newsletter).

252   *Washington*

Refugees International

220 Eye Street NE, Suite 240
Washington, DC 20002
Shephard C. Lowman, Executive Director
(202) 547-3785   Fax: (202) 547-4834

Services Offered: AD, LI, RS. **Established:** 1979. **Staff:** 4. **Budget:** $220,000. **Clientele:** World, Southeast Asia. Advocacy on protection of refugees and public educational programs on the rights of refugees. Monitors refugee situations to ensure that refugees' basic needs for protection and care are honored. Provides information to policymakers and the public through national membership organization. **Publications:** RI NEWSLETTER (quarterly, $25).

253   *Washington*

Salvadoran Refugee Committee (Oscar A. Romero)

Box 43603
Washington, DC 20010
Boris Canjura, Coordinator
(202) 265-6345

Services Offered: AD, CU, CE, RE, RS, SA, SS. **Established:** 1982. **Staff:** 7. **Religious Affiliation:** Catholic. **Clientele:** Central America/Caribbean. Objectives: collect and distribute food and clothing; help refugees secure legal and medical help; orient new arrivals; and provide Salvadoran refugees with emotional and cultural support.

254 *Washington*

Temple Sinai. Sanctuary Committee

3100 Military Road NW
Washington, DC 20015
Rabbi Fred Reiner, Contact
(202) 363-6394

Services Offered: AD, CE, SA. **Religious Affiliation:** Jewish. **Clientele:** Central America/Caribbean. Sanctuary and support services for Salvadoran and Guatemalan refugees.

255 *Washington*

Travelers Aid Society

1015 12th Street NW
Washington, DC 20005
Pauline Dunn, Executive Director
(202) 347-0101

Services Offered: AD, LE, SS. **Established:** 1913. **Staff:** 21. **Budget:** $700,000. **Clientele:** World. Legal assistance, advice and referral as well as limited social services for immigrants and refugees in Metropolitan Washington. **Publications:** TRAVELERS AID NEWS; Annual Report.

256 *Washington*

U.S. Catholic Conference. Migration & Refugee Services

1312 Massachusetts Avenue NW
Washington, DC 20005
Rev. Nicholas DiMarzio, Director
(202) 659-6630   Fax: (202) 614-1211

Services Offered: AD, CU, CE, RE, RS, SS. **Established:** 1920. **Staff:** 150. **Budget:** $22,000,000. **BIA. Religious Affiliation:** Catholic. **Clientele:** World. M&RS is responsible for all immigrant, migrant and refugee activities conducted by the Catholic Church in the United States. The agency coordinates a national network or more than 170 diocesan refugee resettlement offices and 70 local immigration offices. It works with public sector and private sector agencies to resettle and help assimilate individuals and families in American society. In FY 1987, the M&RS network resettled 26,081 refugees, 39.5 percent of the total admitted to the U.S. during that time period. Approximately 80% of the refugees resettled were family reunification cases. M&RS welcomes refugees from all nations, ethnic groups and religions. Besides arranging to meet refugees' basic needs for food and shelter, M&RS provides orientation to the community, ensure that urgent health needs are met, and see that children are registered for school. **Publications:** UPDATE (monthly, $25); LEGISLATIVE MONITOR (irregular, free); Annual Report; List of Publications.

257 *Washington*

U.S. Catholic Conference. Migration & Refugee Services. Regional Immigration Office

1221 Massachusetts Avenue NW
Washington, DC 20005
William O'Brien, Director
(202) 659-6625

Services Offered: AD, CU, LE, RE, SS. **Staff:** 4. **BIA. Religious Affiliation:** Catholic. **Clientele:** World. Regional office responsible for Southeastern United States.

258 *Washington*

U.S. Congress. Congressional Border Caucus

416 CHOB
Washington, DC 20515
Rep. Ronald Coleman, Chair
(202) 225-4831

Clientele: Central America/Caribbean. Bipartisan group of border members from California, Arizona, New Mexico and Texas that address matters of mutual concern, including immigration legislation.

259 *Washington*

U.S. Congress. Congressional Human Rights Caucus

H2-552 HOB Annex II
Washington, DC 20515
Rep. Tom Lantos, Co-Chair
(202) 226-4040   Fax: (202) 225-3127

Clientele: World. 160 members aid individuals denied basic human rights throughout the world.

260 *Washington*

U.S. Congress. House Committee on the Judiciary. Subcommittee on Immigration, Refugees & International Law

2137 RHOB
Washington, DC 20515

Rep. Bruce A. Morrison, Chairman
(202) 225-5727   Fax: (202) 225-1958

Clientele: World. Studies and makes recommendations on immigration and naturalization; citizenship; admission of refugees; treaties and international law; passports; Foreign Sovereign Immunity; and relevant oversight.

---

261   *Washington*

U.S. Congress. Senate Border Caucus

328 HSOB
Washington, DC 20510
Sen. Dennis De Concini, Co-Chair
(202) 224-4521   Fax: (202) 224-8698

Established: 1983. **Clientele**: Central America/Caribbean. Bipartisan group of south and southwestern border state senators holding key committee positions to coordinate legislation and budget issues affecting law enforcement along the southern border from California to Georgia.

---

262   *Washington*

U.S. Congress. Senate Committee on the Judiciary. Subcommittee on Immigration & Refugee Affairs

518 DSOB
Washington, DC 20510
Sen. Edward M. Kennedy, Chairman
(202) 224-7878   Fax: (202) 224-2417

Clientele: World. Studies and makes recommendations on immigration, refugees and naturalization; oversight of INS and BIA; private immigration relief bills; oversight of international migration, refugee laws and policies.

---

263   *Washington*

U.S. Congress. Senate Human Rights Caucus

528 HSOB
Washington, DC 20510
Sen. William Armstrong, Chairman
(202) 224-5941

Clientele: World. Bipartisan group which meets periodically to discuss human rights issues. It seeks to provide a forum within the Senate for the cause of human rights throughout the world. The caucus seeks to integrate important human rights values into the

overall formulation of U.S. foreign policy.

---

264   *Washington*

U.S. Department of Health and Human Services. Family Support Administration. Office of Refugee Resettlement

370 L'Enfant Promenade SW
Washington, DC 20407
Phil Holman, Acting Director
(202) 252-4545   Fax: (202) 252-4683

Services Offered: SS. **Clientele**: World. ORR has primary responsibility for coordinating the domestic resettlement assistance programs. These programs - cash assistance, medical assistance, social services, etc. - are usually administered by state governments. Administers the Refugee Assistance Program which is designed to assimilate refugees and Cuban and Haitian entrants into American society. ORR develops the federal assessment of the likely domestic impacts of the admission of refugees. **Publications**: ANNUAL REPORT TO CONGRESS (free); REFUGEE PROGRAM UPDATE.

---

265   *Washington*

U.S. Department of Justice. Immigration and Naturalization Service

425 Eye Street NW
Washington, DC 20536
James L. Buck, Acting Commissioner
(202) 633-1900   Fax: (202) 633-3296

Clientele: World. Dual mission of providing information and service to the general public, while concurrently exercising its enforcement responsibilities. Responsible for administering and enforcing the immigration and nationality laws of the U.S. relating to the admission, exclusion, deportation and naturalization of aliens; responsible for preventing undocumented entry into the U.S.; investigates, apprehends and removes undocumented aliens; and overseas the operations of the U.S. Border Patrol. Commissioner serves as the principal adviser to the Attorney General and the President on immigration & nationality policy. INS overseas offices interview applicants to determine if they qualify as refugees. **Publications**: INS REPORTER; STATISTICAL YEARBOOK (annual).

U.S. Department of Justice. Office of Special Counsel for Immigration-Related Unfair Employment Practices

Box 65490
Washington, DC 20035
Lawrence J. Siskind, Special Counsel
(800) 255-7688   Fax: (202) 633-4371

Services Offered: Responsible for investigating and prosecuting charges of national origin and citizenship status discrimination in hiring, firing, or recruitment. Jurisdiction over national origin cases is limited to those not covered by the U.S. Equal Employment Opportunity Commission. Special Counsel files complaints before an administrative law judge based on charges filed with this Office, or on its own independent investigations. Coordinates with other federal agencies in promoting public awareness of the antidiscrimination provisions of IRCA through conferences, public service announcements and distribution of information.

---

267   *Washington*

U.S. Department of Labor. Bureau of International Labor Affairs

200 Constitution Avenue NW, Room S2235
Washington, DC 20210
Shellyn McCaffrey, Deputy Under Secretary
(202) 523-6043   Fax: (202) 523-9613

Services Offered: EC. **Clientele**: World. Formulates international economic and trade policies affecting American workers and assists in the development of U.S. immigration policy.

---

268   *Washington*

U.S. Department of Labor. Foreign Labor Certification Division

200 Constitution Avenue NW
Washington, DC 20010
Thomas M. Bruening, Chief
(202) 535-0163   Fax: (202) 523-7312

Services Offered: EC. **Clientele**: World. Sets policies and issues guidelines for regional offices that certify applications for alien employment in the U.S. Determines whether U.S. citizens are also available for those jobs and whether employment of aliens will adversely affect similarly employed U.S. citizens.

---

269   *Washington*

U.S. Department of State. Bureau for Refugee Programs

5824 Main State Building
Washington, DC 20520
Princeton Lyman, Director
(202) 647-3964   Fax: (202) 663-1061

Services Offered: Clientele: World. Administers refugee programs within the Department of State. Responsible for setting priorities for refugee admissions and provides resources for reception and placement in the U.S. BPR contracts with voluntary agencies to pre-screen refugees to determine if they meet U.S. priorities. Develops the country reports and thus affects the basic decisions as to which national origin groups are of special humanitarian concern to the U.S. The INS field offices consult the BPR with regard to cases that seem to warrant special consideration and for a range of administrative decisions that must be referred to Washington. In addition to resettlement activities, the Bureau develops/implements policies related to refugee relief and assistance abroad. The BPR formulates policy for and directs U.S. refugee and migration programs and assists refugees during reception and placement. **Publications**: WORLD REFUGEE REPORT (annual).

---

270   *Washington*

U.S. Department of State. Bureau of Consular Affairs

6811 Main State Building
Washington, DC 20520
Joan M. Clark, Assistant Secretary of State
(202) 647-9576   Fax: (202) 647-0341

Services Offered: Clientele: World. Responsible for administration and enforcement of the provisions of the immigration and nationality laws, insofar as they concern the Department and the Foreign Service, for the issuance of passports, visas and related services. **Publications**: ANNUAL REPORT OF THE VISA OFFICE.

---

271   *Washington*

U.S. Department of State. Bureau of Human Rights and Humanitarian Affairs

Main State Building
Washington, DC 20520
Richard Schifter, Assistant Secretary of State
(202) 647-2126   Fax: (202) 647-9519

Established: 1978. **Staff:** 40. **BIA. Clientele:** World. Responsible for matters pertaining to human rights and humanitarian affairs, including refugees, in the conduct of the foreign policy of the U.S. Provides the Department's advice to the Immigration & Naturalization Service regarding applications for political asylum by foreign nationals. **Publications:** COUNTRY REPORTS ON HUMAN RIGHTS PRACTICES (annual, $36).

---

272   *Washington*

U.S. Department of State. Coordinator for Refugee Affairs

7526 Main State Building
Washington, DC 20520
Jewel S. Lafontant, Ambassador
(202) 647-2118   Fax: (202) 663-1061

Clientele: World. Provides policy guidance and coordination for all U.S. refugee assistance and resettlement programs (both domestic and foreign). Non-operational office whose chief function is to encourage coordination between the public and private sector agencies concerned with refugees and among the various levels of the federal government. Advises the President, Secretary of State and U.S. Attorneys General on refugee admissions policies. Based in the State Department with Ambassadorial rank the Coordinator represents the Executive Branch before Congress and the international community on refugee matters and acts as a clearinghouse on refugee affairs.

---

273   *Washington*

U.S. Office of Management and Budget. Refugee Staff Specialist

725 17th Street NW, Room 7002
Washington, DC 20503
Lisa Guzzi, Staff Specialist
(202) 395-4686

OMB is primarily responsible for assisting the President develop and maintain an effective Federal Government by reviewing organizational structure and management procedures of the executive branch. OMB specialist responsible for the Office of Refugee Resettlement (DHHS) and State Department refugee activities.

---

274   *Washington*

United Nations High Commissioner for Refugees

1718 Connecticut Avenue NW

Washington, DC 20009
John McCallin, Head of Office
(202) 387-8546   Fax: (202) 387-9038

Services Offered: LE, SS, RS. **Established:** 1951. **Clientele:** World. UNHCR was created by the General Assembly of the United Nations which recognized a universal responsibility towards refugees and displaced persons for whom new homes had still to be found as a result of the Second World War. UNHCR's mandate has been extended for five year intervals. Over 1,000 people work in more than 100 offices throughout the world. Headquarters are in Geneva. UNHCR has two main functions: to provide refugees with international protection and, at the request of the host government, assist them towards durable solutions to their problems. Helps refugees survive and get back on their own feet **Publications:** REFUGEES (monthly, free).

---

275   *Washington*

United States Committee for Refugees

1025 Vermont Avenue NW, Suite 920
Washington, DC 20005
Wells Klein, Executive Director
(202) 347-3505   Fax: (202) 347-3418

Services Offered: AD, CE, RS. **Established:** 1958. **Clientele:** World. Public information and advocacy program of the American Council for Nationalities Service. Issues publications and provides information and advocacy about refugees worldwide. Participates actively as refugee advocate in development of U.S. policy with regard to refugees in the U.S. and abroad. Consults with national and international leaders, voluntary organizations and the UN. **Publications:** WORLD REFUGEE SURVEY (annual); REFUGEE REPORTS (monthly).

---

276   *Washington*

Washington Lawyers' Committee for Civil Rights Under Law. Alien Rights Law Project

1400 Eye Street NW
Washington, DC 20005
Carolyn Waller, Director
(202) 682-5900

Services Offered: AD, CE, LE. **Established:** 1978. **Staff:** 6. **Budget:** $200,000. **Clientele:** World. Legal advice and representation in immigration, refugee, political asylum, etc. cases. **Publications:** Annual report.

---

277   *Washington*

Washington Office on Haiti

110 Maryland Avenue NE
Washington, DC 20010
Fritz Longcriame, Executive Director
(202) 543-7095

Services Offered: AD, CE, LI. **Established**:
1984. **Staff**: 3. **Religious Affiliation**: Catholic.
Clientele: Central America/Caribbean. The Office
focuses on public education and advocacy in the belief
that an increased knowledge and awareness of the
Haitian social, economic and political situation would
prompt Americans to work for positive change in that
country. The Office tracks developments in Haiti and
disseminates the information to interested government
bodies, organizations and individuals. Goal is to
prompt U.S. Government to implement more responsible policies which encourages the Haitian government to improve its record of human rights violations. Provides assistance to Haitian refugees in this
country. **Publications**: HAITI BEAT (quarterly
newsletter, $6).

278   *Washington*

Woodrow Wilson International Center

1470 Irving Street NW
Washington, DC 20010
Elaine Grant, Executive Director
(202) 667-0417

Services Offered: AD, EC, ED, LE, SS.
Established: 1969. **Staff**: 11. **Budget**: $300,000.
Clientele: South America, Central
America/Caribbean. Non-profit community agency
serving immigrants with legal aid, information and
referral, vocational training and educational programs.
Provided INS approved classes to satisfy IRCA re-
quirements for second stage.

279   *Washington*

World Relief

118 Third Street SE
Washington, DC 20003
Don Wills, Program Coordinator
(202) 544-5526

Services Offered: AD, CU, CE, RE, SS.
Established: 1980. **Religious Affiliation**:
Ecumenical. **Clientele**: World. Resettle refugees

through cooperation and assistance of local churches.

280 — Apopka

People's Law Office for Organized Workers

64 East Main Street, Suite B
Apopka, FL 32703
Francisco Campos, Attorney
(305) 886-5151

Services Offered: AD, CE, LE. **Established:** 1985. **Clientele:** Central America/Caribbean. Legal assistance and representation of indigent immigrants and refugees.

281 — Belle Glade

Florida Rural Legal Services

572 SW Second Street
Belle Glade, FL 33430
Jim Boon, Attorney
(407) 996-5266

Services Offered: LE. **Clientele:** Central America/Caribbean, World. Advice, representation and referrals in immigration-related matters.

282 — Clearwater

World Relief

Box 12207
Clearwater, FL 34616
Darlene Spears, Program Coordinator
(813) 441-9954

Services Offered: AD, CU, RE, SS. **Established:** 1980. **Religious Affiliation:** Ecumenical. **Clientele:** World. Work with local churches to assist with sponsoring and resettlement of refugees and immigrants.

283 — Fort Lauderdale

First Lutheran Church

441 NE Third Avenue
Fort Lauderdale, FL 33301
Robert Grimm, Pastor
(305) 764-3418

Services Offered: AD, LE, CE, RE, CU, SS. **Established:** 1975. **Religious Affiliation:** Lutheran. **Clientele:** World, Central America/Caribbean. Resettlement and family reunification of refugees and immigrants is coordinated through Lutheran Immigration & Refugee Services.

284 — Gainesville

University of Florida. Caribbean Migration Program

319 Grinter Hall
Gainesville, FL 32611
Helen Safa, Director
(904) 392-0375   Fax: (904) 392-9605

Services Offered: LI, RS. **Established:** 1981. **Staff:** 3. **Clientele:** Central America/Caribbean. Research program concerned with Caribbean migration to the United States, especially the Southeastern United States.

285 — Hollywood

Jewish Family Service of Broward County

4517 Hollywood Boulevard
Hollywood, FL 33021
Sherwin H. Rosenstein, Executive Director
(305) 966-0956

Services Offered: CU, EC, ED, HE, RE, SS. **Established:** 1962. **Staff:** 36. **Budget:** $1,222,000. **Religious Affiliation:** Jewish. **Clientele:** World, USSR, Middle East. The details of daily life, which most Americans take for granted, can be overwhelming to a new immigrant. JFS provides a number of services, in cooperation with the Hebrew Immigrant Aid Society to make the adjustment easier and to help new immigrants become a viable part of the local Jewish community. Services include: housing assistance, orientation to the community, medical/legal referrals, employment assistance, acculturation, Jewish education and short-term financial assistance. **Publications:** FAMILY TIES (newsletter).

286 — Immokalee

Catholic Charities. Immigration Project of Immokalee

Box 156
Immokalee, FL 33934
Joseph Brueggen, Coordinator
(813) 657-6264

Services Offered: AD, LE. **Religious Affiliation:** Catholic. **Clientele:** Central America/Caribbean, World. Legal assistance, advice, representation and referral for immigration-related matters. Assists with Cuban/Haitian applications, photos, tests for English and citizenship, referrals, etc.

287   *Indiantown*

Corn-Maya

Box 147
Indiantown, FL 34956
Andres Casteneda, Director
(407) 597-4151

Services Offered: AD, CU, CE, HE, LE.
Established: 1988. **Staff:** 1. **Clientele:** Central
America/Caribbean. Assistance and support for
refugees and immigrants who are principally Mayan
Indians from Guatemala.

288   *Indiantown*

Holy Cross Service Center

Box 613
Indiantown, FL 34956
Sr. Kathy Fomarek, Director
(407) 597-3382

Services Offered: AD, CU, LE, SS.
Established: 1981. **Staff:** 3. **Budget:** $80,000.
Religious Affiliation: Catholic. **Clientele:**
Central America/Caribbean. Trained volunteers assist
people in obtaining legal status in the United States
and act as advocates if they are detained by INS. Also
provides emergency assistance, language training, etc.
for Hispanics and Haitians.

289   *Jacksonville*

Catholic Charities. Refugee Resettlement Office

Box 1931
Jacksonville, FL 32201
William C. Beitz, Director
(904) 354-3416

Services Offered: AD, CU, CE, LE, RE, SS.
Established: 1965. **Religious Affiliation:**
Catholic. **Clientele:** World. Refugee Resettlement
Program coordinated with US Catholic Conference
Migration & Refugee Services. Program includes
sponsorship development and services that range from
cultural orientation to emergency social services.

290   *Jacksonville*

Florida Baptist Convention

1230 Hendricks Avenue
Jacksonville, FL 32207
Brenda Forlines, Refugee Director
(904) 396-2351

Services Offered: SS. **Religious Affiliation:**
Baptist. **Clientele:** World, Central
America/Caribbean, Southeast Asia. Variety of social
services offered to refugees and immigrants, including
emergency social services and limited educational
programs.

291   *Jacksonville*

Jewish Family and Community Services

1415 Lasalle Street
Jacksonville, FL 32217
Iris Young, Director
(904) 396-2941

Services Offered: SS. **Established:** 1917.
Staff: 16. **Budget:** $468,000. **Religious
Affiliation:** Jewish. **Clientele:** World, USSR.
Assists with the resettlement and family reunification
of refugees and immigrants from throughout the
world, especially the Soviet Union.

292   *Jacksonville*

Lutheran Social Services of Northeast Florida. Refugee and Immigrant Services

134 East Church Street
Jacksonville, FL 32202
Russell J. Bloom, Program Director
(904) 632-0022

Services Offered: AD, CU, EC, ED, HE, SS.
Established: 1980. **Staff:** 12. **BIA. Religious
Affiliation:** Lutheran. **Clientele:** World. Goals
are to: successfully resettle refugees and political
asylees; find employment in order to allow clients to
become self-supporting as soon as possible; and alleviate the stress of culture shock as much as possible.
Publications: Newsletter; Annual Report;
Directory.

293   *Miami*

American Friends Service Committee. Florida Undocumented Workers Program

1205 Sunset Drive
Miami, FL 33143
Jonathan Fried, Director
(305) 665-0022

Services Offered: LE, RE, RS. **Established:**
1983. **Staff:** 5. **Budget:** $170,000. **BIA.**

Religious Affiliation: Quaker. **Clientele:** Central America/Caribbean. Legal services, specifically relating to immigration and refugee law, are provided free of charge to undocumented workers from Mexico and Central America.

---

294 *Miami*

American Immigration Lawyers Association. Pro Bono Project.

1393 SW First Street, Suite 330
Miami, FL 33135
Magda Montiel Davis, Chair
(305) 649-5150

Services Offered: CE, LE. **Established:** 1986. **Staff:** 1. **Budget:** $24,856. **BIA. Clientele:** World. Provides free legal assistance to aliens who are entitled to representation in immigration proceedings but cannot afford a private attorney. Primary focus is to represent aliens of all nationalities who appear before the Immigration Court in deportation or exclusive proceedings, and to assist persons detailed at the Krome North Processing Center. Referral of clients come primarily from the Immigration Court. Clients are also referred by social, charitable, religious and other organizations who cannot serve the clients' needs. Majority of clients are residents of Dade County. Extensive outreach programs include work with the increasing number of Nicaraguans requiring legal assistance. **Publications:** Annual Report.

---

295 *Miami*

Catholic Community Services. Refugee Resettlement Program

1603 SW Eighth Street
Miami, FL 33130
Zita Herrera, Director
(305) 643-2757

Services Offered: AD, EC, RE, SS. **Staff:** 6. **Budget:** $198,000. **Religious Affiliation:** Catholic. **Clientele:** World, Central America/Caribbean. Extensive resettlement program for refugees, asylees and immigrants. Special Placement Sponsorship Program aids Cuban Mariel detainees released from prison to reincorporate with family and community. **Publications:** Annual Report.

---

296 *Miami*

Catholic Immigration Services

970 SW First Street, Suite 210

Miami, FL 33130
Shirley Hart, Director
(305) 326-8400

Services Offered: AD, CU, EC, ED, LE, RE, SS. **BIA. Religious Affiliation:** Catholic. **Clientele:** Central America/Caribbean, World. Advocacy, counseling, employment, social services and legal representation for immigrants.

---

297 *Miami*

Christian Community Service Agency

3360 West Flagler Street
Miami, FL 33135
Mary R. Smith, Executive Director
(305) 442-4202

Services Offered: AD, CU, EC, RE, SS. **Established:** 1965. **Religious Affiliation:** Ecumenical. **Clientele:** World, Central America/Caribbean, South America. Local church agency sponsored by the Protestant Community to serve the needs of individuals and groups striving for self-sufficiency. Serves refugees, principally those from the Caribbean, Central and South America. Provide paralegal immigration assistance. **Publications:** CCSA EVERYONE COUNTS (quarterly newsletter, free); Annual Report.

---

298 *Miami*

Church World Service. Refugee Program

701 SW 27th Avenue
Miami, FL 33135
Michael Pszyk, Director
(305) 541-8040

Services Offered: LE, RS, SS. **Established:** 1945. **BIA. Religious Affiliation:** Church of Christ. **Clientele:** World. Assistance provided to refugees, asylees, immigrants and the undocumented. Services include counseling, emergency assistance, and referral to appropriate agencies when needed.

---

299 *Miami*

Cuban American National Council. Refugee Program

300 SW 12th Avenue
Miami, FL 33130
Guarione Diaz, Executive Director
(305) 642-3484

Services Offered: AD, CU, CE, SS. **Established**: 1988. **Clientele**: Central America/Caribbean. In June, 1988 became the first group in modern times to sponsor refugee admissions to the U.S. without federal fundings. These private placements will number over 1,000 in FY 1989.

---

300   *Miami*

Haitian American Community Association

8037 NE Second Avenue
Miami, FL 33138
John Greenwood, Contact
(305) 751-3429

Services Offered: AD, CU, CE, EC, ED, LE, RE, SS. **Clientele**: Central America/Caribbean. Broad range of services available to the Haitian community, from general advocacy to right of Haitians in the United States to social services.

---

301   *Miami*

Haitian Refugee Center

32 NE 54th Street
Miami, FL 33137
Fr. Gerard Jean-Juste, Executive Director
(305) 757-8538

Services Offered: AD, CU, CE, EC, ED, LE, RS, SS. **Established**: 1974. **BIA**. **Clientele**: Central America/Caribbean. Advocate for the humane treatment of refugees from Haiti. These efforts include: legal advice, counseling and representation in asylum proceedings; class action suits for equal treatment under immigration laws; public education about immigration issues; documentation of human rights abuses to assist in asylum proceedings; building a community advocacy and support system; and networking with other agencies.

---

302   *Miami*

Inmigracion Latina Foundation

Box 521863
Miami, FL 33152
Franklin Chavez, Legal Program Director
(305) 445-0707

Services Offered: AD, CU, CE, LE, SS. **Established**: 1986. **Staff**: 4. **Budget**: $40,000. **BIA**. **Religious Affiliation**: Ecumenical. **Clientele**: South America, Central America/Caribbean. Provides legal and social service

assistance to Hispanic refugees and immigrants. Immigration counseling and legal representation.

---

303   *Miami*

International Rescue Committee

701 SW 27th Avenue
Miami, FL 33135
Grizzel Trellas, Director
(305) 643-2662

Services Offered: AD, CE, CU, EC, SS. **Established**: 1961. **Clientele**: World. IRC provides orientation, reception, general assistance, resettlement, job orientation and placement as part of assisting refugees adapt to life in the United States.

---

304   *Miami*

National Association of Evangelicals. Immigration Program

701 SW 27th Avenue, Suite 714
Miami, FL 33135
Leticia Godoy, Director
(305) 643-9848

Services Offered: AD, LE, SS. **Established**: 1980. **BIA**. **Religious Affiliation**: Ecumenical. **Clientele**: World, Central America/Caribbean. Advocacy and support for refugees and immigrants, including resettlement, family reunification, counseling, information and referral, etc.

---

305   *Miami*

National Council of Jewish Women. Rescue & Migration Service

4200 Biscayne Boulevard
Miami, FL 33137
Charlotte Oliver, Director
(305) 576-4747

Services Offered: AD, CU, LE, SS. **Established**: 1924. **Staff**: 2. **BIA**. **Religious Affiliation**: Jewish. **Clientele**: World, Middle East. Resettlement and familiy reunification assistance to primarily Jews from all over the world fleeing persecution. Has helped over 1,100 individuals.

---

306   *Miami Beach*

Jewish Family Service. Resettlement Program

420 Lincoln Road

Miami Beach, FL 33139
Shuli Klein, Director
(305) 538-0413

Services Offered: AD, CU, RE, SS.
Established: 1970. **Staff:** 2. **BIA. Religious
Affiliation:** Jewish. **Clientele:** USSR, World.
Through coordination with the Hebrew Immigrant
Aid Society assists with the resettlement of refugees
and immigrants.

307   *Miami Beach*
Lutheran Ministries of Florida

225 Second Street
Miami Beach, FL 33138
Marti Walsh, Director
(305) 674-8111

Services Offered: AD, CU, LE, RE, RS, SS.
Established: 1982. **BIA. Religious
Affiliation:** Lutheran. **Clientele:** Central
America/Caribbean, World. Legal, employment and
social services designed to assist refugees (principally
from Central America and the Caribbean) adjust successfully to life in their new land.

308   *North Palm Beach*
Faith Lutheran Church

555 US 1
North Palm Beach, FL 33408
John Frerking, Pastor
(407) 848-4737

Services Offered: CU, RE, SS. **Established:**
1975. **Religious Affiliation:** Lutheran.
Clientele: World. Variety of social services and related assistance to refugees and immigrants establishing a new life in Florida.

309   *Orlando*
Catholic Social Service. Refugee Resettlement Program

1771 North Semoran Boulevard
Orlando, FL 32807
Thomas Aglio, Director
(407) 658-0110

Services Offered: AD, CU, EC, ED, LE, SS.
Established: 1975. **Religious Affiliation:**
Catholic. **Clientele:** World. Refugee resettlement
services include orientation, advocacy, employment
and educational programs, immigration counseling

and social services.

310   *Orlando*
Florida Council of Churches. Refugee Program

924 North Magnolia Avenue, Suite 1236
Orlando, FL 32803
Joyce Voorhees, Director
(407) 839-3454

Services Offered: AD, CU, RE, SS.
Established: 1980. **Staff:** 3. **BIA. Religious
Affiliation:** Ecumenical. **Clientele:** World.
Sponsorship and resettlement of refugees and immi-
grants in coordination with Church World Service.
Publications: Newsletter; Annual Report.

311   *Pensacola*
Catholic Social Services. Refugee and Immigration Services

222 East Government Street
Pensacola, FL 32501
Mary Frances Waite, Director
(904) 438-8564

Services Offered: AD, LE, SS. **Established:**
1979. **BIA. Religious Affiliation:** Catholic.
Clientele: Southeast Asia, Asia, World. Services
include advocacy, legal assistance with all immigration-related matters and social services for refugees
and immigrants.

312   *Saint Petersburg*
Catholic Social Services. Refugee Social Services

6533 Ninth Avenue North
Saint Petersburg, FL 33710
Michael Cook, Director
(813) 345-0953

Services Offered: CU, CE, EC, HE, LE, SS.
Established: 1978. **Staff:** 7. **Budget:** $120,000.
BIA. Religious Affiliation: Catholic.
Clientele: World. Variety of services offered to
refugees and immigrants. They include: medical
screening; legal services; citizenship and other applications and forms; job placement; and general social
and acculturation services.

313   *Sarasota*
Catholic Charities

2015 S. Tuttle Avenue
Sarasota, FL 34239
Arthur G. Granzeier, Executive Director
(813) 957-4496

Services Offered: LE, SS. **Established:** 1984. **Staff:** 5. **Budget:** $7,165. **Religious Affiliation:** Catholic. **Clientele:** Southeast Asia, Central America/Caribbean. Multi-service agency offers refugee resettlement, famility unification and legal services under IRCA.

---

314 *Sarasota*

Jewish Family Service

4370 S. Tamiami Trail, Suite 311
Sarasota, FL 34231
Jerold Stone, Executive Director
(813) 921-7413

Services Offered: AD, CU, LE, RE, CE, RS, SS. **Established:** 1984. **Religious Affiliation:** Jewish. **Clientele:** World, Europe, USSR. Immigrant and refugee resettlement services offered to principally those of the Jewish faith fleeing Eastern Europe and the USSR. **Publications:** Annual Report; Newsletter.

---

315 *Tallahassee*

Florida Department of Health and Rehabilitation Services. Office of Refugee Programs

1317 Winewood Boulevard
Tallahassee, FL 32399
Nancy K. Wittenberg, Administrator
(904) 488-3791   Fax: (904) 487-4272

Services Offered: HE, LE, SS. **Established:** 1979. **Staff:** 7. **Budget:** $26,000,000. **Clientele:** World, Central America/Caribbean. State agency coordinates refugee resettlement in Florida.

---

316 *Tampa*

Catholic Social Services

730 South Sterling
Tampa, FL 33609
Martha Franco, Director
(813) 870-6220

Services Offered: AD, LE, SS. **Established:** 1944. **Staff:** 10. **Budget:** $200,000. **Religious Affiliation:** Catholic. **Clientele:** World. In conjunction with US Catholic Conference Migration & Refugee Services works to resettle refugees and immigrants.

---

317 *Tampa*

Cornerstone Ministries

2708 Central Avenue
Tampa, FL 33602
Brenda Caldwell, Refugee Services
(813) 229-1170

Services Offered: AD, CU, CE, LE, HE, RE, SS. **Established:** 1985. **Staff:** 1. **BIA. Religious Affiliation:** Ecumenical. **Clientele:** Africa, Central America/Caribbean. Services designed to assist acculturation process for refugees and immigrants. These services include counseling, legal and medical assistance, job placement and pastoral support. Principal groups served are Ethiopians and Central Americans.

---

318 *Tampa*

Jewish Family Services

112 South Magnolia
Tampa, FL 33606
Anschel Weiss, Executive Director
(813) 251-0083

Services Offered: AD, CU, CE, EC, ED, HE, LE, RE, SC, SS. **Established:** 1978. **Staff:** 1. **Budget:** $50,000. **Religious Affiliation:** Jewish. **Clientele:** World, USSR, Middle East. Extensive resettlement, educational and social service programs designed to assist refugees, asylees and immigrants in their first few months in the United States. **Publications:** TRUSTLINE (quarterly newsletter); Annual Report.

---

319 *Tampa*

Lutheran Ministries of Florida. Refugee Resettlement Program

3825 Henderson Boulevard
Tampa, FL 33629
Robert Eledge, Director
(813) 831-4449

Services Offered: AD, CU, EC, LE, RE, SS. **Established:** 1982. **Staff:** 3. **Religious Affiliation:** Lutheran. **Clientele:** World. Immigration counseling, employment services, religious liaison and general social services for refugees and immigrants in Florida sponsored through Lutheran Immigration & Refugee Services.

---

320   *West Palm Beach*

Jewish Federation of Palm Beach County

501 South Flagler Drive
West Palm Beach, FL 33401
Jeffrey Klein, Executive Director
(407) 832-2120   Fax: (407) 832-0562

Services Offered: CU, EC, LE, SS. **Staff:** 35.
Religious Affiliation: Jewish. **Clientele:**
World, USSR, Africa. Services are designed to assist
refugees and immigrants successfully adapt to life in a
new land. Services range from legal advice, job
placement as well as traditional social services.
Publications: Newsletter.

321   *West Palm Beach*

Legal Aid Society

224 Datura Street, Room 301
West Palm Beach, FL 33401
Vic Panoff, Attorney
(407) 655-8944

Services Offered: AD, LE. **Clientele:** Central
America/Caribbean, World. Legal representation for
indigent refugees and immigrants in immigration, deportation, asylum, etc. proceedings.

322   *Winter Park*

Jewish Family Services of Greater Orlando

112 Wymore Road
Winter Park, FL 32789
Alvin Gamson, Executive Director
(407) 644-7593

Services Offered: AD, CU, RE, SS.
Established: 1978. **Staff:** 9. **Budget:** $315,040.
BIA. Religious Affiliation: Jewish.
Clientele: World, Europe. Resettlement services for
refugees and immigrants provided primarily to those
of the Jewish faith from all parts of the world.
Publications: Newsletter.

323   *Atlanta*

Catholic Social Services. Refugee Resettlement Program

680 West Peachtree Street NW
Atlanta, GA 30308
Bui Van Tam, Director
(404) 881-6571

Services Offered: SS. **Established:** 1970.
Staff: 3. **Budget:** $95,000. **BIA. Religious
Affiliation:** Catholic. **Clientele:** World. Refugee
resettlement and immigration counseling in coordina-
tion with US Catholic Conference Migration &
Refugee Services.

324   *Atlanta*

Christian Council of Metropolitan Atlanta. Refugee & Immigrant Resettlement Services Program

465 Boulevard SE, Suite 101
Atlanta, GA 30312
Gail Hoffman-Kahler, Director
(404) 622-2235   Fax: (404) 627-6626

Services Offered: AD, CU, EC, ED, HE, LE, LI,
RE, SS. **Established:** 1975. **Staff:** 6. **Religious
Affiliation:** Ecumenical. **Clientele:** World,
Central America/Caribbean, Europe. As an affiliate of
Church World Service helps local denominations and
local sponsors assist refugees who qualify for refugee
status under the Refugee Act of 1980. Services provided by CCMA Refugee Program: orientation and
training to sponsors; assistance to sponsors in providing services to refugees; referral services related to
various needs such as employment, housing, counseling and medical problems; provision of interpretation
and social adjustment counseling; emergency back up
services; assistance in record keeping and case management; and liaison service with national denominational offices. Offers special programs for Eastern
Europeans and Haitian entrants. **Publications:**
Directory ($6).

325   *Atlanta*

Georgia Baptist Convention. Language Missions Department

2930 Flowers Road South
Atlanta, GA 30341
Jerry K. Baker, Director
(404) 455-0404

Services Offered: CU, RE. **Established:** 1965.
Staff: 8. **Budget:** $500,000. **Religious**

Affiliation: Baptist. **Clientele:** World. Services offered include: refugee sponsorship development; emergency follow-up assistance to refugees; creation of ethnic ministries by local congregations; and general resettlement and family reunification. **Publications:** LANGUAGE MISSIONS NEWSLETTER; Directory.

---

326   *Atlanta*

Georgia Department of Human Resources. Refugee Health Program

878 Peachtree Street NE
Atlanta, GA 30309
Barbara Browne, Coordinator
(404) 894-6523

Services Offered: HE. **Established:** 1980. **Staff:** 11. **Budget:** $350,000. **Clientele:** World. Administer health screening programs for newly arrived refugees. Provide interpretation for health screening and follow-up services. Provide seminars, foreign language materials, etc.

---

327   *Atlanta*

Georgia Department of Human Resources. Special Programs Unit

878 Peachtree Street NE, Room 403
Atlanta, GA 30309
Winnie Horton, State Refugee Coordinator
(404) 894-7661

Services Offered: EC, ED, HE, SS. **BIA.** **Clientele:** World. State agency responsible for coordinating refugee resettlement.

---

328   *Atlanta*

Jewish Family Services

1605 Peachtree Road NE
Atlanta, GA 30309
Irving Perlman, Executive Director
(404) 873-2277

Services Offered: AD, CU, LE, RE, SS. **Established:** 1895. **Religious Affiliation:** Jewish. **Clientele:** USSR, Middle East, World. Refugee resettlement coordinated through Hebrew Immigrant Aid Society.

---

329   *Atlanta*

Lutheran Ministries of Georgia

756 West Peachtree Street NW
Atlanta, GA 30308
Henry Wohlgemuth, Executive Director
(404) 875-0201

Services Offered: AD, RE, SS. **Established:** 1981. **Staff:** 15. **Religious Affiliation:** Lutheran. **Clientele:** World. Resettlement and family reunification services offered to those in need.

---

330   *Atlanta*

Save the Children. Refugee Child Care Assistance Project

1340 Spring Street, Suite 200
Atlanta, GA 30309
Nancy Travis, Director
(404) 885-1578

Services Offered: EC, SS. **Established:** 1937. **Staff:** 4. **Budget:** $130,000. **Clientele:** World. The Refugee Child Care Assistance Project has two components. Refugee women are trained to become family day care providers and subsidies are provided for day care for children to those refugees involved in educational programs or work. About 35 women have been trained and annually about 100 children receive assistance. Applicants must have refugee status.

---

331   *Atlanta*

Southern Baptist Immigration and Refugee Resettlement Services

1350 Spring Street NW
Atlanta, GA 30367
William Rutledge, National Consultant
(404) 873-4041   Fax: (404) 898-7228

Services Offered: CU, EC, ED, HE, LE, LI, RE, RS, SS. **Established:** 1961. **Staff:** 4. **Religious Affiliation:** Baptist. **Clientele:** World. Full range of services (from emergency services to legal representation) to refugees and immigrants.

---

332   *Atlanta*

U.S. Department of Health & Human Services. Family Support Administration. Office of Refugee Resettlement

101 Marietta Tower
Atlanta, GA 30323
Perry Childers, Contact
(404) 331-5733

Clientele: World. Regional office of the U.S. Office of Refugee Resettlement responsible for coordinating assistance (cash and medical, demonstration projects, social services, etc.) to refugees.

World Relief

Box 95271
Atlanta, GA 30347
Herbert Snedden, Area Director
(404) 321-6992

Services Offered: AD, CU, RE, RS, SS. Established: 1980. Staff: 6. Budget: $200,000. Religious Affiliation: Ecumenical. Clientele: World. With the assistance of churches reponsible for the resettlement, including processing and counseling, of refugees and immigrants.

334 *Comer*

Jubilee Partners

210 Main Street
Comer, GA 30629
Robbie Bufler, Coordinator
(404) 783-5131

Services Offered: LE, LI. Established: 1979. Staff: 25. Budget: $180,000. Religious Affiliation: Ecumenical. Clientele: Central America/Caribbean. Working with the Canadian Government as well as individuals and church groups all over the United States, Jubilee Partners have helped over 1,000 Central Americans to move legally to new homes in Canada. Most of the refugees live at Jubilee for several months studying English and preparing for their new life in Canada.
Publications: JUBILEE PARTNERS REPORT (bi-monthly); Annual Report.

335 *Decatur*

International Rescue Committee

4303 Memorial Drive, Suite L
Decatur, GA 30032
Margaret Flaherty, Director
(404) 292-7731

Services Offered: AD, CU, CE, LE, SS. Established: 1979. Clientele: World. Voluntary refugee resettlement agency provides services to refugees resettling in the United States.

336 *Decatur*

Lao Community Association

4336 Covington Highway, Suite 103
Decatur, GA 30035
Siong Koua Vanchiasong, Director
(404) 288-4381

Services Offered: EC, SS. Established: 1985. Staff: 7. Clientele: Southeast Asia. Provides the following services and programs: career counseling services; orientation; job development and job placement; and follow-up services. Offer Planned Secondary Resettlement services to refugees who wish to move from the high welfare dependency states, such as California, Wisconsin and Minnesota. The primary goal of this project is to lower the welfare dependency rate by helping these refugees become self-sufficient. All activities designed to help the Hmong and Laotian refugees become self-sufficient.

337 *Marietta*

Americans for International Aid

1370 Murdock Road
Marietta, GA 30062
Jodie Darragh, Director
(404) 973-5909   Fax: (404) 973-4220

Services Offered: RS, SS. Established: 1974. Staff: 1. Budget: $8,000. Religious Affiliation: Ecumenical. Clientele: World, Southeast Asia, Asia. In addition to extensive relief activities overseas, escorting for medical treatment and adoption, AIA since the mid-1970's has offered extensive services to help Amerasian children in Vietnam and Korea emigrate to the United States.
Publications: Newsletter; Annual Report.

338 *Savannah*

St. John's Center. Office of Social Ministry

Grimball Point Road
Savannah, GA 31406
Sr. Patricia Brown, Vicar
(912) 238-2351

Services Offered: AD, SS. Established: 1975. Staff: 1. Religious Affiliation: Catholic. Clientele: Southeast Asia, Central America/Caribbean. Resettle refugees and provide social service assistance through coordination with US Catholic Conference Migration & Refugee Services.

339   *Honolulu*

Catholic Immigration Center

712 North School Street
Honolulu, HI 96817
Cecile Motus, Director
(808) 528-5233

Services Offered: AD, CU, CE, EC, ED, RE, SS. **Established:** 1975. **BIA. Religious Affiliation:** Catholic. **Clientele:** Asia, Southeast Asia. Cultural, educational and social services for refugees and immigrants.

340   *Honolulu*

Child and Family Service. Refugee Employment & Social Assistance Program

200 North Vineyard Boulevard
Honolulu, HI 96817
Daniel Leung, Program Directir
(808) 543-9970

Services Offered: AD, CE, EC, SS. **Established:** 1983. **Staff:** 10. **Budget:** $500,000. **Clientele:** World. Following services offered to promote self-sufficiency among refugees and immigrants: job development and placement; job orientation; case management; counseling referrals and follow-up; and crisis intervention. **Publications:** Annual Report.

341   *Honolulu*

Hawaii Department of Labor & Industrial Relations. Office of Community Services. Refugee Resettlement Program

335 Merchant Street, Room 101
Honolulu, HI 96813
Walter Choy, Executive Director
(808) 548-2014

Services Offered: EC, LE, RS, SS. **Established:** 1985. **Staff:** 2. **Budget:** $1,991,486. **Clientele:** World. Administer state and federal funds for programs serving immigrants and refugees. Variety of services are provided through purchase of service contracts with private, non-profit agencies. **Publications:** REPORT TO THE LEGISLATURE (annual).

342   *Honolulu*

Inter-Agency Council for Immigrant Services

1117 Kaili Street
Honolulu, HI 96819
(808) 847-1535

Services Offered: AD, CE. **Established:** 1973. **Staff:** 4. **Clientele:** World. Provides community organizing and education, advocacy and lobbying for rights of immigrants. Membership consists of about 40 agencies, both private non-profits and state agencies. **Publications:** DIRECTORY OF SERVICES (annual, free).

343   *Honolulu*

International Buddhist Meditation Association

1105 Hind Inuka Drive
Honolulu, HI 96821
Thich Thong Hai, Abbot
(808) 373-4608

Services Offered: CU, RE. **Established:** 1984. **Staff:** 8. **Budget:** $23,000. **BIA. Religious Affiliation:** Buddhist. **Clientele:** Southeast Asia, Asia. Support group for Vietnamese culture, religion and tradition.

344   *Honolulu*

Kalihi-Palama Immigrant Service Center

720 North King Street
Honolulu, HI 96817
Yuk Panglow, Contact
(808) 845-3918

Services Offered: AD, CU, LE, EC, ED, RS, SS. **Established:** 1974. **Clientele:** Southeast Asia, Asia. Create access to existing public and private social services for individuals and families who have limited or no English language and who have immediate needs for housing, employment, education, transportation, legal and immigration support services. Center fingerprints and offers counseling and assistance with immigration forms.

345   *Honolulu*

Na Loio No Na Kanaka. Lawyers for the People of Hawaii

810 North Vineyard Boulevard
Honolulu, HI 96817

William Hoshijo, Executive Director
(808) 847-8828

Services Offered: AD, CE, LE. **Established:** 1983. **BIA. Clientele:** Asia, World. Immigration Law Project provides legal services to indigent in immigration law proceedings, deportation, asylum, etc. Also community outreach and advocacy.

---

346   *Kailua Kona*

Youth With a Mission Relief Services

75-5851 Kuakini Highway
Kailua Kona, HI   96740
Fraser Haug, Coordinator
(808) 326-9567

Services Offered: CU, RE, SS. **Established:** 1979. **Religious Affiliation:** Ecumenical. **Clientele:** Southeast Asia, Asia. Assistance in cultural adaption for refugees and immigrants through a variety of programs.

---

347   *Boise*

Idaho Department of Health and Welfare. Division of Field Operations

450 West State Street
Boise, ID   83720
Molly Trimming, State Refugee Coordinator
(208) 334-2693

Services Offered: AD, EC, ED, HE, SS. **Clientele:** World. Statewide coordination of federal, state and private resources for effective refugee resettlement including cash and medical assistance, support services and such other activities as necessary.

---

348   *Boise*

Sponsors Organized to Assist Refugees

4900 North Five Mile Road
Boise, ID   83704
Tudor Cushman, Contact
(208) 376-4529

Services Offered: AD, CE, LE, SA, SS. **Clientele:** World. Advocacy, cultural, educational and social service support for refugees and immigrants.

---

349   *Emmett*

Catholic Migration and Refugee Services

512 Monroe Street
Emmett, ID   83617
Joanne Gouger, Resettlement Director
(208) 365-5834

Services Offered: SS. **Established:** 1975. **Religious Affiliation:** Catholic. **Clientele:** Southeast Asia, World. Assist with refugee resettlement and family reunification.

---

350 — Belleville

Catholic Social Service

220 West Lincoln
Belleville, IL 62220
John A. Laker, Executive Director
(618) 277-9200

Services Offered: AD, SS. **Established:** 1947.
Staff: 1. **Budget:** $30,000. **BIA. Religious
Affiliation:** Catholic. **Clientele:** World. Refugee
resettlement program is coordinated with US Catholic
Conference Migration & Refugee Services.
Publications: CSS NEWSLETTER; Annual
Report.

351 — Chicago

**Archdiocese of Chicago.
Immigration Services**

1300 South Wabash
Chicago, IL 60605
Zeferino Ochoa, Executive Director
(312) 427-7078

Services Offered: AD, CU, EC, ED, LE, RE, SS.
Established: 1954. **BIA. Religious
Affiliation:** Catholic. **Clientele:** Central
America/Caribbean, World. Offers immigration and
naturalization counseling, employment and educational counseling; and general social service programs.

352 — Chicago

Casa El Salvador

3411 West Diversey Street
Chicago, IL 60647
Robelo Solis, Contact
(312) 489-3567

Services Offered: AD, CU, LE, CE, SS.
Established: 1982. **Clientele:** Central
America/Caribbean. Advocacy, cultural support and
community outreach activities to support refugees
fleeing persecution in El Salvador.

353 — Chicago

Catholic Resettlement Center

721 North La Salle Drive, 7th Floor
Chicago, IL 60610
Mary Wodarczyk, Director
(312) 266-0093

Services Offered: RE, RS, LI, SS. **Established:**
1975. **Religious Affiliation:** Catholic.
Clientele: World. Reception and placement of
refugees coming to Chicago area through the auspices
of the US Catholic Conference Migration & Refugee
Services.

354 — Chicago

**Chicago Commission on Human
Relations. Refugee Liaison**

500 North Peshtigo Court
Chicago, IL 60611
Hayelom Ayala, Contact
(312) 744-4111

Services Offered: AD, CE, LE, LI.
Established: 1947. **Clientele:** World. Provides
technical and legal assistance to refugees and immigrants in Chicago. Analyze and develop City policy
toward immigrants and refugees.

355 — Chicago

**Chicago Committee on Immigrant
Protection**

327 South LaSalle Street, Suite 1500
Chicago, IL 60604
Arturo Jaurequi, Chair
(312) 435-4557

Services Offered: AD, CE, LI, RS, SS.
Established: 1986. **Staff:** 2. **Clientele:** World.
Resources and services for immigrants and refugees.

356 — Chicago

**Chicago Religious Task Force on
Central America.**

59 East Van Buren Street, 14th Floor
Chicago, IL 60605
Robin Semer, Staff
(312) 663-4398

Services Offered: AD, CE, RE, RS, SA.
Established: 1981. **Staff:** 1. **Budget:** $50,000.
Religious Affiliation: Ecumenical. **Clientele:**
Central America/Caribbean. Coordinates information
on Sanctuary Movement and matches Salvadoran
asylees and congregations as well as community
outreach and public information on U.S. policy in
Central America. **Publications:** BASTA
(quarterly).

357   *Chicago*

Chinese American Service League

310 West 24th Place
Chicago, IL   60616
Bernarda Wong, Executive Director
(312) 791-0418

Services Offered: CU, AD, HE, LE, LE, SS.
Established: 1979. **Staff**: 33. **Budget**: $800,000.
Clientele: Southeast Asia, Asia. Establised and ex-
ists as a community based social service agency to
assist Chinese Americans in greater Chicago. Wide
variety of services from immigration counseling to
cultural events. **Publications**: TWENTH FOURTH
PLACE (quarterly newsletter, free); Annual Report.

---

358   *Chicago*

Illinois Conference of Churches. Refugee Resettlement Program

4753 North Broadway, Suite 922
Chicago, IL   60640
May Campbell, Director
(312) 989-5647

Services Offered: AD, CE, LE, RE, SS.
Established: 1980. **Religious Affiliation**:
Ecumenical. **Clientele**: World. Ecumenical resource
in Illinois for national denominational resettlement
work and state judicatory refugee concerns. Advocacy
for and assure provision of direct and indirect services
necessary to meet the needs of Church World Service
refugees resettling in Illinois. Advocacy for fair and
just immigration and refugee policies and practices.

---

359   *Chicago*

International Ladies Garment Workers Union. Immigration Project

323 South Ashland Avenue
Chicago, IL   60607
Amy Dean
(312) 738-6060

Services Offered: AD, CE, LE. **Clientele**:
World. Legal advice, counseling and representation in
immigration-related matters for ILGWU members and
families.

---

360   *Chicago*

International Refugee Center

4750 North Sheridan Avenue
Chicago, IL   60640

Sid L. Mohn, Director
(312) 435-4500

Services Offered: AD, CE, HE, LE, SS. **BIA**.
Clientele: World. Provide counseling and legal ser-
vices in 1987 to over 6,000 individuals and resettle-
ment and support services for over 700 refugees.
Therapy and counseling services available at the
Kovler Center for the Treatment of Victims of
Torture.

---

361   *Chicago*

Japanese American Service Committee of Chicago

4427 North Clark Street
Chicago, IL   60640
Masaru Nambu, Executive Director
(312) 275-7212

Services Offered: SS. **Established**: 1946.
Budget: $620,000. **Clientele**: Asia.
Comprehensive social services for Japanese in need.
Publications: JASC NEWS (quarterly); Annual re-
port.

---

362   *Chicago*

Jewish Family Services. Refugee Services

1 South Franklin Street
Chicago, IL   60606
Martin E. Langer, Executive Director
(312) 444-4001

Services Offered: AD, EC, ED, LE, SS. **BIA**.
Religious Affiliation: Jewish. **Clientele**:
World, USSR. Refugee resettlement and acculturation
programs operated in conjunction with Hebrew
Immigrant Aid Society.

---

363   *Chicago*

Korean American Community Services

4300 North California Avenue
Chicago, IL   60618
Harold H. Shin, Executive Director
(312) 583-5501   Fax: (312) 673-0567

Services Offered: CU, EC, ED, RS, LE, SS.
Established: 1972. **Staff**: 26. **Budget**: $650,000.
Religious Affiliation: Presbyterian. **Clientele**:
Asia. Multi-faceted, not-for-profit social service
agency for uprooted and disadvantaged Koreans and
others. Responds to the needs of Korean immigrants

with a constantly expanding program. Purposes and objectives: to assist immigrants with referral and counseling services; to provide social, recreational and therapeutic services; to provide educational and cultural programs for the advancement of democratic disciplines; to stimulate and implement research and educational projects which will enhance the rights and benefits of immigrants and refugees; and to provide a broad base of social and charitable services. **Publications:** KOREAN AMERICAN (quarterly newsletter, free); Annual Report.

364 *Chicago*
Legal Services Center for Immigrants

1661 South Blue Island Avenue
Chicago, IL 60608
Douglas Schoppert, Supervisory Attorney
(312) 226-0173

Services Offered: AD, CE, LE. **Established:** 1978. **Staff:** 5. **BIA. Clientele:** World. Provides legal representation to clients in deportation and exclusion proceedings and limited visa processing and legalization services.

365 *Chicago*
Lutheran Child and Family Services

6127 South University
Chicago, IL 60637
Peter Conlon, Assistant Director
(312) 753-0600

Services Offered: AD, EC, RE, SS. **Established:** 1975. **Religious Affiliation:** Lutheran. **Clientele:** Central America/Caribbean, Southeast Asia, World. Provides refugee resettlement and family unification program, immigration counseling, acculturation counseling, employment services, and refugee social services.

366 *Chicago*
Midwest Coalition in Defense of Immigrants

1440 West 18th Street
Chicago, IL 60608
Carlos Arango
(312) 226-0819

Services Offered: AD, CU, CE, LE, SS. **Clientele:** Central America/Caribbean. Advocacy and support services designed to assist immigrants

and refugees.

367 *Chicago*
Midwest Immigrant Rights Center

327 South LaSalle Street, Suite 1400
Chicago, IL 60604
Craig Mousin, Contact
(312) 435-4500

Services Offered: AD, CE, LE, SS. **Clientele:** World. Legal and social services for refugees, immigrants and asylees. Legal representation in deportation and assistance with immigration paperwork.

368 *Chicago*
Mutual Aid Association of the New Polish Immigration

5844 North Milwaukee Avenue
Chicago, IL 60646
Tad Szebert, President
(312) 631-3303

Services Offered: AD, CU, CE, EC, LI, SS. **Established:** 1949. **Clientele:** Europe. Services designed to help Polish immigrants with cultural transition, employment and educational programs and social services.

369 *Chicago*
Northside Sanctuary Coalition

17 North State Street, Room 1530
Chicago, IL 60602
Gary Cozette, Coordinator
(312) 899-1805

Services Offered: AD, CE, SA. **Clientele:** Central America/Caribbean. Group of Chicago area publicly declared sanctuaries.

370 *Chicago*
Polish American Immigration Relief Committee

3242 North Pulaski
Chicago, IL 60641
Slawomir Jarcaj, President
(312) 278-7633

Services Offered: AD, CE, LE, RS, SS. **Established:** 1950. **Clientele:** Europe. Provides assistance and support services to Polish refugees resettling in Chicago.

371   *Chicago*

Proyecto Resistencia

59 East Van Buren
Chicago, IL 60605
Secundino Ramirez, Staff
(312) 427-2533

Services Offered: AD, CE, LE, RE, RS, SS.
Established: 1982. **BIA. Clientele:** Central
America/Caribbean. Advocacy, legal assistance and
representation, immigration counseling, social ser-
vices and referrals for asylees and refugees from El
Salvador and Guatemala.

372   *Chicago*

Saura Center

1950 North Milwaukee Avenue
Chicago, IL 60647
Sid L. Mohn, Director
(312) 435-4500

Services Offered: AD, EC, SS. **Budget:**
$881,000. **BIA. Clientele:** Central
America/Caribbean. Resettlement and employment
assistance program for Cuban refugees.

373   *Chicago*

South-East Asia Center

1124 West Ainslie
Chicago, IL 60640
Peter R. Poor, Executive Director
(312) 989-6927

Services Offered: AD, CU, CE, EC, ED, HE,
LE, LI, SS. **Established:** 1979. **Staff:** 5. **Budget:**
$73,000. **Clientele:** Southeast Asia. Mission is to
build bridges between Eastern and Western cultures
and bridges amongst Asian peoples themselves. These
bridges of understanding and cooperation allow Asian
immigrants to better cope with American life and allow American society to better adapt to assist these
newcomers. Specific services include: remedial educational programs; job orientation and training; cultural
orientation; career counseling; and mental health
counseling. Formerly the Association of Chinese
from Indochina. **Publications:** NEW LIFE NEWS
(quarterly, $5).

374   *Chicago*

Synapses. Asian Organizing Program

1821 West Cullerton
Chicago, IL 60608
Reynaldo Lopez, Coordinator
(312) 421-5513

Services Offered: AD, CU, CE, LE, LI, RE, RS,
SS. **Established:** 1985. **Staff:** 5. **Budget:**
$120,000. **Religious Affiliation:** Methodist.
Clientele: Southeast Asia, Asia. Provides a context
for the Asian community in Chicago to discuss and
act on vital issues of survival and well-being. Forums
and community workshops were held on topics like
business and economic development, women, impact
of divorce, housing and anti-Asian violence, In an
attempt to link immigrant problems in the U.S. with
issues in the respective Asian countries an Asian
Human Rights Conference brought together several
ethnic Asian communities of Illincis. Maintains
library resource center. **Publications:**
NEWSLETTER (bi-monthly, $5); Annual report.

375   *Chicago*

Traveler and Immigrants Aid

327 South LaSalle Street
Chicago, IL 60604
Sid L. Mohn, CEO
(312) 435-4500

Services Offered: AD, EC, LE, SS.
Established: 1908. **Staff:** 25. **Budget:** $600,000.
BIA. Clientele: World. Legal counsel and representation for immigrants, refugees and asylees. Provides
advocacy for these groups as well as social services
and employment assistance. **Publications:**
Newsletter; Annual Report.

376   *Chicago*

U.S. Department of Health & Human Services. Family Support Administration. Office of Refugee Resettlement

105 West Adams Street, 20th Floor
Chicago, IL 60603
Dorothea Harrington, Manager
(312) 353-1664

Clientele: World. Regional office of the U.S.
Office of Refugee Resettlement responsible for
coordination of assistance (cash and medical, public
health, social services, etc.) to refugees.

377   *Chicago*

University Church. Sanctuary Project

5655 South University Avenue
Chicago, IL 60637
John Fish, Minister
(312) 363-8142

Services Offered: AD, CE, SA. **Staff:** 1.
Religious Affiliation: Disciples of Christ.
Clientele: Central America/Caribbean. Public sanctuary for Central American refugees in Chicago.

---

378   *Chicago*

Vietnamese Association of Illinois

4833 North Broadway
Chicago, IL 60640
Ngoan Le, Executive Director
(312) 728-3700

Services Offered: AD, CU, EC, ED, SS.
Established: 1976. **Staff:** 22. **Budget:** $600,000.
Clientele: Southeast Asia. Non-profit, tax-exempt organization whose purpose is to promote, support and implement social services, educational and cultural programs to serve the 16,000 Vietnamese in Illinois; to encourage the spirit of mutual assistance among the Vietnamese; and, to foster the development and strength of Vietnamese organizations. Direct services have been provided to 4,000 Vietnamese in Illinois; an additional 5,000 have been reached through cultural programs. **Publications:** BAN TIN NGUOI VIET (monthly newsletter, free); Annual Report.

---

379   *Chicago*

World Relief. Immigration Services

3507 West Lawrence, Suite 206
Chicago, IL 60625
Tim Amstutz, Director
(312) 583-9191 Fax: (312) 267-7227

Services Offered: AD, CU, CE, ED, LE, RE, SS.
Established: 1944. **Clientele:** World. Broad base of social and related services designed to support refugee resettlement and general immigration services. Affiliated with the National Association of Evangelicals.

---

380   *Chicago*

YMCA. Refugee Resettlement Services

101 North Wacker Drive
Chicago, IL 60606
Mike Diamond, Director
(312) 977-0031

Services Offered: AD, CE, CU, ED, SS.
Clientele: World. Coordinates YMCA services for refugees in the United States. Acts as liaison for local U.S. YMCA's and World Alliance of YMCA's. Cooperates with other national voluntary agencies and appropriate government agencies.

---

381   *Evanston*

American Refugee Committee

317 West Howard Street
Evanston, IL 60202
Phyllis J. Handelman, Director
(312) 328-1620

Services Offered: ED, HE, RS. **Established:** 1978. **Staff:** 2. **Budget:** $86,043. **Clientele:** World. ARC is the only agency in Illinois offering programs and workshops that specifically teach bilingual refugees about Western health care and mental health services. ARC offers crosscultural programs to hospitals and other health care institutions to introduce their staff to specific refugee health needs and health-care preferences. ARC also trains volunteers to teach English as a Second Language to refugee groups or individuals. Programs reach 1,100 refugees each year with the assistance of 11 part-time medical professionals and 65 volunteers. **Publications:** AMERICAN REFUGEE COMMITTEE NEWSLETTER; Annual report.

---

382   *Evanston*

Overground Railroad

722 Monroe
Evanston, IL 60202
David H. Janzen, Director
(312) 328-0772

Services Offered: AD, SS. **Established:** 1983.
Staff: 5. **Budget:** $60,000. **Religious Affiliation:** Ecumenical. **Clientele:** Central America/Caribbean. There are two tracks on the Overground Railway. The first track transport Central American refugees to a safe haven in Canada. The refugees are being transported legally. Before traveling, refugees make themselves known to U.S. immigration authorities and apply for asylum, thus becoming temporarily documented in the U.S. Gets refugees to safety and complements the public sanctuary movement whose aim is to boldly challenge the U.S. refugee policy. There is a second track for refugees in detention who do not go to Canada. This program,

called Provisional Legal refuge, helps local churches bond out refugees and resettle them in their community. Then they ofer legal support to their asylum cases in the U.S. Program gives refugees who fear deportation time to work out other options for their lives. **Publications:** Newsletter.

---

383   *Evanston*

Wheadon United Methodist Church. Sanctuary Task Force

2214 Ridge
Evanston, IL 60201
(312) 864-7090

Services Offered: AD, CE, SA. **Religious Affiliation:** Methodist. **Clientele:** Central America/Caribbean. Advocacy, outreach and declared sanctuary for refugees fleeing El Salvador and Guatemala.

---

384   *Glencoe*

Congregation Hakafa. Sanctuary Committee

Box 221
Glencoe, IL 60022
Rabbi Robert Marx, Contact
(312) 835-0410

Services Offered: AD, CE, SA. **Religious Affiliation:** Jewish. **Clientele:** Central America/Caribbean. Declared sanctuary for Salvadoran and Guatemalan refugees.

---

385   *Marion*

Catholic Social Service

100 South Monroe
Marion, IL 62959
Gloria Carmona, Contact
(618) 997-9381

Services Offered: AD, LE, SS. BIA. **Religious Affiliation:** Catholic. **Clientele:** Central America/Caribbean. As of December, 1988 had assisted 300 individuals with applications for the General Amnesty Legalization Program and the Agricultural Amnesty Legalization Program.

---

386   *Peoria*

Catholic Social Service. Tha Huong Program

2900 West Heading Avenue
Peoria, IL 61604
Paul E. Cousin, Administrator
(309) 671-5742

Services Offered: AD, CU, ED, HE, LE, SS. **Established:** 1979. **Staff:** 32. **Budget:** $1,000,000. **Religious Affiliation:** Catholic. **Clientele:** Southeast Asia. This program accepts unaccompanied refugee minors primarily from Southeast Asia. The program is designed to receive boys and girls between the ages of 6 and 18 who are in transition from refugee camps to foster homes in the U.S. Designed to provide an immediate reception/evaluation center for unaccompanied refugee youth upon their arrival. The majority of the minors remain in this residential program an average of six months before placement in a licensed foster home. Residents receive health care and psychological evaluation. Primary goal is to prepare the refugee minors for life in their new country and to make constructive and positive use of the period of transition into mainstream American society. **Publications:** Newsletter; Annual Report.

---

387   *Red Bud*

Posada Sanctuary

Box 115
Red Bud, IL 62278
Kathy McGuire, Coordinator
(618) 549-5255

Services Offered: SA. **Established:** 1986. **Religious Affiliation:** Catholic. **Clientele:** Central America/Caribbean. Provide sanctuary to refugees fleeing Central America and seeking safe haven in North America. **Publications:** UPDATE (quarterly newsletter).

---

388   *Rockford*

United States Catholic Conference

921 West State Street
Rockford, IL 61102
Rev. Thomas E. Burr, Refugee Program
(815) 965-0895

Services Offered: AD, RE, SS. **Established:** 1975. **Religious Affiliation:** Catholic. **Clientele:** World. Orientation and social services offered to new arrivals through Migration & Refugee Services.

---

389   *Springfield*

Illinois Bureau of Naturalization Services

IDPA/OESS
Springfield, IL 62763
Roger J. Mills, Chief
(217) 785-0710

Services Offered: AD, EC, ED, HE, SS.
Clientele: World. Statewide coordination of federal, state and private resources for effective refugee resettlement including cash and medical assistance, support services and such other activities as necessary.

---

390   *Springfield*

Illinois Conference of Churches. Refugee Immigration Program

615 South Fifth Street
Springfield, IL 62704
Mary Caroline Dana, Director
(217) 522-9942   Fax: (312) 989-5642

Services Offered: AD, EC, LE, RE, SS.
Established: 1979. **Staff:** 15. **Budget:** $450,000.
BIA. Religious Affiliation: Ecumenical.
Clientele: World. Program and service objectives: be the ecumenical resource in Illinois for national denominational resettlement work and state judicatory refugee concerns; advocate for and assure the provision of direct and indirect services to meet the needs of refugees; and serve as advocate for fair and just refugee and immigration policies and practices. Activities coordinated with Church World Service.

---

391   *Urbana*

East Central Illinois Refugee Mutual Assistance Center

302 South Birch Street
Urbana, IL 61801
Quyt Nguyen, Director
(217) 344-8455

Services Offered: AD, CU, EC, SS.
Established: 1980. **Staff:** 6. **Budget:** $120,000.
Religious Affiliation: Ecumenical. **Clientele:** World. ECIRMAC provides services essential to refugee resettlement, including job placement and supportive employment services, orientation, translation, liaison, referral, counseling, and advocacy; shares the unique cultural heritage of the refugee community with all interested individuals; and assists refugees and former refugees in the preservation of their language, culture and traditions. **Publications:**

NEWSLETTER (monthly, free).

---

392   *Winfield*

Moob Federation of America

Box 56
Winfield, IL 60190
Djoua X. Xiong, President
(312) 665-6526

Services Offered: AD, CU, CE, RS, SS.
Established: 1983. **Clientele:** Southeast Asia, Asia. Advocacy and support services for Hmong refugees throughout the United States. Goals are the economic and cultural integration of the Hmong into American society. **Publications:** TXOOJ MOOB (semi-annual newsletter).

---

393 — Evansville
Catholic Charities Bureau
603 Court Building
Evansville, IN 47708
Richard C. Rust, Director
(812) 423-5456

Services Offered: AD, SS. **Religious Affiliation**: Catholic. **Clientele**: World. Refugee resettlement operations coordinated through US Catholic Conference Migration & Refugee Services.

394 — Fort Wayne
Catholic Charities. Refugee Office
919 Fairfield Avenue
Fort Wayne, IN 46802
Amy Kreeger, Resettlement Coordinator
(219) 422-7511

Services Offered: AD, EC, ED, LI, RE, SS. **Established**: 1975. **BIA**. **Religious Affiliation**: Catholic. **Clientele**: World. Refugee resettlement with emphasis on early integration into all aspects of society and self-sufficiency.

395 — Fort Wayne
Friends of the Third World
611 West Wayne Street
Fort Wayne, IN 46802
James Goetsch, Administrator
(219) 422-1650

Services Offered: AD, CU, CE, EC, LI. **Established**: 1972. **Staff**: 15. **Budget**: $600,000. **Clientele**: World. Assists refugee groups produce and market their products throughout the United States.

396 — Gary
Catholic Charities. Refugee Assistance
973 West Sixth Avenue
Gary, IN 46402
Rev. Joseph Semancik, Resettlement Director
(219) 882-2720

Services Offered: AD, CU, RE, LI, SS. **Established**: 1975. **BIA**. **Religious Affiliation**: Catholic. **Clientele**: World. Provides services and programs to assist with refugee resettlement and family reunification.

397 — Gary
International Institute of Northwest Indiana
4433 Broadway
Gary, IN 46409
Lawrence Sharp, Director
(219) 980-4636

Services Offered: AD, CU, EC, ED RE, LI. **Established**: 1919. **BIA**. **Clientele**: World. Cultural, educational, and social services are provided to the foreign born. Emphasis is the integration of new arrivals into society while maintaining traditional cultural values.

398 — Indianapolis
Catholic Social Services
1400 North Meridian Street
Indianapolis, IN 46206
Robert H. Riegel, Executive Director
(317) 236-1550

Services Offered: AD, CE, EC, ED, SS. **Established**: 1919. **Staff**: 3. **Budget**: $80,000. **Religious Affiliation**: Catholic. **Clientele**: World. Following services offered: refugee resettlement; sponsor recruitment; job development; translation and interpretation; language training; and information and referral.

399 — Indianapolis
Disciples of Christ. Refugee & Immigration Ministries
Box 1986
Indianapolis, IN 46206
Rev. Jennifer Riggs, Director
(317) 353-1491 Fax: (317) 353-1524

Services Offered: AD, CE, LI, RE, SA, SS. **Established**: 1949. **Staff**: 4. **Religious Affiliation**: Disciples of Christ. **Clientele**: World. National coordinating office for the denomination's ministry to refugees and immigrants in the United States and Canada. Resettle refugees through Church World Service and assist congregations in providing services to undocumented persons. **Publications**: UNDOC: NEWSLETTER FOR PERSONS MINISTERING TO UNDOCUMENTED PERSONS (quarterly); SHARING: NEWSLETTER FOR SPONSORS (quarterly).

400
Indianapolis

Episcopal Refugee Resettlement Commission

Box 1410
Indianapolis, IN 46206
Sylvia Robles, Refugee Coordinator
(317) 236-1556

Services Offered: AD, CU, CE, EC, ED, RE, LI, SS. **Established**: 1982. **Religious Affiliation**: Episcopal. **Clientele**: World. Refugee sponsorship development amongst congregations and direct services and referrals for refugees and families.

401
Indianapolis

Indiana Council of Churches

1100 West 42nd Street, Suite 225
Indianapolis, IN 46208
Sylia Robles, Contact
(317) 923-3674

Services Offered: AD, CE, LE, RE, SS. **Religious Affiliation**: Ecumenical. **Clientele**: World. Advocacy and refugee resettlement xervices coordinated with Church World Service.

402
Indianapolis

Indiana Department of Welfare. Policy & Program Development

238 South Meridian Street
Indianapolis, IN 46204
Robert Igney, State Refugee Coordinator
(317) 232-2002

Services Offered: EC, ED, HE, SS. **Clientele**: World. Statewide coordination of federal, state and private resources for effective refugee resettlement (cash and medical assistance, social services, etc.).

403
Indianapolis

Jewish Family and Children's Services

1717 West 86th Street, Suite 450
Indianapolis, IN 46260
Martin L. Percher, Executive Director
(317) 872-6641

Services Offered: AD, CU, LE, ED, RE, LI, SS. **Religious Affiliation**: Jewish. **Clientele**: USSR, Europe, World. Refugees and immigrants receive assistance with employment, education, cultural orientation, legal services and general social services.

404
North Manchester

Manchester Church of the Brethren. Sanctuary Committee

305 Bond Street
North Manchester, IN 46962
David L. Rogers, Chair
(219) 982-7523

Services Offered: AD, SA. **Established**: 1984. **Staff**: 1. **Budget**: $14,000. **Religious Affiliation**: Brethren. **Clientele**: Central America/Caribbean. Since 1984 provide sanctuary for refugees from Central America. Offer financial, health, educational, religious, etc. assistance until permanent home found. Help with asylum applications and interviews with Canadian authorities. **Publications**: MANCHESTER MEMO (weekly newsletter).

405   *Cedar Rapids*

Faith United Methodist Church. Sanctuary Committee

1010 30th Street NE
Cedar Rapids, IA 52402
Gil Dawes, Coordinator
(319) 363-8454

Services Offered: AD, CE, SA. **Religious Affiliation**: Methodist. **Clientele**: Central America/Caribbean. Declared sanctuary for refugees fleeing from Central America.

406   *Davenport*

Catholic Resettlement and Immigration Office

2706 Gaines Street
Davenport, IA 52804
Betty Anderson, Director
(319) 324-1911

Services Offered: AD, CU, CE, EC, ED, LE, RE, RS, SA, SS. **Established**: 1971. **Religious Affiliation**: Catholic. **Clientele**: World. Reception and placement of refugees through US Catholic Conference Migration & Refugee Services. Legal assistance as well as educational and social service programs available to immigrants and refugees.

407   *Des Moines*

Catholic Council for Social Concern

Box 723
Des Moines, IA 50303
Lawrence Breheny, Refugee Manager
(515) 244-3761

Services Offered: AD, LE, SS. **Established**: 1975. **BIA**. **Religious Affiliation**: Catholic. **Clientele**: Southeast Asia. Services designed to assist refugees adapt to life in Iowa.

408   *Des Moines*

Iowa Department of Human Services. Bureau of Refugee Programs

1200 University Avenue, Suite D
Des Moines, IA 50314
Marvin Weidner, Bureau Chief
(800) 362-2780   Fax: (515) 281-7208

Services Offered: CU, EC, ED, HE, LI, SS. **Established**: 1975. **Staff**: 32. **Budget**: $3,650,000. **Clientele**: Southeast Asia, Europe. BRP serves as both a reception and placement agency and as the State of Iowa's social service provider. One major focus of the Bureau is the recruiting and training of sponsors. The other primary focus is helping refugees move towards self-sufficiency and become productive members of society. The Bureau operates an employment-oriented refugee program utilizing a sophisticated case management system. Program emphasizes job development, early employment and self-sufficiency. Also provides cultural orientation, translation and interpretation, and help with INS. Health related guidance. Maintains media and materials library. Approximately 10,000 refugees (98% from Southeast Asia) have been resettled in Iowa - half of these have been resettled through the Bureau of Refugee Programs. **Publications**: IOWA ORIENTING EXPRESS (bi-monthly, free); List of Publications.

409   *Des Moines*

Lutheran Social Services of Iowa

3116 University Avenue
Des Moines, IA 50311
Dan Norell, Refugee Consultant
(515) 277-4476

Services Offered: AD, CU, EC, ED, HE, LE, RE, SS. **Established**: 1975. **Staff**: 22. **Budget**: $300,000. **BIA**. **Religious Affiliation**: Lutheran. **Clientele**: Southeast Asia, Africa, Europe. Refugee resettlement program includes recruitment of sponsors, placement of refugees and their families and casework management. About 100 refugees annually are placed in Iowa, some 90% of which are sponsored by Lutheran congregations. Also operates programs for unaccompanied minor refugees (foster care) in the U.S. **Publications**: Annual Report.

410   *Dubuque*

Catholic Charities

Box 1309
Dubuque, IA 52001
James Yeast, Executive Director
((319) 588-0558

Services Offered: AD, SS. **Established**: 1930. **Staff**: 1. **Religious Affiliation**: Catholic. **Clientele**: Southeast Asia. Provide reception and placement services for refugees; serve as clearinghouse for information and referral on immigration matters; and general advocate for the needs of refugees and migrants.

411 — Elkhart

Catholic Agency for Migration and Refugee Services

Box 546
Elkhart, KS 67950
Sr. Teresa Orozco, Executive Director
(316) 698-4639

Services Offered: AD, LE, SS. **Established:** 1980. **Staff:** 2. **BIA. Religious Affiliation:** Catholic. **Clientele:** Central America/Caribbean, Southeast Asia. General aid for refugees and immigrants including legal representation.

412 — Garden City

Catholic Agency for Migration & Refugee Services

103 North Ninth
Garden City, KS 67846
Levita Rohlman, Director
(316) 275-2261

Services Offered: SS. **Established:** 1985. **Staff:** 1. **Budget:** $29,000. **Religious Affiliation:** Catholic. **Clientele:** Southeast Asia. Reception and placement of refugees; immigration counseling; assistance with INS paperwork.

413 — Kansas City

Catholic Social Services

229 South Eighth
Kansas City, KS 66044
Diane K. Hentges, Resettlement Director
(913) 621-1504

Services Offered: AD, EC, RE, SS. **Religious Affiliation:** Catholic. **Clientele:** World. Refugee assistance and family reunification. Social services and information and referral during initial placement period.

414 — Salina

Catholic Charities

Box 1366
Salina, KS 67402
Rev. Alfred Wasinger
(913) 825-0208

Services Offered: SS. **Religious Affiliation:** Catholic. **Clientele:** Southeast Asia. Provide aid to refugees and immigrants settling in Kansas.

415 — Topeka

Kansas Department of Social & Rehabilitation Services. Refugee Resettlement Program

Box 30
Topeka, KS 66601
Phillip P. Gutierrez, State Refugee Coordinator
(913) 296-3349

Services Offered: AD, EC, ED, HE, SS. **Clientele:** World. Statewide coordination of federal, state and private resources for effective refugee resettlement (cash and medical assistance, support services, etc.).

416 — Wichita

Catholic Charities. Refugee Program

Box 659
Wichita, KS 67201
Robert Hemberger, Director
(316) 264-0197

Services Offered: AD, CU, EC, RE, SS. **Established:** 1978. **Religious Affiliation:** Catholic. **Clientele:** World. Refugee resettlement and family reunification services available.

417 — Wichita

Lutheran Social Services of Kansas and Oklahoma

1855 North Hillside
Wichita, KS 67214
Rev. Jim Munson, Contact
(316) 686-6645

Services Offered: AD, CU, CE, EC, ED, LE, RE, SS. **Religious Affiliation:** Lutheran. **Clientele:** World. Refugee resettlement and assistance activities coordinated through Lutheran Immigration & Refugee Services.

418   Covington
Catholic Social Services Bureau

3629 Church Street
Covington, KY 41015
Noella Poinsette, Resettlement Director
(606) 581-8974

Services Offered: AD, CU, EC, ED, HE, RE, RS, SS. **Established:** 1975. **BIA. Religious Affiliation:** Catholic. **Clientele:** World. Full range of services and programs, from cultural orientation to job placement, for refugees and immigrants. Goal is making new arrivals as self-sufficient as possible in as short a period of time as possible.

419   Frankfort
Kentucky Cabinet for Human Resources. Office of the State Refugee Coordinator

275 East Main Street, 2nd Floor
Frankfort, KY 40621
James E. Randall, Director
(502) 564-3556

Services Offered: AD, CU, CE, EC, ED, HE, SS. **Clientele:** World. Statewide coordination of public and private resources for effective refugee resettlement including cash and medical assistance, support services, and such other activities as necessary for effective coordinated refugee resettlement.

420   Lexington
Catholic Social Service Bureau. Refugee Resettlement Program

1310 Leestown Road
Lexington, KY 40508
Maria A. Seyedsadr, Coordinator
(606) 253-1993

Services Offered: CU, CE, EC, ED, HE, SS. **Staff:** 2. **Budget:** $90,700. **Religious Affiliation:** Catholic. **Clientele:** World. A professional agency of the Catholic Diocese of Lexington, the Bureau is open to all peoples, regardless of religious beliefs. The Refugee Resettlement Program provides assistance to refugees and immigrants in the Greater Lexington area.

421   Lexington
Central Kentucky Jewish Association

333 Waller Avenue
Lexington, KY 40504
Linda Ravin, Administrator
(606) 252-7622

Services Offered: AD, CU, EC, RE, RS, SS. **Established:** 1977. **Religious Affiliation:** Jewish. **Clientele:** World. Services designed to assist newcomers adapt to life in a new land.

422   Louisville
Jewish Family and Vocational Service

3640 Dutchmans Lane
Louisville, KY 40205
Stephanie Speigel, Executive Director
(502) 452-6341

Services Offered: AD, CU, EC, RE, SS. **Religious Affiliation:** Jewish. **Clientele:** World. Initial resettlement services coordinated through Hebrew Immigrant Aid Society. Counseling, vocational orientation, etc. also offered.

423   Owensboro
Catholic Charities. Refugee Services

4005 Frederica Street
Owensboro, KY 42301
Sr. Theresa Marie Wilkerson, Director
(502) 683-1545

Services Offered: AD, EC, ED, HE, RE, SS. **Established:** 1975. **Staff:** 6. **Budget:** $28,000. **Religious Affiliation:** Catholic. **Clientele:** World. Offer resettlement services, employment services and English language training. Assist with INS paperwork.

424   *Baton Rouge*

Catholic Community Services. Migration & Refugee Services

Box 64688
Baton Rouge, LA 70896
Diane Chisholm-Thomas, Director
(504) 346-0660

Services Offered: EW, CU, CE, EC, ED, HE, LE, LI, SS. **Established:** 1975. **Staff:** 6. **Budget:** $150,000. **Religious Affiliation:** Catholic. **Clientele:** World. Primary mission is to develop and provide resettlement opportunities to incoming refugees, and legalization services to undocumented aliens. Major objective of the program is to assist refugees and immigrants toward economic self-sufficiency through the provision of social services. More than 6,000 refugees have been resettled in the Diocese of Baton Rouge. Operates the Indo-Chinese Resettlement Program.

425   *Baton Rouge*

Louisiana Department of Health & Human Services. Office of Human Development

Box 44367
Baton Rouge, LA 70804
Sybil Willis, State Refugee Coordinator
(504) 342-4017

Services Offered: AD, EC, ED, HE, SS. **Clientele:** World. Statewide coordination of federal, state and private resources for effective refugee resettlement including cash and medical assistance, support services and such other activities as necessary.

426   *Baton Rouge*

Presbytery of Southern Louisiana

928 Rodin Drive
Baton Rouge, LA 70806
James Monroe, General Presbyter
(504) 926-4562

Services Offered: LE, SS. **Religious Affiliation:** Presbyterian. **Clientele:** World. Offers limited assistance to refugees and immigrants. **Publications:** Newsletter.

427   *Houma*

Catholic Social Services

Box 3894

Houma, LA 70361
Miriam Mitchell, Director
(504) 876-0490

Services Offered: AD, RE, RS, SS. **Established:** 1966. **Staff:** 6. **Religious Affiliation:** Catholic. **Clientele:** World. Emergency assistance and services for refugees and immigrants. **Publications:** Annual Report.

428   *Lafayette*

Diocese of Lafayette. Migration & Refugee Services

1408 Carmel Avenue
Lafayette, LA 70503
Tina Davis, Program Director
(318) 261-5535

Services Offered: AD, EC, ED, LE, HE, SS. **Established:** 1975. **Staff:** 7. **Religious Affiliation:** Catholic. **Clientele:** Southeast Asia. Assistance with family reunification, employment services, language training, adjustment of status/asylee paperwork, etc.

429   *New Orleans*

Associated Catholic Charities

8019 Fig Street
New Orleans, LA 70125
Jane M. Foley, Resettlement Director
(504) 866-2537

Services Offered: AD, SS. **Staff:** 7. **BIA. Religious Affiliation:** Catholic. **Clientele:** World, Southeast Asia, Central America/Caribbean. Resettlement services coordinated through US Catholic Conference Migration & Refugee Services. Services include initial placement, casework management, help with immigration/asylum forms, translations, etc.

430   *New Orleans*

Baptist Association of New Orleans

2222 Lakeshore Drive
New Orleans, LA 70122
Rev. Miguel Olmedo, Language Mission
(504) 282-1428

Services Offered: AD, CU, LE, RE, SS. **Established:** 1970. **BIA. Religious Affiliation:** Baptist. **Clientele:** Central America/Caribbean. Legal and social services and

and programs for refugees and immigrants.

applications to the INS.

431 *New Orleans*
Ecumenical Immigration Services

821 General Pershing Drive
New Orleans, LA   70115
Gloribel Rubio, Director
(504) 891-4613

Services Offered: CE, ED, LE, SS.
Established: 1982. **Staff**: 3. **Budget**: $48,335.
BIA. **Religious Affiliation**: Ecumenical.
Clientele: Central America/Caribbean. Provide legal representation in deportation procedures and asylum for Central Americans, particularly refugees from El Salvador and Guatemala.

432 *New Orleans*
Louisiana Department of Health & Human Resources. State Refugee Coordinator

2026 St. Charles Avenue, Room 202
New Orleans, LA   70130
Steven P. Thibodeaux, Coordinator
(504) 342-5116

Services Offered: SS. **Established**: 1982.
Staff: 1. **Clientele**: World. This is the single state agency responsible for the development and administration of the Refugee Resettlement Program.Primary goal is to effectively resettle refugees and to promote economic self-sufficiency for refugees within the shortest possible time. Coordination of federally funded and non-federally funded programs and activities for refugees to assure priority status be given to English language training and employment services and related support services.

433 *New Orleans*
Loyola University. School of Law Clinic

7214 St. Charles Avenue
New Orleans, LA   70118
Evangeline Abriel, Attorney
(504) 865-3131

Services Offered: LE, LI. **Established**: 1974.
BIA. **Clientele**: Central America/Caribbean. Works in all immigration cases with an emphasis on asylum. Client representation at all levels of bond rederterminations, deportation proceedings, BIA appeals and petitions for judicial review as well as administrative

434 *New Orleans*
Naturalization Project

3700 Canal Street
New Orleans, LA   70119
Maxine Lowy, Director
(504) 486-4050

Services Offered: AD, CE, ED, SS.
Established: 1984. **Staff**: 4. **Budget**: $27,000.
Clientele: World, Central America/Caribbean.
Provides orientation and instruction for naturalization and legalization. Processes applications for naturalization, relative petitions and legalization. Serves New Orleans and the Gulf Coast region. **Publications**: Annual Report.

435 *New Orleans*
New Orleans Legal Assistance Corporation

212 Loyola Avenue, Suite 400
New Orleans, LA   70112
Luz Molina, Attorney
(504) 529-1000

Services Offered: LE. **Established**: 1967. **BIA**.
Clientele: World. Serve indigent refugees and immigrants.

436 *Shreveport*
Jewish Family Service

2032 Line Avenue
Shreveport, LA   71104
Monty Pomm, Director
(318) 221-4129

Services Offered: AD, CU, LI, RE, RS, SS.
BIA. **Religious Affiliation**: Jewish.
Clientele: World. Services and programs designed to assist Jewish refugees and immigrants become productive members of the community.

437   *Augusta*

Maine Department of Human Services. Bureau of Social Services

State House Station 11
Augusta, ME 04333
David Stauffer, State Refugee Coordinator
(207) 289-5060

Services Offered: SS. **Established**: 1980.
Staff: 1. **Budget**: $600,000. **Clientele**: World.
Goal of the state agency is to provide services that assist refugees to attain self-sufficiency as soon as possible. Provide cash and medical assistance to needy refugees and a mix of appropriate social services, including employment services and English language training. Coordinates federal, state, local and private agency programs.

---

438   *Hallowell*

Maine Annual Conference of the United Methodist Church

33 Central Avenue
Hallowell, ME 04347
Rev. Jean Marsh, Contact
(207) 622-6636

Services Offered: AD, CE, RE, SS. **Religious Affiliation**: Methodist. **Clientele**: World. Offers ecumenical refugee resettlement and sponsorship services through Church World Service Immigration & Refugee Program.

---

439   *Portland*

Diocesan Refugee Resettlement Program

107 Elm Street
Portland, ME 04101
David Agan, Director
(207) 871-7448

Services Offered: AD, CU, EC, ED, RE, SS.
Established: 1975. **Religious Affiliation**: Catholic. **Clientele**: World. Following resettlement services available: job orientation and placement; housing; language programs; translation and interpretation; and general social services.

---

440   *Portland*

Jewish Family Services

57 Ashmont Street
Portland, ME 04103

Joan Sud Soreff, Administrator
(207) 775-0770

Services Offered: EC, SS. **Established**: 1950.
Religious Affiliation: Jewish. **Clientele**: USSR. Provide assistance and emergency services for the resettlement of Soviet Jews.

---

441 *Baltimore*

Associated Catholic Charities. Refugee Employment Services

6 South Wolfe Street
Baltimore, MD 21231
Tien Thuy Tran, Coordinator
(301) 522-1993

Services Offered: EC, SS. **Established:** 1982. **Staff:** 4. **Budget:** $110,000. **Religious Affiliation:** Catholic. **Clientele:** World. Variety of services geared to preparing the refugee to enter the workplace, such as vocational evaluation and skills assessment, job readiness training, employment counseling, job placement, translation, transportation help, general information and referral services.

442 *Baltimore*

Episcopal Social Ministries

105 West Monument
Baltimore, MD 21201
Beth McNamara, Refugee Coordinator
(301) 837-0300

Services Offered: AD, RE, RS, SS. **Established:** 1981. **Religious Affiliation:** Episcopal. **Clientele:** World. Refugee services and programs designed to assist in transition of refugee to life in the United States.

443 *Baltimore*

Hebrew Immigrant Aid Society of Baltimore

5750 Park Heights Avenue
Baltimore, MD 21215
Ingeborg B. Weinberger, Executive Director
(301) 542-6300

Services Offered: AD, LE, SS. **Established:** 1903. **Staff:** 2. **Budget:** $79,515. **Religious Affiliation:** Jewish. **Clientele:** World. Migration service agency of the Associated Jewish Charities in Baltimore and works in conjunction with the Hebrew Immigrant Aid Society based in New York City. Offers pre-migration, reception and post-migration services including naturalization, asylum, etc. Also operates an indemnification program for Nazi persecutees.

444 *Baltimore*

Jewish Family Service. Resettlement Program

5750 Park Heights Avenue
Baltimore, MD 21215
Lucy Steinitz, Director
(301) 466-9200

Services Offered: AD, CU, ED, RE, LI, SS. **Religious Affiliation:** Jewish. **Clientele:** World. Program designed to assist primarily Jewish refugees with initial needs through social casework process.

445 *Baltimore*

Maryland Department of Human Resources. State Refugee Coordinator

311 West Saratoga Street
Baltimore, MD 21201
Frank J. Bien, Coordinator
(301) 333-1863

Services Offered: AD, EC, ED, HE, SS. **Clientele:** World. Statewide coordination of federal, state and private resources for effective refugee resettlement (cash and medical assistance, social services, etc.).

446 *Baltimore*

National Slavic Convention

16 South Patterson Park Avenue
Baltimore, MD 21231
Rev. Ivan Dornic, Contact
(301) 276-7676

Services Offered: AD, CU, CE, ED, RE, SA, SS. **Established:** 1980. **Staff:** 9. **Budget:** $120,000. **Clientele:** Europe, USSR. Provides variety of services to refugees fleeing from Eastern Europe and the USSR. **Publications:** Newsletter (monthly, free).

447 *Columbia*

Baptist Convention of Maryland

10255 Old Columbia Road
Columbia, MD 21046
Minor Davidson, Director of Missions
(301) 290-5290

Services Offered: AD, CU, RE, SS. **Established:** 1980. **Religious Affiliation:** Baptist. **Clientele:** Central America/Caribbean, Southeast Asia. Refugee resettlement program coordinated through local church sponsorship.

448 *Columbia*
Foreign-Born Information and Referral Network

5999 Harper's Farm Road
Columbia, MD 21044
Patricia A. Hatch, Executive Director
(301) 992-1923

Services Offered: AD, LI, SS. **Established**:
1981. **Staff**: 4. **Budget**: $70,000. **Clientele**:
World. FIRN's goal is to assist refugees and immigrants who are settling in Howard County to attain
economic self-sufficiency and become happy, productive citizens. Provide help in finding jobs, housing,
transportation, day care, health care, consumer assistance, etc. Immigration and naturalization information
and help in filling out forms is also available.
Through the complex and sometimes lengthy resettlement process, FIRN is available to inform, to
guide and to support. **Publications**: FOCUS ON
FIRN (semi-annual, free).

449 *Greenbelt*
Hmong Community Service

7078-B1 Hanover Parkway
Greenbelt, MD 20770
(301) 441-1142

Services Offered: CU, SS. **Religious
Affiliation**: Lutheran. **Clientele**: Southeast Asia.
Referral service for Hmong and Laotian refugees.
Provide limited assistance with translation and interpretation, interaction with government agencies and
acculturation process.

450 *New Windsor*
Church of the Brethren. Refugee Resettlement Program

Box 188
New Windsor, MD 21776
Donna Derr, Director
(301) 635-6464   Fax: (301) 635-6171

Services Offered: AD, SS, SA. **Established**:
1944. **Staff**: 3. **Budget**: $100,140. **Religious
Affiliation**: Brethren. **Clientele**: World. Goals are
to: find sponsors for Church World Service refugee
cases; provide follow-up case management for
refugees who have arrived in the U.S.; provide housing; health screening; English classes for refugees in
their transit center until a sponsor is found; assist
persons with asylum and family reunification applications; and, educate their denominational constituency
on refugee and sanctuary issues. **Publications**:

REFUGEE/DISASTER UPDATE (quarterly, free);
SANCTUARY NEWS (quarterly, free).

451 *Rockville*
Jewish Social Services Agency

6123 Montrose Road
Rockville, MD 20852
Roberta Drucker, Resettlement Coordinator
(301) 770-8741

Services Offered: AD, CU, EC, ED, SS. **BIA**.
Religious Affiliation: Jewish. **Clientele**:
USSR, World. Refugee resettlement program designed to assist refugee become productive member of
society and adjust successfully to life in the U.S.

452 *Rockville*
U.S. Department of Health and Human Services. Public Health Service. Office of Refugee Health

5600 Fishers Lane, 18A-30 Parklawn
Rockville, MD 20857
Clifford Culp, Director
(301) 443-4130

Services Offered: HE. **Clientele**: World.
Coordinate health services for refugees.

453 *Salisbury*
Legal Aid Bureau

111 High Street
Salisbury, MD 21801
Margaret Hennessy, Attorney
(301) 546-5511

Services Offered: LE, LI. **Established**: 1978.
BIA. **Clientele**: Central America/Caribbean. Legal
assistance in immigration matters, particularly relative petitions and asylum.

454 *Silver Spring*
Korean American Community Services

969 Thayer Avenue
Silver Spring, MD 20907
Tae K. Hahn, Executive Director
(301) 589-6470   Fax: (301) 587-4660

Services Offered: CU, ED, LE, SS.
Established: 1979. **Staff**: 3. **Budget**: $70,000.
Religious Affiliation: Ecumenical. **Clientele**:

World, Asia. General assistance to Korean immigrants, including help with INS and other government forms and applications. **Publications**: KACS NEWSLETTER (quarterly); Annual report; Directory.

---

455 *Takoma Park*

Central American Solidarity and Assistance

310 Tulip Avenue
Takoma Park, MD 20912
Lael Parish, Executive Director
(301) 270-0442

Services Offered: AD, CE, CU, EC, ED, RE, SS. **Established**: 1985. **Staff**: 3. **Budget**: $58,000. **Religious Affiliation**: Ecumenical. **Clientele**: Central America/Caribbean. CASA was established in 1985 to help fulfill the essential yet unmet needs of the Central American refugee community in the area. Since then CASA has offered the refugees an array of social services as well as a meeting place to share and confront mutual problems. Provides the following services and programs: legal; food distribution; community garden; clothes closet; medical referral program; emergency housing referral program; survival English classes; job bank; and women's support group. **Publications**: NOTICIAS DE CASA (bi-monthly, free); Annual Report.

---

456 *Takoma Park*

City of Tacoma Park. Office of the Mayor

7500 Naple Avenue
Takoma Park, MD 20912
(301) 270-1700

Services Offered: SA. **Clientele**: Central America/Caribbean. City is a declared public sanctuary for refugees from El Salvador and Guatemala.

---

457 *Amherst*

Pioneer Valley Sanctuary Committee, Mt. Toby Meeting of Friends

RFD 3, Longplain Road
Amherst, MA 01002
(413) 548-9188

Services Offered: SA. **Established**: 1985. **Budget**: $5,000. **Religious Affiliation**: Ecumenical. **Clientele**: Central America/Caribbean. Support the sanctuary of Central American refugees through the assistance of five local religious congregations. Affiliated with the New England Sanctuary Network. Inquiries can be addressed to the Volunteer Steering Committee at the above address.

---

458 *Boston*

Catholic Charities Refugee & Immigration Services

150 Causeway Street
Boston, MA 02114
Mary Diaz, District Director
(617) 262-7806

Services Offered: AD, CE, LE, SS. **Staff**: 10. **BIA**. **Religious Affiliation**: Catholic. **Clientele**: World, Southeast Asia, Central America/Caribbean. The Immigration Services Program is a non-profit service run in conjunction with the Catholic Charitable Bureau of Boston Refugee Resettlement Program. It provides legal assistance to people who have problems with their immigration status. The service is available to all persons of all nationalities, provided they have a low or moderate income and live within the Archdiocese of Boston. Provide a wide range of services from brief advice and help in completing forms to the actual preparation of cases before the INS. The Refugee Sponsor Program assists new arrivals with locating housing, providing emergency services, arranging Social Security visits, encouragement and assistance in finding employment, enrolling children in school, etc.

---

459 *Boston*

Chinese American Civic Association

90 Tyler Street
Boston, MA 02111
Cahu-Ming Lee, Executive Director
(617) 986-9492

Services Offered: AD, EC, ED, SS. **Established**: 1967. **Staff**: 48. **Budget**:

$1,200,000. **BIA. Clientele**: Southeast Asia, Asia. Provides essential human services, including social services, adult education, job training, etc. to facilitate adjustment of new arrivals to the United States. **Publications**: SAMPAN (newspaper); Annual Report.

---

460   *Boston*

Greater Boston Legal Services

68 Essex Street
Boston, MA 02111
Iris Gomez, Attorney
(617) 357-5757

Services Offered: LE, RS. **Clientele**: World. Immigration and naturalization legal services available to indigent clients.

---

461   *Boston*

Immigrant Students Project of the National Coalition of Advocates for Students

100 Boylston Street, Suite 737
Boston, MA 02116
John Willshire Carrera, Director
(617) 357-8507

Services Offered: AD, CE, ED, LE, RS. **Established**: 1986. **Clientele**: World. NCAS is a national coalition of child advocate organizations. The Immigrant Student Project focuses its efforts on immigrant students in the United States public schools. Work on issues involving the right of access to public schools and the right of a quality and equitable public education for immigrant students. **Publications**: STEPS (monographic series); monographs. List of publications available.

---

462   *Boston*

Massachusetts Immigrant & Refugee Advocacy Coalition

178 Tremont Street, 9th Floor
Boston, MA 02111
Muriel Heilberger, Executive Director
(617) 357-6000

Services Offered: AD, CE. **Established**: 1987. **Staff**: 2. **Budget**: $93,000. MIRA advocates for access to city and state-funded services and benefits of documented and undocumented immigrants and refugees and for a more progressive immigration policy. MIRA is a coalition of over 50 groups and individuals - immigrants' rights agencies, labor unions, civil liberties and civil rights advocates, social service agencies, religious groups, lawyers, etc. Objective is to ensure that individuals' rights and benefits are fully protected and dangers and difficulties mimimized in the implementation of the Immigration Reform and Control Act. **Publications**: MIRA News (quarterly newsletter).

---

463   *Boston*

Massachusetts Office for Refugees and Immigrants

2 Boylston Street, 2nd Floor
Boston, MA 02116
Daniel M. Lam, State Refugee Coordinator
(617) 727-7888

Services Offered: AD, EC, ED, HE, SS. **Clientele**: World. Statewide coordination of federal, state and private resources for effective refugee resettlement including cash and medical assistance, support services and such other activities as necessary.

---

464   *Boston*

National Immigration Project of the National Lawyers Guild

14 Beacon Street, Suite 506
Boston, MA 02108
Dan Kesselbrenner, Director
(617) 227-9727

Services Offered: AD, CE, LE. **Established**: 1980. **Staff**: 3. **Budget**: $89,000. **Clientele**: World, Central America/Caribbean. The NIP is a network of lawyers and legal community workers engaged in the legal and political aspects of immigration law and practice. Primary concerns are to protect, defend, and extend the rights of all immigrants in the United States, regardless of status. There are two special sub-projects, the Central American Refugee Defense Fund and the Visa Denial Project. The NIP develops and improves immigration practitioners' legal skills and educates the public about social and political conditions that affect immigrants. To this end, they provide technical assistance, produce materials, and present skills seminars. They defend immigrants' civil and labor rights, work to lessen discrimination, and monitor unlawful law enforcement activity. **Publications**: IMMIGRATION NEWSLETTER (quarterly, $50); CENTRAL AMERICAN REFUGEE DEFENSE FUND (quarterly)

---

465   *Boston*

U.S. Department of Health & Human Services. Family Support Administration. Office of Refugee Resettlement

JFK Federal Building
Boston, MA 02203
Jack Anderson, Contact
(617) 565-2465

Services Offered: Clientele: World. Regional office for U.S. Office of Refugee Resettlement responsible for coordinating federal assistance (cash and medical, social services, health, demonstration grants, etc.) in order to help refugees.

---

466 *Brookline*

Jewish Family and Children's Service

637 Washington Street
Brookline, MA 02165
Ena Feinberg, Migration Counselor
(617) 566-5716   Fax: (617) 566-4667

Services Offered: AD, LE, SS. **Staff:** 35. **BIA. Religious Affiliation:** Jewish. **Clientele:** USSR. Resettlement services for refugees and immigrants coordinated with Hebrew Immigrant Aid Society.

---

467 *Cambridge*

Cambridge and Somerville Legal Services Immigration Unit

264 Third Street
Cambridge, MA 02142
John Willshire Carrera, Staff Attorney
(617) 492-5520

Services Offered: AD, LE. **Staff:** 2. **BIA. Clientele:** World. Represents persons seeking asylum or safe haven in the United States.

---

468 *Cambridge*

Cambridge Organization of Portuguese-Americans

1046 Cambridge Street
Cambridge, MA 02139
Antonio Fontes, Executive Director
(617) 492-5800

Services Offered: AD, CU, CE, SS. **Established:** 1969. **Clientele:** Europe, South America. Programs and services designed to reduce discrimination and promote self-sufficiency among Portuguese-Americans.

---

469 *Cambridge*

Centro Presente

54 Essex Street
Cambridge, MA 02139
Frank Sherry, Director
(617) 497-9080

Services Offered: AD, CU, CE, ED, LI, RE, RS, SS. **Established:** 1981. **BIA. Clientele:** Central America/Caribbean. Offers extensive services and programs to refugees from Central America.

---

470 *Cambridge*

City of Cambridge. Office of the Mayor

154 Berkeley Street
Cambridge, MA 02116
(617) 247-4200

Services Offered: SA. **Clientele:** Central America/Caribbean. Declared public sanctuary for Salvadoran and Guatemalan refugees.

---

471 *Cambridge*

Cultural Survival

11 Divinity Avenue
Cambridge, MA 02138
David Maybury-Lewis, President
(617) 495-2562

Services Offered: AD, CU, HE, CE, LI, RS. **Clientele:** World. Research and analysis on the survival of indigenous peoples and ethnic groups. Examines ethnic persecution as cause of refugees.

---

472 *Cambridge*

Haitian American Association

105 Windsor Street
Cambridge, MA 02139
John Barnes, Director
(617) 492-6622

Services Offered: AD, CU, CE, EC, LE, RE, SS. **Established:** 1978. **Clientele:** Central America/Caribbean. Services offered to Haitian refugees and immigrants.

473   *Cambridge*

Human Rights Internet

Harvard Law School, 401 Pound Hall
Cambridge, MA   02138
Laurie S. Wiseberg, Executive Director
(617) 495-9924   Fax: (617) 495-1110

Services Offered: LI, RS. **Established:** 1976.
Staff: 5. **Clientele:** World. One of the world's major documentation centers on human rights and related topics such as refugees, immigrants, international migration, etc. In addition to publishing a variety of series, HRI provides database searching services, including assisting lawyers prepare asylum cases with background information on the human rights situation in countries from which the refugees have fled. Also offers consultancy services to human rights and refugee/immigrant organizations who are beginning to computerize their documentation collections. Fee schedules for database searching, document reproductuon and computer assistance are available on request. **Publications:** HUMAN RIGHTS INTERNET REPORTER (quarterly, $40-$60); 6 HUMAN RIGHTS DIRECTORIES; monographs.

474   *Dorchester*

Haitian Multi-Service Center

12 Bicknell Street
Dorchester, MA   02121
Frances Laroche, Coordinator
(617) 436-2848

Services Offered: AD, CU, CE, EC, ED, LE, HE, LI, SS. **Clientele:** Central America/Caribbean. Broad range of services and programs designed to assist with cultural, emotional, economic and physical transition for Haitian refugees and immigrants.

475   *Dorchester*

Vietnamese American Civic Association

1486 Dorchester Avenue
Dorchester, MA   02122
Trong Duy Tran, Executive Director
(617) 888-7344

Services Offered: AD, CU, CE, ED, HE, LE, RS, SS. **Staff:** 6. **Budget:** $80,000. **BIA.** **Clientele:** Southeast Asia, Asia. Provides a wide range of services all designed to assist with readjustment to life in the United States. **Publications:** FRIENDSHIP (quarterly magazine, free); Annual Report.

476   *Fall River*

Catholic Social Services of Fall River

Box M - South Station
Fall River, MA   02724
Rev. Peter Graziano, Executive Director
(508) 674-4681

Services Offered: AD, EC, SS. **Established:** 1974. **Staff:** 21. **Budget:** $505,000. **Religious Affiliation:** Catholic. **Clientele:** Southeast Asia. Non-profit, multiservice agency offering a variety of social services and programs, including refugee resettlement.

477   *Jamaica Plains*

Legal Services Center

3529 Washington Street
Jamaica Plains, MA   02130
Antonieta Gimeno, Attorney
(617) 522-3003

Services Offered: LE, RS. **Established:** 1979. **BIA. Clientele:** World. Legal representation of refugees and immigrants in deportation, political asylum and visa petition cases.

478   *Lowell*

Cambodian Mutual Assistance Association of Greater Lowell

125 Perry Street
Lowell, MA   01852
Boran Reth, President
(508) 454-4286

Services Offered: AD, CU, EC, ED, SS. **Established:** 1985. **Staff:** 13. **Budget:** $277,000. **Clientele:** Southeast Asia. Established to enable the Cambodian leadership in Lowell to provide appropriate services to the Cambodian refugee and immigrant community. The goal is to provide programs that will permit refugees to enter the mainstream of society and at the same time maintain their cultural heritage. Affiliated with the Massachusetts Office of Refugees and Immigrants.

479   *Lowell*

International Institute of Lowell

79 High Street
Lowell, MA   01852
Lydia A. Mattei, Executive Director
(508) 459-9031

Services Offered: AD, CU, CE, ED, LE, SS. **Established**: 1928. **Staff**: 8. **BIA**. **Clientele**: World. The International Institute recognizes the contributions all ethnic groups have made, and continue to make to American life. Newcomers are encouraged to retain their native languages and customs while learning the English language and the American way. Provides the following services to immigrants and refugees: translation; interpretation; immigration and naturalization; counseling; referrals; notary public service; ethnic clubs; language courses; and family reunification. Affiliated with the American Council for Nationalities Service.

---

480   *New Bedford*

Immigrants Assistance Center

58 Crapo Street
New Bedford, MA 02740
Ralph Medeiros, President
(508) 996-8113

Services Offered: AD, CE, EC, ED, SS. **Established**: 1971. **Staff**: 6. **Budget**: $130,000. **Clientele**: World, Europe. Primary goals of the IAC is to assist, promote, develop and coordinate civic, educational, charitable, governmental, business, medical and legal organizations and firms to advocate, upgrade and organize the interests of immigrants in the United States, particularly Southeastern Massachusetts. To ease and dissolve the cultural, social and economic barriers faced by persons of any nationality and to provide referral and advocacy services. Though clients come from all parts of the world, most of the clients are Portuguese or Cape Verdean.

---

481   *Somerville*

Somerville Portuguese American League

92 Union Square
Somerville, MA 02143
Jose Moura, Executive Director
(617) 628-6065

Services Offered: AD, CU, CE, LI, RE, RS, SS. **Established**: 1973. **Clientele**: Europe, South America. Advocacy and support group for immigrants from Portugal and Brasil.

---

482   *Springfield*

Diocese of Springfield. Refugee Resettlement Center

11 Pearl Street, Suite 210

Springfield, MA 01103
Elena V. Grechko, Director
(413) 732-6365

Services Offered: AD, CU, CE, EC, ED, LE, SS. **Religious Affiliation**: Catholic. **Clientele**: World. Refugee Resettlement Program provides services and programs to aid refugees in Springfield. Coordination through US Catholic Conference Migration & Refugee Services.

---

483   *Springfield*

Jewish Family Service of Greater Springfield

15 Lenox Street
Springfield, MA 01108
Arthur Weidman, Director
(413) 737-2601

Services Offered: AD, SS. **Established**: 1915. **Staff**: 24. **Budget**: $600,000. **Religious Affiliation**: Jewish. **Clientele**: USSR. "It's a long process, but the end results make it all well worth the effort. It's an obligation rooted in a history that cannot be ignored. It's a unification of distant families in a free country." Each of these statements describes JFS' Russian Resettlement Program. Through coordination with the Hebrew Immigrant Aid Society JFS is an active part of the resettlement process. The refugees are informed about Social Security, Medicare, classes in English, skills training courses, and education for their children. Agency has assisted with the resettlement of over 150 Russian immigrants in the Springfield area. **Publications**: FAMILY MATTERS (quarterly newsletter, free); Annual Report.

---

484   *Springfield*

Sinai Temple. Sanctuary Committee

1100 Dickenson Street
Springfield, MA 01108
Rabbi Shapiro, Contact
(413) 736-3619

Services Offered: AD, CE, SA. **Religious Affiliation**: Jewish. **Clientele**: Central America/Caribbean. Support and sanctuary for Salvadoran and Guatemalan refugees.

---

485   *Watertown*

Lutheran Child & Family Services of Massachusetts

85 Main Street, 3rd Floor

Watertown, MA 02172
Joyce Simon, Contact
(617) 972-6245

Services Offered: AD, CU, EC, ED, RE, SS.
Religious Affiliation: Lutheran. **Clientele**:
World. Refugee resettlement, sponsorship development, family reunification programs and related services offered through Lutheran Immigration &
Refugee Service.

---

486 *Worcester*

Catholic Charities

15 Ripley Street
Worcester, MA 01610
Constance S. Lynch, Refugee Coordinator
(617) 798-0191

Services Offered: AD, CU, RS, SS.
Established: 1960. **Religious Affiliation**:
Catholic. **Clientele**: World. Reception and resettlement of refugees coordinated through US Catholic
Conference Migration & Refugee Services and state
contracts.

---

487 *Worcester*

National Council of Jewish Women. Immigration & Naturalization Office

633 Salisbury Street
Worcester, MA 01609
(508) 791-3438

Services Offered: SS. **Established**: 1935. **BIA.**
Religious Affiliation: Jewish. **Clientele**:
USSR. Resettlement and family reunification services
for Soviet Jews.

---

488 *Ann Arbor*

First Unitarian Church. Sanctuary Committee

1917 Washtenaw Avenue
Ann Arbor, MI 48104
Kenneth Phifer, Contact
(313) 665-6158

Services Offered: AD, CE, SA. **Religious Affiliation**: Unitarian. **Clientele**: Central
America/Caribbean. Advocacy, support, outreach and
declared sanctuary for refugees fleeing Central
America.

---

489 *Clawson*

Vietnamese Catholic Community

581 East Fourteen Mile Road
Clawson, MI 48017
Rev. Vincent Ninh, Pastor
(313) 585-7053

Services Offered: AD, CU, CE, ED, LI, RE, RS,
SS. **Established**: 1976. **Staff**: 12. **Religious Affiliation**: Catholic. **Clientele**: Southeast Asia.
Combination of religious and secular services offered
to provide an atmosphere of community to
Vietnamese Catholics in the Archdiocese of Detroit.
Publications: PHUNG VU LITURGY; TINH
THAN MOI NEWSLETTER (weekly, free); Annual
Report.

---

490 *Detroit*

Archdiocese of Detroit. Office of Refugee Resettlement

305 Michigan Avenue
Detroit, MI 48226
Dennis Scanland, Director
(313) 237-5900

Services Offered: AD, CU, EC, SS.
Established: 1941. **Staff**: 14. **Budget**: $350,000.
BIA. Religious Affiliation: Catholic.
Clientele: World. Assist refugees in attaining economic and cultural self-sufficiency in the Catholic
Archdiocese through airport reception and provision
of basic needs (housing, food, clothing, etc.), orientation, assessment, counseling, employment services,
referral to appropriate community agencies and follow-up for one year from date of arrival.
Publications: VOYAGER (newsletter).

---

491 *Detroit*

Capuchin Mission Secretariat

1820 Mt. Elliot
Detroit, MI 48207
Larry LaCrosse, Director
(313) 579-2100

Services Offered: CE, LI, SA, SS. **Established:**
1983. **BIA. Religious Affiliation:** Catholic.
Clientele: Central America/Caribbean. Work with
local sanctuary churches and solidarity groups to provide community education and assist with the physical, material and other needs of refugees. Assist
undocumented individuals cross into Canada.

---

492 *Detroit*

Detroit Windsor Refugee Coalition

2630 West Lafayette
Detroit, MI 48216
Tim McCabe, Executive Director
(313) 963-0270

Services Offered: LE, SA, SS. **Established:**
1984. **Staff:** 4. **Clientele:** Central
America/Caribbean. Assist political refugees enter
Canada via Detroit/Windsor. **Publications:** Annual
Report.

---

493 *Detroit*

Diocesan Refugee Coordinator

4800 Woodward
Detroit, MI 48201
Evelyn Bayer, Refugee Coordinator
(313) 832-4400

Services Offered: SS. **Established:** 1982.
Staff: 6. **BIA. Religious Affiliation:**
Episcopal. **Clientele:** Europe. Coordinates local
refugee resettlement among congregations.

---

494 *Detroit*

Hmong Community

13560 East McNichols
Detroit, MI 48205
Phia Gao Yang, Coordinator
(313) 372-3600

Services Offered: AD, CU, CE, EC, SS.
Clientele: Southeast Asia. Advocacy and support
for Hmong refugees in the Greater Detroit area.

---

495 *Detroit*

International Institute of Metro Detroit

111 East Kirby
Detroit, MI 48202
Mary G. Ball, Executive Director
(313) 871-8600

Services Offered: AD, CU, CE, EC, ED, LE,
SC, SS. **Established:** 1919. **Staff:** 25. **Budget:**
$453,000. **BIA. Clientele:** World. Services for the
foreign born include: family strengthening and preservation; community and neighborhood development;
supplementary educational programs; assistance with
INS and other immigration and naturalization forms;
job orientation, placement and counseling; and a
broad array of social services. **Publications:**
INTERNATIONAL INSTITUTE NEWSLETTER
(bi-monthly); Annual Report.

---

496 *Detroit*

Michigan Department of Social Services. Office of Refugee Assistance Programs

1200 Sixth Street, Suite 462
Detroit, MI 48226
Joyce Savale, Program Manager
(313) 256-1740

Services Offered: AD, CU, CE, EC, LI, SS.
Established: 1975. **Staff:** 16. **Clientele:** World.
ORAP is the unit within the Department of Social
Services that serves as the lead unit responsible for
the management and administration of federal RAP
grants. The office coordinates various public and private resettlement efforts in order to ensure the cost
effective implementation of refugee resettlement efforts throughout the state; assists in maximizing the
amount of federal participation for cash and medical
assistance payments to refugees; purchases employment and supportive services from private agencies to
assist refugees attain self-sufficiency; administers the
Refugee Unaccompanied Minor Program; interprets
federal policy and directives; and maintains information on statewide resettlement programs and activities.

---

497 *East Lansing*

City of East Lansing. Office of the Mayor

410 Abbott Road
East Lansing, MI 48823
(517) 337-1731

Services Offered: SA. **Clientele:** Central
America/Caribbean. East Lansing is a declared public

sanctuary for Central American refugees.

498 *Ferndale*
Tolstoy Foundation

22750 Woodward Avenue, Suite 211
Ferndale, MI 48220
Virginia Trabold, Coordinator
(313) 546-6008

Services Offered: AD, CU, CE, EC, ED, LE, LI, SS. **Clientele**: Europe, World. Extensive cultural, educational and social services and programs offered to the foreign born in order to facilitate their transition to life in the United States. Emphasis on refugees from Eastern Europe.

499 *Flint*
International Institute of Flint

515 Stevens Street
Flint, MI 48502
Mary Elizabeth Schultz, Executive Director
(313) 767-0720

Services Offered: AD, CU, CE, EC, LE, LI, RS, SS. **Established**: 1922. **Staff**: 12. **Budget**: $298,000. **BIA**. **Clientele**: World. As part of the Flint community for nearly 70 years, the Institute has helped thousands of immigrants resettle in the area, providing the city with an ethnic diversity that has helped make it a unique community. Provides assistance with the problems concerning immigration, repatriation, deportation, as well as information about new laws and advice on documents and procedures. Offers help in filling out applications and clarification of citizenship status. Offers help on such matters as obtaining visas, reuniting separated families, determining citizenship of minor children and similar problems. Provides help with medical, emotional and financial emergencies. Job training and placement services also available. Extensive program of educational services. In 1987 assisted nearly 1,500 clients with immigration problems and served nearly 20,000 through intercultural programs. **Publications**: BULLETIN (monthly, free); Annual Report.

500 *Gaylord*
Community, Family & Children Services. Refugee Foster Care Program

1665 M-32 West, Cabrini Building
Gaylord, MI 49735
Sherry McRill, Coordinator

(313) 732-6761

Services Offered: AD, CU, ED, SS. **Clientele**: Southeast Asia. Provides foster care for unaccompanied refugee youth and related social and educational services.

501 *Grand Rapids*
Bethany Christian Services. Refugee Foster Care Program

3206 Eastern Avenue SE
Grand Rapids, MI 49508
Donna M. Abbott, Coordinator
(616) 245-7100

Services Offered: AD, CU, ED, LE, RE, SS. **Religious Affiliation**: Ecumenical. **Clientele**: Southeast Asia. Foster care program for unaccompanied refugee minors.

502 *Grand Rapids*
Catholic Human Development Office. Refugee Resettlement Program

117 Maple Street SE
Grand Rapids, MI 49503
Dennis Sturtevant, Executive Director
(616) 459-8223

Services Offered: AD, LE, LI, SS. **Established**: 1968. **Staff**: 1. **Budget**: $1,300,000. **Religious Affiliation**: Catholic. **Clientele**: World. The Refugee Resettlement Program provides temporary accomodation for newly-arrived refugees, employment assistance, health care referrals, training referrals and emergency needs. Staff also work to counteract prejudices and ill feelings about refugees as well as assistance in their dealing with immigration, social security, banks and other institutions. Church sponsors and other volunteers are heavily used to meet the many needs. Over 200 refugees are served annually. Participated in the Legalization Program. **Publications**: Annual Report.

503 *Grand Rapids*
Christian Reformed World Relief Committee

2850 Kalamazoo Avenue SE
Grand Rapids, MI 49560
Andrew Ryskamp, Director of U.S. Programs
(616) 246-0739

Services Offered: CE, LI, RE, SS. Established: 1963. Staff: 20. Budget: $7,100,000. BIA. Religious Affiliation: Ecumenical. Clientele: World. Assist churches to sponsor refugee resettlement programs.

---

504   *Grand Rapids*

Freedom Flight Refugee Center

734 Alger SE
Grand Rapids, MI 49507
Norma Smitter, Coordinator
(616) 241-5985

Services Offered: AD, CU, EC, SS. Established: 1975. Staff: 6. Budget: $200,000. Religious Affiliation: Ecumenical. Clientele: World. Employment and social services offered as part of the resettlement program for refugees.

---

505   *Grandville*

Reformed Church in America. Refugee Program

3000 Ivanrest SW
Grandville, MI 49418
Rev. Howard Skipper, Director
(616) 538-3470 Fax: (616) 538-6900

Services Offered: AD, CE, RE, SS. Staff: 2. Clientele: World. Refugee resettlement services coordinated through Church World Services.

---

506   *Kalamazoo*

Kalamazoo Interfaith Sanctuary Project

508 Denner
Kalamazoo, MI 49007
Carol Meyer-Niedzwiecki, Chair
(616) 349-1754

Services Offered: AD, CE, LE, SA. Established: 1983. Religious Affiliation: Ecumenical. Clientele: Central America/Caribbean. Provide sanctuary to refugees in transit through Kalamazoo or temporarily in residence in the city. Also offers community education about sanctuary and conditions in Central America.

---

507   *Lansing*

Lutheran Social Services of Michigan. Refugee Foster Care

801 South Waverly Road, Suite 202
Lansing, MI 48917
Julie Ruhala, Administrator
(517) 321-7663

Services Offered: AD, CU, ED, RE, SS. Religious Affiliation: Lutheran. Clientele: Southeast Asia, World. Provides refugee foster care for unaccompanied minor refugees.

---

508   *Lansing*

Refugee Services

233 North Walnut Street
Lansing, MI 48933
Patricia A. Hepp, Director
(517) 484-1010

Services Offered: AD, CU, CE, EC, ED, HE, SS. Established: 1946. Staff: 10. Budget: $350,000. Religious Affiliation: Catholic. Clientele: World. Agency is a comprehensive resettlement bureau which serves the foreign born by providing immigration, reception and placement, employment and health services, cultural adjustment, and counseling.

---

509   *Marquette*

Catholic Social Services

347 Rock
Marquette, MI 49855
Linda Lynch, Coordinator
(906) 228-8630

Services Offered: SS. Established: 1976. Religious Affiliation: Catholic. Clientele: World. Resettlement activities for the Upper Peninsula coordinated with US Catholic Conference Migration & Refugee Services.

---

510   *Oak Park*

Lutheran Social Services of Michigan. Department of Refugee Services

20700 Greenfield
Oak Park, MI 48237
Jean Post, Director
(313) 968-6800

Services Offered: AD, CU, CE, EC, ED, LE, RE, SS. Religious Affiliation: Lutheran. Clientele: World. Refugee resettlement programs and services, including refugee foster care unit, are offered in coordination with Lutheran Immigration &

Refugee Service.

---

511   *Oak Park*

Refugee Employment Center

13400 Oak Park Boulevard
Oak Park, MI 48237
Lorraine Lavoie, Coordinator
(313) 541-3010

Services Offered: EC. **Clientele:** World.
Orientation, vocational training and job placement for refugees.

---

512   *Southfield*

Assyrian Universal Alliance

Box 2023
Southfield, MI 48037
Afram Rayis, Director
(313) 352-0214

Services Offered: AD, CU, CE, EC, LI, RS, SS.
Established: 1968. **BIA. Clientele:** Middle East.
Provides advocacy and general assistance to refugees
and immigrants from the Middle East.

---

513   *Southfield*

Baptist State Convention

15635 West 12 Mile Road
Southfield, MI 48076
Eugene Bragg, Language Missions
(313) 557-4200

Services Offered: AD, RE, SS. **Established:**
1957. **Religious Affiliation:** Baptist.
Clientele: Southeast Asia. Support church sponsorship of refugee families for resettlement.

---

514   *Southfield*

Jewish Family Service of Detroit

24123 Greenfield Road
Southfield, MI 48075
Samuel Lerner, Executive Director
(313) 559-1500

Services Offered: AD, RE, SS. **Established:**
1939. **Religious Affiliation:** Jewish.
Clientele: World. General resettlement assistance to
refugees.

---

515   *Southfield*

Jewish Vocational Service & Community Workshop

29699 Southfield Road
Southfield, MI 48076
Albert Ascher, Executive Director
(313) 559-5000   Fax: (313) 559-0773

Services Offered: EC, SS. **Established:** 1942.
Staff: 170. **Budget:** $7,000,000. **Religious
Affiliation:** Jewish. **Clientele:** USSR.
Community based social service agency specifically
assisting immigrants and refugees to obtain and retain
employment. Offers assessment of vocational skills,
job training and placement. **Publications:**
Newsletter; Annual Report.

516 — Duluth

Lutheran Social Services

1730 East Superior Street
Duluth, MN 55812
Brenda Otterson, Refugee Coordinator
(218) 728-6839

Services Offered: AD, CE, LE, SS.
Established: 1976. **Religious Affiliation:**
Lutheran. **Clientele:** World. Sponsorship development and refugee resettlement and family reunification coordinated with Lutheran Immigration & Refugee Services.

517 — Mankato

Southern Minnesota Regional Legal Services

Box 3304
Mankato, MN 56001
Francisca Martinez Seigler, Attorney
(507) 387-5588

Services Offered: AD, CE, LE. **Established:**
1977. **Clientele:** Central America/Caribbean.
Immigration counsel and representation for indigent refugees and immigrants.

518 — Minneapolis

American Refugee Committee

2344 Nicollet Avenue
Minneapolis, MN 55404
Jack Soldate, Executive Director
(612) 872-7060

Services Offered: ED, HE. **Established:** 1979.
Staff: 30. **Budget:** $3,000,000. **Clientele:**
Southeast Asia. Program has two components.
Operates five educational projects for refugees in Minnesota and health education program in Chicago.
Also provides medical services and health education in refugee camps overseas. **Publications:** ARC NEWS; Annual Report.

519 — Minneapolis

City of Minneapolis. Office of the Mayor

City Hall, Room 127
Minneapolis, MN 55415
(612) 348-2100

Services Offered: SA. **Clientele:** Central America/Caribbean. Minneapolis is a declared public sanctuary for Salvadoran and Guatemalan refugees.

520 — Minneapolis

Episcopal Diocese of Minnesota. Refugee Resettlement Committee

430 Oak Grove Street
Minneapolis, MN 55403
Lyn Lawyer, Coordinator
(612) 871-5311

Services Offered: AD, CU, RE, SS.
Established: 1984. **Staff:** 1. **Religious Affiliation:** Episcopal. **Clientele:** World.
Refugee resettlement program that works through local churches in Minnesota. **Publications:**
Newsletter; Annual Report.

521 — Minneapolis

Jewish Family and Children's Service. Resettlement Program

1500 South Lilac Drive
Minneapolis, MN 55416
Jeremy Waldman, Executive Director
(612) 546-0616

Services Offered: SS. **Established:** 1911.
Staff: 2. **Budget:** $135,784. **Religious Affiliation:** Jewish. **Clientele:** USSR.
Resettlement services includes: housing; food; access to medical services; job development and placement; referral to cultural, religious and acculturation programs; volunteer assistance; and English language instruction. Activities coordinated with Hebrew Immigrant Aid Society.

522 — Minneapolis

Lutheran Social Services of Minnesota. Refugee & Immigration Services

2414 Park Avenue South
Minneapolis, MN 55404
David G. Jones, Director
(612) 871-0221

Services Offered: AD, CE, EC, RE, SS.
Established: 1963. **Staff:** 51. **Budget:**
$2,562,894. **BIA. Religious Affiliation:**
Lutheran. **Clientele:** World. Sponsor and provide resettlement services to refugees; unaccompanied refugee child foster care program; placement and support services for refugees; and support services, including counseling, advocacy, immigration help, etc.

Publications: REFUGE (quarterly newsletter).

---

523   *Minneapolis*

Pillsbury United Neighborhood Services. Asian Program

2529 13th Avenue South
Minneapolis, MN 55404
Va Lue Vue, Coordinator
(612) 721-1681

Services Offered: AD, CU, CE, EC, ED, LE. Established: 1981. Staff: 2. Budget: $68,000. Clientele: Southeast Asia. Goals are to increase Asian peoples knowledge of resources and opportunities needed for successful integration into American society. Services vary from job counseling to acculturation programs. Publications: Annual Report.

---

524   *Minneapolis*

University of Minnesota. Southeast Asian Refugee Studies Project

330 Humphrey Institute
Minneapolis, MN 55455
Glenn L. Hendricks, Coordinator
(612) 625-5535

Services Offered: LI, RS. Established: 1979. Staff: 3. Budget: $25,000. Clientele: Southeast Asia. The SARS Project was established to encourage, coordinate, and support research related to the people from Southeast Asia who have resettled in the United States. For much of its existence the focus has been on the Hmong people of Laos, but this has been expanded to include people from Cambodia. The research collection includes over 2,000 references in several languages. Publications: SARS NEWSLETTER (quarterly, free).

---

525   *Plymouth*

Vietnamese Evangelical Church

4945 Balsam Lane
Plymouth, MN 55442
Rev. Oan Van Tran, Pastor
(612) 559-3893

Services Offered: CU, CE, ED, RE, SA, SS. Established: 1979. Staff: 5. Religious Affiliation: Ecumenical. Clientele: Southeast Asia, Europe. Sponsorship of refugees in countries of asylum; provides Orderly Departure Program services; sanctuary workshop; and miscellaneous social services. Publications: TIA SANG (newsletter, free).

---

526   *Rochester*

Minnesota - Wisconsin Southern Baptist Convention. Refugee Resettlement Program

519 Sixteenth Street SE
Rochester, MN 55904
Rev. David Turner, Director
(507) 282-3636

Services Offered: SS. Established: 1979. Religious Affiliation: Baptist. Clientele: World. Work with churches to sponsor and resettle refugees.

---

527   *Rochester*

Rochester Refugee Services

517 17th Street NW
Rochester, MN 55901
Sareth Prum, Coordinator
(507) 289-2180

Services Offered: AD, CU, CE, ED, RE, SS. Religious Affiliation: Ecumenical. Clientele: World. Refugee resettlement program and services are coordinated with Church World Service Immigration & Refugee Program.

---

528   *St. Paul*

Catholic Charities. Migration & Refugee Services

215 Old Sixth Street
St. Paul, MN 55102
Msgr. J. Jerome Boxleitner, Director
(612) 222-3001

Services Offered: AD, EC, SS. Established: 1949. Staff: 12. Budget: $250,000. Religious Affiliation: Catholic. Clientele: World. As an affiliate of US Catholic Charities Migration & Refugee Services provides basic reception and placement services for refugees. Additional contracts with government agencies to provide pre-employment case management and employment services. Publications: THE NEWCOMER; Annual Report.

---

529   *St. Paul*

Catholic Charities. Unaccompanied Refugee Minors Program

436 Main Street
St. Paul, MN 55102
Mary Ann Sullivan, Program Supervisor

(612) 224-4805

Services Offered: SS. **Staff:** 4. **Budget:** $120,000. **Religious Affiliation:** Catholic. **Clientele:** Southeast Asia. Foster care for unaccompanied refugee minors.

---

530   *St. Paul*

Central American Resource Center

1407 Cleveland Avenue North
St. Paul, MN 55198
Pam Costain, Director
(612(644-8030)

Services Offered: LI, RS. **Established:** 1983. **Staff:** 6. **Budget:** $100,000. **Clientele:** Central America/Caribbean. Provide limited library assistance to refugees from Central America. Maintains one of the largest libraries on Central America in the Upper Midwest. **Publications:** MINNESOTA CENTRAL AMERICA NEWSLETTER (monthly); EXECUTIVE NEWS SUMMARY; RELIGION REPORT (quarterly); Annual Report.

---

531   *St. Paul*

Centro Legal

179 East Robie Street
St. Paul, MN 55107
Michael Davis, Attorney
(612) 291-0110

Services Offered: AD, LE, LI, RS. **Established:** 1981. **Clientele:** Central America/Caribbean, South America. Comprehensive legal representation in all aspects of immigration, deportation, exclusion, asylum, etc.

---

532   *St. Paul*

Hmong Catholic Center

951 East 5th Street
St. Paul, MN 55106
Rev. Daniel Taillez, Director
(612) 771-4644

Services Offered: CU, ED, LI, RE, SS. **Established:** 1986. **Staff:** 4. **Religious Affiliation:** Catholic. **Clientele:** Southeast Asia. Combination of social, religious and cultural services designed to assist Hmong refugees in St. Paul. **Publications:** TSIM NEEJ TSHIAB (3X/year newsletter); List of Publications.

---

533   *St. Paul*

Immigration History Society

690 Cedar Street
St. Paul, MN 55101
Carlton Qualey, Contact
(612) 296-5662

Services Offered: RS. **Established:** 1965. **Budget:** $15,000. **Clientele:** World. Scholarly group interested in the study and publication of information about immigration to the United States **Publications:** IMMIGRATION HISTORY NEWSLETTER; JOURNAL OF AMERICAN ETHNIC HISTORY.

---

534   *St. Paul*

International Institute of Minnesota

1694 Como Avenue
St. Paul, MN 55108
(612) 647-0191

Services Offered: AD, CU, ED, LE, SS. **Established:** 1920. **Staff:** 32. **Budget:** $1,114,000. **BIA. Clientele:** World. Extensive social, educational, cultural and legal services offered to the foreign born, including immigration counseling and refugee resettlement. **Publications:** Newsletter; Annual Report.

---

535   *St. Paul*

Jewish Family Service

1546 St. Clair
St. Paul, MN 55105
Peter Glick, Executive Director
(612) 698-0767

Services Offered: AD, CU, CE, ED, SS. **Religious Affiliation:** Jewish. **Clientele:** World. Acculturation and adjustment services as well as emergency help for refugees and immigrants.

---

536   *St. Paul*

Minnesota Cambodian Buddhist Society

1821 University Avenue, Suite 360
St. Paul, MN 55104
Mengkruy Ung, Director
(612) 645-7841

Services Offered: AD, CU, ED, RE, SS. **Established:** 1983. **Staff:** 5. **Budget:** $100,000. **Religious Affiliation:** Buddhist. **Clientele:**

Southeast Asia. Goals: to assist refugees in understanding American culture and society; to assist refugees in solving personal and family problems; to help to adjust to life in America and become self-sufficient; to promote friendship and understanding between refugee ethnic groups and the American people. Currently provides support services; social adjustment service; and program for widowed refugee women heads of household. There are about 7,000 Cambodian refugees in Minnesota.

surveys; and publishes bibliographies, conference proceedings, studies based on research in its holdings, and reports to the scholarly and ethnic communities on its activities. Because ethnicity bridges generations, the Center also collects documentation pertaining to the children and grandchildren of the immigrants. One of the major resources for ethnic studies in the U.S. **Publications:** IHRC NEWS (quarterly); SPECTRUM; List of Publications.

---

537   *St. Paul*

Minnesota Council of Churches. Refugee Program

217 MacKubin Street
St. Paul, MN 55102
Shannon Bevans, Coordinator
(612) 298-0069

Services Offered: AD, CE, ED, RE, SS.
Religious Affiliation: Ecumenical. **Clientele:**
World. Ecumenical refugee resettlement program coordinated with Church World Service.

---

538   *St. Paul*

Minnesota Department of Human Services. Refugee Programs

444 Lafayette Road, 2nd Floor
St. Paul, MN 55101
Ann Damon, Coordinator
(612) 296-2754

Services Offered: AD, EC, ED, HE, SS.
Clientele: World. Statewide coordination of federal, state and private resources for effective refugee resettlement including cash and medical assistance, support services and such other activities as necessary.

---

539   *St. Paul*

University of Minnesota. Immigration History Research Center

826 Berry Street
St. Paul, MN 55114
Rudolph J. Vecoli, Director
(612) 627-4208

Services Offered: ED, LI, RS, SC.
Established: 1965. **Staff:** 5. Encourage study of the role of immigration and ethnicity in shaping the society and culture of the United States. Collects the records of 24 American ethnic groups that originate in Europe and the Near East. The Center sponsors conferences, seminars and exhibits; conducts archival

540 *Biloxi*

Catholic Social Services

Box 1457
Biloxi, MS 39533
Martha Milner, Resettlement Coordinator
(601) 374-8316

Services Offered: AD, CU, CE, EC, LE, RE, RS, SS. **Religious Affiliation:** Catholic. **Clientele:** World, Southeast Asia, Asia. Refugee resettlement program is designed to promote early self-sufficiency through employment programs.

541 *Jackson*

Catholic Charities. Refugee Social Service Center

Box 2248
Jackson, MS 39205
Martha Mitternight, Coordinator
(601) 355-8634

Services Offered: AD, CU, EC, RE, SS. **Established:** 1975. **Religious Affiliation:** Catholic. **Clientele:** Southeast Asia. Programs and services for refugees and immigrants designed to attain emotional and economic self-sufficiency for refugees.

542 *Jackson*

Mississippi Baptist Convention. Language Missions Department

Box 530
Jackson, MS 39205
Neron Smith, Director
(601) 968-3800

Services Offered: AD, CU, RE, SS. **Staff:** 3. **Religious Affiliation:** Baptist. **Clientele:** World. Work with Baptist churches in Mississippi to coordinate and support services for refugees. **Publications:** BAPTIST RECORD (weekly); Annual Report.

543 *Jackson*

Mississippi Department of Public Welfare. Refugee Program

Box 352
Jackson, MS 39205
Phoebe Clark, State Refugee Coordinator
(601) 354-0341

Services Offered: EC, ED, HE, SS. **Established:** 1980. **Staff:** 1. **Budget:** $120,000.

Clientele: Southeast Asia. The State Refugee Coordinator, working out of the Department of Public Welfare, is responsible for overall coordination of refugee resettlement in the State. Work with federal government and local social service agencies and contractors.

544   *Jefferson City*

Missouri Division of Family Services. Refugee Assistance Program

Box 88
Jefferson City, MO 65101
Patricia Harris, State Refugee Coordinator
(314) 751-2456

Services Offered: AD, EC, ED, HE, SS.
Clientele: World. Statewide coordination of federal, state and private resources for effective refugee resettlement including cash and medical assistance, support services and such other activities as necessary.

545   *Jefferson City*

Refugee Resettlement Office

Box 417
Jefferson City, MO 65102
Alice Wolters, Director
(314) 635-9127

Services Offered: AD, SS. **Established:** 1975.
Religious Affiliation: Catholic. **Clientele:**
World. Array of social and economic services and programs to assist with refugee resettlement. Primary goal of helping refugees to become self-sufficient and integrated into community.

546   *Kansas City*

Don Bosco Community Center

529 Campbell Street
Kansas City, MO 64106
Lou Rose, Director
(816) 421-0546

Services Offered: EC, ED, SS. **Established:**
1940. **BIA. Clientele:** World. Following services offered to refugees and immigrants: resettlement; assessment; language training; job orientation and placement; document translation and interpretation; and social services.

547   *Kansas City*

Legal Aid of Western Missouri

920 Southwest Boulevard
Kansas City, MO 64108
Suzanne Gladney, Managing Attorney
(816) 474-9868

Services Offered: AD, CE, HE, LE, SA.
Established: 1963. **Staff:** 60. **Budget:**
$1,500,000. **BIA. Clientele:** World. Legal services offered to refugees and immigrants include representation in deportation proceedings.

548   *Kansas City*

U.S. Department of Health & Human Services. Family Support Administration. Office of Refugee Resettlement

601 East 12th Street, Room 515
Kansas City, MO 64106
Larry Laverentz, Refugee Contact
(816) 426-7081   Fax: (816) 867-7081

Established: 1986. **Staff:** 1. **Budget:** $100,000.
Clientele: World. Regional Office of ORR advises and monitors state refugee programs for the region, principally administration and technical assistance, especially in areas of cash, medical and social services. Overall mission to develop and administer refugee programs designed to facilitate timely achievement of economic self-sufficiency, meaningful acculturation, and the full utilization of the human potential of refugees.

549   *Saint Louis*

Emmanuel Lutheran Church. Sanctuary Committee

3540 Marcus
Saint Louis, MO 63115
Ted Schroeder, Contact
(314) 381-8771

Services Offered: AD, CE, SA. **Religious Affiliation:** Lutheran. **Clientele:** Central America/Caribbean. Advocacy, community education and outreach and sanctuary for refugees fleeing El Salvador and Guatemala.

550   *Saint Louis*

International Institute of Metropolitan St. Louis

3800 Park Avenue
Saint Louis, MO 63110
Anna Crosslin, Executive Director
(314) 773-9090

Services Offered: AD, CU, CE, EC, ED, HE, LE, RS, SS. **Established:** 1919. **Staff:** 40.
Budget: $2,000,000. **BIA. Clientele:** World. The Institute specializes in dealing with the problems of immigrants and refugees: helping to reunite families, obtaining visas and citizenship papers, finding jobs

and housing, teaching English as a Second Language, providing translation and interpretor services, and, at all times, helping each individual achieve self-sufficiency and independence. Clients from over 40 countries are served each year. Specific services include: educational services; human services; job placement services; and immigration counseling services. **Publications:** CROSSROADS INTERNATIONAL (newsletter); Annual Report.

---

551   *Saint Louis*

Lutheran Church. Synod Board of Social Ministry Services.

1333 South Kirkwood Road
Saint Louis, MO 63122
Rev. Eugene C. Gunther, Refugee Counselor
(314) 965-9917

Services Offered: AD, ED, RE, SS. **Established:** 1975. **Staff:** 1. **Budget:** $16,200. **Religious Affiliation:** Lutheran. **Clientele:** World. Refugee consultants work with Lutheran congregations to assist them in sponsoring refugees, undocumented persons and immigrants. Goals include information promotion, motivation planning activities designed to augment all elements of resettlement ministry. Activities coordinated through Lutheran Immigration & Refugee Services. **Publications:** WELCOME STRANGER (semi-annual); List of Publications.

---

552   *Springfield*

Council of Churches. Refugee Resettlement Program

Box 3947
Springfield, MO 65808
Jean Elbert, Director
(417) 862-3595

Services Offered: AD, CU, EC, ED, LI, RE, SA, SS. **Established:** 1976. **Religious Affiliation:** Ecumenical. **Clientele:** World. Comprehensive support services for refugees in Southwest Missouri: language development; job orientation and development; counseling services; and assistance with INS documentation.

---

553   *Springfield*

Diocese of Springfield - Cape Girardeau. Resettlement Office

Box 50960
Springfield, MO 65805

Sr. Mary Sax, Director
(417) 866-0841

Services Offered: AD, EC, ED, SS. **Established:** 1975. **Staff:** 3. **Budget:** $40,000. **Religious Affiliation:** Catholic. **Clientele:** Southeast Asia. Goal is to promote successful resettlement of refugees by assisting them to become self-sufficient as early as possible through coordinated and effective use of services. Objectives: core reception and placement services upon arrival; assess refugee needs and provide case management; assist employable refugees find suitable employment by providing a variety of employment services; assist refugees to acquire English language skills; assist refugees to access mainstream services to meet their needs by providing a variety of health-related, outreach, and home management services or referrals; support family reunification; and to encourage refugees to become permanent residents and citizens.

554   *Billings*

Montana Association for Refugee Services

1211 Grand Avenue
Billings, MT 59102
Neng Ky Cha, Executive Director
(406) 252-5601

Services Offered: AD, CU, EC, SS.
Established: 1982. **Staff**: 6. **Budget**: $130,000.
BIA. **Clientele**: World. Private non-profit organization provides a variety of services to refugees within the community. The single purpose of the activities is to achieve successful resettlement of refugee families within Billings. Principal activities include: job placement and job follow-up; social services, medical care coordination, limited transportation and referral activities; refugee sponsorship recruitment; special project activities, such as the Refugee Children Summer Language Program; limited bilingual services and translation services; and other services as needed. **Publications**: Annual Report.

555   *Great Falls*

Lutheran Social Services of Montana

Box 1345
Great Falls, MT 59403
Rev. Kenneth Gjerde, Executive Director
(406) 761-4341

Services Offered: AD, RE, SS. **Established**:
1975. **Religious Affiliation**: Lutheran.
Clientele: Southeast Asia. Resettlement activities coordinated through Lutheran Immigration & Refugee Services. **Publications**: Newsletter.

556   *Helena*

Catholic Social Services. Resettlement Program

Box 907
Helena, MT 59624
Marilyn McKibben, Director
(406) 442-4130

Services Offered: AD, EC, SS. **Established**:
1953. **BIA**. **Religious Affiliation**: Catholic.
Clientele: Southeast Asia. Family reunification program, emphasis on refugees from Southeast Asia. Objective is to assist refugees with financial assistance and initial resettlement expenses. Volunteers help in obtaining furniture and household goods, employment assistance and governmental forms.

557   *Helena*

Montana Department of Family Services. Office of Refugee Resettlement

Box 8005
Helena, MT 59604
Boyce D. Fowler, Program Manager
(406) 444-5900

Services Offered: EC, ED, SS. **Established**:
1975. **Clientele**: World, Southeast Asia. Contracts with private social service agencies to provide refugee services. Coordinate state activities to enhance the rapid integration of refugees in society.

558 — Grand Island

Catholic Charities

Box 996
Grand Island, NE 68802
Jean Ann Molczyck, Resettlement Director
(308) 382-6565

Services Offered: AD, CU, ED, RE, SS. **Staff:** 1. **Religious Affiliation:** Catholic. **Clientele:** World, Central America/Caribbean. Placement and re-settlement services offered to refugees in coordination with U.S. Catholic Conference Migration & Refugee Services.

559 — Lincoln

Catholic Social Services. Refugee Resetlement Office

215 Centennial Mall South
Lincoln, NE 68508
Rev. James Blue, Director
(402) 474-1600

Services Offered: AD, CU, HE, RE, SS. **Established:** 1950. **Staff:** 2. **Budget:** $10,000. **Religious Affiliation:** Catholic. **Clientele:** Southeast Asia, Asia. Offers the following services: coordinate resettlement for refugees; provide orientation to sponsors and assists them to sponsor relatives/friends; initial placement; provides financial assistance to refugees for initial needs; and offer counseling services to refugees concerning adjustment. Have resettled over 500 families in Lincoln.

560 — Lincoln

Nebraska Department of Social Services. Refugee Affairs Program

301 Centennial Mall South
Lincoln, NE 68509
Maria Diaz, State Refugee Coordinator
(402) 471-9200

Services Offered: EC, ED, HE, SS. **Clientele:** World. Statewide coordination of federal, state and private resources for effective refugee resettlement.

561 — North Platte

Immigration Advocacy Service

518 South Jeffers
North Platte, NE 69103
Sr. Theresa McGahan, Director
(308) 534-0550

Services Offered: AD, LE, SS. **Established:** 1988. **Staff:** 1. **Budget:** $30,000. **Religious Affiliation:** Catholic. **Clientele:** World, Central America/Caribbean. Serves people of Western Nebraska by: preparing applications for legalization, waivers and appeals; informing legal temporary residents of the requirements for their application for Legal Permanent Resident status; aiding clients in preparing and filing a variety of immigration related forms; attempting to form a network of service-providers; aiding newly legalized residents in their attempts to move into the mainstream of American society; and serving as a link between US Catholic Conference Migration & Refugee Services and persons who need immigration aid.

562 — Omaha

United Catholic Social Services. Refugee Resettlement Program

Box 2055
Omaha, NE 68120
Maryanne Rouse, Associate Director
(402) 341-4004

Services Offered: AD, CU, CE, SS. **Staff:** 2. **Budget:** $12,000. **BIA. Religious Affiliation:** Catholic. **Clientele:** World. Initial placement and resettlement activities include orientation, emergency services, referrals, etc. Program designed to integrate refugees as quickly as possible.

563   *Carson City*

Nevada Department of Human Resources. State Refugee Coordinator

2527 North Carson Street
Carson City, NV 89710
Michael Willden, Deputy Administrator
(702) 885-4771

Services Offered: CU, EC, ED, SS.
Established: 1982. **Staff:** 5. **Budget:** $712,266.
BIA. Clientele: World, Southeast Asia, Asia.
Coordinate state and federal refugee resettlement in
Nevada. Provide cash and medical assistance and over-
see contracts with private providers. Goal is to en-
hance mechanisms for integration of refugees as pro-
ductive members of the community.

564   *Las Vegas*

Catholic Community Services of Nevada. Immigration & Refugee Services

1501 Las Vegas Boulevard North
Las Vegas, NV 89101
George Soler, Director
(702) 385-2550

Services Offered: SS. **Established:** 1941.
Staff: 7. **Budget:** $80,000. **BIA. Religious
Affiliation:** Catholic. **Clientele:** World. Refugee
resettlement services includes a variety of programs
designed to assist refugees become productive members of society. Activities coordinated through US
Catholic Conference Migration & Refugee Services.

565   *Las Vegas*

Jewish Family Service Agency

1555 East Flamingo, Suite 125
Las Vegas, NV 89119
William Feldman, Executive Director
(702) 732-0304

Services Offered: AD, CU, RE, SS.
Established: 1977. **Staff:** 5. **BIA. Religious
Affiliation:** Jewish. **Clientele:** World. Refugee
resettlement services offered through Hebrew
Immigrant Aid Society. **Publications:** Newsletter;
Annual Report.

566   *Reno*

Catholic Migration and Refugee Service

Box 5415
Reno, NV 89513
Briselda Delgado, Director
(702) 322-7073

Services Offered: AD, EC, RE, SS. **Staff:** 1.
Religious Affiliation: Catholic. **Clientele:**
World. Placement and resettlement services for
refugees that are referred by U.S. Catholic Conference
Migration & Refugee Services.

567   *Reno*

St. Paul's United Methodist Church. Refugee Program

1660 Grandview Avenue
Reno, NV 89503
Rev. Mark Bollwinkel, Coordinator
(702) 747-1431

Services Offered: AD, CE, ED, LE, RE, SS.
Religious Affiliation: Methodist. **Clientele:**
World. Local affiliate of Church World Service
Immigration & Refugee Program.

568   *Concord*

New Hampshire Office of Refugee Resettlement

11 Depot Street
Concord, NH   03301
Patricia Garvin, State Refugee Coordinator
(603) 271-2611

Services Offered: EC, SS. **Established:** 1981.
Staff: 2. **Budget:** $450,000. **Clientele:** World.
Administration of refugee resettlement program at the
state level, with an emphasis on employment services, information and referral and social services.

569   *Manchester*

International Center

102 North Main Street
Manchester, NH   03102
Jackie Whatmough, Director
(603) 668-8602

Services Offered: AD, EC, LE, LI.
Established: 1926. **BIA. Clientele:** World.
Counsel and technical assistance in matters pertaining
to immigration and naturalization, including assistance with naturalization, visa petition, adjustment of
status and related matters; translation and interpretation; and social services designed to assist refugee and
immigrant in transition to life in the United States.

570   *North Hampton*

Episcopal Refugee and Migration Committee

60 Walnut Avenue
North Hampton, NH   03862
Helen McNeil, Refugee Coordinator
(603) 964-6671

Services Offered: AD, LI, RE, SS.
Established: 1980. **Staff:** 2. **Religious
Affiliation:** Episcopal. **Clientele:** World.
Refugee sponsorship and core refugee resettlement
services.

571   *Asbury Park*

Jewish Family and Children's Service

705 Summerfield Avenue
Asbury Park, NJ   07712
Melvin Cohen, Executive Director
(201) 774-6886

Services Offered: AD, CE, RE, SS.
Established: 1976. **Religious Affiliation:**
Jewish. **Clientele:** USSR. Refugee resettlement activities in Monmouth County are coordinated through
the Hebrew Immigrant Aid Society.

572   *Bayonne*

Jewish Family and Counseling Service

1050 Kennedy Boulevard
Bayonne, NJ   07002
Claire Asarnow, Director
(201) 436-1299

Services Offered: SS. **Established:** 1976.
Religious Affiliation: Jewish. **Clientele:**
World. Social services to Jewish refugees and immi-
grants in Jersey City and Bayonne.

573   *Camden*

Catholic Migration and Refugee Services

3098 Pleasant Street
Camden, NJ   08105
Thomas Henkel, Resettlement Director
(609) 541-1145

Services Offered: CU, CE, LE, EC, ED, RE, RS,
SS. **Established:** 1977. **BIA. Religious
Affiliation:** Jewish. **Clientele:** World. Offers following services for refugees and immigrants: vocational training and testing; job orientation, development and placement; legal representation in deportation and other immigration and asylum matters; and
general social services.

574   *Cherry Hill*

Jewish Family Service

100 Park Boulevard
Cherry Hill, NJ   08002
Stephen Rubin, Executive Director
(609) 662-8611

Services Offered: CU, SS. **Established:** 1946.
Religious Affiliation: Jewish. **Clientele:**

USSR. Assist in the resettlement and on-going welfare of Jewish immigrants and refugees.

---

575 *Clifton*

Jewish Family Service

199 Scoles Avenue
Clifton, NJ 07012
Benita M. Burstein, Executive Director
(201) 777-7638

Services Offered: AD, CU, SS. **Established**: 1948. **Religious Affiliation**: Jewish. **Clientele**: USSR, Middle East. Offer orientation, counseling and immigration as part of refugee resettlement program coordinated with Hebrew Immigrant Aid Society.

---

576 *East Brunswick*

Jewish Family Service of Raritan Valley

517 Ryders Lane
East Brunswick, NJ 08816
Ann S. Wexler, Executive Director
(201) 257-4100

Services Offered: SS. **Religious Affiliation**: Jewish. **Clientele**: World. Core services available to immigrants and refugees.

---

577 *East Orange*

Jewish Vocational Service

111 Prospect Street
East Orange, NJ 07017
Morton Schwartz, Emigre Services
(201) 674-3672

Services Offered: EC, LI, RE, SS. **Established**: 1938. **Staff**: 5. **BIA**. **Religious Affiliation**: Jewish. **Clientele**: USSR, World. Vocational orientation, training, counseling and placement as well as limited core social services for refugees and immigrants.

---

578 *Edison*

Jewish Family Service of North Middlesex County

100 Menlo Park
Edison, NJ 08837
Irene Stolzenberg, Executive Director
(201) 494-3923

Services Offered: AD, CU, CE, ED, RE, SS. **Established**: 1980. **Religious Affiliation**: Jewish. **Clientele**: World. Variety of support programs (emergency assistance, therapy, educational programs, etc.) for refugees and immigrants.

---

579 *Elizabeth*

Human Rights Advocates International

1341 North Avenue, Suite 7C
Elizabeth, NJ 07208
Charles F. Printz, Executive Director
(201) 352-6032

Services Offered: AD, CE, LE, RS. **Established**: 1978. **Staff**: 6. **BIA**. **Clientele**: World, Southeast Asia, Middle East. Provide legal assistance in all areas of human rights violations on global scale with special emphasis upon immigration assistance for all refugee and immigrant groups. Presently acts as "guardian ad litem" for Amerasians still within Vietnam with a view to arranging reunions with separated family now in the United States and other countries. Represents cases before the U.S. Orderly Departure Program in respect of Indochinese refugees generally, Vietnamese in particular. Personalized client advocacy via personal sessions with government officials as regards reunions and other legal matters not easily resolved through regular channels of approach. Principal officials hold current accreditation to the U.S. Department of State and the UN Secretariat. **Publications**: Annual Report.

---

580 *Elizabeth*

Jewish Family Service Agency of Central New Jersey

655 Westfield Avenue
Elizabeth, NJ 07208
(201) 352-8375

Services Offered: EC, SS. **Established**: 1913. **Staff**: 24. **Budget**: $650,000. **Religious Affiliation**: Jewish. **Clientele**: Middle East, USSR. Agency provides counseling information and referral, service to the elderly including case management, homemaker and respite care, resettlement of refugees, career counseling, family life education and financial assistance. **Publications**: REACH OUT (3X/year newsletter).

---

581 *Florham Park*

Jewish Family Service of MetroWest

256 Columbia Turnpike
Florham Park, NJ 07932
Elliot R. Rubin, Executive Vice -President
(201) 765-9050 Fax: (201) 765-0195

**Services Offered: SS. Established: 1861.
Staff: 27. Budget: $1,700,00. BIA. Religious
Affiliation:** Jewish. **Clientele:** World, USSR,
Middle East. Variety of services for refugees and im-
migrants includes resettlement and migration assis-
tance, asylum advocacy, change of status, etc.
Resettlement and family reunification coordinated
with the Hebrew Immigrant Aid Society.

---

582   *Highland Park*

Bulgarian National Committee

109 Amherst Street
Highland Park, NJ 08904
Dimitar Petkoff, President
(201) 572-1137

Services Offered: AD, CU, CE, SS.
Established: 1949. **Clientele:** Europe. Advocacy
and support for Bulgarian political refugees throughout the world, including the United States.

---

583   *Jersey City*

Immigration Assistance Service

344 Pacific Avenue
Jersey City, NJ 07304
Rev. William Reily, Coordinator
(201) 333-1971

Services Offered: AD, CE, LE. **BIA. Religious
Affiliation:** Catholic. **Clientele:** World, Central
America/Caribbean. Legal counsel and representation
in immigration matters.

---

584   *Jersey City*

International Institute of New Jersey

880 Bergen Avenue
Jersey City, NJ 07306
Nicholas V. Montalto, Executive Director
(201) 653-3888 Fax: (201) 432-0261

Services Offered: AD, CU, EC, ED, LE, LI, SS.
Established: 1918. **Staff:** 11. **Budget:** $400,000.
BIA. Clientele: World. Within limits set by law
and the capacity of society, the Institute responds to
the plight of the persecuted and displaced. Provides
sponsorship services to hundreds of refugees each
year. In this endeavor, they work closely with religious and civic groups. The following programs are

offered: clearinghouse service; intergroup education;
English language training; case work services; translation services; and resettlement services.
Publications: NEW JERSEY MOSAIC (Irregular
newsletter); Annual Report.

---

585   *New Brunswick*

Middlesex County Legal Services Corporation

78 New Street
New Brunswick, NJ 08901
Paul Mullin, Attorney
(201) 249-7600

Services Offered: LE. **Established:** 1966.
Clientele: World. Immigration and naturalization
counsel for indigent individuals and families.

---

586   *Newark*

Catholic Community Services. Office of Migration

One Summer Avenue
Newark, NJ 07104
Nancy Monti, Executive Director
(201) 482-0100

Services Offered: AD, CU, CE, EC, ED, HE,
LE, SS. **Established:** 1976. **Staff:** 75. **Budget:**
$2,850,000. **BIA. Religious Affiliation:**
Catholic. **Clientele:** World. Extensive program for
refugees and immigrants is all-encompassing in its
concerns. Staff provides advice and expertise on U.S.
immigration laws, legal representation at immigration hearings, and has, collectively, fluency in 21
languages. Staff teach English and offer vocational
and job counseling, since self-sufficiency is the goal
for newcomers. This program has seen the resettlement of over 8,000 people from many nations. Since
1980 Project Haven has provided foster homes for
young Southeast Asian refugees. **Publications:**
NEWSLETTER (quarterly); Annual Report;
Directory.

---

587   *Plainfield*

Center for Central American Refugees

700 Park Avenue, Room 104
Plainfield, NJ 07060
Esther Cruz, Director
(201) 753-8730

Services Offered: AD, CU, CE, LE, SS. **Established**: 1984. **Staff**: 2. **Budget**: $56,110. **Religious Affiliation**: Ecumenical. **Clientele**: Central America/Caribbean. Three areas of programmatic concern are: maintainance and extension of present services, including legal, medical, emergency, educational, and community outreach and integration programs; education of Central Americans and area employers to IRCA, specifically regarding the critical provisions of individual qualification and employer sanctions; and, extension of services and resources for the pressing needs of newly arrived Central Americans. In 1988 the Center assisted over one thousand individuals. **Publications**: VECINO (bimonthly newsletter).

---

588   *Sommerville*

Jewish Family Service of Somerset County

150 West High Street
Sommerville, NJ 08876
Tova Friedman, Executive Director
(201) 725-7799

Services Offered: AD, LE, EC, ED, RE, SS. **Established**: 1980. **Religious Affiliation**: Jewish. **Clientele**: USSR. Resettlement services for refugees and immigrants offers counseling, employment programs, language training and related social and emergency services.

---

589   *South Orange*

Jewish Family Service of Metro West

76 South Orange Avenue
South Orange, NJ 07079
Helen Gottlieb, Migration Coordinator
(201) 761-1166

Services Offered: AD, LE, LI, SS. **BIA**. **Religious Affiliation**: Jewish. **Clientele**: World. Provides counseling and technical services with regard to immigration, asylum, resettlement and naturalization.

---

590   *Teaneck*

Bergen County Sanctuary Committee

687 Larch Avenue
Teaneck, NJ 07666
Joseph Chuman, Chair
(201) 836-5187

Services Offered: AD, CE, ED, RE, SA. **Established**: 1987. **Budget**: $2,000. **Clientele**: Central America/Caribbean. Provide legal, economic, moral and linguistic support for refugees fleeing political violence in El Salvador and Guatemala. Also includes general education on the situation in Central America. **Publications**: SANCTUARY NEWSLETTER (quarterly, free).

---

591   *Trenton*

Jewish Family Service of Delaware Valley

51 Walter Street
Trenton, NJ 08628
Byron L. Pinsky, Executive Director
(609) 882-9317

Services Offered: AD, CU, CE, EC, ED, LE, RE, SS. **Established**: 1937. **Staff**: 11. **Budget**: $500,000. **Religious Affiliation**: Jewish. **Clientele**: USSR. Resettlement and family unification services for Jewish emigres from the Soviet Union. Activities coordinated through the Hebrew Immigrant Aid Society. **Publications**: Annual Report.

---

592   *Trenton*

Lutheran Refugee and Immigration Services

189 South Broad Street
Trenton, NJ 08601
Charles Bergstresser, Director
(609) 393-3442

Services Offered: AD, CU, EC, LE, RE, SS. **Staff**: 7. **Budget**: $275,000. **BIA**. **Religious Affiliation**: Lutheran. **Clientele**: World. Services offered to the immigrant and refugee population of central New Jersey include counseling, job development and social services.

---

593   *Trenton*

Migration and Refugee Services Office

33 West Front Street
Trenton, NJ 08608
Sr. Marion O'Connor, Director
(609) 394-8299

Services Offered: AD, CE, ED, LE. **Religious Affiliation**: Catholic. **Clientele**: World. Advocacy, outreach and legal counsel and representation in immigration matters.

---

594 *Trenton*

New Jersey Department of Human Services. State Refugee Coordinator

1 South Montgomery Street, Room 701
Trenton, NJ 08625
Audrea Dunham
(609) 984-3154

Services Offered: AD, EC, ED, HE, SS.
Clientele: World. Statewide coordination of federal, state and private resources for effective refugee resettlement (cash and medical assistance, support services, etc.).

---

595 *West New York*

International Rescue Committee

6009 Bergenline Avenue, 2nd Floor
West New York, NJ 07093
Guillermo Estevez, Representative
(201) 861-6116

Services Offered: AD, CE, LE, SS. **Clientele**: World. Part of an extensive program that resettles refugees in the United States.

---

596 *West Patterson*

American Fund for Slovak Refugees

870 Rifle Camp Road
West Patterson, NJ 07424
John Holy, Contact
(201) 256-1687

Services Offered: AD, CU, SS. **Established**: 1968. **Budget**: $10,000. **Clientele**: Europe. Coordinates refugee rescue and resettlement work of Slovak ethnic groups in the United States who are interested in assisting Slovak refugees. **Publications**: SLOVAKIA.

---

597 *Albuquerque*

Baptist Convention of New Mexico

Box 485
Albuquerque, NM 87103
Joe Hawn, Refugee Consultant
(505) 247-0586

Services Offered: AD, CU, RE, SS.
Established: 1975. **Religious Affiliation**: Baptist. **Clientele**: World. Promote and coordinate refugee sponsorship and support services among Baptist churches and individuals.

---

598 *Albuquerque*

Catholic Social Services. Refugee Resettlement Program

Box 25405
Albuquerque, NM 87125
Lourdes Martinez, Director
(505) 247-9521

Services Offered: AD, EC, LI, RE, SS.
Established: 1975. **BIA**. **Religious Affiliation**: Catholic. **Clientele**: World. Refugee resettlement and family reunification programs offers orientation and acculturation services, reception and counseling, employment assistance, information and referral, etc.

---

599 *Albuquerque*

Jewish Family Service. Immigration & Resettlement Program

1280 Lomas NE
Albuquerque, NM 87112
Jane Hertz, Executive Director
(505) 292-1521

Services Offered: AD, LE, SS. **Established**: 1985. **Budget**: $56,577. **Religious Affiliation**: Jewish. **Clientele**: Middle East, USSR. Wide range of programs and support systems include reuniting families separated by the necessity of leaving an oppressed country. Local relatives, relatively recent immigrants themselves, are assisted by the agency in bringing their first degree relatives to the local community. Services provided primarily (but not exclusively) to the Jewish population and emigres are generally from Iran and the USSR. **Publications**: Annual Report.

---

600 *Santa Fe*

City of Santa Fe. Office of the Mayor

Box 909
Santa Fe, NM 87504
(505) 984-6521

Services Offered: AD, CE, SA. **Clientele:** Central America/Caribbean. Santa Fe is a declared public sanctuary for Central American refugees fleeing persecution.

---

601 *Santa Fe*

New Mexico Department of Human Services. Social Services Division

Box 2348
Santa Fe, NM 87504
Charmaine Espinosa, State Refugee Coordinator
(505) 827-4201

Services Offered: AD, EC, ED, HE, SS. **Clientele:** World. Statewide coordination of federal, state and private resources for effective refugee resettlement.

---

602 *Albany*

International Center of the Capital Region. Refugee Assistance Program

875 Central Avenue-West Mall
Albany, NY 12206
Helene T. Smith, Executive Director
(518) 459-8812

Services Offered: AD, CU, EC, ED, SS. **Established:** 1965. **Staff:** 9. **Budget:** $232,000. **BIA. Clientele:** World. As the agency coordinating the services refugees need to become self-reliant, the ICCR works with sponsors throughout the ten county area. This cooperative relationship between the resettlement efforts of the sponsors and the supportive services for the refugees is to assure that the refugee families or individuals become contributing members of the community. Refugees sponsored through a variety of organizations such as the US Catholic Conference, Hebrew Immigrant Aid Society and World Relief. **Publications:** Annual Report.

---

603 *Albany*

New York Department of Social Services. State Refugee Coordinator

40 North Pearl Street
Albany, NY 12243
Bruce Bushart
(518) 432-2514

Services Offered: AD, EC, ED, HE, SS. **Clientele:** World. Statewide coordination of federal, state and private resources for effective refugee resettlement including cash and medical assistance, support services and such other activities as necessary.

---

604 *Amityville*

Catholic Charities Migration Office

143 Schliegel Boulevard
Amityville, NY 11701
Paul Paquette, Coordinator
(516) 842-1400

Services Offered: AD, CE, LE, RE, RS, SS. **BIA. Religious Affiliation:** Catholic. **Clientele:** World. Social and legal services available to refugees and immigrants.

---

605 *Astoria*

Catholic Migration Office

23-330 Astoria Boulevard
Astoria, NY   11102
Juan Fernandez, Coordinator
(718) 728-6888

Services Offered: AD, LE, CE, RE, SS.
Established: 1970. **BIA. Religious
Affiliation:** Catholic. **Clientele:** World, Central
America/Caribbean. Broad range of services available
to refugees and immigrants.

---

606   *Astoria*

Federation of Italian-American Societies

33-02 Ditamars Boulevard
Astoria, NY   11105
Antonio Meloni, Contact
(718) 204-2444

Services Offered: AD, CU, CE, ED, LE, SC, SS.
Clientele: Europe. Broad range of services, including immigration assistance, for Italian-American
groups.

---

607   *Bellerose*

American Fund for Slovak Refugees

76-04 252nd Street
Bellerose, NY   11426
George Kantor, Secretary
(718) 347-2749

Services Offered: AD, SS. **Established:** 1968.
Clientele: Europe. Advocacy and support group for
Slovak refugees from Czechoslovakia.

---

608   *Binghampton*

American Civic Association

131 Front Street
Binghampton, NY   13905
Irene Krome, Executive Director
(607) 723-9419

Services Offered: AD, CE, LE, ED.
Established: 1939. **Staff:** 7. **BIA. Clientele:**
World. Advocacy group for citizenship. Offers educational programs and legal counsel in selected immigration matters. Formed by naturalized citizens to
help the foreign born become citizens.
Publications: Newsletter (monthly).

---

609   *Brooklyn*

African American Immigration Service

3011 Avenue J
Brooklyn, NY   11210
Badru I. O. Rabiu
(718) 377-3373

Services Offered: AD, CU, CE, EC, LE, SS.
Staff: 3. **BIA. Clientele:** World. Advocacy, community outreach and legal counsel on all immigration
matters. **Publications:** THE IMMIGRANT
(newsletter).

---

610   *Brooklyn*

Brooklyn Legal Services Corporation

260 Broadway
Brooklyn, NY   11211
Martin Needleman, Chief Counsel
(718) 782-6195

Services Offered: LE. **Established:** 1968. **BIA.
Clientele:** World. Counsel and representation in
immigration related procedures for indigent refugees
and immigrants.

---

611   *Brooklyn*

Caribbean Action Lobby

1534 Bedford Avenue
Brooklyn, NY   11216
Oswald Silvera, Contact
(718) 467-1777

Services Offered: AD, CU, CE, RS.
Established: 1980. **Clientele:** Central
America/Caribbean. Objective is to educate
Caribbeans about U.S. immigration laws and to
lobby in the United States on issues that are of spe-
cial importance to Caribbean immigrants.
Publications: Newsletter (monthly).

---

612   *Brooklyn*

Catholic Migration and Refugee Office

75 Greene Street
Brooklyn, NY   11202
Rev. Ron Marino, Director
(718) 638-5500

Services Offered: AD, LE, CE, RE.
Established: 1971. **BIA. Religious
Affiliation:** Catholic. **Clientele:** World. Services

and programs concentrated on: immigration counseling; technical assistance and representation for clients processing with INS; and legal representation or referrals to qualified attorneys.

---

613   Brooklyn

Central American Legal Assistance

240 Hooper Street
Brooklyn, NY   11211
Anne Pilsbury, Contact
(718) 486-6800

Services Offered: AD, LE. **Established:** 1986. **Clientele:** Central America/Caribbean. Legal counsel and representation in immigration and political asylum cases.

---

614   Brooklyn

Evangelical Crusade of Fishers of Men

1488 New York Avenue
Brooklyn, NY   11210
Rev. Philius Nicolas, Coordinator
(718) 434-7250

Services Offered: AD, CE, ED, LE, RE, SS. **Clientele:** World. Refugee resettlement activities coordinated through Church World Service Immigration & Refugee Program.

---

615   Brooklyn

Haitian Centers Council

50 Court Street, Suite 605
Brooklyn, NY   11201
Joe Etienne, Director
(718) 855-7275

Services Offered: AD, CU, CE, ED, LE, RE, SS. **Clientele:** Central America/Caribbean. Broad based services for Haitian refugees.

---

616   Brooklyn

Long Island Refugee Resettlement Program

1227 Pacific Street
Brooklyn, NY   11216
James Kenyon, Director
(718) 604-3690

Services Offered: SS. **Established:** 1981. **Clientele:** World. Provides counseling for refugees, promotes sponsorship development, and assists with educational, housing, etc.

---

617   Brooklyn

Polish and Slavic Center. Refugee Assistance Center

176 Java Street
Brooklyn, NY   11222
Victor Sasadevsz, Director
(718) 389-4937

Services Offered: AD, CU, EC, RS, SS. **Established:** 1983. **Staff:** 4. **Clientele:** Europe. Refugees from Eastern Europe receive assistance with job orientation, training and placement; advocacy; adjustment services; translation and interpretation; and information and referral. **Publications:** Newsletter (monthly).

---

618   Brooklyn

Rav Tov. International Jewish Rescue Organization

500 Bedford Avenue
Brooklyn, NY   11211
David Niederman, Executive Director
(718) 963-1991

Services Offered: AD, CU, CE, EC, ED, HE, LE, RS, SS. **Established:** 1973. **Staff:** 40. **BIA. Religious Affiliation:** Jewish. **Clientele:** USSR, Middle East, Europe. Provides care and maintenance, medical assistance, visa documentation, and pre-migration planning to refugees while in transit. In countries of resettlement, provides a full range of services including reception, housing, medical care, language training, education, employment counseling and maintenance assistance. **Publications:** ACHIEVEMENT BULLETIN (quarterly).

---

619   Brooklyn

Saint Vincents Services

Box 174
Brooklyn, NY   11202
Msgr. Robert Harris, Director
(718) 522-3700

Services Offered: HE, SS. **Religious Affiliation:** Catholic. **Clientele:** Southeast Asia. Agency maintains over 100 refugee children in foster homes throughout New York State.

---

620 *Brooklyn*

Southside Community Mission

280 Marcy Avenue
Brooklyn, NY 11211
Sr. Peggy Walsh, Refugee Director
(718) 387-3803

Services Offered: AD, LE, SS. **Established**: 1977. **Staff**: 9. **Budget**: $108,000. **BIA**. **Religious Affiliation**: Catholic. **Clientele**: Central America/Caribbean. Provides the following services/assistance to refugees and immigrants: counseling; relative visa petitions; deportation and exclusion hearings; political asylum; human services; and legalization. Work coordinated with the US Catholic Conference Migration & Refugee Services.

621 *Brooklyn*

United Refugee Council

285 Marcy Avenue
Brooklyn, NY 11211
Efraim Friedman, Executive Director
(718) 384-0429

Services Offered: AD, CE, LE, RE, RS, SS. **Established**: 1975. **Staff**: 5. **BIA**. **Religious Affiliation**: Jewish. **Clientele**: World. Provides a variety of services to a predominant Jewish clientele. Works with Rav Tov, the International Jewish Rescue Organization.

622 *Buffalo*

Catholic Charities. Refugee Assistance Program

775 Main Street
Buffalo, NY 14203
Michael Talluto, Director
(716) 842-0270

Services Offered: AD, CE, LI, RE, SS. **Established**: 1945. **BIA**. **Religious Affiliation**: Catholic. **Clientele**: World. Refugee resettlement and family reunification services offered in Western New York through US Catholic Conference Migration & Refugee Services.

623 *Buffalo*

International Institute of Buffalo

864 Delaware Avenue
Buffalo, NY 14209
Hinke Boot, Contact

(716) 883-1900

Services Offered: AD, CU, EC, ED, HE, LE, SS. **Established**: 1934. **Staff**: 14. **Budget**: $390,000. **BIA**. **Clientele**: World. The II is a non-sectarian agency that provides social and educational services to immigrants, non-immigrants, refugees, entrants, non-English speakers and their descendents. Specific services include language assistance in all languages; individual and family counseling; classes in English as a second language; and transportation. **Publications**: INTERNATIONAL INSTITUTE NEWS; Annual Report.

624 *Buffalo*

Jewish Family Service

70 Barker Street
Buffalo, NY 14206
David Gersh, Executive Director
(716) 883-1914

Services Offered: AD, CE, SS. **Established**: 1930. **Religious Affiliation**: Jewish. **Clientele**: World. Comprehensive range of resettlement services.

625 *Commack*

Presbytery of Long Island

50 Hauppauge Road
Commack, NY 11725
Rev. R. Scott Sheldon, Associate Executive
(516) 499-7171

Services Offered: AD, LI, RE. **Religious Affiliation**: Presbyterian. **Clientele**: World. Advocacy for refugees and immigrants from all parts of the world. **Publications**: KAIROS (bi-monthly newsletter); MUTUALITY IN MISSION (bi-monthly newsletter).

626 *Hempstead*

Adelphi University. Refugee Assistance Program

91 North Franklin Street, Room 108
Hempstead, NY 11550
Sheldon Shamitz, Director
(516) 483-1210

Services Offered: AD, CU, EC, ED, HE, RS, SS. **Established**: 1981. **Staff**: 10. **Budget**: $225,000. **Clientele**: World. The Adelphi University Refugee Assistance Program, a program of the Social Services Center of the School of Social

Work, has been set up to ease the difficult transition to American life. It is a resource for refugees on Long Island. The AURAP staff is sensitive to the problems that refugees face in adjusting to a different culture, and the interest the community has in their adaption. RAP offers a variety of free support services, including career planning, job placement, English classes, translation and interpretation, counseling and referrals.

---

627   *Hempstead*

Central American Refugee Center

5 Centre Street, Suite 9
Hempstead, NY 11550
Christopher Gray, Director
(516) 489-8330

Services Offered: AD, CU, CE, EC, ED, LE, SS.
Clientele: Central America/Caribbean. Cultural, educational, legal and general social services available to refugees and immigrants. Affiliated with Church World Service Immigration and Refugee Program.

---

628   *Jamaica*

Afghan Community in America

139-15 95th Avenue
Jamaica, NY 11435
Habib Mayar, Chair
(718) 658-3737

Services Offered: AD, CU, CE, LE, RS, SS.
Established: 1980. **Staff:** 4. **Clientele:** Asia. Provide core social and emergency services to Afghan refugees in the United States as well as informing American public about situation in Afghanistan following Soviet withdrawal.

---

629   *Long Island City*

Irish Immigration Reform Movement

3301 Greenpoint Avenue
Long Island City, NY 11101
Shawn Minihane, Chair
(718) 478-5502

Services Offered: AD, CE. **Established:** 1987. **Staff:** 2. **Clientele:** Europe. Advocacy group and political lobbying to increase immigration quotas for Irish and obtain amnesty for undocumented immigrants in the United States. **Publications:** NEWS BULLETIN (monthly).

---

630   *Mount Vernon*

American Romanian Committee for Assistance to Refugees

63 Oakley Avenue
Mount Vernon, NY 10550
Fr. Florian Galdau, Chair
(914) 699-5511

Services Offered: AD, CU, CE, EC, RS, SS.
Established: 1970. **BIA. Clientele:** Europe. Refugee resettlement activities concentrate on Eastern and Southeastern Europe.

---

631   *New York*

Agudath Israel of America

84 William Street
New York, NY 10038
Morton Avigdor, Contact
(212) 797-9000

Services Offered: AD, CU, CE, LE, LI, RS, SS.
Established: 1939. **BIA. Religious Affiliation:** Jewish. **Clientele:** USSR, Middle East. In 1939 AI established an Immigration & Refugee Division to assist in the rescue of Orthodox Jews from Europe. History of rescue and resettlement since 1939. Programs and services for Jewish refugees, the majority in recent years have come from the USSR and Iran.

---

632   *New York*

American Committee on Italian Migration

352 West 44th Street
New York, NY 10036
Rev. Joseph A. Cogo, Executive Secretary
(212) 247-7373

Services Offered: AD, CU, CE, ED, LE, RE, SS.
Established: 1952. **Staff:** 10. **Budget:** $250,000. **BIA. Religious Affiliation:** Catholic. **Clientele:** Europe. Goals are to promote fair immigration policies and to assist Italian immigrants with problems of resettlement and assimilation.
Publications: NUOVA VIA (bimonthly, free); ACIM NEWSLETTER (bimonthly, free).

---

633   *New York*

American Council for Nationalities Service

95 Madison Avenue
New York, NY 10016

Wells C. Klein, Executive Director
(212) 532-5858   Fax: (212) 532-8558

Services Offered: AD, CE, SS. **Established**: 1958. **Staff**: 60. **Clientele**: World. National non-profit, non-sectarian organization with a network of member agencies (usually called International Institutes) providing resettlement, social, educational and social services for refugees and immigrants. Service organization that advises member agencies and provides technical assistance in immigration, social casework, educational programs, etc. Since 1975 actively engaged in the resettlement of refugees and entrants from Southeast Asia, Cuba, Afghanistan and several African countries. The U.S. Committee for Refugees is an ACNS public information program. **Publications**: WORLD REFUGEE SURVEY (annual); INTERPRETOR RELEASES (weekly); REFUGEE REPORT (bi-monthly).

---

634 *New York*

American Council on International Personnel

510 Madison Avenue
New York, NY   10022
Lucia Trovato, Executive Director
(212) 688-2437

Services Offered: EC. **Established**: 1971. **Clientele**: World. Business association that provides immigration-related personnel assistance to corporations. **Publications**: ACIP NEWSLETTER (bi-monthly); monographs.

---

635 *New York*

American Federation of Jews from Central Europe

570 Seventh Avenue, 16th Floor
New York, NY   10018
K. Peter Lekisch, President
(212) 921-3871

Services Offered: AD, CU, RS, SS. **Established**: 1942. **Religious Affiliation**: Jewish. **Clientele**: Europe. Promotes the interests of American Jews of Central European German-speaking descent, especially in regard to restitution and indemnification. Through its research affiliate, the Research Foundation for Jewish Immigration, sponsors research and publications on the history of German-speaking Central European Jewry and the history of its immigration and acculturation in the United States and world-wide. Through its charitable affiliate, the Jewish Philanthropic Fund of 1933, sponsors social programs for needy Nazi victims in

cooperation with specialized social service agencies. **Publications**: List of Publications.

---

636 *New York*

American Friends Service Committee. Haitian Women's Program

15 Rutherford Place
New York, NY   10003
Patricia Benoit, Director
(212) 598-0971   Fax: (212) 529-4603

Services Offered: AD, CU, CE, EC, LI, SS. **Established**: 1981. **Staff**: 3. **Religious Affiliation**: Quaker. **Clientele**: Central America/Caribbean. Services designed to assist with integration of women from Haiti into American life.

---

637 *New York*

American Fund for Czechoslovak Refugees

1776 Broadway, Suite 2105
New York, NY   10019
Vojtech Jerabek, President
(212) 265-1919

Services Offered: AD, CE, SS. **Established**: 1948. **Staff**: 9. **Budget**: $$950,000. **BIA**. **Clientele**: Europe. Though resettlement services available to refugees from all parts of the world, emphasis is on refugees from Czechoslovakia and Central Europe though in recent years actively participates in the resettlement of Southeast Asians. Maintains offices overseas as well as throughout the U.S.

---

638 *New York*

Archdiocese of New York. Office for Immigrant Services

1011 First Avenue, 7th Floor
New York, NY   10022
Rev. Francisco Dominguez, Director
(212) 371-1000

Services Offered: AD, LE, RE. **Established**: 1978. **BIA**. **Religious Affiliation**: Catholic. **Clientele**: Central America/Caribbean, South America. Provides the following immigration assistance to those in the Archdiocese: extensions of stay; student visas; relative petitions; labor certification; bond redeterminations; release from detention; deportation; political asylum petitions and hearings; and provide information to community about immigration procedures.

639 — New York

Archdiocese of New York. Refugee Resettlement Office

1011 First Avenue, 7th Floor
New York, NY 10022
Paul J. Martin, Director
(212) 371-1000

Services Offered: AD, CU, CE, EC, ED, RE, SS. **BIA. Religious Affiliation**: Catholic. **Clientele**: World. Broad based social, economic and emergency assistance available to refugees within the Archdiocese. Coordinated with US Catholic Conference Migration & Refugee Committee.

640 — New York

Baron de Hirsch Fund

130 East 59th Street
New York, NY 10022
Lauren Katzowitz, Director
(212) 980-1000

Services Offered: RS, SC. **Clientele**: Middle East, Europe, USSR. Funding available to assist with the acculturation of Jewish immigrants in the United States. **Publications**: Guidelines.

641 — New York

Blue Card

2121 Broadway
New York, NY 10023
Florence Smeraldi, Executive Secretary
(212) 873-7400

Services Offered: SS. **Established**: 1940. **Staff**: 3. **Budget**: $274,000. **Religious Affiliation**: Jewish. **Clientele**: Europe. A charitable organization, founded in 1940, Blue Card is dedicated to assisting European Jewish survivors and their descendents who still suffer the after-effects of Nazi oppression, and who have not been able to achieve economic independence and emotional stability. Blue Card provided emergency assistance to meet the uncovered costs of medical care, educational and child care, and a wide variety of financial emergencies. More than 1,000 individuals are assisted annually. The number of those needing help is not declining, since many children of Nazi victims continue to suffer the after-effects of their parents' trauma.

Publications: Annual Report.

642 — New York

Center for Immigrants Rights

48 St. Marks Place
New York, NY 10003
Darlene Kalke, Executive Director
(212) 505-6890

Services Offered: AD, CE, ED, LE, LI. **Established**: 1981. **Staff**: 13. **BIA. Clientele**: World. CIR is an educational organization. It is dedicated to defending, and expanding the rights of immigrants and refugees regardless of their legal status through legal training, defense, and public policy education. Committed to the empowerment of all refugees and immigrants. CIR works to increase public awareness of the plight of immigrants and refugees and the extent to which it is influenced by domestic and foreign policies of the United States government. As an advocate, they work to attain full rights for immigrants and refugees by working alongside their community organizations and by engaging church, labor, civil rights and national organizations to participate in these efforts. Goal is to build a national immigrant and refugee rights movement formed through broad alliances of immigrants, refugees and citizens. **Publications**: CIR REPORT (quarterly newsletter); Annual Report.

643 — New York

Church Refugee Center

105 Chambers Street, 2nd Floor
New York, NY 10007
Linner Delcham, Coordinator
(212) 608-5467

Services Offered: AD, CU, CE, ED, LE, RE, SS. **Staff**: 3. **Religious Affiliation**: Episcopal. **Clientele**: World. Affiliated with Church World Service Immigration & Refugee Program. **Publications**: Annual Report.

644 — New York

Church World Service. Immigration & Refugee Program

475 Riverside Drive
New York, NY 10115
Dale S. de Haan, Director
(212) 870-2164

Services Offered: AD, CE, LE, RE, RS, SS. **Established**: 1946. **BIA. Religious**

Affiliation: Church of Christ. **Clientele**: World. Provides refugee resettlement and first asylum services in the United States and responds to human need throughout the world. Works with denominational offices in the resettlement of refugees and in working on issues of protection of refugees. CWS is the relief, refugee assistance and development arm of the National Council of Churches.

---

645   *New York*

Columbia University. School of Law. Immigration Law Clinic

435 West 116th Street
New York, NY   10027
(212) 854-4291

Services Offered: LE, LI. **Established**: 1980. **Clientele**: World. Supervised law students provide counsel and representation on select immigration related matters.

---

646   *New York*

Conference on Jewish Material Claims Against Germany

15 East 26th Street
New York, NY   10010
Saul L. Kagan, Executive Director
(212) 696-4944

Services Offered: CE, SS. **Established**: 1951. **Religious Affiliation**: Jewish. **Clientele**: Europe. Funds received under agreement from the Federal Republic of Germany used to provide social services for Jewish victims (outside of Israel) of Nazi persecution. Provides special assistance to those Jews who were unable to file by the 1965 deadline for indemnification. Represents about 20 Jewish survivor organizations.

---

647   *New York*

Ellis Island Immigration Museum

New York Harbor
New York, NY   10004
Diana Pardue, Director

Services Offered: LI, RS. **Established**: 1988. **Clientele**: World. Ellis Island was the major federal immigration facility in America. Between 1892 and 1954, 17 million immigrants were processed at Ellis Island. Today, more than forty percent, or over one hundred million, of all living Americans can trace their roots to an ancestor who came through Ellis Island. The new Ellis Island Immigration Museum

tells the story of the largest human migration in modern history. The museum is located in the 200,000-square foot Main Building - the most historically significant structure on Ellis Island. The museum offers visitors a fascinating, complete look at the total immigration experience, using innovative displays that feature historic artifacts and photos, interactive devices, computers and taped reminiscences of the immigrants themselves. The museum includes the American Immigrant Wall of Honor.

---

648   *New York*

Episcopal Migration Ministries

815 Second Avenue
New York, NY   10017
Marion M. Dawson, Executive Director
(212) 687-9454   Fax: (212) 949-6781

Services Offered: AD, LE, RE, SC, SS. **Established**: 1938. **Staff**: 20. **BIA**. **Religious Affiliation**: Episcopal. **Clientele**: World. EMM works to assist refugees, migrants, displaced persons, and asylum seekers in the United States through Episcopal dioceses, and throughout the world through the Anglican Communion and other church partners. In the United States refugees are sponsored for resettlement by individual parishes and through diocesan based programs. Efforts also include advocacy, protection, and support of legal assistance programs for the displaced. Official channel through which the Episcopal Church responds to relief and development needs of refugees, displaced persons and asylum seekers globally. Overseas relief efforts are funded in cooperation with the Presiding Bishop's Fund for World Relief.

---

649   *New York*

Eritrean Relief Committee

475 Riverside Drive, Room 907
New York, NY   10115
Tesfa Seyoum, Executive Director
(212) 870-2727   Fax: (212) 663-4145

Services Offered: AD, CU, CE, ED, EC, LE, RE, SS. **Established**: 1976. **Staff**: 3. **Budget**: $200,000. **Clientele**: Africa. Advocacy and limited services offered to refugees from Ethiopia. **Publications**: Newsletter (quarterly); Annual Report.

---

650   *New York*

Ethiopian Community Mutual Assistance Association

37 Union Square West
New York, NY 10003
Mekonnen Abraha, Executive Director
(212) 627-8358

Services Offered: AD, CU, CE, SS.
Established: 1981. **Clientele**: Africa. Objectives
are to assist in the transition of newly arrived
Ethiopian refugees in their adjustment to life in the
United States. Offers acculturation services, emergency assistance, etc.

---

651   *New York*

Hebrew Immigrant Aid Society

200 Park Avenue South
New York, NY 10003
Ben Zion Leuchter, President
(212) 674-6800   Fax: (212) 460-9242

Services Offered: CU, EC, AD, LI, RS, RE, SC,
SS. **Established**: 1880. **Staff**: 100. **Budget**:
$2,549,000. **BIA**. **Religious Affiliation**:
Jewish. **Clientele**: World, USSR, Middle East.
HIAS is the international migration agency of the organized American Jewish community. Since its inception in the late nineteenth century, HIAS has rescued and resettled more than four million Jews. HIAS
functions through a global network in 47 countries
on six continents. World headquarters are located in
New York City. In 1987 HIAS resettled 7,301
refugees, including 4,000 Soviet Jews and over 500
non-Jewish refugees. HIAS offers its clients a broad
spectrum of assistance and services, including: advice
to relatives of those who contemplate fleeing a country of persecution; arrangement for transit visas; advance planning for resettlement; aid in preparing letters of invitation from the USSR; representations and
interventions with government agencies; coordination
of resettlement activities; counseling for aliens seeking political asylum; advice on changing legal status;
worldwide location of relatives; and other activities to
assist new arrivals. **Publications**: HIAS
REPORTER; STATISTICAL ABSTRACT; Annual
Report.

---

652   *New York*

Human Rights Advocates International

230 Park Avenue, Suite 460
New York, NY 10169
Sanford Mevorah, Chief Legal Counsel
(212) 986-5555

Services Offered: AD, CE, LE, RS.
Established: 1978. **Staff**: 6. **BIA**. **Clientele**:

World, Southeast Asia, Middle East. HRAI is a tax-exempt public service law group providing legal representation and related services "pro bono publico" to
a national & international constituency through a
volunteer network of lawyers in forty countries.
HRAI controls a special expertise in the handling of
immigration/refugee matters, including all types of
visa processing and asylum issues. Actively involved
with Amerasians still in Vietnam and represents cases
before the Orderly Departure Program. Principal officials (all lawyers) hold current accreditation to the
U.S. Department of State and the United Nations
Secretariat. **Publications**: Annual Report.

---

653   *New York*

InterAction (American Council for Voluntary International Action). Migration & Refugee Affairs Committee

200 Park Avenue South
New York, NY 10003
Lynn Belland, Program Officer
(212) 777-8210   Fax: (212) 460-9242

Services Offered: AD, RS. **Established**: 1983.
Staff: 12. **Budget**: $864,000. **Clientele**: World.
InterAction is a broad coalition of 116 U.S. private
and voluntary organizations dedicated to international
humanitarian issues. Members are involved in:
refugee protection, assistance and resettlement; disaster relief; long-term development; public policy; and
educating the American public on international development issues. The Migration & Refugee Affairs
Committee is InterAction's most directly operational
committee, holding frequent meetings to make decisions about refugee resettlement, advocacy, policy,
and other related issues. InterAction is an advocate for
protection and maintenance of first asylum and for the
needs of unaccompanied minors in refugee camps.
Publications: Newsletter; Annual Report; List of
Publications.

---

654   *New York*

International Immigrants Foundation

130 West 42nd Street, 17th Floor
New York, NY 10036
H. Edward Juarez, Executive Director
(212) 221-7255

Services Offered: AD, CE, ED, LE. **Clientele**:
World. Advocacy, educational programs and legal
counsel and representation in immigration, asylum
and labor certification procedures.

---

655 *New York*

International Ladies Garment Workers Union. Immigration Project

275 Seventh Avenue
New York, NY 10001
Muzaffar A. Chishti, Director
(212) 627-0600

Services Offered: AD, CE, ED, LE.
Established: 1982. **Staff:** 7. **Budget:** $400,000.
BIA. Clientele: World. Provide comprehensive immigration legal services to members of the ILGWU and their immediate families.

656 *New York*

International Rescue Committee

386 Park Avenue South, 10th Floor
New York, NY 10016
Robert P. DeVecchi, Executive Director
(212) 679-0010

Services Offered: SS, RS. **Established:** 1933.
Staff: 500. **Budget:** $25,000,000. **BIA.**
Clientele: World. The IRC was founded in 1933, at the request of Albert Einstein, to assist anti-Nazi opponents of Hitler. During the decades that followed, IRC has become one of the leading American non-sectarian voluntary agencies serving people who flee from persecution and violence in totalitarian countries, as well as uprooted victims of civil conflict. The resettlement of refugees fleeing from political, religious and racial persecution, and from war and terror, has been a fundamental concern of the IRC. The goal of resettlement in the United States is the successful absorption of each refugee into the country's diverse social, economic and cultural fabric. During 1988, IRC had the resettlement responsibility for 10,931 refugees from 22 countries admitted to the United States. Since 1975 the IRC has assisted over 100,000 Indochinese refugees. IRC is the largest non-sectarian resettlement agency in the U.S.
Publications: Annual Report.

657 *New York*

International Social Service. American Branch

95 Madison Avenue
New York, NY 10016
Harvey Steinberg, Director
(212) 532-5858   Fax: (212) 532-8558

Services Offered: AD, CE, SS. **Established:** 1924. **Staff:** 4. **Budget:** $163,000. **Clientele:** World. International social services agency (affiliated with American Council for Nationalities Service) assisting individuals and families with casework counseling because of family separation due to international migration. Works with child custody, family reunification, pensions and other socioeconomic problems. Liaison between social agencies in the U.S. and agencies abroad to resolve problems that derive from international migration and the separation of families by national boundaries. Special emphasis on services and protection for children in migration, inter-country adoption planning, and family reunification, including refugee families.

658 *New York*

Jewish Philanthropic Fund of 1933

570 Seventh Avenue, 16th Floor
New York, NY 10018
Herbert A. Strauss, Secretary
(212) 921-3871

Services Offered: CU, HE, SS. **Established:** 1953. **Religious Affiliation:** Jewish.
Clientele: Europe. Provides financial assistance to agencies and institutions of the Jewish emigre community which fled Nazi oppression in German-speaking Central Europe and established themselves in the United States. Offers support to organizations which provide social services, promote the preservation of the German-Jewish cultural heritage, and study the acculturation of German-Jewish immigrants in the United States and world-wide.

659 *New York*

Lawyers Committee for Human Rights. Political Asylum Project

330 Seventh Avenue, 10th Floor
New York, NY 10001
Arthur C. Helton, Director
(212) 629-6170   Fax: (212) 967-0916

Services Offered: AD, ED, LE, SS, CE.
Established: 1978. **Staff:** 20. **Budget:** $1,700,000. **Clientele:** World. For over a decade, the Lawyers Committee for Human Rights has worked to protect and promote fundamental human rights around the world. The Committee has also been at the forefront of efforts to uphold the right of refugees, in flight from political persecution, to seek asylum in the United States. Through the Political Asylum Project, the Lawyers Committee challenges arbitrary or punitive measures that undermine the legal rights of refugees who seek safe haven in the United States. Work in this area is based on the universally recognized norms articulated in the United Nations Convention and Protocol Relating to the

Status of Refugees, as well as standards set by U.S. refugee law. Seeks to uphold the basic rights and freedoms accorded to individuals with refugee status. **Publications:** LCHR NEWSBRIEFS (quarterly); Annual Report; extensive List of Publications which describes monographs and videos on immigration/refugee law.

---

660 *New York*

Lutheran Immigration and Refugee Service

360 Park Avenue South
New York, NY 10010
Rev. Donald H. Larsen, Executive Director
(212) 532-6350

Services Offered: AD, CU, CE, ED, LE, LI, RE, RS, SS. **Established:** 1967. **Budget:** $5,750,000. **BIA. Religious Affiliation:** Lutheran. **Clientele:** World. Provides a full range of services to refugees and their sponsors from pre-arrival through initial resettlement, with a nationwide network of local offices, congregations, and community groups. Also provides immigration counseling. Community building with refugees and immigrants; and public education on behalf of refugees, immigrants and undocumented persons.

---

661 *New York*

Multicultural Immigration Center

Box 200096
New York, NY 10025
Olga Cassis, Director
(212) 663-0753

Services Offered: AD, CU, CE, ED, LE. **Established:** 1977. **Staff:** 7. **BIA. Clientele:** World, Central America/Caribbean. Educational services designed to assist those interested in becoming U.S. citizens. Provide limited legal representation at immigration proceedings.

---

662 *New York*

National Coalition for Haitian Refugees

275 Seventh Avenue, 11th Floor
New York, NY 10001
Jocelyn McCalla, Executive Director
(212) 741-6152   Fax: (212) 691-6171

Services Offered: AD, CE, LE, RS. **Established:** 1982. **Staff:** 3. **BIA. Clientele:** Central America/Caribbean. NCHR is a coalition of

47 U.S. and Haitian religious, labor and human rights organizations which work to assure that Haitian asylum applicants receive fair hearings in the U.S. and to educate the U.S. public about human rights conditions in Haiti as well as their economic, social and political background. **Publications:** HAITI INSIGHT (monthly newsletter, free)

---

663 *New York*

New York Association for New Americans

730 Broadway
New York, NY 10003
Mark Handelman, Executive Vice President
(212) 674-7400

Services Offered: CU, EC, ED, HE, RE, SC, SS. **Established:** 1949. **Staff:** 146. **Budget:** $12,000,000. **Religious Affiliation:** Jewish. **Clientele:** USSR, Southeast Asia, Middle East. NYANA's mission is to assist Jewish refugees (as well as other faiths) who come to New York to achieve financial self-sufficiency and social integration. Provides arrival assistance, food, housing, language training, employment training and referrals, medical services and other emergency services. Acculturation services help the newcomer to adapt to American life while at the same time maintain contact with their cultural and religious heritage. **Publications:** NYANA NEWS (quarterly, free).

---

664 *New York*

New York Circus

Box 37
New York, NY 10108
Rev. David Kalke, Director
(212) 928-7600

Services Offered: AD, CU, CE, LE, EC, ED, SS. **Established:** 1975. **Staff:** 3. **Religious Affiliation:** Ecumenical. **Clientele:** Central America/Caribbean, World. Ecumenical social justice center serving undocumented refugee and immigrant communities (principally Central American). Assistance with housing, emergency support, counseling, educational programs, etc. Advocacy and support to those fleeing Central American persecution. Operates an Immigrants' Rights Project. **Publications:** LUCHA (bi-monthly newsletter); monographs.

---

665 *New York*

New York City. Office of Immigrant Affairs

22 Reade Street, Floor 6N
New York, NY   10007
Elizabeth Bogen, Director
(212) 720-3465

Services Offered: AD, LI, RS. **Established**: 1984. **Staff**: 4. **Clientele**: World. The Office of Immigrant Affairs, located within the New York City Department of City Planning, is an information-gathering and planning arm for public and private agencies, and was set up to help them to do the best possible job of serving immigrant clients. It is not a direct service agency but rather takes a long view of immigrant service issues and policy issues. OIA holds monthly meetings for 30 city agency representatives; coordinates meetings for private immigration counseling agencies; handles the Mayor's immigration-related correspondence; follows legislation in Washington and Albany; provides public speakers; and provides policy analyses and recommendations for city policy on immigration/refugee issues. **Publications**: List of Publications.

---

666 *New York*

New York State Assembly. Task Force on New Americans

270 Broadway, Suite 722
New York, NY   10007
Howard Jordan, Executive Director
(212) 385-6688   Fax: (212) 385-6604

Services Offered: AD, CE, LE, LI, RS. **Established**: 1987. **Staff**: 8. **Budget**: $500,000. **BIA**. **Clientele**: World. Provide services to meet the needs of all New York State residents on immigration related issues. **Publications**: Newsletter; Annual Report.

---

667 *New York*

North Manhattan Coalition for Immigrants' Rights

260 Audabon Avenue
New York, NY   10033
Efrain Frias, Director
(212) 781-0648

Services Offered: AD, CU, CE, ED, LE. **Clientele**: World. Advocacy, cultural and educational support services, and legal counsel regarding immigration matters.

---

668 *New York*

Peylim

3 West 16th Street
New York, NY   10011
Abraham Hirsch, Executive Director
(212) 989-2500

Services Offered: AD, CU, CE, RE, SS. **Established**: 1951. **Religious Affiliation**: Jewish. **Clientele**: World. Assist with resettlement and integration of Jewish refugees in the United States.

---

669 *New York*

Philippine Center for Immigrant Rights

1472 Broadway, Suite 813
New York, NY   10036
Lita Jane Killip, Executive Director
(212) 221-3512

Services Offered: AD, CU, CE, LE, LI, RS, SS. **Established**: 1984. **Staff**: 5. **Budget**: $750,000. **BIA**. **Clientele**: Asia. PHILCIR arose from a shared realization among its organizers of a need for an institutional mechanism that can deliver services or respond to the problems of the Filipino immigrant community. These services are directed to the problems most recurrent among immigrants as well as minority groups, i.e., immigration problems, discrimination, illegal recruitment among Filipino migrant workers, etc. Programs and activities are centered around the concept of self-reliance and community empowerment. **Publications**: OO (quarterly newsletter); Annual Report; monographs.

---

670 *New York*

Polish American Immigration and Relief Committee

140 West 22nd Street, 2nd Floor
New York, NY   10011
Janusz Krzyanowski, Executive Vice President
(212) 254-2240

Services Offered: AD, CU, CE, EC, LE, RS, SS. **Established**: 1948. **Clientele**: Europe. Resettlement and related orientation, employment, counseling and other social services offered to refugees and immigrants from Poland.

---

671 *New York*

Research Foundation for Jewish Immigration

570 Seventh Avenue, 16th Floor
New York, NY 10018
Herbert A. Strauss, Secretary
(212) 921-3871

Services Offered: CU, LI, RS. **Established:** 1971. **Religious Affiliation:** Jewish. **Clientele:** Europe. Studies and records the history of the migration and acculturation of Jewish Nazi persecutees of German-speaking Central Europe in various resettlement countries. **Publications:** INTERNATIONAL BIOGRAPHICAL DICTIONARY OF CENTRAL EUROPEAN EMIGRES, 3v.; JEWISH IMMIGRANTS OF THE NAZI PERIOD IN THE USA, 6v.

---

672 *New York*

Riverside Church. Sanctuary Committee

490 Riverside Drive, Room 122S
New York, NY 10027
Susan Werson, Contact
(212) 222-5900

Services Offered: AD, CE, SA. **Religious Affiliation:** Unitarian. **Clientele:** Central America/Caribbean. Sanctuary services for Salvadoran and Guatemalan refugees.

---

673 *New York*

Tolstoy Foundation

200 Park Avenue South
New York, NY 10003
Leon Marion, Executive Director
(212) 677-7770

Services Offered: AD, CU, CE, LE, SS. **Established:** 1939. **BIA. Clientele:** World. Assist refugees of all nationalities with immigration processing, resettlement counseling, social and economic aid, in countries of asylum and resettlement. Programs to aid indigent Russians and to preserve Russian cultural activities. **Publications:** Newsletter; Annual Report.

---

674 *New York*

Training Program in Human Services for Emigres

75 Varig Street, 2nd Floor

New York, NY 10013
Katherine Schuchman, Program Director
(212) 941-9044

Services Offered: ED, SS. **Established:** 1966. **Staff:** 5. **Clientele:** World. Educational program designed to train refugees and immigrants for entry-level human services positions where their language skills can prove useful. Based on traditional social work education models combining classroom instruction and field work experience. Affiliated with Adelphi University Institute of Child Mental Health.

---

675 *New York*

U. S. Catholic Conference. Migration & Refugee Services. Operational Headquarters

902 Broadway, 8th Floor
New York, NY 10010
Robert G. Wright, Director
(212) 614-1277

Services Offered: AD, CU, CE, EC, ED, LE, LI, RE, RS, SS. **BIA. Religious Affiliation:** Catholic. **Clientele:** World. This is the operational headquarters for a national network of Catholic Migration & Refugee Services offices responsible for assisting all immigrant, migrant and refugee activities. Administrative headquarters located in Washington, D.C.

---

676 *New York*

U.S. Catholic Conference. Migration & Refugee Services. Regional Immigration Office

902 Broadway, 8th Floor
New York, NY 10010
Jim Haggerty, Director
(212) 614-1259

Services Offered: AD, LE, RE, SS. **Staff:** 5. **BIA. Religious Affiliation:** Catholic. **Clientele:** World. Regional office covers northeastern United States.

---

677 *New York*

U.S. Department of Health & Human Services. Family Support Administration. Office of Refugee Resettlement

26 Federal Plaza
New York, NY 10278

Lou Katz, Contact
(212) 264-2890

Clientele: World. Regional office for the U.S. Office of Refugee Resettlement responsible for coordinating assistance (cash & medical, social services, health, etc.) in order to help refugees achieve economic self-sufficiency.

---

678 *New York*

United Church Board for World Ministries. Refugee Resettlement Program

475 Riverside Drive, 16th Floor
New York, NY 10115
Mary Kuenning, Administrator
(212) 870-3369   Fax: (212) 932-1236

Services Offered: AD, SS. **Established**: 1946. **Staff**: 3. **Religious Affiliation**: Church of Christ. **Clientele**: World. Refugee resettlement office in cooperation with Church World Service. Encorages local churches to sponsor refugees. **Publications**: BORDERLINES (semi-annual newsletter).

---

679 *New York*

United Methodist Committee on Relief. Refugee Services Department

475 Riverside Drive, Room 1374
New York, NY 10115
Susan Werson, Contact
(212) 870-3805   Fax: (212) 870-3940

Services Offered: AD, CE, SS. **Staff**: 7. **Religious Affiliation**: Methodist. **Clientele**: World. Resettlement and first asylum assistance to refugees coordinated through Church World Service.

---

680 *New York*

United Nations. High Commissioner for Refugees

Box 20
New York, NY 10017
(212) 963-0074

Services Offered: AD, SS. **Established**: 1951. **Clientele**: World. UNHCR cares for 12 million refugees throughout the world. UNHCR employs 2,000 staff members, working at the Geneva headquarters and in 80 different countries. Expenditures are financed mainly by voluntary contributions from governments. UNHCR is non-political and strictly humanitarian. It has two main functions: to protect refugees and to seek durable solutions to their problems. In order to protect refugees, UNHCR must safeguard their life, security and freedom. It means preventing refugees from being returned to a country where they may be in danger of persecution, and promoting their rights in such vital fields as accomodation, education, employment, and freedom of movement. The High Commissioner, based in Geneva, is Jean-Pierre Hocke. **Publications**: REFUGEES (monthly, free); REFUGEE ABSTRACTS (quarterly).

---

681 *New York*

United Nations. Relief and Works Agency for Palestine Refugees in the Near East

United Nations Building, Room DC2-0550
New York, NY 10017
John Miles, Contact
(212) 963-2255

Services Offered: AD, CU, CE, LE, ED, HE, LI, RS, SS. **Established**: 1950. **Clientele**: Middle East. Provides assistance to registered Palestinian refugees located in the Middle East.

---

682 *New York*

Vietnamese American Cultural Organization

213 West 30th Street, 3rd Floor
New York, NY 10001
Joseph Phan Thanh Hien, Executive Director
(212) 947-2757

Services Offered: CU, EC, ED, HE, SS. **Established**: 1976. **Staff**: 17. **Budget**: $400,000. **Clientele**: Southeast Asia. VACO is a non-profit, multi-social and educational organization serving Indochinese refugees of Cambodian, Laotian, Vietnamese and ethnic Chinese origins residing in the New York Metropolitan area. The overall objectives of VACO's service delivery program are: to enable refugees to become self-sufficient by providing them with needed social and educational services; to prepare refugees for competitive employment; and to facilitate the social adjustment of refugees. Following programs are offered: employment/career orientation and counseling; outreach; assessment; translation and interpretation; social adjustment; skill recertification; mental health services; and domestic violence prevention programs.

---

683   *Nyack*

World Relief

Box WRC
Nyack, NY 10960
Don Hammond, Director
(914) 268-4135   Fax: (914) 268-2271

Services Offered: AD, CU, RS, SS.
Established: 1948. **BIA. Clientele:** World.
Immigration assistance with adjustment of status and
visa applications for refugees and immigrants.
General refugee resettlement agency.

684   *Ogdensburg*

Catholic Charities

Box 296
Ogdensburg, NY 13669
Stephen H. Gratto, Director
(315) 393-2660

Services Offered: SS. **Established:** 1956.
Religious Affiliation: Catholic. **Clientele:**
World. Refugee resettlement activities coordinated
with US Catholic Conference Migration & Refugee
Services.

685   *Plattsburgh*

Plattsburg Interfaith Council

151 South Catherine Street
Plattsburgh, NY 12901
Margot Zeglis, Coordinator
(518) 561-0470

Services Offered: AD, CU, CE, RE, SS.
Religious Affiliation: Ecumenical. **Clientele:**
World. Advocacy and support services for refugees and
immigrants.

686   *Rochester*

Catholic Family Center. Refugee Department

50 Chestnut Street
Rochester, NY 14604
Edward Patane, Manager
(716) 546-7220

Services Offered: AD, CU, EC, SS.
Established: 1912. **Staff:** 15. **Budget:** $350,000.
Religious Affiliation: Catholic. **Clientele:**
World. Assists with the resettlement and reunification
of refugees and immigrants. Activities coordinated
through US Catholic Conference Migration and

Refugee Services.

687   *Rochester*

Corpus Christi Church. Sanctuary Committee

80 Prince Street
Rochester, NY 14605
(716) 325-2424

Services Offered: AD, CE, SA. **Religious
Affiliation:** Catholic. **Clientele:** Central
America/Caribbean. Declared sanctuary for Central
American refugees.

688   *Rochester*

Jewish Family Service

441 East Avenue
Rochester, NY 14607
Gregory Langen, Executive Director
(716) 461-0110

Services Offered: AD, CU, SS. **Religious
Affiliation:** Jewish. **Clientele:** Europe, USSR.
Resettle Soviet Jews and other political or religious
refugee groups interested in emigrating to the United
States and choosing to settle in Rochester.

689   *Staten Island*

Center for Migration Studies

209 Flagg Place
Staten Island, NY 10304
Lydio F. Tomasi, Executive Director
(718) 351-8800

Services Offered: CU, ED, LE, LI, RS.
Established: 1964. **Staff:** 17. **Budget:** $550,000.
Clientele: World. CMS encourages the interdisci-
plinary study of human migration and refugee move-
ments everywhere through scientific research projects.
Sponsors the CMS Annual National Legal
Conference on Immigration and Refugee Policy in
Washington, DC. Major contributor to the scholar-
ship of migration and refugee/immigrant affairs.
Publications: CMS NEWSLETTER (seimi-an-
nual, free); INTERNATIONAL MIGRATION
REVIEW (quarterly, $27.50); MIGRATION WORLD
MAGAZINE (5X/year, $19); List of Publications.

690   *Staten Island*

College of Staten Island. Center for Immigrant and Population Studies

130 Stuyvestant Place, Room 932
Staten Island, NY 10301
Roy S. Bryce-Laporte, Director
(718) 390-7946 Fax: (718) 273-5031

Services Offered: RS. Established: 1987.
Staff: 4. CIPS is an organized research unit of the College of Staten Island (City University of New York) established in 1987 to organize, promote, coordinate, conduct and disseminate research on immigrants and implications of population dynamics. At present the Center's principal concern and on-going studies are on the study of foreign-born and immigrant populations of New York State and its implications for the State and City of New York with selected areas of emphasis.

691   *Syracuse*

Americanization League

725 Harrison Street
Syracuse, NY 13210
Helga Kolek, Nationality Director
(315) 425-4120

Services Offered: AD, LE, SS. Established: 1916. **Staff:** 3. **Budget:** $55,000. **Clientele:** World. Extensive services for immigrants and refugees include: counseling on personal, social and cultural adjustment problems; counseling on all immigration and naturalization matters; applications for naturalization; help with petitions, affidavits, invitations and applications; translations and certifications of documents in 6 languages; notary services; and general assistance regarding immigration and citizenship matters. **Publications:** Annual Statistical Report.

692   *Syracuse*

Syracuse Interreligious Council. Refugee Assistance Program

910 Madison Avenue
Syracuse, NY 13210
Nona Stewart, Refugee Coordinator
(315) 474-1261

Services Offered: AD, CU, CE, EC, ED, HE, LI, RE, SS. Established: 1981. **Religious Affiliation:** Ecumenical. **Clientele:** World. Extensive services offered include: community education and outreach; advocacy; sponsorship development; church and judicatory contacts; support ser-

vices; job orientation and employment assistance; language programs; health care; orientation and acculturation; and other social services coordinated with Church World Service Immigration & Refugee Services.

693   *Utica*

Mohawk Valley Resource Center for Refugees

249 Bleecker Street
Utica, NY 13501
Rose Marie Battisti, Executive Director
(315) 738-1083

Services Offered: AD, CE, EC, ED, HE, SS. Established: 1979. **Staff:** 16. **Budget:** $426,000. **Religious Affiliation:** Lutheran. **Clientele:** Southeast Asia, Europe. MVRCR is a non-profit organization, located in central New York, whose aim is to resettle refugees from around the world and aid them in becoming self-sufficient in the United States. Since the Center was established in 1979, it has assisted refugees from Eastern Europe and Southeast Asia.

694   *Cary*

New Hope Presbytery

1104 Askhan Drive
Cary, NC 27511
Wendy Segreti, Coordinator
(919) 467-4944

Services Offered: AD, CE, SS. **Religious Affiliation:** Ecumenical. **Clientele:** World. Ecumenical refugee resettlement and sponsorship development affiliated with Church World Service.

695   *Cary*

North Carolina Baptist State Convention

Box 1107
Cary, NC 27512
Burke Holland, Language Missions
(919) 467-5100

Services Offered: AD, CU, CE, LE, RE, RS. **Established:** 1977. **BIA. Religious Affiliation:** Baptist. **Clientele:** World. Refugee resettlement and outreach services.

696   *Charlotte*

Catholic Social Service. Refugee Office

1524 East Morehead Street
Charlotte, NC 28207
Barbara Bazluki, Director
(704) 331-1720

Services Offered: AD, CU, EC, ED, HE, SS. **Established:** 1975. **Staff:** 10. **Budget:** $400,000. **Religious Affiliation:** Catholic. **Clientele:** World. Resettlement agency with social service contracts with the principal goal of bringing refugees to rapid self-sufficiency, self reliance and wholeness.

697   *Charlotte*

Jewish Family Services

Box 13369
Charlotte, NC 28211
Adrienne J. Rosenberg, Director
(704) 364-6594

Services Offered: AD, EC, SS, CU. **Established:** 1980. **Staff:** 3. **Budget:** $78,363. **Religious Affiliation:** Jewish. **Clientele:** World, USSR, Middle East. Social service programs designed to assist refugees and immigrants resettle and adjust to life in the Charlotte area. Majority of refugees and immigrants from the USSR and Middle East.

698   *Charlotte*

Mecklenburg Presbytery Refugee Resettlement Office

1830 Queens Road
Charlotte, NC 28207
Dora Lee Brown
(704) 372-3805

Services Offered: AD, CU, CE, LE, RE, SS. **Religious Affiliation:** Ecumenical. **Clientele:** World. Ecumenical refugee resettlement and sponsorship development coordinated with Church World Service.

699   *Fayetteville*

Catholic Social Ministries. Refugee Resettlement

111 Boone Trail
Fayetteville, NC 28306
Sr. Dorothy Ann Pyle, Director
(919) 424-2020

Services Offered: AD, SS. **Staff:** 1. **Budget:** $13,500. **Religious Affiliation:** Catholic. **Clientele:** Southeast Asia, Middle East, Europe. Advocacy and assistance to refugees, especially with family reunification. Provide caseworker 90-day follow-up. This entails assistance and information relating to social security, health, employment, school enrollment, language training, etc.

700   *Greensboro*

Lutheran Family Services. Refugee Resettlement Services

131 Manley Avenue
Greensboro, NC 27415
Raleigh Bailey, Director
(919) 855-0390

Services Offered: AD, CU, ED, LE, LI, RE, SS. **Established:** 1979. **BIA. Religious Affiliation:** Lutheran. **Clientele:** World. Sponsorship development, advocacy and refugee resettlement services.

701   *Hipoint*

World Relief

910 Eastchester Drive
Hipoint, NC 27260
Wayme Wingfield, Program Coordinator
(919) 887-9007

Services Offered: AD, CU, RE, SS.
Established: 1980. **Religious Affiliation:**
Ecumenical. **Clientele:** World. Working with
churches to assist in the sponsoring and resettlment
of refugees and immigrants.

---

702 *Montreat*

Asheville Presbytery. Refugee Resettlement Office

Box 7
Montreat, NC 28757
Lilian Fountain, Coordinator
(704) 669-5803

Services Offered: AD, CE, SS. **Religious
Affiliation:** Ecumenical. **Clientele:** World.
Ecumenical refugee resettlement and sponsorship de-
velopment coordinated with Church World Service.

---

703 *Morganton*

Hmong Natural Association of North Carolina

Box 1709
Morganton, NC 28655
Kue Chaw, Director
(704) 433-8475

Services Offered: SS. **Established:** 1980.
Staff: 5. **Budget:** $150,000. **Religious
Affiliation:** Baptist. **Clientele:** Southeast Asia.
Provide social services and resettlement assistance.

---

704 *Raleigh*

Diocese of Raleigh. Refugee Resettlement Office

300 Cardinal Gibbons Drive
Raleigh, NC 27606
John Carey, Director
(919) 821-9700

Services Offered: AD, CU, RE, SS.
Established: 1975. **Religious Affiliation:**
Catholic. **Clientele:** World. Advocacy, support and
social services as part of refugee resettlement program.

---

705 *Raleigh*

Episcopal Diocese of North Carolina. Refugee Committee

Box 17025
Raleigh, NC 27619
Rev. Jim Lewis, Chair
(919) 787-6313

Services Offered: AD, SS. **Staff:** 8. **Budget:**
$1,000. **Religious Affiliation:** Episcopal.
Clientele: World. Works with parishes to encourage
refugee sponsorship and occasionally assists with
family reunification. Provides materials to parishes
and relatives to assist with resettlement, though limited financial assistance available to refugees.

---

706 *Raleigh*

North Carolina Department of Human Resources. Family Services Section

325 North Salisbury Street
Raleigh, NC 27611
George W. Fleming, State Refugee Coordinator
(919) 733-4650

Services Offered: AD, EC, ED, HE, SS.
Clientele: World. Statewide coordination of federal,
state and private resources for effective refugee resettlement including cash and medical assistance, support services and such other activities as necessary.

---

707 *Raleigh*

North Carolina Refugee Health Program

Box 2091
Raleigh, NC 27602
Ronald N. Goodson, Program Manager
(919) 733-7081

Services Offered: HE. **Established:** 1979.
Staff: 1. **Budget:** $140,587. **BIA. Clientele:**
World. Purpose of the RHP is to assure speedy health
assessments of newly arrived refugees and to promote
the integration of refugees in the existing health care
delivery system. The program service categories include: translation services, outreach services, administrative services, and health assessments. Program services are available to all newly arrived refugees.
Publications: Annual Report; Directory.

---

708   *Bismarck*

North Dakota Department of Human Services. Refugee Resettlement Program

State Capitol, New Office Wing
Bismarck, ND 58505
Donald L. Schmid, State Refugee Coordinator
(701) 224-4809

Services Offered: AD, EC, ED, HE, SS.
Clientele: World. Statewide coordination of federal, state and private resources for effective refugee resettlement (cash and medical assistance, support services, etc.).

---

709   *Fargo*

Lutheran Social Services of North Dakota. Refugee Program

Box 389
Fargo, ND 58107
Barry Nelson, Director
(701) 235-7341

Services Offered: AD, CU, EC, LI, RE, SS.
Established: 1936. **Staff:** 7. **Budget:** $260,000.
Religious Affiliation: Lutheran. **Clientele:** World. Includes recruitment of sponsors for refugee resettlement, follow-up services to refugees. Has federal contracts to provide case management for refugees, job development, job upgrading, and manages the Unaccompanied Refugee Minor Program. Assists on a more limited basis with immigration matters, including adjustment of status, filing for family reunifications and referrals. Activities coordinated with Lutheran Immigration & Refugee Services. **Publications:** Annual Report.

---

710   *Fargo*

Vietnamese Mutual Assistance Association of North Dakota

Box 1633
Fargo, ND 58107
Hung Le, Contact
(701) 235-1311

Services Offered: CU, LI, SS. **Established:** 1981. **Staff:** 6. **Budget:** $6,000. **Clientele:** Southeast Asia. Advocacy, social and cultural services to Vietnamese refugees in North Dakota.
Publications: Newsletter (monthly, free).

---

711   *Akron*

International Institute

207 East Tallmadge Avenue
Akron, OH 44310
Maxine Floreani, Executive Director
(216) 376-5106

Services Offered: AD, CU, CE, EC, ED, SS.
Established: 1916. **Staff:** 12. **Budget:** $350,000.
BIA. Clientele: World. Offers extensive services to the foreign born, including: immigration and adjustment counseling; educational programs; intercultural and ethnic information center; and core services for refugee resettlement. In September 1988 over 50 Hmong were assisted by the Refugee Resettlement Department. Affiliated with the American Council for Nationalities Service. **Publications:** NEWSLETTER (quarterly); Annual Report.

---

712   *Akron*

Jewish Family Service

3085 West Market Street, Room 102
Akron, OH 44313
Cathy Weiss, Executive Director
(216) 867-3388

Services Offered: AD, CU, SS. **Established:** 1914. **Religious Affiliation:** Jewish. **Clientele:** World. Refugee and immigrant resettlement services assist new arrivals with transition to life in the U.S. Professionals and volunteers offer counseling, social adjustment services as well as other social services.

---

713   *Beachwood*

Jewish Vocational Service

21403 Chagrin Boulevard
Beachwood, OH 44122
Richard Binenfeld, Director
(216) 751-3103

Services Offered: EC, SC, SS. **Established:** 1938. **Staff:** 42. **Budget:** $550,000. **Religious Affiliation:** Jewish. **Clientele:** USSR, Middle East. Operates a variety of programs aimed at meeting the employment-related needs of the recently arrived Russian and Eastern European immigrants and refugees. Services include: job placement; vocational guidance and counseling; internships; resume writing; and college & career services. **Publications:** JVS TODAY (bi-monthly, free).

---

714   *Cincinnati*

Catholic Social Service. Resettlement Program

100 East Eighth Street
Cincinnati, OH 45202
Raymond Egan, Director
(513) 241-7745

Services Offered: AD, CU, LE, RE, RS, SS.
Established: 1910. **BIA. Religious
Affiliation:** Catholic. **Clientele:** World.
Programs and services designed to assist newcomers
adapt to life in the U.S. and become productive members of society.

---

715   *Cincinnati*

Community Friends Meeting. Sanctuary Committee

3960 Winding Way
Cincinnati, OH 45229
(513) 861-4353

Services Offered: AD, CE, SA. **Religious
Affiliation:** Quaker. **Clientele:** Central
America/Caribbean. Sanctuary services for Salvadoran
and Guatemalan refugees.

---

716   *Cincinnati*

Travelers Aid International Institute. Refugee Resource Center

632 Vine Street, Suite 505
Cincinnati, OH 45202
Nancy Minson, Coordinator
(513) 721-7660

Services Offered: AD, CU, CE, EC, ED, LE,
RS, SS. **Established:** 1980. **BIA. Clientele:**
World. Educational, employment and social programs
designed for the foreign born to become self-suficient
productive members of society as quickly as possible.

---

717   *Cleveland*

Catholic Social Services. Migration & Refugee Services

3409 Woodland Avenue
Cleveland, OH 44115
Rev. Augustine Lan, Resettlement Director
(216) 881-1600

Services Offered: SS. **Established:** 1975.
Staff: 5. **Budget:** $132,000. **BIA. Religious
Affiliation:** Catholic. **Clientele:** World. CSS assists refugees in various phases of resettlement including: sponsor recruitment - enlisting local people
who are interested in helping refugees; sponsor orientation - orienting people to the specific needs of the
refugee, including finding housing, clothing, health
care, education and employment; reception services -
welcoming newly arrived refugees at the airport; and,
referral services - referrals to appropriate social service
agencies. CSS also provides the following immigration services: family reunification; and adjustment of
status. In FY 1987 nearly 600 individuals were assisted. **Publications:** Annual Report.

---

718   *Cleveland*

Nationalities Services Center

1715 Euclid Avenue
Cleveland, OH 44115
Algis Ruksenas, Executive Director
(216) 781-4560

Services Offered: CU, EC, ED, SS.
Established: 1916. **Staff:** 13. **Budget:** $400,000.
BIA. Clientele: World. Help immigrants and
refugees with survival, educational and social services
which enable them to achieve economic and social
self-sufficiency. Assist newcomers in taking advantage of and fully participating in the social, cultural,
educational and economic opportunities available and
to promote understanding, awareness, communication
and cooperation among the many diverse ethnic, racial
and nationality groups. **Publications:** Annual
Report.

---

719   *Cleveland Heights*

Jewish Family Service Association

2060 South Taylor Road
Cleveland Heights, OH 44118
Burton Rubin, Executive Director
(216) 371-2600

Services Offered: AD, CU, RE, SS. **Religious
Affiliation:** Jewish. **Clientele:** USSR, Southeast
Asia. Services designed to assist in the resettlement
of refugees, primarily from the Soviet Union.

---

720   *Columbus*

Cambodian Mutual Assistance Association

648 South Ohio Avenue
Columbus, OH 43205
Vuthy Keo, Executive Director
(614) 252-3372

Services Offered: AD, CU, CE, EC, ED, HE, LE, SS. Established: 1980. Staff: 11. Budget: $225,000. Clientele: Southeast Asia, Africa. CMAA is a non-profit, self-help refugee resettlement and service organization. Provides the following services: resettlement program; employment services; English language training; housing assistance; social services referral; refugee child welfare services; and resource development and outreach. Though principal group served are Cambodians, CMAA assists all newly arrived refugees.

---

721 *Columbus*

Catholic Migration and Refugee Resettlement Services

197 East Gay Street
Columbus, OH 43215
Jim Smith, Resettlement Director
(614) 228-1121

Services Offered: RE, SS. Religious Affiliation: Catholic. Clientele: World. Social services to assist new arrivals.

---

722 *Columbus*

Lutheran Social Services. Unaccompanied Minor Refugee Program

57 East Main Street
Columbus, OH 43215
Rev. Nelson Meyer, President
(614) 228-5209

Services Offered: AD, CU, EC, SS. Established: 1980. Staff: 6. BIA. Religious Affiliation: Lutheran. Clientele: Southeast Asia. UMRP is a foster care program for Vietnamese adolescents who escaped from Southeast Asia and entered the United States without parents or guardians. Special educational and cultural enrichment programs. Activities coordinated through Lutheran Immigration & Refugee Services.

---

723 *Columbus*

Neil Avenue Mennonite Church. Sanctuary Committee

251 West Sixth Avenue
Columbus, OH 43201
Don Nofziger, Pastor
(614) 299-7970

Services Offered: AD, LE, SA. Established: 1985. Staff: 3. Budget: $2,000. Religious Affiliation: Mennonite. Clientele: Central America/Caribbean. In 1985 declared sanctuary and agreed to assist Central American refugees seeking a safe haven in the U.S.

---

724 *Columbus*

Ohio Council of Churches. Refugee Services

89 East Wilson Bridge Road
Columbus, OH 43085
Grace Johnson, Director
(614) 885-9590

Services Offered: AD, CU, ED, LI, RE, RS, SS. Established: 1979. Religious Affiliation: Ecumenical. Clientele: World. Sponsorship recruitment and development; cross-cultural programs; initial and follow-up services; and general advocacy for refugees and asylees.

---

725 *Columbus*

Ohio Department of Human Services. Program Development Division

30 East Broad Street
Columbus, OH 43215
Michael M. Seidemann, Refugee Coordinator
(614) 466-5848

Services Offered: AD, EC, ED, HE, SS. Clientele: World. Statewide coordination of federal, state and private resources for effective refugee resettlement including cash and medical assistance, support services and such other activities as necessary.

---

726 *Columbus*

Ohio State Convention of Baptists

1680 East Broad Street
Columbus, OH 43203
Dennis Kaz, Associat Director
(614) 258-8491

Services Offered: RE, SS. Established: 1954. Staff: 1. Religious Affiliation: Baptist. Clientele: World. Social service support for church sponsored refugee resettlement programs. Publications: Annual Report.

---

727 *Cuyahoga Falls*

Redeemer Lutheran Church. Hmong Farm Project

2141 Fifth Street
Cuyahoga Falls, OH 44221
Lavada Harnapp, Secretary
(216) 928-4603

Services Offered: SS. **Established:** 1982. **Budget:** $5,000. **Religious Affiliation:** Lutheran. **Clientele:** Southeast Asia. Unusual project that provides garden plots for Hmong refugee families to use to raise vegetables.

---

728   *Dayton*

Cambodia's of Ohio

1450 Sherwood Forest Drive
Dayton, OH 45449
Vi Houi, Executive Director
(513) 866-8731

Services Offered: AD, CU, CE, EC, SS. **Established:** 1979. **Clientele:** Southeast Asia. Social and cultural services designed to assist Cambodian refugees integrate into U.S. society and become financially productive members of society.

---

729   *Dayton*

Catholic Social Services

922 West Riverview Avenue
Dayton, OH 45407
Ronald Eckerk, Executive Director
(513) 223-7217

Services Offered: AD, RE, SS. **Established:** 1921. **Staff:** 1. **Budget:** $26,000. **Religious Affiliation:** Catholic. **Clientele:** World, Africa, Asia. Assess sponsors, complete paperwork for refugees in camps overseas, and provide resettlement and follow-up services to incoming refugees. Also assist U.S. relatives in completing required paperwork for the Orderly Departure Program. Work coordinated through US Catholic Conference Migration & Refugee Services. **Publications:** Annual Report.

---

730   *Dayton*

Miami Presbytery

1541 South Smithville Road
Dayton, OH 45410
Rev. David L. Fleming, Executive for Congregations
(513) 258-8118

Services Offered: AD, SS. **Established:** 1973. **Religious Affiliation:** Presbyterian. **Clientele:** World. Assist and coordinate activities among Presbyterian congregations in Ohio. **Publications:** Newsletter.

---

731   *Toledo*

Catholic Social Services

Box 985
Toledo, OH 43696
Donna Therkelsen, Director
(419) 244-6711

Services Offered: AD, CU, CE, EC, ED, RE, SS. **BIA. Religious Affiliation:** Catholic. **Clientele:** World. Advocate, sponsor and provider of direct services (and referrals) for the resettlement of refugees.

---

732   *Toledo*

International Institute of Toledo

2040 Scottwodd Avenue
Toledo, OH 43620
Patricia Vance, Coordinator
(419) 241-9178

Services Offered: AD, CU, CE, EC, ED, LE, LI, SS. **BIA. Clientele:** World. Extensive cultural, social, economic, legal and related services for immigrants and refugees. Objectives are the successful integration of newcomers in American society.

---

733   *Toledo*

Project Deliverance

444 Floyd Street
Toledo, OH 43620
Marcena Upp, Coordinator
(419) 242-7401

Services Offered: AD, CU, CE, LE, RE, SA, SS. **Religious Affiliation:** Ecumenical. **Clientele:** Central America/Caribbean, World. Ecumenical refugee resettlement and sponsorship development programs affiliated with Church World Service.

---

734   *Wooster*

Christ Church of the Brethren. Sanctuary Committee

1068 Country Club Drive
Wooster, OH 44691

Wayne Hochstetter, Clerk
(216) 262-1771

Services Offered: AD, EC, ED, HE, LE, RE, SA. **Established:** 1983. **Religious Affiliation:** Brethren. **Clientele:** Central America/Caribbean. Provide public sanctuary to Guatemalans and Salvadorans fleeing life-threatening situations in their own countries. Affiliated with the Wooster Coalition for Public Sanctuary. **Publications:** Newsletter.

---

735   *Wooster*

Coalition for Public Sanctuary

Box 751
Wooster, OH   44691

Services Offered: AD, CE, SA. **Clientele:** Central America/Caribbean. Support and sanctuary for refugees fleeing El Salvador and Guatemala.

---

736   *Youngstown*

Jewish Family and Children's Service

Box 449
Youngstown, OH   44505
Alvin Weinberg, Executive Director
(216) 746-7926

Services Offered: SS. **Established:** 1935. **Religious Affiliation:** Jewish. **Clientele:** Europe, USSR, Middle East. Resettlement services primarily for Jewish immigrants coordinated through Hebrew Immigrant Aid Society.

---

737   *Oklahoma City*

American Immigration Lawyers Association. Texas Chapter

911 NW 57th
Oklahoma City, OK   73118
E. Vance Winningham, Jr., Chairman
(405) 843-1037   Fax: (405) 848-2463

Services Offered: LE. **Established:** 1946. **Budget:** $25,000. **Clientele:** World. Provide services to immigration attorneys and coordinate available Pro Bono legal services of members to immigrants and refugees. Regional affiliate of AILA. **Publications:** AILA TEXAS CHAPTER NEWSLETTER (bi-monthly, $75).

---

738   *Oklahoma City*

Baptist General Convention of Oklahoma

1141 North Robinson
Oklahoma City, OK   73103
Bob Lovejoy, Missions Department
(405) 236-4341

Services Offered: SS. **Established:** 1975. **Staff:** 1. **Religious Affiliation:** Baptist. **Clientele:** World. Clearinghouse and sponsorship development for the resettlement of refugees.

---

739   *Oklahoma City*

Catholic Social Ministries. Migration & Resettlement Services Department

Box 1516
Oklahoma City, OK   73101
Timothy O'Connor, Executive Director
(405) 232-9801

Services Offered: AD, LE, SS. **Established:** 1975. **Staff:** 7. **Budget:** $141,395. **Religious Affiliation:** Catholic. **Clientele:** World. Attempts to enhance the chances of refugees who are granted permission to enter the U.S. by the INS, to become well-adjusted, productive residents. In 1988 the staff assisted 183 arrivals by finding sponsors for families; working with sponsor families to provide housing, clothing, and food to refugees; assisting refugees in applying for social programs; enrolling children in school; enrolling adults in English language classes; arranging for health assessment; orienting refugees; and aiding refugees in the search for suitable employment. **Publications:** SEVENTH STREET SENTINEL (quarterly newsletter, free); Annual Report.

---

740   *Oklahoma City*

Central American Refugee Project

431 SW Eleventh Street
Oklahoma City, OK 73109
Rick Rhodes, Coordinator
(405) 236-0413

Services Offered: AD, CU, CE, LE, SA, SS.
Religious Affiliation: Ecumenical. **Clientele:**
World. Ecumenical resettlement and support services
coordinated with Church World Service.

---

741   *Oklahoma City*

New Lao Friendship Club of Oklahoma

1805 NW 33rd Street
Oklahoma City, OK 73118
Phoukhong Thephachanh, President
(405) 525-9179

Services Offered: SS. **Established:** 1983.
Staff: 15. **Budget:** $12,728. **BIA. Religious
Affiliation:** Buddhist. **Clientele:** Southeast Asia.
Private non-profit mutual assistance association
established in order to intercede, advocate and facilitate
to further meet the needs of Laotians, new arrivals and
the limited English-speaking by providing direct
emergency services and crisis intervention.
Publications: NEW LAO FRIENDSHIP
NEWSLETTER.

---

742   *Oklahoma City*

Oklahoma Department of Human Services. Refugee Unit

Box 25352
Oklahoma City, OK 73125
Phil Watson, Director
(405) 521-4091

Services Offered: EC, ED, SS. **Established:**
1936. **Staff:** 1. **Clientele:** World. State agency coordinates refugee activities. Goal is to help refugees
achieve self-sufficiency as soon as possible through
employment services, language training programs and
social services. **Publications:** Annual Report.

---

743   *Oklahoma City*

Vietnamese American Association. Refugee Center

3121 North Classen, Room 201
Oklahoma City, OK 73118

Truong Khanh Tao, Executive Director
(405) 524-3088

Services Offered: AD, CU, CE, EC, ED, LE,
HE, SS. **Staff:** 20. **Clientele:** World, Southeast
Asia. Extensive services ranging from general advocacy and cultural preservation to educational and employment programs as well as traditional social service support network.

---

744   *Stillwater*

Interfaith Refugee Assistance Project

Box 1352
Stillwater, OK 74074
Dolly Warden, Treasurer
(405) 377-4531

Services Offered: AD, EC, ED, HE, LE, SA, SS.
Established: 1986. **BIA. Religious
Affiliation:** Unitarian. **Clientele:** Central
America/Caribbean. Voluntary organization affiliated
with the Unitarian Universalist Service Committee.
Assists refugees from Central America and is a de-
clared sanctuary. Foster parent program for refugee
children held in detention in South Texas.

---

745   *Stillwater*

Legal Aid of Western Oklahoma

920 South Main Street
Stillwater, OK 74074
Judy Newbold, Directing Attorney
(405) 624-1734

Services Offered: LE. **Established:** 1980.
Clientele: World. Legal counsel and representation
for indigents in immigration related matters.

---

746   *Tulsa*

Catholic Migration and Refugee Service

739 North Denver Street
Tulsa, OK 74106
Hazel Leitch, Refugee Director
(918) 585-8167

Services Offered: AD, CU, LE, RE, RS, SS.
Established: 1951. **BIA. Religious
Affiliation:** Catholic. **Clientele:** World. Services
and programs as part of diocesan support programs for
refugees and immigrants.

---

747   *Tulsa*

College Hill Presbyterian Church. Sanctuary Committee

700 South Columbia
Tulsa, OK 74105
Rev. David Caldwell, Coordinator
(918) 592-5800

Services Offered: AD, CE, SA. **Religious Affiliation:** Presbyterian. **Clientele:** Central America/Caribbean. Advocacy, public education and sanctuary services for refugees from El Salvador and Guatemala.

---

748   Baker

Catholic Migration & Refugee Services

Box 68
Baker, OR 97814
Marguerite Reed, Director
(503) 523-2902

Services Offered: AD, EC, ED, HE, LE, RE, SS. **Established:** 1975. **Staff:** 1. **BIA. Religious Affiliation:** Catholic. **Clientele:** World, Southeast Asia. Primarily work with sponsoring refugees, finding them homes, sponsors, meeting emergency needs and helping with assimilation.

---

749   Eugene

Holt International Children's Services

Box 2880
Eugene, OR 97402
David Kim, Executive Director
(503) 687-2202   Fax: (503) 683-6175

Services Offered: CU, LI, RE, SS. **Established:** 1956. **Staff:** 35. **Budget:** $6,500,000. **Clientele:** World. Provides adoption services in the United States for homeless children from throughout the world as well as assist foreign social service agencies improve their services to children.

---

750   Hood River

Hood River Valley Immigration Project

Box 830
Hood River, OR 97031
Kathy McGregor, Coordinator
(503) 386-3433

Services Offered: AD, CE, SS. **Established:** 1987. **Staff:** 2. **Clientele:** World, Central America/Caribbean. Provide immigration counseling, including assistance with documentation, referrals for appeals as well as educational outreach assistance and liaison with community on the plight of refugees and immigrants.

---

751   Lake Oswego

Diocese of Oregon

Box 467
Lake Oswego, OR 97034
Jenny Stewart, Refugee Coordinator

(503) 224-7582

Services Offered: AD, CE, RE, SS.
Established: 1979. **Religious Affiliation:**
Episcopal. **Clientele:** World. Promotes refugee
sponsorship of refugee individual's and families
amongst Episcopal parishes.

---

752 *Portland*

Archdiocese of Portland. Immigration Counseling Service

434 NW Sixth Avenue
Portland, OR 97209
Margaret Godfrey, Director
(503) 221-1689

Services Offered: AD, LE. **Established:** 1978.
BIA. Religious Affiliation: Catholic.
Clientele: Central America/Caribbean, World.
Provide legal counsel and representation for indigent
individuals in immigration and asylum matters.

---

753 *Portland*

Catholic Resettlement Services

231 SE 12th Avenue
Portland, OR 97214
Dan Jordan, Resettlement Director
(503) 231-4866

Services Offered: CU, RS, SS. **Established:**
1948. **Religious Affiliation:** Catholic.
Clientele: World. Reception and resettlement of
refugees and asylees coordinated with US Catholic
Conference Migration & Refugee Services.

---

754 *Portland*

Jewish Family and Child Service

1130 SW Morrison
Portland, OR 97205
Alvin Rackner, Executive Director
(503) 226-7079

Services Offered: AD, CU, LE, RE, SS.
Established: 1905. **Religious Affiliation:**
Jewish. **Clientele:** USSR. Refugee resettlement activities concentrated on the integration of Soviet Jews
and programs in order to attain self-sufficiency as
quickly as possible.

---

755 *Portland*

Lutheran Family Service. Refugee Services

605 Southeast 39th Street
Portland, OR 97214
Salah Ansary, Coordinator
(503) 233-0042

Services Offered: AD, CU, LE, RE, SS.
Religious Affiliation: Lutheran. **Clientele:**
World. Refugee resettlement and family reunification
in the Pacific Northwest coordinated with Lutheran
Immigration & Refugee Services. Operates small re-
settlement office in Edmonds, Washington.

---

756 *Portland*

Sponsors Organized to Assist Refugees

5404 NE Alameda Drive
Portland, OR 97213
Ellen Martin, Director
(503) 284-3002

Services Offered: AD, CU, RE, SS.
Established: 1979. **Staff:** 11. **Budget:** $250,000.
Religious Affiliation: Ecumenical. **Clientele:**
World. SOAR is an interdenominational, ecumenical
project to recruit and train sponsors for refugees.
Provides support and resources to sponsors. Program
of ecumenical ministries of Oregon and is the local
office of Church World Service. SOAR helps refugees
file papers for relatives still overseas, translates documents for the INS, helps complete change of status
forms and other immigration-related matters.
Bilingual casework staff provides variety of social
services. Services provided to refugees in Oregon,
Idaho and Southwest Washington.

---

757 *Portland*

Vietnamese Seventh-Day Adventist Church

7604 SE Clinton
Portland, OR 97206
Lao Duong, Minister
(503) 771-4219

Services Offered: AD, RE, SA, SS.
Established: 1980. **Staff:** 3. **Budget:** $30,000.
Religious Affiliation: Seventh Day Adventist.
Clientele: Southeast Asia. Refugee resettlement
services including sponsorship of Vietnamese fami-
lies as well as support services upon arrival.
Publications: NIEW TIN (newsletter).

758   *Portland*

Yiu Mienh Association of Oregon

3105 NE 108th
Portland, OR 97266
San Seng Saephan, President
(503) 252-8709

Services Offered: AD, CU, CE, SS.
Established: 1982. **Staff:** 6. **Budget:** $3,000.
Clientele: Southeast Asia. Provide services to assist Mien refugees to become assimilated while preserving traditional values and culture. Maintain linkages with Mien people in Thailand and China.

---

759   *Salem*

Oregon Department of Human Resources. Refugee Program

100 Public Service Building
Salem, OR 97310
Ron Spendal, State Refugee Coordinator
(503) 373-7177

Services Offered: AD, EC, ED, HE, SS.
Clientele: World. Statewide coordination of federal, state and private resources for effective refugee resettlement.

---

760   *Akron*

Mennonite Central Committee. Immigration & Refugee Program

21 South 12th Street
Akron, PA 17501
Don Sensenig, Director
(717) 859-1151

Services Offered: RE, SA, SS. **Established:**
1979. **Staff:** 2. **Religious Affiliation:**
Mennonite. **Clientele:** World. IRP strives to meet the needs of persons migrating to the United States to escape persecution, conflict and poverty, while attempting to educate the constituency on the root causes underlying these migrations, and working to change US policies and practices that contribute to injustice and discrimination. Works with the Overground Railway to assist persons fleeing Central America to find haven. **Publications:** Annual Report.

---

761   *Allentown*

Catholic Social Agency. Migration Services

928 Union Boulevard
Allentown, PA 18103
Sr. Anne Towey, Supervisor
(215) 435-1541

Services Offered: AD, CU, ED, RE, SS. **Staff:**
10. **BIA. Religious Affiliation:** Catholic.
Clientele: World. Participates through Catholic Migration & Refugee Services in the resettlement and family reunification of refugees and immigrants.

---

762   *Clifton Heights*

PRIME Ecumenical Commitment to Refugees

360 North Oak Avenue
Clifton Heights, PA 19018
Janet Shabon, Coordinator
(215) 259-4500

Services Offered: AD, CU, CE, ED, RE, SS.
Religious Affiliation: Ecumenical. **Clientele:**
World. Ecumenical refugee resettlement and sponsorship development affiliated with Church World Service.

---

763   *Erie*

Catholic Social Services

329 West Tenth Street
Erie, PA 16502
Sr. Teresa Marie Bohren, Executive Director
(814) 456-2091

Services Offered: SS. **Established:** 1955.
Religious Affiliation: Catholic. **Clientele:**
World. Sponsorship development and refugee resettlement services.

---

764 *Erie*

International Institute of Erie

330 Holland Street
Erie, PA 16512
Margaret Rex, Executive Director
(814) 452-3935

Services Offered: AD, CU, EC, ED, SS.
Established: 1938. **Staff:** 26. **BIA. Clientele:**
World. The immediate purpose of the II is to act as a
bureau of information and service to foreign speaking
peoples and to aid the foreign born in adjustment to
American life. Broader purpose is to interest people of
native and foreign birth to work together on an equal
basis for the development of fellowship and mutual
understanding and a high type of citizenship for all.
Following are some services/programs available for
refugees: case management; vocational training; translation and interpretation; English language training;
employment counseling; job placement; immigration
and naturalization counseling; legalization counseling; and information and referral. **Publications:**
INTERNATIONAL INSTITUTE NEWSLETTER.

---

765 *Harrisburg*

Catholic Charities. Immigration & Refugee Services

1500 Herr Street
Harrisburg, PA 17103
Beverly J. Smith, Program Director
(717) 232-0568

Services Offered: EC, ED, LE, SS.
Established: 1975. **Staff:** 25. **Budget:** $350,000.
BIA. Religious Affiliation: Catholic.
Clientele: World. Following services are offered:
refugee resettlement; immigration services; English
language training; case management; and translation
and interpretation.

---

766 *Harrisburg*

International Service Center

21 South River Street

Harrisburg, PA 17101
Truong Ngoc Phuong, Coordinator
(717) 236-9401

Services Offered: AD, ED, CE, LE, SS.
Clientele: World. Refugee and immigrant services
range from legal representation to educational programs to adjustment counseling.

---

767 *Harrisburg*

Pennsylvania Department of Public Welfare. Office of Policy, Planning & Evaluation

Health Welfare Building 529
Harrisburg, PA 17120
Ronald Kirby, Refugee Contact
(717) 783-7535

Services Offered: EC, ED, HE, SS. **Clientele:**
World. Statewide coordination of federal, state and
private resources for effective refugee resettlement including cash and medical assistance, support services
and such other activities as necessary.

---

768 *Hazelton*

Lutheran Welfare Service

Box 310
Hazelton, PA 18201
Lawrence House, Development Director
(717) 454-5300

Services Offered: SS. **Established:** 1974.
Religious Affiliation: Lutheran. **Clientele:**
Southeast Asia. Refugee resettlement activities coordinated through Lutheran Immigration & Refugee
Services.

---

769 *Lancaster*

Nationalities Service Center

10 South Prince Street
Lancaster, PA 17603
Ann Carr, Accredited Representative
(717) 291-4454

Services Offered: CE, ED, LE. **Established:**
1985. **Staff:** 2. **Budget:** $50,000. **BIA.**
Clientele: World. Professional multi-lingual staff
offers assistance in the field of immigration and naturalization law and procedure. Services include representing clients in deportation proceedings and in all
types of immigration cases (except labor certification), processing legalization appeals, offering
ESL/Civics classes, conducting community education

and translating documents. NSC creates mutual understandings between individuals, among groups by building upon the strength that pluralism offers society.

---

770   *Mechanicsburg*

Tressler Lutheran Services. Refugee Services Program

960 Century Drive
Mechanicsburg, PA 17055
Alan Dudley, Director
(717) 795-0300

Services Offered: AD, CU, CE, RE, SS. **Established:** 1971. **Staff:** 7. **Religious Affiliation:** Lutheran. **Clientele:** World. Social services provided to refugees sponsored and resettled through Lutheran Immigration & Refugee Services. Advocacy on behalf of all refugees, whether of not affiliated with LIRS. **Publications:** TLS VIEWS (quarterly newsletter, free); Annual Report.

---

771   *Overbrook Hills*

CASA

1408 Dorset Lane
Overbrook Hills, PA 19151
Elizabeth Abrams-Morley, Coordinator
(215) 642-8852

Services Offered: AD, CE, SA. **Clientele:** Central America/Caribbean. Sanctuary services for Salvadoran and Guatemalan refugees.

---

772   *Philadelphia*

Balch Institute for Ethnic Studies

18 South Seventh Street
Philadelphia, PA 19106
M. Mark Stolarik, President
(215) 925-8090

Services Offered: LI, RS. **Established:** 1971. **Staff:** 19. **Budget:** $1,000,000. **Clientele:** World. The Institute documents and interprets America's multicultural heritage. Unique in the concern for all books, documents and artifacts that relate to America's more than 100 ethnic groups. Planned collections provide excellent opportunities for crosscultural and interdisciplinary research. Maintains research library and ethnographic museum and offers a variety of educational programs. Recently established its own press as well as an annual prize for manuscripts on any aspect of immigration or ethnicity in America. **Publications:** NEW DIMENSIONS (semi-annual

newsletter, free); monographs.

---

773   *Philadelphia*

Catholic Social Services. Migration & Refugee Resettlement Department

222 North 17th Street
Philadelphia, PA 19103
Elena A. Santora, Administrator
(215) 587-3794

Services Offered: AD, CU, CE, EC, ED, LE, RE, SS. **Established:** 1975. **Staff:** 16. **BIA**. **Religious Affiliation:** Catholic. **Clientele:** World. Serve refugees sponsored by the US Catholic Conferebce in their resettlement by providing case management, employment, ESL and status adjustment and immigration assistance in family reunification, deportation, asylum, visa processing, labor certification, etc. Advocate in the community for refugees and immigrants. **Publications:** Newsletter; Annual Report.

---

774   *Philadelphia*

Community Legal Services

5219 Chestnut Street
Philadelphia, PA 19139
Sam Gomez, Directing Attorney
(215) 471-2200

Services Offered: AD, CE, LE, SS. **BIA**. **Clientele:** World. Provide legal representation in all aspects of immigration law. Also community outreach and education about public benefits for refugees. **Publications:** Annual Report; Directory.

---

775   *Philadelphia*

Federation of Jewish Agencies of Greater Philadelphia

226 South 16th Street
Philadelphia, PA 19102
Robert P. Forman, Executive Vice President
(215) 893-5600   Fax: (215) 735-7977

Services Offered: CE. **Established:** 1901. **Staff:** 110. **Religious Affiliation:** Jewish. **Clientele:** Middle East, Europe, USSR. FJA is an umbrella organization of the Philadelphia Jewish community. Regarding the area of refugee resettlement, the Federation is responsible for overseeing and coordinating service provision through the listed agencies to Jewish refugees. The majority of refugees are from the USSR. Works with the Hebrew Immigrant Aid Society to advocate on behalf of

---

refugees and to secure funding for their resettlement and family reunification. **Publications:** JEWISH EXPONENT (weekly, $25); NORTHEAST JEWISH TIMES (weekly, $25); Annual Report.

---

776   *Philadelphia*

Hebrew Immigrant Aid Society

1315 Walnut Street, Lower Level
Philadelphia, PA   19107
Robert L. Klotz, Executive Director
(215) 735-1670

Services Offered: AD, CU, CE, LE, RE, RS, SS. **Staff:** 7. **Budget:** $200,000. **BIA. Religious Affiliation:** Jewish. **Clientele:** USSR, World. Advocacy, legal representation and social service support to individuals and families resettling in the U.S. Provides immigrant and resettlement programs. **Publications:** Newsletter (bi-monthly, free); Annual Report.

---

777   *Philadelphia*

Jewish Family and Children's Agency

1610 Spruce Street
Philadelphia, PA   19115
Harold Goldman, Resettlement Director
(215) 545-3290

Services Offered: AD, CU, RE, SS. **Religious Affiliation:** Jewish. **Clientele:** USSR. Social services designed to assist resettlement of Soviet Jews.

---

778   *Philadelphia*

Lutheran Children and Family Service

2900 Green Lane
Philadelphia, PA   19129
Gamechise Guja, Refugee Director
(215) 951-6850

Services Offered: CU, LI, RS, SS. **Established:** 1922. **Religious Affiliation:** Lutheran. **Clientele:** World. Social adjustment and social service programs to assist in relocation and resettlement of refugees.

---

779   *Philadelphia*

National Lawyers Guild. Central American Refugee Defense

4812 Florence Avenue
Philadelphia, PA   19143
Peter Schneider, Coordinator
(215) 893-5306

Services Offered: LE. **Clientele:** Central America/Caribbean. Coordination of pro bono attorneys primarily for immigration and asylum representation of Central Americans.

---

780   *Philadelphia*

Nationalities Service Center

1300 Spruce Street
Philadelphia, PA   19107
Gabriella Labella, Coordinator
(215) 893-8432

Services Offered: AD, CU, EC, ED, LE, SS. **Established:** 1921. **BIA. Clientele:** World. Cultural, educational, legal and social services for the entire immigrant community.

---

781   *Philadelphia*

Philadelphia Refugee Service Center

4047 Sansom Street
Philadelphia, PA   19104
Evelyn Hidalgo, Executive Director
(215) 386-1298

Services Offered: AD, CU, EC, SS. **Established:** 1979. **Staff:** 20. **BIA. Clientele:** World. Advocacy, cultural, educational, employment and social services for refugees and immigrants.

---

782   *Philadelphia*

U.S. Department of Health & Human Services. Family Support Administration. Office of Refugee Resettlement

Box 8436
Philadelphia, PA   19101
Dick Gilbert, Contact
(215) 596-1320

Clientele: World. Regional office of the U.S. Office of Refugee Resettlement responsible for coordinating assistance (cash and medical, social services, health, etc.) to refugees.

---

783   *Pittsburgh*

Catholic Charities. Refugee Service Program

307 Fourth Avenue, Suite 300
Pittsburgh, PA 15222
Amy P. Deak, Supervisor
(412) 471-1120

Services Offered: EC, SS. **Established:** 1975. **Staff:** 5. **Religious Affiliation:** Catholic. **Clientele:** Africa, Middle East, Southeast Asia. RSP provides resettlement services for refugees in the Diocese of Pittsburgh and social services for refugees in the Western Region of Pennsylvania. The philosophy of the RSP has been that successful resettlement is a combination of a carefully planned sponsorship undertaken by committed volunteers and the provision of professional support services. The RSP views refugees as survivors who need basic transitional services to help them become active, productive members of their local communities; its programs are designed to help refugees achieve economic self-sufficiency and social adjustment as soon as possible. The following services are provided: sponsorship, recruitment and orientation; case management and service planning; employment services and job development; translation and interpretation; and English language training.

---

784   *Pittsburgh*

Interfaith Sanctuary Movement

7211 Thomas Boulevard
Pittsburgh, PA 15208
(412) 242-3167

Services Offered: AD, CE, SA. **Religious Affiliation:** Mennonite. **Clientele:** Central America/Caribbean. Services and sanctuary for Salvadoran and Guatemalan refugees.

---

785   *Reading*

Jewish Family Service

1700 City Line Street
Reading, PA 19604
Dan Tannenbaum, Executive Director
(215) 921-2766

Services Offered: CU, LE, RE, RS, SS. **Established:** 1945. **Religious Affiliation:** Jewish. **Clientele:** World, USSR. Central fundraising and planning agency of the Jewish community provides resettlement services.

---

786   *Scranton*

Catholic Social Services

400 Wyoming Avenue
Scranton, PA 18503
Kenneth Horan, Resettlement Director
(717) 346-8936

Services Offered: CU, LE, SS. **Established:** 1975. **BIA. Religious Affiliation:** Catholic. **Clientele:** World. Refugee resettlement program.

---

787   *Scranton*

Jewish Family Service

615 Jefferson Avenue, Suite 204
Scranton, PA 18510
Thomas Goldenson, Executive Director
(717) 344-1186

Services Offered: SS. **Established:** 1915. **Religious Affiliation:** Jewish. **Clientele:** USSR, Europe. Resettlement activities coordinated through Hebrew Immigrant Aid Society.

---

788   *Valley Forge*

American Baptist Churches. Immigration & Refugee Services

Box 851
Valley Forge, PA 19482
Matthew R. Giuffrida, Director
(215) 768-2425   Fax: (215) 768-2470

Services Offered: AD, EC, HE, LE, RE, SA, SS. **Established:** 1919. **Staff:** 12. **Budget:** $49,225. **Religious Affiliation:** Baptist. **Clientele:** World. The Office of Immigration & Refugee Services encourages resettlement and other appropriate services for refugees, undocumented and "overstayed" aliens, migrants, legally admitted immigrants, and legalization applicants/recipients. It initiates denominational resolutions to implement Church policy documents as emerging events direct and as determined by the Church Resolution on Church Sanctuary. In 1987 sponsored 1,208 individuals from 17 countries. Since 1948 have sponsored almost 65,000 individuals.

---

789   *Wayne*

Central Baptist Church. Sanctuary Group

Box 309
Wayne, PA 19087
Ellen Green, Coordinator
(215) 688-0664

Services Offered: AD, CE, LI, RE, SA. **Established**: 1984. **Budget**: $4,500. **Religious Affiliation**: Baptist. **Clientele**: Central America/Caribbean. Sanctuary at CBC was begun in 1984 when the congregation voted to offer housing and support to undocumented refugees. Advocacy on behalf of Central Americans and the cause of justice and peace for that troubled area of the world. Support of refugees, locally and nationally.

---

790 *West Chester*
Concord Friends Meeting Sanctuary

1712 Boot Road
West Chester, PA 19380
Beth Burger, Chair
(215) 644-0316

Services Offered: SA. **Established**: 1986. **Religious Affiliation**: Quaker. **Clientele**: Central America/Caribbean. Offers sanctaury for Central American refugees and public information on events in Central America.

---

791 *Willow Grove*
Coalition for Haitian Concerns

Box 95
Willow Grove, PA 19090
Gerard A. Ferere, President
(215) 657-3193

Services Offered: AD, CU, CE, EC, ED, HE, LE, LI, RE, RS, SA, SC, SS. **Established**: 1980. **Clientele**: Central America/Caribbean. Works for the well-being of the Haitian community, the Haitian refugees, and other refugee groups, and to provide the following services: employment; housing; educational and legal assistance, etc. Organization for advocacy, and all other activities stem from the need to support their position as advocates for Haitian refugees. **Publications**: DRUM BEAT (irregular newsletter).

---

792 *Lincoln*
Southeast Asian Center

Community College of RI
Lincoln, RI 2865
Laurice Girouard, Director
(401) 333-7244   Fax: (401) 333-7111

Services Offered: CU, ED, LI, SS. **Established**: 1988. **Staff**: 8. **Budget**: $200,000. **Clientele**: Southeast Asia. The Southeast Asian Center recruits and retains for the Community College members of RI's Southeast Asian community. Provides counseling and monitoring services, general referral, sponsorship of cross-cultural workshops for college and community. Maintains resource library.

---

793 *Providence*
Brown University. Population Studies & Training Center

Brown University
Providence, RI 2912
Sidney Goldstein, Director
(401) 863-2668

Services Offered: ED, RS. **Established**: 1965. **Staff**: 20. **Budget**: $500,000. Educational institution training demographers for work in universities, government agencies, international institutions, private foundations and enterprises. The Demography Library and Data Bank are major resources for international migration and socio-economic conditions in various countries. **Publications**: UPDATE (semiannual newsletter); Annual Report.

---

794 *Providence*
Catholic Social Services

433 Elmwood Avenue
Providence, RI 2907
Gerard A. Noel, Resettlement Director
(401) 467-7200

Services Offered: SS. **Established**: 1926. **BIA**. **Religious Affiliation**: Catholic. **Clientele**: World. Basic resettlement services offered through US Catholic Conference Migration & Refugee Services.

---

795 *Providence*
Diocese of Rhode Island

271 North Main Street
Providence, RI 2903
Ida Johnston, Refugee Coordinator

(401) 331-4622

Services Offered: SS. **Religious Affiliation**: Episcopal. **Clientele**: World. Work with parishes in sponsoring of refugees.

---

796 *Providence*

International Institute of Rhose Island

421 Elmwood Avenue
Providence, RI 2907
Bill Shuey, Executive Director
(401) 461-5940

Services Offered: AD, CU, CE, EC, ED, LE, HE, LI, SS. **BIA**. **Clientele**: World. Extensive services for the foreign born include: job orientation, training and placement; health and legal assistance; educational programs; translation and interpretation; refugee resettlement services for newly arrived; immigration services; cultural programs; and information and referrals.

---

797 *Providence*

Jewish Family Service

229 Waterman Street
Providence, RI 2906
Paul Segal, Executive Director
(401) 331-1244

Services Offered: AD, CU, EC, ED, LI, SS. **Established**: 1929. **BIA**. **Religious Affiliation**: Jewish. **Clientele**: World. Broad based services to assist refugees and immigrations in tranition to life in the U.S.

---

798 *Providence*

Khmer Buddhist Society of New England

178 Hanover Street
Providence, RI 2907
Maha Ghosanandra, Venerable
(401) 273-0969

Services Offered: CU, LI, RE. **Established**: 1980. **Religious Affiliation**: Buddhist. **Clientele**: Southeast Asia. This is the spiritual and cultural center for the local Cambodian community. Services designed to assist with orientation to life in the United States while maintaining traditional values and beliefs.

---

799 *Providence*

Rhode Island Department of Human Services. State Refugee Coordinator

275 Westminster Mall, 5th Floor
Providence, RI 2881
Lynn August, Refugee Coordinator
(401) 277-2551

Services Offered: AD, EC, ED, HE, SS. **Clientele**: World. Statewide coordination of federal, state and private resources for effective refugee resettlement including cash and medical assistance, support services and such other activities as necessary.

---

800 *Providence*

Socio-Economic Development Center for Southeast Asians

620 Potters Avenue
Providence, RI 2907
Tia N. Kha, Program Director
(401) 941-8422

Services Offered: AD, CE, EC, ED, SS. **Established**: 1987. **Staff**: 10. **Budget**: $225,000. **Clientele**: Southeast Asia. Provides the following services for Southeast Asians: family reunification; local advocacy; citizenship information; job orientation, development and training; counseling and guidance for school age population; and full range of social programs for elderly. **Publications**: Newsletter (planned for early 1990).

---

801 *Woonsocket*

Vietnamese Society of Rhode Island

43 Federal Street, Room 21
Woonsocket, RI 2895
Joseph R. Le, Executive Director
(401) 762-0343

Services Offered: CU. **Established**: 1982. **Staff**: 1. **Budget**: $1,000. **Clientele**: Southeast Asia. To assist refugees in Rhode Island with regard to charitable, educational, social, and cultural concerns. To promote communication within the Vietnamese community. To develop relationships between Vietnamese community and other communities and organizations in the state, and to maintain links outside Rhode Island.

802   *Columbia*

Migration & Refugee Services

Box 5287
Columbia, SC 29250
Peggy Sookikian, Director
(803) 798-5124

Services Offered: AD, LI, RE, SS.
Established: 1979. **Staff:** 1. **Budget:** $13,000.
Religious Affiliation: Catholic. **Clientele:**
World. In coordination with US Catholic Conference
Migration & Refugee Services resettle refugees with
family members and to help second migration
refugees to find jobs. Refer all refugees and immi-
grants to proper agencies for additional assistance.
One staff member covers the entire state.

803   *Columbia*

South Carolina Department of Social Services. Refugee Resettlement Program

Box 1469
Columbia, SC 29202
Bernice Scott, State Refugee Coordinator
(803) 253-6338

Services Offered: AD, EC, ED, HE, SS.
Clientele: World. Statewide coordination of federal,
state and private resources for effective refugee resettlement including cash and medical assistance, support services and such other activities as necessary.

804   *Pierre*

South Dakota Department of Social Services. Refugee Resettlement Program

700 North Governors Drive
Pierre, SD 57501
Vern Guericke, State Refugee Coordinator
(605) 773-3493

Services Offered: AD, EC, ED, HE, SS.
Clientele: World. Statewide coordination of federal,
state and private resources for effective refugee resettlement including cash and medical assistance, support services and such other activities as necessary.

805   *Sioux Falls*

Lutheran Social Services of South Dakota. Refugee Resettlement

601 West 11th Street
Sioux Falls, SD 57104
Barbara Day Greenlee, Director
(605) 336-9136

Services Offered: SS. **Established:** 1975.
Staff: 7. **Budget:** $215,000. **Religious
Affiliation:** Lutheran. **Clientele:** World. LSS is
the only voluntary agency resettling refugees in
South Dakota and the sole recipient of federal Office
of Refugee Resettlement funds. Comprehensive
refugee resettlement services: sponsorship development; language training; employment; general case
work; mental health counseling; case management
services; and general immigration counseling.
Publications: SPONSORSHIP NEWSLETTER
(quarterly); NEWS AND VIEWS: REFUGEE
NEWSLETTER (quarterly).

806 *Chattanooga*

Family and Children's Services of Chattanooga. Services for Refugees

317 Oak Street
Chattanooga, TN 37403
Glenn Hughes, Director, Special Services
(615) 755-2865

Services Offered: AD, CU, EC, CE, SS. **Established:** 1981. **Staff:** 1. **Budget:** $27,000. **Clientele:** Southeast Asia. Private non-profit agency with a service contract to the State of Tennessee to provide the following services to refugees: manpower employment services and social adjustment services.

807 *Knoxville*

Bridge Refugee Services

200 Lockett Road
Knoxville, TN 37919
Sue Corsano-Hoffer, Director
(615) 588-2754

Services Offered: SS. **Established:** 1983. **Staff:** 2. **Budget:** $28,000. **Religious Affiliation:** Ecumenical. **Clientele:** World, Europe. Work with churches to sponsor refugees. Training and monitoring of sponsorship programs. **Publications:** BRIDGE NOTES (bi-monthly, free).

808 *Knoxville*

Tennessee Valley Unitarian Church. Sanctuary Committee

3219 Kingston Pike West
Knoxville, TN 37919
(615) 523-4176

Services Offered: AD, CE, SA. **Religious Affiliation:** Unitarian. **Clientele:** Central America/Caribbean. Advocacy, community outreach and sanctuary for Salvadoran and Guatemalan refugees.

809 *Memphis*

Cambodian Association of Memphis

1624 Hartland Street
Memphis, TN 38108
Heng Hory, President
(901) 682-3997

Services Offered: CU, ED, SS. **Established:** 1983. **Staff:** 10. **Budget:** $3,500. **Religious Affiliation:** Ecumenical. **Clientele:** Southeast Asia. General array of services for Cambodian refugees and their families.

810 *Memphis*

Catholic Charities. Refugee Resettlement Program

Box 41679
Memphis, TN 38174
Carolyn Tisdale, Resettlement Director
(901) 722-4700

Services Offered: CU, EC, SS. **Established:** 1975. **Religious Affiliation:** Catholic. **Clientele:** Southeast Asia. Initial sponsorship and resettlement of legally admitted refugees in affiliation with US Catholic Conference.

811 *Nashville*

Association of Vietnamese in Nashville

1038 Percy Warner Boulevard
Nashville, TN 37205
Anh H. Dao, President
(615) 356-6918

Services Offered: CU, SS. **Established:** 1977. **Religious Affiliation:** Ecumenical. **Clientele:** Southeast Asia. Voluntary self-help organization designed to assist with the adjustment process of Vietnamese in Nashville. Mutual assistance regarding housing, employment and general social and educational services.

812 *Nashville*

Diocese of Nashville. Refugee Resettlement Program

30 White Bridge Road
Nashville, TN 37205
Margot Deschenes, Resettlement Director
(615) 352-3052

Services Offered: AD, CU, EC, ED, LE, SS. **Established:** 1975. **Religious Affiliation:** Catholic. **Clientele:** World. Advocacy, economic, educational and social services for refugees.

813 *Nashville*

Jewish Family Service

801 Percy Warner Boulevard
Nashville, TN 37205
Jay Pilzer, Executive Director
(615) 356-4234

Services Offered: AD, CU, LE, LI, SS.
Established: 1973. **Religious Affiliation**: Jewish. **Clientele**: World, USSR. Refugee resettlement services primarily for Jewish emigres.

814 *Nashville*

Metropolitan Social Services. Refugee Program

25 Middleton
Nashville, TN 37210
Margaret Pollard, Director
(615) 259-5381

Services Offered: AD, CE, ED, LE, SS.
Clientele: Southeast Asia, World. Broad range of social service programs designed to assist refugees and immigrants adjust to life in the United States.

815 *Nashville*

Mid-Cumberland Refugee Assistance Ministry

3900 West End Avenue
Nashville, TN 37205
Rev. Kerry Hird, Coordinator
(615) 383-3772

Services Offered: AD, CU, CE, RE, SS.
Religious Affiliation: Ecumenical. **Clientele**: World. Ecumenical refugee resettlement and sponsorship development program affiliated with Church World Service.

816 *Nashville*

Tennessee Department of Human Services. Refugee Program

400 Deaderick Street
Nashville, TN 37219
Martha Roupas, State Coordinator
(615) 741-2587

Services Offered: EC, ED, HE, SS. **Clientele**: World. This is the state agency assigned primary responsibility for refugees and state legalization impact assistance grants. The universe of services includes cash assistance, medical assistance, language training, social adjustment, language training and adult educa-

tion programs.

817 *Nashville*

World Relief

2605 Lincoya Drive
Nashville, TN 37214
Debi Stephens, Program Coordinator
(615) 885-1018

Services Offered: AD, CU, RE, SS.
Established: 1980. **Religious Affiliation**: Ecumenical. **Clientele**: World. Work with local churches to help with sponsoring and resettlement of refugees and immigrants.

818   *Amarillo*

Catholic Family Services. Refugee & Citizenship Division

Box 15127
Amarillo, TX   79105
Al Bednorz, Supervisor
(806) 376-4571

Services Offered: AD, CU, EC, HE, SS.
Established: 1935. **Staff**: 8. **Budget**: $230,000.
BIA. **Religious Affiliation**: Catholic.
Clientele: World. Assist sponsors file for refugee
relatives, reception and placement of refugees, cultural
orientation, employee development, and refugee
health screening. Provide all facets of family reunification immigration, including help with I-130, Visa
packets 3 and 4, application for permanent residence,
application for citizenship, replacement of lost immigration documents, etc. Referrals for those who need
to appear before an immigration judge.
Publications: Annual Report.

819   *Austin*

Caritas of Austin

308 East Seventh Street
Austin, TX   78701
Jerry Eichorn, Director
(512) 472-4135

Services Offered: AD, CE, SS. **Established**:
1976. **Religious Affiliation**: Catholic.
Clientele: Central America/Caribbean. Refugee resettlement services for primarily Central Americans
in the Diocese of Austin.

820   *Austin*

Casa Marianella

821 Gunter Street
Austin, TX   78702
(512) 385-5571

Services Offered: AD, CU, ED, HE, LE, SS.
Established: 1986. **Staff**: 3. **Budget**: $65,000.
Religious Affiliation: Ecumenical. **Clientele**:
Central America/Caribbean. Mission of Casa
Marianella is to provide emergency humanitarian aid
(shelter, food, clothing, medical and legal assistance,
etc.) to Central American refugees. Also community
outreach activities to inform the population about
conditions in Central America and the conditions
refugees face in the U.S. **Publications**: AMIGOS
DE CASA MARIANELLA (quarterly, free); CASA
MARIANELLA LIGHT (monthly, free).

821   *Austin*

Central America Resource Center

Box 2327
Austin, TX   78768
Jill Gronquist, Director
(512) 476-9841

Services Offered: LI, RS. **Established**: 1983.
Staff: 5. **Clientele**: Central America/Caribbean.
The Refugee Legal Support Service provides docu-
mentation of human rights abuses in Central America
to attorneys and direct service organizations working
to gain asylum for Central Americans. Principally in-
formation/documentation and research center. Major
clearinghouse on refugee information for Central
Americans. **Publications**: DIRECTORY OF
CENTRAL AMERICAN ORGANIZATIONS;
NEWSPAK (bi-weekly, $30); CENTRAL
AMERICA WRITERS' BULLETIN (semi-annual).

822   *Austin*

East Side Group

3101 French Place
Austin, TX   78722
Jennifer Long, Coordinator
(512) 474-4782

Services Offered: AD, CE, LE, SS.
Established: 1982. **Staff**: 20. **Clientele**: Central
America/Caribbean. Assist with bond redetermina-
tion, refugee sponsorship and work with Canadian
Consulate in Dallas for refugees seeking a safe haven
in Canada.

823   *Austin*

Friends Meeting of Austin. Sanctuary Committee

3014 Washington Square
Austin, TX   78705
(512) 452-1841

Services Offered: AD, CE, SA. **Religious
Affiliation**: Quaker. **Clientele**: Central
America/Caribbean. Advocacy, public outreach and
sanctuary for refugees fleeing from Central America.

824   *Austin*

Immigration and Legalization Service

Box 13327, Capitol Station
Austin, TX   78711

Rev. Darald Chatham, Director
(512) 756-7760

Services Offered: AD, CE, ED, LE, RE, SS.
Established: 1987. **Staff:** 3. **Budget:** $64,000.
Religious Affiliation: Catholic. **Clientele:**
World. Combination of services designed to assist
refugees and immigrants with integration into life in
the U.S. Activities coordinated with US Catholic
Conference.

---

825   Austin

Texas Department of Human Service. Refugee Program

Box 2960
Austin, TX   78769
Lee Russell, State Refugee Coordinator
(512) 450-4172

Services Offered: AD, EC, ED, HE, SS.
Clientele: World. Statewide coordination of federal,
state and private resources for effective refugee resettlement including cash and medical assistance, support services and such other activities as necessary.

---

826   Beaumont

Partnership for Human Development. Resettlement Office.

Box 6610
Beaumont, TX   77705
Pat Morgan, Director
(409) 832-7994

Services Offered: AD, CE, SS. **Established:**
1975. **Clientele:** Central America/Caribbean,
World. Human services offered to refugees and immigrants in Southeast Texas.

---

827   Brownsville

Catholic Social Services. Central American Refugee Services

1254 East Tyler
Brownsville, TX   78520
Fr. Don Rickard, Coordinator
(512) 541-0220

Services Offered: AD, CE, RS, SS.
Established: 1982. **Clientele:** Central
America/Caribbean. Advocacy and support services to
Central American refugees.

---

828   Brownsville

South Texas Immigration Council

845 East 13th Street
Brownsville, TX   78520
Anna Duran, Coordinator
(512) 542-1991

Services Offered: LE, SS. **Established:** 1976.
BIA. Clientele: Central America/Caribbean. Social
and legal services for immigrants and refugees.

---

829   Corpus Christi

Catholic Social Services

1322 Comanche
Corpus Christi, TX   78401
Robert E. Freeman, Administrator
(512) 884-0651

Services Offered: AD, CE, LE. **Established:**
1985. **Religious Affiliation:** Catholic.
Clientele: Southeast Asia. Legal counsel and services in immigration matters.

---

830   Corpus Christi

Coastal Bend Friends Meeting

1121 Rickey
Corpus Christi, TX   78412
Charles Arguell, Clerk
(512) 991-2505

Services Offered: ED, HE, LI, SA. **Staff:** 3.
Religious Affiliation: Quaker. **Clientele:**
Central America/Caribbean. Provide sanctuary for
Central American refugees and general assistance to
refugees in order to move out of South Texas.

---

831   Dallas

Catholic Charities. Immigration Counseling Services

3845 Oak Lawn Avenue
Dallas, TX   75219
Vanna Slaughter, Program Director
(214) 528-4870

Services Offered: AD, CE, ED, LE, SS.
Established: 1975. **Staff:** 5. **Budget:** $150,000.
BIA. Religious Affiliation: Catholic.
Clientele: World, Central America/Caribbean.
Services for refugees, undocumented and immigrants
include: community education and immigrant rights;
relative visa petitions; citizenship petitions; legal representation in immigration court (deportations, asylum, voluntary departure, etc.); and general legal as-

sistance.

---

832   *Dallas*

Dallas-Fort Worth Refugee Interagency

4113 Junius
Dallas, TX 75246
Mimi Chao, Executive Director
(214) 821-4883

Services Offered: AD, CU, CE, EC, ED, RS, SS. **Established:** 1977. **Clientele:** World. Broad range of services includes sponsorship, job development and placement, family reunification, cultural orientation, translation and interpretation, counseling and other social services.

---

833   *Dallas*

International Rescue Committee

1514 Pecos Street
Dallas, TX 75204
Deedee Underhill, Director
(214) 824-8140

Services Offered: AD, CE, SS. **Established:** 1976. **Clientele:** World. Core resettlement services for refugees from all parts of the world.

---

834   *Dallas*

Jewish Family Services

7800 Northaven Road, Suite 8
Dallas, TX 75230
Arnold S. Marks, Resettlement Director
(214) 696-6400

Services Offered: AD, CU, RE, RS, SS. **Established:** 1977. **Clientele:** World. Resettlement of Jewish immigrants and refugees through Hebrew Immigrant Aid Society.

---

835   *Dallas*

Mennonite International Refugee Assistance

Box 223641
Dallas, TX 75222
Brad Ginter, Contact
(214) 941-3784

Services Offered: LE, SS. **Established:** 1982. **Staff:** 2. **Religious Affiliation:** Mennonite. **Clientele:** Central America/Caribbean. Assist

refugees in a five state area served by the Canadian Consulate (Dallas) apply for permanent residence in Canada. MIRA provides limited legal and social services for these Central American refugees.

---

836   *Dallas*

North Texas Immigration Coalition

3845 Oak Lawn Avenue
Dallas, TX 75219
Vanna Slaughter, Executive Committee
(214) 528-4870

Services Offered: AD, CU, CE, LE. **Established:** 1986. **Budget:** $4,000. **Clientele:** World, Central America/Caribbean. Community education regarding the consequences of U.S. refugee and immigration policy and the monitoring of INS enforcement/abuses of detainees, applicants, asylees, etc. **Publications:** MEMBERSHIP DIRECTORY.

---

837   *Dallas*

Proyecto Adelante

Box 223641
Dallas, TX 75222
Vicky Stifter, Outreach Director
(214) 941-3784

Services Offered: AD, CU, ED, CE, LE, RS, SS. **Established:** 1982. **Clientele:** Central America/Caribbean. Counseling, legal, educational and social services to assist refugees from Central America. Community outreach programs to inform community about plight of refugees.

---

838   *Dallas*

Southern Methodist University. Law School. Political Asylum Project

3315 Daniel
Dallas, TX 75275
Joe W. Pitts, Assistant Professor
(214) 692-2564

Services Offered: LE. **Established:** 1988. **Clientele:** World. Provides legal representation to indigent refugees fleeing persecution in their home countries; educational program to inform law students about the legal theory of political asylum.

---

839   *Dallas*

U.S. Department of Health & Human Services. Family Support

Administration. Office of Refugee Resettlement

1200 Main Tower, Room 1700
Dallas, TX 75202
Russ Jewert, Specialist
(214) 767-4155

Services Offered: EC. **Established:** 1982.
Clientele: World. Regional office of the Office of Refugee Resettlement responsible for coordination of federal and state refugee resettlement activities.

---

840   *Dallas*

Vietnamese Mutual Assistance Association

Box 64625
Dallas, TX 75206
Bob Booker, Executive Director
(214) 826-6181   Fax: (214) 823-9153

Services Offered: AD, CU, ED, HE, LE, SC, SS.
Established: 1987. **Staff:** 1. **Budget:** $20,000.
Clientele: Southeast Asia. Help Vietnamese and Amerasian families with language training, acculturation, clothing, food, and referrals and information.

---

841   *Del Rio*

Texas Rural Legal Aid. Clinica de Inmigracion

Box 964
Del Rio, TX 78840
Alpha Hernandez, Directing Attorney
(512) 775-1535

Services Offered: AD, CE, LE, LI, RS.
Established: 1980. **BIA. Clientele:** Central America/Caribbean. Legal counsel and representation in immigration related matters.

---

842   *Edinburg*

Border Association for Refugees from Central America

Box 715
Edinburg, TX 78540
Ninfa Ochoa-Krueger, Executive Director
(512) 631-7447   Fax: (512) 687-7468

Services Offered: AD, CE, EC, LE, RE, SS.
Established: 1981. **Staff:** 6. **Religious Affiliation:** Ecumenical. **Clientele:** Central America/Caribbean. Objectives are to provide an array of services to assist refugees fleeing Central America, e.g., legal representtation, social services, and community awareness programs. **Publications:** BARCA NEWSLETTER.

---

843   *Edinburg*

Texas Rural Legal Aid

316 South Closner
Edinburg, TX 78539
(512) 383-5673

Services Offered: LE. BIA. **Clientele:** World, Central America/Caribbean. Legal representation to clients in immigration matters.

---

844   *El Paso*

Annunciation House

1003 East San Antonio
El Paso, TX 79901
Ruven Garcia, Director
(915) 545-4509

Services Offered: AD, CE, LE, SS.
Established: 1978. **Clientele:** Central America/Caribbean, South America. Legal counsel with immigration and asylum litigation as well as social and outreach services.

---

845   *El Paso*

Diocesan Migrant & Refugee Services

1013 East San Antonio
El Paso, TX 79901
Rev. Richard A. Matty, Director
(915) 532-3975

Services Offered: AD, CE, LE, LI.
Established: 1987. **Staff:** 10. **Religious Affiliation:** Catholic. **Clientele:** World, Central America/Caribbean. Offers legal services in terms of immigration counseling to low income and the poor. This includes the entire spectrum of immigration law. Also operates the refugee resettlement program through US Catholic Conference Migration & Refugee Services.Over 38,000 individuals served annually.

---

846   *El Paso*

El Paso Legal Assistance Society

1220 North Stanten
El Paso, TX 79901
Cathy Barnes, Directing Attorney

(915) 544-3022

Services Offered: CE, LE. **BIA. Clientele:** Central America/Caribbean. Immigration counsel to indigent individuals and families.

---

847 *El Paso*

Jewish Family and Children's Services

5831 North Mesa
El Paso, TX 79912
Sidney Dictor, Executive Director
(915) 581-3256

Services Offered: SS. **Established:** 1979. **Religious Affiliation:** Jewish. **Clientele:** USSR, Southeast Asia. Refugee resettlement services offered through Hebrew Immigrant Aid Society.

---

848 *El Paso*

U.S. Catholic Conference. Migration & Refugee Services. Regional Immigration Office

1200 North Mesa
El Paso, TX 79902
Luis Alfonso Velarde, Jr., Director
(915) 533-3971

Services Offered: AD, CU, LE, RE, SS. **Staff:** 8. **BIA. Religious Affiliation:** Catholic. **Clientele:** Central America/Caribbean, World. Regional office for Southwestern United States.

---

849 *Fort Worth*

Catholic Charities. Migration and Refugee Services

1404 Hemphill Street
Fort Worth, TX 76104
Eldon Hager, Director
(817) 921-5381

Services Offered: LE, RE, SS. **Established:** 1975. **BIA. Religious Affiliation:** Catholic. **Clientele:** World. Refugee resettlement services in the Fort Worth area.

---

850 *Fort Worth*

Fort Worth Independent School District. Survival English & Orientation for Refugees Program

705 South Henderson Street
Fort Worth, TX 76104
Steven Blostein, Coordinator
(817) 332-7544

Services Offered: ED. **Clientele:** World, Southeast Asia, Central America/Caribbean. Special English language evening classes (free) only for refugees.

---

851 *Fort Worth*

Immigration Counseling Migration & Refugee Services

118 NW 24th Street
Fort Worth, TX 76106
Blanca L. Partida, Immigration Caseworker
(817) 624-8037

Services Offered: AD, CE, LE, RE, RS, SS. **Established:** 1980. **BIA. Religious Affiliation:** Catholic. **Clientele:** World. General immigration and counseling assistance.

---

852 *Fort Worth*

Jewish Social Services

6801 Dan Danciger Road
Fort Worth, TX 76133
Howard Hirsch, Coordinator
(817) 294-2660

Services Offered: CU, RE, SS. **Religious Affiliation:** Jewish. **Clientele:** USSR. Refugee resettlement services in Tarrant County.

---

853 *Fort Worth*

World Relief

5000 James Avenue
Fort Worth, TX 76115
John Parsons, Area Director
(817) 924-0748

Services Offered: AD, CU, CE, EC, ED, LE, HE, RE. **Established:** 1980. **Staff:** 8. **Clientele:** World. Provides following services to refugees and immigrants: immigration counseling and advocacy; sponsorship services; acculturation and orientation services; housing services; case management; employment and economic development; and pastoral care.

---

854 *Grand Prairie*

Hmong-American Planning & Development Center

921 West Highway 303, Suite P
Grand Prairie, TX 75051
Thao Phia Xaykao, Executive Director
(214) 988-0502

Services Offered: EC, SS. **Established:** 1985.
Staff: 4. **Budget:** $100,000. **Religious
Affiliation:** Ecumenical. **Clientele:** Southeast
Asia. Planned secondary resettlement program for Lao
highlander refugees from impacted areas. Also promote economic self-sufficiency amongst Hmong
community. **Publications:** VOICE OF HAPDC
(newsletter).

---

855   *Harlingen*

Casa de Proyecto Libertad

110A East Jackson
Harlingen, TX 78550
Sr. Alice Lawler, Executive Director
(512) 425-9552

Services Offered: AD, CE, LE, SS.
Established: 1982. **Staff:** 12. **Budget:** $240,000.
Clientele: Central America/Caribbean. Major goals
include providing direct legal services to refugees,
immigrants and migrants in South Texas; to promote
refugee rights; assist clientele in self-empowerment;
and promote change in U.S. foreign policy in Central
America and Latin America. **Publications:** CASA
DE PROYECTO LIBERTAD BULLETIN (quarterly,
free).

---

856   *Harlingen*

South Texas Immigration Council

107 North Third
Harlingen, TX 78550
Nati Ayala, Coordinator
(512) 425-6987

Services Offered: EW, CU, CE, ED, LE.
Clientele: Central America/Caribbean, World.
Advocacy, community outreach, educational programs
and legal counsel and representation in deportation,
visa petitioning, etc.

---

857   *Houston*

Casa Juan Diego

Box 70113
Houston, TX 77270
Mark Zwick, Director

(713) 869-7376

Services Offered: AD, EC, ED, HE, LE, SA, SS.
Established: 1980. **Staff:** 10. **Budget:** $300,000.
Religious Affiliation: Ecumenical. **Clientele:**
Central America/Caribbean. This is a Catholic
Worker House of Hospitality for refugees from
Central America. Provides hospitality and sanctuary,
medical, legal and educational services, and related so-
cial services. **Publications:** HOUSTON
CATHOLIC WORKER (English and Spanish lan-
guage versions, monthly).

---

858   *Houston*

Catholic Charities. Resettlement Services

3520 Montrose Boulevard
Houston, TX 77006
Pauline Van Tho, Administrator
(713) 526-5812

Services Offered: CU, LE, RE, SS.
Established: 1975. **BIA. Religious
Affiliation:** Catholic. **Clientele:** World.
Sponsorship and resettlement services for refugees and
families.

---

859   *Houston*

Central American Refugee Center

4001 Caroline
Houston, TX 77004
Frances Tobin, Coordinator
(713) 522-3611

Services Offered: AD, CE, LE. **Clientele:**
Central America/Caribbean. Legal counsel and representation in deportation, asylum and other immigration and refugee law.

---

860   *Houston*

Centro de Ayuda Para Immigrantes

101 North St. Charles
Houston, TX 77003
Harvey Orozco, Director
(713) 228-5200

Services Offered: AD, CU, CE, LE, RS, SS.
Established: 1985. **Staff:** 12. **Budget:** $350,000.
Religious Affiliation: Catholic. **Clientele:**
Central America/Caribbean, World. Dedicated to the
defense of immigrant rights. Legal counsel and representation in all areas of immigrant law, including
naturalization, visas, deportation defense and federal

court actions. Community advocacy, refugee resettlement and other outreach activities.

---

861   *Houston*

Houston Metropolitan Ministries

3217 Montrose Boulevard, Suite 200
Houston, TX   77006
William Thomas, Coordinator
(713) 522-3955

Services Offered: AD, CU, CE, RE, SS.
Religious Affiliation: Ecumenical. **Clientele**:
Central America/Caribbean, World. Ecumenical
refugee resettlement and sponsorship services offered
through Church World Service.

---

862   *Houston*

Immigration Counseling Center

945 Lathrop
Houston, TX   77020
Rose Lopez, Executive Director
(713) 924-6045

Services Offered: AD, CE, LE. **Established**:
1975. **BIA**. **Clientele**: Central America/Caribbean,
World. Provides immigration assistance and counsel
to the undocumented. Legal help as well as accompanying
clients to INS, etc.

---

863   *Houston*

Immigration Institute

2102 Austin
Houston, TX   77002
Leonel Castillo, Director
(713) 951-9401

Services Offered: AD, CE, LE. **Established**:
1983. **Staff**: 3. **Budget**: $60,000. **Clientele**:
Central America/Caribbean. Advocacy, counsel and
assistance in immigration matters. Formerly affiliated
with Houston International University.

---

864   *Houston*

Immigration Law Enforcement Monitoring Project

3635 West Dallas
Houston, TX   77019
Maria Jimenez, Director
(713) 524-5428

Services Offered: AD, CE, RS, LI.
Established: 1987. **Staff**: 2. **Budget**: $159,000.
Religious Affiliation: Quaker. **Clientele**:
Central America/Caribbean. National police accountability
project working toward more humane law enforcement
of immigration laws. Goal is to reduce
level of abuse of authority in the enforcement of
immigration laws. Specific objectives are: changing
policies that foster such abuses; increasing public
awareness of abuses and public understanding of the
humanity of undocumented persons; and assisting undocumented
people in exercising their rights and utilizing
existing procedures for their protection. Assist
victims of immigration law enforcement abuse and
serve as civil rights advocates. Library and research
component.

---

865   *Houston*

International Community Services

1112 Kipling Street
Houston, TX   77006
Alan P. Swanniutt, Director
(713) 521-9083

Services Offered: AD, CU, CE, EC, ED, LE, SS.
Established: 1980. **BIA**. **Clientele**: World.
Refugee services include programs dealing with cultural
orientation, outreach, education, employment as
well as general counseling.

---

866   *Houston*

Jewish Family Service. Refugee Resettlement Program

Box 20548
Houston, TX   77225
Mallory Robinson, Supervisor
(713) 667-9336

Services Offered: CU, EC, SS. **Established**:
1913. **Staff**: 5. **Budget**: $20,000. **Religious
Affiliation**: Jewish. **Clientele**: Middle East,
Europe, USSR. Officially designated resettlement
agency for the Houston Jewish Community. The responsibility
for the initial adjustment of newcomers
from foreign lands includes provisions for housing,
job placement, financial assistance, medical and dental
care. In addition, these refugees are assisted in aculturation
and integration services, all on a relatively
short-term basis. Long-term assistance to the foreign
born ranges from dealing with technical immigration
problems, citizenship and naturalization to English
classes. The goal is to help these newcomers become
productive members of the community. Activities
coordinated through Hebrew Immigrant Aid Society.

Refugees principally from Iran, Eastern Europe and the USSR.

867   *Houston*

Lutheran Immigration and Refugee Service

3131 West Alabama, Suite 124
Houston, TX   77098
Robert Palm, Director
(713) 521-0110

Services Offered: AD, CU, RE, SS. **Religious Affiliation**: Lutheran. **Clientele**: World. Resettlement and social service program available to refugees and immigrants.

868   *Houston*

Texan Training & Employment Center

8282 Bellaire, Suite 153
Houston, TX   77036
Nguyen Ngoc Linh, Executive Director
(713) 779-4515   Fax: (713) 779-5464

Services Offered: EC, SS. **Established**: 1986. **Staff**: 30. **Budget**: $1,500,000. **Clientele**: Southeast Asia. Extensive array of employment services for Vietnamese refugees.

869   *Houston*

World Relief

Box 11366
Houston, TX   77293
Rita Loera, Contact
(713) 864-2306

Services Offered: AD, CE, ED, SS. **Clientele**: Central America/Caribbean, World. Variety of services offered to refugees and immigrants.

870   *Houston*

YMCA International Services

3635 West Dallas
Houston, TX   77019
Nancy Falgout, Director
(713) 527-8690

Services Offered: AD, EC, ED, LE, LI, SS. **Established**: 1983. **Staff**: 30. **Budget**: $650,000. **BIA. Clientele**: World. Refugee resettlement program assists 350 refugees annually. Services include job placement, immigration counseling and representation, pro bono program for asylees, language classes, and general social services.

871   *Laredo*

Catholic Social Services. Servicios Para Inmigrantes

Box 3305
Laredo, TX   78044
Daniel Martinez, Supervisor
(512) 724-3604

Services Offered: AD, CE, LE, LI, RE, RS, SS. **Established**: 1984. **BIA. Religious Affiliation**: Catholic. **Clientele**: Central America/Caribbean. Broad range of social service support system as well as legal counsel to immigrants.

872   *Lubbock*

Catholic Family Service. Immigration Service

123 North Avenue N
Lubbock, TX   79401
Stephen Hay, Supervisor
(806) 765-8475

Services Offered: AD, CE, LE, RS, RE. **Established**: 1985. **BIA. Religious Affiliation**: Catholic. **Clientele**: Central America/Caribbean. Counseling, advocacy, outreach and educational programs designed to help individuals and families in all aspects of immigration services.

873   *McAllen*

South Texas Immigration Council

1201 Erie
McAllen, TX   78501
LaVara Solis, Administrator
(512) 682-5397

Services Offered: LE. **Established**: 1976. **BIA. Clientele**: Central America/Caribbean. Counsel and representation in all aspects of immigration law.

874   *San Antonio*

Catholic Services for Immigrants

2903 West Salinas
San Antonio, TX   78207
Victor Madrigal, Jr., Program Director

(512) 432-6091

Services Offered: AD, CE, EC, ED, HE, LE, LI, RE, RS, SS. **Established:** 1976. **Staff:** 12. **Budget:** $350,000. **BIA. Religious Affiliation:** Catholic. **Clientele:** World, Central America/Caribbean. Extensive immigration services provided in order to help those individuals seeking benefits under the immigration laws of the United States. Goal is to assist all individuals entitled to a benefit under the immigration laws. Includes: relative petitions; occupational petitioning; Board of Immigration appeals; and other services for immigrants and refugees.

---

875   *San Antonio*

Immigration Law Project

434 South Main, Suite 300
San Antonio, TX 78204
John Carte, Directing Attorney
(512) 227-0111

Services Offered: LE. **Established:** 1987. **Staff:** 3. **Budget:** $45,000. **Clientele:** World, Central America/Caribbean. Cooperative venture of the Pro Bono Law Project, San Antonio Young Lawyers Association, San Antonio Bar Association and the Texas Chapter of the American Immigration Lawyers Association. Legal counseling and assistance provided to refugees and immigrants.

---

876   *San Antonio*

Jewish Family Service

8438 Ahern Drive
San Antonio, TX 78245
Richard Ney, Executive Director
(512) 349-5481

Services Offered: AD, CU, EC, ED, RE, SS. **Established:** 1972. **Staff:** 28. **Budget:** $350,000. **Religious Affiliation:** Jewish. **Clientele:** USSR, Southeast Asia. Refugee resettlement services offered through Hebrew Immigrant Aid Society. **Publications:** CHAI LITES (quarterly newsletter, free); Annual Report.

---

877   *San Antonio*

Khmer Society of San Antonio. Refugee SOS

1154 East Commerce
San Antonio, TX 78205
Thida Khus, Executive Director
(512) 227-0990

Services Offered: EC, ED, SS. **Established:** 1982. **Clientele:** World, Southeast Asia. Main goal of KSSA is to assist members adjust to life in the United States. Refugee SOS believes this goal is best accomplished through the participation of individuals, families, counselors, the private sector of the community and business, regardless of which ethnic group they represent, who desire to increase the total well-being of refugees in their new environment. Extends culturally sensitive, personal and professional support to aid in the transition process. **Publications:** Newsletter.

---

878   *San Antonio*

San Antonio Literacy Council

1101 West Woodlawn Avenue
San Antonio, TX 78201
Margarita Huantes, Executive Director
(512) 732-9711

Services Offered: CU, CE, RS, SS. **Established:** 1960. **BIA. Clientele:** Central America/Caribbean. Assist Central Americans with citizenship problems, including counseling and help with INS documentation.

---

879   *San Benito*

Rio Grande Defense Committee

Box 2066
San Benito, TX 78586
(512) 428-8418

Services Offered: AD, CE, LE, RE, SS. **Clientele:** Central America/Caribbean. Advocacy and support group for the humane treatment of Central Americans seeking a safe haven in the United States.

---

880   *San Juan*

American Civil Liberties Union. South Texas Project

Box 188
San Juan, TX 78589
Carter C. White, Contact
(512) 787-8171

Services Offered: AD, CE, LE. **Established:** 1972. **Clientele:** Central America/Caribbean. Legal representation and services to refugees, immigrants and asylees in the Rio Grande Valley. Advocate for rights of newly arrived.

---

881   *Waco*

Heart of Texas Legal Services

Box 2304
Waco, TX 76703
Pat Clarke, Attorney
(817) 752-5596

Services Offered: AD, CE, LE. **Clientele:** Central America/Caribbean. Legal counsel and representation for indigent individuals and families in immigration law.

882   *Salt Lake City*

Catholic Community Services of Utah. Refugee Resettlement Program

333 East South Temple Street
Salt Lake City, UT 84111
Thomas J. Ivory, Director
(801) 328-9100

Services Offered: AD, CU, CE, EC, ED, HE, LE, RE, RS, SS. **Established:** 1979. **Staff:** 7. **Budget:** $412,000. **Religious Affiliation:** Catholic. **Clientele:** Southeast Asia. Extensive services to assist refugees attain self-sufficiency and social adjustment. Program components include: pre-arrival and reception services, orientation, sponsorship, employment services, case management, and immigration assistance. Also operates the Refugee Foster Care Program which aids 70 unaccompanied refugee minors. **Publications:** Newsletter (quarterly, free).

883   *Salt Lake City*

Intermountain Health Care. Refugee Clinic

1102 West 400 North
Salt Lake City, UT 84116
Mike Englebert-Benton, Physician Assistant
(801) 363-4955

Services Offered: HE. **Established:** 1987. **Staff:** 1. **Clientele:** World, Southeast Asia. Refugee free medical clinic.

884   *Salt Lake City*

Jewish Family Services

2416 East 1700 South
Salt Lake City, UT 84108
Helene Leta, Executive Director
(801) 581-0098

Services Offered: SS. **Staff:** 1. **Budget:** $25,000. **Religious Affiliation:** Jewish. **Clientele:** World, Middle East, USSR. Refugee resetlement program is coordinated through Hebrew Immigrant Aid Society.

885   *Salt Lake City*

Utah Department of Social Services. Refugee & Alien Legalization Program

Box 45500

Salt Lake City, UT 84145
Sherman K. Roquiero, Coordinator
(801) 538-4100

Services Offered: EC, ED, HE, SS.
Established: 1978. **Staff:** 3. **Budget:**
$3,000,000. **Clientele:** World. Administer the state
refugee resettlement and state legalization impact assistance grant programs in Utah.

---

886   *Salt Lake City*

Utah Immigration Project

344 Goshen Street
Salt Lake City, UT 84104
Rev. Tony Lopez, Director
(801) 531-1177

Services Offered: AD, CE, ED, LE.
Established: 1981. **BIA. Clientele:** World.
Advocacy, community education and outreach and legal counsel and representation in all immigration
matters.

---

887   *West Jordan*

Lao Family Community

3516 West 8280 South
West Jordan, UT 84084
Vuc Yang, President
(801) 566-4893

Services Offered: AD, CU, CE, EC, ED, HE,
LE, LI, RE, RS, SA, SC, SS. **Established:** 1980.
Staff: 15. **BIA. Clientele:** Southeast Asia, Asia.
Extensive services offered to Laotian refugees and
other refugees from Asia. **Publications:** LAO
FAMILY NEWS JOURNAL; Annual Report.

---

888   *Brattleboro*

Experiment in International Living

Kipling Road
Brattleboro, VT 05301
Charles F. MacCormack, President
(802) 257-4628   Fax: (802) 257-9274

Services Offered: EC, ED. **Established:** 1932.
Staff: 500. **Budget:** $38,000,000. **Clientele:**
World. Mission is to educate participants and students
from throughout the world with the necessary knowledge, attitudes and skills needed to contribute personally to international understanding and global development. Participants include refugees and development professionals. **Publications:** ODYSSEY
(3/year magazine, free); Annual Report.

---

889   *Burlington*

City of Burlington. Office of the Mayor

City Hall
Burlington, VT 05401
(802) 658-9300

Services Offered: SA. **Clientele:** Central
America/Caribbean. Burlington is a publicly declared
sanctuary for refugees from El Salvador and
Guatemala.

---

890   *Burlington*

Vermont Catholic Charities. Refugee Resettlement Program

351 North Avenue
Burlington, VT 05401
Rev. Roland Rivard, Director
(802) 658-6110

Services Offered: SS. **Established:** 1929.
Religious Affiliation: Catholic. **Clientele:**
Southeast Asia, Europe. The Refugee Resettlement
Program is designed to assist individuals and families
to resolve or alleviate problems encountered with resettlement in a new country. The program uses casework and teaching procedures and is operated by professional and volunteer staff.

---

891   *Springfield*

Vermont State Refugee Coordinator

Charlestown Road
Springfield, VT 05156

Judith May
(802) 885-9602

Services Offered: AD, EC, ED, HE, SS.
Clientele: World. Statewide coordination of federal, state and private resources for effective refugee resettlement (cash and medical assistance, social services, etc.).

892   *Alexandria*

Lao Consultant Firm

5520 North Morgan Street
Alexandria, VA 22312
Somsanith Khamvongsa, Director
(703) 256-7081

Services Offered: CU, CE, EC, ED, HE, LE, LI, RE, RS, SA, SC, SS. **Established**: 1984. **Staff**: 3. **Budget**: $24,000. **Religious Affiliation**: Ecumenical. **Clientele**: Southeast Asia. Provide assistance principally to Southeast Asian refugees in Virginia.

893   *Arlington*

Catholic Migration & Refugee Services

915 South Wakefield
Arlington, VA 22204
Have Herrmann, Director
(703) 979-7010

Services Offered: AD, CU, LE, EC, RE, SS. **Established**: 1975. **Religious Affiliation**: Catholic. **Clientele**: World. Core resettlement services range from sponsorship development and orientation to employment assistance and immigration counseling.

894   *Arlington*

Christian Refugee Outreach

2315 South Grant Street
Arlington, VA 22202
Nancy Lanman, Coordinator
(703) 979-5180

Services Offered: AD, CU, CE, LE, RE, SS. **Religious Affiliation**: Ecumenical. **Clientele**: World. Ecumenical refugee resettlement and sponsorship services coordinated with Church World Service.

895   *Arlington*

Ethiopian Community Development Council

3213 Columbia Pike, Suite 101
Arlington, VA 22204
Tsehaye Teferra, Director
(703) 685-0510

Services Offered: AD, CU, CE, EC, ED, LI, RS, SS. **Established**: 1983. **Staff**: 7. **Budget**: $150,000. **Clientele**: Africa. The primary purpose of ECDC is to enhance the economic, educational and social development of the Ethiopian community in the United States. Goals are to: initiate economic development programs; offer extensive employment services; expand public awareness of the Ethiopian community and their contributions; and distribute educational materials related to Ethiopians and Ethiopia. **Publications:** Directory.

896   *Arlington*

Unitarian Church of Arlington

4444 Arlington Boulevard
Arlington, VA   22204
George Beach, Minister
(703) 892-2565

Services Offered: AD, CU, CE, ED, LI, RE, SA. **Established:** 1949. **Staff:** 4. **Religious Affiliation:** Unitarian. **Clientele:** World. Support measures to protect and assist refugees seeking a safe haven in the United States. A sanctuary church. **Publications:** ARLINGTARIAN (weekly, free); Annual Report; Directory.

897   *Fairfax*

George Mason University. Indochina Institute.

4400 University Drive
Fairfax, VA   22030
Nguyen Manh Hung, Director
(703) 323-2272

Services Offered: AD, CU, CE, ED, LI, RS. **Established:** 1979. **Clientele:** Southeast Asia. Advocate for Vietnamese refugees as well as offering educational and research projects, for example, the Center for the Study of the Vietnam Generation. Resource for Vietnamese community. **Publications:** Newsletter.

898   *Falls Church*

Northern Virginia Family Service. Multicultural (Refugee) Program

100 North Washington Street
Falls Church, VA   22046
Judy Basham, Director
(703) 536-2066

Services Offered: AD, CU, CE, SS. **Established:** 1979. **Clientele:** World. Multicultural programs offered to refugee community center on community outreach, cross-cultural consultation, and broad range of traditional social services.

899   *Falls Church*

U.S. Department of Justice. Executive Office for Immigration Review

1609 Skyline
Falls Church, VA   22041
David L. Milhollan, Director
(703) 756-6171

Services Offered: LE. **Clientele:** World. The Attorney General has delegated certain aspects of his power and authority for the administration and interpretation of the immigration laws to the EOIR. EOIR is independent of the INS, the body charged with the enforcement of the immigration laws. The EOIR includes the Board of Immigration Appeal, the Office of the Chief Immigration Judge and the Office of the Chief Administrative Officer. BIA is the highest administrative tribunal charged with interpreting the immigration laws. Primary mission of the BIA is to ensure that immigration laws receive uniform application. BIA Chairman is David Milhollan. The Office of the Chief Immigration Judge is responsible for the general supervision and direction of the immigration judges in the performance of their duties. Chief Immigration Judge is William R. Robie. Office of Chief Administrative Officer (William Tyson) supervises and administers law judges who are concerned with allegations of unlawful employment of aliens and immigration-related employment discrimination.

900   *McLean*

Vietnam Refugee Fund

1850 Patton Terrace
McLean, VA   22101
Tanya Dang, President
(703) 734-0028

Services Offered: AD, CU, CE, EC, LI. **Established:** 1971. **Clientele:** Southeast Asia. Advocacy and support services for the resettlement of Vietnamese refugees.

901   *Norfolk*

Diocese of Richmond. Office of Refugee Resettlement

1802 Ash Avenue
Norfolk, VA   23509
Kathleen Garske, Regional Director
(804) 623-9131

Services Offered: AD, CU, CE, EC, ED, HE, LI, SS. **Established:** 1976. **Staff:** 10. **Religious Affiliation:** Catholic. **Clientele:** World, Southeast Asia. Newcomers face a number of confusing situations when they first come to the U.S. The Refugee Resettlement Office has services that can help new arrivals understand American culture and prepare to participate effectively in American life. Social adjustment services are provided in the refugee's native language whenever possible. The services offered include: orientation; employment assistance; interpretation and translation; English instruction; support counseling; and information and referral. These services are available to all refugees, regardless of their voluntary agency. Affiliated with U.S. Catholic Conference. **Publications:** NEW LIFE (irregular, free).

---

902   *Richmond*

Cambodian Association of Virginia

7825 Midlothian Turnpike
Richmond, VA 23235
Jeffrey T. Poch, Contact
(804) 323-4401

Services Offered: AD, ED, HE, SS. **Established:** 1979. **Staff:** 4. **Budget:** $68,000. **Religious Affiliation:** Ecumenical. **Clientele:** Southeast Asia. Provide a variety of services to refugees designed to make them as self-sufficient as quickly as possible, from job and language training to mental health counseling.

---

903   *Richmond*

Ecumenical Refugee Resettlement Services

1212 Wilmer Avenue
Richmond, VA 23237
Dorothy France, Director
(804) 262-8155

Services Offered: AD, CU, CE, EC, ED, SS. **Established:** 1982. **Staff:** 5. **Religious Affiliation:** Episcopal. **Clientele:** World. Resettlement services include: advocacy for refugees and undocumented; sponsorship development; job orientation and development; immigration assistance; and counseling, referral and a myriad of social services. **Publications:** Newsletter (irregular); Annual Report.

---

904   *Richmond*

Jewish Family Service

7027 Three Chopt Road
Richmond, VA 23226
Peter Opper, Executive Director
(804) 282-5644

Services Offered: CU, RE, SS. **Religious Affiliation:** Jewish. **Clientele:** USSR, Southeast Asia. Resettlement program for refugees encompasses wide range of social service options.

---

905   *Richmond*

Vietnamese Community in Virginia

4504 Whale Rock Road
Richmond, VA 23234
Giac Haquang, President
(804) 226-5611

Services Offered: CU, CE, LE, RE, SS. **Established:** 1980. **Religious Affiliation:** Ecumenical. **Clientele:** Southeast Asia, Oceania, World. Provide assistance to Vietnamese refugees in Virginia. Services include: promote patriotic friendship among Vietnamese; promote mutual assistance among Vietnamese and to protect their rights against discrimination; preserve Vietnamese customs, way of life and traditions; and preserve Vietnamese culture in order to enrich life for all in the U.S. **Publications:** THONG TIN (newsletter, free).

---

906   *Richmond*

Virginia Baptist General Board. Division of Missions Ministries

Box 8568
Richmond, VA 23226
Phillip E. Rodgerson, Director
(804) 672-2100

Services Offered: RE, SS. **Established:** 1969. **Religious Affiliation:** Baptist. **Clientele:** World. In addition to coordinating the placement of refugees with sponsoring churches, the Division assists with counseling and general religious support for the refugees.

---

907   *Richmond*

Virginia Council of Churches. Refugee Program

1212 Wilmer Avenue
Richmond, VA 23227
Rev. Dorothy France, Coordinator
(804) 262-8155

Services Offered: AD, CU, CE, ED, LE, RE, SS.
Religious Affiliation: Ecumenical. Clientele:
World. Ecumenical refugee resettlement and sponsor-
ship services coordinated through Church World
Service.

---

908 *Richmond*

Virginia Department of Social Services. State Refugee Coordinator

8007 Discovery Drive
Richmond, VA 23229
Anne H. Hamrick
(804) 281-9029

Services Offered: AD, EC, ED, HE, SS.
Clientele: World. Statewide coordination of federal,
state and private resources for effective refugee resettlement.

---

909 *Roanoke*

Diocese of Richmond. Office of Refugee Resetlement

824 Campbell Avenue, Room 7
Roanoke, VA 240116
Jere Wrightsman, Director
(703) 342-7561

Services Offered: AD, CU, CE, EC, ED, RS,
SS. Established: 1975. Religious Affiliation:
Catholic. Clientele: World. Resettlement services
from orientation and sponsorship development to educational and employment programs.

---

910 *Grandview*

Catholic Family and Child Services. Family Reunification & Immigration Counseling Center

Box 22
Grandview, WA 98930
Dario Ybarra, Director
(509) 837-5548

Services Offered: AD, CU, LE, SS. Staff: 3.
BIA. Religious Affiliation: Catholic.
Clientele: Central America/Caribbean, World.
Assistance with immigration counseling and family
reunification, including general counseling and refer-
rals.

---

911 *Grandview*

EPIC Immigration Project

225 Division
Grandview, WA 98930
Oralia Torrez, Contact
(509) 882-4122

Services Offered: AD, CU, CE, ED, LE.
Clientele: Central America/Caribbean. Advocacy,
outreach and legal services to refugees and immigrants.

---

912 *Granger*

Centro Campesino. Projecto de Inmigracion

120 Sunnyside Avenue
Granger, WA 98932
Pedro Herrera, Attorney
(509) 854-2100

Services Offered: AD, CE, ED, LE, SS.
Clientele: Central America/Caribbean. Provides legal advice, counsel and representation in a variety of
immigration matters as well as community outreach
and limited social service programs.

---

913 *Olympia*

City of Olympia. Office of the Mayor

Box 1967
Olympia, WA 98507
(206) 753-8450

Services Offered: SA. Clientele: Central
America/Caribbean. Declared public sanctuary city.

---

914   *Olympia*

Washington Bureau of Refugee Assistance

OB-31B
Olympia, WA 98504
Thuy Vu, Director
(206) 753-3086 Fax: (206) 753-6745

Services Offered: EC, ED, HE, SS.
Established: 1975. **Staff:** 11. **Clientele:** World, Southeast Asia. The goal of the Refugee Assistance Program is to promote the economic self-sufficiency of refugees within the shortest period after entrance into the state through effective use of social services and financial and medical assistance. Washington State's current refugee population is approximately 50,000, with about 80% coming from Southeast Asia. The Bureau Director is designated as State Coordinator. Funds are provided for several types of services: cash and medical assistance, health screening, social services and foster care. **Publications:** Annual Report.

915   *Renton*

King County Rape Relief. Southeast Asian Child Sexual Assault Prevention Project

1025 South Third
Renton, WA 98055
Mary Ellen Stone, Executive Director
(206) 226-5062

Services Offered: AD, CE, LE, SS.
Established: 1972. **Staff:** 13. **Budget:** $500,000.
Clientele: Southeast Asia. Developed culturally sensitive materials for use in the Southeast Asian communities regarding child sexual abuse. Also operates the Southeast Asian Sexual Assault Helpline [(206) 322-0382]. **Publications:** List of Publications; Annual Report.

916   *Seattle*

Asian Counseling and Referral Service

1032 South Jackson Street
Seattle, WA 98104
Theresa Fujiwara, Executive Director
(206) 447-3606

Services Offered: AD, CU, EC, LE, RE, RS, SS.
Established: 1973. **Staff:** 40. **Clientele:** Asia, Southeast Asia, Oceania. Services and programs range from refugee job training and advocacy to general so-

cial services and referral. **Publications:** Newsletter (quarterly); Annual Report.

917   *Seattle*

Catholic Refugee Services

810 18th Avenue
Seattle, WA 98122
Jhari Michelson, Coordinator
(206) 323-9450

Services Offered: AD, CU, CE, SS.
Established: 1979. **Staff:** 4. **Budget:** $100,000.
Religious Affiliation: Catholic. **Clientele:** World. Refugee resettlement, sponsorship development, limited immigration assistance, limited job placement, etc.

918   *Seattle*

Central American Refugee Program

225 North 70th
Seattle, WA 98103
Hermelinda Gonzales, Director
(206) 789-7297

Services Offered: AD, CU, CE, LE, SS.
Established: 1983. **Staff:** 3. **Religious Affiliation:** Ecumenical. **Clientele:** Central America/Caribbean. Offers the following services to refugees from Central America: emergency shelter; housing; employment counseling; legal representation and follow-up legal services; translation and interpretation; and general social services. Formerly the Salvadoran and Guatemalan Refugee Program. **Publications:** Newsletter (quarterly); Annual Report.

919   *Seattle*

Committee in Defense of Immigrant Rights

Box 1196
Seattle, WA 98111
Juan Bocanegra, Director
(206) 725-5440

Services Offered: AD, CE, SS. **Staff:** 2.
Clientele: World. Advocacy and support services to immigrants and refugees.

920   *Seattle*

Hispanic Immigration Counseling Program

3600 South Graham Street
Seattle, WA 98118
Irene Gutierrez, Immigration Counselor
(206) 721-4752

Services Offered: AD, CU, CE, LE, RE.
Established: 1982. **BIA. Clientele**: Central
America/Caribbean, South America. Legal representation at deportation and bond redetermination hearings; assistance with visa applications; and outreach services to immigrants and refugees.

---

921   *Seattle*

International Rescue Committee

318 First Avenue South, Suite 120
Seattle, WA 98104
Bob Johnson, Director
(206) 623-2105

Services Offered: AD, CE, LE, RS, SS.
Clientele: World. Refugee resettlement office covering Pacific Northwest.

---

922   *Seattle*

Jewish Family Service

1214 Boylston Avenue
Seattle, WA 98101
Kenneth Weinberr, Executive Director
(206) 461-3240

Services Offered: AD, EC, RE, SS.
Established: 1892. **Staff**: 25. **Budget**:
$1,200,000. **Religious Affiliation**: Jewish.
Clientele: World. Resettlement services for all immigrants and refugees (emphasis on those of Jewish faith) sponsored by Hebrew Immigrant Aid Society.

---

923   *Seattle*

Joint Legal Task Force on Central American Refugees

909 Eighth Avenue
Seattle, WA 98104
Sarah Ignatius, Staff Attorney
(206) 587-4009

Services Offered: AD, CE, LE. **Established**:
1982. **Staff**: 2. **Budget**: $75,000. **Clientele**:
Central America/Caribbean. Non-profit organization that works with indigent refugees from El Salvador and Guatemala. The JLTF represents these refugees in asylum proceedings and assists them in obtaining legal status under IRCA. Without the intervention of the JLTF, it is likely that these people would have

been deported to face grave dangers, even death, in their homelands. In 1987 represented or advised nearly 400 clients and worked with about 130 volunteer attorneys. JLTF activities include: asylum representation; legalization; community education; documentation; and advice and referrals.

---

924   *Seattle*

Seattle - King County Bar Association. Legalization, Education and Advocacy Project

810 Third Avenue, Suite 330
Seattle, WA 98104
Barbara Green, Coordinator
(206) 382-2519

Services Offered: AD, CE, LE. **Established**:
1987. **Staff**: 3. **Budget**: $92,000. **Clientele**:
Central America/Caribbean. Provided bro bono representation to legalization applicants whose initial applications denied. **Publications**: LEAP LINES:
NEWSLETTER OF THE LEAP IMMIGRATION
PROJECT (monthly).

---

925   *Seattle*

U.S. Department of Health & Human Services. Family Support Administration. Office of Refugee Resettlement

2901 Third Avenue, MS 305
Seattle, WA 98212
Bob Burkhart, Contact
(206) 442-2680

Clientele: World. ORR regional office responsible for coordinating assistance (cash and medical, social services, demonstration projects, etc.) to refugee population.

---

926   *Seattle*

University Unitarian Church. Sanctuary Committee

6556 35th Avenue NE
Seattle, WA 98115
Rev. Peter Raible, Contact
(206) 525-8400

Services Offered: SA. **Religious Affiliation**:
Unitarian. **Clientele**: Central America/Caribbean.
Declared public sanctuary for refugees from Central America.

927 *Seattle*

Vietnamese Lutheran Ministry

7727 Mary Avenue NW
Seattle, WA 98117
Rev. John T. Dovinh, President
(206) 783-6041

Services Offered: AD, RE, SS. **Established:** 1988. **Staff:** 5. **Religious Affiliation:** Lutheran. **Clientele:** Southeast Asia. Operates refugee resetlement program for Southeast Asians.

---

928 *Seattle*

Washington Association of Churches. Immigration & Refugee Program

3902 South Ferdinand Street
Seattle, WA 98118
Sally Mackey, Director
(206) 721-5288

Services Offered: AD, CE, EC, ED, LE, SS. **Established:** 1975. **Staff:** 13. **Budget:** $200,000. **Religious Affiliation:** Ecumenical. **Clientele:** World. Sponsor development with local and affiliate congregations for refugees and their families. Services include: orientation; placement; employment services; legal assistance for immigration, political asylum and deportation hearings and proceedings. Operates the Washington Immigration Project. **Publications:** Newsletter (quarterly).

---

929 *Seattle*

World Relief

316 Maynard Avenue South
Seattle, WA 98104
Cal Uomoto, Director
(206) 587-0234

Services Offered: CE, SS. **Established:** 1979. **Staff:** 6. **BIA. Clientele:** World. Refugee resetlement program in the Greater Seattle area.

---

930 *Spokane*

Refugee and Immigrant Multi-Service Center

South 130 Arthur
Spokane, WA 99202
Minh Van Tran, Director
(509) 456-7153

Services Offered: AD, CE, LE, SS. **Established:** 1975. **Staff:** 4. **Budget:** $60,000.

BIA. Religious Affiliation: Catholic. **Clientele:** World. Goals: to increase the quality of life for refugees; to assist refugees to start a new life and become self-sufficient; to assist churches, groups and individuals in response to refugee needs; and to provide education on refugee cultures to the community. Immigration Services provides limited representation in deportation proceedings; conducts community education and training; and referrals for complex immigration cases.

---

931 *Spokane*

Spokane Bar Association. Pro Bono Program

Box 470
Spokane, WA 99260
Mary Wardrop, Directing Attorney
(509) 456-6036

Services Offered: LE. **BIA. Clientele:** World. Advice, counsel and legal representation in immigration and asylum matters through panel of consulting attorneys.

---

932 *Spokane*

Washington Association of Churches. Refugee Resettlement Office

North 2319 Monroe, Suite 202
Spokane, WA 99205
Susan MacIntyre, Director
(509) 325-2591

Services Offered: AD, CU, CE, LE, ED, RE, LI, SS. **Established:** 1980. **BIA. Religious Affiliation:** Ecumenical. **Clientele:** World. Ecumenical association assists religious, community and organizations respond to the needs of refugees. Programs and services include: refugee resettlement; sponsorship development; community education; language training and interpretation; and information and referral.

---

933 *Tacoma*

Catholic Refugee Services

1304 Yakima Avenue South
Tacoma, WA 98405
Dennis Hunthausen, Coordinator
(206) 383-5526

Services Offered: AD, EC, SS. **Established:** 1980. **Religious Affiliation:** Catholic. **Clientele:** World. Primary purpose is to provide permanent refuge and to reunite refugee families and friends who have been forced to flee their homeland due to war and persecution. Program has provided reception and placement services to over 1,000 newly arrived refugees to Pierce County since 1980. As a voluntary resettlement agency processes sponsorship papers for refugees; assist relatives and sponsors in preparing for new arrivals; and upon arrival provide orientation and support for their initial resettlement. Also provide employment services to help refugees become self-reliant members of the community. Outreach services such as interpretation and translation, notary public assistance, information and referral and some assistance with clothing and household needs.

---

934   Tacoma

Tacoma Community House

Box 5107
Tacoma, WA 98405
Robert M. Yamashita, Executive Director
(206) 383-3951

Services Offered: CU, EC, ED, LI, SS.
Established: 1911. **Staff:** 35. **Budget:** $860,000.
Religious Affiliation: Methodist. **Clientele:** World, Southeast Asia, Asia. Resettlement services for refugees, principally from Southeast Asia. Services include: interpretation and translation; employment orientation, counseling and placement; English language training; counseling; and recreational activities. Includes numerous specialized programs for refugees, e.g., homebound English for refugee women. **Publications:** VOLUNTEER VOICE (quarterly); TCH NEWSLETTER (quarterly).

---

935   Yakima

Catholic Family and Child Service

5301-C Tieton Drive
Yakima, WA 98908
Rev. Thomas Champoux, Director
(509) 965-7100

Services Offered: AD, ED, RE, SS.
Established: 1975. **Religious Affiliation:** Catholic. **Clientele:** World. Coordinates refugee resettlement with US Catholic Conference Migration & Refugee Services.

---

936   Charleston

Catholic Community Services. Office of Migration & Refugee Services

1033 Quarrier Street
Charleston, WV 25301
George Smoulder, Executive Director
(304) 343-1036

Services Offered: AD, CU, CE, EC, ED, SS.
Established: 1975. **Staff:** 3. **Budget:** $75,000.
Religious Affiliation: Catholic. **Clientele:** World. Provide an array of translation, outreach, counseling and social services to refugees entering West Virginia.

---

937   Charleston

West Virginia Department of Human Services

1900 Washington Street East
Charleston, WV 25305
Cheryl Posey, Refugee Coordinator
(304) 348-8290

Services Offered: AD, EC, ED, HE, SS.
Clientele: World. Statewide coordination of federal, private and state resources for effective refugee resettlement including cash and medical assistance, support services and such other activities as necessary.

---

938 *Eau Claire*

Eau Claire Area Hmong Mutual Assistance Association

1624 Bellinger Street
Eau Claire, WI 54703
Kay Moua, Executive Director
(715) 832-8420

Services Offered: AD, CU, CE, ED, LI, SS. **Established:** 1983. **Staff:** 6. **Budget:** $120,000. **Clientele:** Southeast Asia. Aid refugees in resettlement process, provide acculturation and orientation services, help solve refugee community problems, counseling, job and educational referrals and job placement facilities. The aim of the state and federal funding is to strive for economic self-sufficiency.

939 *Green Bay*

Diocese of Green Bay. Department of Refugee, Migration & Hispanic Services

Box 1825
Green Bay, WI 54305
Barbara B. Biebel, Director
(414) 437-7531

Services Offered: AD, CU, CE, LI, RE, SS. **Established:** 1975. **Staff:** 8. **Budget:** $246,000. **Religious Affiliation:** Catholic. **Clientele:** Southeast Asia. Advocate for refugees and immigrants to lessen discrimination and negative attitudes. Work to achieve family reunification through resettlement activities. Refugees are resettled into four cities for greater community support. Assist with filing for immigration status for refugees after one year and for naturalization after five years. Goal is to resettle through sponsorship network and coordinate efforts with volunteers and relatives so a support network is established. Information and referral services.

940 *Green Bay*

Hmong Association of Brown County. Refugee Community Center

617 North Irwin Avenue
Green Bay, WI 54302
Koua S. Yang, Director
(414) 432-8900

Services Offered: AD, CU, CE, EC, ED, SS. **Established:** 1982. **Staff:** 15. **Budget:** $260,000. **Clientele:** Southeast Asia. Goal is to make the refugee population self-sufficient by providing outreach, translation, English language training and employment services to all Hmong and Laotian refugees. **Publications:** ASSOCIATION NEWS (bi-monthly newsletter).

941 *La Crosse*

La Crosse Area Hmong Mutual Assistance Association

326 South Seventh
La Crosse, WI 54601
Denis Tucker, Associate Executive Director
(608) 784-2704

Services Offered: AD, CU, EC, HE, SS. **Established:** 1982. **Staff:** 16. **Budget:** $250,000. **Clientele:** Southeast Asia. Goal is to assist refugees in adjusting to life in the United States. Services include: employment training and job placement; language instruction; basics skills; advocacy; and case management. **Publications:** HMAA NEWSLETTER (quarterly).

942 *Madison*

Catholic Social Services

4905 Schofield Street
Madison, WI 53716
Mary Sobota, Refugee Program
(608) 221-2000

Services Offered: SS. **Established:** 1975. **Religious Affiliation:** Catholic. **Clientele:** World. Refugee Program provides social service support services to refugees and immigrants.

943 *Madison*

Jewish Social Services

310 North Midvale Boulevard, Suite 325
Madison, WI 53705
Steven H. Morrison, Executive Director
(608) 231-3426

Services Offered: AD, CU, CE, ED, RE, SS. **Established:** 1978. **Staff:** 3. **Budget:** $150,000. **Religious Affiliation:** Jewish. **Clientele:** USSR, Middle East. Refugee resettlement services provided by social workers. These activities coordinated through the Hebrew Immigrant Aid Society. **Publications:** Annual Report.

944 *Madison*

Temple Beth El. Sanctuary Committee

2702 Arbor Drive
Madison, WI 53711
(608) 238-3123

Services Offered: AD, CE, SA. **Religious Affiliation**: Jewish. **Clientele**: Central America/Caribbean. Declared sanctuary for refugees fleeing from El Salvador and Guatemala.

---

945   *Madison*

University of Wisconsin. Center for Demography and Ecology

4430 Social Science Building
Madison, WI 53706
Robert Hauser, Director
(608) 262-2182   Fax: (608) 262-0123

Services Offered: LI, RS. **Established**: 1962. **Staff**: 42. Research areas include immigrants and refugees entering the United States and migration patterns.

---

946   *Madison*

Wisconsin Division of Community Services. Refugee Assistance Office

Box 7851
Madison, WI 53707
Jules F. Bader, State Coordinator
(608) 266-8354

Services Offered: SS. **Established**: 1975. **Staff**: 7. **Budget**: $6,000,000. **Clientele**: World. WRAO is federally funded state agency responsible for social services and cash and medical assistance funds designed to facilitate refugees and legalized aliens attain self-sufficiency. Provide indirect services through contract for employment training, case management, language training, and health and supportive services.

---

947   *Milwaukee*

Cross Lutheran Church

1821 North 16th Street
Milwaukee, WI 53205
Joseph Ellwanger, Pastor
(414) 344-1746

Services Offered: AD, SA, SS. **Established**: 1870. **Religious Affiliation**: Lutheran. **Clientele**: Central America/Caribbean, Africa.

Resettlement services to refugees coordinated through Lutheran Immigration & Refugee Services. Sanctuary for Central American refugees.

---

948   *Milwaukee*

Ecumenical Refugee Council

2510 North Frederick Avenue
Milwaukee, WI 53211
Robert Pettit, Contact
(414) 332-5381

Services Offered: AD, CE, SS. **Established**: 1979. **Staff**: 4. **Budget**: $40,000. **BIA**. **Religious Affiliation**: Ecumenical. **Clientele**: World, Central America/Caribbean. Emergency social services to refugees in Wisconsin. Also provides aid to refugees at border in South Texas and places homeless Central American children in foster homes in Wisconsin.

---

949   *Milwaukee*

Hmong/American Friendship Association

2414 West Vliet Street
Milwaukee, WI 53205
Chia Thao, Executive Director
(414) 344-6575

Services Offered: AD, CU, EC, HE, SS. **Established**: 1983. **Staff**: 9. **Budget**: $200,000. **Clientele**: Southeast Asia. Following services offered to Hmong and Laotian refugees: employment; housing; health; advocacy; emergency services; cultural orientation; and information and referral. **Publications**: NTAWV XOV XWM (irregular newsletter, free); Annual Report.

---

950   *Milwaukee*

International Institute of Wisconsin

2810 West Highland Boulevard
Milwaukee, WI 53208
Alexander P. Durtka, Jr., Executive Director
(414) 933-0521

Services Offered: AD, CU, SS. **Established**: 1936. **Staff**: 20. **Budget**: $1,034,000. **BIA**. **Clientele**: World. Social service agency that provides a broad range of services. These services include immigration and naturalization; counseling and technical assistance for the foreign-born; educational programs designed to promote increased cultural understanding; language training; citizenship classes; professional and social programming for international visitors; and a friendship family program for international university students. Committment to helping the immigrant and refugee become an integral part of the community and a productive member of society. **Publications:** Newsletter; Annual Report.

---

951 *Milwaukee*

Jewish Family Services

1360 North Prospect Avenue
Milwaukee, WI 53202
Ralph Sherman, Resettlement Worker
(414) 273-6515

Services Offered: AD, CU, CE, SS. **Religious Affiliation:** Jewish. **Clientele:** Europe, USSR. Resettlement services assist newcomer to become independent and self-supporting and educate the local community about refugees and immigrants.

---

952 *Milwaukee*

Lao Family Community

1420 West Scott Street
Milwaukee, WI 53204
Ger Vang, President
(414) 383-4180

Services Offered: AD, EC, SS. **Established:** 1981. **Staff:** 9. **Budget:** $220,000. **Clientele:** Southeast Asia. Non-profit membership organization whose primary mission is to aid refugees in their adjustment to life in the United States. Goal is to assist Laotian and Hmong refugees reduce or alleviate the problems encountered in the cultural transition process and to provide education and support resources necessary to assist refugees become independent and self-sufficient citizens.

---

953 *Milwaukee*

Lutheran Social Services of Wisconsin & Upper Michigan

Box 08520
Milwaukee, WI 53208
Lowell Grottveit, Vice President
(414) 342-7175   Fax: (414) 342-2933

Services Offered: AD, CU, RE, RS, SS. **Established:** 1975. **Staff:** 8. **Budget:** $200,000. **Religious Affiliation:** Lutheran. **Clientele:** World. Broad based resettlement services, coordinated with Lutheran Immigration & Refugee Services, include the following: secure and train sponsors for refugees; case management services for refugees; cooperate and consult with other agencies; and assist

with family reunification. **Publications:** Newsletter; Annual Report.

---

954 *Oshkosh*

Oshkosh Lao Hmong Association

2929 Harrison Street
Oshkosh, WI 54901
Pao Yang
(414) 426-0150

Services Offered: AD, CU, EC. **Staff:** 3. **Budget:** $94,000. **Religious Affiliation:** Buddhist. **Clientele:** Southeast Asia. Services designed to assist with the refugee's integration into society and the ability to become economically self-sufficient in as short a period as possible. Activities coordinated with numerous government and social service agencies. **Publications:** Newsletter (quarterly); Annual Report.

---

955 *Sheboygan*

Hmong Mutual Assistance Association

901 Superior Avenue, Room 350
Sheboygan, WI 53081
Song Yang, Executive Director
(414) 458-0808

Services Offered: AD, CU, CE, EC, ED, SC, SS. **Established:** 1981. **Staff:** 8. **Budget:** $175,809. **Religious Affiliation:** Ecumenical. **Clientele:** Southeast Asia. Provide employment assistance, job development and career counseling, case management services, etc. to newly arrived families from Thailand. Also provide support services, through coordination with public and private agencies, to existing refugee families. **Publications:** XA XOU (bi-monthly newsletter); Annual Report.

---

956 *Superior*

Catholic Charities Bureau. Resettlement Program

Box 219
Superior, WI 54880
Brian Soland, Director
(715) 394-6617

Services Offered: CU, SS. **Religious Affiliation:** Catholic. **Clientele:** World. Wide range of social services as well as referrals for medical care for refugees as part of resettlement services.

---

957   *Casper*

Catholic Social Services

Box 2247
Casper, WY 82602
Tom Cotterill, Executive Director
(307) 237-2723

Services Offered: AD, LI, RE, SS.
Established: 1980. **BIA**. **Religious
Affiliation**: Catholic. **Clientele**: World. Refugee
and immigration services to assist with transition to
new life in the United States.

---

958   *Cheyenne*

Wyoming Department of Health & Social Services. Refugee Relocation Program

390 Hathaway Building
Cheyenne, WY 82002
Steve Vajda, Coordinator
(307) 777-6081

Services Offered: AD, EC, ED, HE, SS.
Clientele: World. Responsible for statewide coordination of federal, state and private resources for effective refugee resettlement.

Appendices

Appendix A

United States Immigration and Refugee Policy: Entering the 1990's

United States Immigration and Refugee Policy: Entering the 1990's

Essay prepared by the Refugee Policy Group

INTRODUCTION

Millions of foreigners come to the United States each year. The vast majority are temporary visitors, or nonimmigrants. Included in this category are tourists, business persons, students, diplomats, temporary workers and others. In 1987 alone more than 12 million nonimmigrants visited the United States, and it is projected that the annual number of temporary visitors to this country will exceed 18 million per year within the next five years. About 600,000 foreigners are admitted each year for permanent residence as well. They arrive under several different admissions categories: some for family reunification; others for employment; and still others as refugees. In addition to these legal arrivals are individuals who come illegally to the United States. During the past two years, more than 3 million illegal aliens applied to adjust their status to legal residence under the Immigration Reform and Control Act of 1986. There are, however, an estimated 1.5 to 3 million aliens still residing illegally in this country. [1]

The 1980s has been an eventful decade in the development of U.S. immigration and refugee policy. The decade began with passage of the Refugee Act of 1980 which, for the first time in U.S. immigration history, provided permanent legislation governing both admission of and assistance to refugees. Almost immediately upon enactment, the Refugee Act was tested, both in the resettlement of record numbers of Southeast Asian refugees and the direct arrival of Cuban and Haitian boat people.

In the next year, the U.S. Select Commission on Immigration and Refugee Policy reported its recommendations on reforms in the handling of both legal and illegal immigration to the United States. Based on two years of hearings, research and policy analysis, the blue ribbon panel recommended that the front door to this country be opened modestly to allow for additional legal migration and that the back door of illegal migration be closed by the imposition of sanctions on employers who hired aliens who did not have work authorization. The Select Commission also recommended that illegal aliens currently in the country be given legal status as the increased enforcement took place.

Congress and the Administration took these recommendations under advisement, beginning what turned out to be a five year process of controversial legislative development. Finally, in November 1986, the Immigration Reform and Control Act passed both houses of Congress. This legislation focused on the illegal migration issue, putting into place employers sanctions, a program to legalize long-resident undocumented aliens, and a seasonal agricultural worker program.

Mexico has long been and continues to be the principal source of illegal (as well as legal) migration to the United States. Almost 70 percent of those legalized under the IRCA amnesty program were from Mexico. Mexicans still account for the majority of apprehensions at the Southern land border. During the past decade, however, newer, large-scale migrations from Central America have also been seen. Prompted by civil wars and civil strife, as well as devastated economies, people from El Salvador, Nicaragua and Guatemala have come to the United States in record numbers.

The arrival of the Central Americans, along with migrants from other troubled countries such as Iran, Afghanistan, Haiti and Poland, has placed tremendous pressure during the 1980s on the system for dealing with politically-generated migration. Large numbers of people sought relief from deportation because they feared return to their home countries. Small numbers have proved to the satisfaction of the U.S. government that they had a well-founded fear of persecution and have been granted refugee status. Most have been denied asylum, however. Among those who have not been granted refugee status are individuals who have left life threatening situations. Some of these individuals have been granted Extended Voluntary Departure, that is, permission to remain indefinitely in the United States until conditions change sufficiently in their home countries to permit return. Others—primarily Central Americans—remain without any protection from deportation.

At the same time, new pressures have also been building relating to the admission of political migrants from overseas. In recent years, there has been an opening of emigration possibilities from the Soviet Union and Eastern bloc countries. Traditionally, those leaving the Soviet Union have been treated as refugees and have been admitted to the United States almost without exception. As conditions change in the East, however, questions have been raised about the advisability and appropriateness of admitting the emigres as refugees. Yet, most do not qualify for entry as legal immigrants. Since, for foreign policy reasons, the United States is unwilling to close its doors to these migrants, the inadequacy of current immigration policies is becoming increasingly apparent.

The 1990s are likely to see as significant developments in immigration and refugee policy as did the 1980s. Early on the agenda will be the need for reform in the legal immigration system as well as improved mechanisms for handling politically- generated migration. Also likely is continuing review and refinement of the provisions of the Immigration Reform and Control Act, in particular its implications for these undocumented aliens who did not qualify for the "amnesty program."

In order to better plan for the changes needed in U.S. immigration and refugee policy, a firm understanding is needed of the existing and complex set of policies, procedures and institutions that relate to immigration and refugee issues. What follows is a brief introduction to the immigration and refugee system of the United States. Included in this paper is information about current and proposed admissions policies; the characteristics of immigrants, refugees and legalized aliens; the federal, state and private agencies that work with aliens; and the programs for which different categories of immigrants are eligible. Because some of the policies and programs for refugees and legalized aliens differ from those pertaining to other migrants, separate information is provided on these groups where applicable. The paper concludes with thoughts on immigration and refugee issues that are still to be addressed.

Appendix A

ADMISSIONS POLICIES AND PROCEDURES

Legal Immigrants

Legal immigration to the United States is governed by the Immigration and Nationality Act, as amended in 1965, 1976 and 1978. The 1965 amendments abolished the national origins quotas that had been used to admit permanent residents since the 1920s. The national origins quotas greatly favored immigration from Western Europe because the individual country quotas were based on the U.S. population distribution in 1890, when most Americans were descended from the British and other Western Europeans.

The 1965 amendments provided for unlimited immigration of the immediate family of U.S. citizens and a ceiling of 160,000 on numerically limited immigration from the Eastern Hemisphere and a 120,000 ceiling on such immigration from the Western Hemisphere. The 1965 amendments also established a preference system (applicable only to those from the Eastern Hemisphere until the amendments of 1976) which gave priority to aliens seeking family reunification and those with needed occupational skills and abilities. Further, no country in the Eastern Hemisphere was to exceed a quota of 20,000 admissions per year. In 1976, the preference system and the per country limitation were applied to the Western Hemisphere as well. Then, in 1978, the last major change occurred in legal immigration policies, with the elimination of separate Western and Eastern Hemisphere ceilings. Under the 1978 amendments, there would be a worldwide ceiling of 290,000 visas (reduced to 270,000 after the refugee preference category was removed in 1980—see below).

At present, then, legal immigrants are admitted to the United States for permanent residence under two broad categories: 1) immediate relatives of U.S. citizens and members of special admission groups; and 2) others admitted for family reunification and immigrants admitted on basis of their employment profile.

The first category, immediate relatives and other numerically exempt immigrants, are exempted from numerical restrictions. The immediate relatives of U.S. citizens include spouses, unmarried minor children, and parents of adult citizens. About 225,000 aliens are admitted for this type of family reunification, with more than half being spouses and the rest evenly divided between children and parents of U.S. citizens. The number of other numerically exempt categories are much smaller, averaging only several thousand per year. These include ministers of religions and their families, employees of the U.S. government abroad, and certain retired employees of international organizations and their families.

The second type of potential immigrants are subject to a worldwide annual ceiling for 270,000 and a single country ceiling of 20,000. They are also subject to a categorical preference system which further limits the numbers of individuals within prescribed categories allowed to enter the United States. Each preference has a specified percentage allocated, as shown in Table I. Because unused numbers in one category can be applied to others, the actual proportion of admissions differs from the ceiling. More than 100,000 immigrants (instead of the allotted 70,200) enter under the second preference—the spouses and minor children of permanent residents while only 10,000 (instead of the allotted 54,000) come in under first preference—the unmarried adult children of U.S. citizens.

Table 2 shows the total number of immigrants admitted to the United States in 1987 and 1988 by major category of admissions.

During the past few years, there have been a number of proposals made to improve the existing immigration system. At present, the major emphasis of U.S. legal immigration is on family reunification. There are few avenues of legal immigration available to those without family ties in the United States. Included in recent legislative proposals generating from both the Congress and the Administration are procedures through which "independent" immigrants can more freely enter the country. Most of these proposals would modestly increase overall immigration in order to stimulate new movements without endangering the ability of immediate families to reunify. There are variations, however, in the proposed mechanisms (a point system, for example, which would give priority to those with transferable skills and English language ability among other characteristics). There is also debate about the need for establishing an overall cap on immigration by placing the now numerically exempt categories under a single worldwide ceiling.

TABLE I

CATEGORY	PERCENTAGE LIMIT
First: Unmarried adult children of U.S. citizens and their children	20
Second: Spouses and unmarried sons and daughters of permanent resident aliens	26
Third: Professors, scientists, and artists of exceptional ability and their spouses and children	10
Fourth: Married children of U.S. citizens and their spouses and children	10
Fifth: Brothers and sisters of adult U.S. citizens and their spouses and children	24
Sixth: Skilled and unskilled workers in occupations where labor is needed in the U.S. and their spouses and children	10

Nonpreference: Other qualified applicants Unused Quotas

Taken from: U.S. Immigration and Naturalization Service, 1983 *Statistical Yearbook of the Immigration and Naturalization Service* (Washington D.C.: U.S. Government Printing office, 1983)

TABLE II

Immigrants Admitted by Major Category of Admission
FY 1988

Category of admission	1988	1987	Change	
			Number	Percent
Total	643,025	601,516	41,509	6.9
Subject to limitations	264,148	271,135	-6,987	-2.6
Relative preferences	200,772	211,809	-11,037	-5.2
Occupational preferences	53,607	53,873	-266	-0.5
Nonpreference	6,029	3,040	2,989	98.3
Other	3,740	2,413	1,327	55.0
Exempt from limitations	378,877	330,381	48,496	14.7
Immediate relatives of U.S. citizens	219,340	218,575	765	0.3
Spouses [1]	130,977	132,452	-1,475	-1.1
Parents	47,500	45,183	2,317	5.1
Children [2]	40,863	40,940	-77	-0.2
Refugee and asylee adjustments ...	110,721	96,474	14,247	14.8
1972 Registry	39,999	8,060	31,939	396.3
Other	8,817	7,272	1,545	21.2

[1] Includes fiances(ees) of U.S. citizens.   [2] Includes children of fiances(ees) of U.S. citizens.

Refugees and Asylees

Although the United States has been a place of permanent refuge for people fleeing persecution since the arrival of the Pilgrims, the adoption of a formal refugee policy is a recent development. Until 1980, refugee resettlement was based on temporary legislation or ad hoc administrative actions. The Refugee Act of 1980 was designed to provide permanent authority both for the admission of and assistance to refugees.

Prior to the passage of the Refugee Act, refugees were admitted to the United States in three ways:

- In the aftermath of World War II, a large number of refugees were brought to the U.S. by means of special temporary legislation enacted independently of existing immigration law;

- A few thousand refugees were qualified under the conditional entry provision of the Immigration and Nationality Act; and

- After 1956, the majority of refugees were admitted through the administrative parole power of the Attorney General.

The Refugee Act provided mechanisms for determining who is a refugee and, among those determined to be refugees, who and how many should be admitted. The act removed refugees as the seventh preference category previously defined in the Immigration and Nationality Act as amended in 1965. The act incorporated into U.S. law a definition of a refugee similar to the one contained in the U.N. Convention on the Status of Refugees:

> ...any person who is outside any country of such person's nationality or, in the case of a person having no nationality, is outside any country in which such a person last habitually resided, and who is unable or unwilling to return to, and is unable or unwilling to avail himself or herself of the protection of that country because of persecution or a well-founded fear of persecution on account of race, religion, nationality, membership in a particular social group, or political opinion. ...(Refugee Act of 1980, Section 201).

This definition pertains to refugees resettled from overseas as well as those applying for political asylum within the United States.

The number of refugees from overseas to be admitted in any given year is determined by the President, in consultation with the Judiciary Committees of the House of Representatives and the Senate. If an emergency occurs, the President can ask for an emergency consultation and adjust admission numbers accordingly. During the general and emergency consultations, the President also indicates the anticipated geographic distribution of refugee admissions during the fiscal year.

In determining admission levels, both international and domestic concerns are taken into account. The State Department issues a report annually that outlines the need for resettlement among various groups throughout the world and the extent to which other countries will admit and assist in the resettlement of refugees. The report includes the analysis of the impact of refugee resettlement on the foreign policy interests of the United States. In addition, the report also contains information about the anticipated social, demographic, and economic impact of refugee resettlement on the United States. Based on this information, the administration proposes ceilings for the admission of refugees by geographic area.

Applicants for admission must meet several criteria. First, they have to demonstrate that they are refugees within the meaning of the definition contained in the Refugee Act. They are interviewed by officers of the Immigration and Naturalization Service to determine the reasons that they left their countries of origin and their likely fate should they return. These are processing guidelines to assist INS officers judge whether applicants meet their statutory definition.

Second, applicants must meet certain processing priorities. First priority is given to exceptional cases of refugees in immediate danger of loss of life and to political prisoners and dissidents. Beyond these compelling cases, priority is given to refugees with direct ties to the United States because they worked for the U.S. government or American firms, received training in the United States, or have close family members already living in the country. The number of refugee admissions has fluctuated during the past decade. At the height of the Indochinese refugee crisis of 1980 - 1981, more than 200,000 refugees were admitted to the United States. The level of admissions decreased steadily until 1983 when it leveled off to about 60-70,000 per year. During the past two years, the admission level has begun to increase once more, largely in response to more liberalized emigration policies in the Soviet Union and Eastern Europe that have permitted thousands to exit their countries.

A smaller number of people are granted political asylum in the United States each year. These are individuals who enter the United States illegally or on nonimmigrant visas. They then tell immigration authorities that they are unable to return to their home countries because they fear persecution on the grounds contained in the Refugee Act. If they demonstrate that their fear is well-founded, they will be granted temporary permission to remain in the United States. After one year, they may adjust their status to permanent residence. No more than 5,000 asylees may adjust their status in any given year.

Both the resettlement and asylum systems are under close scrutiny at present, largely because of the growing number of individuals who have been denied refugee status because they do not meet the international definition of a refugee. Many of these individuals are, nevertheless, of interest to the United States.

For those denied refugee status abroad and for whom legal immigration is not an option, admission can be provided under the parole authority of the Attorney General. For those denied asylum in the United States, relief from deportation through Extended Voluntary Departure (EVD) is possible. Neither option is particularly desirable, however, because they are ad hoc responses to what have been recurrent situations. In addition, both provide a degree of Executive branch autonomy—since the decisions on parole and EVD can be made without consultation with Congress—that has been of concern to the legislature. In fact, the Refugee Act specifically bars use of parole in admitting refugees.

Recently, the inadequacies in refugee admissions provisions have become particularly apparent because of the high rate of denials of Soviet applicants for refugee resettlement. For foreign policy reasons, the United States would prefer to admit these individuals even if they do not meet the refugee definition since it has been a major objective of this country to encourage more open emigration from the Soviet Union. As a result, there is discussion of new legislation to provide for the admission of "special interest" immigrants as a new category.

The direct arrival of Central Americans citing concerns about civil violence in their countries has put similar pressures on the asylum system. Most Central Americans have been denied asylum, with the government claiming that they do not meet the refugee definition. The Administration has also been unwilling to provide EVD to those coming from El Salvador, Guatemala and Nicaragua although it is available to Poles, Afghans, Ethiopians, and some Ugandans. Legislation has been proposed for a new "safe haven" category to accommodate those leaving conditions of civil war, civil strife and generalized human rights violations.

Legalization Programs

The third major type of recent immigration has been the legalization of individuals who had previously resided illegally in the United States. Immigration legislation has always contained provisions for the legalization of individuals—through registry or suspension of deportation—who had been residing illegally within the United States for a long period of time. Very small numbers have generally been able to avail themselves of these provisions, however, since the illegal aliens had to have been residing in this country since 1948 (to avail themselves of the registry provision) or had to have shown that their deportation would have caused undue hardship to a U.S. citizen (to avail themselves of the suspension of deportation provision).

In 1986 the Immigration Reform and Control Act of 1986 (IRCA) was enacted. IRCA provided for the legalization of large numbers of undocumented aliens through two major programs. The major vehicle for legalization covers undocumented aliens who could establish continuous residence in the United states since January 1, 1982 and meet other criteria for admissibility as immigrants. Under the legislation, these aliens were able to apply to adjust their status to lawful temporary residence if they applied between May 5, 1987 and May 4, 1988. They may then adjust temporary residence within the 12 months following completion of 18 months of temporary residence. Permanent residence is contingent on passing an English language and civics examination that is comparable to the current citizenship examination or enrollment in an approved course of instruction. Nearly 1.8 million aliens applied for legal status under this program. It is estimated that 90 percent or more of these applications will be approved.

The second program is for Special Agricultural Workers (SAW program). The SAW program permits illegal alien workers who have done at least 90 days of qualifying agricultural work between May 1, 1985 and May 1, 1986 to apply for temporary legal status. The SAW program lasted from June 1, 1987 to November 30, 1988. More than 1.2 million agricultural workers applied for the SAW program. It is expected that a far lower proportion of these cases will be approved. The Immigration and Naturalization Service estimates that approximately 850,000 will qualify for permanent residence under this program.

A smaller legalization program, enacted after passage of IRCA, covers people granted Extended Voluntary Departure because they are nationals of Poland, Ethiopia, Afghanistan, or Uganda. Under EVD, residents of these countries are permitted to remain temporarily in this country, presumably until conditions change in their country of origin and their safe return is possible. Aliens from these countries who have been in the United States since July 21, 1984 were given two years, until December 1989, to apply for adjustment to temporary legal residence. Thereafter, they will be eligible to become permanent residents. EVDs are still applying for legalization and no count to date was available.

Despite the large legalization programs that have been implemented during the past two years, there are still sizeable numbers of illegal aliens resident in the United States. Many have been residing in this country for several years, but they came after the 1982 cut-off date for the amnesty program. Some are the spouses and children of the legalized. In the years ahead, the futures of these individuals will need to be addressed.

CHARACTERISTICS OF IMMIGRANTS, REFUGEES AND LEGALIZED ALIENS

Immigrants

The largest number of immigrants admitted to the United States come from Asia and North America, with smaller numbers from Europe, Africa, Oceania and South America. The countries providing the largest numbers of immigrants are: Mexico, the Philippines, Korea, Cuba, India, China, Dominican Republic, Vietnam, Jamaica and Haiti. Together, these ten countries account for almost half of all legal immigration to the United States.

Once in the United States, the immigrants tend to settle in a few states and localities. The six states cited by new arrivals as their state of intended residence are California, New York, Florida, Texas, New Jersey and Illinois. These states, which account for 38.4 percent of the overall U.S. population, are the intended state of residence for 71.4 percent of the immigrants. Within these states, immigrants are located in a few metropolitan areas. The major sites of intended residence are New York, NY; Los Angeles, CA.; Miami-Hialeah, FL.; Chicago, IL; and Washington, DC metropolitan area. These five metropolitan areas received between 35 and 40 percent of all immigrants during the past few years.

The new immigrants are evenly divided between men and women. They are a young population, with a median age of 27.9 years. The median age for male immigrants is 27.7 and for female immigrants is 28.0. By contrast, the median age for the U.S. population is higher, with 30.9 years for males and 33.2 years for females.

Based on information collected at the time of entry, 50.2 percent of immigrants who arrived from 1985-1987 had occupations. There were significant differences between men and women, with about two-thirds of the men reporting occupations and only 36 percent of immigrant women. In each case, the proportion is lower than for the overall U.S. population, where 76 percent of men and 55 percent of women report involvement in the labor force. According to the Labor Department, however, these data understate the proportion of subsequent labor force participation for immigrants, particularly among women.

Immigrants have an occupational structure that is similar to the overall U.S. population, with a few exceptions. About one fourth of the immigrants, as is true of the overall population, are in managerial or professional specialties. About 12 percent of each group are in precision production, craft and repair. By contrast, a smaller proportion of immigrants (16.2) than other U.S. residents (31.2) are in technical, sales and administrative support. And, a higher proportion of immigrants are in service occupations (20.0 % as compared to 13.4 %) or work as operators, fabricators, and laborers (22.5 % as compared to 15.6 %).

Upon entry into the U.S. labor force, the distribution of occupations shows even greater similarity. According to data in the 1983 *Current Population Survey*, the occupational distribution of native born and foreign born workers remains similar in most categories, although the foreign born continue to hold a higher proportion of jobs as operatives, fabricators and laborers and a lower proportion of jobs in sales and administrative support.

Some of the continuing occupational differences can be explained by educational differences. There are a greater proportion of native born clustered at the high school level than is true of recently arrived immigrants. The foreign born, by contrast, are concentrated at both ends of the educational spectrum with larger proportions with little or no education and higher proportions with four or more years of college.

Refugees

During the past decade, the largest number of refugees entering the United States came from Southeast Asia. Other sizeable groups include Soviets, Poles, Afghans, Ethiopians, and Rumanians.

As with other immigrants, refugees tend to cluster in a few locations. Refugees are more dispersed, however, than other newcomers, in part because of an explicit federal policy to encourage resettlement of refugees in a way that would impede the formation of large concentrations. For example, the government has sought favorable alternative sites, providing additional social service funding in order to increase the likelihood that refugees would remain where they were initially placed. Nevertheless, several states remain the favored destination of most refugees because their families already live there. The states with the largest numbers of refugee arrivals are: California, New York, Texas, Illinois and Minnesota.[2]

The gender distribution of refugees vary by nationality. Among Southeast Asians, about 55 percent are male and 45 percent are female. Men and women are about equally represented in the Soviet refugee population. By contrast, the majority of Ethiopian refugees are men.

Newly arriving refugees have been younger on average than both the U.S. population and other immigrants. The median age of arriving Southeast Asian refugees has been between 18 and 22 for most of this decade. Other recent refugee groups have had an average age of mid-twenties. The major exceptions to this pattern are Soviet refugees whose median age has been late thirties to early forties. At least 20 percent of the Soviet refugees are in their sixties or older.

A recent national survey on refugee participation in the labor force (October 1987) shows that 39 percent of all Southeast Asian refugees over the age of 16 were employed or actively seeking work. Included in this statistic are refugees who entered the United States between 1975 and 1987. The longer refugees are in the country, the more likely they are to participate in the work force.

As with labor force participation, employment increases with time in the United States. According to the surveys conducted by the Office of Refugee Resettlement, for 1983 arrivals, the unemployment rate decreased from 55 percent in 1983 to 36 percent in 1984, to 17 percent in 1985, and to 10 percent in 1986. For 1984 arrivals, it decreased from 41 percent in 1984, to 36 percent in 1985, and to 18 percent in 1986. The figures for 1986 arrivals are especially notable, with a 31 percent labor force participation rate being at the high end of the range for a first-year group, while the unemployment rate of 25 percent is about half of that historically found for the Southeast Asian refugees.

A recent survey found that 40 percent of refugees worked in manufacturing, with almost 25 percent employed in retail trade. Professionals accounted for 15 percent of the employed. More specifically, four occupational categories employed the vast majority of the refugees: technical, sales and administrative support (24.4 percent), service (21.9 percent), precision production, craft and repair (21.4 percent), and operators and fabricators (19.3 percent). Within these occupations, refugees tend to hold low-skilled positions. More than one-fourth of those in the service sector are janitors and cleaners, with another 40 percent working in food preparation and distribution (cooks, kitchen workers, waiters and waitresses and their assistants). Another large percentage of refugees work in the electronics industry, generally in unskilled support positions.

For refugees, unlike immigrants, use of welfare programs is significant during the first few years after arrival. As discussed below, immigrants are generally unable to avail themselves of these programs during their first three years in the country while refugees are given special eligibility for public assistance. As of the end of FY 1987, about 52 percent of refugees who had been in the United States for three years or less were receiving some form of cash assistance. Welfare utilization rates vary greatly from state to state; they also differ by nationality. Dependency rates calculated by nationality range between 12 and 72 percent of time-eligible refugees. These calculations show relatively high dependency among the Southeast Asians compared with most other groups. According to the Office of Refugee Resettlement, the best estimates are that 64 percent of Vietnamese and 72 percent of Lao, and 58 percent of Khmer refugees, in the United States for less than three years, receive cash assistance.

The capacity to become independent of public assistance programs, as with employment, improves over time. The annual survey of Southeast Asian refugees shows that about 70 percent of those in the U.S. for less than six months live in households receiving cash assistance; for those in the country for over 36 months, this group has dropped to 39 percent.

Legalized Aliens

While there are legalized aliens from virtually every country in the world, the vast majority (including the regular amnesty program as well as the SAW program) are from Mexico. Other countries with major legalized populations include El Salvador, Guatemala, Philippines, Columbia, Haiti, Nicaragua, Poland, Iran and Jamaica. [3]

The legalized population tends to cluster in a few states, with California having more than 50 percent. Other states with sizeable populations include Texas, Florida, Illinois and New York.

Nationally, 54 percent of the aliens legalized under the regular amnesty program are male and 46 percent are female. The SAW program population tends to be more male dominated, with 83 percent being men. The majority legalized under both programs are adults of employment age. The median age of the amnesty legalized is 30 years, with 77 percent falling into the 15 to 44 age group. For the SAWs, the median age is 28 with 90 percent falling into the 15 to 44 age bracket.

A very high proportion of the legalized aliens are now in the work force. They are represented in all job categories, but the largest proportion are employed in jobs in the laboring and service sectors of the economy. There are professional and technical workers within the population as well. The type and quality of their U.S. jobs varies considerably. At one end of the spectrum are those who have reestablished their professional standing in this country, while at the other end are highly educated legalized aliens who are working in menial jobs.

ASSISTANCE PROGRAMS

Special assistance programs are generally not made available to recently arrived legal immigrants. For the first three years of their residence in the United States, immigrants generally cannot avail themselves of federal public assistance programs. When a newly arrived immigrant applies for Aid to Families with Dependent Children, his or her sponsor's income and resources are deemed to be available to the alien according to a prescribed formula. Immigrants are eligible for any state funded programs that may be available to the general population, but these vary considerably within states and are generally for individuals with extremely low incomes. Beyond the three year period, immigrants are eligible for public assistance programs under the same eligibility rules used for the U.S. citizen population.

Legalized aliens also are ineligible for federal benefits, in this case, for the first five years of their legal residence in the United States. States and localities have the option of permitting or disqualifying legalized aliens from their programs during this period of time. There are federal funds available to help defray the costs to states of providing cash and medical assistance, public health services, and educational services. These funds can only be used to reimburse costs incurred in programs available to other populations within the state. An exception is funding available for language training and civics courses needed by the legalized aliens to adjust to permanent residence.

By contrast, the Refugee Act provides legislative authority for a program of special assistance to refugees. Unlike other immigrants, refugees are forced to leave their home countries and seek new homes. They generally do not have the time to prepare for their relocation and are therefore unable to bring resources with them. Often, they do not have families in the United States who are able to provide economic assistance. The goal of the resettlement program then is to provide needed transitional assistance to promote their rapid achievement of economic self- sufficiency.

Under current regulations and program guidelines, the following assistance and services are available for refugees:

- **Reception and Placement Grants.** Grants are provided by the Bureau for Refugee Programs to voluntary resettlement agencies, on the basis of cooperative agreements, to support pre-arrival activities (identification and orientation of sponsors, travel arrangements to bring refugees to their final destination); reception (assistance in obtaining initial housing, furnishings, food, and clothing); and orientation and referral services in the areas of health, employment and training.

- **Cash Assistance**. Refugees who are categorically eligible for Aid to Families with Dependent Children (AFDC), Supplemental Security Income (SSI) or state and local General Assistance programs (GA) may receive such assistance with full federal reimbursement of all state costs during the refugees' first 24 months in the United States. Refugees who meet income eligibility requirements but not family composition requirements for AFDC may receive Refugee Cash Assistance during their first 12 months in the United States, with full federal reimbursement of all state costs.

- **Medical Assistance**. Refugees who are categorically eligible for Medicaid may receive such assistance, with full federal reimbursement of all state costs during the refugees' first 24 months in the United States. Refugees who meet income eligibility requirements but not family composition requirements for Medicaid may receive Refugee Medical Assistance during their first 12 months in the United States, with full federal reimbursement of all state costs.

- **Social Services**. States receive funds, based on the number of refugee residents in the state who have been in the United States for 36 months or less, to support a range of services, including employment services, English-as-a-second language training programs, health referral services, translating and interpreting services, and social adjustment services. Priority is given to those employment and language services that promote economic self-sufficiency.

- **Targeted Assistance**. "Impacted Areas" (localities with high concentration of welfare-dependent refugees) receive funds to support supplemental services to promote self-sufficiency.

- **Transitional Assistance to Refugee Children**. Administered by the Department of Education, this program provides funds to the states for educational services for refugee children.

- **Health Program for Refugees**. Administered through the Centers for Disease Control, this program awards grants to states and localities to identify health problems that might impede effective resettlement of refugees and refer refugees for appropriate diagnosis and treatment.

- **English-as-a-Second-Language and Cultural Orientation Program**. Administered by the Bureau for Refugee Programs, this program provides training to U.S.-bound refugees in processing centers; for the Southeast Asian refugees these programs are provided in Thailand and the Philippines.

As in the admission program, the assistance policies related to refugees have come under criticism in recent years. While the refugee program has had considerable success in resettling many refugees, there are a number of issues that present problems for the program now and lessen its ability to meet the challenges ahead. The problems include:

- continued utilization of public assistance programs by some refugees;

- reliance by the federal, state and local governments on public assistance mechanisms, procedures, and regulations for providing transitional assistance to refugees;

- reliance on formulas and pro forma approaches in developing resettlement plans for individual clients;

- the erosion of effective private sector involvement in and funding for refugee programs;

- failures to respond adequately to the needs of smaller refugee groups such as Ethiopians, Afghans and Romanians; to a diverse array of skill levels; or to a variety of household sizes and compositions; and

- high costs that may limit the capacity of the United States, given budgetary constraints, to continue to admit large numbers of refugees.

The challenge then faced by the resettlement system is two fold: 1) strengthening the capacity to assist a heterogeneous mix of refugees in their social and economic adjustment to life in the United States while, at the same time, 2) tightening and in some cases reducing the scope of the federal resettlement effort in response to budget pressures.

INSTITUTIONAL ROLES

Agencies at the federal, state and local levels in both public and private organizations are involved in the immigration system. A brief description of the roles and responsibilities of the groups follows.

Federal Government

Four federal departments have primary responsibilities for the programs dealing with admission of and assistance to refugees and legal immigrants into the United States: the Justice Department, the State Department, the Department of Health and Human Services, and the Labor Department.

The *Immigration and Naturalization Service* (INS), an agency of the United States Department of Justice, is charged with administration of the Immigration and Nationality Act. Thus, this agency has responsibilities concerning both immigrants and refugees. The INS determines the admissibility of all immigrants and nonimmigrants seeking entry into the United States. The INS adjudicates asylum claims and processes refugees for admission to the United States, determining if an individual meets the statutory definition of a refugee. The INS also has an enforcement responsibility, to apprehend, detain and deport illegal aliens as necessary.

The *Bureau of Consular Affairs, U.S. Department of State* is responsible for controlling the number of immigrant visas issued. The State Department issues two-thirds of all immigrant visas abroad. The rest go to nonimmigrants and refugees in the United States who adjust to permanent resident status through the INS. The Bureau of Consular Affairs has complete discretion over who receives a visa—either as a visitor or as an immigrant.

The *Office of the U.S. Coordinator for Refugee Affairs* is the principal policy coordination mechanism within the U.S. government for refugee-related matters. It is a non-operational office, whose function is to encourage coordination between the public and private sector agencies concerned with refugees, and between various levels of government. The Coordinator is based in the State Department, and, with regard to his international responsibilities, has Ambassadorial status.

The *Bureau for Refugee Programs* administers the State Department's refugee programs. It is responsible for the development and implementation of policies related to refugee relief and assistance overseas and U.S. contributions to international refugee organizations. It is also responsible for setting priorities for admission of refugees to the United States and providing resources for their processing and training overseas, reception and placement in U.S. communities. These last activities are performed through cooperative agreements and contracts with voluntary agencies.

The *Office of Refugee Resettlement* in the Department of Health and Human Services (DHHS) is charged with chief operational responsibility for the domestic assistance program. Domestic assistance policy making is invested in the Secretary of DHHS in consultation with the U.S. Coordinator. ORR funds and monitors a range of programs, most of which are administered by state governments—cash assistance, medical assistance, social services, and targeted assistance, for example. In addition, DHHS is responsible for public health related services and provides matching grants to private agencies that serve non-Indochinese refugees. ORR is also responsible for administration of the State Legalization Impact Assistance Grants (SLIAG) program implemented under IRCA as discussed below.

The *Office of Refugee Health* in the Public Health Service, DHHS coordinates the activities of those PHS agencies involved in refugee health programs, the major one of which is the *Center for Disease Control*. It is responsible for the medical screening of refugees and administration of the domestic health assessment program.

The *U.S. Department of Labor* is responsible for foreign labor certifications. Section 212(a)(14) of the Immigration and Nationality Act requires that each alien intending to migrate to the United States for the purpose of employment must first obtain a certification from the Secretary of Labor that: 1) there are not sufficient U.S. workers who are able, willing, qualified and available at the place of intended employment; and 2) the employment of the alien will not adversely affect the wages and working conditions of U.S. workers similarly employed. To oversee policy development related to immigration, there is an Immigration Policy Group in addition to the Office of Foreign Labor Certification.

State Agencies

States also play an important role in immigration matters, particularly with regard to assistance to refugees and legalized aliens. State officials have been given responsibility for administering assistance programs and social services for refugees. States also coordinate the delivery of other services, in cooperation with voluntary agencies and other public authorities. Most states contract with private language training programs and employment services, while public welfare offices provide cash assistance.

In order to qualify for federal refugee funds, states are required to file an annual plan with the Office of Refugee Resettlement. The plan must contain a description of how the state intends to encourage economic self-sufficiency, designation of an individual who will be responsible for ensuring coordination of public and private resources, plans for the care and supervision of unaccompanied minors, and plans for the identification of refugees who have medical problems. States are also required to establish advisory councils composed of voluntary agencies, refugees, and others interested in resettlement issues.

States also have a significant role in relationship to the legalized aliens. IRCA established the SLIAG Program "to alleviate the financial impact on States and local governments that may result from the adjustment of immigrant status" through the legalization program. Under SLIAG $1 billion per year will be made available during the four fiscal years beginning in FY 1988 in grants to states to reimburse certain federal costs of providing assistance to eligible legalized aliens (ELAs).

States may use SLIAG funds to cover the costs associated with three types of assistance: public assistance, public health assistance, and educational services. Thirty percent of the funds are to be allocated equally among these three areas with the remaining 70 percent allocated as states desire given local impacts and priorities. The program is intended to cover additional costs to states resulting from the enactment of IRCA, with the recognition that the funds may not allow for reimbursement of 100 percent of those costs. With the exception of certain educational programs, SLIAG is not to be used to establish programs but rather to offset costs incurred in ongoing service programs because of legalization. At the state level, responsibility for SLIAG has been assigned to the refugee office in some cases and to newly created SLIAG offices in others.

Private Voluntary Organizations

Private voluntary organizations have had a longstanding role in the immigration system, particularly in facilitating the resettlement of refugees. Through local offices and affiliates throughout the country, the voluntary agencies have participated in the resettlement activities accompanying every major refugee flow into the United States.

Voluntary agency operational activities are numerous. They participate in overseas relief activities; they assist the government in processing refugees for admission; they arrange for sponsorships and placement of refugees in the United States; they receive refugees at their places of resettlement; they offer a range of services through their own resources, reception and placement grants, matching grants, or state administered social service contracts; and they provide income support to refugees during their first 30 days in the country.

Many voluntary agencies also have immigration counseling services and provide other support to both legal and illegal aliens. Some were designated as Qualified Designated Entities (QDEs) for the purposes of helping illegal aliens apply for legalization. The agencies received federal grants under which they counseled applicants, collected the documentation needed to prove their eligibility for legalization, and prepared the necessary paperwork. Many of these agencies are continuing to assist the legalized aliens apply for permanent residence.

Ethnic Associations

Members of the ethnic groups comprising immigration to the United States are the final component in immigration and refugee programs. They often form ethnic associations that provide services and/or advocate on behalf of their members. For example, associations of recently arrived refugees have been enlisted to assist newcomers. Mutual Assistance Associations (MAAs) formed by refugees now provide a full range of services, including translation and interpretation, social adjustment services, employment services, and economic development activities.

CONCLUSIONS

Immigration and refugee issues are likely to remain major public policy concerns of the 1990s. The world is certainly on the move, and there are indications that new migration possibilities will be opening up in the decade ahead. The United States is already facing the challenge of handling population movements from a diverse range of countries: Mexico, El Salvador, Nicaragua, Poland, Ethiopia, Afghanistan—to name only a few. At the same time, the Soviet Union and Eastern European countries are reexamining their emigration policies, promising liberalization in the months and years ahead.

These new migration patterns—from South to North, from East to West—will require a variety of new approaches. Existing legislative and administrative mechanisms have already been found wanting. The legal immigration system has been unable to accommodate the admission of the range of individuals in whom the United States has a humanitarian, political or economic interest in admitting. Although it is too soon to know the ultimate effectiveness of IRCA's enforcement provisions, illegal migration—particularly of Central Americans who have left their countries, in part at least for political reasons—continues to be a problem.

Understanding the system we currently have is a first step towards improving it. It is with this goal in mind that this brief introduction to U.S. immigration and refugee policy and programs has been presented.

Notes

[1] Unless otherwise indicated statistics in this article are from *The President's Comprehensive Triennial Report on Immigration*, 1989.

[2] Statistics on refugees come from *Refugee Resettlement Program—Report to Congress*, U.S. Department of Health and Human Services, Office of Refugee Resettlement.

[3] Statistics on the characteristics of the legalized aliens are taken from *Serving the Newly Legalized: Their Characteristics and Cuirrent Needs*, Refugee Policy Group, 1988.

Appendix B

Directories

Immigration and Naturalization Service Directory

Regional Offices

Eastern Region

Stanley McKinley
Reginal Commissioner
Federal Building
Burlington, VT 05401
(802) 951-6201
FAX (802) 832-6266

Northern Region

Gerald Coyle
Regional Commissioner
Federal Building
Twin Cities, MN 55111
(612) 725-3851
FAX (612) 725-3248

Southern Region

Steve Martin
Regional Commissioner
311 N. Stemmons Frwy
Dallas, TX 75207
(214) 767-6001
FAX (214) 729-6025

Western Region

Robert Moschorak
Regional Commissioner
Box 30080
Laguna Niguel, CA 92677
(714) 643-4236
FAX (714) 796-4883

District Offices

Walter Cadman
Garmatz Federal Bldg.
Baltimore, MD 21201
(301) 962-2010

Charles Cobb
JFK Federal Bldg.
Boston, MA 02203
(617) 565-3131

Benedict Ferro
68 Court St.
Buffalo, NY 14202
(716) 846-4741
FAX (716) 437-4440

James Pomeroy
970 Broad St.
Newark, NJ 07102
(201) 645-2298

Charles Sava
26 Federal Plaza
New York, NY 10278
(212) 264-5943

Lyle Karn
601 Market St.
Philadelphia, PA 19101
(215) 597-7305

Eugene Fitzpatrick
741 Warren Ave.
Portland, ME 04101
(207) 780-3352

James Walker
Box 5068
San Juan, PR 00936
(809) 753-4343

William Carroll
4420 N. Fairfax
Arlington, VA 22203
(703) 235-4002
FAX (703) 235-9075

Gary Johnson
701 C St.
Anchorage, AK 99513
(907) 271-5029

A.D. Moyer
219 S. Dearborn St.
Chicago, IL 60604
(312) 353-7300
FAX (312) 888-3644

Robert Brown
1240 E. 9th St.
Cleveland, OH 44199
(216) 522-4766

Donald Russell
1961 Stout St.
Denver, CO 80294
(303) 844-4801

James Montgomery
333 Mt. Elliott St.
Detroit, MI 48207
(313) 226-3250

Marvin Mohrman
301 S. Park
Helena, MT 59626
(406) 449-5288

Ronald Sanders
9747 N. Conant
Kansas City, MO 64153
(816) 891-9314

James Cole
106 S. 15th St.
Omaha, NE 68102
(402) 221-4653

David Beebe
511 NW Broadwat
Portland, OR 97209
(503) 221-2155

Tom Schilgen
180 E. Kellog Blvd.
St. Paul, MN 55101
(612) 290-3793

Richard Smith
815 Airport Way S.
Seattle, WA 98134
(206) 442-5950
FAX (206) 399-1464

Tom Fischer
50 Spring St.
Atlanta, GA 30303
(404) 331-2788
FAX (404) 242-7931

Ron Chandler
1100 Commerce St.
Dallas, TX 75242
(214) 767-0514

Al Guigni
700 E. San Antonio
El Paso, TX 79901
(915) 534-6334

Omar Seweel
2102 Teege Ave.
Harlingen, TX 78550
(512) 427-8592
FAX (512) 423-7147

Ronald Parra
509 N. Belt
Houston, TX 77060
(713) 847-7950

Perry Rivkind
7880 Biscayne Blvd.
Miami, FL 33138
(305) 536-4787
FAX (305) 751-6986

John Caplinger
701 Loyola Ave.
New Orleans, LA 70113
(504) 589-6521

Richard Casillas
727 E. Durango
San Antonio, TX 78206
(512) 229-6356

Walter Craig
595 Ala Moana Blvd.
Honolulu, HI 96809
(808) 541-1389

Ernest Gustafson
300 N. Los Angeles St.
Los Angeles, CA 90012
(213) 894-2780

Patrick Kane
230 N. First Ave.
Phoenix, AZ 85025
(602) 261-3114

James Turnage
880 Front Street
San Diego, CA 92188
(619) 293-5645

David Ilchert
630 Sansome St,
San Francisco, CA 94111
(415) 556-5711

Foreign District Offices

James Foster
American Embassy
Bangkok, Thailand
APO San Francisco, CA 96346

Diana Pickett
American Embassy
Rome, Italy
APO New York, NY 09794

Ernest Trominski
American Embassy
Mexico City, Mexico
Box 3087
Laredo, TX 78044
(905) 528-6335

Chief Patrol Agents

Eastern Region

William Dickman
231 Grand Island Blvd.
Tonawanda, NY 14150
(716) 846-4101

Wayne Preston
Grand Avenue
Swanton, VT 05488
(902) 868-3229

Border Patrol HQ
Route 1
Houlton, ME 04730
(207) 532-6521

Northern Region

Stephen Williams
1590 H St.
Blaine, WA 98230
(206) 332-8781

Gene Rutledge
10710 Newport Hwy.
Spokane, WA 99208
(509) 456-4626

Norman Mercer
2605 5th Ave. S.
Havre, MT 59501
(406) 265-6781

Donald Worth
2320 S. Washington
Grand Forks, ND 58206
(701) 775-6250

Edwin Earl
333 Mt. Elliot
Detroit, MI 48207
(313) 226-3566

Southern Region

Michael Williams
Border Patrol HQ
El Paso, TX 79925
(915) 541-7850

Hugh Rushton
300 Madrid St.
Marfa, TX 79843
(915) 729-4353

Jose Garza
207 W. Del Mar
Laredo, TX 78041
(512) 723-8197

Silvestre Reyes
2301 S. Main St.
McAllen, TX 78502
(512) 686-5496

William Gibson
Qualia Drive
Del Rio, TX 78840
(512) 774-4681

Jessee Tabor
3819 Patterson
New Orleans, LA 70114
(504) 589-6107

Marshall Metzgar
7201 Pembroke Rd.
Pembroke Pines, FL
33024
(305) 963-9807

Joe Bennett
Box 467 Raney
Aguadilla, PR 00604
(809) 890-5060

Western Region

J.W. Carter
6102 9th St.
Dublin, CA 94568
(415) 828-3770

Dale Cozart
3752 Beyer Blvd.
San Ysidro, CA 92073
(619) 428-7251
FAX (619) 428-7029

Dale Musegades
1111 N. Imperial
El Centro, CA 92243
(619) 357-2441

L. Gene Corder
350 First St.
Yuma, AZ 85364
(602) 726-2587

Ronald Dowdy
1970 W. Ajo Way
Tucson, AZ 85713
(602) 629-6871

Office of the Immigration Judge

William R. Robie
Chief Immigration Judge
5201 Leesburg Pike
Falls Church, VA 22041
(703) 756-6247

Joan Arrowsmith
Office of the Immigration Judge
4420 N. Fairfax Drive
Arlington, VA 22203
(703) 235-9024

Charles Auslander
Office of the Immigration Judge
77 Forsythe St., Rm. 392
Atlanta, GA 30303
(404) 331-4377

John Gossart Jr.
Office of the Immigration Judge
103 S. Gay St., Rm. 316
Baltimore, MD 21202
(301) 962-3092

Star Pacitto
Office of the Immigration Judge
JFK Federal Bldg., Rm. 510-A
Boston, MA 02203
(617) 565-3083

Patricia Baker
Office of the Immigration Judge
219 S. Dearborn St., Rm. 423
Chicago, IL 60604
(312) 353-7313

Thomas Hetrick
Office of the Immigration Judge
1100 Commerce St., Rm. 2C12
Dallas, TX 75242
(214) 767-1814

Jesse Sellers
Office of the Immigration Judge
1961 Stout St., Rm. 1708
Denver, CO 80202
(303) 844-5815

Brent Perkins
Office of the Immigration Judge
1115 N. Imperial Ave.
El Centro, CA 92243
(619) 353-2860

George Spreyne
Office of the Immigration Judge
511 E. San Angelo
El Paso, TX 79901
(915) 534-6513

Howard Schtsam
Office of the Immigration Judge
222 E. Van Buren, Suite 600
Harlingen, TX 78550
(512) 427-8582

Brenda Cook
Office of the Immigration Judge
2320 La Branch St., Rm. 2235
Houston, TX 77004
(713) 750-1870

Evelyn Diaz Brown
Office of the Immigration Judge
Box 711
Los Angeles, CA 90053
(213) 894-2811

Brian Karth
Office of the Immigration Judge
7880 Biscayne Blvd., 8th Fl.
Miami, FL 33138
(305) 536-5008

Keith Williams
Krome North Processing Cntr.
Box 160327
Snapper Creek Station
Miami, FL 33116
(305) 552-1844

Thomas Bonita
Office of the Immigration Judge
970 Broad St.
Newark, NJ 07102
(201) 645-3524

Anthony DeGaeto
Office of the Immigration Judge
26 Federal Plaza, Rm. 13130
New York, NY 10278
(212) 264-5958

Howard Cohen
Office of the Immigration Judge
201 Varick St., Rm. 350
New York, NY 10014
(212) 620-3243

Edwin Hughes
Office of the Immigration Judge
211 Highway 165 South
Oakdale, LA 71463
(318) 335-0757

John Zastrow
Office of the Immigration Judge
230 N. First Ave.
Phoenix, AZ 85025
(602) 261-4233

Antoinette Bonacci
Office of the Immigration Judge
727 E. Durango Blvd.
San Antonio, TX 78206
(512) 229-6637

John Williams
Office of the Immigration Judge
950 Sixth Ave.
San Diego, CA 92101
(619) 557-6052

Bernard Hornbach
Office of the Immigration Judge
Box 2326
San Francisco, CA 94126
(415) 556-1560

William Nail, Jr.
Office of the Immigration Judge
1000 Second Ave., Suite 3150
Seattle, WA 98104
(206) 442-5953

United Nations High Commissioner for Refugees

Headquarters

UNHCR
P.O. Box 2500
CH-1211 Geneva 2 Dépôt
Switzerland

Europe

Austria: UNHCR Branch Office,
P.O. Box 550, 1400 Vienna.

Belgium: UNHCR Branch Office,
11a, rue Van Eyck, 1050 Brussels.

Cyprus: Office of the UNHCR
Chief of Mission, P.O. Box 1642,
Nicosia.

France: UNHCR Branch Office,
159, avenue Charles-de-Gaulle,
92521 Neuilly-sur-Seine.

Germany, Fed. Republic of:
UNHCR Branch Office,
Rheinallee 6, 5300 Bonn 2.
UNHCR Sub-Office,
Postfach 1129, 8502 Zirndorf 1.

Greece: UNHCR Branch Office,
59, Skoufa Street, Athens.

Italy: UNHCR Branch Office,
19, Via Caroncini, 00197 Rome.

Luxembourg: Office of the UNHCR
Correspondent, 34, rue de Crécey,
Luxembourg.

The Netherlands: UNHCR Branch
Office, Stadhouderslaan 28,
2517 HZ The Hague.

Portugal: UNHCR Branch Office,
Rua Latino Coelho 1, Edificio Avis,
Bloco A3-17 Esq., Lisbon.

Spain: UNHCR Branch Office,
P.O. Box 36-121, 28020 Madrid.

Sweden: UNHCR Regional Office,
Styrmansgatan 4, 3rd floor,
11454 Stockholm.

Turkey: UNHCR Branch Office,
17 Abidin Daver Sokak, Cankaya,
Ankara.

United Kingdom:
UNHCR Branch Office,
36, Westminster Palace Gardens,
Artillery Row,
London SWIP IRR.

Yugoslavia: Office of the UNHCR
Honorary Representative,
58 Proleterskih Brigada,
11000 Belgrade.

Americas

Argentina: UNHCR Regional Office,
Bartolomé Mitre 699, 8 Piso,
1357 Capital, Buenos Aires.

Belize: UNHCR Sub-Office,
Belmopan.

Brazil: UNHCR Sub-Office,
P.O. Box 02-0052, CEP 7000 Brasilia.

Canada: UNHCR Branch Office,
280, Albert Street, Suite 401,
Ottawa, Ontario K1P 5G8.

Chile: UNHCR Sub-Office,
c/o UNDP, Casilla 197-D, Santiago.

Costa Rica: UNHCR Regional Office,
Apartado Postal 12, Ferrocarril Pacifico,
1009 San José.

El Salvador:
UNHCR Chargé de Mission,
c/o UNDP, P.O. Box 1114,
San Salvador.

Guatemala:
UNHCR Chargé de Mission,
c/o UNDP, Apartado Postal 23-A,
Guatemala City.

Honduras:
UNHCR Branch Office,
c/o UNDP, P.O. Box 976, Tegucigalpa.
UNHCR Sub-Office, Mocorón
UNHCR Sub-Office, San Marcos.

Mexico:
UNHCR Regional Office,
c/o UNDP, Apartado Postal, 6-719,
06600 Mexico D.F.
UNHCR Sub-Office, Campeche.

Nicaragua: UNHCR
Chargé de Mission, ACNUR
Apartado Postal 5151, Managua.
UNHCR Sub-Office, Puerto Cabezas.

Peru: UNHCR Sub-Office,
Apartado Postal 4480, Lima.

USA: UNHCR Branch Office,
United Nations, Grand Central,
P.O. Box 20, New York, N.Y. 10017.
UNHCR Liaison Office,
1718 Connecticut Avenue, N.W.,
2nd floor, Washington D.C. 20009.

Asia & Oceania

Afghanistan: UNHCR
Chargé de Mission, P.O. Box 3232,
Kabul.

Australia:
UNHCR Regional Office,
G.P.O. Box 1983,
Canberra City A.C.T. 2601.

China:
UNHCR Chargé de Mission,
c/o UNDP, 2, Dongqijie Sanlitun,
Beijing.

Hong Kong: UNHCR
Chief of Mission, P.O. Box 73887,
Kowloon Central Post Office,
Kowloon, Hong Kong.

India: UNHCR
Chargé de Mission, c/o UNDP,
P.O. Box 3059, New Delhi 110003.

Indonesia:
UNHCR Branch Office,
P.O. Box 4505, Jakarta.
UNHCR Sub-Office, P.O. Box 20,
Tanjung Pinang, Riau.

Japan: UNHCR Branch Office,
Shin Aoyama Building Nishikan,
19th Floor, 1-1 Minami Aoyama
1-chome, Minato-ku, Tokyo 107.

Kampuchea: UNHCR
Chargé de Mission, Phnom Penh.

Laos: UNHCR Branch Office in the
Lao People's Democratic Republic,
B.P. 760, Vientiane.

Malaysia:
UNHCR Branch Office,
P.O. Box 10185, 50706 Kuala Lumpur.
UNHCR Sub-Office, P.O. Box 78,
20700 Kuala Trengganu.

Pakistan: Office of the UNHCR
Chief of Mission, P.O. Box 1263,
Islamabad.

UNHCR Sub-Office, P.O. Box 767,
University Post Office, Peshawar.
UNHCR Sub-Office, P.O. Box 30,
Quetta.
UNHCR Sub-Office, P.O. Box 12274,
Karachi 46.
UNHCR Sub-Office, 8-A Ali Block,
New Garden Town, Lahore.

Papua New Guinea:
UNHCR Branch Office,
P.O. Box 631, Port Moresby.

The Philippines:
UNHCR Branch Office,
P.O. Box 828 (MCPO) 1299 Makati,
Metro Manila.

Singapore:
UNHCR Branch Office,
P.O. Box 1403, Maxwell Road Post
Office, Singapore 9028.

Sri Lanka:
UNHCR Branch Office
No. 20 Torrington Avenue,
Colombo 7.

Thailand:
UNHCR Branch Office,
P.O. Box 2-121, Rajdamnern,
Bangkok 10200.

Viet Nam:
UNHCR Branch Office,
257, rue Hoang Thai Hoc, Hanoi.

Africa & Middle East

Algeria:
UNHCR Branch Office,
B.P. 823,
Algiers-Gare.

Angola: UNHCR Branch Office,
C.P. 1342, Luanda.

Bahrain: UNHCR Regional Office,
P.O. Box 10155, Um Al-Hassam.
Manama.

Botswana:
UNHCR Branch Office,
P.O. Box 288, Gaborone.

Burundi: UNHCR Branch Office,
B.P. 307, Bujumbura.

Cameroon, Rep. of:
UNHCR Branch Office,
B.P. 7077, Yaoundé.
UNHCR Sub-Office, B.P. 299,
Garoua.

Central African Republic:
UNHCR Chargé de Mission,
c/o UNDP, B.P. 950,
Bangui.

Djibouti: UNHCR Branch Office,
B.P. 1885, Djibouti.

Egypt: UNHCR Branch Office,
8 Shari Dar el Shifa, Garden City,
P.O. Box 1844, Cairo.

Ethiopia:
UNHCR Regional Liaison
Office, P.O. Box 1076, Addis Ababa.
UNHCR Sub-Office, Asmara.
UNHCR Sub-Office, Aman.
UNHCR Sub-Office, Awasa.
UNHCR Sub-Office, P.O. Box 426,
Dire Dawa.
UNHCR Sub-Office, Gambella.

Iran, Islamic Republic of: UNHCR
Chargé de Mission,
No. 21 Corner of Leyli Alley,
Vanak Street, 19919 Tehran.

Iraq: UNHCR Chargé de Mission,
c/o UNDP, P.O. Box 2048
(Alwiyah), Baghdad.

Israel: Office of the UNHCR
Honorary Correspondent,
P.O. Box 3489, Jerusalem.

Kenya: UNHCR Branch Office,
P.O. Box 43801, Nairobi.

Lebanon: UNHCR Branch Office,
P.O. Box 7332, Beirut.

Lesotho: UNHCR Branch Office,
P.O. Box MS 746, Maseru.

Malawi: UNHCR Branch Office,
P.O. Box 30230, /
City Centre Lilongwe 3.
UNHCR Sub-Office, P.O. Box 2274,
Blantyre.

Morocco: Office of the UNHCR
Honorary Representative, B.P. 13434,
Casablanca-Principale.

Mozambique: UNHCR Branch Office,
P.O. Box 1198, Maputo.
UNHCR Sub-Office, B.P. 375, Tete.

Nigeria: UNHCR
Chargé de Mission,
P.O. Box 53874, Ikoyi, Lagos.

Rwanda: UNHCR Branch Office,
B.P. 867, Kigali.

Saudi Arabia: UNHCR Liaison Office,
c/o UNDP, P.O. Box 558, Riyadh 11421.

Senegal: UNHCR Regional
Office, B.P. 3125, Dakar.

Somalia: UNHCR Branch Office,
P.O. Box 2925, Mogadishu.
UNHCR Sub-Office, Hargeisa.
UNHCR Sub-Office, Belet
Weyne-Hiran.
UNHCR Sub-Office, Qorioley.
UNHCR Sub-Office, Garba Hare.
UNHCR Sub-Office, Luuq.

Sudan: UNHCR Branch Office,
P.O. Box 2560, Khartoum.
UNHCR Sub-Office, El Geneina.
UNHCR Sub-Office, Es Showak.
UNHCR Sub-Office, Juba.
UNHCR Sub-Office, P.O. Box 220,
Port Sudan.

Swaziland: UNHCR Branch Office,
P.O. Box 83, Mbabane.

Tanzania, United Rep. of:
UNHCR Branch Office,
P.O. Box 2666, Dar-es-Salaam.
UNHCR Sub-Office,
P.O. Box 1052, Kigoma.
UNHCR Sub-Office, Songea.

Tunisia: Office of the UNHCR
Honorary Representative, B.P. 220,
Tunis.

Uganda: UNHCR Branch Office,
P.O. Box 3813, Kampala.
UNHCR Sub-Office, Arua.

Yemen Arab Republic: UNHCR
Chargé de Mission, P.O. Box 12093,
Sana'a.

Zaire: UNHCR Regional Office,
B.P. 7248, Kinshasa.
UNHCR Sub-Office,
B.P. 381, Lubumbashi.

Zambia: UNHCR Branch Office,
P.O. Box 32542, Lusaka.

Zimbabwe: UNHCR Branch Office,
P.O. Box 4565, Harare.

Appendix C

Documents

Glossary

Acquired Citizenship—Citizenship conferred at birth on children born abroad to a U.S. citizen parent(s). Data for a fiscal year cover the number of certificates of citizenship issued during the year, regardless of when citizenship was acquired. The data are not necessarily a complete accounting of individuals who have acquired citizenship, since only those individuals who acquired citizenship and subsequently requested and were issued a certificate of citizenship from the Immigration and Naturalization Service are included in the data.

Adjustment to Immigrant Status—Procedure allowing certain aliens already in the United States to apply for immigrant status. Aliens admitted to the United States in a nonimmigrant or other capacity may have their status changed to that of lawful permanent resident if they are eligible to receive an immigrant visa as a permanent resident and an immigrant visa is immediately available. In such cases, the alien is counted as an immigrant as of the date of adjustment, even though the alien may have been in the United States for an extended period of time.

Agricultural Workers—As a nonimmigrant class of admission, an alien coming temporarily to the United States to perform agricultural labor or services, as defined by the Secretary of Labor. This nonimmigrant category was established as a separate class of admission by the Immigration Reform and Control Act of 1986.

Alien—Any person not a citizen or national of the United States.

Alien Address Report Program—A now-defunct annual registration program for aliens. Until Public Law 97-116 (Act of 12/29/81) eliminated the stipulation, all aliens in the United States were required to register with the Immigration and Naturalization Service each January. Nationality and state of residence data were compiled annually on the alien population reporting under the program. The last year for which data are available is 1980.

Amerasian Act—Public Law 97-359 (Act of 10/22/82) provides for the immigration to the United States of certain Amerasian children. In order to qualify for benefits under this law, an alien must have been born in Cambodia, Korea, Laos, Thailand, or Vietnam after December 31, 1950 and before October 22, 1982 and have been fathered by a U.S. citizen.

Apprehension—The arrest of a deportable alien by the Immigration and Naturalization Service. Each apprehension of the same alien in a fiscal year is counted separately.

Area Control—Enforcement operations conducted by the Immigration and Naturalization Service's Investigations Division to locate and apprehend aliens illegally in the United States. Area Control surveys focus on places of employment where illegal aliens are concentrated.

Asylee—An alien in the United States or at a port of entry unable or unwilling to return to his or her country of nationality, or to seek the protection of that country because of persecution or a well-founded fear of persecution. Persecution or the fear thereof may be based on the alien's race, religion, nationality, membership in a particular social group, or political opinion. For persons with no nationality, the country of nationality is considered to be the country in which the alien last habitually resided. Asylees are eligible to adjust to lawful permanent resident status after one year of continuous presence in the United States. These immigrants are exempt from the worldwide numerical limitation of 270,000; however, the Immigration and Nationality Act stipulates that only 5,000 asylees can adjust per fiscal year.

Beneficiaries—Those aliens who receive immigration benefits from petitions filed with the U.S. Immigration and Naturalization Service. Beneficiaries generally derive privilege or status as a result of their relationship (including that of employer-employee) to a U.S. citizen or lawful permanent resident.

Border Crosser—An alien or citizen resident of the United States reentering the country after an absence of less than six months in Canada or Mexico, *or* a nonresident alien entering the United States across the Canadian border for stays of no more that six months or across the Mexican border for stays of no more than 72 hours, *or* a U.S. citizen residing in Canada or Mexico who enters the United States frequently for business or pleasure, *or* an individual entering the United States on any flight originating in Canada or Mexico.

Border Patrol Sector—Any one of 22 geographic areas into which the United States is divided for the Immigration and Naturalization Service's Border Patrol activities. Of the 22 sectors, all but 3 are located along the northern and southern borders of the United States.

Business Nonimmigrant—An alien coming temporarily to the United States to engage in commercial transactions which do not involve gainful employment in the United States, i.e., engaged in international commerce on behalf of a foreign firm, not employed in the U.S. labor market, and receives no salary from U.S. sources.

Certificate of Citizenship—Identity document proving U.S. citizenship. Certificates of citizenship are issued to derivative citizens and to persons who acquired U.S. citizenship (see definitions for Acquired and Derivative Citizenship).

Child—An unmarried person under 21 years of age who is: a legitimate child; a stepchild provided that the child was *under 18 years of age* at the time that the marriage creating the stepchild status occurred; a legitimated child provided that the child was legitimate while in the legal custody of the legitimating parent; a child adopted while *under 16 years of age* who has resided since adoption in the legal custody of the adopting parents for at least *2 years*; or an orphan, *under 16 years of age*, who has been adopted abroad by a U.S. citizen or has an immediate-relative visa petition submitted in his/her behalf and is coming to the United States for adoption by a U.S. citizen.

Conditional Immigrant—See Immigration Marriage Fraud Amendments of 1986.

Country of Former Allegiance—The previous country of citizenship of a naturalized U.S. citizen or of a person who derived U.S. citizenship.

Country of Last Residence—The country in which the alien habitually resided prior to entering the United States.

Crewman—A foreign national serving in any capacity on board a vessel or aircraft. Crewmen are admitted for twenty-nine days, with no extensions. Crewmen required to depart on the same vessel on which they arrived are classified as D-1s. Crewmen who depart on a vessel different than the one on which they arrived are classified as D-2s. Although these aliens are technically nonimmigrants, crewmen are not included in nonimmigrant admission data.

Crewman Technical (or Nonwillful) Violator—Any crewman who through no fault of his or her own remains in the United States more than 29 days (e.g., a crewman hospitalized beyond the 29-day admission period).

Cuban/Haitian Entrant—Status accorded 1) Cubans who entered the United States illegally between April 15, 1980 and October 10, 1980 and 2) Haitians who entered the country illegally before January 1, 1981. Cubans and Haitians meeting these criteria who have continuously resided in the United States since before January 1, 1982 may adjust to permanent resident status under a provision of the Immigration Control and Reform Act of 1986.

Deferred Inspection—See Parolee.

Departure Under Safeguards—The departure of an illegal alien whose departure from the United States is physically observed by an Immigration and Naturalization Service official.

Dependent—Spouse, unmarried dependent child under 21 years of age, unmarried dependent child under 25 years of age who is in full-time attendance at a postsecondary educational institution, or unmarried child who is physically or mentally disabled.

Deportable Alien—An alien in the United States subject to any of the 19 grounds of deportation specified in the Immigration and Nationality Act. This includes any alien illegally in the United States, regardless of whether the alien entered the country illegally or entered legally but subsequently violated the terms of his or her visa.

Deportation—The formal removal of an alien from the United States when the presence of that alien is deemed inconsistent with the public welfare. Deportation is ordered by an immigration judge without any punishment being imposed or contemplated. Data for a fiscal year cover the deportations verified during that fiscal year. Airlines, ship companies, or port officials provide the Immigration and Naturalization Service with the departure data on aliens who are deported.

Derivative Citizenship—Citizenship conveyed to children through the naturalization of parents or, under certain circumstances, to spouses of citizens at or during marriage or to foreign-born children adopted by U.S. citizen parents, provided certain conditions are met. Data for a fiscal year cover the number of certificates of U.S. citizenship issued during the year, regardless of when citizenship was derived. The data are not necessarily a complete accounting of individuals who have derived citizenship, since only those individuals who derived citizenship, requested, and were issued a certificate of citizenship from the Immigration and Naturalization Service are covered by the data.

District—Any one of thirty-three geographic areas into which the United States and its territories are divided for the Immigration and Naturalization Service's field operations or one of three overseas offices located in Rome, Bangkok, or Mexico City. Operations are supervised by a district director located at a district office within the district's geographic boundaries.

Employer Sanctions—The employer sanctions provision of the Immigration Reform and Control Act of 1986 prohibits employers from hiring, recruiting, or referring for a fee aliens known to be unauthorized to work in the United States. Violators of the law are subject to a series of civil fines or criminal penalties when there is a pattern or practice of violations.

Exchange Visitor—An alien coming temporarily to the United States as a participant in a program approved by the Secretary of State for the purpose of teaching, instructing or lecturing, studying, observing, conducting research, consulting, demonstrating special skills, or receiving training.

Exclusion—The formal denial of an alien's entry into the United States. The exclusion of the alien is made by an immigration judge after an exclusion hearing. Data for a fiscal year cover the exclusions verified during that fiscal year. Airlines, ship companies, or port officials provide the Immigration and Naturalization Service with the departure data on aliens who are excluded.

Exempt from Numerical Limitations—Those aliens accorded lawful permanent residence who are exempt from the provisions of the preference system set forth in immigration law. Exempt categories include immediate relatives of U.S. citizens, refugees, special immigrants, and certain other groups of immigrants.

Fiance(ee) of U.S. Citizen—A nonimmigrant alien coming to the United States to conclude a valid marriage with a U.S. citizen within ninety days after entry.

Files Control Office—An Immigration and Naturalization Service field office — either a district (including INS overseas offices) or a suboffice of that district — where alien case files are maintained and controlled.

Fiscal Year—Currently, the twelve-month period beginning October 1 and ending September 30. Historically, until 1831 and from 1843-49, the twelve-month period ending September 30 of the respective year; from 1832-42 and 1850-67, ending December 31 of the respective year; from 1868-1976, ending June 30 of the respective year. The transition quarter (TQ) for 1976 covers the three-month period, July-September 1976.

Foreign Government Official—As a nonimmigrant class of admission, an alien coming temporarily to the United States who has been accredited by a foreign government to function as an ambassador, public minister, career diplomatic or consular officer, other accredited official, or an attendant, servant or personal employee of an accredited official, and all above aliens' spouses and unmarried minor (or dependent) children.

Foreign Information Media Representative—As a nonimmigrant class of admission, an alien coming temporarily to the United States as a bona fide representative of foreign press, radio, film, or other foreign information media and the alien's spouse and unmarried minor (or dependent) children.

Foreign Medical School Graduate—An immigrant who has graduated from a medical school or has qualified to practice medicine in a foreign state, who was licensed and practicing medicine on January 9, 1978, and who entered the United States as a nonimmigrant on a temporary worker or exchange visitor visa before January 10, 1978. The alien must meet the requirements set forth in Public Law 97-116 (Act of 12/29/81) in order to qualify for this immigrant classification. These immigrants and their spouses and children are exempt from the worldwide numerical limitation of 270,000. However, if the sum of these immigrant classes plus the investor immigrant classes and the numerically restricted classes exceeds the limitations (for a dependency, an independent country, or worldwide) in any fiscal year, the respective limitation of that area is reduced by that excess for the following year.

Foreign State of Chargeability—The independent country to which an immigrant entering under the preference system is accredited. No more than 20,000 immigrant visas may be issued to natives of independent countries in a fiscal year. Dependencies of independent countries cannot exceed 600 of the 20,000 limit. Since these limits are based on visa issuance rather than entries into the United States, and immigrant visas are valid for 4 months, there is not total correspondence between these two occurrences. Chargeability is usually determined by country of birth. Exceptions are made to prevent the separation of family members when the limitation for the country of birth has been met.

General Naturalization Provisions—The basic requirements for naturalization that every applicant must meet, unless a member of a special class. General provisions require an applicant to be at least 18 years of age, a lawful permanent resident with 5 years of continuous residence in the United States, and to have been physically present in the country for half that period.

Geographic Area of Chargeability—Any one of 5 regions — Africa, East Asia, Latin America and the Caribbean, Near East and South Asia, and the U.S.S.R. and Eastern Europe — into which the world is divided for the initial admission of refugees to the United States. Annual consultations between the Executive Branch and the Congress determine the ceiling on the number of refugees that can be admitted to the United States from each area. In fiscal year 1987, an unallocated reserve was incorporated into the admission ceilings, requiring private sector funding.

Hemispheric Ceilings—Statutory limits on immigration to the United States in effect from 1968 to October 1978. Mandated by the Immigration and Nationality Act Amendments of 1965, the ceiling on immigration from the Eastern Hemisphere was set at 170,000, with a per-country limit of 20,000. Immigration from the Western Hemisphere was held to 120,000, without a per-country limit until January 1, 1977. The Western Hemisphere was then subject to a 20,000 per country limit. Effective October 1978, the separate hemisphere limits were abolished in favor of a worldwide limit of 290,000. This limit was lowered to 280,000 for fiscal year 1980, and to 270,000 for fiscal year 1981 and subsequent years, because refugees were no longer subject to these limitations based on the Refugee Act of 1980.

Immediate Relatives—Certain immigrants who because of their close relationship to U.S. citizens are exempt from the numerical limitations imposed on immigration to the United States. Immediate relatives are: spouses of citizens, children (under 21 years of age) of citizens, parents of citizens 21 years of age or older, and orphans adopted by U.S. citizens who are at least 21 years of age.

Immigrant—An alien admitted to the United States as a lawful permanent resident. Immigrants are those persons lawfully accorded the privilege of residing permanently in the United States. They may be issued immigrant visas by the Department of State overseas or adjusted to permanent resident status by the Immigration and Naturalization Service in the United States.

Immigration Marriage Fraud Amendments of 1986—Public Law 99-639 (Act of 11/14/86), which was passed in order to deter immigration-related marriage fraud. Its major provision stipulates that aliens deriving their immigrant status based on a marriage of less than two years are conditional immigrants. To remove their conditional status the immigrants must apply at an Immigration and Naturalization Service office within 90 days after their second-year anniversary of receiving conditional status. If the aliens cannot show that the marriage through which the status was obtained was and is a valid one, their conditional immigrant status is terminated and they become deportable.

Immigration Reform and Control Act (IRCA) of 1986—Public Law 99-603 (Act of 11/6/86), which was passed in order to control and deter illegal immigration to the United States. Its major provisions stipulate legalization of undocumented aliens, legalization of certain agricultural workers, sanctions for employers who knowingly hire undocumented workers, and increased enforcement at U.S. borders.

Indefinite Parolee—See Parolee.

International Representative—As a nonimmigrant class of admission, an alien coming temporarily to the United States as a principal or other accredited representative of a foreign government (whether officially recognized or not recognized by the United States) to an international organization, an international organization officer or employee, and all above aliens' spouses and unmarried minor (or dependent) children.

Intracompany Transferee—An alien, employed by an international firm or corporation, who seeks to enter the United States temporarily in order to continue to work for the same employer, or a subsidiary or affiliate, in a capacity that is primarily managerial, executive, or involves specialized knowledge.

Investor—An immigrant who is present in the United States and who, on or before June 1, 1978, qualified as a nonpreference immigrant because the alien had invested capital (before June 1, 1978) in a business in the United States in which the alien was one of the principal managers, and had applied for adjustment to lawful permanent resident status. These immigrants and their spouses and children are exempt from the worldwide numerical limitation of 270,000. However, if the sum of these immigrant classes plus the foreign medical graduate classes plus the numerically restricted classes exceeds the limitations (for a dependency, an independent country, or worldwide) in any fiscal year, the respective limitation of the area is reduced by that excess for the following year. As a nonimmigrant class of admission, see Treaty Trader or Investor.

IRCA—See Immigration Reform and Control Act of 1986.

Labor Certification—Requirement falling on 1) those persons whose immigration to the United States is based on job skills (third, sixth, and nonpreference immigrant categories) and 2) nonimmigrant temporary workers (H-2s) coming to perform services unavailable in the United States. Labor certification is awarded by the Secretary of Labor when there are insufficient numbers of U.S. workers available to undertake the employment sought by an applicant and when the alien's employment will not have an adverse affect on the wages and working conditions of U.S. workers similarly employed. Determination of labor availability in the United States is made at the time of a visa application and at the location where the applicant wishes to work.

Legalized Aliens—Certain illegal aliens are eligible to apply for temporary resident status under the legalization provision of the Immigration Reform and Control Act of 1986. To be eligible, aliens must have continuously resided in the United States in an unlawful status since January 1, 1982, not be excludable, and have entered the United States either 1) illegally before January 1, 1982 or 2) as temporary visitors before January 1, 1982, with their authorized stay expiring before that date or with the Government's knowledge of their unlawful status before that date. Legalization consists of two stages — temporary and then permanent residency. The one-year application period for temporary residency began on May 5, 1987 and ended May 4, 1988. The application period for permanent residency begins on December 5, 1988 and ends on December 4, 1990. Those granted temporary residence must apply for permanent residence within a one-year period beginning in the 19th month after their initial application. In order to adjust to permanent status, aliens must have had continuous residence in the United States, be admissible as an immigrant, and demonstrate minimal understanding and knowledge of the English language and U.S. history and government.

Median age—The age which divides the population into two equal sized groups, one younger and one older than the median.

Medical and Legal Parolee—See Parolee.

Nationality—The country of a person's citizenship. For nonimmigrant data, citizenship refers to the alien's claimed country of citizenship.

NATO Official—As a nonimmigrant class of admission, an alien coming temporarily to the United States as a member of the armed forces, or as a civilian employed by the armed forces, on assignment with a foreign government signatory to NATO (North Atlantic Treaty Organization), and the alien's spouse and unmarried minor (or dependent) children.

Naturalization—The conferring, by any means, of citizenship upon a person after birth.

Naturalization Court—Any court authorized to award U.S. citizenship. Jurisdiction for naturalization has been conferred upon the following courts: U.S. District Courts of all states, the District of Columbia, and Puerto Rico; the District Courts of Guam and the Virgin Islands; and state courts. Generally, naturalization courts are authorized to award citizenship only to those persons who reside within their territorial jurisdiction.

Naturalization Petition—The form used by a lawful permanent resident to apply for U.S. citizenship. The petition is filed with a naturalization court through the Immigration and Naturalization Service.

New Arrival—A lawful permanent resident alien who enters the United States at a port of entry. The alien is generally required to present an immigrant visa issued outside the United States by a consular officer of the Department of State. Three classes of immigrants, however, need not have an immigrant visa to enter the United States — children born abroad to lawful permanent resident aliens, children born subsequent to the issuance of an immigrant visa to accompanying parents, and American Indians born in Canada.

Nonimmigrant—An alien who seeks temporary entry to the United States for a specific purpose. The alien must have a permanent residence abroad and qualify for the nonimmigrant classification sought. The nonimmigrant classifications are: foreign government officials, visitors for business and for pleasure, aliens in transit through the United States, treaty traders and investors, students, international representatives, temporary workers and trainees, representatives of foreign information media, exchange vistors, fiances(ees) of U.S. citizens, Intracompany transferees, and NATO officials. Most nonimmigrant classes can be accompanied or joined by spouses and unmarried minor (or dependent) children. Although refugees, parolees, withdrawals, and stowaways are considered nonimmigrants upon arrival to the United States, these classes as well as crewmen, are not included in nonimmigrant admission data. See other sections of Glossary for detailed descriptions of classes of nonimmigrant admission.

Nonpreference Category—Nonpreference visas are available to any qualified applicant not entitled to one under the other preferences. Nonpreference numbers have been unavailable since September 1978 because of high demand in the preference categories. An additional 5,000 nonpreference visas are available in fiscal years 1987 and 1988 under a provision of the Immigration Reform and Control Act of 1986. Aliens born in countries from which immigration was adversely affected by the Immigration and Nationality Act Amendments of 1965 (P.L. 89-236) are eligible for the 5,000 visas, which are issued above the worldwide limitation of 270,000.

Occupation—For an alien entering the United States or adjusting without a labor certification, occupation refers to the employment held in the country of last or legal residence or in the United States. For an alien with a labor certification, occupation is the employment for which certification has been issued. Labor certification would be issued to third, sixth, and nonpreference immigrants or to nonimmigrant temporary workers (H-2s) performing labor or services unavailable in the United States.

Occupational Preferences—The third and sixth categories of the immigrant preference system. Third preference allows for the admission of members of the professions, and scientists or artists of exceptional ability. Sixth preference covers skilled or unskilled occupations for which labor is in short supply in the United States.

Orphans—For immigration purposes, a child whose parents have died or disappeared, or who has been abandoned or otherwise separated from both parents. An orphan may also be a child whose sole surviving parent is incapable of providing that child with proper care and who has, in writing, irrevocably released the child for emigration and adoption. In order to qualify as an immediate relative, the orphan must be under the age of sixteen at the time a petition is filed on his or her behalf. To enter the United States, an orphan must have been adopted abroad by a U.S. citizen or be coming to the United States for adoption by a citizen.

Panama Canal Act Immigrants—Three categories of special immigrants established by Public Law 96-70 (Act of 9/27/79): 1) certain former employees of the Panama Canal Company or Canal Zone Government, their spouses and children; 2) certain former employees of the U.S. government in the Panama Canal Zone, their spouses and children; and 3) certain former employees of the Panama Canal Company or Canal Zone Government on April 1, 1979, their spouses and children. The Act provides for admission of a maximum of 15,000 immigrants, at a rate of no more than 5,000 a year. They are not, however, subject to the worldwide limitation.

Parolee—An alien, appearing to be inadmissable to the inspecting officer, allowed to enter the United States under emergency (humanitarian) conditions or when that alien's entry is determined to be in the public interest. Parole does not constitute a formal admission to the United States and confers temporary admission status only, requiring parolees to leave when the conditions supporting their parole cease to exist. Although these aliens are technically considered nonimmigrants upon arrival, parolees are not included in nonimmigrant admission data. Definitions of parolees include:

1) Indefinite parolee—Parole is usually set for a specified period of time according to the conditions of parole. In some cases, as conditions warrant, the period of parole is specified as indefinite.

2) Deferred inspection—Parole may be granted to an alien who appears not to be clearly admissible to the inspecting officer. An appointment will be made for the alien's appearance at another Service office where more information is available and the inspection can be completed.

3) Medical and legal parolee—Parole may be granted to an alien who has a serious medical condition which would make detention or return inappropriate or who is to serve as a witness in legal proceedings or is subject to prosecution in the United States.

Per-Country Limit—The maximum number of immigrant visas that can be issued to any one country in a fiscal year. Natives of independent countries can currently be issued no more than 20,000 visa numbers and natives of their dependencies no more than 600 of that total. The per-country limit does not indicate, however, that a country will be given 20,000 visa numbers each year, just that it cannot receive more than that number. Because of the combined workings of the preference system and per-country limits, most countries do not reach this level of visa issuance.

Port of Entry—Any location in the United States or its territories which is designated as a point of entry for aliens and U.S. citizens. All district and files control offices are also considered ports since they become locations of entry for aliens adjusting to immigrant status.

Preinspection—Complete immigration inspection of airport passengers before departure from a foreign country. No further immigration inspection is required upon arrival in the United States other than submission of INS Form I-94 for nonimmigrant aliens.

Preference System—The six categories among which 270,000 immigrant visa numbers are distributed each year: unmarried sons and daughters (over 21 years of age) of U.S. citizens (20 percent); spouses and unmarried sons and daughters of aliens lawfully admitted for permanent residence (26 percent); members of the professions or persons of exceptional ability in the sciences and arts (10 percent); married sons and daughters of U.S. citizens (10 percent); brothers and sisters of U.S. citizens over 21 years of age (24 percent); and needed skilled or unskilled workers (10 percent). A seventh nonpreference category, historically open to immigrants not entitled to a visa number under one of the six preferences just listed, has had no numbers available since September 1978.

Principal Alien—The alien from whom another alien derives a privilege or status under immigration law or regulations (usually spouses and minor children).

Refugee—Any person who is outside his or her country of nationality who is unable or unwilling to return to that country because of persecution or a well-founded fear of persecution. Persecution or the fear thereof may be based on the alien's race, religion, nationality, membership in a particular social group, or political opinion. People with no nationality must be outside their country of last habitual residence to qualify as a refugee. Refugees are exempt from numerical limitation and are eligible to adjust to lawful permanent residence after one year of continuous presence in the United States. Although these aliens are considered nonimmigrants when initially admitted to the United States, refugees are not included in nonimmigrant admission data.

Refugee Approvals—The number of refugees approved for admission to the United States during a fiscal year. Refugee approvals are made by Immigration and Naturalization Service officers in overseas offices.

Refugee Arrivals—The number of refugees the Immigration and Naturalization Service initially admits to the United States through ports of entry during a fiscal year.

Refugee Authorized Admissions—The maximum number of refugees allowed to enter the United States in a given fiscal year. As set forth in the Refugee Act of 1980 (Public Law 96-212) the annual figure is determined by the President after consultations with Congress.

Refugee Conditional Entrant—An alien who entered the United States or who adjusted to lawful permanent resident status under the seventh preference category of Public Law 89-236 (Act of 10/3/65). Visa numbers for conditional entrants were limited to six percent of the total numerical limitation. The seventh preference was abolished by the Refugee Act of 1980 (P.L. 96-212) and the six percent limitation assigned to second preference. At the same time, the worldwide numerical limit for immigrants was reduced from 290,000 to 270,000 per fiscal year.

Refugee-Parolee—A qualified applicant for conditional entry, between February 1970 and April 1980, whose application for admission to the United States could not be approved because of inadequate numbers of seventh preference visas. As a result, the applicant was paroled into the United States under the parole authority granted the Attorney General.

Region—Any one of four areas of the United States into which the Immigration and Naturalization Service divides jurisdiction for administrative purposes — Eastern Region, Southern Region, Northern Region, and Western Region.

Registry Date—Aliens who have continuously resided in the United States in an unlawful status since January 1, 1972 are eligible to adjust to legal permanent resident status under the registry provision. Before the date was amended by the Immigration Reform and Control Act of 1986, aliens had to have been in the country continuously since June 30, 1948 to qualify.

Relative Preferences—The first, second, fourth, and fifth categories of the immigrant preference system. The first preference allows the entry of unmarried sons and daughters (over 21 years of age) of U.S. citizens. The second preference covers spouses and unmarried sons and daughters of aliens lawfully admitted for permanent residence. The fourth preference allows for the entry of married sons and daughters of U. S. citizens. The fifth preference deals with the brothers and sisters of U.S. citizens, provided such citizens are at least 21 years of age.

Required Departure—The directed departure of an alien from the United States without an order of deportation. The departure may be voluntary or involuntary on the part of the alien, and may or may not have been preceded by a hearing before an immigration judge. Data for a fiscal year cover the required departures verified in that fiscal year. Airlines, ship companies, or port officials provide the Immigration and Naturalization Service with the departure data on aliens required to depart. Detailed required departure data cover only those aliens placed under docket control. The data do not include aliens who are required to depart directly under safeguards, i.e., those aliens who immediately are turned out of the United States. The latter cases are counted for workload purposes and are included in required departure tables 59 and 70.

Silva Immigrants—Immigrants from independent Western Hemisphere countries and their spouses and children who were issued preference numbers under the Silva Program (1977-81). The Silva Program was instituted by court order to provide for the recapture of 144,999 preference visa numbers originally used for Cuban refugee adjustments. Silva numbers, although subject to an overall numerical limitation, were assigned in addition to the annual worldwide ceiling.

Special Agricultural Workers (SAW)—Aliens who have performed labor in perishable agricultural commodities for a specified period of time and are admissible as immigrants may become temporary and then permanent residents under a provision of the Immigration Reform and Control Act of 1986. The 18- month application period began June 1, 1987 and ends November 30, 1988. Up to 350,000 aliens who have worked at least 90 days in each of the 3 years preceding May 1, 1986 are eligible for Group I temporary resident status. Eligible aliens who qualify under this requirement but apply after the 350,000 limit has been met and aliens who performed labor in perishable agricultural commodities for at least 90 days during the year ending May 1, 1986 are eligible for Group II temporary resident status. Adjustment to permanent resident status is essentially automatic for both groups; however, aliens in Group I are eligible on December 1, 1989 and those in Group II are eligible one year later on December 1, 1990.

Special Immigrants—Certain categories of immigrants exempt from numerical limitations on visa issuance: persons who lost citizenship by marriage; persons who lost citizenship by serving in foreign armed forces; ministers of religion, their spouses and children; certain employees and former employees of the U.S. Government abroad, their spouses and children; Panama Canal Act immigrants; certain foreign medical school graduates, their spouses and children; and certain retired employees of international orgainzations, their spouses and children.

Special Naturalization Provisions—Provisions covering special classes of persons who may be naturalized even though they do not meet all the general requirements for naturalization. Such special provisions allow: 1) wives or husbands of U.S. citizens to be naturalized in three years instead of the prescribed five years; 2) a surviving spouse of a U.S. citizen who served in the armed forces to file in any naturalization court instead of where he/she resides; 3) children of U.S. citizen parents to be naturalized without meeting the literacy or government-knowledge requirements or taking the oath, if too young to understand the meaning. Other classes of persons who may qualify for special consideration are former U.S. citizens, servicemen, seamen, and employees of organizations promoting U.S. interests abroad.

Stateless—Having no nationality.

Stowaway—An alien coming to the United States surreptitiously on an airplane or vessel without legal status of admission who, therefore, is subject to denial of formal admission and return to the point of embarkation by the transportation carrier.

Student—As a nonimmigrant class of admission, an alien coming temporarily to the United States to pursue a full course of study in an approved program in either an academic (college, university, seminary, conservatory, academic high school, elementary school, other institution, or language training program) or a vocational or other recognized nonacademic institution.

Subject to Numerical Limitations—Condition imposed on all immigration to the United States, except for the immediate relatives of U.S. citizens and certain special immigrants. The number of aliens accorded lawful permanent residence under the provisions of the preference system must not exceed 270,000 in any fiscal year. The preference system provides for the admission of relatives of citizens (other than immediate relatives), immediate relatives of lawful permanent resident aliens, aliens in specified occupations, as well as other immigrants.

Suspension of Deportation—A discretionary benefit adjusting an alien's status from that of deportable alien to one lawfully admitted for permanent residence. Application for suspension of deportation is made during the course of a deportation hearing before an immigration judge.

Temporary Worker—Temporary workers consist of three categories of nonimmigrant alien workers: 1) aliens of distinguished merit and ability coming temporarily to the United States to perform services of an exceptional nature; 2) aliens coming to the United States to perform temporary sevices or labor, if unemployed persons capable of performing the service or labor cannot be found in the United States (see also Agricultural Workers); and 3) aliens coming temporarily to the United States as trainees, other than to receive graduate medical education or training.

Transit Alien—An alien in immediate and continuous transit through the United States, with or without a visa, including 1) aliens who qualify as persons entitled to pass in transit to and from the United Nations Headquarters District and foreign countries and 2) foreign government officials and their spouses and unmarried minor (or dependent) children in transit.

Transition Quarter—The three-month period—July 1 through September 30, 1976 — between fiscal year 1976 and fiscal year 1977. At that time, the fiscal year definition shifted from July 1 - June 30 to October 1 - September 30.

Transit Without Visa (TWOV)—An alien traveling without a nonimmigrant visa under section 238 of the immigration law.

Treaty Trader or Investor—As a nonimmigrant class of admission, an alien coming temporarily to the United States, under the provisions of a treaty of commerce and navigation between the United States and the foreign state of such alien, to carry on substantial trade or to direct the operations of an enterprise in which he has invested a substantial amount of capital, and the alien's spouse and unmarried minor (or dependent) children.

Unmarried Alien—An alien, who is not married at the time an application is filed.

Virgin Islands Adjustment Act—Public Law 97-271 (Act of 9/30/82) provides for the adjustment to lawful permanent resident status of certain nonimmigrants who entered the Virgin Islands as temporary workers or as the spouse or child of such a worker. Aliens who are eligible to adjust under this act must have resided in the Virgin Islands since June 30, 1975.

Withdrawal—An alien's voluntary removal of an application for admission to the United States in lieu of an exclusion hearing before an immigration judge. Although these aliens are technically considered nonimmigrants when applying for entry, withdrawals are not included in the nonimmigrant admission data.

Worldwide Ceiling—The numerical limit imposed on immigrant visa issuance worldwide beginning in fiscal year 1979. The current ceiling totals 270,000 visa numbers. Prior to enactment of Public Law 96-212 on March 17, 1980, the worldwide ceiling was 290,000. The ceiling in fiscal year 1980 was 280,000.

Source: INS *Statistical Yearbook*

U.S. Visa Symbols

The following symbols are used in issuing visas to immigrants and nonimmigrants proceeding to the United States. Unless otherwise stated, the section of law cited refers to the Immigration and Nationality Act, as amended. (66 Stat. 163, 8 U.S.C. 1101; 79 Stat. 911; 90 Stat. 2703.)

Immediate Relatives

Visa Symbol	Class	Section of Law
IR-1	Spouse of U.S. citizen	201(b)
IR-2	Child of U.S. citizen	201(b)
IR-3	Orphan adopted abroad by U.S. citizen	201(b)
IR-4	Orphan to be adopted in the United States by U.S. citizen	201(b)
IR-5	Parent of U.S. citizen at least 21 years of age	201(b)
CR-1	Spouse of U.S. citizen (conditional status)	201(b) & 216
CR-2	Child of U.S. citizen (conditional status)	201(b) & 216
VI-5	Parent of U.S. citizen who acquired permanent resident status under the Virgin Islands Nonimmigrant Alien Adjustment Act	201(b) & Sec. 2 of the Virgin Islands Nonimmigrant Alien Adjustment Act (P.L. 97-271)

Special K Classes

Visa Symbol	Class	Section of Law
K-21	Beneficiary of 2d preference petition filed prior to July 1, 1961	25(a), Act of Sept. 26, 1961
K-22	Beneficiary of 3d preference petition filed prior to July 1, 1961	Do.
K-23	Beneficiary of 1st preference petition filed prior to April 1,1962	2, Act of Oct. 24, 1962
K-24	Spouse or child of alien classified K-23	Do.
K-25	Beneficiary of 4th preference petition filed prior to January 1, 1962, who is registered prior to March 31, 1954	1, Act of Oct. 24, 1962
K-26	Spouse or child of alien classified K-25	Do.

Special Immigrants

Visa Symbol	Class	Section of Law
SB-1	Returning resident	101(a)(27)(A)
SC-1	Person who lost U.S. citizenship by marriage	101(a)(27)(B) & 324(a)
SC-2	Person who lost U.S. citizenship by serving in foreign armed forces	101(a)(27)(B) & 327
SD-1	Minister of religion	101(a)(27)(C)
SD-2	Spouse of alien classified SD-1	101(a)(27)(C)
SD-3	Child of alien classified SD-1	101(a)(27)(C)
SE-1	Certain employees or former employees of the U.S. Government abroad	101(a)(27)(D)
SE-2	Accompanying spouse of alien classified SE-1	101(a)(27)(D)
SE-3	Accompanying child of alien classified SE-1	101(a)(27)(D)
SF-1	Certain former employees of the Panama Canal Company or Canal Zone Government	101(a)(27)(E)
SF-2	Accompanying spouse or child of alien classified SF-1	101(a)(27)(E)
SG-1	Certain former employees of the U.S. Government in the Panama Canal Zone	101(a)(27)(F)
SG-2	Accompanying spouse or child of alien classified SG-1	101(a)(27)(F)
SH-1	Certain former employees of the Panama Canal Company or Canal Zone Government on April 1, 1979	101(a)(27)(G)
SH-2	Accompanying spouse or child of alien classified SH-1	101(a)(27)(G)
SJ-2	Accompanying spouse or child of an alien classified SJ (certain foreign medical graduates)	101(a)(27)(H)
SK-1	Certain retired international organization employees	101(a)(27)(I)(iii)
SK-2	Spouse of alien classified SK-1	101(a)(27)(I)(iv)
SK-3	Certain unmarried sons or daughters of international organization employees	101(a)(27)(I)(i)
SK-4	Certain surviving spouses of deceased international organization employees	101(a)(27)(I)(ii)

Visa Symbol		Class	Section of Law
P1-1	First preference:	Unmarried son or daughter of U.S. citizen	203(a)(1)
P1-2	First preference:	Child of alien classified P1-1	203(a)(8)
P2-1	Second preference:	Spouse of alien resident	203(a)(2)
P2-2	Second preference:	Unmarried son or daughter of alien resident	203(a)(2)
P2-3	Second preference:	Child of alien classified P2-1 or P2-2	203(a)(8)
P3-1	Third preference:	Professional, scientist, or artist	203(a)(3)
P3-2	Third preference:	Spouse of alien classified P3-1	203(a)(8)
P3-3	Third preference:	Child of alien classified P3-1	203(a)(8)
P4-1	Fourth preference:	Married son or daughter of U.S. citizen	203(a)(4)
P4-2	Fourth preference:	Spouse of alien classified P4-1	203(a)(8)
P4-3	Fourth preference:	Child of alien classified P4-1	203(a)(8)
P5-1	Fifth preference:	Brother or sister of U.S. citizen over 21 years of age	203(a)(5)
P5-2	Fifth preference:	Spouse of alien classified P5-1	203(a)(8)
P5-3	Fifth preference:	Child of alien classified P5-1	203(a)(8)
P6-1	Sixth preference:	Needed skilled or unskilled worker	203(a)(6)
P6-2	Sixth preference:	Spouse of alien classified P6-1	203(a)(8)
P6-3	Sixth preference:	Child of alien classified P6-1	203(a)(8)
C2-1	Second preference:	Spouse of alien resident (conditional)	203(a)(2) & 216
C2-2	Second preference:	Unmarried son or daughter of alien resident (conditional)	203(a)(2) & 216
C2-3	Second preference:	Child of alien, classified C2-1 or C2-2 (conditional)	203(a)(8) & 216
C4-1	Fourth preference:	Married son or daughter of U.S. citizen (conditional)	203(a)(4) & 216
C4-2	Fourth preference:	Spouse of alien classified C4-1 (conditional)	203(a)(8) & 216
C4-3	Fourth preference:	Child of alien classified C4-1 (conditional)	203(a)(8) & 216

Nonpreference

NP-1	Nonpreference immigrant	203(a)(7)
NP-5	Nonpreference immigrant under Section 314 of P.L. 99-603	203(a)(7) & Sec. 314 of P.L. 99-603

Special Agricultural Workers

S1W	Special Agricultural Worker Group 1	210(a)(2)(A)
S2W	Special Agricultural Worker Group 2	210(a)(2)(B)

Nonimmigrants

A-1	Ambassador, public minister, career diplomat or consular officer, and immediate family	101(a)(15)(A)(i)
A-2	Other foreign government official or employee, and immediate family	101(a)(15)(A)(ii)
A-3	Attendant, servant, or personal employee of A-1 or A-2, and immediate family	101(a)(15)(A)(iii)
B-1	Temporary visitor for business	101(a)(15)(B)
B-2	Temporary visitor for pleasure	101(a)(15)(B)
B-1/B-2	Temporary visitor for business and pleasure	101(a)(15)(B)
C-1	Alien in transit	101(a)(15)(C)
C-2	Alien in transit to United Nations Headquarters district under Section 11(3), (4), or (5) of the Headquarters Agreement.	101(a)(15)(C)
C-3	Foreign government official, immediate family, attendant, servant or personal employee, in transit	212(d)(8)
D	Crewmember (sea or air)	101(a)(15)(D)
E-1	Treaty trader, spouse and children	101(a)(15)(E)(i)
E-2	Treaty investor, spouse and children	101(a)(15)(E)(ii)
F-1	Student	101(a)(15)(F)(i)
F-2	Spouse or child of student	101(a)(15)(F)(ii)
G-1	Principal resident representative of recognized foreign member government to international organization, staff, and immediate family	101(a)(15)(G)(i)
G-2	Other representative of recognized foreign member government to international organization, and immediate family	101(a)(15)(G)(ii)
G-3	Representative of nonrecognized or nonmember foreign government to international organization, and immediate family	101(a)(15)(G)(iii)
G-4	International organization officer or employee, and immediate family	101(a)(15)(G)(iv)
G-5	Attendant, servant, or personal employee of G-1 through G-4 and immediate family	101(a)(15)(G)(v)

Visa Symbol	Class	Section of Law
H-1	Temporary worker of distinguished merit and ability	101(a)(15)(H)(i)
H-2	Temporary worker performing services unavailable in the United States	101(a)(15)(H)(ii)
H-2A	Temporary agricultural workers performing services unavailable in the United States (Petitions filed on or after June 1, 1987)	101(a)(15)(H)(ii)(a)
H-2B	Other temporary workers performing services unavailable in the United States (Petitions filed on or after June 1, 1987)	101(a)(15)(H)(ii)(b)
H-3	Trainee	101(a)(15)(H)(iii)
H-4	Spouse or child of alien classified H-1, H-2 or H-3	101(a)(15)(H)(iv)
I	Representative of foreign information media, spouse and children	101(a)(15)(I)
J-1	Exchange visitor	101(a)(15)(J)
J-2	Spouse or child of exchange visitor	101(a)(15)(J)
K-1	Fiance(e) of United States citizen	101(a)(15)(K)
K-2	Child of fiance(e) of U.S. citizen	101(a)(15)(K)
L-1	Intracompany transferee (executive, managerial, and specialized personnel continuing employment with international firm or corporation)	101(a)(15)(L)
L-2	Spouse or child of intracompany transferee	101(a)(15)(L)
M-1	Vocational student or other nonacademic student	101(a)(15)(M)
M-2	Spouse or Child of an alien classified M-1	101(a)(15)(M)
N-8	Parent of an alien classified SK-3 special immigrant	101(a)(15)(N)(i)
N-9	Child of N-8 or of an SK-1, SK-2 or SK-4 special immigrant	101(a)(15)(N)(ii)

NATO-1	Principal permanent representative of member state to NATO (including any of its subsidiary bodies) resident in the U.S. and resident members of official staff; Secretary General, Assistant Secretaries General, and Executive Secretary of NATO; other permanent NATO officials of similar rank, and members of immediate family.	Art. 12, 5 UST 1094 Art. 20, 5 UST 1098
NATO-2	Other representatives of member states to NATO (including any of its subsidiary bodies) including representatives, advisers, and technical experts of delegations, and members of immediate family; dependents of members of a force entering in accordance with the provisions of the NATO Status-of-Forces Agreement or in accordance with provisions of the "Protocol on the Status of International Military Headquarters"; members of such a force if issued visas.	Art. 13, 5 UST 1094; Art. 1, 4 UST 1794 Art. 3, 4 UST 1796
NATO-3	Official clerical staff accompanying a representative of member state to NATO (including any of its subsidiary bodies) and members of immediate family	Art. 14, 5 UST 1096
NATO-4	Officials of NATO (other than those classifiable as NATO-1) and members of immediate family.	Art. 18, 5 UST 1098
NATO-5	Experts, other than officials classifiable under the symbol NATO-4, employed in missions on behalf of NATO, and their dependents.	Art. 21, 5 UST 1100
NATO-6	Members of a civilian component accompanying a force entering in accordance with the provisions of the NATO Status-of-Forces agreement members of a civilian component attached to or employed by an Allied Headquarters under the "Protocol on the Status of International Military Headquarters" set up pursuant to the North Atlantic Treaty, and their dependents.	Art. 1, 4 UST 1794 Art. 3, 5 UST 877
NATO-7	Attendant, servant, or personal employee of NATO-1 through NATO-6 classes, and immediate family.	Arts. 12-20, 5 UST 1094-1098

Note: Pursuant to Articles 3, 12, 13, 14, 18, and 20 of the Agreement on the Status of the North Atlantic Treaty Organization, National Representatives and International Staff, (5 UST 877, 1094), 22 CFR 41.70 provides as follows: Section 41.70 NATO representatives, officials and employees.

(a) (1) An alien shall be classifiable under the symbol NATO-1, NATO-2, NATO-3, NATO-4, or NATO-5 (See Section 41.12 for classes of aliens entitled to classification under each symbol) if he establishes to the satisfaction of the consular officer that he is seeking admission to the United States under the applicable provision of the Agreement on the Status of the North Atlantic Treaty Organization, National Representatives and International Staff, or that he is a member of the immediate family of an alien classified under the symbol NATO-1, NATO-2, NATO-3, NATO-4, or NATO-5.

    (2) Armed services personnel entering the United States in accordance with the provisions of the NATO Status-of-Forces Agreement or in accordance with the provisions of the Protocol on the Status of International Military Headquarters enter the United States under the appropriate treaty waiver of documentary requirements contained in Section 41.5(d) or (e), but if issued visas shall be classifiable under the symbol NATO-2.

    (3) Dependents of armed services personnel referred to in paragraph (a)(2) shall be classifiable under the symbol NATO-2.

(b) An alien member of a civilian component accompanying a force entering in accordance with the provisions of the NATO Status-of-Forces Agreement, and his dependents, or an alien member of a civilian component attached to or employed by an Allied Headquarters under the Protocol on the Status of International Military Headquarters set up pursuant to the North Atlantic Treaty, and his dependents, shall be classificable under the symbol NATO-6.

(c) An alien attendant, servant, or personal employee of an alien classified under the symbol NATO-1, NATO-2, NATO-3, NATO-4, NATO-5, or NATO-6, and the members of the immediate family of such attendant, servant, or personal employee, shall be classifiable under the symbol NATO-7.

Chronology of U.S. Immigration Policy

1875   First federal restriction on immigration prohibits prostitutes and convicts.

1882   First general immigration law enacted which curbs Chinese immigration. Congress excludes convicts, the insane and persons likely to become public charges, and places a head tax on each immigrant.

1891   Ellis Island opens as immigrant processing center.

1903   List of excluded immigrants expands to include polygamists and political radicals.

1917   Congress requires literacy in some language for immigrants and virtually bans all immigration from Asia.

1921   Quotas are established limiting the number of immigrants of each nationality.

1924   Johnson-Reed Act (National Origins Law) sets temporary annual quotas at two percent of the country's U.S. population based on the 1890 Census and establishes immigration limit of 150,000 in any one year from non-Western Hemisphere countries.

1943   Chinese Exclusion Laws repealed.

1952   Immigration and Nationality Act of 1952 (McCarran-Walter) reaffirms national origins system and sets immigration limits.

1965   Immigration and Nationality Act amendments abolish national origins system, and establish preference system and annual ceilings for countries.

1980   Immigration and Nationality Act amended by the passage of the Refugee Act establishing a regular process of refugee admissions and resettlement.

1986   Immigration Reform and Control Act imposes sanctions on employers who hire illegal aliens and grants amnesty to illegal aliens in the U.S. since 1982.

Key Dates in the Immigration Reform and Control Act of 1986

November 6, 1986   President Reagan signs IRCA granting amnesty and providing for employer sanctions for knowingly hiring undocumented immigrants. To be eligible, aliens must have continuously resided in the U.S. in an unlawful status since January 1, 1982.

May 5, 1987   INS began accepting applications for amnesty.

June 1, 1987   Special legalization program for farmworkers (SAW) began.

August 21, 1987   INS began issuing citations for employer's knowingly hiring undocumented workers.

May 4, 1988   Deadline to apply for amnesty.

June 1, 1988   Fines replace citations for hiring undocumented workers.

November 30, 1988   End of application for SAW program.

December 1, 1988   INS begins full enforcement, including agricultural growers.

November 6, 1993   First of the amnesty applicants begin qualifying for U.S. citizenship.

U.S. Refugee and Asylum Programs and Policies: A 1988 Chronology

The following is a chronology of U.S. programs, policy and legislative decisions affecting refugees and asylum seekers during 1988.

January 1   Beginning today, and lasting through February 28, 1989, the government is temporarily prohibited from deporting, excluding, or denying visas to aliens based solely on "beliefs, statements, or associations which, if engaged in by a U.S. citizen in the United States, would be protected under the Constitution." The prohibition is a result of legislation temporarily repealing sections of the McCarren-Walter Act of 1952, which have permitted the government to bar the admission of foreigners on various grounds, including political beliefs, "sexual deviation," polygamy, and insanity.

January 4   The FBI begins reviewing the detention status of 2,100 Cubans at six federal detention facilities to determine each inmate's level of involvement in the rioting and hostage-taking at the federal detention center at Oakdale, Louisiana, and at the Atlanta Federal Penitentiary.

February 1   As of this date, and for the duration of FY 88, federal reimbursement to states for refugee cash and medical assistance costs will only be provided for a refugee's first 24 months in the U.S., rather than 31 months.

March 3   The Office of Refugee Resettlement (ORR) tells state refugee coordinators that in FY 88, there will be a 38 percent cut in funding for state administration of refugee programs. The result, according to state refugee officials, will be the closing of state refugee programs in up to 11 states, the elimination of key services in others, and an overall increase in welfare dependency rates, which had fallen in FY 87.

March 15   By a vote of 88-4, the Senate approves a legal immigration bill that would provide for an annual ceiling of 590,000 immigrant visas, of which 470,000 would be reserved for family immigration and 120,000 for "independent" immigrants. Refugee admissions would not be subject to the immigration ceiling.

March 21   The Department of Justice announces that Polish, Afghan, Ugandan, and Ethiopian nationals who have been protected by extended voluntary departure (EVD), a temporary reprieve from deportation granted by the Attorney General, will be able to adjust their status to that of temporary resident aliens, if they have been present in the United States since July 21, 1984.

April 6   Ambassador Jonathan Moore, the U.S. Coordinator for Refugees, reported to Congress the President's proposal to raise the FY 88 refugee admissions ceiling based on "an unforseen refugee emergency" requiring an additional 15,000 places for refugees from the Soviet Union and Eastern Europe.

April 29   Ruling in a class action suit, *Orantes-Hernandez v. Meese*, a U.S. District Court judge orders the INS to stop employing threats, misrepresentations, subterfuge, or other forms of coercion to induce Salvadorans to accept "voluntary departure" to El Salvador.

May 4
: The INS receives more than 1.5 million legalization applications prior to May 4, the end of the general amnesty registration. Voluntary agency personnel estimate that more than 80 percent of Salvadorans in the U.S. were not eligible for the legalization.

May 24
: The Western Region of INS is ordered by a California federal court judge to release any child under its detention to his parent, guardian, or "other responsible adult party," if the child is otherwise eligible for release on bond or recognizance. The judge stipulates that any minor taken into INS custody must be afforded a hearing to determine probable cause in his arrest and on the need for any restrictions placed on his release.

June 13
: The Cuban-American National Foundation (CANF) signs an agreement with the U.S. government under which CANF will privately sponsor up to 600 refugees for admission to the U.S. this fiscal year, the first group in modern times to sponsor refugee admissions to the U.S. without federal funding.

July 4
: The U.S. abruptly suspends refugee processing out of the Moscow Embassy, which has been the route of entry for almost all Armenians leaving the Soviet Union under the U.S. refugee program. Less than two weeks later, however, the State Department partially reverses its position to allow an additional 400 people to emigrate.

July 27
: INS proposes a revision in asylum procedure allowing immigration judges to limit the scope of evidentiary hearings on certain asylum claims in exclusion or deportation proceedings. If any asylum applicant had "participated in the persecution" of others, committed a "serious crime" in the U.S., or poses a "danger to the security of the U.S.", immigration judges would not need to consider evidence of the applicant's fear of persecution if returned to his home country.

August 14
: An emergency supplemental appropriations bill (P.L. 100-393) is signed into law, which provides an additional $24 million for emergency refugee migration and assistance in FY 88. Of this, $6 covers admission of another 3,000 Soviet refugees in FY 88. The remainder supplements overseas assistance programs, primarily in Africa.

August 24
: ORR reduces the period of eligibility for refugee cash assistance (RCA) and refugee medical assistance (RMA) from 18 months to 12 months.

September 30
: For the first time since 1976, Congress passes all 13 federal budget appropriations bills prior to the start of the new fiscal year. Included is $794,306,000 for refugee assistance overseas, admissions, and domestic resettlement assistance.

October 5
: President Reagan authorizes the admission of up to 94,000 refugees in FY 89, 10,000 of whom would enter the country with either partial or no funding from the government.

October 5
: The House of Representatives passes the Temporary Safe Haven Act of 1988, which would establish criteria by which the Attorney General can grant temporary safe haven

in the U.S. to nationals of countries experiencing armed conflict or other dangerous conditions.

October 13   The Family Support Act of 1988 (P.L. 100-485) is signed into law. Among other provisions, it requires states to provide 12 months of both transitional childcare assistance and Medicaid benefits for most families who leave public assistance rolls as a result of employment.

November 1   President Reagan signs into law the Genocide Convention Implementation Act of 1988, making genocide or attempted genocide a federal crime.

December 8   U.S. Attorney General Thornburgh announces he has expanded his parole authority to admit up to 2,000 Soviet emigres per month from Moscow plus all Soviet emigres in Rome who cannot be admitted to the U.S. as refugees.

December 13   The Reagan Administration announces that it has removed 7,000 refugee admissions numbers from Southeast Asian and Near Eastern regional allocations and transferred them to the Soviet Union, to accomodate growing backlogs in Jewish and Armenian applications.

December 16   Facing a dramatic increase in the number of Nicaraguan and other Central American asylum seekers passing through Harlingen, Texas, INS decides to revise its policy and begin extraordinary measures to ajudicate claims at the Mexican border.

December 24   About 400 Haitians are sent home after being intercepted by the U.S. Coast Guard as they attempted to sail to the U.S.

Source: *Refugee Reports*, January 27, 1989, p. 8-9.

Interfaith Committee for Central American Refugee Protection
Joint Statement of the Interfaith Delegation to South Texas

May 17, 1989

Despite the expenditure of a large sum of money (millions of dollars) by the Immigration and Naturalization Service (INS) during the past sixty days, we saw no convincing evidence that the policy of increased enforcement, detention, and rapid deportation has resulted in any significant decrease in the flow of Central American refugees across the border.

In fact, all indications are that this movement of people began as early as 1981 and has continued at a steady rate. Its ebbs and flows appear to be influenced much more by the level of civil war and political repression in Central America than any policy of the INS. All the current INS policy has succeeded in doing is to remove the refugees and the problem from public view and create serious obstacles to the filing of legitimate asylum claims.

It seems to us that our country has a strong moral responsibility to aid Central American refugees, the overwhelming majority of whom have fled war-like conditions of violence and deprivation. *We are convinced that political asylum alone is not an adequate instrument for protecting the lives of these people.* For this reason we strongly support prompt enactment of the Moakley-DeConcini bill extending voluntary departure status to Salvadorans and Nicaraguans, as an important first step toward resolving this crisis. Moreover, we strongly support the safe haven concept of a temporary protected status for individuals fleeing civil unrest throughout the Central American region.

As to the current policy, we condemn the detention of Central American refugees, men, women and children who are not criminals, as inhumane and as a violation of due process. We echo the call for providing asylum seekers with full information on rights and procedures to apply for asylum and unrestricted access to legal counsel; and for the provision of full due process guarantees in the ajudication of their asylum claims, including the right to appeal. We support reinstatement of an Administration policy allowing Central American asylum seekers to leave the Rio Grande Valley and file their asylum claims in other areas of the country, and to obtain work authorization while their claims are being ajudicated.

We believe that, in the long run, a lasting solution to the continuing flow of Central American refugees across our borders can best be achieved by working for peace and economic stability in Central America.

Member Organizations: American Friends Service Committee; Church World Service Immigration and Refugee Program; Episcopal Migration Ministries; HIAS (Hebrew Immigrant Aid Society); Lutheran Immigration and Refugee Service; Mennonite Central Committee, Immigration and Refugee Program; U.S. Catholic Conference, Migration and Refugee Services; United Church Board for World Ministries.

Jewish Covenant of Sanctuary (1989)

For the past several years the United States has become a place of uncertain refuge for men, women and children who are fleeing for their lives from the vicious and devastating wars in Central America. Many of these refugees have chosen to leave their country only after witnessing the murder of close friends and relatives.

The United Nations has declared these people legitimate refugees of war; by every moral and legal standard, they ought to be received as such by the government of the United States. The 1951 United Nations Convention and the 1967 Protocol Agreements on Refugees - both signed by the United States - established the rights of refugees *not* to be sent back to their countries of origin. Thus far, however, our government has been unwilling to meet its obligations under these agreements. The refugees among us are consequently threatened with the prospect of deportation back to El Salvador and Guatemala, where they face the likelihood of severe reprisals, perhaps including death.

The plight of these refugees powerfully reminds us of our own history. Hundreds of thousands of Jews who could have been saved from Hitler's ovens did not meet the U.S. immigration requirements, nor those of virtually any other land. With all sanctuary denied them, our people were forced to wander as illegal aliens. Their return to Hitler's Europe almost always meant their death. Against this denial of safety there were a few courageous voices - the righteous gentiles - who followed their consciences and provided safe haven.

Our historical experience of the Diaspora has given us a profound appreciation for the exiled and the homeless among all people: black slaves who fled north to freedom, all the immigrants who fled desperate oppression. In their name we now seek to answer the call from our own tradition.

When a stranger sojourns with you in your land, you shall do him no wrong. The stranger who sojourns with you shall be as the native among you, and you shall love him as yourself; for you were strangers in the land of Egypt. LEVITICUS 19:33-34

Give council, grant justice; make your shade like night at the height of noon; hide the outcasts, betray not the fugitive. Let the outcasts of Moab sojourn among you; be a refuge to them from the destroyer. ISAIAH 16:3-4

The words of the Torah, the demands of the prophets, the ethics of the Talmud and the centuries of Jewish response are clear. Therefore we join in covenant to provide sanctuary - support, protection and advocacy - to Central American refugees who request safe haven out of fear of persecution upon return to their homeland. We do this out of concern for the welfare of these refugees, regardless of their official immigrant status. We understand that sanctuary is a serious responsibility for all persons involved. Although we recognize that legal consequences may result from our action, we do not acknowledge that the provision of sanctuary is an illegal act. We enter this covenant as an act of conscience and moral imperative.

Statement on Principles for Legal Immigration Policy

September 13, 1988

The Catholic Church in the United States has long maintained a strong concern for immigrants. That commitment stems directly from the Church's belief in the dignity of labor systematically articulated by Pope Leo XIII in his 1891 encyclical *Rerum Novarum*. Since then a substantial body of church documents, including the encyclicals *Exsul Familia, Mater et Magistra, Pacem in Terris, Octogesima Adveniens, Laborem Exercens* and *Sollicitudo Rei Socialis*, have all affirmed the right of individuals and families to migrate in order to secure work can be viewed as a necessary corollary. The right to migrate for work should never be displaced by the exercise of a nation's sovereign right to control its own borders. Protecting the public interests of our own society and recognizing the right to immigrate are determinations that should be made in the context of the universal common good.

The Church's traditional position was clearly expressed by the Vatican in the 1969 *Instruction on the Pastoral Care of People Who Migrate*:

> Public authorities unjustly deny the rights of human persons if they block or impede emigration or immigration except where grave requirements of the common good, considered objectively, demand it.

Over the years, the Church's position—often balancing the demands of the common good with the right to migrate—has been stated many times by the U.S. bishops in response to changes in immigration policy and law.

Currently, major new proposals to reform the U.S. legal immigration system are under discussion. We recognize that there is a need to reshape our immigration system, but we strongly encourage Congress to engage in extensive, thoughtful and public debate before any new immigration law is enacted.

As a contributor to this debate, the Church draws on her long experience in protecting the rights of immigrants. From that experience we offer the following principles to guide the development of any legal immigration policy.

- First, family reunification must be affirmed as the basic precept driving a just immigration system.

- Second, our fundamental tradition is fair treatment to all nations and their emigrants.

- Third, temporary labor programs should be gradually eliminated. Permanent workers should receive full rights. Those temporary worker categories that are necessary ought to offer full labor market rights.

- Fourth, every effort should be made to discourage illegal immigration by promoting just immigration law.

- Fifth, the endangerment of any nation's valuable human resources must be avoided; this is especially true in the case of developing counties.

Passed unanimously by the Administrative Board of the National Conference of Catholic Bishops on September 13, 1988.

Refugees and Human Rights

Ghassan Arnaout
Director, Division of Refugee Law and Doctrine
United Nations High Commissioner for Refugees

March 2, 1989

The protection of refugees operates within a broader framework of individual rights and the responsibilities of states. These rights and responsibilities have, at their origin, a philosophy recognizing the uniqueness and worth of the individual person and the imperative of preserving life and promoting human development in a just society. Human rights law, which derives from the same origins, is the source of many existing refugee protection principles and structures, and also complements them. Among the fundamental human rights which are at issue in this Commission: the right to life, liberty and security of person, the right not to be subjected to torture or to cruel, inhuman or degrading treatment or punishment, the right not to be subjected to arbitrary arrest, detention or exile, the right to fredom of movement and the right to leave and to return to one's country, are all of particular relevance to the refugee situation. The right not to be discriminated against on the grounds of race, religion, nationality, social origin or political opinion is, of course, at the heart of the refugee issue.

Enjoyment by a refugee of the right to security of person or freedom from torture requires, for example, a right to seek and enjoy asylum. Although millions of refugees worldwide continue to benefit from asylum and are treated in accordance with internationally accepted standards, this essential basic need is increasingly being challenged by many States. This challenge takles many different forms, including outright denial of any refuge; implementations of procedures or mechanisms blocking access to asylum opportunities; *refoulement*, or expulsion of refugees. The closer scrutiny being given by members of this Commission to particular situations where the grant or conditions of asylum are at issue, is both timely and welcome.

The individual's right to leave and to return voluntarily to the country of origin has, over recent years, taken on a higher significance for lasting solutions to refugee problems. We would encourage further discussion to focus not only on the right itself, vitally linked as it is to the concept of asylum, but also on the consequences of return, including the very important aspects of non-discrimination and physical safety.

In another area, the *International Covenant on Civil and Political Rights* is quite specific in the minimum rights it envisages in relation to detention: it must not be arbitrary; it must be in accordance with established legal procedure; it must be followed by court proceedings without delay; and it must be under conditions of humanity and repect for human dignity. The Executive Committee of the High Commissioner's Program reached much the same position. This Committee agreed that detention should be considered an exceptional reposnse in an asylum situation. Moreover, it placed considerable emphasis on detention being under acceptable, humane conditions. Yet the experience of UNHCR is that lengthy periods of detention for refugees, sometimes under conditions which defy basic standards of decency and common humanity, has become a routine occurrence. It occurs in all continents.

UNHCR has documented over past months a depressingly long list of acts of expulsion or forcible return to countries of origin by a number of States receiving asylum-seekers. There have been instances of *refoulement* very recently where the refugees concerned have been executed on return. Increasingly over recent years the security of refugees has been seriously endangered through physical attacks against their person, military and armed attacks against their camps and settlements, militarization of their camps and their forcible recruitment into regular or irregular armed forces.

Direct assaults on refugees are the most dramatic illustration of violation of basic rights leading to major protection problems. There are also, however, problems of serious human dimensions resulting from less obvious curtailing of rights on a daily basis. The 1951 *Convention Relating to the Status of Refugees* contains a number of provisions dealing with juridical status, welfare, social security and employment rights. These provisions in part parallel similar provisions in human rights instruments, including, for example, the *International Covenant on Economic, Social and Cultural Rights*. At the most recent session of UNHCR's Executive Committee, the Commission called on all States hosting refugees to consider ways in which refugee employment might be facilitated and to examine their laws and practices, with a view to identifying and to removing, to the extent possible, existing obstacles to refugee employment.

Much has been said about violations of human rights as a cause of mass exodus of refugees. UNHCR's Executive Committee, at its last session, went further in drawing specific attention to what it described as "the direct relationship between observance of human rights standards, refugee movements and problems of protection." Human rights violations range across the spectrum of the refugee problem. We believe there could be value in the debate on human rights and mass exoduses being broadened to reflect the relevance of human rights issues to all facets of the refugee problem.

For UNHCR, non-governmental agencies provide an invaluable support structure for the promotion of refugee protection. The challenge for all of us in this area is to separate humanitarian and human rights problems from the often complex political situations in which they are generated. Such an approach offers as well the best promise for resolution of outstanding and difficult refugee situations. This has most recently been explicitly recognized by governments participating in ongoing preparations for the May 1989 Conference on Central American Refugees. While UNHCR must be cognisant of the political factors surrounding refugee issues, it nevertheless remains steadfastly humanitarian and non-political in its responses.

Excerpts from a speech by Mr. Ghassan Arnaout before the 45th Session of the United Nations Commission on Human Rights, Geneva, Switzerland on March 2, 1989.

City of Refuge Resolution
Takoma Park, Maryland

October 28, 1985

A. The Situation in El Salvador and Guatemala

WHEREAS   the nations of El Salvador and Guatemala are in the midst of crisis of civil war and gross human rights violations; and

WHEREAS   the United Nations General Assembly has recognized a state of civil war existing in El Salvador for the past five years and has repeatedly deplored the widespread human rights abuses in both countries; and

WHEREAS   respected international human rights organizations continue to report that the fundamental human rights situation is not improving:

a.   in El Salvador the security and armed forces have been repeatedly incriminated in torture, disappearances and murder, resulting in some 50,000 civilian deaths and disappearances since 1979, and the abuses continue to the present; and

b.   in Guatemala an average of 130 suspected and actual opponents of the military dictatorship continue to be slaughtered or disappeared each moth, often in a most brutal manner; and

WHEREAS   a deliberate policy of aerial bombardments, strafings, mortarings and army operations by the Salvadoran government against civilians in opposition-held areas of El Salvador have caused thousands of casualities and forced thousands more to flee El Salvador in 1984 and 1985; for the practices, Americas Watch has concluded, "the government of El Salvador may be fairly charged with committing war crimes"; and

WHEREAS   the military government of Guatemala has systematically instilled a pervasive fear of relocating the rural indigenous population, taking their land, and forcing some 800,000 peasants to participate in so-called "civilian patrols", which actually are organized and controlled by the army; thus, Guatemala has become what human rights observers call "A Nation of Prisoners"; and

B. These Situations Have Produced Countless Refugees

WHEREAS   approximately 800,000 Salvadorans (15% of the country's five milion people) have fled their homeland since 1979, about 500,000 of whom have sought temporary haven in the United States -- including some 80,000 in the metropolitan Washington D.C. area; and some 100,000 Guatemalans have sought temporary refuge in the United States; and

WHEREAS   approximately 20,000 Salvadorans and Guatemalan refugees have sought refuge in Takoma Park and neighboring Maryland counties and are actively contributing to the well-being of our city; and

C. The U.S. Government Sends These Refugees Back to Their War-Torn Homelands Against Their Will

WHEREAS   the U.S. Department of State considers the Salvadorans and Guatemalans in the U.S. to be nothing more than migrants seeking economic advantage in this country, and the Immigration and Naturalization Service (INS) therefore arrests them and deports them to their war-torn homelands; and

WHEREAS   these refugees face the grave risk of persecution and war-related atrocities in the countries they have fled, and numerous cases of murders and disappearances of deportees have been documented; and

D. These Deportations Violate National and International Law

WHEREAS   the U.S. government's forcible repatriation of these refugees at this time violate the following legal and humanitarian norms:

a. *Refugees fleeing persecution*: The U.S. Refugee Act of 1980 and the U.N. Protocol on the Status of Refugees (signed by the U.S. in 1968) allows political asylum for those who have a well-founded fear of persecution upon return to their country;

However, in spite of the widespread persecution in El Salvador and Guatemala, and in spite of a determination by the U.N. High Commissioner for Refugees that *all* Salvadorans who have fled their country since 1979 are *prima facie* refugees of the persecution, the INS in 1984 denied 97.6% of Salvadoran asylum applicants and 99.7% of Guatemalan applicants;

b. *Refugees fleeing civil strife:* The Immigration and Nationality Act allows the Justice Department to temporarily halt repatriations of refugees whose countries are undergoing "civil strife"; this right called "extended voluntary departure" or EVD is currently granted on a country-wide basis to all nationals from Poland, Uganda, Ethiopia, and Afghanistan without their having to show individual fears of persecution;

However, the Justice Department has continually refused to grant EVD to Salvadorans and Guatemalans in spite of Congressional resolutions requesting it, and in spite of the overwhelming evidence of civil strife in those countries;

c. *Refugees fleeing war*: customary international law prohibits the forced repatriation of refugees fleeing war until the war ceases;

However, the U.S. actively deports Salvadorans and Guatemalans while war rages in their countries, this denying them a fundamental internationally recognized right;

d. *Refugees fleeing war-crimes*: The Geneva Conventions of 1949 allow individuals to flee their country to avoid becoming victims of war crimes, and to demand the temporary protection of any other High Contracting Party to the Conventions (both the U.S. and El Salvador are High Contracting Parties);

However, by expelling people to a country that is guilty of war crimes, the U.S. itself may be committing grave breaches of the Geneva Conventions.

E. The American People Are Acting in Opposition to These Unjust Policies

WHEREAS   over 200 U.S. churches, synagogues, and other community organizations have publicly declared themselves sanctuaries for Salvadoran and Guatemalan refugees as a public witness against the morally and legally unjustifiable deportation of those people; and

WHEREAS   the cities of Berkeley, CA; St. Paul, MN; Cambridge, MA; Chicago, IL; Madison, WI; San Jose, CA; and Ithaca, NY in independent actions have recently enacted resulutions defending the rights of Salvadoran and Guatemalan refugees in their communities and manifesting their solidarity with the Sanctuary Movement; and

WHEREAS   the citizens of Takoma Park share this concern for the plight of their Salvadoran and Guatemalan neighbors, and many of them have assisted these refugees with shelter, food, friendship, and other essentials; and

WHEREAS   the principles of international law and the best of American traditions not only permit but require that we aid refugees seeking safe haven here; and

WHEREAS   the citizens of Takoma Park desire to maintain and protect those high traditions and duties; and

WHEREAS   neither Maryland nor federal law requires any city to enforce the federal immigration laws;

NOW BE IT THEREFORE RESOLVED that the City of Takoma Park hereby declares itself a City of Refuge for Salvadorans and Guatemalans fleeing the persecution, war and atrocities in their respective countries, and welcomes them to the City; and

BE IT FURTHER RESOLVED that the City of Takoma Park condemns the unjust expulsions of Salvadorans and Guatemalans to their countries at this time by the federal government; and

BE IT FURTHER RESOLVED that the City of Takoma Park applauds the actions of Takoma Park residents who have acted to help Salvadoran and Guatemalan refugees in the City; it commends the work done by Casa de Maryland, a voluntary agency in the City which has seen to the needs of many refugees here; and it stands in solidarity with churches and other organizations throughout the country who have provided public sanctuary for Central American refugees; and

BE IT FURTHER RESOLVED that the City of Takoma Park urges the Maryland Congressional Delegation and Maryland's U.S. Senators to press for immediate action to stop the deportation of Salvadoran refugees for up to two years; and that they take steps to investigate the discriminatory practices of INS's enforcement of immigration laws with respect to refugees from Central America; and

BE IT FURTHER RESOLVED that a copy of this resolution be sent to Maryland's Congressional Delegation and U.S. Senators, to the U.S. Attorney General, to the Chicago

Religious Task Force on Central America and to Cong. Moakley and Sen. DeConcini; and

BE IT FURTHER RESOLVED that the intent of this resolution shall be given further practical effect by passage of an appropriate ordinance which will become law in Takoma Park upon enactment.

Appendix D

Statistical Data

Table 1	Immigration to the U.S.: FY 1820-1987	237
Table 2	Percent of Immigrants Admitted to the U.S. by Region & Period: FY 1955-1987	238
Chart 1	Immigrants Admitted to the U.S. 1970-1979 by Region of Birth & Naturalization: FY 1970-1987	239
Table 3	Immigrants Admitted to the U.S. from Top Fifteen Countries of Birth: FY 1987	240
Table 4	Immigrant Visas Issued at Foreign Service Posts by Geographic Areas: FY 1984-1988	241
Chart 2	Number and Percent of Immigrants Admitted to the U.S. as Refugees for Top Twenty Refugee Countries of Birth: FY 1946-1987	242
Table 5	Summary of U.S. Refugee Admissions: FY 1975- FY 1989	243
Table 6	Southeast Asian Refugees: Cumulative State Populations from 1975 through April 30, 1989	244
Table 7	Amerasian Arrivals in the U.S.: April 1989 & FY 89	245
Table 8	Refugees Resettled & Persons Granted Asylum: U.S., FY 1986-1987	246
Table 9	U.S. Refugee Admission Levels: FY 1988 and FY 1989	247
Table 10	U.S. Refugee Arrivals: April,1989 & FY 1989	248
Table 11	U.S. Refugee Arrivals by Voluntary/Sponsoring Agency: April,1989 & FY 1989	249
Table 12	U.S. Refugee-Status Applications: FY 1980-1987	250
Table 13	U.S. Refugee-Status Applications by Geographic Area and Selected Country of Chargeability: FY 1987	250
Table 14	Refugees Granted Lawful U.S. Permanent Resident Status in FY 1987 by Calendar Year of Entry and Region and Selected Country of Birth	251
Table 15	Asylum Cases Filed With INS District Directors by Selected Nationality: FY 1987	252
Table 16	U.S. Asylum Rates of Approval: FY 1988	253
Chart 3	Legalization Applications (IRCA) by Type of Application for Top Fifteen States: FY 1987	253
Table 17	Aliens Deported by Cause and Region and Selected Country of Nationality: FY 1987	255
Table 18	Refugees in Need of Protection and Assistance, By Country and Region: 1988	256
Table 19	Major Resettlement Countries: Refugees Resettled and Persons Granted Asylum, 1986 and 1987	257
Table 20	Contributions to the UNHCR: 1987	258
Table 21	Largest Projected UNHCR General Programs for 1989	259
Table 22	Contributions to the International Committee for Migration: 1987	260

Table 1

Immigration to the U.S.: FY 1820-1987

Year	Number	Year	Number	Year	Number	Year	Number
1820 - 1987	**53,723,582**						
1820	8,385	**1871 - 80**	**2,812,191**	**1921 - 30**	**4,107,209**	**1971 - 80**	**4,493,314**
		1871	321,350	1921	805,228	1971	370,478
		1872	404,806	1922	309,556	1972	384,685
1821 - 30	**143,439**	1873	459,803	1923	522,919	1973	400,063
1821	9,127	1874	313,339	1924	706,896	1974	394,861
1822	6,911	1875	227,498	1925	294,314	1975	386,194
1823	6,354	1876	169,986	1926	304,488	1976	398,613
1824	7,912	1877	141,857	1927	335,175	1976, TQ	103,676
1825	10,199	1878	138,469	1928	307,255	1977	462,315
1826	10,837	1879	177,826	1929	279,678	1978	601,442
1827	18,875	1880	457,257	1930	241,700	1979	460,348
1828	27,382					1980	530,639
1829	22,520	**1881 - 90**	**5,246,613**	**1931 - 40**	**528,431**		
1830	23,322	1881	669,431	1931	97,139	**1981 - 87**	**4,067,630**
		1882	788,992	1932	35,576	1981	596,600
1831 - 40	**599,125**	1883	603,322	1933	23,068	1982	594,131
1831	22,633	1884	518,592	1934	29,470	1983	559,763
1832	60,482	1885	395,346	1935	34,956	1984	543,903
1833	58,640	1886	334,203	1936	36,329	1985	570,009
1834	65,365	1887	490,109	1937	50,244	1986	601,708
1835	45,374	1888	546,889	1938	67,895	1987	601,516
1836	76,242	1889	444,427	1939	82,998		
1837	79,340	1890	455,302	1940	70,756		
1838	38,914						
1839	68,069	**1891 - 1900**	**3,687,564**	**1941 - 50**	**1,035,039**		
1840	84,066	1891	560,319	1941	51,776		
		1892	579,663	1942	28,781		
1841 - 50	**1,713,251**	1893	439,730	1943	23,725		
1841	80,289	1894	285,631	1944	28,551		
1842	104,565	1895	258,536	1945	38,119		
1843	52,496	1896	343,267	1946	108,721		
1844	78,615	1897	230,832	1947	147,292		
1845	114,371	1898	229,299	1948	170,570		
1846	154,416	1899	311,715	1949	188,317		
1847	234,968	1900	448,572	1950	249,187		
1848	226,527						
1849	297,024	**1901 - 10**	**8,795,386**	**1951 - 60**	**2,515,479**		
1850	369,980	1901	487,918	1951	205,717		
		1902	648,743	1952	265,520		
1851 - 60	**2,598,214**	1903	857,046	1953	170,434		
1851	379,466	1904	812,870	1954	208,177		
1852	371,603	1905	1,026,499	1955	237,790		
1853	368,645	1906	1,100,735	1956	321,625		
1854	427,833	1907	1,285,349	1957	326,867		
1855	200,877	1908	782,870	1958	253,265		
1856	200,436	1909	751,786	1959	260,686		
1857	251,306	1910	1,041,570	1960	265,398		
1858	123,126						
1859	121,282	**1911 - 20**	**5,735,811**	**1961 - 70**	**3,321,677**		
1860	153,640	1911	878,587	1961	271,344		
		1912	838,172	1962	283,763		
1861 - 70	**2,314,824**	1913	1,197,892	1963	306,260		
1861	91,918	1914	1,218,480	1964	292,248		
1862	91,985	1915	326,700	1965	296,697		
1863	176,282	1916	298,826	1966	323,040		
1864	193,418	1917	295,403	1967	361,972		
1865	248,120	1918	110,618	1968	454,448		
1866	318,568	1919	141,132	1969	358,579		
1867	315,722	1920	430,001	1970	373,326		
1868	138,840						
1869	352,768						
1870	387,203						

NOTE: The numbers shown are as follows: from 1820-67, figures represent alien passengers arrived at seaports; from 1868-91 and 1895-97, immigrant aliens arrived; from 1892-94 and 1898-1987, immigrant aliens admitted for permanent residence. From 1892-1903, aliens entering by cabin class were not counted as immigrants. Land arrivals were not completely enumerated until 1908.

Table 2

Percent of Immigrants Admitted to the U.S. by Region & Period: FY 1955-1987

Region	1955-64	1965-74	1975-84	1985	1986	1987
All regions	100.0	100.0	100.0	100.0	100.0	100.0
Europe	50.2	29.8	13.4	11.1	10.4	10.2
North and West	28.6	11.0	5.2	5.0	5.0	5.2
South and East	21.6	18.7	8.1	6.0	5.4	5.0
Asia	7.7	22.4	43.3	46.4	44.6	42.8
Africa	.7	1.5	2.4	3.0	2.9	2.9
Oceania	.4	.7	.8	.7	.6	.7
North America	36.0	39.6	33.6	31.9	34.5	36.0
Caribbean	7.1	18.0	15.1	14.6	16.9	17.1
Central America	2.5	2.6	3.7	4.6	4.7	4.9
Other N. America	26.4	19.0	14.8	12.7	12.9	14.0
South America	5.1	6.0	6.6	6.9	7.0	7.4

Chart 1

Immigrants Admitted to the U.S. 1970-1979 by Region of Birth & Naturalization: FY 1970-1987

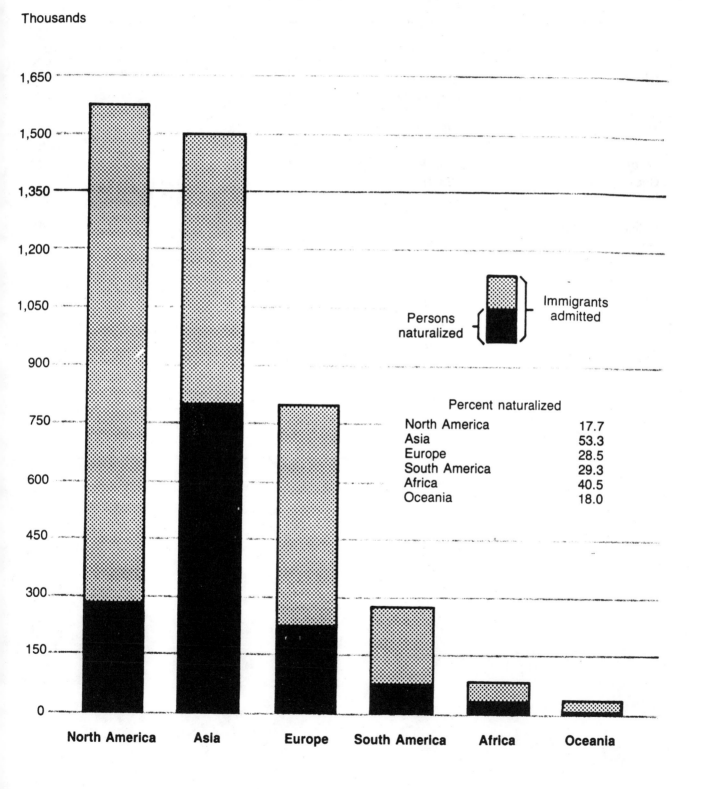

Thousands

Percent naturalized

North America	17.7
Asia	53.3
Europe	28.5
South America	29.3
Africa	40.5
Oceania	18.0

Table 3

Immigrants Admitted to the U.S. from Top Fifteen Countries of Birth: FY 1987

Country of birth	1987	1986	Change	
			Number	Percent
Total	601,516	601,708	−192	—
1) Mexico	72,351	66,533	5,818	8.7
2) Philippines	50,060	52,558	−2,498	−4.8
3) Korea	35,849	35,776	73	.2
4) Cuba	28,916	33,114	−4,198	−12.7
5) India	27,803	26,227	1,576	6.0
6) China, Mainland	25,841	25,106	735	2.9
7) Dominican Republic	24,858	26,175	−1,317	−5.0
8) Vietnam	24,231	29,993	−5,762	−19.2
9) Jamaica	23,148	19,595	3,553	18.1
10) Haiti	14,819	12,666	2,153	17.0
11) Iran	14,426	16,505	−2,079	−12.6
12) United Kingdom	13,497	13,657	−160	−1.2
13) Cambodia	12,460	13,501	−1,041	−7.7
14) Taiwan	11,931	13,424	−1,493	−11.1
15) Canada	11,876	11,039	837	7.6
Other	209,450	205,839	3,611	1.8

Table 4

Immigrant Visas Issued at Foreign Service Posts By Geographic Areas
FY 1984-1988

Region of Birth or Chargeability	1984	1985	1986	1987	1988
Europe	31,757	31,823	31,753	36,268	38,279
Asia	145,095	153,337	157,735	161,266	165,228
Africa	6,204	6,411	7,387	8,124	8,040
North America	133,325	138,122	147,138	150,180	148,090
South America	27,568	28,935	31,651	34,863	29,964
Oceania	2,197	2,411	2,307	2,565	2,233
TOTAL	346,146	361,039	377,971	393,266	391,834

Source: *Visa Bulletin*, March 1989

Chart 2

Number and Percent of Immigrants Admitted to the U.S. as Refugees for Top Twenty Refugee Countries of Birth: FY 1946-1987

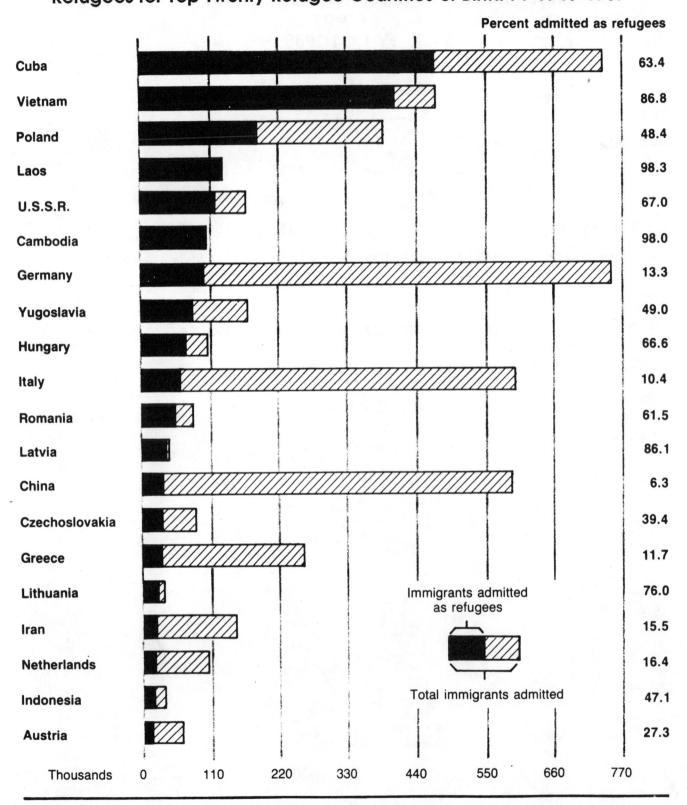

Percent admitted as refugees

Country	Percent
Cuba	63.4
Vietnam	86.8
Poland	48.4
Laos	98.3
U.S.S.R.	67.0
Cambodia	98.0
Germany	13.3
Yugoslavia	49.0
Hungary	66.6
Italy	10.4
Romania	61.5
Latvia	86.1
China	6.3
Czechoslovakia	39.4
Greece	11.7
Lithuania	76.0
Iran	15.5
Netherlands	16.4
Indonesia	47.1
Austria	27.3

Immigrants admitted
as refugees

Total immigrants admitted

Thousands   0   110   220   330   440   550   660   770

NOTE: Germany includes the Federal Republic of Germany and the German Democratic Republic. China includes Mainland China and Taiwan.

Table 5

Summary of U.S. Refugee Admissions
Cumulative FY 1975-FY 1989

FY	Africa	Asia	E. Europe	USSR	Latin America	Near East Asia	TOTAL
1975	0	135,000	1,947	6,211	3,000	0	146,158
1976	0	15,000	1,756	7,450	3,000	0	27,206
1977	0	7,000	1,755	8,191	3,000	0	19,946
1978	0	20,574	2,245	10,688	3,000	0	36,507
1979	0	76,521	3,393	24,449	7,000	0	111,363
1980	955	163,799	5,025	28,444	6,662	2,231	207, 116
1981	2,119	131,139	6,704	13,444	2,017	3,829	159,252
1982	3,326	73,522	10,780	2,756	602	6,369	97,355
1983	2,648	39,408	12,083	1,409	668	5,465	61,681
1984	2,747	51,960	10,285	715	160	5,246	71,113
1985	1,953	49,970	9,350	640	138	5,994	68,045
1986	1,315	45,454	8,713	787	173	5,998	62,440
1987	1,994	40,112	8,606	3,694	315	10,107	64,828
1988	1,588	35,015	7,818	20,421	2,497	8,415	75,754
1989	1,014	30,726	5,688	22,462	1,313	5,873	67,076
TOTAL	19,659	915,525	96,148	151,761	33,545	59,527	1,276,165

Source: U.S. Bureau For Refugee Programs

Table 6

Southeast Asian Refugees
Cumulative State Populations From 1975 Through April 30, 1989

State	Estimated Total	State	Estimated Total
Alabama	3,300	Montana	1,000
Alaska	100	Nebraska	2,600
Arizona	7,400	Nevada	2,500
Arkansas	3,200	New Hampshire	900
California	356,300	New Jersey	8,100
Colorado	12,200	New Mexico	2,300
Connecticut	8,100	New York	32,700
Delaware	300	North Carolina	6,700
District of Columbia	1,700	North Dakota	1,000
Florida	15,400	Ohio	12,400
Georgia	11,800	Oklahoma	9,100
Hawaii	7,900	Oregon	20,400
Idaho	1,900	Pennsylvania	28,800
Illinois	28,900	Rhode Island	7,400
Indiana	4,400	South Carolina	2,500
Iowa	9,900	South Dakota	1,100
Kansas	10,600	Tennessee	6,200
Kentucky	3,100	Texas	67,400
Louisiana	15,200	Utah	9,200
Maine	1,700	Vermont	700
Maryland	10,500	Virginia	22,800
Massachusetts	29,000	Washington	42,400
Michigan	12,300	West Virginia	400
Minnesota	32,700	Wisconsin	14,300
Mississippi	1,800	Wyoming	200
Missouri	8,200	Guam	300

Total   901,300

Source: U.S. Office of Refugee Resettlement

Table 7

Amerasian Arrivals in the U.S.
April 1989 & FY 89

State	April 1989	Year To Date FY 89	State	April 1989	Year To Date FY 89
Alabama	38	69	Montana	0	0
Alaska	0	0	Nebraska	0	0
Arizona	15	60	Nevada	0	3
Arkansas	2	4	New Hampshire	0	1
California	126	456	New Jersey	21	61
Colorado	6	13	New Mexico	0	0
Connecticut	0	0	New York	79	235
Delaware	0	2	North Carolina	8	51
District of Columbia	52	141	North Dakota	3	3
Florida	24	63	Ohio	0	17
Georgia	20	74	Oklahoma	4	25
Hawaii	4	23	Oregon	8	50
Idaho	0	1	Pennsylvania	34	105
Illinois	16	76	Rhode Island	0	0
Indiana	6	9	South Carolina	0	0
Iowa	6	21	South Dakota	3	3
Kansas	1	10	Tennessee	0	6
Kentucky	5	39	Texas	61	173
Louisiana	0	9	Utah	6	42
Maine	5	7	Vermont	0	0
Maryland	17	73	Virginia	29	84
Massachusetts	38	101	Washington	21	51
Michigan	23	57	West Virginia	0	0
Minnesota	17	75	Wisconsin	0	3
Mississippi	0	0	Wyoming	0	0
Missouri	39	73	Puerto Rico	0	0

Total   737   2,369

Source: U.S. Office of Refugee Resettlement

Table 8

Refugees Resettled & Persons Granted Asylum: U.S., FY 1986-1987

	Refugees	FY 86 Asylees	Total	Refugees	FY 87 Asylees	Total
Country						
United States						
from						
Africa						
Ethiopia	1,268	217	1,485	1,831	205	2,036
Other	47	49	96	163	53	216
Subtotal	*1,315*	*266*	*1,581*	*1,994*	*258*	*2,252*
East Asia						
Vietnam	22,796	8	22,804	14,509	20	14,529
Cambodia	9,789	6	9,795	1,539	0	1,539
Laos-Lowlanders	9,201	2	9,203	7,257	2	7,259
Laos-Highlanders	3,668	0	3,668	8,307	0	8,307
Other	0	0	0	0	32	32
Subtotal	*45,454*	*16*	*45,470*	*31,612*	*54*	*31,634*
Eastern Europe						
Poland	3,735	456	4,191	3,626	558	4,184
Romania	2,373	152	2,525	3,075	137	3,212
Czechoslovakia	1,589	39	1,628	1,072	13	1,085
Soviet Union	787	44	831	3,694	33	3,727
Hungary	754	26	780	669	14	683
Other	262	104	366	164	25	189
Subtotal	*9,500*	*821*	*10,321*	*12,300*	*780*	*13,080*
Latin America						
Cuba	173	17	190	273	73	346
Nicaragua	0	1,284	1,284	36	2,213	2,249
Other	0	0	0	6	78	84
Subtotal	*173*	*1,301*	*1,474*	*315*	*2,364*	*2,679*
Near East/South Asia						
Afghanistan	2,535	4,284	6,819	3,220	24	3,244
Iran	3,148	1,568	4,716	6,681	1,346	8,027
Iraq	307	12	319	202	16	218
Other	8	123	131	4	250	254
Subtotal	*5,998*	*5,987*	*11,985*	*10,107*	*1,636*	*11,743*
Stateless	0	NA	NA	0	1	1
Subtotal	*0*	*NA*	*NA*	*0*	*1*	*1*
Grand Total	*62,440*	*8,391*	*70,831*	*64,828*	*5,093*	*69,921*

Table 9

U.S. Refugee Admission Levels: FY 1988 and FY 1989

Region		FY 88 Actual	FY 89 Allocations (Revised April, 1989)
East Asia			
	First Asylum	28,313	28,000
	ODP	6,702	22,000
	Subtotal	35,015	50,000
Eastern Europe/USSR			
	USSR	20,421	43,500
	Eastern Europe	7,818	6,500
	Subtotal	28,239	50,000
Near East/South Asia		8,415	7,000
Latin America/Caribbean		2,497	3,500
Africa		1,588	2,000
TOTAL		**75,754**	**112,500**

Source: U.S. Bureau of Refugee Programs

Table 10

U.S. Refugee Arrivals
April, 1989 & FY 1989

State	April 1989	Year To Date FY 89	State	April 1989	Year To Date FY 89
Alabama	17	50	Montana	2	5
Alaska	1	10	Nebraska	8	175
Arizona	56	419	Nevada	16	122
Arkansas	5	76	New Hampshire	4	110
California	1830	15,591	New Jersey	86	882
Colorado	48	470	New Mexico	0	59
Connecticut	70	515	New York	878	7950
Delaware	2	24	North Carolina	28	226
District of Columbia	38	282	North Dakota	17	60
Florida	335	2449	Ohio	49	390
Georgia	51	512	Oklahoma	16	150
Hawaii	41	138	Oregon	85	661
Idaho	10	127	Pennsylvania	171	1365
Illinois	194	2005	Rhode Island	28	216
Indiana	17	99	South Carolina	8	33
Iowa	18	363	South Dakota	8	70
Kansas	40	194	Tennessee	18	305
Kentucky	14	104	Texas	214	1694
Louisiana	23	194	Utah	20	263
Maine	6	73	Vermont	12	73
Maryland	118	819	Virginia	121	638
Massachusetts	197	1957	Washington	169	1607
Michigan	75	573	West Virginia	1	8
Minnesota	122	1174	Wisconsin	53	594
Mississippi	5	59	Wyoming	16	16
Missouri	45	350	Puerto Rico	0	1

Total   5,408   46,304

Source: U.S. Office of Refugee Resettlement

Table 11

U.S. Refugee Arrivals by Voluntary/Sponsoring Agency
April,1989 & FY 1989

Voluntary/Sponsoring Agency	April 1989	YTD FY 89
American Council for Nationalities Service	284	2511
American Fund for Czechoslovak Refugees	37	547
Cuban American National Foundation	0	913
Church World Service	372	3311
Hebrew Immigrant Aid Society	1330	11,291
International Rescue Committee	508	4541
Iowa Refugee Service Center	15	217
Lutheran Immigration & Refugee Service	380	3481
Polish-American Immigration & Relief Committee	6	180
Presiding Bishop's Fund	117	955
Tolstoy Foundation	141	1380
U.S. Catholic Conference	1389	13,249
World Relief Refugee Service	266	1861
Unknown/None	563	1867
Total	**5,408**	**46,304**

Source: U.S. Office of Refugee Resettlement

Table 12

U.S. Refugee-Status Applications
FY 1980-1987

Year	Applications pending beginning of year	Applications filed during year	Applications approved during year	Applications denied during year	Applications otherwise closed during year	Applications pending end of year
1980 (April-September) .	16,642	111,883	89,580	6,149	1,197	14,957
1981	14,957	193,230	155,291	15,322	3,998	18,619
1982	18,619	94,769	61,527	14,943	6,631	11,668
1983	11,668	104,190	73,645	20,255	2,489	7,801
1984	7,801	107,437	77,932	16,220	604	12,681
1985	12,681	93,415	59,436	18,430	1,842	13,707
1986	13,707	81,017	52,081	9,679	3,362	15,895
1987	15,895	101,718	61,529	13,911	6,126	20,152

NOTE: The Refugee Act of 1980 went into effect on April 1, 1980.

Table 13

U.S. Refugee-Status Applications by Geographic Area and
Selected Country of Chargeability
FY 1987

Geographic area and country of chargeability	Applications pending beginning of year	Applications filed during year	Applications approved during year	Applications denied during year	Applications otherwise closed during year	Applications pending end of year
All countries	**15,895**	**101,718**	**61,529**	**13,911**	**6,126**	**20,152**
Africa	**1,305**	**4,395**	**1,974**	**892**	**176**	**1,353**
Angola	91	98	41	1	–	56
Ethiopia	938	3,858	1,808	868	174	1,008
Lesotho	32	37	4	–	–	33
Namibia	35	42	3	–	1	38
South Africa	87	147	70	4	–	73
Uganda	7	63	25	–	–	38
Zaire	91	111	12	13	1	85
Other Africa	24	39	11	6	–	22
East Asia	**50**	**45,710**	**37,082**	**8,451**	**16**	**161**
Cambodia	4	1,800	1,187	604	1	8
Hong Kong	–	41	15	14	5	7
Laos	10	22,440	17,518	4,913	–	9
Vietnam	36	21,429	18,362	2,920	10	137
Eastern Europe and U.S.S.R.	**8,457**	**29,278**	**12,290**	**2,305**	**2,662**	**12,021**
Albania	51	151	48	29	42	32
Bulgaria	96	312	116	14	26	156
Czechoslovakia	1,051	2,971	1,060	210	350	1,351
Hungary	840	2,968	695	335	430	1,508
Poland	4,437	11,971	3,568	1,384	1,345	5,674
Romania	1,849	6,101	3,105	310	439	2,247
U.S.S.R	86	4,741	3,695	7	11	1,028
Yugoslavia	47	63	3	16	19	25
Latin America	**2**	**352**	**99**	**49**	**192**	**12**
Chile	–	4	–	4	–	–
Cuba	2	80	69	2	3	6
Nicaragua	–	268	30	43	189	6
Near East	**6,081**	**21,983**	**10,084**	**2,214**	**3,080**	**6,605**
Afghanistan	2,061	7,756	3,221	959	1,991	1,585
Iran	3,815	13,919	6,658	1,230	1,053	4,978
Iraq	196	296	203	25	36	32
Other Near East	9	12	2	–	–	10

- Represents zero.

Table 14

Refugees Granted Lawful U.S. Permanent Resident Status in FY 1987 by Calendar Year of Entry and Region and Selected Country of Birth

Region and country of birth	Total	1986	1985	1984	1983	1982	1981	1980	Before 1980	Unknown or not re-ported
All countries	**91,474**	**15,090**	**26,758**	**8,311**	**2,654**	**1,567**	**1,882**	**30,187**	**1,704**	**3,321**
Europe	**9,037**	**2,719**	**3,890**	**823**	**264**	**166**	**106**	**139**	**123**	**807**
Bulgaria	102	51	42	2	-	-	-	-	1	6
Czechoslovakia	1,027	459	398	78	32	6	5	7	2	40
Germany, Federal Rep.	69	18	33	8	-	3	-	-	-	7
Hungary	540	187	237	52	14	10	1	4	2	33
Poland	3,019	958	1,166	352	99	88	19	11	5	321
Romania	2,876	725	1,586	253	74	23	17	12	2	184
Spain	45	-	3	4	1	-	2	27	6	2
U.S.S.R.	1,171	263	365	54	32	31	57	72	99	198
Other Europe	188	58	60	20	12	5	5	6	6	16
Asia	**49,237**	**11,945**	**21,871**	**7,238**	**2,220**	**1,315**	**1,141**	**928**	**444**	**2,135**
Afghanistan	2,019	802	849	136	54	27	5	4	-	142
Cambodia	12,205	1,228	5,532	2,941	1,071	351	386	123	80	493
China, Mainland	497	169	281	21	4	1	2	5	2	12
Hong Kong	102	38	39	9	2	3	2	2	-	7
Indonesia	138	32	66	21	3	11	-	2	-	3
Iran	2,514	826	1,421	111	31	1	3	3	4	114
Iraq	266	93	123	9	8	12	9	1	4	7
Laos	6,559	2,293	1,473	1,065	242	294	-273	475	166	278
Malaysia	67	23	27	11	1	1	1	1	-	2
Philippines	367	72	165	80	24	13	5	-	-	8
Thailand	3,745	588	1,800	768	199	86	52	58	30	164
Vietnam	20,596	5,738	10,030	2,047	581	512	401	244	154	889
Other Asia	162	43	65	19	-	3	2	10	4	16
Africa	**1,483**	**334**	**819**	**173**	**59**	**14**	**29**	**3**	**4**	**48**
Ethiopia	1,292	310	710	150	46	13	21	2	2	38
Sudan	83	10	57	10	3	1	1	-	-	1
Other Africa	108	14	52	13	10	-	7	1	2	9
Oceania	**3**	**1**	**1**	**1**	**-**	**-**	**-**	**-**	**-**	**-**
North America	**31,569**	**89**	**169**	**69**	**105**	**65**	**599**	**29,040**	**1,112**	**321**
Caribbean	**31,438**	**84**	**157**	**65**	**88**	**60**	**591**	**28,979**	**1,105**	**309**
Cuba	26,927	48	152	62	82	46	59	25,711	488	279
Haiti	4,419	36	1	1	4	14	530	3,215	588	30
Other Caribbean	92	-	4	2	2	-	2	53	29	-
Central America	**94**	**3**	**3**	**4**	**16**	**5**	**5**	**45**	**6**	**7**
Other North America	37	2	9	-	1	-	3	16	1	5
South America	**143**	**2**	**7**	**6**	**6**	**7**	**7**	**77**	**21**	**10**
Unknown or not reported	2	-	1	1	-	-	-	-	-	-

- Represents zero.

Table 15

Asylum Cases Filed With INS District Directors by Selected Nationality
FY 1987

Nationality	Applications pending beginning of year	Applications received during year	Applications granted during year	Individuals granted asylum during year	Applications denied during year	Applications otherwise closed during year	Applications pending end of year
All nationalities	99,408	26,107	4,062	5,093	3,454	37,269	80,730
Afghanistan	123	102	22	24	62	39	102
Bangladesh	8	13	–	–	8	4	9
Bulgaria	2	10	4	4	3	–	5
Chile	9	12	4	5	7	5	5
China, Mainland	32	75	21	27	12	22	52
Colombia	5	15	1	4	3	7	9
Cuba	89,606	3,684	70	73	110	33,057	60,053
Czechoslovakia	38	37	11	13	17	10	37
Egypt	22	51	5	8	32	8	28
El Salvador	997	2,684	29	39	776	483	2,393
Ethiopia	122	519	165	205	184	51	241
Ghana	8	22	4	4	9	3	14
Guatemala	245	640	7	7	178	89	611
Haiti	2,042	75	–	–	69	1,180	868
Honduras	128	134	2	2	39	49	172
Hungary	69	116	14	14	56	41	74
India	65	39	–	–	51	20	33
Iran	744	1,675	967	1,346	468	198	786
Iraq	28	24	12	16	10	7	23
Jordan	11	12	–	–	10	6	7
Lebanon	118	168	23	48	64	48	151
Liberia	20	32	7	7	20	7	18
Libya	67	109	86	115	20	15	55
Mexico	6	42	5	9	1	7	35
Nicaragua	3,926	13,377	1,867	2,213	357	1,519	13,560
Pakistan	42	64	5	7	26	5	70
Peru	14	38	1	1	12	6	33
Philippines	43	94	1	1	45	31	60
Poland	346	1,284	447	558	497	143	543
Romania	83	339	126	137	85	36	175
Sierra Leone	12	7	–	–	3	–	16
Somalia	44	67	14	14	24	17	56
South Africa	30	27	8	17	14	9	26
Sri Lanka	22	35	–	–	17	6	34
Syria	74	66	47	67	9	17	67
U.S.S.R.	17	62	32	33	8	9	30
Uganda	31	26	1	1	23	10	23
Venezuela	7	13	1	1	1	2	16
Vietnam	7	21	10	20	5	6	7
Yugoslavia	62	104	16	17	36	34	80
Other	133	193	27	36	83	63	153

– Represents zero.
NOTE: Cuban asylum applicants who have adjusted to lawful permanent resident status under the Cuban Refugee Adjustment Act of 1966 appear as cases otherwise closed in asylum data.

Table 16

U.S. Asylum Rates of Approval
FY 1988

	Country	Approval Rate For Cases Decided	Cases Granted	Cases Denied
1	Romania	82.9%	345	71
2	Vietnam	80.0%	8	2
3	Ethiopia	77.00%	441	131
4	Iran	75.0%	764	254
5	China	69.7%	60	26
6	Somalia	67.9%	55	26
7	Syria	65.7%	25	13
8	Pakistan	57.8%	33	24
9	Poland	53.7%	433	373
10	Nicaragua	53.1%	2,786	2,455
11	Uganda	51.7%	15	14
12	Czechoslovakia	44.8%	13	16
13	Afghanistan	39.5%	36	55
14	Lebanon	36.6%	56	97
15	Cuba	31.9%	30	64
16	Haiti	31.5%	6	13
17	Hungary	28.9%	24	59
18	Bangladesh	16.6%	1	5
19	India	15.0%	3	17
20	Liberia	15.0%	3	17
21	Philippines	10.0%	4	36
22	Yugoslavia	9.2%	6	59
23	Honduras	7.4%	10	125
24	Guatemala	5.0%	24	447
25	El Salvador	2.7%	110	3,822
TOTAL		**39.1%**	**5,530**	**8,577**

Source: Immigration and Naturalization Service

Chart 3

Legalization Applications (IRCA) by Type of Application for Top Fifteen States: FY 1987

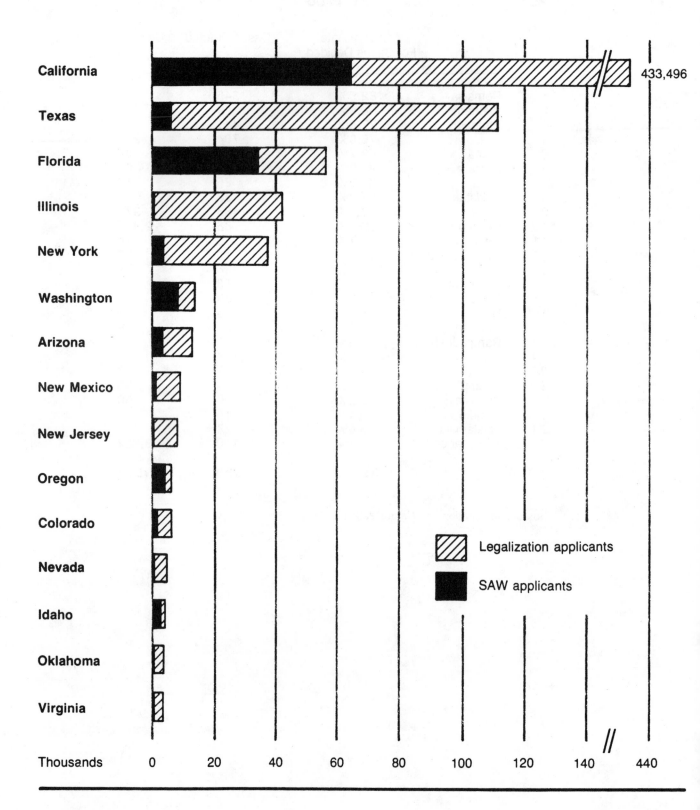

Table 17

Aliens Deported by Cause and Region and Selected Country of Nationality
FY 1987

Region and country of nationality	Total	Criminal	Violation of narcotic laws	Previously excluded or deported	Entered without proper documents	Failed to maintain or comply with conditions of nonimmigrant status	Entered without inspection or by false statements	Miscellaneous
All countries	**22,579**	**1,646**	**2,631**	**343**	**358**	**1,374**	**16,186**	**39**
Europe	**347**	**38**	**38**	**4**	**9**	**164**	**91**	**3**
France	32	4	3	-	-	16	9	-
Germany, Federal Rep.	37	5	4	1	2	17	7	1
Greece	22	-	2	-	1	16	3	-
Spain	21	2	1	-	-	6	12	-
United Kingdom	100	12	18	2	4	46	18	-
Yugoslavia	23	2	3	-	-	8	10	-
Other Europe	112	13	7	1	2	55	32	2
Asia	**435**	**27**	**39**	**4**	**23**	**258**	**81**	**2**
India	45	1	-	-	1	30	13	-
Iran	41	4	4	-	-	24	8	1
Israel	27	4	1	3	1	11	7	-
Japan	21	3	2	1	4	7	4	-
Korea	21	-	1	-	4	12	4	-
Lebanon	26	-	8	-	-	15	3	-
Pakistan	44	1	10	-	-	23	10	-
Philippines	87	7	2	-	7	57	13	-
Other Asia	123	7	11	-	6	79	19	1
Africa	**350**	**22**	**38**	**3**	**8**	**231**	**47**	**1**
Niger	35	1	7	1	-	21	5	-
Nigeria	216	17	27	1	7	138	26	-
Other Africa	99	4	4	1	1	72	16	1
Oceania	**46**	**6**	**1**	**-**	**-**	**29**	**10**	**-**
Tonga	21	2	-	-	-	17	2	-
Other Oceania	25	4	1	-	-	12	8	-
North America	**19,943**	**1,521**	**2,272**	**321**	**301**	**490**	**15,005**	**32**
Canada	243	49	51	9	14	64	53	3
Mexico	13,229	1,310	1,852	274	241	197	9,334	20
Caribbean	**712**	**57**	**193**	**6**	**27**	**155**	**269**	**5**
Bahamas, The	21	4	7	-	-	7	3	-
Dominican Republic	255	19	54	2	9	37	134	-
Haiti	108	8	33	-	4	19	43	1
Jamaica	255	16	82	2	12	65	75	3
Trinidad & Tobago	34	3	9	-	-	15	7	-
Other Caribbean	39	7	8	2	2	12	7	1
Central America	**5,759**	**105**	**176**	**32**	**19**	**74**	**5,349**	**4**
Belize	89	5	9	1	5	7	62	-
Costa Rica	42	2	3	-	-	3	34	-
El Salvador	2,585	62	106	14	6	16	2,379	2
Guatemala	1,881	18	31	8	3	12	1,807	2
Honduras	1,033	12	19	8	2	16	976	-
Nicaragua	87	-	3	-	1	3	80	-
Panama	42	6	5	1	2	17	11	-
South America	**1,458**	**32**	**243**	**11**	**17**	**202**	**952**	**1**
Argentina	30	1	3	1	-	11	14	-
Bolivia	54	-	17	-	-	19	18	-
Brazil	62	2	4	-	1	18	37	-
Chile	22	1	1	-	-	7	13	-
Colombia	988	18	168	9	14	86	692	1
Ecuador	109	4	13	-	-	20	72	-
Peru	109	1	16	-	1	16	75	-
Uruguay	22	-	1	-	-	6	15	-
Venezuela	37	1	17	1	-	14	4	-
Other South America	25	4	3	-	1	5	12	-

Table 18

Refugees in Need of Protection and Assistance
By Country and Region: 1988

Africa

Angola	95,000
Benin	3,000
Botswana	2,700
Burkina Faso	200
Burundi	75,000
Cameroon	4,500
Central African Republic	3,000
Congo	2,100
Djibouti	2,000
Ethiopia	700,000
Gabon	400
Ghana	100
Ivory Coast	800
Kenya	10,700
Lesotho	3,800
Liberia	300
Malawi	625,000
Mozambique	400
Nigeria	5,000
Rwanda	20,000
Senegal	5,600
Sierra Leone	200
Somalia	366,500
South Africa	175,000
Sudan	700,000
Swaziland	70,000
Tanzania	264,100
Togo	500
Uganda	125,000
Zaire	325,000
Zambia	146,000
Zimbabwe	171,000
TOTAL	3,902,700

East Asia

Hong Kong	25,000
Indonesia	2,200
Japan	500
Korea	100
Macau	500
Malaysia	101,500
New Guinea	8,300
Philippines	20,000
Singapore	300
Taiwan	200
Thailand	438,300
Vietnam	25,000
TOTAL	621,900

Near East, South Asia, and North Africa

Algeria	167,500
Egypt	5,500
Gaza Strip	460,000
India	245,500
Iran	2,800,000
Jordan	873,000
Lebanon	294,000
Morocco	600
Nepal	12,000
Pakistan	3,591,000
Saudia Arabia	221,100
Syria	260,800
Tunisia	100
West Bank	385,000
Yemen Arab Republic	61,500
TOTAL	9,452,600

Western Hemisphere

Argentina	4,700
Belize	4,200
Bolivia	300
Brazil	300
Chile	300
Colombia	500
Costa Rica	38,800
Dominican Republic	5,000
Ecuador	700
El Salvador	400
French Guiana	9,000
Guatemala	2,100
Honduras	40,800
Mexico	161,500
Nicaragua	7,000
Panama	2,400
Peru	700
Uruguay	200
Venezuela	500
TOTAL	279,400

GRAND TOTAL   **14,256,600**

Source: U.S. Bureau of Refugee Programs and UN High Commissioner for Refugees.

Table 19

Major Resettlement Countries
Refugees Resettled and Persons Granted Asylum, 1986 and 1987

Country	1986	1987
Australia	12,000	11,092
Austria	1,432	1,113
Canada	21,508	23,348
Denmark	9,299	2,726
France	10,645	12,848
Germany (Federal Republic)	8,893	8,231
Japan	358	579
Netherlands	2,027	2,381
New Zealand	685	799
Norway	835	1,043
Spain	683	4,182
Sweden	13,419	16,545
Switzerland	820	830
United Kingdom	2,067	813

Source: U.S. Bureau of Refugee Programs

Table 20

Contributions to the UNHCR: 1987

Donor	Amount in U.S.$	Percent of Total Contributions
A. *Governments and Intergovernmental Organizations*		
1. United States	$ 108,479,128	26.69
2. Japan	57,486,996	13.08
3. European Economic Community	46,592,964	10.60
4. Federal Republic of Germany	42,656,695	9.71
5. United Kingdom	28,454,393	6.48
6. Denmark	22,577,174	5.14
7. Italy	19,843,932	4.43
8. Sweden	19,232,703	4.38
9. Switzerland	18,309,963	4.17
10. Netherlands	16,242,308	3.70
11. Norway	15,629,870	3.56
12. Canada	14,618,082	3.33
13. Finland	6,961,172	1.58
14. Australia	5,032,434	1.15
15. Belgium	3,182,318	0.72
16. France	2,377,573	0.54
17. Spain	808,097	0.18
18. New Zealand	518,975	0.12
19. China	398,248	0.09
20. Ireland	348,980	0.08
21. Arab Gulf Program for U.N. Development	305,000	0.07
22. Luxembourg	139,280	0.03
Other Governments and Intergovernmental Organizations	980,937	0.22
Subtotal, Governmental Contributions	$ 431,177,222	98.24
B. *United Nations System*	405,715	0.09
C. *Nongovernmental Organizations and Other Donors*	7,743,414	1.76
Grand Total	$ 439,326,351	100

Source: UNHCR.

Table 21

Largest Projected UNHCR General Programs for 1989

Country	US$ (Million)
Pakistan	46.3
Ethiopia	42.9
Sudan	37.6
Somalia	34.5
Malawi	22.9
Thailand	21.4
Iran	19.7
Honduras	12.7
Mexico	8.3
Hong Kong	6.8
Philippines	6.4
Angola	5.2
Zimbabwe	5.1

Source: *Refugees*, November, 1988, p. 8.

Table 22

Contributions to the International Committee for Migration: 1987

(in U.S. dollars)

Donor		Amount in U.S.$	Percent of Total Contributions
A.	*Member Governments*		
1.	United States	$ 6,972,958	30.44
2.	Federal Republic of Germany	5,021,906	21.92
3.	Italy	1,946,919	8.50
4.	Switzerland	1,516,103	6.62
5.	Denmark	1,084,908	4.74
6.	Norway	855,094	3.73
7.	Belgium	797,863	3.48
8.	Israel	598,457	2.61
9.	Netherlands	502,780	2.19
10.	Portugal	407,638	1.78
11.	Australia	371,620	1.62
12.	Argentina	289,380	1.26
13.	Austria	212,717	0.93
14.	Luxembourg	196,347	0.86
15.	Colombia	166,938	0.73
16.	Greece	158,798	0.69
17.	Chile	128,440	0.56
18.	Venezuela	98,370	0.43
19.	Ecuador	68,364	0.30
20.	Peru	43,720	0.19
21.	Paraguay	36,925	0.16
22.	Costa Rica	36,003	0.16
23.	El Salvador	34,685	0.15
24.	Uruguay	30,604	0.13
25.	Honduras	30,450	0.13
26.	Bolivia	27,325	0.12
27.	Cyprus	27,325	0.12
28.	Dominican Republic	27,325	0.12
29.	Guatemala	27,325	0.12
30.	Kenya	27,325	0.12
31.	Nicaragua	27,325	0.12
32.	Panama	27,325	0.12
33.	Thailand	27,325	0.12
	Subtotal, Member Governments	*$ 21,826,587*	*95.27*
B.	*Others*		
1.	European Economic Community	584,386	2.55
2.	Japan	328,243	1.43
3.	UNHCR	163,752	0.71
4.	Canada	7,200	0.03
	Subtotal	*$1,083,581*	*4.73*
	Grand Total	*$ 22,910,168*	*100*

Source: ICM.

Indices

Index I

Organizational Names

Access	CA	123
Adelphi Univ. Refugee Assistance Program	NY	626
Adult and Child Guidance Center. Indochinese	CA	159
Adventist Community Services	DC	222
Afghan Center	CA	190
Afghan Community in Amer.	NY	628
Afghan Refugee Fund	CA	63
AFL/CIO Immigration Project	CA	64
African Amer. Immigration Service	NY	609
Agudath Israel of Amer.	NY	631
Aid To Refugee Children Without Parents	CA	160
Alabama Baptist State Conv.	AL	4
Alabama Dept. of Human Resources. Refugee R	AL	5
All Culture Friendship Center Refugee & Immi	CA	55
All Culture Friendship Center Refugee & Immi	CA	65
Amer. Arab Anti-Discrimination Comm.	DC	223
Amer. Baptist Churches. Immigration & Refug	PA	788
Amer. Civic Assoc.	NY	608
Amer. Civil Liberties Union. South Texas Proj	TX	880
Amer. Comm. on Italian Migration	NY	632
Amer. Council for Nationalities Service	NY	633
Amer. Council on Intl. Personnel	NY	634
Amer. Fed. of Jews from Central Europe	NY	635
Amer. Friends Service Comm. Florida Undocum	FL	293
Amer. Friends Service Comm. Haitian Women'	NY	636
Amer. Friends Service Comm. Immigration Pro	CA	108
Amer. Fund for Czechoslovak Refugees	NY	637
Amer. Fund for Slovak Refugees	NJ	596
Amer. Fund for Slovak Refugees	NY	607
Amer. Immigrant Foundation	CA	164
Amer. Immigration Lawyers Assoc.	DC	224
Amer. Immigration Lawyers Assoc. Pro Bono	FL	294
Amer. Immigration Lawyers Assoc. Texas Cha	OK	737
Amer. Public Welfare Assoc. Task Force on Im	DC	225
Amer. Red Cross. Intl. Services	DC	226
Amer. Refugee Comm.	IL	381
Amer. Refugee Comm.	MN	518
Amer. Romanian Comm. for Assistance to Ref	NY	630
Americanization League	NY	691
Amer. For Immigration Control	DC	227
Amer. for Intl. Aid	GA	337
Amnesty Intl.	CA	66
Amnesty Intl. USA	CA	132
Anaheim Independencia Center	CA	27
Annunciation House	TX	844
Archdiocese of Chicago. Immigration Services	IL	351
Archdiocese of Detroit. Office of Refugee Rese	MI	490
Archdiocese of New York. Office for Immigran	NY	638
Archdiocese of New York. Refugee Resettlemen	NY	639
Archdiocese of Portland. Immigration Counsel	OR	752
Arizona Center for Immigrants	AZ	7
Arizona Dept. of Economic Security. Refugee	AZ	8
Arkansas Dept. of Human Services. Refugee Re	AR	25
Armenian Assembly of Amer.	DC	228
Asheville Presbytery. Refugee Resettlement Of	NC	702
Asia Pacific Concerns Comm.	CA	181
Asian Counseling and Referral Service	WA	916
Asian Immigrant Womens Advocates	CA	93
Asian Legal Services Outreach	CA	112
Asian Pacific Amer. Legal Center of Southern	CA	67
Asian Resources	CA	113
Associated Catholic Charities	LA	429
Associated Catholic Charities. Refugee Employ	MD	441
Assoc. of Vietnamese in Nashville	TN	811
Assyrian Universal Alliance	MI	512
Balch Institute for Ethnic Studies	PA	772
Baptist Assoc. of New Orleans	LA	430
Baptist Conv. of Maryland	MD	447
Baptist Conv. of New Mexico	NM	597
Baptist General Conv. of Oklahoma	OK	738
Baptist State Conv.	MI	513
Baron de Hirsch Fund	NY	640
Bergen County Sanctuary Comm.	NJ	590
Bethany Christian Services. Refugee Foster Ca	MI	501
Blue Card	NY	641
Boat People SOS	CA	124
Border Assoc. for Refugees from Central Amer	TX	842
Bridge Refugee Services	TN	807
Brooklyn Legal Services Corp.	NY	610
Brown Univ. Population Studies & Training C	RI	793
Buddhist Council for Refugee Rescue and Reset	CA	133
Bulgarian Natl. Comm.	NJ	582
California Dept. of Social Services. Office of	CA	114
California Southern Baptist Conv. Refugee Re	CA	43
Cambodia's of Ohio	OH	728
Cambodian Assoc. of Amer.	CA	57
Cambodian Assoc. of Memphis	TN	809
Cambodian Assoc. of Mobile	AL	2
Cambodian Assoc. of Virginia	VA	902
Cambodian Business Assoc.	CA	58
Cambodian Family	CA	165
Cambodian Mutual Assistance Assoc.	OH	720
Cambodian Mutual Assistance Assoc. of Greate	MA	478
Cambridge and Somerville Legal Services Imm	MA	467
Cambridge Organization of Portuguese-Amer.	MA	468
Capuchin Mission Secretariat	MI	491
Caribbean Action Lobby	NY	611
Caritas of Austin	TX	819
CASA	PA	771
Casa de la Esperanza	DC	229
Casa de Proyecto Libertad	TX	855
Casa El Salvador	IL	352
Casa Juan Diego	TX	857
Casa Marianella	TX	820
Catholic Agency for Migration & Refugee Serv	KS	412
Catholic Agency for Migration and Refugee Se	KS	411
Catholic Charities	FL	313
Catholic Charities	IA	410
Catholic Charities	KS	414
Catholic Charities	MA	486
Catholic Charities	NE	558
Catholic Charities	NY	684
Catholic Charities Bureau	IN	393
Catholic Charities Bureau. Resettlement Prog	WI	956
Catholic Charities Migration Office	NY	604
Catholic Charities Refugee & Immigration Se	MA	458

Catholic Charities. Immigration & Refugee D	CA	68
Catholic Charities. Immigration & Refugee P	CA	174
Catholic Charities. Immigration & Refugee S	PA	765
Catholic Charities. Immigration Counseling C	CA	161
Catholic Charities. Immigration Counseling S	TX	831
Catholic Charities. Immigration Program	CA	134
Catholic Charities. Immigration Project	CA	94
Catholic Charities. Immigration Project of Im	FL	286
Catholic Charities. Immigration Services	CA	106
Catholic Charities. Migration & Refugee Serv	MN	528
Catholic Charities. Migration and Refugee Se	CT	211
Catholic Charities. Migration and Refugee Se	TX	849
Catholic Charities. Refugee Assistance	IN	396
Catholic Charities. Refugee Assistance Progra	NY	622
Catholic Charities. Refugee Office	IN	394
Catholic Charities. Refugee Program	KS	416
Catholic Charities. Refugee Resettlement Offi	CA	182
Catholic Charities. Refugee Resettlement Offi	FL	289
Catholic Charities. Refugee Resettlement Pro	CA	35
Catholic Charities. Refugee Resettlement Pro	DE	220
Catholic Charities. Refugee Resettlement Pro	TN	810
Catholic Charities. Refugee Service Center	DC	230
Catholic Charities. Refugee Service Program	PA	783
Catholic Charities. Refugee Services	KY	423
Catholic Charities. Refugee Social Service Ce	MS	541
Catholic Charities. Resettlement Program	CA	44
Catholic Charities. Resettlement Services	CA	166
Catholic Charities. Resettlement Services	TX	858
Catholic Charities. Unaccompanied Refugee M	MN	529
Catholic Community Services of Nevada. Imm	NV	564
Catholic Community Services of Utah. Refug	UT	882
Catholic Community Services. Migration & R	LA	424
Catholic Community Services. Office of Migr	NJ	586
Catholic Community Services. Office of Migr	WV	936
Catholic Community Services. Refugee Reset	FL	295
Catholic Community Services. Resettlement &	CA	125
Catholic Council for Social Concern	IA	407
Catholic Family and Child Service	WA	935
Catholic Family and Child Services. Family R	WA	910
Catholic Family Center. Refugee Dept.	NY	686
Catholic Family Service. Immigration Service	TX	872
Catholic Family Services. Refugee & Citizens	TX	818
Catholic Human Development Office. Refugee	MI	502
Catholic Immigration & Resettlement Office	CA	177
Catholic Immigration and Refugee Services	CO	199
Catholic Immigration Center	HI	339
Catholic Immigration Services	FL	296
Catholic Migration & Refugee Services	OR	748
Catholic Migration & Refugee Services	VA	893
Catholic Migration and Refugee Office	NY	612
Catholic Migration and Refugee Resettlement	OH	721
Catholic Migration and Refugee Service	NV	566
Catholic Migration and Refugee Service	OK	746
Catholic Migration and Refugee Services	ID	349
Catholic Migration and Refugee Services	NJ	573
Catholic Migration Office	NY	605
Catholic Refugee Services	WA	917
Catholic Refugee Services	WA	933
Catholic Resettlement and Immigration Office	IA	406
Catholic Resettlement Center	IL	353
Catholic Resettlement Services	OR	753
Catholic Services for Immigrants	TX	874
Catholic Social Agency. Migration Services	PA	761
Catholic Social Ministries. Migration & Rese	OK	739
Catholic Social Ministries. Refugee Resettlem	NC	699
Catholic Social Service	IL	350
Catholic Social Service	IL	385
Catholic Social Service Bureau. Refugee Resett	KY	420
Catholic Social Service of Phoenix	AZ	9
Catholic Social Service. Refugee Office	NC	696
Catholic Social Service. Refugee Resettlement	FL	309
Catholic Social Service. Refugee Resettlement	CA	115
Catholic Social Service. Resettlement Program	CO	207
Catholic Social Service. Resettlement Program	OH	714
Catholic Social Service. Tha Huong Program	IL	386
Catholic Social Services	AK	6
Catholic Social Services	FL	316
Catholic Social Services	IN	398
Catholic Social Services	KS	413
Catholic Social Services	LA	427
Catholic Social Services	MI	509
Catholic Social Services	MS	540
Catholic Social Services	OH	729
Catholic Social Services	OH	731
Catholic Social Services	PA	763
Catholic Social Services	PA	786
Catholic Social Services	RI	794
Catholic Social Services	TX	829
Catholic Social Services	WI	942
Catholic Social Services	WY	957
Catholic Social Services Bureau	KY	418
Catholic Social Services of Fall River	MA	476
Catholic Social Services. Central Amer. Refug	TX	827
Catholic Social Services. Immigration Service	CA	29
Catholic Social Services. Migration & Refugee	PA	773
Catholic Social Services. Migration & Refugee	AZ	16
Catholic Social Services. Migration & Refugee	OH	717
Catholic Social Services. Refugee and Immigra	FL	311
Catholic Social Services. Refugee Program	AL	3
Catholic Social Services. Refugee Resetlement	NE	559
Catholic Social Services. Refugee Resettlemen	CA	179
Catholic Social Services. Refugee Resettlemen	GA	323
Catholic Social Services. Refugee Resettlemen	NM	598
Catholic Social Services. Refugee Social Servi	FL	312
Catholic Social Services. Resettlement Progra	CA	87
Catholic Social Services. Resettlement Progra	MT	556
Catholic Social Services. Servicios Para Inmig	TX	871
Center for Applied Linguistics. Refugee Servic	DC	231
Center for Central Amer. Refugees	NJ	587
Center for Immigrants Rights	NY	642
Center for Immigration Studies	DC	232
Center for Migration Studies	NY	689
Central Amer. Resource Center	TX	821
Central Amer. Legal Assistance	NY	613
Central Amer. Refugee Center	CA	69
Central Amer. Refugee Center	DC	233

Central Amer. Refugee Center	NY	627
Central Amer. Refugee Center	TX	859
Central Amer. Refugee Program	WA	918
Central Amer. Refugee Project	AZ	10
Central Amer. Refugee Project	CO	200
Central Amer. Refugee Project	OK	740
Central Amer. Resource Center	MN	530
Central Amer. Solidarity and Assistance	MD	455
Central Baptist Church. Sanctuary Group	PA	789
Central Coast Sanctuary	CA	175
Central Kentucky Jewish Assoc.	KY	421
Centro Campesino. Projecto de Inmigracion	WA	912
Centro de Ayuda Para Immigrantes	TX	860
Centro Legal	MN	531
Centro Presente	MA	469
Chicago Commission on Human Relations. Re	IL	354
Chicago Comm. on Immigrant Protection	IL	355
Chicago Religious Task Force on Central Amer	IL	356
Child and Family Service. Refugee Employmen	HI	340
Chinatown Service Center	CA	70
Chinese Amer. Civic Assoc.	MA	459
Chinese Amer. Service League	IL	357
Chinese Newcomer Service Center	CA	135
Christ Church of the Brethren. Sanctuary Com	OH	734
Christian Community Service Agency	FL	297
Christian Community Services	CO	197
Christian Council of Metropolitan Atlanta. Ref	GA	324
Christian Reformed World Relief Comm.	MI	503
Christian Refugee Outreach	VA	894
Church of the Brethren. Refugee Resettlement	MD	450
Church Refugee Center	NY	643
Church World Service. Immigration & Refugee	NY	644
Church World Service. Refugee Program	FL	298
City of Berkeley. Public Sanctuary	CA	32
City of Burlington. Office of the Mayor	VT	889
City of Cambridge. Office of the Mayor	MA	470
City of Davis. Office of the Mayor	CA	37
City of East Lansing. Office of the Mayor	MI	497
City of Minneapolis. Office of the Mayor	MN	519
City of Olympia. Office of the Mayor	WA	913
City of Sacramento. Office of the Mayor	CA	116
City of Santa Fe. Office of the Mayor	NM	600
City of Tacoma Park. Office of the Mayor	MD	456
City of West Hollywood. City Council	CA	196
Clinica Msr. Oscar A. Romero	CA	71
Coalition for Haitian Concerns	PA	791
Coalition for Immigrant and Refugee Rights	CA	136
Coalition for Public Sanctuary	OH	735
Coastal Bend Friends Meeting	TX	830
College Hill Presbyterian Church. Sanctuary	OK	747
College of Staten Island. Center for Immigran	NY	690
Colorado Refugee and Immigrant Services Pro	CO	201
Columbia Univ. School of Law. Immigration	NY	645
Comite de Refugiados Salvadorenos	CA	40
Comite en Defensa de los Immigrantes	CA	110
Commission for the Study of Intl. Migration	DC	234
Comm. in Defense of Immigrant Rights	WA	919
Comm. to Defend Immigrant & Refugee Righ	CA	95
Community Friends Meeting. Sanctuary Com	OH	715
Community Law Center	CA	167
Community Legal Services	CA	36
Community Legal Services	CA	92
Community Legal Services	PA	774
Community, Family & Children Services. Re	MI	500
Concord Friends Meeting Sanctuary	PA	790
Conference on Jewish Material Claims Again	NY	646
Congregation Hakafa. Sanctuary Comm.	IL	384
Connecticut Dept. of Human Resources. State	CT	212
Conscientious Alliance for Peace	AL	1
Corn-Maya	FL	287
Cornerstone Ministries	FL	317
Corpus Christi Church. Sanctuary Comm.	NY	687
Council of Churches. Refugee Resettlement P	MO	552
Cross Lutheran Church	WI	947
Cuban Amer. Natl. Council. Refugee Program	FL	299
Cultural Survival	MA	471
Dallas-Fort Worth Refugee Interagency	TX	832
Datacenter	CA	96
Delaware Dept. of Health & Social Services.	DE	219
Delaware Dept. of Justice. Service for Foreign	DE	221
Detroit Windsor Refugee Coalition	MI	492
Diocesan Migrant & Refugee Services	TX	845
Diocesan Refugee Coordinator	MI	493
Diocesan Refugee Resettlement Program	ME	439
Diocese of Green Bay. Dept. of Refugee, Mig	WI	939
Diocese of Lafayette. Migration & Refugee S	LA	428
Diocese of Nashville. Refugee Resettlement P	TN	812
Diocese of Oregon	OR	751
Diocese of Raleigh. Refugee Resettlement Of	NC	704
Diocese of Rhode Island	RI	795
Diocese of Richmond. Office of Refugee Rese	VA	909
Diocese of Richmond. Office of Refugee Rese	VA	901
Diocese of Springfield - Cape Girardeau. Rese	MO	553
Diocese of Springfield. Refugee Resettlement	MA	482
Disciples of Christ. Refugee & Immigration M	IN	399
District of Columbia Dept. of Human Service	DC	235
Don Bosco Community Center	MO	546
Downtown Legalization Project	CA	72
East Bay Sanctuary Covenant	CA	33
East Central Illinois Refugee Mutual Assistan	IL	391
East Side Group	TX	822
Eau Claire Area Hmong Mutual Assistance As	WI	938
Ecumenical Immigration Services	LA	431
Ecumenical Refugee Council	WI	948
Ecumenical Refugee Resettlement Services	VA	903
Ecumenical Refugee Services	CO	202
El Centro Asylum Project	CA	42
El Concilio. Immigration Project	CA	45
El Paso Legal Assistance Society	TX	846
El Rescate	CA	73
Ellis Island Immigration Museum	NY	647
Emmanuel Lutheran Church. Sanctuary Comm	MO	549
EPIC Immigration Project	WA	911
Episcopal Diocese of Minnesota. Refugee Re	MN	520
Episcopal Diocese of North Carolina. Refuge	NC	705
Episcopal Migration Ministries	NY	648

Episcopal Refugee and Migration Comm.	NH	570
Episcopal Refugee Resettlement Commission	IN	400
Episcopal Social Ministries	MD	442
Episcopal Social Service	CT	208
Eritrean Relief Comm.	NY	649
Ethiopian Community Center	DC	236
Ethiopian Community Development Council	VA	895
Ethiopian Community Mutual Assistance Ass	NY	650
Evangelical Crusade of Fishers of Men	NY	614
Experiment in Intl. Living	VT	888
Faith Lutheran Church	FL	308
Faith United Methodist Church. Sanctuary Co	IA	405
Family and Children's Services of Chattanooga	TN	806
Father Moriarty Asylum Program	CA	137
Fed. for Amer. Immigration Reform	DC	237
Fed. of Italian-Amer. Societies	NY	606
Fed. of Jewish Agencies of Greater Philadelphi	PA	775
Fed. of Vietnamese & Allied Veterans	CA	56
Filipinos for Affirmative Action	CA	97
First Lutheran Church	FL	283
First Unitarian Church	CA	183
First Unitarian Church. Sanctuary Comm.	MI	488
Florida Baptist Conv.	FL	290
Florida Council of Churches. Refugee Program	FL	310
Florida Dept. of Health and Rehabilitation Ser	FL	315
Florida Rural Legal Services	FL	281
Foreign-Born Information and Referral Networ	MD	448
Fort Worth Independent School District. Survi	TX	850
Freedom Flight Refugee Center	MI	504
Fresno Ecumenical Resettlement Project	CA	46
Friendly House	AZ	11
Friends Meeting of Austin. Sanctuary Comm.	TX	823
Friends of the Third World	IN	395
General Conference of Seventh-Day Adventists	DC	238
George Mason Univ. Indochina Institute.	VA	897
George Washington Univ. Natl. Law Center. I	DC	239
Georgia Baptist Conv. Language Missions Dep	GA	325
Georgia Dept. of Human Resources. Refugee He	GA	326
Georgia Dept. of Human Resources. Special Pr	GA	327
Good Samaritan Community Center	CA	138
Greater Boston Legal Services	MA	460
Greater Hartford Jewish Fed.	CT	216
Guatemala Human Rights Commission/USA	DC	240
Haitian Amer. Assoc.	MA	472
Haitian Amer. Community Assoc.	FL	300
Haitian Centers Council	NY	615
Haitian Multi-Service Center	MA	474
Haitian Refugee Center	FL	301
Hawaii Dept. of Labor & Industrial Relations.	HI	341
Heart of Texas Legal Services	TX	881
Hebrew Immigrant Aid Society	NY	651
Hebrew Immigrant Aid Society	PA	776
Hebrew Immigrant Aid Society of Baltimore	MD	443
Hispanic Immigration Counseling Program	WA	920
Hmong Amer. Human Rights Comm.	CA	47
Hmong Assoc. of Brown County. Refugee Com	WI	940
Hmong Catholic Center	MN	532
Hmong Community	MI	494
Hmong Community Service	MD	449
Hmong Council	CA	48
Hmong Mutual Assistance Assoc.	WI	955
Hmong Natural Assoc. of North Carolina	NC	703
Hmong-Amer. Planning & Development Center	TX	854
Hmong/Amer. Friendship Assoc.	WI	949
Holt Intl. Children's Services	OR	749
Holy Cross Mission	CA	184
Holy Cross Service Center	FL	288
Hood River Valley Immigration Project	OR	750
Houston Metropolitan Ministries	TX	861
Human Rights Advocates Intl.	NJ	579
Human Rights Advocates Intl.	NY	652
Human Rights Internet	MA	473
Human Services Assoc.	CA	31
Humboldt Congregations for Sanctuary	CA	28
Humboldt Unitarian-Universalist Fellowship	CA	30
Idaho Dept. of Health and Welfare. Div. of Fiel	ID	347
Illinois Bureau of Naturalization Services	IL	389
Illinois Conference of Churches. Refugee Immi	IL	390
Illinois Conference of Churches. Refugee Reset	IL	358
Immigrant Assistance Line	CA	139
Immigrant Legal Resource Center	CA	41
Immigrant Legal Resource Center	CA	140
Immigrant Students Project of the Natl. Coaliti	MA	461
Immigrants Assistance Center	MA	480
Immigrants' Rights Office	CA	74
Immigration Advocacy Service	NE	561
Immigration and Legalization Service	TX	824
Immigration Assistance Service	NJ	583
Immigration Counseling Center	TX	862
Immigration Counseling Migration & Refugee	TX	851
Immigration History Society	MN	533
Immigration Institute	TX	863
Immigration Law Enforcement Monitoring Proj	TX	864
Immigration Law Project	TX	875
Immigration Project	CA	75
Immigration Project	CA	194
Immigration Service of Santa Rosa	CA	189
Immigration Services of Santa Rosa	CA	131
Impact	CA	126
Indiana Council of Churches	IN	401
Indiana Dept. of Welfare. Policy & Program De	IN	402
Indochina Resource Action Center	DC	241
Indochinese Assistance Center	CA	117
Inland Counties Legal Services	CA	111
Inmigracion Latina Foundation	FL	302
Inter-Agency Council for Immigrant Services	HI	342
InterAction (Amer. Council for Voluntary Intl.	NY	653
Intercultural Action Center	CA	178
Interfaith Refugee Assistance Project	OK	744
Interfaith Sanctuary Movement	PA	784
Intermountain Health Care. Refugee Clinic	UT	883
Intl. Buddhist Meditation Assoc.	HI	343
Intl. Catholic Migration Commission	DC	242
Intl. Center	NH	569
Intl. Center of the Capital Region. Refugee As	NY	602
Intl. Community Services	TX	865

Intl. Immigrants Foundation	NY	654	Jewish Family and Community Services	FL	291
Intl. Institute	OH	711	Jewish Family and Counseling Service	NJ	572
Intl. Institute of Buffalo	NY	623	Jewish Family and Voc. Service	KY	422
Intl. Institute of Connecticut	CT	209	Jewish Family Service	AZ	17
Intl. Institute of Connecticut	CT	213	Jewish Family Service	CA	51
Intl. Institute of Erie	PA	764	Jewish Family Service	CA	99
Intl. Institute of Flint	MI	499	Jewish Family Service	CT	215
Intl. Institute of Los Angeles	CA	191	Jewish Family Service	FL	314
Intl. Institute of Los Angeles. Immigrant & Re	CA	76	Jewish Family Service	LA	436
Intl. Institute of Los Angeles. Refugee Relocat	CA	158	Jewish Family Service	MN	535
Intl. Institute of Lowell	MA	479	Jewish Family Service	NJ	574
Intl. Institute of Metro Detroit	MI	495	Jewish Family Service	NJ	575
Intl. Institute of Metropolitan St. Louis	MO	550	Jewish Family Service	NY	624
Intl. Institute of Minnesota	MN	534	Jewish Family Service	NY	688
Intl. Institute of New Jersey	NJ	584	Jewish Family Service	OH	712
Intl. Institute of Northwest Indiana	IN	397	Jewish Family Service	PA	785
Intl. Institute of Rhose Island	RI	796	Jewish Family Service	PA	787
Intl. Institute of San Francisco	CA	141	Jewish Family Service	RI	797
Intl. Institute of the East Bay	CA	98	Jewish Family Service	TN	813
Intl. Institute of Toledo	OH	732	Jewish Family Service	TX	876
Intl. Institute of Wisconsin	WI	950	Jewish Family Service	VA	904
Intl. Ladies Garment Workers Union. Immigrat	CA	77	Jewish Family Service	WA	922
Intl. Ladies Garment Workers Union. Immigrat	NY	655	Jewish Family Service Agency	NV	565
Intl. Ladies Garment Workers Union. Immigrat	IL	359	Jewish Family Service Agency of Central New	NJ	580
Intl. Refugee Center	IL	360	Jewish Family Service Assoc.	OH	719
Intl. Rescue Comm.	CA	49	Jewish Family Service of Broward County	FL	285
Intl. Rescue Comm.	CA	78	Jewish Family Service of Delaware Valley	NJ	591
Intl. Rescue Comm.	CA	118	Jewish Family Service of Detroit	MI	514
Intl. Rescue Comm.	CA	127	Jewish Family Service of Greater Springfield	MA	483
Intl. Rescue Comm.	CA	142	Jewish Family Service of Metro West	NJ	589
Intl. Rescue Comm.	CA	162	Jewish Family Service of MetroWest	NJ	581
Intl. Rescue Comm.	CA	168	Jewish Family Service of North Middlesex Cou	NJ	578
Intl. Rescue Comm.	CA	185	Jewish Family Service of Raritan Valley	NJ	576
Intl. Rescue Comm.	DC	243	Jewish Family Service of Somerset County	NJ	588
Intl. Rescue Comm.	FL	303	Jewish Family Service. Immigration & Resettl	NM	599
Intl. Rescue Comm.	GA	335	Jewish Family Service. Refugee Resettlement P	TX	866
Intl. Rescue Comm.	NJ	595	Jewish Family Service. Refugee Services	CA	79
Intl. Rescue Comm.	NY	656	Jewish Family Service. Resettlement Program	CA	128
Intl. Rescue Comm.	TX	833	Jewish Family Service. Resettlement Program	FL	306
Intl. Rescue Comm.	WA	921	Jewish Family Service. Resettlement Program	MD	444
Intl. Service Center	PA	766	Jewish Family Service. Resettlement Services	CT	210
Intl. Social Service. Amer. Branch	NY	657	Jewish Family Services	FL	318
Iowa Dept. of Human Services. Bureau of Refug	IA	408	Jewish Family Services	GA	328
Irish Immigration Reform Movement	NY	629	Jewish Family Services	ME	440
Japanese Amer. Service Comm. of Chicago	IL	361	Jewish Family Services	NC	697
Japanese Newcomer Service	CA	143	Jewish Family Services	TX	834
Jesuit Refugee Service	DC	244	Jewish Family Services	UT	884
Jewish Family & Children Services	CA	144	Jewish Family Services	WI	951
Jewish Family & Children's Service	AZ	12	Jewish Family Services of Greater Orlando	FL	322
Jewish Family and Child Service	OR	754	Jewish Family Services. Refugee Services	IL	362
Jewish Family and Children's Agency	PA	777	Jewish Fed. of Palm Beach County	FL	320
Jewish Family and Children's Service	CO	203	Jewish Philanthropic Fund of 1933	NY	658
Jewish Family and Children's Service	MA	466	Jewish Social Services	TX	852
Jewish Family and Children's Service	NJ	571	Jewish Social Services	WI	943
Jewish Family and Children's Service	OH	736	Jewish Social Services Agency	MD	451
Jewish Family and Children's Service. Resettle	MN	521	Jewish Voc. & Career Counseling Service	CA	145
Jewish Family and Children's Services	IN	403	Jewish Voc. Service	NJ	577
Jewish Family and Children's Services	TX	847	Jewish Voc. Service	OH	713

Jewish Voc. Service & Community Workshop	MI	515
Joint Legal Task Force on Central Amer. Refug	WA	923
Jubilee Partners	GA	334
Kalamazoo Interfaith Sanctuary Project	MI	506
Kalihi-Palama Immigrant Service Center	HI	344
Kansas Dept. of Social & Rehabilitation Servi	KS	415
Kentucky Cabinet for Human Resources. Office	KY	419
Khemara Buddhikarma - The Cambodian Buddhi	CA	59
Khmer Buddhist Society of New England	RI	798
Khmer Health Advocates	CT	217
Khmer Society of San Antonio. Refugee SOS	TX	877
King County Rape Relief. Southeast Asian Chi	WA	915
Korean Amer. Community Services	IL	363
Korean Amer. Community Services	MD	454
La Crosse Area Hmong Mutual Assistance Asso	WI	941
Lao Community Assoc.	GA	336
Lao Consultant Firm	VA	892
Lao Family Community	CA	88
Lao Family Community	CA	89
Lao Family Community	CA	91
Lao Family Community	CA	100
Lao Family Community	CA	119
Lao Family Community	CA	169
Lao Family Community	UT	887
Lao Family Community	WI	952
Lao Khmu Assoc.	CA	186
Lawyers Comm. for Human Rights. Political A	NY	659
Legal Aid Bureau	MD	453
Legal Aid of Western Missouri	MO	547
Legal Aid of Western Oklahoma	OK	745
Legal Aid Society	FL	321
Legal Aid Society. Alien Rights Unit	CA	129
Legal Services Center	MA	477
Legal Services Center for Immigrants	IL	364
Legal Services of Northern California	CA	120
Long Island Refugee Resettlement Program	NY	616
Los Angeles County Bar Assoc. Immigration L	CA	80
Louisiana Dept. of Health & Human Resources.	LA	432
Louisiana Dept. of Health & Human Services.	LA	425
Loyola Univ. School of Law Clinic	LA	433
Lutheran Child & Family Services of Massachu	MA	485
Lutheran Child and Family Services	IL	365
Lutheran Children and Family Service	PA	778
Lutheran Church. Synod Board of Social Minis	MO	551
Lutheran Family Service. Refugee Services	OR	755
Lutheran Family Services. Refugee Resettlemen	NC	700
Lutheran Immigration & Refugee Services	DC	245
Lutheran Immigration and Refugee Service	NY	660
Lutheran Immigration and Refugee Service	TX	867
Lutheran Ministries of Florida	FL	307
Lutheran Ministries of Florida. Refugee Resettl	FL	319
Lutheran Ministries of Georgia	GA	329
Lutheran Refugee and Immigration Services	NJ	592
Lutheran Refugee Resettlement	CO	204
Lutheran Social Ministry of the Southwest. Re	AZ	13
Lutheran Social Services	MN	516
Lutheran Social Services of Iowa	IA	409
Lutheran Social Services of Kansas and Oklaho	KS	417
Lutheran Social Services of Michigan. Dept. o	MI	510
Lutheran Social Services of Michigan. Refugee	MI	507
Lutheran Social Services of Minnesota. Refuge	MN	522
Lutheran Social Services of Montana	MT	555
Lutheran Social Services of North Dakota. Refu	ND	709
Lutheran Social Services of Northeast Florida.	FL	292
Lutheran Social Services of Northern Californi	CA	146
Lutheran Social Services of South Dakota. Refu	SD	805
Lutheran Social Services of Wisconsin & Uppe	WI	953
Lutheran Social Services. Immigration & Refug	CA	81
Lutheran Social Services. Unaccompanied Min	OH	722
Lutheran Welfare Service	PA	768
Maine Annual Conference of the United Metho	ME	438
Maine Dept. of Human Services. Bureau of Soc	ME	437
Manchester Church of the Brethren. Sanctuary	IN	404
Maryland Dept. of Human Resources. State Ref	MD	445
Massachusetts Immigrant & Refugee Advocacy	MA	462
Massachusetts Office for Refugees and Immigra	MA	463
Mecklenburg Presbytery Refugee Resettlement	NC	698
Mennonite Central Comm. Immigration & Ref	PA	760
Mennonite Immigration and Refugee Services	DC	246
Mennonite Intl. Refugee Assistance	TX	835
Metropolitan Social Services. Refugee Program	TN	814
Miami Presbytery	OH	730
Michigan Dept. of Social Services. Office of R	MI	496
Mid-Cumberland Refugee Assistance Ministry	TN	815
Middlesex County Legal Services Corp.	NJ	585
Midwest Coalition in Defense of Immigrants	IL	366
Midwest Immigrant Rights Center	IL	367
Migration & Refugee Services	SC	802
Migration and Refugee Services Office	NJ	593
Minnesota - Wisconsin Southern Baptist Conv	MN	526
Minnesota Cambodian Buddhist Society	MN	536
Minnesota Council of Churches. Refugee Progr	MN	537
Minnesota Dept. of Human Services. Refugee P	MN	538
Mission Community Legal Defense	CA	147
Mississippi Baptist Conv. Language Missions	MS	542
Mississippi Dept. of Public Welfare. Refugee P	MS	543
Missouri Div. of Family Services. Refugee Ass	MO	544
Mohawk Valley Resource Center for Refugees	NY	693
Montana Assoc. for Refugee Services	MT	554
Montana Dept. of Family Services. Office of R	MT	557
Monterey County Sanctuary	CA	103
Moob Fed. of Amer.	IL	392
Multicultural Immigration Center	NY	661
Mutual Aid Assoc. of the New Polish Immigrat	IL	368
Na Loio No Na Kanaka. Lawyers for the People	HI	345
Natl. Assoc. for Vietnamese Amer. Education	CA	170
Natl. Assoc. of Evangelicals. Immigration Pro	FL	304
Natl. Center For Immigrants' Rights	CA	82
Natl. Coalition for Haitian Refugees	NY	662
Natl. Council of Jewish Women. Immigration	MA	487
Natl. Council of Jewish Women. Rescue & Mi	FL	305
Natl. Immigration Project of the Natl. Lawyers	MA	464
Natl. Immigration, Refugee, and Citizenship F	DC	247
Natl. Lawyers Guild. Central Amer. Refugee De	PA	779
Natl. Network for Immigrant & Refugee Rights	CA	101
Natl. Slavic Conv.	MD	446

Nationalities Service Center	PA	769
Nationalities Service Center	PA	780
Nationalities Service of Central California	CA	50
Nationalities Services Center	OH	718
Naturalization Project	LA	434
Nebraska Dept. of Social Services. Refugee Aff	NE	560
Neil Avenue Mennonite Church. Sanctuary Co	OH	723
Nevada Dept. of Human Resources. State Refug	NV	563
New Hampshire Office of Refugee Resettlement	NH	568
New Hope Presbytery	NC	694
New Jersey Dept. of Human Services. State Ref	NJ	594
New Lao Friendship Club of Oklahoma	OK	741
New Mexico Dept. of Human Services. Social	NM	601
New Orleans Legal Assistance Corp.	LA	435
New York Assoc. for New Amer.	NY	663
New York Circus	NY	664
New York City. Office of Immigrant Affairs	NY	665
New York Dept. of Social Services. State Refu	NY	603
New York State Assembly. Task Force on New	NY	666
North Carolina Baptist State Conv.	NC	695
North Carolina Dept. of Human Resources. Fa	NC	706
North Carolina Refugee Health Program	NC	707
North Dakota Dept. of Human Services. Refuge	ND	708
North Manhattan Coalition for Immigrants' Ri	NY	667
North Texas Immigration Coalition	TX	836
Northern Virginia Family Service. Multicultura	VA	898
Northside Sanctuary Coalition	IL	369
O.L.A. Immigration Rights Center	CA	193
O.L.A. Raza	CA	109
Ohio Council of Churches. Refugee Services	OH	724
Ohio Dept. of Human Services. Program Devel	OH	725
Ohio State Conv. of Baptists	OH	726
Oklahoma Dept. of Human Services. Refugee U	OK	742
One Stop Immigration & Educational Center	CA	83
Orange County Coalition for Immigrant Rights	CA	171
Orange County Community Consortium	CA	172
Oregon Dept. of Human Resources. Refugee Pr	OR	759
Organization of Chinese Amer.	DC	248
Oshkosh Lao Hmong Assoc.	WI	954
Overground Railroad	IL	382
Palo Alto Friends Meeting	CA	107
Partnership for Human Development. Resettle	TX	826
Pennsylvania Dept. of Public Welfare. Office o	PA	767
People's Immigration Service	CA	195
People's Law Office for Organized Workers	FL	280
Peylim	NY	668
Philadelphia Refugee Service Center	PA	781
Philippine Center for Immigrant Rights	NY	669
Pillsbury United Neighborhood Services. Asian	MN	523
Pioneer Valley Sanctuary Comm., Mt. Toby M	MA	457
Plattsburg Interfaith Council	NY	685
Plenty USA	CA	38
Polish Amer. Immigration and Relief Comm.	NY	670
Polish Amer. Immigration Relief Comm.	IL	370
Polish and Slavic Center. Refugee Assistance	NY	617
Posada Sanctuary	IL	387
Presbyterian Synod of Southern California and	CA	84
Presbytery of Long Island	NY	625
Presbytery of Southern Louisiana	LA	426
PRIME Ecumenical Commitment to Refugees	PA	762
Project Deliverance	OH	733
Proyecto Adelante	TX	837
Proyecto Resistencia	IL	371
Rav Tov. Intl. Jewish Rescue Organization	NY	618
Redeemer Lutheran Church. Hmong Farm Proje	OH	727
Reformed Church in Amer. Refugee Program	MI	505
Refugee and Immigrant Multi-Service Center	WA	930
Refugee Assistance Program	CA	130
Refugee Employment Assistance Project	CA	148
Refugee Employment Center	MI	511
Refugee Policy Group	DC	249
Refugee Resettlement Comm.	CA	90
Refugee Resettlement Office	AR	24
Refugee Resettlement Office	MO	545
Refugee Resettlement Program	AR	26
Refugee Services	MI	508
Refugee Voices	DC	250
Refugee Women in Development	DC	251
Refugees Intl.	DC	252
Research Foundation for Jewish Immigration	NY	671
Rhode Island Dept. of Human Services. State R	RI	799
Rio Grande Defense Comm.	TX	879
Riverside Church. Sanctuary Comm.	NY	672
Rochester Refugee Services	MN	527
Rosenberg Foundation	CA	149
Saint Vincents Services	NY	619
Salvadoran Refugee Comm. (Oscar A. Romero)	DC	253
San Antonio Literacy Council	TX	878
San Francisco Lawyers' Comm. Immigrant & R	CA	150
San Francisco Lawyers' Comm. Political Asylu	CA	151
San Juan Bautista Lutheran Church. Sanctuary	AZ	18
San Juan Macias Immigrant Center	CA	104
Sanctuary Covenant of San Francisco	CA	152
Sandigan California	CA	121
Santa Clara County Health Dept. Refugee Heal	CA	163
Sarrlano Chirino Amaya Central Amer. Refuge	CA	85
Saura Center	IL	372
Save the Children. Refugee Child Care Assista	GA	330
Seattle - King County Bar Assoc. Legalization	WA	924
Sepulveda Unitarian Universalist Society	CA	180
Sinai Temple. Sanctuary Comm.	MA	484
Socio-Economic Development Center for Sout	RI	800
Somerville Portuguese Amer. League	MA	481
South and Meso-Amer. Indian Information Cen	CA	34
South Carolina Dept. of Social Services. Refug	SC	803
South Dakota Dept. of Social Services. Refuge	SD	804
South Texas Immigration Council	TX	828
South Texas Immigration Council	TX	856
South Texas Immigration Council	TX	873
South-East Asia Center	IL	373
Southeast Asian Center	RI	792
Southern Arizona Legal Aid	AZ	19
Southern Baptist Immigration and Refugee Res	GA	331
Southern California Interfaith Task Force on C	CA	86
Southern Methodist Univ. Law School. Politic	TX	838
Southern Minnesota Regional Legal Services	MN	517

Southside Community Mission	NY	620
Spokane Bar Assoc. Pro Bono Program	WA	931
Sponsors Organized to Assist Refugees	ID	348
Sponsors Organized to Assist Refugees	OR	756
St. Anselm's Immigrant & Refugee Community	CA	52
St. John's Center. Office of Social Ministry	GA	338
St. Paul's United Methodist Church. Refugee P	NV	567
St. Teresa's Church. Sanctuary Comm.	CA	153
Sunyvale Community Services	CA	188
Synapses. Asian Organizing Program	IL	374
Syracuse Interreligious Council. Refugee Assis	NY	692
Tacoma Community House	WA	934
TECHO Central Amer. Education Center	AZ	20
Temple Beth El. Sanctuary Comm.	WI	944
Temple Emanu-El. Sanctuary Comm.	AZ	21
Temple Israel. Sanctuary Comm.	CA	60
Temple Sinai. Sanctuary Comm.	CA	102
Temple Sinai. Sanctuary Comm.	DC	254
Tennessee Dept. of Human Services. Refugee P	TN	816
Tennessee Valley Unitarian Church. Sanctuary	TN	808
Texan Training & Employment Center	TX	868
Texas Dept. of Human Service. Refugee Progra	TX	825
Texas Rural Legal Aid	TX	843
Texas Rural Legal Aid. Clinica de Inmigracion	TX	841
Tolstoy Foundation	AZ	14
Tolstoy Foundation	CA	192
Tolstoy Foundation	MI	498
Tolstoy Foundation	NY	673
Training Program in Human Services for Emig	NY	674
Traveler and Immigrants Aid	IL	375
Travelers Aid Intl. Institute. Refugee Resource	OH	716
Travelers Aid Society	DC	255
Tressler Lutheran Services. Refugee Services P	PA	770
Tucson Ecumenical Council. Central Amer. Tas	AZ	22
Tucson Ecumenical Council. Legal Assistance	AZ	23
U. S. Catholic Conference. Migration & Refug	NY	675
U.S. Catholic Conference. Migration & Refug	DC	256
U.S. Catholic Conference. Migration & Refug	CA	154
U.S. Catholic Conference. Migration & Refug	DC	257
U.S. Catholic Conference. Migration & Refug	NY	676
U.S. Catholic Conference. Migration & Refug	TX	848
U.S. Congress. Congressional Border Caucus	DC	258
U.S. Congress. Congressional Human Rights	DC	259
U.S. Congress. House Comm. on the Judiciary	DC	260
U.S. Congress. Senate Border Caucus	DC	261
U.S. Congress. Senate Comm. on the Judiciary	DC	262
U.S. Congress. Senate Human Rights Caucus	DC	263
U.S. Dept. of Health & Human Services. Fami	CA	155
U.S. Dept. of Health & Human Services. Fami	CO	205
U.S. Dept. of Health & Human Services. Fami	GA	332
U.S. Dept. of Health & Human Services. Fami	IL	376
U.S. Dept. of Health & Human Services. Fami	MA	465
U.S. Dept. of Health & Human Services. Fami	MO	548
U.S. Dept. of Health & Human Services. Fami	NY	677
U.S. Dept. of Health & Human Services. Fami	PA	782
U.S. Dept. of Health & Human Services. Fami	TX	839
U.S. Dept. of Health & Human Services. Fami	WA	925
U.S. Dept. of Health and Human Services. Fam	DC	264
U.S. Dept. of Health and Human Services. Publ	MD	452
U.S. Dept. of Justice. Executive Office for Imm	VA	899
U.S. Dept. of Justice. Immigration and Naturali	DC	265
U.S. Dept. of Justice. Office of Special Counse	DC	266
U.S. Dept. of Labor. Bureau of Intl. Labor Affa	DC	267
U.S. Dept. of Labor. Foreign Labor Certificati	DC	268
U.S. Dept. of State. Bureau for Refugee Progra	DC	269
U.S. Dept. of State. Bureau of Consular Affairs	DC	270
U.S. Dept. of State. Bureau of Human Rights a	DC	271
U.S. Dept. of State. Coordinator for Refugee A	DC	272
U.S. Office of Management and Budget. Refuge	DC	273
Ukrainian Research Foundation	CO	206
Unitarian Church of Arlington	VA	896
Unitarian Church. Sanctuary Comm.	CT	218
Unitarian Society of Sacramento. Sanctuary Co	CA	122
Unitarian Universalist Church	CA	61
United Cambodian Community	CA	62
United Catholic Social Services. Refugee Reset	NE	562
United Church Board for World Ministries. Ref	NY	678
United Methodist Church. Refugee Concerns C	CA	156
United Methodist Comm. on Relief. Refugee S	NY	679
United Nations High Commissioner for Refuge	DC	274
United Nations. High Commissioner for Refug	NY	680
United Nations. Relief and Works Agency for	NY	681
United Refugee Council	NY	621
U.S. Catholic Conference	IL	388
U.S. Comm. for Refugees	DC	275
Univ. Church. Sanctuary Project	IL	377
Univ. of California. School of Law. Immigrati	CA	39
Univ. of Florida. Caribbean Migration Progra	FL	284
Univ. of Minnesota. Immigration History Rese	MN	539
Univ. of Minnesota. Southeast Asian Refugee	MN	524
Univ. of Wisconsin. Center for Demography a	WI	945
Univ. Unitarian Church. Sanctuary Comm.	WA	926
Utah Dept. of Social Services. Refugee & Alie	UT	885
Utah Immigration Project	UT	886
Valley Immigrants Rights Center	CA	105
Valley Religious Task Force on Central Amer.	AZ	15
Vermont Catholic Charities. Refugee Resettlem	VT	890
Vermont State Refugee Coordinator	VT	891
Vietnam Refugee Fund	VA	900
Vietnamese Amer. Assoc. Refugee Center	OK	743
Vietnamese Amer. Civic Assoc.	MA	475
Vietnamese Amer. Cultural Alliance of Colorad	CO	198
Vietnamese Amer. Cultural Organization	NY	682
Vietnamese Assoc. of Illinois	IL	378
Vietnamese Catholic Community	MI	489
Vietnamese Catholic Community in Connectic	CT	214
Vietnamese Community in Virginia	VA	905
Vietnamese Community of Orange County	CA	173
Vietnamese Evangelical Church	MN	525
Vietnamese Lutheran Ministry	WA	927
Vietnamese Mutual Assistance Assoc.	TX	840
Vietnamese Mutual Assistance Assoc. of North	ND	710
Vietnamese Service Center	CA	53
Vietnamese Seventh-Day Adventist Church	OR	757
Vietnamese Society of Rhode Island	RI	801
Virginia Baptist General Board. Div. of Missio	VA	906

Virginia Council of Churches. Refugee Progra	VA	907
Virginia Dept. of Social Services. State Refuge	VA	908
Washington Assoc. of Churches. Immigration	WA	928
Washington Assoc. of Churches. Refugee Rese	WA	932
Washington Bureau of Refugee Assistance	WA	914
Washington Lawyers' Comm. for Civil Rights	DC	276
Washington Office on Haiti	DC	277
West Virginia Dept. of Human Services	WV	937
Westside Legal Services	CA	176
Wheadon United Methodist Church. Sanctuary	IL	383
Wisconsin Div. of Community Services. Refug	WI	946
Woodrow Wilson Intl. Center	DC	278
World Relief	CA	54
World Relief	CA	157
World Relief	CA	187
World Relief	DC	279
World Relief	FL	282
World Relief	GA	333
World Relief	NY	683
World Relief	NC	701
World Relief	TN	817
World Relief	TX	853
World Relief	TX	869
World Relief	WA	929
World Relief. Immigration Services	IL	379
Wyoming Dept. of Health & Social Services.	WY	958
Yiu Mienh Assoc. of Oregon	OR	758
YMCA Intl. Services	TX	870
YMCA. Refugee Resettlement Services	IL	380
Youth With a Mission Relief Services	HI	346

Index II

Contact Persons

Abbott, Donna M.	501	Boon, Jim	281	Chuman, Joseph	590

Abbott, Donna M. — 501
Abraha, Mekonnen — 650
Abrams-Morley, Elizabeth — 771
Abriel, Evangeline — 433
Acosta, Frank — 72
Agan, David — 439
Aglio, Thomas — 309
Aguirre, Raquel — 94
Amstutz, Tim — 379
Anderson, Betty — 406
Anderson, Jack — 465
Andres, Rev. Justo — 184
Ansary, Salah — 755
Arango, Carlos — 366
Arguell, Charles — 830
Armstrong, Sen. William — 263
Asarnow, Claire — 572
Ascher, Albert — 515
Asencio, Diego C. — 234
August, Lynn — 799
Avigdor, Morton — 631
Ayala, Hayelom — 354
Ayala, Nati — 856
Azhocar, Ernesto — 126
Baccam, Kham — 182
Bader, Jules F. — 946
Bagan, Laurel — 201
Bailey, Raleigh — 700
Baker, Jerry K. — 325
Ball, Mary G. — 495
Barnes, Cathy — 846
Barnes, John — 472
Barnes, Walter — 114
Basham, Judy — 898
Battisti, Rose Marie — 693
Bayer, Evelyn — 493
Bazluki, Barbara — 696
Beach, George — 896
Bednorz, Al — 818
Beitz, William C. — 289
Belland, Lynn — 653
Benoit, Patricia — 636
Bergstresser, Charles — 592
Beruman, Guadalupe — 110
Betts, Nancy — 148
Bevans, Shannon — 537
Biebel, Barbara B. — 939
Bien, Frank J. — 445
Binenfeld, Richard — 713
Blank, Marianne — 52
Bloom, Russell J. — 292
Blostein, Steven — 850
Blue, Rev. James — 559
Bocanegra, Juan — 919
Bogen, Elizabeth — 665
Bohren, Sr. Teresa Marie — 763
Bollwinkel, Rev. Mark — 567
Booker, Bob — 840

Boon, Jim — 281
Boot, Hinke — 623
Borkowski, Zoe — 98
Boxleitner, Msgr. J. Jerome — 528
Bragg, Eugene — 513
Brassard, Eugene — 11
Breheny, Lawrence — 407
Brown, Carol — 23
Brown, Dora Lee — 698
Brown, Sr. Patricia — 338
Browne, Barbara — 326
Brueggen, Joseph — 286
Bruening, Thomas M. — 268
Bryce-Laporte, Roy S. — 690
Buck, James L. — 265
Bufler, Robbie — 334
Burger, Beth — 790
Burkhart, Bob — 925
Burr, Rev. Thomas E. — 388
Burstein, Benita M. — 575
Bushart, Bruce — 603
Bustamante, Andres — 64
Caldwell, Brenda — 317
Caldwell, Rev. David — 747
Campbell, May — 358
Campos, Francisco — 280
Campos, Sara — 151
Canales, Rita — 36
Canjura, Boris — 253
Carey, John — 704
Carmona, Gloria — 385
Carr, Ann — 769
Carr, Barbara — 199
Carrera, John Willshire — 461
Carrera, John Willshire — 467
Carte, John — 875
Cassis, Olga — 661
Castentan, Andres — 287
Castillo, Angella — 69
Castillo, Herb — 177
Castillo, Leonel — 863
Cayuqco, Nilo — 34
Cha, Neng Ky — 554
Champoux, Rev. Thomas — 935
Chao, Chaosarn S. — 100
Chao, Mimi — 832
Charlow, Bart — 159
Chatham, Rev. Darald — 824
Chavez, Franklin — 302
Chavez, Roberto — 54
Chaw, Kue — 703
Chen, Thongsy — 158
Chhean, Rev. Kong — 59
Childers, Perry — 332
Chisholm-Thomas, Diane — 424
Chishti, Muzaffar A. — 655
Choy, Walter — 341
Chu, Irene K. — 70

Chuman, Joseph — 590
Clark, Joan M. — 270
Clark, Phoebe — 543
Clarke, Pat — 881
Climent, Don — 142
Cogo, Rev. Joseph A. — 632
Cohen, Melvin — 571
Coleman, Rep. Ronald — 258
Conlon, Peter — 365
Cook, Michael — 312
Cooper, Alicia — 168
Cooper, Don — 216
Coronado, Ramiro — 87
Corsano-Hoffer, Sue — 807
Costain, Pam — 530
Cotterill, Tom — 957
Cousin, Paul E. — 386
Cozette, Gary — 369
Crosslin, Anna — 550
Cruz, Esther — 587
Culp, Clifford — 452
Cumbee, Judy — 1
Curtain, Ron — 157
Cushman, Tudor — 348
Damon, Ann — 538
Dana, Mary Caroline — 390
Dang, Tanya — 900
Dang, Ywyet — 230
Dao, Anh H. — 811
Darragh, Jodie — 337
Davidson, Minor — 447
Davis, Magda Montiel — 294
Davis, Michael — 531
Davis, Tina — 428
Dawes, Gil — 405
Dawson, Marion M. — 648
De Concini, Sen. Dennis — 261
de Haan, Dale S. — 644
De la Rosa, Roberto — 109
Deak, Amy P. — 783
Dean, Amy — 359
Debs, Sr. Annette — 167
Delcham, Linner — 643
Delgado, Briselda — 566
Derr, Donna — 450
Deschenes, Margot — 812
DeVecchi, Robert P. — 656
Diamond, Mike — 380
Diaz, Guarione — 299
Diaz, Maria — 560
Diaz, Mary — 458
Dictor, Sidney — 847
Dieck, Ruth — 204
DiMarzio, Rev. Nicholas — 256
Dominguez, Rev. Francisco — 638
Dorman, Joy — 187
Dornic, Rev. Ivan — 446
Dovinh, Rev. John T. — 927

Drucker, Roberta	451	Gallagher, Dennis	249	Gunther, Rev. Eugene C.	551
Dudley, Alan	770	Gamson, Alvin	322	Gutierrez, Irene	920
Dunham, Audrea	594	Garcia, Mike	104	Gutierrez, Jose	83
Dunn, Pauline	255	Garcia, Ruven	844	Gutierrez, Phillip P.	415
Duong, Lao	757	Garske, Kathleen	901	Guzzi, Lisa	273
Duran, Anna	828	Garvin, Patricia	568	Ha, Vo Van	205
Durtka, Jr., Alexander P.	950	Geminiani, Victor M.	120	Hager, Eldon	849
Eckerk, Ronald	729	Gersh, David	624	Haggerty, Jim	676
Edwards, Dorothy	164	Ghosanandra, Maha	798	Hahn, Tae K.	454
Egan, Raymond	714	Gilbert, Dick	782	Hai, Lee	91
Eichler, Thomas P.	219	Gimeno, Antonieta	477	Hai, Thich Thong	343
Eichorn, Jerry	819	Ginsberg, Elliot	212	Hall, Heidi	103
Eiten, Don	141	Ginter, Brad	835	Hall, Rev. Frank	218
Elbert, Jean	552	Girouard, Laurice	792	Hammond, Don	683
Eledge, Robert	319	Giuffrida, Matthew R.	788	Hamrick, Anne H.	908
Ellwanger, Joseph	947	Gjerde, Rev. Kenneth	555	Handelman, Mark	663
Englebert-Benton, Mike	883	Gladney, Suzanne	547	Handelman, Phyllis J.	381
Entz, Rosemary	238	Glick, Peter	535	Haquang, Giac	905
Espinosa, Charmaine	601	Godfrey, Margaret	752	Harnapp, Lavada	727
Espitia, Joseph	29	Godoy, Leticia	304	Harrington, Dorothea	376
Estevez, Guillermo	595	Goeke, Mary Lou	134	Harris, Msgr. Robert	619
Etienne, Joe	615	Goetsch, James	395	Harris, Patricia	544
Evans, Ray	243	Goff, Fred	96	Hart, Shirley	296
Falgout, Nancy	870	Goldenson, Thomas	787	Hatch, Patricia A.	448
Feinberg, Ena	466	Goldfarb, Emily	136	Haug, Fraser	346
Feldman, William	565	Goldman, Harold	777	Hauser, Robert	945
Ferere, Gerard A.	791	Goldstein, Sidney	793	Hawn, Joe	597
Fernandez, Juan	605	Gomez, Iris	460	Hay, Stephen	872
Ferrin, Gretchen	28	Gomez, Sam	774	Healy, Sr. Kathleen	152
Field, Jane	145	Gonzales, Hermelinda	918	Healy, Sr. Kathleen	153
Fischberg, Jane	137	Gonzalez, Silvia	76	Heilberger, Muriel	462
Fish, John	377	Goodson, Ronald N.	707	Helmer, Brigitte	35
Flaherty, Margaret	335	Gottlieb, Helen	589	Helton, Arthur C.	659
Fleming, George W.	706	Gouger, Joanne	349	Hemberger, Robert	416
Fleming, Rev. David L.	730	Grant, Elaine	278	Hendricks, Glenn L.	524
Floreani, Maxine	711	Grant, James	208	Henkel, Thomas	573
Foley, Jane M.	429	Granzeier, Arthur G.	313	Hennessy, Margaret	453
Fomarek, Sr. Kathy	288	Gratto, Stephen H.	684	Henry, Tony	108
Fontes, Antonio	468	Gray, Christopher	627	Hentges, Diane K.	413
Forlines, Brenda	290	Graziano, Rev. Peter	476	Hepp, Patricia A.	508
Forman, Robert P.	775	Grechko, Elena V.	482	Hernandez, Alpha	841
Fountain, Lilian	702	Green, Barbara	924	Hernandez, Barbara	31
Fowler, Boyce D.	557	Green, Ellen	789	Herrera, Pedro	912
France, Dorothy	903	Green, Rev. Robert Edward	183	Herrera, Zita	295
France, Rev. Dorothy	907	Greene, David	106	Herrmann, Have	893
Franco, Martha	316	Greenlee, Barbara Day	805	Hertz, Jane	599
Freeman, Robert E.	829	Greenspan, Benjamin	215	Hidalgo, Evelyn	781
Frerking, John	308	Greenwood, John	300	Hird, Rev. Kerry	815
Frias, Efrain	667	Grimm, Robert	283	Hirsch, Abraham	668
Fried, Jonathan	293	Grognet, Allene	231	Hirsch, Howard	852
Friedman, Anita	144	Gronquist, Jill	821	Hirsch, Rifka	165
Friedman, Efraim	621	Grossfeld, Jerry	203	Hochstetter, Wayne	734
Friedman, Tova	588	Grottveit, Lowell	953	Hoffman, James	154
Friendly, Ana Zeledon	71	Grussendorf, Paul	239	Hoffman-Kahler, Gail	324
Fujiwara, Theresa	916	Gueckguezian, Knar	46	Holland, Burke	695
Furman, Sima	79	Guericke, Vern	804	Holman, Phil	264
Galdau, Fr. Florian	630	Guja, Gamechise	778	Holy, John	596
Galedo, Lillian	97	Gundrum, Janet	188	Horan, Kenneth	786

Horton, Winnie	327	Klein, Jeffrey	320	Lowman, Shephard C.	252
Hory, Heng	809	Klein, Shuli	306	Lowy, Maxine	434
Hoshijo, William	345	Klein, Wells	275	Luangpraseut, Khamchong	170
Houi, Vi	728	Klein, Wells C.	633	Lynch, Constance S.	486
House, Lawrence	768	Klotz, Robert L.	776	Lynch, Linda	509
Howe, Kathleen	81	Knafelc, Shirley	207	MacCormack, Charles F.	888
Huantes, Margarita	878	Kolek, Helga	691	MacIntyre, Susan	932
Hughes, Glenn	806	Kreeger, Amy	394	Mackey, Sally	928
Hul, Nil	57	Krome, Irene	608	Madrigal, Jr., Victor	874
Hung, Nguyen Manh	897	Krzyanowski, Janusz	670	Marder, Rabbi Sheldon	60
Hunt, Jan S.	117	Kuenning, Mary	678	Marino, Rev. Ron	612
Hunthausen, Dennis	933	Kwoh, Stewart	67	Marion, Leon	673
Ignatius, Sarah	923	Labella, Gabriella	780	Marks, Arnold S.	834
Igney, Robert	402	LaCrosse, Larry	491	Marmis, Fern	17
Ivory, Thomas J.	882	Lafontant, Jewel S.	269	Marsh, Rev. Jean	438
Janzen, David H.	382	Lafontant, Jewel S.	272	Martin, Ellen	756
Jarcaj, Slawomir	370	Laker, John A.	350	Martin, Paul J.	639
Jaurequi, Arturo	355	Lam, Daniel M.	463	Martinez, Cheryl	200
Jean-Juste, Fr. Gerard	301	Lan, Rev. Augustine	717	Martinez, Daniel	871
Jensen, Cindy	127	Langen, Gregory	688	Martinez, Lourdes	598
Jerabek, Vojtech	637	Langer, Martin E.	362	Martinez, Sara	85
Jewert, Russ	839	Lanman, Nancy	894	Martinez-Chavez, Laura	175
Jimenez, Maria	864	Lantos, Rep. Tom	259	Marx, Rabbi Robert	384
Johnson, Bob	921	Lao, Cau	115	Masserman, Jay	51
Johnson, Gladys C.	221	Laroche, Frances	474	Mattei, Lydia A.	479
Johnson, Grace	724	Larsen, Rev. Donald H.	660	Matty, Rev. Richard A.	845
Johnston, Ida	795	Laverentz, Larry	548	May, Eliza	225
Jones, David G.	522	Lavoie, Lorraine	511	May, Judith	891
Jones, Hilda	139	Lawler, Sr. Alice	855	Mayar, Habib	628
Jordan, Dan	753	Lawyer, Lyn	520	Maybury-Lewis, David	471
Jordan, Howard	666	Le, Hung	710	McCabe, Tim	492
Juarez, H. Edward	654	Le, Joseph R.	801	McCaffrey, Shellyn	267
Kagan, Saul L.	646	Le, Ngoan	378	McCalla, Jocelyn	662
Kalke, Darlene	642	Lee, Cahu-Ming	459	McCallin, John	274
Kalke, Rev. David	664	Lee, May O.	113	McGahan, Sr. Theresa	561
Kanthoul, Vora	58	Leiden, Warren	224	McGregor, Kathy	750
Kantor, George	607	Leitch, Hazel	746	McGuire, Kathy	387
Karpeles, Rev. Eileen	122	Lekisch, K. Peter	635	McKibben, Marilyn	556
Katz, Lou	677	Lerner, Samuel	514	McLean, Ruth	245
Katzowitz, Lauren	640	Leta, Helene	884	McMahan, Lauren	73
Kaz, Dennis	726	Leuchter, Ben Zion	651	McNamara, Beth	442
Kellman, Sharon R.	55	Leung, Daniel	340	McNeil, Helen	570
Kennedy, Sen. Edward M.	262	Lewis, Rev. Jim	705	McRill, Sherry	500
Kennon, Ken	22	Lieu, Dang Thi	162	McSpadden, Lucia Ann	156
Kenyon, James	616	Linh, Nguyen Ngoc	868	Medeiros, Ralph	480
Keo, Vuthy	720	Litherland, Irene	33	Meloni, Antonio	606
Kesselbrenner, Dan	464	Lockey, David	14	Mercado, Milagros	191
Kha, Tia N.	800	Locks, Amy	195	Mevorah, Sanford	652
Khamvongsa, Somsanith	892	Locson, Leni	121	Meyer, Rev. Nelson	722
Khang, By	118	Loera, Rita	869	Meyer-Niedzwiecki, Carol	506
Khoa, Le Xuan	241	Long, Jennifer	822	Michelson, Jhari	917
Khoonsrivong, Boon H.	186	Longcriame, Fritz	277	Miles, John	681
Khus, Thida	877	Lopez, Rev. Tony	886	Milhollan, David L.	899
Killip, Lita Jane	669	Lopez, Reynaldo	374	Mills, Roger J.	389
Kim, David	749	Lopez, Rose	862	Milner, Martha	540
Kirby, Ronald	767	Lopez-Perez, Alice	27	Minihane, Shawn	629
Kirsnis, Elizabeth	68	Loue, Sana	129	Minson, Nancy	716
Kitawaki, Yoshiko	143	Lovejoy, Bob	738	Mitchell, Miriam	427

Mitternight, Martha	541	Ornstein, Robert	63	Rabin, Dave	42
Moan, Rev. Frank	250	Orozco, Harvey	860	Rabiu, Badru I. O.	609
Mohn, Sid L.	375	Orozco, Sr. Teresa	411	Rackner, Alvin	754
Mohn, Sid L.	360	Ortiz, Leonore	6	Raible, Rev. Peter	926
Mohn, Sid L.	372	Ortiz, Michael J.	74	Ramirez, Secundino	371
Mokhiber, Al	223	Otterson, Brenda	516	Randall, James E.	419
Molczyck, Jean Ann	558	Palacios, Eduardo	189	Rascon, Juan	10
Molina, Luz	435	Palacios, Eduardo R.	131	Rascon, Susan	7
Money, Robert	213	Palm, Robert	867	Ravin, Linda	421
Monroe, James	426	Panglow, Yuk	344	Rayis, Afram	512
Montalto, Nicholas V.	584	Panoff, Vic	321	Reed, Marguerite	748
Monti, Nancy	586	Paquette, Paul	604	Reily, Rev. William	583
Morales, Irene C.	111	Pardue, Diana	647	Reiner, Rabbi Fred	254
Morgan, Pat	826	Paris, Harvey	210	Reth, Boran	478
Morris, Betty	24	Parish, Lael	455	Rex, Margaret	764
Morrison, Rep. Bruce A.	260	Parsons, John	853	Rezvani, Mahtb	66
Morrison, Steven H.	943	Partida, Blanca L.	851	Rhodes, Rick	740
Moses, Lincoln	107	Patane, Edward	686	Rickard, Fr. Don	827
Motus, Cecile	339	Patterson, Walt	25	Riegel, Robert H.	398
Moua, Kay	938	Peer, Robert	123	Riggs, Rev. Jennifer	399
Moura, Jose	481	Peichel, Donna	197	Rivard, Rev. Roland	890
Mousin, Craig	367	Percher, Martin L.	403	Rizza, Nicholas J.	132
Mucha, Mary	80	Perlman, Irving	328	Robertson, Mary Ekise	179
Mullin, Paul	585	Petkoff, Dimitar	582	Robinson, Mallory	866
Munson, Rev. Jim	417	Pettit, Robert	948	Robles, Sylia	401
Myers, Carmen	90	Pham, Henry Tuoc	198	Robles, Sylvia	400
Nambu, Masaru	361	Phan Thanh Hien, Joseph	682	Rodgerson, Phillip E.	906
Nava, Beatrice	77	Phifer, Kenneth	488	Rodriguez, Alfredo	147
Needleman, Martin	610	Phuong, Truong Ngoc	766	Rodriguez, Antonio	75
Negussie, Lissane	236	Picetti, Maria	161	Rogers, David L.	404
Nelson, Barry	709	Pihl, Rev. Carl H.	146	Rohlman, Levita	412
Neuschwander, Carlos	246	Pilsbury, Anne	613	Roquiero, Sherman K.	885
Newbold, Judy	745	Pilzer, Jay	813	Rosa, Teresa de la	193
Ney, Richard	876	Pinsky, Byron L.	591	Rosales, Sylvia	233
Nguon, Hilda	13	Pitts, Joe W.	838	Rose, Lou	546
Nguyen, Duc X.	53	Plank, Gwen W.	125	Rosenberg, Adrienne J.	697
Nguyen, Huu D.	160	Poch, Jeffrey T.	902	Rosenstein, Sherwin H.	285
Nguyen, Quyt	391	Poinsette, Noella	418	Roupas, Martha	816
Nguyen, Tam	44	Pok, Than	62	Rouse, Maryanne	562
Nguyen, Tuong	173	Pollard, Margaret	814	Rubin, Burton	719
Nicolas, Rev. Philius	614	Pomm, Monty	436	Rubin, Elliot R.	581
Niederman, David	618	Poor, Peter R.	373	Rubin, Robert	150
Ninh, Rev. Vincent	489	Popal, Zalmy	190	Rubin, Stephen	574
Noel, Gerard A.	794	Popov, Michael	192	Rubio, Gloribel	431
Nofziger, Don	723	Popp, Elena	176	Ruhala, Julie	507
Norell, Dan	409	Posey, Cheryl	937	Ruiz, Hiram	235
O'Brien, William	257	Post, Jean	510	Ruksenas, Algis	718
O'Connor, Sr. Marion	593	Potts, Earl	4	Russell, Lee	825
O'Connor, Timothy	739	Powell, James	163	Rust, Richard C.	393
O'Kelly, Michael	61	Powers, Douglas	133	Rutledge, William	331
Ochoa, Zeferino	351	Printz, Charles F.	579	Ryskamp, Andrew	503
Ochoa-Krueger, Ninfa	842	Prockup, Michelle Johnson	3	Saephan, San Seng	758
Oines, James A.	15	Prum, Sareth	527	Safa, Helen	284
Oliver, Charlotte	305	Pryor, Richard V.	220	Sahlin, Monte	222
Oliver, Myra M.	209	Pszyk, Michael	298	Salamida, Mary Ann	172
Olmedo, Rev. Miguel	430	Purcell, James M.	174	Sanders, Joel	5
Olson, Ronald G.	16	Pyle, Sr. Dorothy Ann	699	Sanfran, San	99
Opper, Peter	904	Qualey, Carlton	533	Santora, Elena A.	773

Sasadevsz, Victor	617	Sobota, Mary	942	Towey, Sr. Anne	761
Savale, Joyce	496	Soland, Brian	956	Trabold, Virginia	498
Sax, Sr. Mary	553	Soldate, Jack	518	Tran, Jack Nhuan N.	56
Scanland, Dennis	490	Soler, George	564	Tran, Minh Van	930
Schifter, Richard	271	Solis, LaVara	873	Tran, Thus	166
Schmid, Donald L.	708	Solis, Robelo	352	Tran, Tien Thuy	441
Schneider, Peter	779	Sookikian, Peggy	802	Tran, Tri H.	8
Schoppert, Douglas	364	Soreff, Joan Sud	440	Tran, Trong Duy	475
Schroeder, Ted	549	Soto, Fr. Jaime	171	Travis, Nancy	330
Schubert, Richard	226	Spear, Rick	155	Trease, Nancy	19
Schuchman, Katherine	674	Spears, Darlene	282	Trellas, Grizzel	303
Schultz, Gus	32	Speigel, Stephanie	422	Trimming, Molly	347
Schultz, Mary Elizabeth	499	Spendal, Ron	759	Trovato, Lucia	634
Schwartz, Morton	577	Spitzer, Jill Borg	128	Tucker, Denis	941
Schweitzer, Peter	38	Stacy, Palmer A.	227	Turner, Rev. David	526
Scott, Bernice	803	Stauffer, David	437	Underhill, Deedee	833
Scully, Mary	217	Stauffer, Howard	30	Ung, Mengkruy	536
Segal, Paul	797	Stein, Dan	237	Uomoto, Cal	929
Segreti, Wendy	694	Steinberg, Harvey	657	Upp, Marcena	733
Seidberg, Carol	12	Steinitz, Lucy	444	Vajda, Steve	958
Seidemann, Michael M.	725	Stephens, Debi	817	Van Tran, Rev. Oan	525
Seigler, Francisca Martinez	517	Stewart, Jenny	751	Vance, Patricia	732
Semancik, Rev. Joseph	396	Stewart, Nona	692	Vanchiasong, Siong Koua	336
Semer, Robin	356	Stifter, Vicky	837	Vang, Dang	47
Sensenig, Don	760	Stolarik, M. Mark	772	Vang, Ger	952
Seyedsadr, Maria A.	420	Stolzenberg, Irene	578	Vartian, Ross	228
Seyoum, Tesfa	649	Stone, Jerold	314	Vecoli, Rudolph J.	539
Shabon, Janet	762	Stone, Mary Ellen	915	Velarde, Jr., Luis Alfonso	848
Shamitz, Sheldon	626	Strauss, Herbert A.	658	Voorhees, Joyce	310
Shapiro, Rabbi	484	Strauss, Herbert A.	671	Vorwerk, Patricia	202
Sharp, Lawrence	397	Strelchun, Sr. Dorothy	211	Vu, Thuy	914
Shavvers, Rev. Charlotte	180	Sturtevant, Dennis	502	Vue, Phen	48
Shea, Helen	9	Sullivan, Mary Ann	529	Vue, Va Lue	523
Sheldon, Rev. R. Scott	625	Suon, Sanh	2	Waite, Mary Frances	311
Sherman, Ralph	951	Swanniutt, Alan P.	865	Waldman, Jeremy	521
Sherry, Frank	469	Swartz, Dale Frederick	247	Wali, Sima	251
Shin, Harold H.	363	Szebert, Tad	368	Waller, Carolyn	276
Shuey, Bill	796	Taillez, Rev. Daniel	532	Walsh, Marti	307
Silvera, Oswald	611	Talluto, Michael	622	Walsh, Sr. Peggy	620
Silverman, Mark	140	Tam, Bui Van	323	Waltermire, Mary	185
Simcox, David	232	Tamayo, Bill	101	Warden, Dolly	744
Simon, Joyce	485	Tannenbaum, Dan	785	Wardrop, Mary	931
Siskind, Lawrence J.	266	Tao, Truong Khanh	743	Wasinger, Rev. Alfred	414
Skipper, Rev. Howard	505	Teague, Pam	178	Watson, Phil	742
Slaughter, Vanna	831	Teferra, Tschaye	895	Wauters, Rev. Will	138
Slaughter, Vanna	836	Thao, Cheu	169	Wehrli, Mary Brent	86
Smeraldi, Florence	641	Thao, Chia	949	Weidman, Arthur	483
Smith, Beverly J.	765	Thephachanh, Phoukhong	741	Weidner, Marvin	408
Smith, Donald	84	Therkelsen, Donna	731	Weinberg, Alvin	736
Smith, Helene T.	602	Thibodeaux, Steven P.	432	Weinberger, Ingeborg B.	443
Smith, James F.	39	Thien, Do	130	Weinberr, Kenneth	922
Smith, Jim	721	Tho, Pauline Van	858	Weiss, Anschel	318
Smith, Mary R.	297	Thomas, William	861	Weiss, Cathy	712
Smith, Neron	542	Tisdale, Carolyn	810	Weizenbaum, Rabbi Joseph	21
Smith, Rev. Simon	244	Tobin, Frances	859	Werson, Susan	672
Smitter, Norma	504	Tomasi, Lydio F.	689	Werson, Susan	679
Smoulder, George	936	Torres, Lily	45	Wexler, Ann S.	576
Snedden, Herbert	333	Torrez, Oralia	911	Whatmough, Jackie	569

Wheeler, Charles	82
Whipple, Bruce	78
White, Carter C.	880
Wilkerson, Sr. Theresa Marie	423
Willden, Michael	563
Willis, Sybil	425
Wills, Don	279
Wilson, Kirke	149
Wingfield, Wayme	701
Winningham, Jr., E. Vance	737
Wiseberg, Laurie S.	473
Wittenberg, Nancy K.	315
Wodarczyk, Mary	353
Wohlgemuth, Henry	329
Wolters, Alice	545
Wong, Bernarda	357
Wong, Po S.	135
Wong, Susana	112
Wright, Robert G.	675
Wrightsman, Jere	909
Wynar, Bodhan S.	206
Xaykao, Thao Phia	854
Xiong, Djoua X.	392
Xuong, Nguyen Huu	124
Ya, Raj Rama	181
Yamashita, Robert M.	934
Yang, Chou	89
Yang, Chu Ning	49
Yang, Houa	88
Yang, Koua S.	940
Yang, Pao	954
Yang, Phia Gao	494
Yang, Song	955
Yang, Vuc	887
Yang, Yia B.	119
Ybarra, Dario	910
Yeast, James	410
Yeast, Mark	43
Yee, Melinda	248
Yokoyama, Jane	194
Young, Iris	291
Young, Rev. Peter D.	214
Zachmann, Alice	240
Zavala, Graciela	92
Zeglis, Margot	685
Zwick, Mark	857

Index III

Services

ADVOCACY

Access	CA	123	Border Assoc. for Refugees from Central Amer	TX	842
Adelphi Univ. Refugee Assistance Program	NY	626	Bulgarian Natl. Comm.	NJ	582
Adult and Child Guidance Center. Indochinese	CA	159	California Dept. of Social Services. Office of	CA	114
Adventist Community Services	DC	222	California Southern Baptist Conv. Refugee Re	CA	43
Afghan Center	CA	190	Cambodia's of Ohio	OH	728
Afghan Community in Amer.	NY	628	Cambodian Assoc. of Virginia	VA	902
Afghan Refugee Fund	CA	63	Cambodian Business Assoc.	CA	58
AFL/CIO Immigration Project	CA	64	Cambodian Family	CA	165
African Amer. Immigration Service	NY	609	Cambodian Mutual Assistance Assoc.	OH	720
Agudath Israel of Amer.	NY	631	Cambodian Mutual Assistance Assoc. of Greate	MA	478
Aid To Refugee Children Without Parents	CA	160	Cambridge and Somerville Legal Services Imm	MA	467
All Culture Friendship Center Refugee & Immi	CA	55	Cambridge Organization of Portuguese-Amer.	MA	468
All Culture Friendship Center Refugee & Immi	CA	65	Caribbean Action Lobby	NY	611
Amer. Arab Anti-Discrimination Comm.	DC	223	Caritas of Austin	TX	819
Amer. Baptist Churches. Immigration & Refug	PA	788	CASA	PA	771
Amer. Civic Assoc.	NY	608	Casa de la Esperanza	DC	229
Amer. Civil Liberties Union. South Texas Proj	TX	880	Casa de Proyecto Libertad	TX	855
Amer. Comm. on Italian Migration	NY	632	Casa El Salvador	IL	352
Amer. Council for Nationalities Service	NY	633	Casa Juan Diego	TX	857
Amer. Fed. of Jews from Central Europe	NY	635	Casa Marianella	TX	820
Amer. Friends Service Comm. Haitian Women'	NY	636	Catholic Agency for Migration and Refugee Se	KS	411
Amer. Friends Service Comm. Immigration Pro	CA	108	Catholic Charities	IA	410
Amer. Fund for Czechoslovak Refugees	NY	637	Catholic Charities	MA	486
Amer. Fund for Slovak Refugees	NJ	596	Catholic Charities	NE	558
Amer. Fund for Slovak Refugees	NY	607	Catholic Charities Bureau	IN	393
Amer. Immigrant Foundation	CA	164	Catholic Charities Migration Office	NY	604
Amer. Public Welfare Assoc. Task Force on Im	DC	225	Catholic Charities Refugee & Immigration Ser	MA	458
Amer. Romanian Comm. for Assistance to Ref	NY	630	Catholic Charities. Immigration & Refugee Di	CA	68
Americanization League	NY	691	Catholic Charities. Immigration Counseling C	CA	161
Amnesty Intl.	CA	66	Catholic Charities. Immigration Counseling S	TX	831
Anaheim Independencia Center	CA	27	Catholic Charities. Immigration Program	CA	134
Annunciation House	TX	844	Catholic Charities. Immigration Project of Im	FL	286
Archdiocese of Chicago. Immigration Services	IL	351	Catholic Charities. Immigration Services	CA	106
Archdiocese of Detroit. Office of Refugee Rese	MI	490	Catholic Charities. Migration & Refugee Servi	MN	528
Archdiocese of New York. Office for Immigran	NY	638	Catholic Charities. Migration and Refugee Ser	CT	211
Archdiocese of New York. Refugee Resettlemen	NY	639	Catholic Charities. Refugee Assistance	IN	396
Archdiocese of Portland. Immigration Counsel	OR	752	Catholic Charities. Refugee Assistance Progra	NY	622
Arizona Center for Immigrants	AZ	7	Catholic Charities. Refugee Office	IN	394
Arizona Dept. of Economic Security. Refugee	AZ	8	Catholic Charities. Refugee Program	KS	416
Armenian Assembly of Amer.	DC	228	Catholic Charities. Refugee Resettlement Offic	CA	182
Asheville Presbytery. Refugee Resettlement Of	NC	702	Catholic Charities. Refugee Resettlement Offic	FL	289
Asia Pacific Concerns Comm.	CA	181	Catholic Charities. Refugee Resettlement Prog	CA	35
Asian Counseling and Referral Service	WA	916	Catholic Charities. Refugee Resettlement Prog	DE	220
Asian Immigrant Womens Advocates	CA	93	Catholic Charities. Refugee Service Center	DC	230
Asian Legal Services Outreach	CA	112	Catholic Charities. Refugee Services	KY	423
Associated Catholic Charities	LA	429	Catholic Charities. Refugee Social Service Cen	MS	541
Assyrian Universal Alliance	MI	512	Catholic Charities. Resettlement Program	CA	44
Baptist Assoc. of New Orleans	LA	430	Catholic Charities. Resettlement Services	CA	166
Baptist Conv. of Maryland	MD	447	Catholic Community Services of Utah. Refuge	UT	882
Baptist Conv. of New Mexico	NM	597	Catholic Community Services. Office of Migra	NJ	586
Baptist State Conv.	MI	513	Catholic Community Services. Office of Migra	WV	936
Bergen County Sanctuary Comm.	NJ	590	Catholic Community Services. Refugee Resettl	FL	295
Bethany Christian Services. Refugee Foster Ca	MI	501	Catholic Community Services. Resettlement &	CA	125
Boat People SOS	CA	124	Catholic Council for Social Concern	IA	407

Catholic Family and Child Service	WA	935
Catholic Family and Child Services. Family R	WA	910
Catholic Family Center. Refugee Dept.	NY	686
Catholic Family Service. Immigration Service	TX	872
Catholic Family Services. Refugee & Citizensh	TX	818
Catholic Human Development Office. Refugee	MI	502
Catholic Immigration & Resettlement Office	CA	177
Catholic Immigration Center	HI	339
Catholic Immigration Services	FL	296
Catholic Migration & Refugee Services	OR	748
Catholic Migration & Refugee Services	VA	893
Catholic Migration and Refugee Office	NY	612
Catholic Migration and Refugee Service	NV	566
Catholic Migration and Refugee Service	OK	746
Catholic Migration Office	NY	605
Catholic Refugee Services	WA	917
Catholic Refugee Services	WA	933
Catholic Resettlement and Immigration Office	IA	406
Catholic Services for Immigrants	TX	874
Catholic Social Agency. Migration Services	PA	761
Catholic Social Ministries. Migration & Reset	OK	739
Catholic Social Ministries. Refugee Resettleme	NC	699
Catholic Social Service	IL	350
Catholic Social Service	IL	385
Catholic Social Service of Phoenix	AZ	9
Catholic Social Service. Refugee Office	NC	696
Catholic Social Service. Refugee Resettlement	FL	309
Catholic Social Service. Resettlement Program	CO	207
Catholic Social Service. Resettlement Program	OH	714
Catholic Social Service. Tha Huong Program	IL	386
Catholic Social Services	AK	6
Catholic Social Services	FL	316
Catholic Social Services	IN	398
Catholic Social Services	KS	413
Catholic Social Services	LA	427
Catholic Social Services	MS	540
Catholic Social Services	OH	729
Catholic Social Services	OH	731
Catholic Social Services	TX	829
Catholic Social Services	WY	957
Catholic Social Services Bureau	KY	418
Catholic Social Services of Fall River	MA	476
Catholic Social Services. Central Amer. Refuge	TX	827
Catholic Social Services. Immigration Services	CA	29
Catholic Social Services. Migration & Refugee	PA	773
Catholic Social Services. Refugee and Immigra	FL	311
Catholic Social Services. Refugee Reselement	NE	559
Catholic Social Services. Refugee Resettlemen	CA	179
Catholic Social Services. Refugee Resettlemen	NM	598
Catholic Social Services. Resettlement Progra	CA	87
Catholic Social Services. Resettlement Progra	MT	556
Catholic Social Services. Servicios Para Inmig	TX	871
Center for Central Amer. Refugees	NJ	587
Center for Immigrants Rights	NY	642
Central Amer. Legal Assistance	NY	613
Central Amer. Refugee Center	CA	69
Central Amer. Refugee Center	DC	233
Central Amer. Refugee Center	NY	627
Central Amer. Refugee Center	TX	859
Central Amer. Refugee Program	WA	918
Central Amer. Refugee Project	AZ	10
Central Amer. Refugee Project	CO	200
Central Amer. Refugee Project	OK	740
Central Amer. Solidarity and Assistance	MD	455
Central Baptist Church. Sanctuary Group	PA	789
Central Kentucky Jewish Assoc.	KY	421
Centro Campesino. Projecto de Inmigracion	WA	912
Centro de Ayuda Para Immigrantes	TX	860
Centro Legal	MN	531
Centro Presente	MA	469
Chicago Commission on Human Relations. Re	IL	354
Chicago Comm. on Immigrant Protection	IL	355
Chicago Religious Task Force on Central Ame	IL	356
Child and Family Service. Refugee Employmen	HI	340
Chinese Amer. Civic Assoc.	MA	459
Chinese Amer. Service League	IL	357
Chinese Newcomer Service Center	CA	135
Christ Church of the Brethren. Sanctuary Com	OH	734
Christian Community Service Agency	FL	297
Christian Community Services	CO	197
Christian Council of Metropolitan Atlanta. Re	GA	324
Christian Refugee Outreach	VA	894
Church of the Brethren. Refugee Resettlement	MD	450
Church Refugee Center	NY	643
Church World Service. Immigration & Refugee	NY	644
City of Santa Fe. Office of the Mayor	NM	600
City of West Hollywood. City Council	CA	196
Coalition for Haitian Concerns	PA	791
Coalition for Immigrant and Refugee Rights &	CA	136
Coalition for Public Sanctuary	OH	735
College Hill Presbyterian Church. Sanctuary C	OK	747
Comite de Refugiados Salvadorenos	CA	40
Comite en Defensa de los Immigrantes	CA	110
Comm. in Defense of Immigrant Rights	WA	919
Comm. to Defend Immigrant & Refugee Rights	CA	95
Community Friends Meeting. Sanctuary Comm	OH	715
Community Legal Services	CA	92
Community Legal Services	PA	774
Community, Family & Children Services. Refu	MI	500
Congregation Hakafa. Sanctuary Comm.	IL	384
Connecticut Dept. of Human Resources. State	CT	212
Conscientious Alliance for Peace	AL	1
Corn-Maya	FL	287
Cornerstone Ministries	FL	317
Corpus Christi Church. Sanctuary Comm.	NY	687
Council of Churches. Refugee Resettlement Pro	MO	552
Cross Lutheran Church	WI	947
Cuban Amer. Natl. Council. Refugee Program	FL	299
Cultural Survival	MA	471
Dallas-Fort Worth Refugee Interagency	TX	832
Delaware Dept. of Health & Social Services. D	DE	219
Delaware Dept. of Justice. Service for Foreign	DE	221
Diocesan Migrant & Refugee Services	TX	845
Diocesan Refugee Resettlement Program	ME	439
Diocese of Green Bay. Dept. of Refugee, Migra	WI	939
Diocese of Lafayette. Migration & Refugee Ser	LA	428

Diocese of Nashville. Refugee Resettlement Pr	TN	812
Diocese of Oregon	OR	751
Diocese of Raleigh. Refugee Resettlement Offi	NC	704
Diocese of Richmond. Office of Refugee Resetl	VA	909
Diocese of Richmond. Office of Refugee Resett	VA	901
Diocese of Springfield - Cape Girardeau. Resett	MO	553
Diocese of Springfield. Refugee Resettlement	MA	482
Disciples of Christ. Refugee & Immigration M	IN	399
District of Columbia Dept. of Human Services	DC	235
Downtown Legalization Project	CA	72
East Bay Sanctuary Covenant	CA	33
East Central Illinois Refugee Mutual Assistanc	IL	391
East Side Group	TX	822
Eau Claire Area Hmong Mutual Assistance Ass	WI	938
Ecumenical Refugee Council	WI	948
Ecumenical Refugee Resettlement Services	VA	903
Ecumenical Refugee Services	CO	202
El Centro Asylum Project	CA	42
El Concilio. Immigration Project	CA	45
El Rescate	CA	73
Emmanuel Lutheran Church. Sanctuary Comm.	MO	549
EPIC Immigration Project	WA	911
Episcopal Diocese of Minnesota. Refugee Res	MN	520
Episcopal Diocese of North Carolina. Refugee	NC	705
Episcopal Migration Ministries	NY	648
Episcopal Refugee and Migration Comm.	NH	570
Episcopal Refugee Resettlement Commission	IN	400
Episcopal Social Ministries	MD	442
Eritrean Relief Comm.	NY	649
Ethiopian Community Center	DC	236
Ethiopian Community Development Council	VA	895
Ethiopian Community Mutual Assistance Asso	NY	650
Evangelical Crusade of Fishers of Men	NY	614
Faith United Methodist Church. Sanctuary Com	IA	405
Family and Children's Services of Chattanoog	TN	806
Father Moriarty Asylum Program	CA	137
Fed. of Italian-Amer. Societies	NY	606
Filipinos for Affirmative Action	CA	97
First Lutheran Church	FL	283
First Unitarian Church	CA	183
First Unitarian Church. Sanctuary Comm.	MI	488
Florida Council of Churches. Refugee Program	FL	310
Foreign-Born Information and Referral Networ	MD	448
Freedom Flight Refugee Center	MI	504
Fresno Ecumenical Resettlement Project	CA	46
Friends Meeting of Austin. Sanctuary Comm.	TX	823
Friends of the Third World	IN	395
George Mason Univ. Indochina Institute.	VA	897
George Washington Univ. Natl. Law Center. I	DC	239
Good Samaritan Community Center	CA	138
Guatemala Human Rights Commission/USA	DC	240
Haitian Amer. Assoc.	MA	472
Haitian Amer. Community Assoc.	FL	300
Haitian Centers Council	NY	615
Haitian Multi-Service Center	MA	474
Haitian Refugee Center	FL	301
Heart of Texas Legal Services	TX	881
Hebrew Immigrant Aid Society	NY	651
Hebrew Immigrant Aid Society	PA	776
Hebrew Immigrant Aid Society of Baltimore	MD	443
Hispanic Immigration Counseling Program	WA	920
Hmong Amer. Human Rights Comm.	CA	47
Hmong Assoc. of Brown County. Refugee Com	WI	940
Hmong Community	MI	494
Hmong Council	CA	48
Hmong Mutual Assistance Assoc.	WI	955
Hmong/Amer. Friendship Assoc.	WI	949
Holy Cross Mission	CA	184
Holy Cross Service Center	FL	288
Hood River Valley Immigration Project	OR	750
Houston Metropolitan Ministries	TX	861
Human Rights Advocates Intl.	NJ	579
Human Rights Advocates Intl.	NY	652
Human Services Assoc.	CA	31
Idaho Dept. of Health and Welfare. Div. of Fie	ID	347
Illinois Bureau of Naturalization Services	IL	389
Illinois Conference of Churches. Refugee Imm	IL	390
Illinois Conference of Churches. Refugee Rese	IL	358
Immigrant Assistance Line	CA	139
Immigrant Students Project of the Natl. Coalit	MA	461
Immigrants Assistance Center	MA	480
Immigrants' Rights Office	CA	74
Immigration Advocacy Service	NE	561
Immigration and Legalization Service	TX	824
Immigration Assistance Service	NJ	583
Immigration Counseling Center	TX	862
Immigration Counseling Migration & Refugee	TX	851
Immigration Institute	TX	863
Immigration Law Enforcement Monitoring Pro	TX	864
Immigration Project	CA	75
Immigration Project	CA	194
Immigration Service of Santa Rosa	CA	189
Impact	CA	126
Indiana Council of Churches	IN	401
Indochina Resource Action Center	DC	241
Inmigracion Latina Foundation	FL	302
Inter-Agency Council for Immigrant Services	HI	342
InterAction (Amer. Council for Voluntary Intl.	NY	653
Intercultural Action Center	CA	178
Interfaith Refugee Assistance Project	OK	744
Interfaith Sanctuary Movement	PA	784
Intl. Catholic Migration Commission	DC	242
Intl. Center	NH	569
Intl. Center of the Capital Region. Refugee As	NY	602
Intl. Community Services	TX	865
Intl. Immigrants Foundation	NY	654
Intl. Institute	OH	711
Intl. Institute of Buffalo	NY	623
Intl. Institute of Connecticut	CT	209
Intl. Institute of Connecticut	CT	213
Intl. Institute of Erie	PA	764
Intl. Institute of Flint	MI	499
Intl. Institute of Los Angeles	CA	191
Intl. Institute of Los Angeles. Immigrant & R	CA	76
Intl. Institute of Los Angeles. Refugee Reloca	CA	158
Intl. Institute of Lowell	MA	479

Intl. Institute of Metro Detroit	MI	495
Intl. Institute of Metropolitan St. Louis	MO	550
Intl. Institute of Minnesota	MN	534
Intl. Institute of New Jersey	NJ	584
Intl. Institute of Northwest Indiana	IN	397
Intl. Institute of Rhose Island	RI	796
Intl. Institute of San Francisco	CA	141
Intl. Institute of the East Bay	CA	98
Intl. Institute of Toledo	OH	732
Intl. Institute of Wisconsin	WI	950
Intl. Ladies Garment Workers Union. Immigra	CA	77
Intl. Ladies Garment Workers Union. Immigra	NY	655
Intl. Ladies Garment Workers Union. Immigra	IL	359
Intl. Refugee Center	IL	360
Intl. Rescue Comm.	CA	49
Intl. Rescue Comm.	CA	78
Intl. Rescue Comm.	CA	118
Intl. Rescue Comm.	CA	127
Intl. Rescue Comm.	CA	142
Intl. Rescue Comm.	CA	185
Intl. Rescue Comm.	DC	243
Intl. Rescue Comm.	FL	303
Intl. Rescue Comm.	GA	335
Intl. Rescue Comm.	NJ	595
Intl. Rescue Comm.	TX	833
Intl. Rescue Comm.	WA	921
Intl. Service Center	PA	766
Intl. Social Service. Amer. Branch	NY	657
Irish Immigration Reform Movement	NY	629
Japanese Newcomer Service	CA	143
Jesuit Refugee Service	DC	244
Jewish Family & Children Services	CA	144
Jewish Family & Children's Service	AZ	12
Jewish Family and Child Service	OR	754
Jewish Family and Children's Agency	PA	777
Jewish Family and Children's Service	CO	203
Jewish Family and Children's Service	MA	466
Jewish Family and Children's Service	NJ	571
Jewish Family and Children's Services	IN	403
Jewish Family and Voc. Service	KY	422
Jewish Family Service	AZ	17
Jewish Family Service	CA	51
Jewish Family Service	CA	99
Jewish Family Service	CT	215
Jewish Family Service	FL	314
Jewish Family Service	LA	436
Jewish Family Service	MN	535
Jewish Family Service	NJ	575
Jewish Family Service	NY	624
Jewish Family Service	NY	688
Jewish Family Service	OH	712
Jewish Family Service	RI	797
Jewish Family Service	TN	813
Jewish Family Service	TX	876
Jewish Family Service	WA	922
Jewish Family Service Agency	NV	565
Jewish Family Service Assoc.	OH	719
Jewish Family Service of Delaware Valley	NJ	591
Jewish Family Service of Detroit	MI	514
Jewish Family Service of Greater Springfield	MA	483
Jewish Family Service of Metro West	NJ	589
Jewish Family Service of North Middlesex Co	NJ	578
Jewish Family Service of Somerset County	NJ	588
Jewish Family Service. Immigration & Resettl	NM	599
Jewish Family Service. Refugee Services	CA	79
Jewish Family Service. Resettlement Program	CA	128
Jewish Family Service. Resettlement Program	FL	306
Jewish Family Service. Resettlement Program	MD	444
Jewish Family Service. Resettlement Services	CT	210
Jewish Family Services	FL	318
Jewish Family Services	GA	328
Jewish Family Services	NC	697
Jewish Family Services	TX	834
Jewish Family Services	WI	951
Jewish Family Services of Greater Orlando	FL	322
Jewish Family Services. Refugee Services	IL	362
Jewish Social Services	WI	943
Jewish Social Services Agency	MD	451
Joint Legal Task Force on Central Amer. Refu	WA	923
Kalamazoo Interfaith Sanctuary Project	MI	506
Kalihi-Palama Immigrant Service Center	HI	344
Kansas Dept. of Social & Rehabilitation Servi	KS	415
Kentucky Cabinet for Human Resources. Office	KY	419
Khmer Health Advocates	CT	217
King County Rape Relief. Southeast Asian Ch	WA	915
La Crosse Area Hmong Mutual Assistance Ass	WI	941
Lao Family Community	CA	88
Lao Family Community	CA	100
Lao Family Community	CA	119
Lao Family Community	UT	887
Lao Family Community	WI	952
Lao Khmu Assoc.	CA	186
Lawyers Comm. for Human Rights. Political A	NY	659
Legal Aid of Western Missouri	MO	547
Legal Aid Society	FL	321
Legal Services Center for Immigrants	IL	364
Legal Services of Northern California	CA	120
Louisiana Dept. of Health & Human Services.	LA	425
Lutheran Child & Family Services of Massach	MA	485
Lutheran Child and Family Services	IL	365
Lutheran Church. Synod Board of Social Minis	MO	551
Lutheran Family Service. Refugee Services	OR	755
Lutheran Family Services. Refugee Resettleme	NC	700
Lutheran Immigration & Refugee Services	DC	245
Lutheran Immigration and Refugee Service	NY	660
Lutheran Immigration and Refugee Service	TX	867
Lutheran Ministries of Florida	FL	307
Lutheran Ministries of Florida. Refugee Resett	FL	319
Lutheran Ministries of Georgia	GA	329
Lutheran Refugee and Immigration Services	NJ	592
Lutheran Refugee Resettlement	CO	204
Lutheran Social Ministry of the Southwest. Re	AZ	13
Lutheran Social Services	MN	516
Lutheran Social Services of Iowa	IA	409
Lutheran Social Services of Kansas and Oklaho	KS	417
Lutheran Social Services of Michigan. Dept. o	MI	510

Lutheran Social Services of Michigan. Refugee	MI	507	Northern Virginia Family Service. Multicultura	VA	898
Lutheran Social Services of Minnesota. Refuge	MN	522	Northside Sanctuary Coalition	IL	369
Lutheran Social Services of Montana	MT	555	O.L.A. Immigration Rights Center	CA	193
Lutheran Social Services of North Dakota. Ref	ND	709	O.L.A. Raza	CA	109
Lutheran Social Services of Northeast Florida.	FL	292	Ohio Council of Churches. Refugee Services	OH	724
Lutheran Social Services of Northern Californi	CA	146	Ohio Dept. of Human Services. Program Devel	OH	725
Lutheran Social Services of Wisconsin & Upp	WI	953	Orange County Coalition for Immigrant Rights	CA	171
Lutheran Social Services. Immigration & Refu	CA	81	Orange County Community Consortium	CA	172
Lutheran Social Services. Unaccompanied Min	OH	722	Oregon Dept. of Human Resources. Refugee Pr	OR	759
Maine Annual Conference of the United Metho	ME	438	Oshkosh Lao Hmong Assoc.	WI	954
Manchester Church of the Brethren. Sanctuary	IN	404	Overground Railroad	IL	382
Maryland Dept. of Human Resources. State Re	MD	445	Palo Alto Friends Meeting	CA	107
Massachusetts Immigrant & Refugee Advocacy	MA	462	Partnership for Human Development. Resettle	TX	826
Massachusetts Office for Refugees and Immigr	MA	463	People's Immigration Service	CA	195
Mennonite Immigration and Refugee Services	DC	246	People's Law Office for Organized Workers	FL	280
Metropolitan Social Services. Refugee Program	TN	814	Peylim	NY	668
Miami Presbytery	OH	730	Philadelphia Refugee Service Center	PA	781
Michigan Dept. of Social Services. Office of R	MI	496	Philippine Center for Immigrant Rights	NY	669
Mid-Cumberland Refugee Assistance Ministry	TN	815	Pillsbury United Neighborhood Services. Asian	MN	523
Midwest Coalition in Defense of Immigrants	IL	366	Plattsburg Interfaith Council	NY	685
Midwest Immigrant Rights Center	IL	367	Polish Amer. Immigration and Relief Comm.	NY	670
Migration & Refugee Services	SC	802	Polish Amer. Immigration Relief Comm.	IL	370
Migration and Refugee Services Office	NJ	593	Polish and Slavic Center. Refugee Assistance	NY	617
Minnesota Cambodian Buddhist Society	MN	536	Presbyterian Synod of Southern California and	CA	84
Minnesota Council of Churches. Refugee Prog	MN	537	Presbytery of Long Island	NY	625
Minnesota Dept. of Human Services. Refugee	MN	538	PRIME Ecumenical Commitment to Refugees	PA	762
Mississippi Baptist Conv. Language Missions	MS	542	Project Deliverance	OH	733
Missouri Div. of Family Services. Refugee As	MO	544	Proyecto Adelante	TX	837
Mohawk Valley Resource Center for Refugees	NY	693	Proyecto Resistencia	IL	371
Montana Assoc. for Refugee Services	MT	554	Rav Tov. Intl. Jewish Rescue Organization	NY	618
Monterey County Sanctuary	CA	103	Reformed Church in Amer. Refugee Program	MI	505
Moob Fed. of Amer.	IL	392	Refugee and Immigrant Multi-Service Center	WA	930
Multicultural Immigration Center	NY	661	Refugee Assistance Program	CA	130
Mutual Aid Assoc. of the New Polish Immigra	IL	368	Refugee Resettlement Comm.	CA	90
Na Loio No Na Kanaka. Lawyers for the Peopl	HI	345	Refugee Resettlement Office	MO	545
Natl. Assoc. of Evangelicals. Immigration Pro	FL	304	Refugee Services	MI	508
Natl. Coalition for Haitian Refugees	NY	662	Refugee Voices	DC	250
Natl. Council of Jewish Women. Rescue & Mi	FL	305	Refugee Women in Development	DC	251
Natl. Immigration Project of the Natl. Lawyers	MA	464	Refugees Intl.	DC	252
Natl. Immigration, Refugee, and Citizenship F	DC	247	Rhode Island Dept. of Human Services. State R	RI	799
Natl. Network for Immigrant & Refugee Right	CA	101	Rio Grande Defense Comm.	TX	879
Natl. Slavic Conv.	MD	446	Riverside Church. Sanctuary Comm.	NY	672
Nationalities Service Center	PA	780	Rochester Refugee Services	MN	527
Nationalities Service of Central California	CA	50	Salvadoran Refugee Comm. (Oscar A. Romero)	DC	253
Naturalization Project	LA	434	San Francisco Lawyers' Comm. Immigrant & R	CA	150
Neil Avenue Mennonite Church. Sanctuary Co	OH	723	San Juan Bautista Lutheran Church. Sanctuary	AZ	18
New Hope Presbytery	NC	694	Sanctuary Covenant of San Francisco	CA	152
New Jersey Dept. of Human Services. State Re	NJ	594	Sandigan California	CA	121
New Mexico Dept. of Human Services. Social	NM	601	Santa Clara County Health Dept. Refugee Healt	CA	163
New York Circus	NY	664	Sarrlano Chirino Amaya Central Amer. Refugee	CA	85
New York City. Office of Immigrant Affairs	NY	665	Saura Center	IL	372
New York Dept. of Social Services. State Refu	NY	603	Seattle - King County Bar Assoc. Legalization,	WA	924
New York State Assembly. Task Force on New	NY	666	Sepulveda Unitarian Universalist Society	CA	180
North Carolina Baptist State Conv.	NC	695	Sinai Temple. Sanctuary Comm.	MA	484
North Carolina Dept. of Human Resources. Fa	NC	706	Socio-Economic Development Center for South	RI	800
North Dakota Dept. of Human Services. Refuge	ND	708	Somerville Portuguese Amer. League	MA	481
North Manhattan Coalition for Immigrants' Ri	NY	667	South and Meso-Amer. Indian Information Cet	CA	34
North Texas Immigration Coalition	TX	836	South Carolina Dept. of Social Services. Refug	SC	803

South Dakota Dept. of Social Services. Refuge	SD	804
South-East Asia Center	IL	373
Southern Arizona Legal Aid	AZ	19
Southern California Interfaith Task Force on C	CA	86
Southern Minnesota Regional Legal Services	MN	517
Southside Community Mission	NY	620
Sponsors Organized to Assist Refugees	ID	348
Sponsors Organized to Assist Refugees	OR	756
St. Anselm's Immigrant & Refugee Community	CA	52
St. John's Center. Office of Social Ministry	GA	338
St. Paul's United Methodist Church. Refugee Pr	NV	567
Synapses. Asian Organizing Program	IL	374
Syracuse Interreligious Council. Refugee Assist	NY	692
TECHO Central Amer. Education Center	AZ	20
Temple Beth El. Sanctuary Comm.	WI	944
Temple Emanu-El. Sanctuary Comm.	AZ	21
Temple Israel. Sanctuary Comm.	CA	60
Temple Sinai. Sanctuary Comm.	DC	254
Tennessee Valley Unitarian Church. Sanctuary	TN	808
Texas Dept. of Human Service. Refugee Progra	TX	825
Texas Rural Legal Aid. Clinica de Inmigracion	TX	841
Tolstoy Foundation	AZ	14
Tolstoy Foundation	MI	498
Tolstoy Foundation	NY	673
Traveler and Immigrants Aid	IL	375
Travelers Aid Intl. Institute. Refugee Resource	OH	716
Travelers Aid Society	DC	255
Tressler Lutheran Services. Refugee Services Pr	PA	770
Tucson Ecumenical Council. Central Amer. Tas	AZ	22
Tucson Ecumenical Council. Legal Assistance	AZ	23
U. S. Catholic Conference. Migration & Refug	NY	675
U.S. Catholic Conference. Migration & Refuge	DC	256
U.S. Catholic Conference. Migration & Refuge	CA	154
U.S. Catholic Conference. Migration & Refuge	DC	257
U.S. Catholic Conference. Migration & Refuge	NY	676
U.S. Catholic Conference. Migration & Refuge	TX	848
Unitarian Church of Arlington	VA	896
Unitarian Church. Sanctuary Comm.	CT	218
United Cambodian Community	CA	62
United Catholic Social Services. Refugee Reset	NE	562
United Church Board for World Ministries. Ref	NY	678
United Methodist Church. Refugee Concerns C	CA	156
United Methodist Comm. on Relief. Refugee S	NY	679
United Nations. High Commissioner for Refug	NY	680
United Nations. Relief and Works Agency for	NY	681
United Refugee Council	NY	621
U.S. Catholic Conference	IL	388
U.S. Comm. for Refugees	DC	275
Univ. Church. Sanctuary Project	IL	377
Utah Immigration Project	UT	886
Valley Immigrants Rights Center	CA	105
Valley Religious Task Force on Central Amer.	AZ	15
Vermont State Refugee Coordinator	VT	891
Vietnam Refugee Fund	VA	900
Vietnamese Amer. Assoc. Refugee Center	OK	743
Vietnamese Amer. Civic Assoc.	MA	475
Vietnamese Assoc. of Illinois	IL	378
Vietnamese Catholic Community	MI	489
Vietnamese Catholic Community in Connectic	CT	214
Vietnamese Lutheran Ministry	WA	927
Vietnamese Mutual Assistance Assoc.	TX	840
Vietnamese Service Center	CA	53
Vietnamese Seventh-Day Adventist Church	OR	757
Virginia Council of Churches. Refugee Progra	VA	907
Virginia Dept. of Social Services. State Refuge	VA	908
Washington Assoc. of Churches. Immigration	WA	928
Washington Assoc. of Churches. Refugee Rese	WA	932
Washington Lawyers' Comm. for Civil Rights	DC	276
Washington Office on Haiti	DC	277
West Virginia Dept. of Human Services	WV	937
Wheadon United Methodist Church. Sanctuary	IL	383
Woodrow Wilson Intl. Center	DC	278
World Relief	CA	54
World Relief	CA	187
World Relief	DC	279
World Relief	FL	282
World Relief	GA	333
World Relief	NY	683
World Relief	NC	701
World Relief	TN	817
World Relief	TX	853
World Relief	TX	869
World Relief. Immigration Services	IL	379
Wyoming Dept. of Health & Social Services.	WY	958
Yiu Mienh Assoc. of Oregon	OR	758
YMCA Intl. Services	TX	870
YMCA. Refugee Resettlement Services	IL	380

COMMUNITY EDUCATION/POLITICAL ORGANIZING

Afghan Community in Amer.	NY	628
AFL/CIO Immigration Project	CA	64
African Amer. Immigration Service	NY	609
Agudath Israel of Amer.	NY	631
Amer. Arab Anti-Discrimination Comm.	DC	223
Amer. Civic Assoc.	NY	608
Amer. Civil Liberties Union. South Texas Proj	TX	880
Amer. Comm. on Italian Migration	NY	632
Amer. Council for Nationalities Service	NY	633
Amer. Friends Service Comm. Haitian Women'	NY	636
Amer. Friends Service Comm. Immigration Pro	CA	108
Amer. Fund for Czechoslovak Refugees	NY	637
Amer. Immigrant Foundation	CA	164
Amer. Immigration Lawyers Assoc. Pro Bono	FL	294
Amer. Romanian Comm. for Assistance to Ref	NY	630
Amer. For Immigration Control	DC	227
Amnesty Intl.	CA	66
Annunciation House	TX	844
Archdiocese of New York. Refugee Resettlemen	NY	639
Arizona Center for Immigrants	AZ	7
Armenian Assembly of Amer.	DC	228
Asheville Presbytery. Refugee Resettlement Of	NC	702
Asia Pacific Concerns Comm.	CA	181
Asian Immigrant Womens Advocates	CA	93
Asian Legal Services Outreach	CA	112
Assyrian Universal Alliance	MI	512
Bergen County Sanctuary Comm.	NJ	590
Boat People SOS	CA	124
Border Assoc. for Refugees from Central Amer.	TX	842
Bulgarian Natl. Comm.	NJ	582
Cambodia's of Ohio	OH	728
Cambodian Business Assoc.	CA	58
Cambodian Mutual Assistance Assoc.	OH	720
Cambridge Organization of Portuguese-Amer.	MA	468
Capuchin Mission Secretariat	MI	491
Caribbean Action Lobby	NY	611
Caritas of Austin	TX	819
CASA	PA	771
Casa de la Esperanza	DC	229
Casa de Proyecto Libertad	TX	855
Casa El Salvador	IL	352
Catholic Charities Migration Office	NY	604
Catholic Charities Refugee & Immigration Ser	MA	458
Catholic Charities. Immigration & Refugee Di	CA	68
Catholic Charities. Immigration Counseling Se	TX	831
Catholic Charities. Immigration Program	CA	134
Catholic Charities. Immigration Services	CA	106
Catholic Charities. Refugee Assistance Progra	NY	622
Catholic Charities. Refugee Resettlement Offic	CA	182
Catholic Charities. Refugee Resettlement Offic	FL	289
Catholic Community Services of Utah. Refugee	UT	882
Catholic Community Services. Migration & Re	LA	424
Catholic Community Services. Office of Migra	NJ	586
Catholic Community Services. Office of Migra	WV	936
Catholic Family Service. Immigration Service	TX	872
Catholic Immigration & Resettlement Office	CA	177
Catholic Immigration Center	HI	339
Catholic Migration and Refugee Office	NY	612
Catholic Migration and Refugee Services	NJ	573
Catholic Migration Office	NY	605
Catholic Refugee Services	WA	917
Catholic Resettlement and Immigration Office	IA	406
Catholic Services for Immigrants	TX	874
Catholic Social Service Bureau. Refugee Resett	KY	420
Catholic Social Services	IN	398
Catholic Social Services	MS	540
Catholic Social Services	OH	731
Catholic Social Services	TX	829
Catholic Social Services. Central Amer. Refuge	TX	827
Catholic Social Services. Migration & Refugee	PA	773
Catholic Social Services. Refugee Program	AL	3
Catholic Social Services. Refugee Social Servi	FL	312
Catholic Social Services. Servicios Para Inmig	TX	871
Center for Central Amer. Refugees	NJ	587
Center for Immigrants Rights	NY	642
Center for Immigration Studies	DC	232
Central Amer. Refugee Center	DC	233
Central Amer. Refugee Center	NY	627
Central Amer. Refugee Center	TX	859
Central Amer. Refugee Program	WA	918
Central Amer. Refugee Project	AZ	10
Central Amer. Refugee Project	CO	200
Central Amer. Refugee Project	OK	740
Central Amer. Solidarity and Assistance	MD	455
Central Baptist Church. Sanctuary Group	PA	789
Centro Campesino. Projecto de Inmigracion	WA	912
Centro de Ayuda Para Immigrantes	TX	860
Centro Presente	MA	469
Chicago Commission on Human Relations. Re	IL	354
Chicago Comm. on Immigrant Protection	IL	355
Chicago Religious Task Force on Central Amer	IL	356
Child and Family Service. Refugee Employmen	HI	340
Chinatown Service Center	CA	70
Chinese Newcomer Service Center	CA	135
Christian Community Services	CO	197
Christian Reformed World Relief Comm.	MI	503
Christian Refugee Outreach	VA	894
Church Refugee Center	NY	643
Church World Service. Immigration & Refugee	NY	644
City of Santa Fe. Office of the Mayor	NM	600
City of West Hollywood. City Council	CA	196
Clinica Msr. Oscar A. Romero	CA	71
Coalition for Haitian Concerns	PA	791
Coalition for Immigrant and Refugee Rights &	CA	136
Coalition for Public Sanctuary	OH	735
College Hill Presbyterian Church. Sanctuary C	OK	747
Comite de Refugiados Salvadorenos	CA	40
Comite en Defensa de los Immigrantes	CA	110

Comm. in Defense of Immigrant Rights   WA   919
Comm. to Defend Immigrant & Refugee Rights   CA   95
Community Friends Meeting. Sanctuary Comm   OH   715
Community Law Center   CA   167
Community Legal Services   CA   92
Community Legal Services   PA   774
Conference on Jewish Material Claims Against   NY   646
Congregation Hakafa. Sanctuary Comm.   IL   384
Conscientious Alliance for Peace   AL   1
Corn-Maya   FL   287
Cornerstone Ministries   FL   317
Corpus Christi Church. Sanctuary Comm.   NY   687
Cuban Amer. Natl. Council. Refugee Program   FL   299
Cultural Survival   MA   471
Dallas-Fort Worth Refugee Interagency   TX   832
Diocesan Migrant & Refugee Services   TX   845
Diocese of Green Bay. Dept. of Refugee, Migra WI   939
Diocese of Oregon   OR   751
Diocese of Richmond. Office of Refugee Resetl VA   909
Diocese of Richmond. Office of Refugee Resett VA   901
Diocese of Springfield. Refugee Resettlement   MA   482
Disciples of Christ. Refugee & Immigration M   IN   399
Downtown Legalization Project   CA   72
East Bay Sanctuary Covenant   CA   33
East Side Group   TX   822
Eau Claire Area Hmong Mutual Assistance Ass   WI   938
Ecumenical Immigration Services   LA   431
Ecumenical Refugee Council   WI   948
Ecumenical Refugee Resettlement Services   VA   903
El Centro Asylum Project   CA   42
El Concilio. Immigration Project   CA   45
El Paso Legal Assistance Society   TX   846
Emmanuel Lutheran Church. Sanctuary Comm.   MO   549
EPIC Immigration Project   WA   911
Episcopal Refugee Resettlement Commission   IN   400
Eritrean Relief Comm.   NY   649
Ethiopian Community Center   DC   236
Ethiopian Community Development Council   VA   895
Ethiopian Community Mutual Assistance Asso   NY   650
Evangelical Crusade of Fishers of Men   NY   614
Faith United Methodist Church. Sanctuary Com   IA   405
Family and Children's Services of Chattanooga TN   806
Father Moriarty Asylum Program   CA   137
Fed. for Amer. Immigration Reform   DC   237
Fed. of Italian-Amer. Societies   NY   606
Fed. of Jewish Agencies of Greater Philadelphi PA 775
Filipinos for Affirmative Action   CA   97
First Lutheran Church   FL   283
First Unitarian Church   CA   183
First Unitarian Church. Sanctuary Comm.   MI   488
Friends Meeting of Austin. Sanctuary Comm.   TX   823
Friends of the Third World   IN   395
George Mason Univ. Indochina Institute.   VA   897
Good Samaritan Community Center   CA   138
Greater Hartford Jewish Fed.   CT   216
Haitian Amer. Assoc.   MA   472
Haitian Amer. Community Assoc.   FL   300
Haitian Centers Council   NY   615

Haitian Multi-Service Center   MA   474
Haitian Refugee Center   FL   301
Heart of Texas Legal Services   TX   881
Hebrew Immigrant Aid Society   PA   776
Hispanic Immigration Counseling Program   WA   920
Hmong Assoc. of Brown County. Refugee Com   WI   940
Hmong Community   MI   494
Hmong Mutual Assistance Assoc.   WI   955
Hood River Valley Immigration Project   OR   750
Houston Metropolitan Ministries   TX   861
Human Rights Advocates Intl.   NJ   579
Human Rights Advocates Intl.   NY   652
Human Services Assoc.   CA   31
Illinois Conference of Churches. Refugee Reset IL 358
Immigrant Assistance Line   CA   139
Immigrant Legal Resource Center   CA   41
Immigrant Students Project of the Natl. Coaliti MA 461
Immigrants Assistance Center   MA   480
Immigration and Legalization Service   TX   824
Immigration Assistance Service   NJ   583
Immigration Counseling Center   TX   862
Immigration Counseling Migration & Refugee   TX   851
Immigration Institute   TX   863
Immigration Law Enforcement Monitoring Proj   TX   864
Immigration Project   CA   194
Immigration Services of Santa Rosa   CA   131
Indiana Council of Churches   IN   401
Indochina Resource Action Center   DC   241
Indochinese Assistance Center   CA   117
Inmigracion Latina Foundation   FL   302
Inter-Agency Council for Immigrant Services   HI   342
Intercultural Action Center   CA   178
Interfaith Sanctuary Movement   PA   784
Intl. Catholic Migration Commission   DC   242
Intl. Community Services   TX   865
Intl. Immigrants Foundation   NY   654
Intl. Institute   OH   711
Intl. Institute of Connecticut   CT   213
Intl. Institute of Flint   MI   499
Intl. Institute of Los Angeles   CA   191
Intl. Institute of Los Angeles. Refugee Relocat CA 158
Intl. Institute of Lowell   MA   479
Intl. Institute of Metro Detroit   MI   495
Intl. Institute of Metropolitan St. Louis   MO   550
Intl. Institute of Rhose Island   RI   796
Intl. Institute of San Francisco   CA   141
Intl. Institute of the East Bay   CA   98
Intl. Institute of Toledo   OH   732
Intl. Ladies Garment Workers Union. Immigrat   CA   77
Intl. Ladies Garment Workers Union. Immigrat   NY   655
Intl. Ladies Garment Workers Union. Immigrat   IL   359
Intl. Refugee Center   IL   360
Intl. Rescue Comm.   FL   303
Intl. Rescue Comm.   GA   335
Intl. Rescue Comm.   NJ   595
Intl. Rescue Comm.   TX   833
Intl. Rescue Comm.   WA   921
Intl. Service Center   PA   766

Intl. Social Service. Amer. Branch	NY	657
Irish Immigration Reform Movement	NY	629
Jesuit Refugee Service	DC	244
Jewish Family and Children's Service	NJ	571
Jewish Family Service	FL	314
Jewish Family Service	MN	535
Jewish Family Service	NY	624
Jewish Family Service of Delaware Valley	NJ	591
Jewish Family Service of North Middlesex Cou	NJ	578
Jewish Family Services	FL	318
Jewish Family Services	WI	951
Jewish Social Services	WI	943
Joint Legal Task Force on Central Amer. Refug	WA	923
Kalamazoo Interfaith Sanctuary Project	MI	506
Kentucky Cabinet for Human Resources. Office	KY	419
King County Rape Relief. Southeast Asian Chi	WA	915
Lao Consultant Firm	VA	892
Lao Family Community	CA	88
Lao Family Community	CA	100
Lao Family Community	CA	119
Lao Family Community	UT	887
Lao Khmu Assoc.	CA	186
Lawyers Comm. for Human Rights. Political A	NY	659
Legal Aid of Western Missouri	MO	547
Legal Services Center for Immigrants	IL	364
Legal Services of Northern California	CA	120
Lutheran Immigration & Refugee Services	DC	245
Lutheran Immigration and Refugee Service	NY	660
Lutheran Refugee Resettlement	CO	204
Lutheran Social Services	MN	516
Lutheran Social Services of Kansas and Oklaho	KS	417
Lutheran Social Services of Michigan. Dept. of	MI	510
Lutheran Social Services of Minnesota. Refuge	MN	522
Maine Annual Conference of the United Metho	ME	438
Massachusetts Immigrant & Refugee Advocacy	MA	462
Mennonite Immigration and Refugee Services	DC	246
Metropolitan Social Services. Refugee Program	TN	814
Michigan Dept. of Social Services. Office of R	MI	496
Mid-Cumberland Refugee Assistance Ministry	TN	815
Midwest Coalition in Defense of Immigrants	IL	366
Midwest Immigrant Rights Center	IL	367
Migration and Refugee Services Office	NJ	593
Minnesota Council of Churches. Refugee Progr	MN	537
Mohawk Valley Resource Center for Refugees	NY	693
Monterey County Sanctuary	CA	103
Moob Fed. of Amer.	IL	392
Multicultural Immigration Center	NY	661
Mutual Aid Assoc. of the New Polish Immigrat	IL	368
Na Loio No Na Kanaka. Lawyers for the People	HI	345
Natl. Coalition for Haitian Refugees	NY	662
Natl. Immigration Project of the Natl. Lawyers	MA	464
Natl. Immigration, Refugee, and Citizenship F	DC	247
Natl. Network for Immigrant & Refugee Rights	CA	101
Natl. Slavic Conv.	MD	446
Nationalities Service Center	PA	769
Naturalization Project	LA	434
New Hope Presbytery	NC	694
New York Circus	NY	664
New York State Assembly. Task Force on New	NY	666
North Carolina Baptist State Conv.	NC	695
North Manhattan Coalition for Immigrants' Ri	NY	667
North Texas Immigration Coalition	TX	836
Northern Virginia Family Service. Multicultura	VA	898
Northside Sanctuary Coalition	IL	369
O.L.A. Immigration Rights Center	CA	193
O.L.A. Raza	CA	109
Orange County Coalition for Immigrant Rights	CA	171
Orange County Community Consortium	CA	172
Palo Alto Friends Meeting	CA	107
Partnership for Human Development. Resettle	TX	826
People's Immigration Service	CA	195
People's Law Office for Organized Workers	FL	280
Peylim	NY	668
Philippine Center for Immigrant Rights	NY	669
Pillsbury United Neighborhood Services. Asian	MN	523
Plattsburg Interfaith Council	NY	685
Polish Amer. Immigration and Relief Comm.	NY	670
Polish Amer. Immigration Relief Comm.	IL	370
PRIME Ecumenical Commitment to Refugees	PA	762
Project Deliverance	OH	733
Proyecto Adelante	TX	837
Proyecto Resistencia	IL	371
Rav Tov. Intl. Jewish Rescue Organization	NY	618
Reformed Church in Amer. Refugee Program	MI	505
Refugee and Immigrant Multi-Service Center	WA	930
Refugee Assistance Program	CA	130
Refugee Resettlement Comm.	CA	90
Refugee Resettlement Program	AR	26
Refugee Services	MI	508
Refugee Voices	DC	250
Rio Grande Defense Comm.	TX	879
Riverside Church. Sanctuary Comm.	NY	672
Rochester Refugee Services	MN	527
Salvadoran Refugee Comm. (Oscar A. Romero)	DC	253
San Antonio Literacy Council	TX	878
San Juan Bautista Lutheran Church. Sanctuary	AZ	18
Sanctuary Covenant of San Francisco	CA	152
Sarrlano Chirino Amaya Central Amer. Refugee	CA	85
Seattle - King County Bar Assoc. Legalization,	WA	924
Sepulveda Unitarian Universalist Society	CA	180
Sinai Temple. Sanctuary Comm.	MA	484
Socio-Economic Development Center for South	RI	800
Somerville Portuguese Amer. League	MA	481
South and Meso-Amer. Indian Information Cen	CA	34
South Texas Immigration Council	TX	856
South-East Asia Center	IL	373
Southern Arizona Legal Aid	AZ	19
Southern California Interfaith Task Force on C	CA	86
Southern Minnesota Regional Legal Services	MN	517
Sponsors Organized to Assist Refugees	ID	348
St. Anselm's Immigrant & Refugee Community	CA	52
St. Paul's United Methodist Church. Refugee Pr	NV	567
Synapses. Asian Organizing Program	IL	374
Syracuse Interreligious Council. Refugee Assist	NY	692
TECHO Central Amer. Education Center	AZ	20
Temple Beth El. Sanctuary Comm.	WI	944

Temple Emanu-El. Sanctuary Comm.	AZ	21
Temple Israel. Sanctuary Comm.	CA	60
Temple Sinai. Sanctuary Comm.	DC	254
Tennessee Valley Unitarian Church. Sanctuary	TN	808
Texas Rural Legal Aid. Clinica de Inmigracion	TX	841
Tolstoy Foundation	AZ	14
Tolstoy Foundation	MI	498
Tolstoy Foundation	NY	673
Travelers Aid Intl. Institute. Refugee Resource	OH	716
Tressler Lutheran Services. Refugee Services Pr	PA	770
Tucson Ecumenical Council. Central Amer. Tas	AZ	22
U. S. Catholic Conference. Migration & Refug	NY	675
U.S. Catholic Conference. Migration & Refuge	DC	256
Ukrainian Research Foundation	CO	206
Unitarian Church of Arlington	VA	896
Unitarian Church. Sanctuary Comm.	CT	218
United Cambodian Community	CA	62
United Catholic Social Services. Refugee Reset	NE	562
United Methodist Comm. on Relief. Refugee S	NY	679
United Nations. Relief and Works Agency for	NY	681
United Refugee Council	NY	621
U.S. Comm. for Refugees	DC	275
Univ. Church. Sanctuary Project	IL	377
Utah Immigration Project	UT	886
Valley Immigrants Rights Center	CA	105
Valley Religious Task Force on Central Amer.	AZ	15
Vietnam Refugee Fund	VA	900
Vietnamese Amer. Assoc. Refugee Center	OK	743
Vietnamese Amer. Civic Assoc.	MA	475
Vietnamese Amer. Cultural Alliance of Colorad	CO	198
Vietnamese Catholic Community	MI	489
Vietnamese Community in Virginia	VA	905
Vietnamese Evangelical Church	MN	525
Virginia Council of Churches. Refugee Progra	VA	907
Washington Assoc. of Churches. Immigration	WA	928
Washington Assoc. of Churches. Refugee Rese	WA	932
Washington Lawyers' Comm. for Civil Rights	DC	276
Washington Office on Haiti	DC	277
Wheadon United Methodist Church. Sanctuary	IL	383
World Relief	DC	279
World Relief	TX	853
World Relief	TX	869
World Relief	WA	929
World Relief. Immigration Services	IL	379
Yiu Mienh Assoc. of Oregon	OR	758
YMCA. Refugee Resettlement Services	IL	380

CULTURAL

Adelphi Univ. Refugee Assistance Program	NY	626
Adult and Child Guidance Center. Indochinese	CA	159
Afghan Center	CA	190
Afghan Community in Amer.	NY	628
African Amer. Immigration Service	NY	609
Agudath Israel of Amer.	NY	631
Aid To Refugee Children Without Parents	CA	160
Amer. Arab Anti-Discrimination Comm.	DC	223
Amer. Comm. on Italian Migration	NY	632
Amer. Fed. of Jews from Central Europe	NY	635
Amer. Friends Service Comm. Haitian Women'	NY	636
Amer. Fund for Slovak Refugees	NJ	596
Amer. Romanian Comm. for Assistance to Ref	NY	630
Archdiocese of Chicago. Immigration Services	IL	351
Archdiocese of Detroit. Office of Refugee Rese	MI	490
Archdiocese of New York. Refugee Resettlemen	NY	639
Arizona Dept. of Economic Security. Refugee	AZ	8
Armenian Assembly of Amer.	DC	228
Asia Pacific Concerns Comm.	CA	181
Asian Counseling and Referral Service	WA	916
Asian Legal Services Outreach	CA	112
Assoc. of Vietnamese in Nashville	TN	811
Assyrian Universal Alliance	MI	512
Baptist Assoc. of New Orleans	LA	430
Baptist Conv. of Maryland	MD	447
Baptist Conv. of New Mexico	NM	597
Bethany Christian Services. Refugee Foster Ca	MI	501
Bulgarian Natl. Comm.	NJ	582
California Southern Baptist Conv. Refugee Re	CA	43
Cambodia's of Ohio	OH	728
Cambodian Assoc. of Amer.	CA	57
Cambodian Assoc. of Memphis	TN	809
Cambodian Assoc. of Mobile	AL	2
Cambodian Business Assoc.	CA	58
Cambodian Family	CA	165
Cambodian Mutual Assistance Assoc.	OH	720
Cambodian Mutual Assistance Assoc. of Greate	MA	478
Cambridge Organization of Portuguese-Amer.	MA	468
Caribbean Action Lobby	NY	611
Casa de la Esperanza	DC	229
Casa El Salvador	IL	352
Casa Marianella	TX	820
Catholic Charities	MA	486
Catholic Charities	NE	558
Catholic Charities Bureau. Resettlement Progra	WI	956
Catholic Charities. Immigration & Refugee Di	CA	68
Catholic Charities. Refugee Assistance	IN	396
Catholic Charities. Refugee Program	KS	416
Catholic Charities. Refugee Resettlement Offic	CA	182
Catholic Charities. Refugee Resettlement Offic	FL	289
Catholic Charities. Refugee Resettlement Prog	DE	220
Catholic Charities. Refugee Resettlement Prog	TN	810
Catholic Charities. Refugee Service Center	DC	230
Catholic Charities. Refugee Social Service Cen	MS	541
Catholic Charities. Resettlement Program	CA	44
Catholic Charities. Resettlement Services	CA	166
Catholic Charities. Resettlement Services	TX	858
Catholic Community Services of Utah. Refuge	UT	882
Catholic Community Services. Migration & R	LA	424
Catholic Community Services. Office of Migra	NJ	586
Catholic Community Services. Office of Migra	WV	936
Catholic Family and Child Services. Family R	WA	910
Catholic Family Center. Refugee Dept.	NY	686
Catholic Family Services. Refugee & Citizensh	TX	818
Catholic Immigration Center	HI	339
Catholic Immigration Services	FL	296
Catholic Migration & Refugee Services	VA	893
Catholic Migration and Refugee Service	OK	746
Catholic Migration and Refugee Services	NJ	573
Catholic Refugee Services	WA	917
Catholic Resettlement and Immigration Office	IA	406
Catholic Resettlement Services	OR	753
Catholic Social Agency. Migration Services	PA	761
Catholic Social Service Bureau. Refugee Resett	KY	420
Catholic Social Service. Refugee Office	NC	696
Catholic Social Service. Refugee Resettlement	FL	309
Catholic Social Service. Resettlement Program	CO	207
Catholic Social Service. Resettlement Program	OH	714
Catholic Social Service. Tha Huong Program	IL	386
Catholic Social Services	AK	6
Catholic Social Services	MS	540
Catholic Social Services	OH	731
Catholic Social Services	PA	786
Catholic Social Services Bureau	KY	418
Catholic Social Services. Immigration Service	CA	29
Catholic Social Services. Migration & Refugee	PA	773
Catholic Social Services. Refugee Program	AL	3
Catholic Social Services. Refugee Resetlement	NE	559
Catholic Social Services. Refugee Resettlemen	CA	179
Catholic Social Services. Refugee Social Servi	FL	312
Catholic Social Services. Resettlement Progra	CA	87
Center for Central Amer. Refugees	NJ	587
Center for Migration Studies	NY	689
Central Amer. Refugee Center	CA	69
Central Amer. Refugee Center	DC	233
Central Amer. Refugee Center	NY	627
Central Amer. Refugee Program	WA	918
Central Amer. Refugee Project	OK	740
Central Amer. Solidarity and Assistance	MD	455
Central Kentucky Jewish Assoc.	KY	421
Centro de Ayuda Para Immigrantes	TX	860
Centro Presente	MA	469
Chinatown Service Center	CA	70
Chinese Amer. Service League	IL	357
Chinese Newcomer Service Center	CA	135
Christian Community Service Agency	FL	297
Christian Community Services	CO	197
Christian Council of Metropolitan Atlanta. Re	GA	324

Christian Refugee Outreach	VA	894
Church Refugee Center	NY	643
Clinica Msr. Oscar A. Romero	CA	71
Coalition for Haitian Concerns	PA	791
Coalition for Immigrant and Refugee Rights &	CA	136
Comite de Refugiados Salvadorenos	CA	40
Comite en Defensa de los Immigrantes	CA	110
Community, Family & Children Services. Refu	MI	500
Corn-Maya	FL	287
Cornerstone Ministries	FL	317
Council of Churches. Refugee Resettlement Pro	MO	552
Cuban Amer. Natl. Council. Refugee Program	FL	299
Cultural Survival	MA	471
Dallas-Fort Worth Refugee Interagency	TX	832
Diocesan Refugee Resettlement Program	ME	439
Diocese of Green Bay. Dept. of Refugee, Migr	WI	939
Diocese of Nashville. Refugee Resettlement Pr	TN	812
Diocese of Raleigh. Refugee Resettlement Offi	NC	704
Diocese of Richmond. Office of Refugee Reset	VA	909
Diocese of Richmond. Office of Refugee Reset	VA	901
Diocese of Springfield. Refugee Resettlement	MA	482
Downtown Legalization Project	CA	72
East Central Illinois Refugee Mutual Assistanc	IL	391
Eau Claire Area Hmong Mutual Assistance Ass	WI	938
Ecumenical Refugee Resettlement Services	VA	903
Ecumenical Refugee Services	CO	202
El Concilio. Immigration Project	CA	45
El Rescate	CA	73
EPIC Immigration Project	WA	911
Episcopal Diocese of Minnesota. Refugee Res	MN	520
Episcopal Refugee Resettlement Commission	IN	400
Episcopal Social Service	CT	208
Eritrean Relief Comm.	NY	649
Ethiopian Community Center	DC	236
Ethiopian Community Development Council	VA	895
Ethiopian Community Mutual Assistance Asso	NY	650
Faith Lutheran Church	FL	308
Family and Children's Services of Chattanoog	TN	806
Fed. of Italian-Amer. Societies	NY	606
Fed. of Vietnamese & Allied Veterans	CA	56
Filipinos for Affirmative Action	CA	97
First Lutheran Church	FL	283
Florida Council of Churches. Refugee Program	FL	310
Freedom Flight Refugee Center	MI	504
Fresno Ecumenical Resettlement Project	CA	46
Friendly House	AZ	11
Friends of the Third World	IN	395
George Mason Univ. Indochina Institute.	VA	897
Georgia Baptist Conv. Language Missions De	GA	325
Good Samaritan Community Center	CA	138
Greater Hartford Jewish Fed.	CT	216
Haitian Amer. Assoc.	MA	472
Haitian Amer. Community Assoc.	FL	300
Haitian Centers Council	NY	615
Haitian Multi-Service Center	MA	474
Haitian Refugee Center	FL	301
Hebrew Immigrant Aid Society	NY	651
Hebrew Immigrant Aid Society	PA	776
Hispanic Immigration Counseling Program	WA	920
Hmong Assoc. of Brown County. Refugee Com	WI	940
Hmong Catholic Center	MN	532
Hmong Community	MI	494
Hmong Community Service	MD	449
Hmong Council	CA	48
Hmong Mutual Assistance Assoc.	WI	955
Hmong/Amer. Friendship Assoc.	WI	949
Holt Intl. Children's Services	OR	749
Holy Cross Mission	CA	184
Holy Cross Service Center	FL	288
Houston Metropolitan Ministries	TX	861
Human Services Assoc.	CA	31
Indochina Resource Action Center	DC	241
Inmigracion Latina Foundation	FL	302
Intercultural Action Center	CA	178
Intl. Buddhist Meditation Assoc.	HI	343
Intl. Center of the Capital Region. Refugee As	NY	602
Intl. Community Services	TX	865
Intl. Institute	OH	711
Intl. Institute of Buffalo	NY	623
Intl. Institute of Connecticut	CT	209
Intl. Institute of Connecticut	CT	213
Intl. Institute of Erie	PA	764
Intl. Institute of Flint	MI	499
Intl. Institute of Los Angeles	CA	191
Intl. Institute of Los Angeles. Refugee Reloca	CA	158
Intl. Institute of Lowell	MA	479
Intl. Institute of Metro Detroit	MI	495
Intl. Institute of Metropolitan St. Louis	MO	550
Intl. Institute of Minnesota	MN	534
Intl. Institute of New Jersey	NJ	584
Intl. Institute of Northwest Indiana	IN	397
Intl. Institute of Rhose Island	RI	796
Intl. Institute of San Francisco	CA	141
Intl. Institute of the East Bay	CA	98
Intl. Institute of Toledo	OH	732
Intl. Institute of Wisconsin	WI	950
Intl. Rescue Comm.	CA	162
Intl. Rescue Comm.	CA	168
Intl. Rescue Comm.	FL	303
Intl. Rescue Comm.	GA	335
Iowa Dept. of Human Services. Bureau of Refu	IA	408
Japanese Newcomer Service	CA	143
Jewish Family & Children Services	CA	144
Jewish Family and Child Service	OR	754
Jewish Family and Children's Agency	PA	777
Jewish Family and Children's Service	CO	203
Jewish Family and Children's Services	IN	403
Jewish Family and Voc. Service	KY	422
Jewish Family Service	AZ	17
Jewish Family Service	CA	51
Jewish Family Service	CT	215
Jewish Family Service	FL	314
Jewish Family Service	LA	436
Jewish Family Service	MN	535
Jewish Family Service	NJ	574
Jewish Family Service	NJ	575

Jewish Family Service	NY	688	Lutheran Social Services of Northeast Florida.	FL	292
Jewish Family Service	OH	712	Lutheran Social Services of Wisconsin & Upp	WI	953
Jewish Family Service	PA	785	Lutheran Social Services. Immigration & Refu	CA	81
Jewish Family Service	RI	797	Lutheran Social Services. Unaccompanied Min	OH	722
Jewish Family Service	TN	813	Mennonite Immigration and Refugee Services	DC	246
Jewish Family Service	TX	876	Michigan Dept. of Social Services. Office of R	MI	496
Jewish Family Service	VA	904	Mid-Cumberland Refugee Assistance Ministry	TN	815
Jewish Family Service Agency	NV	565	Midwest Coalition in Defense of Immigrants	IL	366
Jewish Family Service Assoc.	OH	719	Minnesota Cambodian Buddhist Society	MN	536
Jewish Family Service of Broward County	FL	285	Mississippi Baptist Conv. Language Missions	MS	542
Jewish Family Service of Delaware Valley	NJ	591	Montana Assoc. for Refugee Services	MT	554
Jewish Family Service of North Middlesex Co	NJ	578	Monterey County Sanctuary	CA	103
Jewish Family Service. Refugee Resettlement	TX	866	Moob Fed. of Amer.	IL	392
Jewish Family Service. Refugee Services	CA	79	Multicultural Immigration Center	NY	661
Jewish Family Service. Resettlement Program	FL	306	Mutual Aid Assoc. of the New Polish Immigra	IL	368
Jewish Family Service. Resettlement Program	MD	444	Natl. Assoc. for Vietnamese Amer. Education	CA	170
Jewish Family Services	FL	318	Natl. Council of Jewish Women. Rescue & Mi	FL	305
Jewish Family Services	GA	328	Natl. Slavic Conv.	MD	446
Jewish Family Services	NC	697	Nationalities Service Center	PA	780
Jewish Family Services	TX	834	Nationalities Service of Central California	CA	50
Jewish Family Services	WI	951	Nationalities Services Center	OH	718
Jewish Family Services of Greater Orlando	FL	322	Nevada Dept. of Human Resources. State Refug	NV	563
Jewish Fed. of Palm Beach County	FL	320	New York Assoc. for New Amer.	NY	663
Jewish Philanthropic Fund of 1933	NY	658	New York Circus	NY	664
Jewish Social Services	TX	852	North Carolina Baptist State Conv.	NC	695
Jewish Social Services	WI	943	North Manhattan Coalition for Immigrants' Ri	NY	667
Jewish Social Services Agency	MD	451	North Texas Immigration Coalition	TX	836
Kalihi-Palama Immigrant Service Center	HI	344	Northern Virginia Family Service. Multicultura	VA	898
Kentucky Cabinet for Human Resources. Office	KY	419	O.L.A. Immigration Rights Center	CA	193
Khemara Buddhikarma - The Cambodian Buddh	CA	59	Ohio Council of Churches. Refugee Services	OH	724
Khmer Buddhist Society of New England	RI	798	Orange County Community Consortium	CA	172
Korean Amer. Community Services	IL	363	Oshkosh Lao Hmong Assoc.	WI	954
Korean Amer. Community Services	MD	454	Peylim	NY	668
La Crosse Area Hmong Mutual Assistance Ass	WI	941	Philadelphia Refugee Service Center	PA	781
Lao Consultant Firm	VA	892	Philippine Center for Immigrant Rights	NY	669
Lao Family Community	CA	88	Pillsbury United Neighborhood Services. Asia	MN	523
Lao Family Community	CA	91	Plattsburg Interfaith Council	NY	685
Lao Family Community	CA	100	Polish Amer. Immigration and Relief Comm.	NY	670
Lao Family Community	CA	119	Polish and Slavic Center. Refugee Assistance	NY	617
Lao Family Community	CA	169	Presbyterian Synod of Southern California and	CA	84
Lao Family Community	UT	887	PRIME Ecumenical Commitment to Refugees	PA	762
Lutheran Child & Family Services of Massach	MA	485	Project Deliverance	OH	733
Lutheran Children and Family Service	PA	778	Proyecto Adelante	TX	837
Lutheran Family Service. Refugee Services	OR	755	Rav Tov. Intl. Jewish Rescue Organization	NY	618
Lutheran Family Services. Refugee Resettleme	NC	700	Refugee Resettlement Comm.	CA	90
Lutheran Immigration & Refugee Services	DC	245	Refugee Resettlement Office	AR	24
Lutheran Immigration and Refugee Service	NY	660	Refugee Services	MI	508
Lutheran Immigration and Refugee Service	TX	867	Research Foundation for Jewish Immigration	NY	671
Lutheran Ministries of Florida	FL	307	Rochester Refugee Services	MN	527
Lutheran Ministries of Florida. Refugee Resett	FL	319	Salvadoran Refugee Comm. (Oscar A. Romero)	DC	253
Lutheran Refugee and Immigration Services	NJ	592	San Antonio Literacy Council	TX	878
Lutheran Refugee Resettlement	CO	204	Sandigan California	CA	121
Lutheran Social Ministry of the Southwest. Re	AZ	13	Sarrlano Chirino Amaya Central Amer. Refuge	CA	85
Lutheran Social Services of Iowa	IA	409	Sepulveda Unitarian Universalist Society	CA	180
Lutheran Social Services of Kansas and Oklaho	KS	417	Somerville Portuguese Amer. League	MA	481
Lutheran Social Services of Michigan. Dept. o	MI	510	South and Meso-Amer. Indian Information Cen	CA	34
Lutheran Social Services of Michigan. Refugee	MI	507	South Texas Immigration Council	TX	856
Lutheran Social Services of North Dakota. Ref	ND	709	South-East Asia Center	IL	373

Southeast Asian Center   RI   792
Southern Baptist Immigration and Refugee Res   GA   331
Southern California Interfaith Task Force on C   CA   86
Sponsors Organized to Assist Refugees   OR   756
St. Anselm's Immigrant & Refugee Community   CA   52
Synapses. Asian Organizing Program   IL   374
Syracuse Interreligious Council. Refugee Assis NY   692
Tacoma Community House   WA   934
TECHO Central Amer. Education Center   AZ   20
Tolstoy Foundation   AZ   14
Tolstoy Foundation   MI   498
Tolstoy Foundation   NY   673
Travelers Aid Intl. Institute. Refugee Resource OH   716
Tressler Lutheran Services. Refugee Services P PA   770
U. S. Catholic Conference. Migration & Refug   NY   675
U.S. Catholic Conference. Migration & Refug   DC   256
U.S. Catholic Conference. Migration & Refug   DC   257
U.S. Catholic Conference. Migration & Refuge   TX   848
Ukrainian Research Foundation   CO   206
Unitarian Church of Arlington   VA   896
United Cambodian Community   CA   62
United Catholic Social Services. Refugee Reset NE   562
United Methodist Church. Refugee Concerns C   CA   156
United Nations. Relief and Works Agency for   NY   681
Valley Religious Task Force on Central Amer.   AZ   15
Vietnam Refugee Fund   VA   900
Vietnamese Amer. Assoc. Refugee Center   OK   743
Vietnamese Amer. Civic Assoc.   MA   475
Vietnamese Amer. Cultural Alliance of Colorad   CO   198
Vietnamese Amer. Cultural Organization   NY   682
Vietnamese Assoc. of Illinois   IL   378
Vietnamese Catholic Community   MI   489
Vietnamese Catholic Community in Connectic   CT   214
Vietnamese Community in Virginia   VA   905
Vietnamese Community of Orange County   CA   173
Vietnamese Evangelical Church   MN   525
Vietnamese Mutual Assistance Assoc.   TX   840
Vietnamese Mutual Assistance Assoc. of North   ND   710
Vietnamese Service Center   CA   53
Vietnamese Society of Rhode Island   RI   801
Virginia Council of Churches. Refugee Progra   VA   907
Washington Assoc. of Churches. Refugee Rese   WA   932
World Relief   CA   54
World Relief   DC   279
World Relief   FL   282
World Relief   GA   333
World Relief   NY   683
World Relief   NC   701
World Relief   TN   817
World Relief   TX   853
World Relief. Immigration Services   IL   379
Yiu Mienh Assoc. of Oregon   OR   758
YMCA. Refugee Resettlement Services   IL   380
Youth With a Mission Relief Services   HI   346

ECONOMIC

Adelphi Univ. Refugee Assistance Program	NY	626
Adult and Child Guidance Center. Indochinese	CA	159
Afghan Center	CA	190
Afghan Community in Amer.	NY	628
African Amer. Immigration Service	NY	609
Agudath Israel of Amer.	NY	631
Aid To Refugee Children Without Parents	CA	160
Amer. Arab Anti-Discrimination Comm.	DC	223
Amer. Comm. on Italian Migration	NY	632
Amer. Fed. of Jews from Central Europe	NY	635
Amer. Friends Service Comm. Haitian Women'	NY	636
Amer. Fund for Slovak Refugees	NJ	596
Amer. Romanian Comm. for Assistance to Ref	NY	630
Archdiocese of Chicago. Immigration Services	IL	351
Archdiocese of Detroit. Office of Refugee Rese	MI	490
Archdiocese of New York. Refugee Resettlemen	NY	639
Arizona Dept. of Economic Security. Refugee	AZ	8
Armenian Assembly of Amer.	DC	228
Asia Pacific Concerns Comm.	CA	181
Asian Counseling and Referral Service	WA	916
Asian Legal Services Outreach	CA	112
Assoc. of Vietnamese in Nashville	TN	811
Assyrian Universal Alliance	MI	512
Baptist Assoc. of New Orleans	LA	430
Baptist Conv. of Maryland	MD	447
Baptist Conv. of New Mexico	NM	597
Bethany Christian Services. Refugee Foster Ca	MI	501
Bulgarian Natl. Comm.	NJ	582
California Southern Baptist Conv. Refugee Re	CA	43
Cambodia's of Ohio	OH	728
Cambodian Assoc. of Amer.	CA	57
Cambodian Assoc. of Memphis	TN	809
Cambodian Assoc. of Mobile	AL	2
Cambodian Business Assoc.	CA	58
Cambodian Family	CA	165
Cambodian Mutual Assistance Assoc.	OH	720
Cambodian Mutual Assistance Assoc. of Greate	MA	478
Cambridge Organization of Portuguese-Amer.	MA	468
Caribbean Action Lobby	NY	611
Casa de la Esperanza	DC	229
Casa El Salvador	IL	352
Casa Marianella	TX	820
Catholic Charities	MA	486
Catholic Charities	NE	558
Catholic Charities Bureau. Resettlement Progra	WI	956
Catholic Charities. Immigration & Refugee Di	CA	68
Catholic Charities. Refugee Assistance	IN	396
Catholic Charities. Refugee Program	KS	416
Catholic Charities. Refugee Resettlement Offic	CA	182
Catholic Charities. Refugee Resettlement Offic	FL	289
Catholic Charities. Refugee Resettlement Prog	DE	220
Catholic Charities. Refugee Resettlement Prog	TN	810
Catholic Charities. Refugee Service Center	DC	230
Catholic Charities. Refugee Social Service Cen	MS	541
Catholic Charities. Resettlement Program	CA	44
Catholic Charities. Resettlement Services	CA	166
Catholic Charities. Resettlement Services	TX	858
Catholic Community Services of Utah. Refuge	UT	882
Catholic Community Services. Migration & R	LA	424
Catholic Community Services. Office of Migra	NJ	586
Catholic Community Services. Office of Migra	WV	936
Catholic Family and Child Services. Family R	WA	910
Catholic Family Center. Refugee Dept.	NY	686
Catholic Family Services. Refugee & Citizensh	TX	818
Catholic Immigration Center	HI	339
Catholic Immigration Services	FL	296
Catholic Migration & Refugee Services	VA	893
Catholic Migration and Refugee Service	OK	746
Catholic Migration and Refugee Services	NJ	573
Catholic Refugee Services	WA	917
Catholic Resettlement and Immigration Office	IA	406
Catholic Resettlement Services	OR	753
Catholic Social Agency. Migration Services	PA	761
Catholic Social Service Bureau. Refugee Resett	KY	420
Catholic Social Service. Refugee Office	NC	696
Catholic Social Service. Refugee Resettlement	FL	309
Catholic Social Service. Resettlement Program	CO	207
Catholic Social Service. Resettlement Program	OH	714
Catholic Social Service. Tha Huong Program	IL	386
Catholic Social Services	AK	6
Catholic Social Services	MS	540
Catholic Social Services	OH	731
Catholic Social Services	PA	786
Catholic Social Services Bureau	KY	418
Catholic Social Services. Immigration Service	CA	29
Catholic Social Services. Migration & Refugee	PA	773
Catholic Social Services. Refugee Program	AL	3
Catholic Social Services. Refugee Resetlement	NE	559
Catholic Social Services. Refugee Resettlemen	CA	179
Catholic Social Services. Refugee Social Servi	FL	312
Catholic Social Services. Resettlement Progra	CA	87
Center for Central Amer. Refugees	NJ	587
Center for Migration Studies	NY	689
Central Amer. Refugee Center	CA	69
Central Amer. Refugee Center	DC	233
Central Amer. Refugee Center	NY	627
Central Amer. Refugee Program	WA	918
Central Amer. Refugee Project	OK	740
Central Amer. Solidarity and Assistance	MD	455
Central Kentucky Jewish Assoc.	KY	421
Centro de Ayuda Para Immigrantes	TX	860
Centro Presente	MA	469
Chinatown Service Center	CA	70
Chinese Amer. Service League	IL	357
Chinese Newcomer Service Center	CA	135
Christian Community Service Agency	FL	297
Christian Community Services	CO	197
Christian Council of Metropolitan Atlanta. Re	GA	324

Christian Refugee Outreach	VA	894
Church Refugee Center	NY	643
Clinica Msr. Oscar A. Romero	CA	71
Coalition for Haitian Concerns	PA	791
Coalition for Immigrant and Refugee Rights &	CA	136
Comite de Refugiados Salvadorenos	CA	40
Comite en Defensa de los Immigrantes	CA	110
Community, Family & Children Services. Refu	MI	500
Corn-Maya	FL	287
Cornerstone Ministries	FL	317
Council of Churches. Refugee Resettlement Pro	MO	552
Cuban Amer. Natl. Council. Refugee Program	FL	299
Cultural Survival	MA	471
Dallas-Fort Worth Refugee Interagency	TX	832
Diocesan Refugee Resettlement Program	ME	439
Diocese of Green Bay. Dept. of Refugee, Migr	WI	939
Diocese of Nashville. Refugee Resettlement Pr	TN	812
Diocese of Raleigh. Refugee Resettlement Offi	NC	704
Diocese of Richmond. Office of Refugee Reset	VA	909
Diocese of Richmond. Office of Refugee Reset	VA	901
Diocese of Springfield. Refugee Resettlement	MA	482
Downtown Legalization Project	CA	72
East Central Illinois Refugee Mutual Assistanc	IL	391
Eau Claire Area Hmong Mutual Assistance Ass	WI	938
Ecumenical Refugee Resettlement Services	VA	903
Ecumenical Refugee Services	CO	202
El Concilio. Immigration Project	CA	45
El Rescate	CA	73
EPIC Immigration Project	WA	911
Episcopal Diocese of Minnesota. Refugee Rese	MN	520
Episcopal Refugee Resettlement Commission	IN	400
Episcopal Social Service	CT	208
Eritrean Relief Comm.	NY	649
Ethiopian Community Center	DC	236
Ethiopian Community Development Council	VA	895
Ethiopian Community Mutual Assistance Asso	NY	650
Faith Lutheran Church	FL	308
Family and Children's Services of Chattanooga	TN	806
Fed. of Italian-Amer. Societies	NY	606
Fed. of Vietnamese & Allied Veterans	CA	56
Filipinos for Affirmative Action	CA	97
First Lutheran Church	FL	283
Florida Council of Churches. Refugee Program	FL	310
Freedom Flight Refugee Center	MI	504
Fresno Ecumenical Resettlement Project	CA	46
Friendly House	AZ	11
Friends of the Third World	IN	395
George Mason Univ. Indochina Institute.	VA	897
Georgia Baptist Conv. Language Missions Dep	GA	325
Good Samaritan Community Center	CA	138
Greater Hartford Jewish Fed.	CT	216
Haitian Amer. Assoc.	MA	472
Haitian Amer. Community Assoc.	FL	300
Haitian Centers Council	NY	615
Haitian Multi-Service Center	MA	474
Haitian Refugee Center	FL	301
Hebrew Immigrant Aid Society	NY	651
Hebrew Immigrant Aid Society	PA	776
Hispanic Immigration Counseling Program	WA	920
Hmong Assoc. of Brown County. Refugee Com	WI	940
Hmong Catholic Center	MN	532
Hmong Community	MI	494
Hmong Community Service	MD	449
Hmong Council	CA	48
Hmong Mutual Assistance Assoc.	WI	955
Hmong/Amer. Friendship Assoc.	WI	949
Holt Intl. Children's Services	OR	749
Holy Cross Mission	CA	184
Holy Cross Service Center	FL	288
Houston Metropolitan Ministries	TX	861
Human Services Assoc.	CA	31
Indochina Resource Action Center	DC	241
Inmigracion Latina Foundation	FL	302
Intercultural Action Center	CA	178
Intl. Buddhist Meditation Assoc.	HI	343
Intl. Center of the Capital Region. Refugee As	NY	602
Intl. Community Services	TX	865
Intl. Institute	OH	711
Intl. Institute of Buffalo	NY	623
Intl. Institute of Connecticut	CT	209
Intl. Institute of Connecticut	CT	213
Intl. Institute of Erie	PA	764
Intl. Institute of Flint	MI	499
Intl. Institute of Los Angeles	CA	191
Intl. Institute of Los Angeles. Refugee Relocat	CA	158
Intl. Institute of Lowell	MA	479
Intl. Institute of Metro Detroit	MI	495
Intl. Institute of Metropolitan St. Louis	MO	550
Intl. Institute of Minnesota	MN	534
Intl. Institute of New Jersey	NJ	584
Intl. Institute of Northwest Indiana	IN	397
Intl. Institute of Rhose Island	RI	796
Intl. Institute of San Francisco	CA	141
Intl. Institute of the East Bay	CA	98
Intl. Institute of Toledo	OH	732
Intl. Institute of Wisconsin	WI	950
Intl. Rescue Comm.	CA	162
Intl. Rescue Comm.	CA	168
Intl. Rescue Comm.	FL	303
Intl. Rescue Comm.	GA	335
Iowa Dept. of Human Services. Bureau of Refug	IA	408
Japanese Newcomer Service	CA	143
Jewish Family & Children Services	CA	144
Jewish Family and Child Service	OR	754
Jewish Family and Children's Agency	PA	777
Jewish Family and Children's Service	CO	203
Jewish Family and Children's Services	IN	403
Jewish Family and Voc. Service	KY	422
Jewish Family Service	AZ	17
Jewish Family Service	CA	51
Jewish Family Service	CT	215
Jewish Family Service	FL	314
Jewish Family Service	LA	436
Jewish Family Service	MN	535
Jewish Family Service	NJ	574
Jewish Family Service	NJ	575

Jewish Family Service	NY	688
Jewish Family Service	OH	712
Jewish Family Service	PA	785
Jewish Family Service	RI	797
Jewish Family Service	TN	813
Jewish Family Service	TX	876
Jewish Family Service	VA	904
Jewish Family Service Agency	NV	565
Jewish Family Service Assoc.	OH	719
Jewish Family Service of Broward County	FL	285
Jewish Family Service of Delaware Valley	NJ	591
Jewish Family Service of North Middlesex Cou	NJ	578
Jewish Family Service. Refugee Resettlement P	TX	866
Jewish Family Service. Refugee Services	CA	79
Jewish Family Service. Resettlement Program	FL	306
Jewish Family Service. Resettlement Program	MD	444
Jewish Family Services	FL	318
Jewish Family Services	GA	328
Jewish Family Services	NC	697
Jewish Family Services	TX	834
Jewish Family Services	WI	951
Jewish Family Services of Greater Orlando	FL	322
Jewish Fed. of Palm Beach County	FL	320
Jewish Philanthropic Fund of 1933	NY	658
Jewish Social Services	TX	852
Jewish Social Services	WI	943
Jewish Social Services Agency	MD	451
Kalihi-Palama Immigrant Service Center	HI	344
Kentucky Cabinet for Human Resources. Office	KY	419
Khemara Buddhikarma - The Cambodian Buddh	CA	59
Khmer Buddhist Society of New England	RI	798
Korean Amer. Community Services	IL	363
Korean Amer. Community Services	MD	454
La Crosse Area Hmong Mutual Assistance Asso	WI	941
Lao Consultant Firm	VA	892
Lao Family Community	CA	88
Lao Family Community	CA	91
Lao Family Community	CA	100
Lao Family Community	CA	119
Lao Family Community	CA	169
Lao Family Community	UT	887
Lutheran Child & Family Services of Massachu	MA	485
Lutheran Children and Family Service	PA	778
Lutheran Family Service. Refugee Services	OR	755
Lutheran Family Services. Refugee Resettlemen	NC	700
Lutheran Immigration & Refugee Services	DC	245
Lutheran Immigration and Refugee Service	NY	660
Lutheran Immigration and Refugee Service	TX	867
Lutheran Ministries of Florida	FL	307
Lutheran Ministries of Florida. Refugee Resett	FL	319
Lutheran Refugee and Immigration Services	NJ	592
Lutheran Refugee Resettlement	CO	204
Lutheran Social Ministry of the Southwest. Re	AZ	13
Lutheran Social Services of Iowa	IA	409
Lutheran Social Services of Kansas and Oklaho	KS	417
Lutheran Social Services of Michigan. Dept. o	MI	510
Lutheran Social Services of Michigan. Refugee	MI	507
Lutheran Social Services of North Dakota. Ref	ND	709
Lutheran Social Services of Northeast Florida.	FL	292
Lutheran Social Services of Wisconsin & Uppe	WI	953
Lutheran Social Services. Immigration & Refug	CA	81
Lutheran Social Services. Unaccompanied Min	OH	722
Mennonite Immigration and Refugee Services	DC	246
Michigan Dept. of Social Services. Office of R	MI	496
Mid-Cumberland Refugee Assistance Ministry	TN	815
Midwest Coalition in Defense of Immigrants	IL	366
Minnesota Cambodian Buddhist Society	MN	536
Mississippi Baptist Conv. Language Missions	MS	542
Montana Assoc. for Refugee Services	MT	554
Monterey County Sanctuary	CA	103
Moob Fed. of Amer.	IL	392
Multicultural Immigration Center	NY	661
Mutual Aid Assoc. of the New Polish Immigrat	IL	368
Natl. Assoc. for Vietnamese Amer. Education	CA	170
Natl. Council of Jewish Women. Rescue & Mi	FL	305
Natl. Slavic Conv.	MD	446
Nationalities Service Center	PA	780
Nationalities Service of Central California	CA	50
Nationalities Services Center	OH	718
Nevada Dept. of Human Resources. State Refug	NV	563
New York Assoc. for New Amer.	NY	663
New York Circus	NY	664
North Carolina Baptist State Conv.	NC	695
North Manhattan Coalition for Immigrants' Ri	NY	667
North Texas Immigration Coalition	TX	836
Northern Virginia Family Service. Multicultura	VA	898
O.L.A. Immigration Rights Center	CA	193
Ohio Council of Churches. Refugee Services	OH	724
Orange County Community Consortium	CA	172
Oshkosh Lao Hmong Assoc.	WI	954
Peylim	NY	668
Philadelphia Refugee Service Center	PA	781
Philippine Center for Immigrant Rights	NY	669
Pillsbury United Neighborhood Services. Asian	MN	523
Plattsburg Interfaith Council	NY	685
Polish Amer. Immigration and Relief Comm.	NY	670
Polish and Slavic Center. Refugee Assistance	NY	617
Presbyterian Synod of Southern California and	CA	84
PRIME Ecumenical Commitment to Refugees	PA	762
Project Deliverance	OH	733
Proyecto Adelante	TX	837
Rav Tov. Intl. Jewish Rescue Organization	NY	618
Refugee Resettlement Comm.	CA	90
Refugee Resettlement Office	AR	24
Refugee Services	MI	508
Research Foundation for Jewish Immigration	NY	671
Rochester Refugee Services	MN	527
Salvadoran Refugee Comm. (Oscar A. Romero)	DC	253
San Antonio Literacy Council	TX	878
Sandigan California	CA	121
Sarrlano Chirino Amaya Central Amer. Refuge	CA	85
Sepulveda Unitarian Universalist Society	CA	180
Somerville Portuguese Amer. League	MA	481
South and Meso-Amer. Indian Information Cen	CA	34
South Texas Immigration Council	TX	856
South-East Asia Center	IL	373

Southeast Asian Center	RI	792
Southern Baptist Immigration and Refugee Res	GA	331
Southern California Interfaith Task Force on C	CA	86
Sponsors Organized to Assist Refugees	OR	756
St. Anselm's Immigrant & Refugee Community	CA	52
Synapses. Asian Organizing Program	IL	374
Syracuse Interreligious Council. Refugee Assis	NY	692
Tacoma Community House	WA	934
TECHO Central Amer. Education Center	AZ	20
Tolstoy Foundation	AZ	14
Tolstoy Foundation	MI	498
Tolstoy Foundation	NY	673
Travelers Aid Intl. Institute. Refugee Resource	OH	716
Tressler Lutheran Services. Refugee Services P	PA	770
U. S. Catholic Conference. Migration & Refug	NY	675
U.S. Catholic Conference. Migration & Refuge	DC	256
U.S. Catholic Conference. Migration & Refuge	DC	257
U.S. Catholic Conference. Migration & Refuge	TX	848
Ukrainian Research Foundation	CO	206
Unitarian Church of Arlington	VA	896
United Cambodian Community	CA	62
United Catholic Social Services. Refugee Rese	NE	562
United Methodist Church. Refugee Concerns C	CA	156
United Nations. Relief and Works Agency for	NY	681
Valley Religious Task Force on Central Amer.	AZ	15
Vietnam Refugee Fund	VA	900
Vietnamese Amer. Assoc. Refugee Center	OK	743
Vietnamese Amer. Civic Assoc.	MA	475
Vietnamese Amer. Cultural Alliance of Colorad	CO	198
Vietnamese Amer. Cultural Organization	NY	682
Vietnamese Assoc. of Illinois	IL	378
Vietnamese Catholic Community	MI	489
Vietnamese Catholic Community in Connectic	CT	214
Vietnamese Community in Virginia	VA	905
Vietnamese Community of Orange County	CA	173
Vietnamese Evangelical Church	MN	525
Vietnamese Mutual Assistance Assoc.	TX	840
Vietnamese Mutual Assistance Assoc. of North	ND	710
Vietnamese Service Center	CA	53
Vietnamese Society of Rhode Island	RI	801
Virginia Council of Churches. Refugee Progra	VA	907
Washington Assoc. of Churches. Refugee Rese	WA	932
World Relief	CA	54
World Relief	DC	279
World Relief	FL	282
World Relief	GA	333
World Relief	NY	683
World Relief	NC	701
World Relief	TN	817
World Relief	TX	853
World Relief. Immigration Services	IL	379
Yiu Mienh Assoc. of Oregon	OR	758
YMCA. Refugee Resettlement Services	IL	380
Youth With a Mission Relief Services	HI	346

EDUCATION

Adelphi Univ. Refugee Assistance Program	NY	626
Adult and Child Guidance Center. Indochinese	CA	159
AFL/CIO Immigration Project	CA	64
All Culture Friendship Center Refugee & Immi	CA	55
All Culture Friendship Center Refugee & Immi	CA	65
Amer. Arab Anti-Discrimination Comm.	DC	223
Amer. Civic Assoc.	NY	608
Amer. Comm. on Italian Migration	NY	632
Amer. Immigrant Foundation	CA	164
Amer. Refugee Comm.	IL	381
Amer. Refugee Comm.	MN	518
Anaheim Independencia Center	CA	27
Archdiocese of Chicago. Immigration Services	IL	351
Archdiocese of New York. Refugee Resettlemen	NY	639
Arizona Dept. of Economic Security. Refugee	AZ	8
Asia Pacific Concerns Comm.	CA	181
Asian Resources	CA	113
Bergen County Sanctuary Comm.	NJ	590
Bethany Christian Services. Refugee Foster Ca	MI	501
Brown Univ. Population Studies & Training C	RI	793
Buddhist Council for Refugee Rescue and Reset	CA	133
California Dept. of Social Services. Office of	CA	114
Cambodian Assoc. of Memphis	TN	809
Cambodian Assoc. of Mobile	AL	2
Cambodian Assoc. of Virginia	VA	902
Cambodian Family	CA	165
Cambodian Mutual Assistance Assoc.	OH	720
Cambodian Mutual Assistance Assoc. of Greate	MA	478
Casa de la Esperanza	DC	229
Casa Juan Diego	TX	857
Casa Marianella	TX	820
Catholic Charities	NE	558
Catholic Charities. Immigration & Refugee Di	CA	68
Catholic Charities. Immigration & Refugee Pro	CA	174
Catholic Charities. Immigration & Refugee Se	PA	765
Catholic Charities. Immigration Counseling S	TX	831
Catholic Charities. Migration and Refugee Ser	CT	211
Catholic Charities. Refugee Office	IN	394
Catholic Charities. Refugee Resettlement Offic	CA	182
Catholic Charities. Refugee Resettlement Prog	CA	35
Catholic Charities. Refugee Services	KY	423
Catholic Charities. Resettlement Program	CA	44
Catholic Community Services of Utah. Refuge	UT	882
Catholic Community Services. Migration & R	LA	424
Catholic Community Services. Office of Migra	NJ	586
Catholic Community Services. Office of Migra	WV	936
Catholic Family and Child Service	WA	935
Catholic Immigration Center	HI	339
Catholic Immigration Services	FL	296
Catholic Migration & Refugee Services	OR	748
Catholic Migration and Refugee Services	NJ	573
Catholic Resettlement and Immigration Office	IA	406
Catholic Services for Immigrants	TX	874
Catholic Social Agency. Migration Services	PA	761
Catholic Social Service Bureau. Refugee Resett	KY	420
Catholic Social Service of Phoenix	AZ	9
Catholic Social Service. Refugee Office	NC	696
Catholic Social Service. Refugee Resettlement	FL	309
Catholic Social Service. Resettlement Program	CO	207
Catholic Social Service. Tha Huong Program	IL	386
Catholic Social Services	IN	398
Catholic Social Services	OH	731
Catholic Social Services Bureau	KY	418
Catholic Social Services. Immigration Service	CA	29
Catholic Social Services. Migration & Refugee	PA	773
Catholic Social Services. Refugee Program	AL	3
Catholic Social Services. Refugee Resettlemen	CA	179
Catholic Social Services. Resettlement Progra	CA	87
Center for Applied Linguistics. Refugee Servic	DC	231
Center for Immigrants Rights	NY	642
Center for Migration Studies	NY	689
Central Amer. Refugee Center	NY	627
Central Amer. Solidarity and Assistance	MD	455
Centro Campesino. Projecto de Inmigracion	WA	912
Centro Presente	MA	469
Chinese Amer. Civic Assoc.	MA	459
Christ Church of the Brethren. Sanctuary Com	OH	734
Christian Community Services	CO	197
Christian Council of Metropolitan Atlanta. Re	GA	324
Church Refugee Center	NY	643
Clinica Msr. Oscar A. Romero	CA	71
Coalition for Haitian Concerns	PA	791
Coalition for Immigrant and Refugee Rights &	CA	136
Coastal Bend Friends Meeting	TX	830
Colorado Refugee and Immigrant Services Prog	CO	201
Comm. to Defend Immigrant & Refugee Rights	CA	95
Community Legal Services	CA	92
Community, Family & Children Services. Refu	MI	500
Connecticut Dept. of Human Resources. State	CT	212
Council of Churches. Refugee Resettlement Pro	MO	552
Dallas-Fort Worth Refugee Interagency	TX	832
Delaware Dept. of Health & Social Services. D	DE	219
Diocesan Refugee Resettlement Program	ME	439
Diocese of Lafayette. Migration & Refugee Ser	LA	428
Diocese of Nashville. Refugee Resettlement Pr	TN	812
Diocese of Richmond. Office of Refugee Reset	VA	909
Diocese of Richmond. Office of Refugee Reset	VA	901
Diocese of Springfield - Cape Girardeau. Reset	MO	553
Diocese of Springfield. Refugee Resettlement	MA	482
District of Columbia Dept. of Human Services.	DC	235
Don Bosco Community Center	MO	546
Downtown Legalization Project	CA	72
East Bay Sanctuary Covenant	CA	33
Eau Claire Area Hmong Mutual Assistance Ass	WI	938
Ecumenical Immigration Services	LA	431
Ecumenical Refugee Resettlement Services	VA	903
Ecumenical Refugee Services	CO	202
El Concilio. Immigration Project	CA	45

EPIC Immigration Project	WA	911
Episcopal Refugee Resettlement Commission	IN	400
Eritrean Relief Comm.	NY	649
Ethiopian Community Development Council	VA	895
Evangelical Crusade of Fishers of Men	NY	614
Experiment in Intl. Living	VT	888
Fed. of Italian-Amer. Societies	NY	606
Fed. of Vietnamese & Allied Veterans	CA	56
Fort Worth Independent School District. Survi	TX	850
Friendly House	AZ	11
George Mason Univ. Indochina Institute.	VA	897
Georgia Dept. of Human Resources. Special Pr	GA	327
Guatemala Human Rights Commission/USA	DC	240
Haitian Amer. Community Assoc.	FL	300
Haitian Centers Council	NY	615
Haitian Multi-Service Center	MA	474
Haitian Refugee Center	FL	301
Hmong Assoc. of Brown County. Refugee Com	WI	940
Hmong Catholic Center	MN	532
Hmong Council	CA	48
Hmong Mutual Assistance Assoc.	WI	955
Holy Cross Mission	CA	184
Human Services Assoc.	CA	31
Idaho Dept. of Health and Welfare. Div. of Fie	ID	347
Illinois Bureau of Naturalization Services	IL	389
Immigrant Students Project of the Natl. Coalit	MA	461
Immigrants Assistance Center	MA	480
Immigration and Legalization Service	TX	824
Immigration Project	CA	75
Indiana Dept. of Welfare. Policy & Program D	IN	402
Interfaith Refugee Assistance Project	OK	744
Intl. Center of the Capital Region. Refugee As	NY	602
Intl. Community Services	TX	865
Intl. Immigrants Foundation	NY	654
Intl. Institute	OH	711
Intl. Institute of Buffalo	NY	623
Intl. Institute of Connecticut	CT	209
Intl. Institute of Connecticut	CT	213
Intl. Institute of Erie	PA	764
Intl. Institute of Los Angeles	CA	191
Intl. Institute of Lowell	MA	479
Intl. Institute of Metro Detroit	MI	495
Intl. Institute of Metropolitan St. Louis	MO	550
Intl. Institute of Minnesota	MN	534
Intl. Institute of New Jersey	NJ	584
Intl. Institute of Northwest Indiana	IN	397
Intl. Institute of Rhose Island	RI	796
Intl. Institute of San Francisco	CA	141
Intl. Institute of the East Bay	CA	98
Intl. Institute of Toledo	OH	732
Intl. Ladies Garment Workers Union. Immigrat	CA	77
Intl. Ladies Garment Workers Union. Immigrat	NY	655
Intl. Service Center	PA	766
Iowa Dept. of Human Services. Bureau of Refug	IA	408
Japanese Newcomer Service	CA	143
Jewish Family and Children's Services	IN	403
Jewish Family Service	MN	535
Jewish Family Service	RI	797
Jewish Family Service	TX	876
Jewish Family Service of Broward County	FL	285
Jewish Family Service of Delaware Valley	NJ	591
Jewish Family Service of North Middlesex Cou	NJ	578
Jewish Family Service of Somerset County	NJ	588
Jewish Family Service. Refugee Services	CA	79
Jewish Family Service. Resettlement Program	CA	128
Jewish Family Service. Resettlement Program	MD	444
Jewish Family Services	FL	318
Jewish Family Services. Refugee Services	IL	362
Jewish Social Services	WI	943
Jewish Social Services Agency	MD	451
Kalihi-Palama Immigrant Service Center	HI	344
Kansas Dept. of Social & Rehabilitation Servi	KS	415
Kentucky Cabinet for Human Resources. Office	KY	419
Khmer Society of San Antonio. Refugee SOS	TX	877
Korean Amer. Community Services	IL	363
Korean Amer. Community Services	MD	454
Lao Consultant Firm	VA	892
Lao Family Community	CA	88
Lao Family Community	CA	119
Lao Family Community	CA	169
Lao Family Community	UT	887
Lawyers Comm. for Human Rights. Political A	NY	659
Louisiana Dept. of Health & Human Services.	LA	425
Lutheran Child & Family Services of Massachu	MA	485
Lutheran Church. Synod Board of Social Minis	MO	551
Lutheran Family Services. Refugee Resettlemen	NC	700
Lutheran Immigration and Refugee Service	NY	660
Lutheran Refugee Resettlement	CO	204
Lutheran Social Services of Iowa	IA	409
Lutheran Social Services of Kansas and Oklaho	KS	417
Lutheran Social Services of Michigan. Dept. of	MI	510
Lutheran Social Services of Michigan. Refugee	MI	507
Lutheran Social Services of Northeast Florida.	FL	292
Maryland Dept. of Human Resources. State Ref	MD	445
Massachusetts Office for Refugees and Immigra	MA	463
Metropolitan Social Services. Refugee Program	TN	814
Migration and Refugee Services Office	NJ	593
Minnesota Cambodian Buddhist Society	MN	536
Minnesota Council of Churches. Refugee Progr	MN	537
Minnesota Dept. of Human Services. Refugee P	MN	538
Mississippi Dept. of Public Welfare. Refugee P	MS	543
Missouri Div. of Family Services. Refugee Ass	MO	544
Mohawk Valley Resource Center for Refugees	NY	693
Montana Dept. of Family Services. Office of R	MT	557
Monterey County Sanctuary	CA	103
Multicultural Immigration Center	NY	661
Natl. Assoc. for Vietnamese Amer. Education	CA	170
Natl. Slavic Conv.	MD	446
Nationalities Service Center	PA	769
Nationalities Service Center	PA	780
Nationalities Service of Central California	CA	50
Nationalities Services Center	OH	718
Naturalization Project	LA	434
Nebraska Dept. of Social Services. Refugee Aff	NE	560
Nevada Dept. of Human Resources. State Refug	NV	563
New Jersey Dept. of Human Services. State Ref	NJ	594

New Mexico Dept. of Human Services. Social	NM	601
New York Assoc. for New Amer.	NY	663
New York Circus	NY	664
New York Dept. of Social Services. State Refu	NY	603
North Carolina Dept. of Human Resources. Fa	NC	706
North Dakota Dept. of Human Services. Refuge	ND	708
North Manhattan Coalition for Immigrants' Ri	NY	667
Ohio Council of Churches. Refugee Services	OH	724
Ohio Dept. of Human Services. Program Devel	OH	725
Oklahoma Dept. of Human Services. Refugee U	OK	742
Orange County Community Consortium	CA	172
Oregon Dept. of Human Resources. Refugee Pr	OR	759
Organization of Chinese Amer.	DC	248
Pennsylvania Dept. of Public Welfare. Office o	PA	767
Pillsbury United Neighborhood Services. Asian	MN	523
PRIME Ecumenical Commitment to Refugees	PA	762
Proyecto Adelante	TX	837
Rav Tov. Intl. Jewish Rescue Organization	NY	618
Refugee Assistance Program	CA	130
Refugee Resettlement Comm.	CA	90
Refugee Resettlement Office	AR	24
Refugee Resettlement Program	AR	26
Refugee Services	MI	508
Rhode Island Dept. of Human Services. State R	RI	799
Rochester Refugee Services	MN	527
Sandigan California	CA	121
Santa Clara County Health Dept. Refugee Healt	CA	163
Socio-Economic Development Center for South	RI	800
South and Meso-Amer. Indian Information Cen	CA	34
South Carolina Dept. of Social Services. Refug	SC	803
South Dakota Dept. of Social Services. Refuge	SD	804
South Texas Immigration Council	TX	856
South-East Asia Center	IL	373
Southeast Asian Center	RI	792
Southern Baptist Immigration and Refugee Res	GA	331
Southern California Interfaith Task Force on C	CA	86
St. Anselm's Immigrant & Refugee Community	CA	52
St. Paul's United Methodist Church. Refugee Pr	NV	567
Syracuse Interreligious Council. Refugee Assist	NY	692
Tacoma Community House	WA	934
TECHO Central Amer. Education Center	AZ	20
Tennessee Dept. of Human Services. Refugee P	TN	816
Texas Dept. of Human Service. Refugee Progra	TX	825
Tolstoy Foundation	CA	192
Tolstoy Foundation	MI	498
Training Program in Human Services for Emigr	NY	674
Travelers Aid Intl. Institute. Refugee Resource	OH	716
Tucson Ecumenical Council. Central Amer. Tas	AZ	22
U. S. Catholic Conference. Migration & Refug	NY	675
Unitarian Church of Arlington	VA	896
United Cambodian Community	CA	62
United Nations. Relief and Works Agency for	NY	681
Univ. of Minnesota. Immigration History Rese	MN	539
Utah Dept. of Social Services. Refugee & Alie	UT	885
Utah Immigration Project	UT	886
Valley Religious Task Force on Central Amer.	AZ	15
Vermont State Refugee Coordinator	VT	891
Vietnamese Amer. Assoc. Refugee Center	OK	743
Vietnamese Amer. Civic Assoc.	MA	475
Vietnamese Amer. Cultural Alliance of Colorad	CO	198
Vietnamese Amer. Cultural Organization	NY	682
Vietnamese Assoc. of Illinois	IL	378
Vietnamese Catholic Community	MI	489
Vietnamese Catholic Community in Connectic	CT	214
Vietnamese Community of Orange County	CA	173
Vietnamese Evangelical Church	MN	525
Vietnamese Mutual Assistance Assoc.	TX	840
Virginia Council of Churches. Refugee Progra	VA	907
Virginia Dept. of Social Services. State Refuge	VA	908
Washington Assoc. of Churches. Immigration	WA	928
Washington Assoc. of Churches. Refugee Rese	WA	932
Washington Bureau of Refugee Assistance	WA	914
West Virginia Dept. of Human Services	WV	937
Woodrow Wilson Intl. Center	DC	278
World Relief	CA	157
World Relief	TX	853
World Relief	TX	869
World Relief. Immigration Services	IL	379
Wyoming Dept. of Health & Social Services.	WY	958
YMCA Intl. Services	TX	870
YMCA. Refugee Resettlement Services	IL	380

HEALTH

Adelphi Univ. Refugee Assistance Program	NY	626
Amer. Baptist Churches. Immigration & Refug	PA	788
Amer. Refugee Comm.	IL	381
Amer. Refugee Comm.	MN	518
Anaheim Independencia Center	CA	27
Arizona Dept. of Economic Security. Refugee	AZ	8
Asia Pacific Concerns Comm.	CA	181
California Dept. of Social Services. Office of	CA	114
Cambodian Assoc. of Mobile	AL	2
Cambodian Assoc. of Virginia	VA	902
Cambodian Mutual Assistance Assoc.	OH	720
Casa Juan Diego	TX	857
Casa Marianella	TX	820
Catholic Charities. Refugee Services	KY	423
Catholic Community Services of Utah. Refugee	UT	882
Catholic Community Services. Migration & Re	LA	424
Catholic Community Services. Office of Migra	NJ	586
Catholic Family Services. Refugee & Citizensh	TX	818
Catholic Migration & Refugee Services	OR	748
Catholic Services for Immigrants	TX	874
Catholic Social Service Bureau. Refugee Resett	KY	420
Catholic Social Service. Refugee Office	NC	696
Catholic Social Service. Tha Huong Program	IL	386
Catholic Social Services Bureau	KY	418
Catholic Social Services. Refugee Program	AL	3
Catholic Social Services. Refugee Resetlement	NE	559
Catholic Social Services. Refugee Social Servi	FL	312
Central Amer. Refugee Center	DC	233
Chinatown Service Center	CA	70
Chinese Amer. Service League	IL	357
Christ Church of the Brethren. Sanctuary Com	OH	734
Christian Community Services	CO	197
Christian Council of Metropolitan Atlanta. Re	GA	324
Clinica Msr. Oscar A. Romero	CA	71
Coalition for Haitian Concerns	PA	791
Coalition for Immigrant and Refugee Rights &	CA	136
Coastal Bend Friends Meeting	TX	830
Colorado Refugee and Immigrant Services Prog	CO	201
Connecticut Dept. of Human Resources. State	CT	212
Corn-Maya	FL	287
Cornerstone Ministries	FL	317
Cultural Survival	MA	471
Delaware Dept. of Health & Social Services. D	DE	219
Diocese of Lafayette. Migration & Refugee Ser	LA	428
Diocese of Richmond. Office of Refugee Resett	VA	901
District of Columbia Dept. of Human Services.	DC	235
East Bay Sanctuary Covenant	CA	33
Florida Dept. of Health and Rehabilitation Ser	FL	315
Georgia Dept. of Human Resources. Refugee He	GA	326
Georgia Dept. of Human Resources. Special Pr	GA	327
Good Samaritan Community Center	CA	138
Haitian Multi-Service Center	MA	474
Hmong Council	CA	48
Hmong/Amer. Friendship Assoc.	WI	949
Idaho Dept. of Health and Welfare. Div. of Fie	ID	347
Illinois Bureau of Naturalization Services	IL	389
Indiana Dept. of Welfare. Policy & Program De	IN	402
Interfaith Refugee Assistance Project	OK	744
Intermountain Health Care. Refugee Clinic	UT	883
Intl. Institute of Buffalo	NY	623
Intl. Institute of Metropolitan St. Louis	MO	550
Intl. Institute of Rhose Island	RI	796
Intl. Institute of San Francisco	CA	141
Intl. Institute of the East Bay	CA	98
Intl. Refugee Center	IL	360
Iowa Dept. of Human Services. Bureau of Refug	IA	408
Jewish Family Service of Broward County	FL	285
Jewish Family Service. Resettlement Program	CA	128
Jewish Family Services	FL	318
Jewish Philanthropic Fund of 1933	NY	658
Kansas Dept. of Social & Rehabilitation Servi	KS	415
Kentucky Cabinet for Human Resources. Office	KY	419
Khmer Health Advocates	CT	217
La Crosse Area Hmong Mutual Assistance Asso	WI	941
Lao Consultant Firm	VA	892
Lao Family Community	CA	88
Lao Family Community	UT	887
Legal Aid of Western Missouri	MO	547
Louisiana Dept. of Health & Human Services.	LA	425
Lutheran Social Services of Iowa	IA	409
Lutheran Social Services of Northeast Florida.	FL	292
Maryland Dept. of Human Resources. State Ref	MD	445
Massachusetts Office for Refugees and Immigra	MA	463
Minnesota Dept. of Human Services. Refugee P	MN	538
Mississippi Dept. of Public Welfare. Refugee P	MS	543
Missouri Div. of Family Services. Refugee Ass	MO	544
Mohawk Valley Resource Center for Refugees	NY	693
Nebraska Dept. of Social Services. Refugee Aff	NE	560
New Jersey Dept. of Human Services. State Ref	NJ	594
New Mexico Dept. of Human Services. Social	NM	601
New York Assoc. for New Amer.	NY	663
New York Dept. of Social Services. State Refu	NY	603
North Carolina Dept. of Human Resources. Fa	NC	706
North Carolina Refugee Health Program	NC	707
North Dakota Dept. of Human Services. Refuge	ND	708
Ohio Dept. of Human Services. Program Devel	OH	725
Orange County Community Consortium	CA	172
Oregon Dept. of Human Resources. Refugee Pr	OR	759
Organization of Chinese Amer.	DC	248
Pennsylvania Dept. of Public Welfare. Office o	PA	767
Rav Tov. Intl. Jewish Rescue Organization	NY	618
Refugee Resettlement Program	AR	26
Refugee Services	MI	508
Rhode Island Dept. of Human Services. State R	RI	799
Saint Vincents Services	NY	619
Santa Clara County Health Dept. Refugee Healt	CA	163
South Carolina Dept. of Social Services. Refug	SC	803
South Dakota Dept. of Social Services. Refuge	SD	804

South-East Asia Center   IL   373
Southern Baptist Immigration and Refugee Res GA   331
Syracuse Interreligious Council. Refugee Assis NY   692
Tennessee Dept. of Human Services. Refugee P TN   816
Texas Dept. of Human Service. Refugee Progra TX   825
U.S. Dept. of Health and Human Services. Publ MD   452
United Cambodian Community   CA   62
United Nations. Relief and Works Agency for   NY   681
Utah Dept. of Social Services. Refugee & Alie UT   885
Valley Religious Task Force on Central Amer.   AZ   15
Vermont State Refugee Coordinator   VT   891
Vietnamese Amer. Assoc. Refugee Center   OK   743
Vietnamese Amer. Civic Assoc.   MA   475
Vietnamese Amer. Cultural Organization   NY   682
Vietnamese Mutual Assistance Assoc.   TX   840
Virginia Dept. of Social Services. State Refuge VA 908
Washington Bureau of Refugee Assistance   WA   914
West Virginia Dept. of Human Services   WV   937
World Relief   TX   853
Wyoming Dept. of Health & Social Services.   WY   958

LEGAL

Afghan Community in Amer.	NY	628
AFL/CIO Immigration Project	CA	64
African Amer. Immigration Service	NY	609
Agudath Israel of Amer.	NY	631
Amer. Arab Anti-Discrimination Comm.	DC	223
Amer. Baptist Churches. Immigration & Refug	PA	788
Amer. Civic Assoc.	NY	608
Amer. Civil Liberties Union. South Texas Proj	TX	880
Amer. Comm. on Italian Migration	NY	632
Amer. Friends Service Comm. Florida Undocum	FL	293
Amer. Immigrant Foundation	CA	164
Amer. Immigration Lawyers Assoc.	DC	224
Amer. Immigration Lawyers Assoc. Pro Bono	FL	294
Amer. Immigration Lawyers Assoc. Texas Cha	OK	737
Americanization League	NY	691
Amnesty Intl. USA	CA	132
Anaheim Independencia Center	CA	27
Annunciation House	TX	844
Archdiocese of Chicago. Immigration Services	IL	351
Archdiocese of New York. Office for Immigran	NY	638
Archdiocese of Portland. Immigration Counseli	OR	752
Arizona Center for Immigrants	AZ	7
Asian Counseling and Referral Service	WA	916
Asian Immigrant Womens Advocates	CA	93
Asian Legal Services Outreach	CA	112
Asian Pacific Amer. Legal Center of Southern	CA	67
Baptist Assoc. of New Orleans	LA	430
Bethany Christian Services. Refugee Foster Ca	MI	501
Border Assoc. for Refugees from Central Amer.	TX	842
Brooklyn Legal Services Corp.	NY	610
Cambodian Mutual Assistance Assoc.	OH	720
Cambridge and Somerville Legal Services Imm	MA	467
Casa de la Esperanza	DC	229
Casa de Proyecto Libertad	TX	855
Casa El Salvador	IL	352
Casa Juan Diego	TX	857
Casa Marianella	TX	820
Catholic Agency for Migration and Refugee Se	KS	411
Catholic Charities	FL	313
Catholic Charities Migration Office	NY	604
Catholic Charities Refugee & Immigration Ser	MA	458
Catholic Charities. Immigration & Refugee Di	CA	68
Catholic Charities. Immigration & Refugee Ser	PA	765
Catholic Charities. Immigration Counseling C	CA	161
Catholic Charities. Immigration Counseling S	TX	831
Catholic Charities. Immigration Program	CA	134
Catholic Charities. Immigration Project	CA	94
Catholic Charities. Immigration Project of Im	FL	286
Catholic Charities. Immigration Services	CA	106
Catholic Charities. Migration and Refugee Ser	TX	849
Catholic Charities. Refugee Resettlement Offic	CA	182
Catholic Charities. Refugee Resettlement Offic	FL	289
Catholic Charities. Refugee Resettlement Prog	CA	35
Catholic Charities. Resettlement Services	TX	858
Catholic Community Services of Utah. Refuge	UT	882
Catholic Community Services. Migration & R	LA	424
Catholic Community Services. Office of Migra	NJ	586
Catholic Community Services. Resettlement &	CA	125
Catholic Council for Social Concern	IA	407
Catholic Family and Child Services. Family R	WA	910
Catholic Family Service. Immigration Service	TX	872
Catholic Human Development Office. Refugee	MI	502
Catholic Immigration & Resettlement Office	CA	177
Catholic Immigration and Refugee Services	CO	199
Catholic Immigration Services	FL	296
Catholic Migration & Refugee Services	OR	748
Catholic Migration & Refugee Services	VA	893
Catholic Migration and Refugee Office	NY	612
Catholic Migration and Refugee Service	OK	746
Catholic Migration and Refugee Services	NJ	573
Catholic Migration Office	NY	605
Catholic Resettlement and Immigration Office	IA	406
Catholic Services for Immigrants	TX	874
Catholic Social Ministries. Migration & Reset	OK	739
Catholic Social Service	IL	385
Catholic Social Service. Refugee Resettlement	FL	309
Catholic Social Service. Resettlement Program	CO	207
Catholic Social Service. Resettlement Program	OH	714
Catholic Social Service. Tha Huong Program	IL	386
Catholic Social Services	FL	316
Catholic Social Services	MS	540
Catholic Social Services	PA	786
Catholic Social Services	TX	829
Catholic Social Services. Immigration Service	CA	29
Catholic Social Services. Migration & Refugee	PA	773
Catholic Social Services. Refugee and Immigra	FL	311
Catholic Social Services. Refugee Social Servi	FL	312
Catholic Social Services. Servicios Para Inmig	TX	871
Center for Central Amer. Refugees	NJ	587
Center for Immigrants Rights	NY	642
Center for Migration Studies	NY	689
Central Amer. Legal Assistance	NY	613
Central Amer. Refugee Center	CA	69
Central Amer. Refugee Center	DC	233
Central Amer. Refugee Center	NY	627
Central Amer. Refugee Center	TX	859
Central Amer. Refugee Program	WA	918
Central Amer. Refugee Project	AZ	10
Central Amer. Refugee Project	CO	200
Central Amer. Refugee Project	OK	740
Centro Campesino. Projecto de Inmigracion	WA	912
Centro de Ayuda Para Immigrantes	TX	860
Centro Legal	MN	531
Chicago Commission on Human Relations. Re	IL	354
Chinese Amer. Service League	IL	357
Christ Church of the Brethren. Sanctuary Com	OH	734
Christian Community Services	CO	197
Christian Council of Metropolitan Atlanta. Re	GA	324

Christian Refugee Outreach	VA	894	Human Rights Advocates Intl.	NY	652
Church Refugee Center	NY	643	Human Services Assoc.	CA	31
Church World Service. Immigration & Refugee	NY	644	Illinois Conference of Churches. Refugee Imm	IL	390
Church World Service. Refugee Program	FL	298	Illinois Conference of Churches. Refugee Rese	IL	358
Coalition for Haitian Concerns	PA	791	Immigrant Assistance Line	CA	139
Coalition for Immigrant and Refugee Rights &	CA	136	Immigrant Legal Resource Center	CA	41
Columbia Univ. School of Law. Immigration L	NY	645	Immigrant Legal Resource Center	CA	140
Comite de Refugiados Salvadorenos	CA	40	Immigrant Students Project of the Natl. Coalit	MA	461
Comite en Defensa de los Immigrantes	CA	110	Immigrants' Rights Office	CA	74
Comm. to Defend Immigrant & Refugee Rights	CA	95	Immigration Advocacy Service	NE	561
Community Law Center	CA	167	Immigration and Legalization Service	TX	824
Community Legal Services	CA	36	Immigration Assistance Service	NJ	583
Community Legal Services	CA	92	Immigration Counseling Center	TX	862
Community Legal Services	PA	774	Immigration Counseling Migration & Refugee	TX	851
Corn-Maya	FL	287	Immigration Institute	TX	863
Cornerstone Ministries	FL	317	Immigration Law Project	TX	875
Detroit Windsor Refugee Coalition	MI	492	Immigration Project	CA	75
Diocesan Migrant & Refugee Services	TX	845	Immigration Project	CA	194
Diocese of Lafayette. Migration & Refugee Ser	LA	428	Immigration Service of Santa Rosa	CA	189
Diocese of Nashville. Refugee Resettlement Pr	TN	812	Immigration Services of Santa Rosa	CA	131
Diocese of Springfield. Refugee Resettlement	MA	482	Impact	CA	126
Downtown Legalization Project	CA	72	Indiana Council of Churches	IN	401
East Bay Sanctuary Covenant	CA	33	Indochina Resource Action Center	DC	241
East Side Group	TX	822	Inland Counties Legal Services	CA	111
Ecumenical Immigration Services	LA	431	Inmigracion Latina Foundation	FL	302
Ecumenical Refugee Services	CO	202	Intercultural Action Center	CA	178
El Centro Asylum Project	CA	42	Interfaith Refugee Assistance Project	OK	744
El Concilio. Immigration Project	CA	45	Intl. Center	NH	569
El Paso Legal Assistance Society	TX	846	Intl. Community Services	TX	865
El Rescate	CA	73	Intl. Immigrants Foundation	NY	654
EPIC Immigration Project	WA	911	Intl. Institute of Buffalo	NY	623
Episcopal Migration Ministries	NY	648	Intl. Institute of Connecticut	CT	209
Eritrean Relief Comm.	NY	649	Intl. Institute of Connecticut	CT	213
Evangelical Crusade of Fishers of Men	NY	614	Intl. Institute of Flint	MI	499
Father Moriarty Asylum Program	CA	137	Intl. Institute of Los Angeles. Immigrant & Re	CA	76
Fed. of Italian-Amer. Societies	NY	606	Intl. Institute of Lowell	MA	479
First Lutheran Church	FL	283	Intl. Institute of Metro Detroit	MI	495
Florida Dept. of Health and Rehabilitation Ser	FL	315	Intl. Institute of Metropolitan St. Louis	MO	550
Florida Rural Legal Services	FL	281	Intl. Institute of Minnesota	MN	534
Friendly House	AZ	11	Intl. Institute of New Jersey	NJ	584
George Washington Univ. Natl. Law Center. I	DC	239	Intl. Institute of Rhose Island	RI	796
Good Samaritan Community Center	CA	138	Intl. Institute of San Francisco	CA	141
Greater Boston Legal Services	MA	460	Intl. Institute of the East Bay	CA	98
Haitian Amer. Assoc.	MA	472	Intl. Institute of Toledo	OH	732
Haitian Amer. Community Assoc.	FL	300	Intl. Ladies Garment Workers Union. Immigrat	CA	77
Haitian Centers Council	NY	615	Intl. Ladies Garment Workers Union. Immigrat	NY	655
Haitian Multi-Service Center	MA	474	Intl. Ladies Garment Workers Union. Immigrat	IL	359
Haitian Refugee Center	FL	301	Intl. Refugee Center	IL	360
Hawaii Dept. of Labor & Industrial Relations.	HI	341	Intl. Rescue Comm.	CA	142
Heart of Texas Legal Services	TX	881	Intl. Rescue Comm.	CA	162
Hebrew Immigrant Aid Society	PA	776	Intl. Rescue Comm.	CA	168
Hebrew Immigrant Aid Society of Baltimore	MD	443	Intl. Rescue Comm.	GA	335
Hispanic Immigration Counseling Program	WA	920	Intl. Rescue Comm.	NJ	595
Hmong Amer. Human Rights Comm.	CA	47	Intl. Rescue Comm.	WA	921
Hmong Council	CA	48	Intl. Service Center	PA	766
Holy Cross Mission	CA	184	Jewish Family and Child Service	OR	754
Holy Cross Service Center	FL	288	Jewish Family and Children's Service	MA	466
Human Rights Advocates Intl.	NJ	579	Jewish Family and Children's Services	IN	403

Jewish Family Service	CT	215
Jewish Family Service	FL	314
Jewish Family Service	PA	785
Jewish Family Service	TN	813
Jewish Family Service of Delaware Valley	NJ	591
Jewish Family Service of Metro West	NJ	589
Jewish Family Service of Somerset County	NJ	588
Jewish Family Service. Immigration & Resettl	NM	599
Jewish Family Service. Resettlement Program	CA	128
Jewish Family Services	FL	318
Jewish Family Services	GA	328
Jewish Family Services. Refugee Services	IL	362
Jewish Fed. of Palm Beach County	FL	320
Joint Legal Task Force on Central Amer. Refug	WA	923
Jubilee Partners	GA	334
Kalamazoo Interfaith Sanctuary Project	MI	506
Kalihi-Palama Immigrant Service Center	HI	344
King County Rape Relief. Southeast Asian Ch	WA	915
Korean Amer. Community Services	IL	363
Korean Amer. Community Services	MD	454
Lao Consultant Firm	VA	892
Lao Family Community	CA	88
Lao Family Community	CA	100
Lao Family Community	UT	887
Lawyers Comm. for Human Rights. Political A	NY	659
Legal Aid Bureau	MD	453
Legal Aid of Western Missouri	MO	547
Legal Aid of Western Oklahoma	OK	745
Legal Aid Society	FL	321
Legal Aid Society. Alien Rights Unit	CA	129
Legal Services Center	MA	477
Legal Services Center for Immigrants	IL	364
Legal Services of Northern California	CA	120
Los Angeles County Bar Assoc. Immigration L	CA	80
Loyola Univ. School of Law Clinic	LA	433
Lutheran Family Service. Refugee Services	OR	755
Lutheran Family Services. Refugee Resettlemen	NC	700
Lutheran Immigration and Refugee Service	NY	660
Lutheran Ministries of Florida	FL	307
Lutheran Ministries of Florida. Refugee Resett	FL	319
Lutheran Refugee and Immigration Services	NJ	592
Lutheran Refugee Resettlement	CO	204
Lutheran Social Services	MN	516
Lutheran Social Services of Iowa	IA	409
Lutheran Social Services of Kansas and Oklaho	KS	417
Lutheran Social Services of Michigan. Dept. o	MI	510
Lutheran Social Services. Immigration & Refug	CA	81
Mennonite Immigration and Refugee Services	DC	246
Mennonite Intl. Refugee Assistance	TX	835
Metropolitan Social Services. Refugee Program	TN	814
Middlesex County Legal Services Corp.	NJ	585
Midwest Coalition in Defense of Immigrants	IL	366
Midwest Immigrant Rights Center	IL	367
Migration and Refugee Services Office	NJ	593
Mission Community Legal Defense	CA	147
Monterey County Sanctuary	CA	103
Multicultural Immigration Center	NY	661
Na Loio No Na Kanaka. Lawyers for the Peopl	HI	345
Natl. Assoc. of Evangelicals. Immigration Pro	FL	304
Natl. Center For Immigrants' Rights	CA	82
Natl. Coalition for Haitian Refugees	NY	662
Natl. Council of Jewish Women. Rescue & Mi	FL	305
Natl. Immigration Project of the Natl. Lawyers	MA	464
Natl. Lawyers Guild. Central Amer. Refugee De	PA	779
Nationalities Service Center	PA	769
Nationalities Service Center	PA	780
Neil Avenue Mennonite Church. Sanctuary Co	OH	723
New Orleans Legal Assistance Corp.	LA	435
New York Circus	NY	664
New York State Assembly. Task Force on New	NY	666
North Carolina Baptist State Conv.	NC	695
North Manhattan Coalition for Immigrants' Ri	NY	667
North Texas Immigration Coalition	TX	836
O.L.A. Immigration Rights Center	CA	193
O.L.A. Raza	CA	109
One Stop Immigration & Educational Center	CA	83
Organization of Chinese Amer.	DC	248
People's Immigration Service	CA	195
People's Law Office for Organized Workers	FL	280
Philippine Center for Immigrant Rights	NY	669
Pillsbury United Neighborhood Services. Asian	MN	523
Polish Amer. Immigration and Relief Comm.	NY	670
Polish Amer. Immigration Relief Comm.	IL	370
Presbytery of Southern Louisiana	LA	426
Project Deliverance	OH	733
Proyecto Adelante	TX	837
Proyecto Resistencia	IL	371
Rav Tov. Intl. Jewish Rescue Organization	NY	618
Refugee and Immigrant Multi-Service Center	WA	930
Refugee Assistance Program	CA	130
Refugee Resettlement Comm.	CA	90
Rio Grande Defense Comm.	TX	879
San Francisco Lawyers' Comm. Immigrant & R	CA	150
San Francisco Lawyers' Comm. Political Asylu	CA	151
San Juan Macias Immigrant Center	CA	104
Seattle - King County Bar Assoc. Legalization	WA	924
South Texas Immigration Council	TX	828
South Texas Immigration Council	TX	856
South Texas Immigration Council	TX	873
South-East Asia Center	IL	373
Southern Arizona Legal Aid	AZ	19
Southern Baptist Immigration and Refugee Res	GA	331
Southern Methodist Univ. Law School. Politic	TX	838
Southern Minnesota Regional Legal Services	MN	517
Southside Community Mission	NY	620
Spokane Bar Assoc. Pro Bono Program	WA	931
Sponsors Organized to Assist Refugees	ID	348
St. Paul's United Methodist Church. Refugee P	NV	567
Synapses. Asian Organizing Program	IL	374
Texas Rural Legal Aid	TX	843
Texas Rural Legal Aid. Clinica de Inmigracion	TX	841
Tolstoy Foundation	MI	498
Tolstoy Foundation	NY	673
Traveler and Immigrants Aid	IL	375
Travelers Aid Intl. Institute. Refugee Resource	OH	716
Travelers Aid Society	DC	255

Tucson Ecumenical Council. Central Amer. Tas	AZ	22
Tucson Ecumenical Council. Legal Assistance	AZ	23
U. S. Catholic Conference. Migration & Refug	NY	675
U.S. Catholic Conference. Migration & Refuge	CA	154
U.S. Catholic Conference. Migration & Refuge	DC	257
U.S. Catholic Conference. Migration & Refuge	NY	676
U.S. Catholic Conference. Migration & Refuge	TX	848
U.S. Dept. of Justice. Executive Office for Imm	VA	899
United Nations High Commissioner for Refuge	DC	274
United Nations. Relief and Works Agency for	NY	681
United Refugee Council	NY	621
Univ. of California. School of Law. Immigrati	CA	39
Utah Immigration Project	UT	886
Valley Immigrants Rights Center	CA	105
Valley Religious Task Force on Central Amer.	AZ	15
Vietnamese Amer. Assoc. Refugee Center	OK	743
Vietnamese Amer. Civic Assoc.	MA	475
Vietnamese Community in Virginia	VA	905
Vietnamese Mutual Assistance Assoc.	TX	840
Virginia Council of Churches. Refugee Progra	VA	907
Washington Assoc. of Churches. Immigration	WA	928
Washington Assoc. of Churches. Refugee Rese	WA	932
Washington Lawyers' Comm. for Civil Rights	DC	276
Westside Legal Services	CA	176
Woodrow Wilson Intl. Center	DC	278
World Relief	TX	853
World Relief. Immigration Services	IL	379
YMCA Intl. Services	TX	870

LIBRARY & INFORMATION

Agudath Israel of Amer.	NY	631
Amer. Arab Anti-Discrimination Comm.	DC	223
Amer. Friends Service Comm. Haitian Women'	NY	636
Amer. Friends Service Comm. Immigration Pro	CA	108
Amer. Immigrant Foundation	CA	164
Amnesty Intl.	CA	66
Amnesty Intl. USA	CA	132
Asia Pacific Concerns Comm.	CA	181
Assyrian Universal Alliance	MI	512
Balch Institute for Ethnic Studies	PA	772
Capuchin Mission Secretariat	MI	491
Catholic Charities. Immigration & Refugee Di	CA	68
Catholic Charities. Immigration Counseling C	CA	161
Catholic Charities. Immigration Program	CA	134
Catholic Charities. Refugee Assistance	IN	396
Catholic Charities. Refugee Assistance Progra	NY	622
Catholic Charities. Refugee Office	IN	394
Catholic Community Services. Migration & R	LA	424
Catholic Human Development Office. Refugee	MI	502
Catholic Resettlement Center	IL	353
Catholic Services for Immigrants	TX	874
Catholic Social Services	WY	957
Catholic Social Services. Refugee Program	AL	3
Catholic Social Services. Refugee Resettlemen	NM	598
Catholic Social Services. Servicios Para Inmig	TX	871
Center for Applied Linguistics. Refugee Servic	DC	231
Center for Immigrants Rights	NY	642
Center for Immigration Studies	DC	232
Center for Migration Studies	NY	689
Central Amer. Resource Center	TX	821
Central Amer. Refugee Center	DC	233
Central Amer. Resource Center	MN	530
Central Baptist Church. Sanctuary Group	PA	789
Centro Legal	MN	531
Centro Presente	MA	469
Chicago Commission on Human Relations. Re	IL	354
Chicago Comm. on Immigrant Protection	IL	355
Christian Council of Metropolitan Atlanta. Re	GA	324
Christian Reformed World Relief Comm.	MI	503
Coalition for Haitian Concerns	PA	791
Coalition for Immigrant and Refugee Rights &	CA	136
Coastal Bend Friends Meeting	TX	830
Columbia Univ. School of Law. Immigration L	NY	645
Council of Churches. Refugee Resettlement Pro	MO	552
Cultural Survival	MA	471
Datacenter	CA	96
Delaware Dept. of Justice. Service for Foreign	DE	221
Diocesan Migrant & Refugee Services	TX	845
Diocese of Green Bay. Dept. of Refugee, Migr	WI	939
Diocese of Richmond. Office of Refugee Reset	VA	901
Disciples of Christ. Refugee & Immigration M	IN	399
East Bay Sanctuary Covenant	CA	33
Eau Claire Area Hmong Mutual Assistance Ass	WI	938
El Rescate	CA	73
Ellis Island Immigration Museum	NY	647
Episcopal Refugee and Migration Comm.	NH	570
Episcopal Refugee Resettlement Commission	IN	400
Ethiopian Community Development Council	VA	895
Father Moriarty Asylum Program	CA	137
Fed. for Amer. Immigration Reform	DC	237
Foreign-Born Information and Referral Networ	MD	448
Friends of the Third World	IN	395
George Mason Univ. Indochina Institute.	VA	897
Good Samaritan Community Center	CA	138
Guatemala Human Rights Commission/USA	DC	240
Haitian Multi-Service Center	MA	474
Hebrew Immigrant Aid Society	NY	651
Hmong Catholic Center	MN	532
Holt Intl. Children's Services	OR	749
Human Rights Internet	MA	473
Immigrant Legal Resource Center	CA	41
Immigrant Legal Resource Center	CA	140
Immigrants' Rights Office	CA	74
Immigration Law Enforcement Monitoring Pro	TX	864
Indochina Resource Action Center	DC	241
Intl. Center	NH	569
Intl. Institute of Connecticut	CT	213
Intl. Institute of Flint	MI	499
Intl. Institute of New Jersey	NJ	584
Intl. Institute of Northwest Indiana	IN	397
Intl. Institute of Rhose Island	RI	796
Intl. Institute of Toledo	OH	732
Intl. Rescue Comm.	CA	118
Intl. Rescue Comm.	CA	168
Intl. Rescue Comm.	CA	185
Iowa Dept. of Human Services. Bureau of Refug	IA	408
Japanese Newcomer Service	CA	143
Jewish Family & Children Services	CA	144
Jewish Family and Children's Services	IN	403
Jewish Family Service	LA	436
Jewish Family Service	RI	797
Jewish Family Service	TN	813
Jewish Family Service of Metro West	NJ	589
Jewish Family Service. Resettlement Program	MD	444
Jewish Voc. Service	NJ	577
Jubilee Partners	GA	334
Khmer Buddhist Society of New England	RI	798
Khmer Health Advocates	CT	217
Lao Consultant Firm	VA	892
Lao Family Community	UT	887
Legal Aid Bureau	MD	453
Loyola Univ. School of Law Clinic	LA	433
Lutheran Children and Family Service	PA	778
Lutheran Family Services. Refugee Resettlemen	NC	700
Lutheran Immigration and Refugee Service	NY	660
Lutheran Social Services of North Dakota. Ref	ND	709
Michigan Dept. of Social Services. Office of R	MI	496
Migration & Refugee Services	SC	802

Mission Community Legal Defense   CA   147
Mutual Aid Assoc. of the New Polish Immigrat   IL   368
Natl. Immigration, Refugee, and Citizenship F   DC   247
Natl. Network for Immigrant & Refugee Rights   CA   101
Nationalities Service of Central California   CA   50
New York City. Office of Immigrant Affairs   NY   665
New York State Assembly. Task Force on New   NY   666
Ohio Council of Churches. Refugee Services   OH   724
Philippine Center for Immigrant Rights   NY   669
Presbyterian Synod of Southern California and   CA   84
Presbytery of Long Island   NY   625
Refugee Policy Group   DC   249
Refugee Resettlement Office   AR   24
Refugees Intl.   DC   252
Research Foundation for Jewish Immigration   NY   671
San Francisco Lawyers' Comm. Political Asylu   CA   151
Sarrlano Chirino Amaya Central Amer. Refuge   CA   85
Somerville Portuguese Amer. League   MA   481
South and Meso-Amer. Indian Information Cen   CA   34
South-East Asia Center   IL   373
Southeast Asian Center   RI   792
Southern Arizona Legal Aid   AZ   19
Southern Baptist Immigration and Refugee Res   GA   331
Synapses. Asian Organizing Program   IL   374
Syracuse Interreligious Council. Refugee Assis   NY   692
Tacoma Community House   WA   934
TECHO Central Amer. Education Center   AZ   20
Texas Rural Legal Aid. Clinica de Inmigracion   TX   841
Tolstoy Foundation   AZ   14
Tolstoy Foundation   MI   498
Tucson Ecumenical Council. Legal Assistance   AZ   23
U. S. Catholic Conference. Migration & Refug   NY   675
Ukrainian Research Foundation   CO   206
Unitarian Church of Arlington   VA   896
United Methodist Church. Refugee Concerns C   CA   156
United Nations. Relief and Works Agency for   NY   681
Univ. of Florida. Caribbean Migration Progra   FL   284
Univ. of Minnesota. Immigration History Res   MN   539
Univ. of Minnesota. Southeast Asian Refugee   MN   524
Univ. of Wisconsin. Center for Demography a   WI   945
Valley Religious Task Force on Central Amer.   AZ   15
Vietnam Refugee Fund   VA   900
Vietnamese Amer. Cultural Alliance of Colorad   CO   198
Vietnamese Catholic Community   MI   489
Vietnamese Mutual Assistance Assoc. of North   ND   710
Washington Assoc. of Churches. Refugee Rese   WA   932
Washington Office on Haiti   DC   277
YMCA Intl. Services   TX   870

RELIGION

Adventist Community Services	DC	222
Afghan Center	CA	190
Alabama Baptist State Conv.	AL	4
All Culture Friendship Center Refugee & Immi	CA	55
All Culture Friendship Center Refugee & Immi	CA	65
Amer. Baptist Churches. Immigration & Refug	PA	788
Amer. Comm. on Italian Migration	NY	632
Amer. Friends Service Comm. Florida Undocum	FL	293
Archdiocese of Chicago. Immigration Services	IL	351
Archdiocese of New York. Office for Immigran	NY	638
Archdiocese of New York. Refugee Resettlemen	NY	639
Asian Counseling and Referral Service	WA	916
Baptist Assoc. of New Orleans	LA	430
Baptist Conv. of Maryland	MD	447
Baptist Conv. of New Mexico	NM	597
Baptist State Conv.	MI	513
Bergen County Sanctuary Comm.	NJ	590
Bethany Christian Services. Refugee Foster Ca	MI	501
Border Assoc. for Refugees from Central Amer	TX	842
California Southern Baptist Conv. Refugee Re	CA	43
Catholic Charities	NE	558
Catholic Charities Migration Office	NY	604
Catholic Charities. Immigration Counseling C	CA	161
Catholic Charities. Immigration Program	CA	134
Catholic Charities. Migration and Refugee Ser	CT	211
Catholic Charities. Migration and Refugee Ser	TX	849
Catholic Charities. Refugee Assistance	IN	396
Catholic Charities. Refugee Assistance Progra	NY	622
Catholic Charities. Refugee Office	IN	394
Catholic Charities. Refugee Program	KS	416
Catholic Charities. Refugee Resettlement Offic	CA	182
Catholic Charities. Refugee Resettlement Offic	FL	289
Catholic Charities. Refugee Resettlement Prog	CA	35
Catholic Charities. Refugee Resettlement Prog	DE	220
Catholic Charities. Refugee Service Center	DC	230
Catholic Charities. Refugee Services	KY	423
Catholic Charities. Refugee Social Service Cen	MS	541
Catholic Charities. Resettlement Program	CA	44
Catholic Charities. Resettlement Services	CA	166
Catholic Charities. Resettlement Services	TX	858
Catholic Community Services of Utah. Refuge	UT	882
Catholic Community Services. Refugee Resettl	FL	295
Catholic Community Services. Resettlement &	CA	125
Catholic Family and Child Service	WA	935
Catholic Family Service. Immigration Service	TX	872
Catholic Immigration Center	HI	339
Catholic Immigration Services	FL	296
Catholic Migration & Refugee Services	OR	748
Catholic Migration & Refugee Services	VA	893
Catholic Migration and Refugee Office	NY	612
Catholic Migration and Refugee Resettlement	OH	721
Catholic Migration and Refugee Service	NV	566
Catholic Migration and Refugee Service	OK	746
Catholic Migration and Refugee Services	NJ	573
Catholic Migration Office	NY	605
Catholic Resettlement and Immigration Office	IA	406
Catholic Resettlement Center	IL	353
Catholic Services for Immigrants	TX	874
Catholic Social Agency. Migration Services	PA	761
Catholic Social Service. Resettlement Program	OH	714
Catholic Social Services	AK	6
Catholic Social Services	KS	413
Catholic Social Services	LA	427
Catholic Social Services	MS	540
Catholic Social Services	OH	729
Catholic Social Services	OH	731
Catholic Social Services	WY	957
Catholic Social Services Bureau	KY	418
Catholic Social Services. Migration & Refugee	PA	773
Catholic Social Services. Refugee Resetlement	NE	559
Catholic Social Services. Refugee Resettlemen	NM	598
Catholic Social Services. Resettlement Progra	CA	87
Catholic Social Services. Servicios Para Inmig	TX	871
Central Amer. Refugee Center	DC	233
Central Amer. Solidarity and Assistance	MD	455
Central Baptist Church. Sanctuary Group	PA	789
Central Kentucky Jewish Assoc.	KY	421
Centro Presente	MA	469
Chicago Religious Task Force on Central Ame	IL	356
Christ Church of the Brethren. Sanctuary Com	OH	734
Christian Community Service Agency	FL	297
Christian Council of Metropolitan Atlanta. Re	GA	324
Christian Reformed World Relief Comm.	MI	503
Christian Refugee Outreach	VA	894
Church Refugee Center	NY	643
Church World Service. Immigration & Refugee	NY	644
Coalition for Haitian Concerns	PA	791
Conscientious Alliance for Peace	AL	1
Cornerstone Ministries	FL	317
Council of Churches. Refugee Resettlement Pro	MO	552
Diocesan Refugee Resettlement Program	ME	439
Diocese of Green Bay. Dept. of Refugee, Migr	WI	939
Diocese of Oregon	OR	751
Diocese of Raleigh. Refugee Resettlement Offi	NC	704
Disciples of Christ. Refugee & Immigration M	IN	399
Ecumenical Refugee Services	CO	202
El Centro Asylum Project	CA	42
Episcopal Diocese of Minnesota. Refugee Rese	MN	520
Episcopal Migration Ministries	NY	648
Episcopal Refugee and Migration Comm.	NH	570
Episcopal Refugee Resettlement Commission	IN	400
Episcopal Social Ministries	MD	442
Eritrean Relief Comm.	NY	649
Evangelical Crusade of Fishers of Men	NY	614
Faith Lutheran Church	FL	308
Father Moriarty Asylum Program	CA	137
First Lutheran Church	FL	283
First Unitarian Church	CA	183

Florida Council of Churches. Refugee Program	FL	310
Georgia Baptist Conv. Language Missions Dep	GA	325
Greater Hartford Jewish Fed.	CT	216
Haitian Amer. Assoc.	MA	472
Haitian Amer. Community Assoc.	FL	300
Haitian Centers Council	NY	615
Hebrew Immigrant Aid Society	NY	651
Hebrew Immigrant Aid Society	PA	776
Hispanic Immigration Counseling Program	WA	920
Hmong Catholic Center	MN	532
Holt Intl. Children's Services	OR	749
Holy Cross Mission	CA	184
Houston Metropolitan Ministries	TX	861
Humboldt Unitarian-Universalist Fellowship	CA	30
Illinois Conference of Churches. Refugee Imm	IL	390
Illinois Conference of Churches. Refugee Rese	IL	358
Immigration and Legalization Service	TX	824
Immigration Counseling Migration & Refugee	TX	851
Indiana Council of Churches	IN	401
Intl. Buddhist Meditation Assoc.	HI	343
Intl. Institute of Northwest Indiana	IN	397
Jesuit Refugee Service	DC	244
Jewish Family & Children Services	CA	144
Jewish Family & Children's Service	AZ	12
Jewish Family and Child Service	OR	754
Jewish Family and Children's Agency	PA	777
Jewish Family and Children's Service	NJ	571
Jewish Family and Children's Services	IN	403
Jewish Family and Voc. Service	KY	422
Jewish Family Service	AZ	17
Jewish Family Service	CA	51
Jewish Family Service	CA	99
Jewish Family Service	CT	215
Jewish Family Service	FL	314
Jewish Family Service	LA	436
Jewish Family Service	PA	785
Jewish Family Service	TX	876
Jewish Family Service	VA	904
Jewish Family Service	WA	922
Jewish Family Service Agency	NV	565
Jewish Family Service Assoc.	OH	719
Jewish Family Service of Broward County	FL	285
Jewish Family Service of Delaware Valley	NJ	591
Jewish Family Service of Detroit	MI	514
Jewish Family Service of North Middlesex Cou	NJ	578
Jewish Family Service of Somerset County	NJ	588
Jewish Family Service. Refugee Services	CA	79
Jewish Family Service. Resettlement Program	CA	128
Jewish Family Service. Resettlement Program	FL	306
Jewish Family Service. Resettlement Program	MD	444
Jewish Family Services	FL	318
Jewish Family Services	GA	328
Jewish Family Services	TX	834
Jewish Family Services of Greater Orlando	FL	322
Jewish Social Services	TX	852
Jewish Social Services	WI	943
Jewish Voc. Service	NJ	577
Khemara Buddhikarma - The Cambodian Buddh	CA	59
Khmer Buddhist Society of New England	RI	798
Lao Consultant Firm	VA	892
Lao Family Community	UT	887
Lutheran Child & Family Services of Massachu	MA	485
Lutheran Child and Family Services	IL	365
Lutheran Church. Synod Board of Social Minis	MO	551
Lutheran Family Service. Refugee Services	OR	755
Lutheran Family Services. Refugee Resettlemen	NC	700
Lutheran Immigration & Refugee Services	DC	245
Lutheran Immigration and Refugee Service	NY	660
Lutheran Immigration and Refugee Service	TX	867
Lutheran Ministries of Florida	FL	307
Lutheran Ministries of Florida. Refugee Resett	FL	319
Lutheran Ministries of Georgia	GA	329
Lutheran Refugee and Immigration Services	NJ	592
Lutheran Refugee Resettlement	CO	204
Lutheran Social Ministry of the Southwest. Re	AZ	13
Lutheran Social Services of Iowa	IA	409
Lutheran Social Services of Kansas and Oklaho	KS	417
Lutheran Social Services of Michigan. Dept. o	MI	510
Lutheran Social Services of Michigan. Refugee	MI	507
Lutheran Social Services of Minnesota. Refuge	MN	522
Lutheran Social Services of Montana	MT	555
Lutheran Social Services of North Dakota. Ref	ND	709
Lutheran Social Services of Wisconsin & Uppe	WI	953
Maine Annual Conference of the United Metho	ME	438
Mennonite Central Comm. Immigration & Ref	PA	760
Mid-Cumberland Refugee Assistance Ministry	TN	815
Migration & Refugee Services	SC	802
Minnesota Cambodian Buddhist Society	MN	536
Minnesota Council of Churches. Refugee Prog	MN	537
Mississippi Baptist Conv. Language Missions	MS	542
Natl. Slavic Conv.	MD	446
New York Assoc. for New Amer.	NY	663
North Carolina Baptist State Conv.	NC	695
Ohio Council of Churches. Refugee Services	OH	724
Ohio State Conv. of Baptists	OH	726
One Stop Immigration & Educational Center	CA	83
Peylim	NY	668
Plattsburg Interfaith Council	NY	685
Presbyterian Synod of Southern California and	CA	84
Presbytery of Long Island	NY	625
PRIME Ecumenical Commitment to Refugees	PA	762
Project Deliverance	OH	733
Proyecto Resistencia	IL	371
Reformed Church in Amer. Refugee Program	MI	505
Rio Grande Defense Comm.	TX	879
Rochester Refugee Services	MN	527
Salvadoran Refugee Comm. (Oscar A. Romero)	DC	253
San Juan Macias Immigrant Center	CA	104
Sanctuary Covenant of San Francisco	CA	152
Sepulveda Unitarian Universalist Society	CA	180
Somerville Portuguese Amer. League	MA	481
Southern Baptist Immigration and Refugee Res	GA	331
Southern California Interfaith Task Force on C	CA	86
Sponsors Organized to Assist Refugees	OR	756
St. Anselm's Immigrant & Refugee Community	CA	52
St. Paul's United Methodist Church. Refugee Pr	NV	567

Synapses. Asian Organizing Program	IL	374
Syracuse Interreligious Council. Refugee Assis	NY	692
Tressler Lutheran Services. Refugee Services Pr	PA	770
Tucson Ecumenical Council. Central Amer. Tas	AZ	22
U. S. Catholic Conference. Migration & Refug	NY	675
U.S. Catholic Conference. Migration & Refuge	DC	256
U.S. Catholic Conference. Migration & Refuge	DC	257
U.S. Catholic Conference. Migration & Refuge	NY	676
U.S. Catholic Conference. Migration & Refuge	TX	848
Unitarian Church of Arlington	VA	896
United Methodist Church. Refugee Concerns C	CA	156
United Refugee Council	NY	621
U.S. Catholic Conference	IL	388
Valley Religious Task Force on Central Amer.	AZ	15
Vietnamese Catholic Community	MI	489
Vietnamese Catholic Community in Connectic	CT	214
Vietnamese Community in Virginia	VA	905
Vietnamese Evangelical Church	MN	525
Vietnamese Lutheran Ministry	WA	927
Vietnamese Seventh-Day Adventist Church	OR	757
Virginia Baptist General Board. Div. of Missio	VA	906
Virginia Council of Churches. Refugee Progra	VA	907
Washington Assoc. of Churches. Refugee Rese	WA	932
World Relief	DC	279
World Relief	FL	282
World Relief	GA	333
World Relief	NC	701
World Relief	TN	817
World Relief	TX	853
World Relief. Immigration Services	IL	379
Youth With a Mission Relief Services	HI	346

RESEARCH

Adelphi Univ. Refugee Assistance Program	NY	626	Dallas-Fort Worth Refugee Interagency	TX	832
Afghan Community in Amer.	NY	628	Datacenter	CA	96
Agudath Israel of Amer.	NY	631	Diocese of Richmond. Office of Refugee Resetl	VA	909
Amer. Arab Anti-Discrimination Comm.	DC	223	Downtown Legalization Project	CA	72
Amer. Fed. of Jews from Central Europe	NY	635	El Rescate	CA	73
Amer. Friends Service Comm. Florida Undocu	FL	293	Ellis Island Immigration Museum	NY	647
Amer. Refugee Comm.	IL	381	Episcopal Social Ministries	MD	442
Amer. Romanian Comm. for Assistance to Ref	NY	630	Episcopal Social Service	CT	208
Amer. For Immigration Control	DC	227	Ethiopian Community Development Council	VA	895
Amer. for Intl. Aid	GA	337	Fed. for Amer. Immigration Reform	DC	237
Amnesty Intl.	CA	66	Filipinos for Affirmative Action	CA	97
Amnesty Intl. USA	CA	132	George Mason Univ. Indochina Institute.	VA	897
Asia Pacific Concerns Comm.	CA	181	Greater Boston Legal Services	MA	460
Asian Counseling and Referral Service	WA	916	Greater Hartford Jewish Fed.	CT	216
Assyrian Universal Alliance	MI	512	Guatemala Human Rights Commission/USA	DC	240
Balch Institute for Ethnic Studies	PA	772	Haitian Refugee Center	FL	301
Baron de Hirsch Fund	NY	640	Hawaii Dept. of Labor & Industrial Relations.	HI	341
Boat People SOS	CA	124	Hebrew Immigrant Aid Society	NY	651
Brown Univ. Population Studies & Training Ce	RI	793	Hebrew Immigrant Aid Society	PA	776
Caribbean Action Lobby	NY	611	Human Rights Advocates Intl.	NJ	579
Catholic Charities	MA	486	Human Rights Advocates Intl.	NY	652
Catholic Charities Migration Office	NY	604	Human Rights Internet	MA	473
Catholic Charities. Immigration & Refugee Di	CA	68	Human Services Assoc.	CA	31
Catholic Community Services of Utah. Refugee	UT	882	Immigrant Legal Resource Center	CA	140
Catholic Family Service. Immigration Service	TX	872	Immigrant Students Project of the Natl. Coalit	MA	461
Catholic Migration and Refugee Service	OK	746	Immigration Counseling Migration & Refugee	TX	851
Catholic Migration and Refugee Services	NJ	573	Immigration History Society	MN	533
Catholic Resettlement and Immigration Office	IA	406	Immigration Law Enforcement Monitoring Pro	TX	864
Catholic Resettlement Center	IL	353	Immigration Service of Santa Rosa	CA	189
Catholic Resettlement Services	OR	753	InterAction (Amer. Council for Voluntary Intl.	NY	653
Catholic Services for Immigrants	TX	874	Intl. Institute of Flint	MI	499
Catholic Social Service. Resettlement Program	OH	714	Intl. Institute of Metropolitan St. Louis	MO	550
Catholic Social Services	LA	427	Intl. Rescue Comm.	CA	78
Catholic Social Services	MS	540	Intl. Rescue Comm.	CA	127
Catholic Social Services Bureau	KY	418	Intl. Rescue Comm.	NY	656
Catholic Social Services. Central Amer. Refuge	TX	827	Intl. Rescue Comm.	WA	921
Catholic Social Services. Servicios Para Inmig	TX	871	Japanese Newcomer Service	CA	143
Center for Applied Linguistics. Refugee Servic	DC	231	Jesuit Refugee Service	DC	244
Center for Immigration Studies	DC	232	Jewish Family Service	FL	314
Center for Migration Studies	NY	689	Jewish Family Service	LA	436
Central Amer. Resource Center	TX	821	Jewish Family Service	PA	785
Central Amer. Resource Center	MN	530	Jewish Family Services	TX	834
Central Kentucky Jewish Assoc.	KY	421	Kalihi-Palama Immigrant Service Center	HI	344
Centro de Ayuda Para Immigrantes	TX	860	Khmer Health Advocates	CT	217
Centro Legal	MN	531	Korean Amer. Community Services	IL	363
Centro Presente	MA	469	Lao Consultant Firm	VA	892
Chicago Comm. on Immigrant Protection	IL	355	Lao Family Community	UT	887
Chicago Religious Task Force on Central Ame	IL	356	Legal Services Center	MA	477
Church World Service. Immigration & Refugee	NY	644	Lutheran Children and Family Service	PA	778
Church World Service. Refugee Program	FL	298	Lutheran Immigration and Refugee Service	NY	660
Coalition for Haitian Concerns	PA	791	Lutheran Ministries of Florida	FL	307
College of Staten Island. Center for Immigrant	NY	690	Lutheran Social Services of Wisconsin & Uppe	WI	953
Commission for the Study of Intl. Migration a	DC	234	Mission Community Legal Defense	CA	147
Cultural Survival	MA	471	Moob Fed. of Amer.	IL	392

Natl. Center For Immigrants' Rights   CA   82
Natl. Coalition for Haitian Refugees   NY   662
Natl. Immigration, Refugee, and Citizenship F DC 247
Natl. Network for Immigrant & Refugee Rights CA   101
New York City. Office of Immigrant Affairs   NY   665
New York State Assembly. Task Force on New   NY   666
North Carolina Baptist State Conv.   NC   695
Ohio Council of Churches. Refugee Services   OH   724
One Stop Immigration & Educational Center   CA   83
Orange County Coalition for Immigrant Right CA   171
Orange County Community Consortium   CA   172
Philippine Center for Immigrant Rights   NY   669
Polish Amer. Immigration and Relief Comm.   NY   670
Polish Amer. Immigration Relief Comm.   IL   370
Polish and Slavic Center. Refugee Assistance NY   617
Presbyterian Synod of Southern California and CA   84
Proyecto Adelante   TX   837
Proyecto Resistencia   IL   371
Rav Tov. Intl. Jewish Rescue Organization   NY   618
Refugee Policy Group   DC   249
Refugee Voices   DC   250
Refugee Women in Development   DC   251
Refugees Intl.   DC   252
Research Foundation for Jewish Immigration   NY   671
Rosenberg Foundation   CA   149
Salvadoran Refugee Comm. (Oscar A. Romero)   DC   253
San Antonio Literacy Council   TX   878
San Francisco Lawyers' Comm. Immigrant & R   CA   150
Sarrlano Chirino Amaya Central Amer. Refuge CA   85
Somerville Portuguese Amer. League   MA   481
South and Meso-Amer. Indian Information Cen CA   34
Southern Baptist Immigration and Refugee Res GA   331
Synapses. Asian Organizing Program   IL   374
Texas Rural Legal Aid. Clinica de Inmigracion TX 841
Travelers Aid Intl. Institute. Refugee Resource OH 716
U. S. Catholic Conference. Migration & Refug NY   675
U.S. Catholic Conference. Migration & Refuge DC   256
Ukrainian Research Foundation   CO   206
United Nations High Commissioner for Refuge DC   274
United Nations. Relief and Works Agency for NY   681
United Refugee Council   NY   621
U.S. Comm. for Refugees   DC   275
Univ. of Florida. Caribbean Migration Progra FL   284
Univ. of Minnesota. Immigration History Res MN   539
Univ. of Minnesota. Southeast Asian Refugee MN   524
Univ. of Wisconsin. Center for Demography a WI   945
Vietnamese Amer. Civic Assoc.   MA   475
Vietnamese Amer. Cultural Alliance of Colorad CO 198
Vietnamese Catholic Community   MI   489
World Relief   GA   333
World Relief   NY   683

SANCTUARY

Amer. Baptist Churches. Immigration & Refug	PA	788
Bergen County Sanctuary Comm.	NJ	590
Capuchin Mission Secretariat	MI	491
CASA	PA	771
Casa Juan Diego	TX	857
Catholic Charities. Immigration Program	CA	134
Catholic Resettlement and Immigration Office	IA	406
Central Amer. Refugee Project	OK	740
Central Baptist Church. Sanctuary Group	PA	789
Central Coast Sanctuary	CA	175
Chicago Religious Task Force on Central Ame	IL	356
Christ Church of the Brethren. Sanctuary Com	OH	734
Church of the Brethren. Refugee Resettlement	MD	450
City of Berkeley. Public Sanctuary	CA	32
City of Burlington. Office of the Mayor	VT	889
City of Cambridge. Office of the Mayor	MA	470
City of Davis. Office of the Mayor	CA	37
City of East Lansing. Office of the Mayor	MI	497
City of Minneapolis. Office of the Mayor	MN	519
City of Olympia. Office of the Mayor	WA	913
City of Sacramento. Office of the Mayor	CA	116
City of Santa Fe. Office of the Mayor	NM	600
City of Tacoma Park. Office of the Mayor	MD	456
City of West Hollywood. City Council	CA	196
Coalition for Haitian Concerns	PA	791
Coalition for Public Sanctuary	OH	735
Coastal Bend Friends Meeting	TX	830
College Hill Presbyterian Church. Sanctuary C	OK	747
Community Friends Meeting. Sanctuary Comm	OH	715
Concord Friends Meeting Sanctuary	PA	790
Congregation Hakafa. Sanctuary Comm.	IL	384
Corpus Christi Church. Sanctuary Comm.	NY	687
Council of Churches. Refugee Resettlement Pro	MO	552
Cross Lutheran Church	WI	947
Detroit Windsor Refugee Coalition	MI	492
Disciples of Christ. Refugee & Immigration M	IN	399
East Bay Sanctuary Covenant	CA	33
Emmanuel Lutheran Church. Sanctuary Comm.	MO	549
Faith United Methodist Church. Sanctuary Com	IA	405
First Unitarian Church	CA	183
First Unitarian Church. Sanctuary Comm.	MI	488
Friends Meeting of Austin. Sanctuary Comm.	TX	823
Humboldt Congregations for Sanctuary	CA	28
Humboldt Unitarian-Universalist Fellowship	CA	30
Immigrant Legal Resource Center	CA	41
Interfaith Refugee Assistance Project	OK	744
Interfaith Sanctuary Movement	PA	784
Kalamazoo Interfaith Sanctuary Project	MI	506
Lao Consultant Firm	VA	892
Lao Family Community	UT	887
Legal Aid of Western Missouri	MO	547
Manchester Church of the Brethren. Sanctuary	IN	404
Mennonite Central Comm. Immigration & Ref	PA	760
Mennonite Immigration and Refugee Services	DC	246
Monterey County Sanctuary	CA	103
Natl. Slavic Conv.	MD	446
Neil Avenue Mennonite Church. Sanctuary Co	OH	723
Northside Sanctuary Coalition	IL	369
Palo Alto Friends Meeting	CA	107
Pioneer Valley Sanctuary Comm., Mt. Toby M	MA	457
Posada Sanctuary	IL	387
Project Deliverance	OH	733
Riverside Church. Sanctuary Comm.	NY	672
Salvadoran Refugee Comm. (Oscar A. Romero)	DC	253
San Juan Bautista Lutheran Church. Sanctuary	AZ	18
Sanctuary Covenant of San Francisco	CA	152
Sepulveda Unitarian Universalist Society	CA	180
Sinai Temple. Sanctuary Comm.	MA	484
South and Meso-Amer. Indian Information Cen	CA	34
Southern California Interfaith Task Force on C	CA	86
Sponsors Organized to Assist Refugees	ID	348
St. Teresa's Church. Sanctuary Comm.	CA	153
Temple Beth El. Sanctuary Comm.	WI	944
Temple Emanu-El. Sanctuary Comm.	AZ	21
Temple Israel. Sanctuary Comm.	CA	60
Temple Sinai. Sanctuary Comm.	CA	102
Temple Sinai. Sanctuary Comm.	DC	254
Tennessee Valley Unitarian Church. Sanctuary	TN	808
Tucson Ecumenical Council. Central Amer. Tas	AZ	22
Unitarian Church of Arlington	VA	896
Unitarian Church. Sanctuary Comm.	CT	218
Unitarian Society of Sacramento. Sanctuary Co	CA	122
Unitarian Universalist Church	CA	61
Univ. Church. Sanctuary Project	IL	377
Univ. Unitarian Church. Sanctuary Comm.	WA	926
Valley Religious Task Force on Central Amer.	AZ	15
Vietnamese Evangelical Church	MN	525
Vietnamese Seventh-Day Adventist Church	OR	757
Wheadon United Methodist Church. Sanctuary	IL	383

SCHOLARSHIPS

Baron de Hirsch Fund	NY	640
Coalition for Haitian Concerns	PA	791
Episcopal Migration Ministries	NY	648
Fed. of Italian-Amer. Societies	NY	606
Hebrew Immigrant Aid Society	NY	651
Hmong Mutual Assistance Assoc.	WI	955
Intl. Institute of Metro Detroit	MI	495
Jewish Family Services	FL	318
Jewish Voc. Service	OH	713
Lao Consultant Firm	VA	892
Lao Family Community	CA	100
Lao Family Community	UT	887
New York Assoc. for New Amer.	NY	663
O.L.A. Raza	CA	109
United Methodist Church. Refugee Concerns	CA	156
Univ. of Minnesota. Immigration History Re	MN	539
Vietnamese Mutual Assistance Assoc.	TX	840

SOCIAL SERVICES

Access	CA	123
Adelphi Univ. Refugee Assistance Program	NY	626
Adult and Child Guidance Center. Indochinese	CA	159
Adventist Community Services	DC	222
Afghan Center	CA	190
Afghan Community in Amer.	NY	628
Afghan Refugee Fund	CA	63
African Amer. Immigration Service	NY	609
Agudath Israel of Amer.	NY	631
Aid To Refugee Children Without Parents	CA	160
Alabama Baptist State Conv.	AL	4
Alabama Dept. of Human Resources. Refugee R	AL	5
All Culture Friendship Center Refugee & Immi	CA	55
All Culture Friendship Center Refugee & Immi	CA	65
Amer. Arab Anti-Discrimination Comm.	DC	223
Amer. Baptist Churches. Immigration & Refug	PA	788
Amer. Comm. on Italian Migration	NY	632
Amer. Council for Nationalities Service	NY	633
Amer. Fed. of Jews from Central Europe	NY	635
Amer. Friends Service Comm. Haitian Women'	NY	636
Amer. Fund for Czechoslovak Refugees	NY	637
Amer. Fund for Slovak Refugees	NJ	596
Amer. Fund for Slovak Refugees	NY	607
Amer. Red Cross. Intl. Services	DC	226
Amer. Romanian Comm. for Assistance to Ref	NY	630
Americanization League	NY	691
Amer. for Intl. Aid	GA	337
Anaheim Independencia Center	CA	27
Annunciation House	TX	844
Archdiocese of Chicago. Immigration Services	IL	351
Archdiocese of Detroit. Office of Refugee Rese	MI	490
Archdiocese of New York. Refugee Resettlemen	NY	639
Arizona Center for Immigrants	AZ	7
Arizona Dept. of Economic Security. Refugee	AZ	8
Armenian Assembly of Amer.	DC	228
Asheville Presbytery. Refugee Resettlement Of	NC	702
Asian Counseling and Referral Service	WA	916
Asian Legal Services Outreach	CA	112
Asian Resources	CA	113
Associated Catholic Charities	LA	429
Associated Catholic Charities. Refugee Employ	MD	441
Assoc. of Vietnamese in Nashville	TN	811
Assyrian Universal Alliance	MI	512
Baptist Assoc. of New Orleans	LA	430
Baptist Conv. of Maryland	MD	447
Baptist Conv. of New Mexico	NM	597
Baptist General Conv. of Oklahoma	OK	738
Baptist State Conv.	MI	513
Bethany Christian Services. Refugee Foster Ca	MI	501
Blue Card	NY	641
Border Assoc. for Refugees from Central Amer	TX	842
Bridge Refugee Services	TN	807
Buddhist Council for Refugee Rescue and Reset	CA	133
Bulgarian Natl. Comm.	NJ	582

California Dept. of Social Services. Office of	CA	114
California Southern Baptist Conv. Refugee Re	CA	43
Cambodia's of Ohio	OH	728
Cambodian Assoc. of Amer.	CA	57
Cambodian Assoc. of Memphis	TN	809
Cambodian Assoc. of Mobile	AL	2
Cambodian Assoc. of Virginia	VA	902
Cambodian Mutual Assistance Assoc.	OH	720
Cambodian Mutual Assistance Assoc. of Greate	MA	478
Cambridge Organization of Portuguese-Amer.	MA	468
Capuchin Mission Secretariat	MI	491
Caritas of Austin	TX	819
Casa de la Esperanza	DC	229
Casa de Proyecto Libertad	TX	855
Casa El Salvador	IL	352
Casa Juan Diego	TX	857
Casa Marianella	TX	820
Catholic Agency for Migration & Refugee Serv	KS	412
Catholic Agency for Migration and Refugee Se	KS	411
Catholic Charities	FL	313
Catholic Charities	IA	410
Catholic Charities	KS	414
Catholic Charities	MA	486
Catholic Charities	NE	558
Catholic Charities	NY	684
Catholic Charities Bureau	IN	393
Catholic Charities Bureau. Resettlement Progra	WI	956
Catholic Charities Migration Office	NY	604
Catholic Charities Refugee & Immigration Ser	MA	458
Catholic Charities. Immigration & Refugee Di	CA	68
Catholic Charities. Immigration & Refugee Pro	CA	174
Catholic Charities. Immigration & Refugee Se	PA	765
Catholic Charities. Immigration Counseling C	CA	161
Catholic Charities. Immigration Counseling S	TX	831
Catholic Charities. Immigration Program	CA	134
Catholic Charities. Immigration Services	CA	106
Catholic Charities. Migration & Refugee Servi	MN	528
Catholic Charities. Migration and Refugee Ser	CT	211
Catholic Charities. Migration and Refugee Ser	TX	849
Catholic Charities. Refugee Assistance	IN	396
Catholic Charities. Refugee Assistance Progra	NY	622
Catholic Charities. Refugee Office	IN	394
Catholic Charities. Refugee Program	KS	416
Catholic Charities. Refugee Resettlement Offic	CA	182
Catholic Charities. Refugee Resettlement Offic	FL	289
Catholic Charities. Refugee Resettlement Prog	CA	35
Catholic Charities. Refugee Resettlement Prog	DE	220
Catholic Charities. Refugee Resettlement Prog	TN	810
Catholic Charities. Refugee Service Center	DC	230
Catholic Charities. Refugee Service Program	PA	783
Catholic Charities. Refugee Services	KY	423
Catholic Charities. Refugee Social Service Cen	MS	541
Catholic Charities. Resettlement Program	CA	44
Catholic Charities. Resettlement Services	CA	166

Catholic Charities. Resettlement Services	TX	858
Catholic Charities. Unaccompanied Refugee M	MN	529
Catholic Community Services of Nevada. Imm	NV	564
Catholic Community Services of Utah. Refuge	UT	882
Catholic Community Services. Migration & R	LA	424
Catholic Community Services. Office of Migra	NJ	586
Catholic Community Services. Office of Migra	WV	936
Catholic Community Services. Refugee Resettl	FL	295
Catholic Community Services. Resettlement &	CA	125
Catholic Council for Social Concern	IA	407
Catholic Family and Child Service	WA	935
Catholic Family and Child Services. Family R	WA	910
Catholic Family Center. Refugee Dept.	NY	686
Catholic Family Services. Refugee & Citizensh	TX	818
Catholic Human Development Office. Refugee	MI	502
Catholic Immigration & Resettlement Office	CA	177
Catholic Immigration and Refugee Services	CO	199
Catholic Immigration Center	HI	339
Catholic Immigration Services	FL	296
Catholic Migration & Refugee Services	OR	748
Catholic Migration & Refugee Services	VA	893
Catholic Migration and Refugee Resettlement	OH	721
Catholic Migration and Refugee Service	NV	566
Catholic Migration and Refugee Service	OK	746
Catholic Migration and Refugee Services	ID	349
Catholic Migration and Refugee Services	NJ	573
Catholic Migration Office	NY	605
Catholic Refugee Services	WA	917
Catholic Refugee Services	WA	933
Catholic Resettlement and Immigration Office	IA	406
Catholic Resettlement Center	IL	353
Catholic Resettlement Services	OR	753
Catholic Services for Immigrants	TX	874
Catholic Social Agency. Migration Services	PA	761
Catholic Social Ministries. Migration & Reset	OK	739
Catholic Social Ministries. Refugee Resettleme	NC	699
Catholic Social Service	IL	350
Catholic Social Service	IL	385
Catholic Social Service Bureau. Refugee Resett	KY	420
Catholic Social Service of Phoenix	AZ	9
Catholic Social Service. Refugee Office	NC	696
Catholic Social Service. Refugee Resettlement	FL	309
Catholic Social Service. Refugee Resettlement	CA	115
Catholic Social Service. Resettlement Program	CO	207
Catholic Social Service. Resettlement Program	OH	714
Catholic Social Service. Tha Huong Program	IL	386
Catholic Social Services	AK	6
Catholic Social Services	FL	316
Catholic Social Services	IN	398
Catholic Social Services	KS	413
Catholic Social Services	LA	427
Catholic Social Services	MI	509
Catholic Social Services	MS	540
Catholic Social Services	OH	729
Catholic Social Services	OH	731
Catholic Social Services	PA	763
Catholic Social Services	PA	786
Catholic Social Services	RI	794
Catholic Social Services	WI	942
Catholic Social Services	WY	957
Catholic Social Services Bureau	KY	418
Catholic Social Services of Fall River	MA	476
Catholic Social Services. Central Amer. Refuge	TX	827
Catholic Social Services. Immigration Services	CA	29
Catholic Social Services. Migration & Refugee	PA	773
Catholic Social Services. Migration & Refugee	AZ	16
Catholic Social Services. Migration & Refugee	OH	717
Catholic Social Services. Refugee and Immigra	FL	311
Catholic Social Services. Refugee Program	AL	3
Catholic Social Services. Refugee Resetlement	NE	559
Catholic Social Services. Refugee Resettlemen	CA	179
Catholic Social Services. Refugee Resettlemen	GA	323
Catholic Social Services. Refugee Resettlemen	NM	598
Catholic Social Services. Refugee Social Servi	FL	312
Catholic Social Services. Resettlement Progra	CA	87
Catholic Social Services. Resettlement Progra	MT	556
Catholic Social Services. Servicios Para Inmig	TX	871
Center for Central Amer. Refugees	NJ	587
Central Amer. Refugee Center	CA	69
Central Amer. Refugee Center	DC	233
Central Amer. Refugee Center	NY	627
Central Amer. Refugee Program	WA	918
Central Amer. Refugee Project	AZ	10
Central Amer. Refugee Project	CO	200
Central Amer. Refugee Project	OK	740
Central Amer. Solidarity and Assistance	MD	455
Central Kentucky Jewish Assoc.	KY	421
Centro Campesino. Projecto de Inmigracion	WA	912
Centro de Ayuda Para Immigrantes	TX	860
Centro Presente	MA	469
Chicago Comm. on Immigrant Protection	IL	355
Child and Family Service. Refugee Employmen	HI	340
Chinatown Service Center	CA	70
Chinese Amer. Civic Assoc.	MA	459
Chinese Amer. Service League	IL	357
Chinese Newcomer Service Center	CA	135
Christian Community Service Agency	FL	297
Christian Community Services	CO	197
Christian Council of Metropolitan Atlanta. Re	GA	324
Christian Reformed World Relief Comm.	MI	503
Christian Refugee Outreach	VA	894
Church of the Brethren. Refugee Resettlement	MD	450
Church Refugee Center	NY	643
Church World Service. Immigration & Refugee	NY	644
Church World Service. Refugee Program	FL	298
Clinica Msr. Oscar A. Romero	CA	71
Coalition for Haitian Concerns	PA	791
Coalition for Immigrant and Refugee Rights &	CA	136
Colorado Refugee and Immigrant Services Prog	CO	201
Comite en Defensa de los Immigrantes	CA	110
Comm. in Defense of Immigrant Rights	WA	919
Community Legal Services	PA	774
Community, Family & Children Services. Refu	MI	500
Conference on Jewish Material Claims Against	NY	646
Connecticut Dept. of Human Resources. State	CT	212
Conscientious Alliance for Peace	AL	1

Cornerstone Ministries	FL	317	Friendly House	AZ	11
Council of Churches. Refugee Resettlement Pro	MO	552	General Conference of Seventh-Day Adventists	DC	238
Cross Lutheran Church	WI	947	Georgia Dept. of Human Resources. Special Pr	GA	327
Cuban Amer. Natl. Council. Refugee Program	FL	299	Good Samaritan Community Center	CA	138
Dallas-Fort Worth Refugee Interagency	TX	832	Greater Hartford Jewish Fed.	CT	216
Delaware Dept. of Health & Social Services. D	DE	219	Haitian Amer. Assoc.	MA	472
Detroit Windsor Refugee Coalition	MI	492	Haitian Amer. Community Assoc.	FL	300
Diocesan Refugee Coordinator	MI	493	Haitian Centers Council	NY	615
Diocesan Refugee Resettlement Program	ME	439	Haitian Multi-Service Center	MA	474
Diocese of Green Bay. Dept. of Refugee, Migra	WI	939	Haitian Refugee Center	FL	301
Diocese of Lafayette. Migration & Refugee Ser	LA	428	Hawaii Dept. of Labor & Industrial Relations.	HI	341
Diocese of Nashville. Refugee Resettlement Pr	TN	812	Hebrew Immigrant Aid Society	NY	651
Diocese of Oregon	OR	751	Hebrew Immigrant Aid Society	PA	776
Diocese of Raleigh. Refugee Resettlement Offi	NC	704	Hebrew Immigrant Aid Society of Baltimore	MD	443
Diocese of Rhode Island	RI	795	Hmong Assoc. of Brown County. Refugee Com	WI	940
Diocese of Richmond. Office of Refugee Resetl	VA	909	Hmong Catholic Center	MN	532
Diocese of Richmond. Office of Refugee Resett	VA	901	Hmong Community	MI	494
Diocese of Springfield - Cape Girardeau. Resett	MO	553	Hmong Community Service	MD	449
Diocese of Springfield. Refugee Resettlement	MA	482	Hmong Council	CA	48
Disciples of Christ. Refugee & Immigration M	IN	399	Hmong Mutual Assistance Assoc.	WI	955
District of Columbia Dept. of Human Services.	DC	235	Hmong Natural Assoc. of North Carolina	NC	703
Don Bosco Community Center	MO	546	Hmong-Amer. Planning & Development Center	TX	854
East Bay Sanctuary Covenant	CA	33	Hmong/Amer. Friendship Assoc.	WI	949
East Central Illinois Refugee Mutual Assistanc	IL	391	Holt Intl. Children's Services	OR	749
East Side Group	TX	822	Holy Cross Mission	CA	184
Eau Claire Area Hmong Mutual Assistance Ass	WI	938	Holy Cross Service Center	FL	288
Ecumenical Immigration Services	LA	431	Hood River Valley Immigration Project	OR	750
Ecumenical Refugee Council	WI	948	Houston Metropolitan Ministries	TX	861
Ecumenical Refugee Resettlement Services	VA	903	Human Services Assoc.	CA	31
Ecumenical Refugee Services	CO	202	Idaho Dept. of Health and Welfare. Div. of Fiel	ID	347
El Centro Asylum Project	CA	42	Illinois Bureau of Naturalization Services	IL	389
El Concilio. Immigration Project	CA	45	Illinois Conference of Churches. Refugee Immi	IL	390
El Rescate	CA	73	Illinois Conference of Churches. Refugee Reset	IL	358
Episcopal Diocese of Minnesota. Refugee Rese	MN	520	Immigrants Assistance Center	MA	480
Episcopal Diocese of North Carolina. Refugee	NC	705	Immigration Advocacy Service	NE	561
Episcopal Migration Ministries	NY	648	Immigration and Legalization Service	TX	824
Episcopal Refugee and Migration Comm.	NH	570	Immigration Counseling Migration & Refugee	TX	851
Episcopal Refugee Resettlement Commission	IN	400	Immigration Project	CA	75
Episcopal Social Ministries	MD	442	Immigration Project	CA	194
Episcopal Social Service	CT	208	Immigration Service of Santa Rosa	CA	189
Eritrean Relief Comm.	NY	649	Immigration Services of Santa Rosa	CA	131
Ethiopian Community Center	DC	236	Indiana Council of Churches	IN	401
Ethiopian Community Development Council	VA	895	Indiana Dept. of Welfare. Policy & Program De	IN	402
Ethiopian Community Mutual Assistance Asso	NY	650	Indochina Resource Action Center	DC	241
Evangelical Crusade of Fishers of Men	NY	614	Indochinese Assistance Center	CA	117
Faith Lutheran Church	FL	308	Inmigracion Latina Foundation	FL	302
Family and Children's Services of Chattanooga	TN	806	Intercultural Action Center	CA	178
Father Moriarty Asylum Program	CA	137	Interfaith Refugee Assistance Project	OK	744
Fed. of Italian-Amer. Societies	NY	606	Intl. Catholic Migration Commission	DC	242
Fed. of Vietnamese & Allied Veterans	CA	56	Intl. Center of the Capital Region. Refugee As	NY	602
Filipinos for Affirmative Action	CA	97	Intl. Community Services	TX	865
First Lutheran Church	FL	283	Intl. Institute	OH	711
Florida Baptist Conv.	FL	290	Intl. Institute of Buffalo	NY	623
Florida Council of Churches. Refugee Program	FL	310	Intl. Institute of Connecticut	CT	209
Florida Dept. of Health and Rehabilitation Ser	FL	315	Intl. Institute of Connecticut	CT	213
Foreign-Born Information and Referral Networ	MD	448	Intl. Institute of Erie	PA	764
Freedom Flight Refugee Center	MI	504	Intl. Institute of Flint	MI	499
Fresno Ecumenical Resettlement Project	CA	46	Intl. Institute of Los Angeles	CA	191

Intl. Institute of Los Angeles. Immigrant & Re	CA	76
Intl. Institute of Los Angeles. Refugee Relocat	CA	158
Intl. Institute of Lowell	MA	479
Intl. Institute of Metro Detroit	MI	495
Intl. Institute of Metropolitan St. Louis	MO	550
Intl. Institute of Minnesota	MN	534
Intl. Institute of New Jersey	NJ	584
Intl. Institute of Rhose Island	RI	796
Intl. Institute of San Francisco	CA	141
Intl. Institute of the East Bay	CA	98
Intl. Institute of Toledo	OH	732
Intl. Institute of Wisconsin	WI	950
Intl. Refugee Center	IL	360
Intl. Rescue Comm.	CA	49
Intl. Rescue Comm.	CA	78
Intl. Rescue Comm.	CA	118
Intl. Rescue Comm.	CA	127
Intl. Rescue Comm.	CA	142
Intl. Rescue Comm.	CA	162
Intl. Rescue Comm.	CA	168
Intl. Rescue Comm.	CA	185
Intl. Rescue Comm.	DC	243
Intl. Rescue Comm.	FL	303
Intl. Rescue Comm.	GA	335
Intl. Rescue Comm.	NJ	595
Intl. Rescue Comm.	NY	656
Intl. Rescue Comm.	TX	833
Intl. Rescue Comm.	WA	921
Intl. Service Center	PA	766
Intl. Social Service. Amer. Branch	NY	657
Iowa Dept. of Human Services. Bureau of Refug	IA	408
Japanese Amer. Service Comm. of Chicago	IL	361
Japanese Newcomer Service	CA	143
Jewish Family & Children Services	CA	144
Jewish Family & Children's Service	AZ	12
Jewish Family and Child Service	OR	754
Jewish Family and Children's Agency	PA	777
Jewish Family and Children's Service	CO	203
Jewish Family and Children's Service	MA	466
Jewish Family and Children's Service	NJ	571
Jewish Family and Children's Service	OH	736
Jewish Family and Children's Service. Resettle	MN	521
Jewish Family and Children's Services	IN	403
Jewish Family and Children's Services	TX	847
Jewish Family and Community Services	FL	291
Jewish Family and Counseling Service	NJ	572
Jewish Family and Voc. Service	KY	422
Jewish Family Service	AZ	17
Jewish Family Service	CA	51
Jewish Family Service	CA	99
Jewish Family Service	CT	215
Jewish Family Service	FL	314
Jewish Family Service	LA	436
Jewish Family Service	MN	535
Jewish Family Service	NJ	574
Jewish Family Service	NJ	575
Jewish Family Service	NY	624
Jewish Family Service	NY	688
Jewish Family Service	OH	712
Jewish Family Service	PA	785
Jewish Family Service	PA	787
Jewish Family Service	RI	797
Jewish Family Service	TN	813
Jewish Family Service	TX	876
Jewish Family Service	VA	904
Jewish Family Service	WA	922
Jewish Family Service Agency	NV	565
Jewish Family Service Agency of Central New	NJ	580
Jewish Family Service Assoc.	OH	719
Jewish Family Service of Broward County	FL	285
Jewish Family Service of Delaware Valley	NJ	591
Jewish Family Service of Detroit	MI	514
Jewish Family Service of Greater Springfield	MA	483
Jewish Family Service of Metro West	NJ	589
Jewish Family Service of MetroWest	NJ	581
Jewish Family Service of North Middlesex Cou	NJ	578
Jewish Family Service of Raritan Valley	NJ	576
Jewish Family Service of Somerset County	NJ	588
Jewish Family Service. Immigration & Resettl	NM	599
Jewish Family Service. Refugee Resettlement P	TX	866
Jewish Family Service. Refugee Services	CA	79
Jewish Family Service. Resettlement Program	CA	128
Jewish Family Service. Resettlement Program	FL	306
Jewish Family Service. Resettlement Program	MD	444
Jewish Family Service. Resettlement Services	CT	210
Jewish Family Services	FL	318
Jewish Family Services	GA	328
Jewish Family Services	ME	440
Jewish Family Services	NC	697
Jewish Family Services	TX	834
Jewish Family Services	UT	884
Jewish Family Services	WI	951
Jewish Family Services of Greater Orlando	FL	322
Jewish Family Services. Refugee Services	IL	362
Jewish Fed. of Palm Beach County	FL	320
Jewish Philanthropic Fund of 1933	NY	658
Jewish Social Services	TX	852
Jewish Social Services	WI	943
Jewish Social Services Agency	MD	451
Jewish Voc. & Career Counseling Service	CA	145
Jewish Voc. Service	NJ	577
Jewish Voc. Service	OH	713
Jewish Voc. Service & Community Workshop	MI	515
Kalihi-Palama Immigrant Service Center	HI	344
Kansas Dept. of Social & Rehabilitation Serv	KS	415
Kentucky Cabinet for Human Resources. Offic	KY	419
Khmer Health Advocates	CT	217
Khmer Society of San Antonio. Refugee SOS	TX	877
King County Rape Relief. Southeast Asian Ch	WA	915
Korean Amer. Community Services	IL	363
Korean Amer. Community Services	MD	454
La Crosse Area Hmong Mutual Assistance Ass	WI	941
Lao Community Assoc.	GA	336
Lao Consultant Firm	VA	892
Lao Family Community	CA	88
Lao Family Community	CA	89

Lao Family Community	CA	91
Lao Family Community	CA	119
Lao Family Community	CA	169
Lao Family Community	UT	887
Lao Family Community	WI	952
Lao Khmu Assoc.	CA	186
Lawyers Comm. for Human Rights. Political A	NY	659
Long Island Refugee Resettlement Program	NY	616
Louisiana Dept. of Health & Human Resources	LA	432
Louisiana Dept. of Health & Human Services.	LA	425
Lutheran Child & Family Services of Massach	MA	485
Lutheran Child and Family Services	IL	365
Lutheran Children and Family Service	PA	778
Lutheran Church. Synod Board of Social Mini	MO	551
Lutheran Family Service. Refugee Services	OR	755
Lutheran Family Services. Refugee Resettleme	NC	700
Lutheran Immigration & Refugee Services	DC	245
Lutheran Immigration and Refugee Service	NY	660
Lutheran Immigration and Refugee Service	TX	867
Lutheran Ministries of Florida	FL	307
Lutheran Ministries of Florida. Refugee Resett	FL	319
Lutheran Ministries of Georgia	GA	329
Lutheran Refugee and Immigration Services	NJ	592
Lutheran Refugee Resettlement	CO	204
Lutheran Social Ministry of the Southwest. Re	AZ	13
Lutheran Social Services	MN	516
Lutheran Social Services of Iowa	IA	409
Lutheran Social Services of Kansas and Oklah	KS	417
Lutheran Social Services of Michigan. Dept. o	MI	510
Lutheran Social Services of Michigan. Refuge	MI	507
Lutheran Social Services of Minnesota. Refug	MN	522
Lutheran Social Services of Montana	MT	555
Lutheran Social Services of North Dakota. Ref	ND	709
Lutheran Social Services of Northeast Florida.	FL	292
Lutheran Social Services of Northern Californ	CA	146
Lutheran Social Services of South Dakota. Ref	SD	805
Lutheran Social Services of Wisconsin & Upp	WI	953
Lutheran Social Services. Immigration & Refu	CA	81
Lutheran Social Services. Unaccompanied Min	OH	722
Lutheran Welfare Service	PA	768
Maine Annual Conference of the United Metho	ME	438
Maine Dept. of Human Services. Bureau of So	ME	437
Maryland Dept. of Human Resources. State Re	MD	445
Massachusetts Office for Refugees and Immigr	MA	463
Mennonite Central Comm. Immigration & Re	PA	760
Mennonite Immigration and Refugee Services	DC	246
Mennonite Intl. Refugee Assistance	TX	835
Metropolitan Social Services. Refugee Program	TN	814
Miami Presbytery	OH	730
Michigan Dept. of Social Services. Office of R	MI	496
Mid-Cumberland Refugee Assistance Ministry	TN	815
Midwest Coalition in Defense of Immigrants	IL	366
Midwest Immigrant Rights Center	IL	367
Migration & Refugee Services	SC	802
Minnesota - Wisconsin Southern Baptist Con	MN	526
Minnesota Cambodian Buddhist Society	MN	536
Minnesota Council of Churches. Refugee Prog	MN	537
Minnesota Dept. of Human Services. Refugee	MN	538
Mississippi Baptist Conv. Language Mission	MS	542
Mississippi Dept. of Public Welfare. Refugee	MS	543
Missouri Div. of Family Services. Refugee As	MO	544
Mohawk Valley Resource Center for Refugees	NY	693
Montana Assoc. for Refugee Services	MT	554
Montana Dept. of Family Services. Office of R	MT	557
Monterey County Sanctuary	CA	103
Moob Fed. of Amer.	IL	392
Mutual Aid Assoc. of the New Polish Immigra	IL	368
Natl. Assoc. for Vietnamese Amer. Education	CA	170
Natl. Assoc. of Evangelicals. Immigration Pro	FL	304
Natl. Center For Immigrants' Rights	CA	82
Natl. Council of Jewish Women. Immigration	MA	487
Natl. Council of Jewish Women. Rescue & Mi	FL	305
Natl. Slavic Conv.	MD	446
Nationalities Service Center	PA	780
Nationalities Service of Central California	CA	50
Nationalities Services Center	OH	718
Naturalization Project	LA	434
Nebraska Dept. of Social Services. Refugee Af	NE	560
Nevada Dept. of Human Resources. State Refug	NV	563
New Hampshire Office of Refugee Resettlemen	NH	568
New Hope Presbytery	NC	694
New Jersey Dept. of Human Services. State Re	NJ	594
New Lao Friendship Club of Oklahoma	OK	741
New Mexico Dept. of Human Services. Social	NM	601
New York Assoc. for New Amer.	NY	663
New York Circus	NY	664
New York Dept. of Social Services. State Refu	NY	603
North Carolina Dept. of Human Resources. Fa	NC	706
North Dakota Dept. of Human Services. Refug	ND	708
Northern Virginia Family Service. Multicultur	VA	898
O.L.A. Raza	CA	109
Ohio Council of Churches. Refugee Services	OH	724
Ohio Dept. of Human Services. Program Deve	OH	725
Ohio State Conv. of Baptists	OH	726
Oklahoma Dept. of Human Services. Refugee U	OK	742
Orange County Coalition for Immigrant Right	CA	171
Orange County Community Consortium	CA	172
Oregon Dept. of Human Resources. Refugee Pr	OR	759
Overground Railroad	IL	382
Palo Alto Friends Meeting	CA	107
Partnership for Human Development. Resettle	TX	826
Pennsylvania Dept. of Public Welfare. Office	PA	767
Peylim	NY	668
Philadelphia Refugee Service Center	PA	781
Philippine Center for Immigrant Rights	NY	669
Plattsburg Interfaith Council	NY	685
Plenty USA	CA	38
Polish Amer. Immigration and Relief Comm.	NY	670
Polish Amer. Immigration Relief Comm.	IL	370
Polish and Slavic Center. Refugee Assistance	NY	617
Presbyterian Synod of Southern California and	CA	84
Presbytery of Southern Louisiana	LA	426
PRIME Ecumenical Commitment to Refugees	PA	762
Project Deliverance	OH	733
Proyecto Adelante	TX	837
Proyecto Resistencia	IL	371

Rav Tov. Intl. Jewish Rescue Organization	NY	618
Redeemer Lutheran Church. Hmong Farm Proje	OH	727
Reformed Church in Amer. Refugee Program	MI	505
Refugee and Immigrant Multi-Service Center	WA	930
Refugee Employment Assistance Project	CA	148
Refugee Resettlement Comm.	CA	90
Refugee Resettlement Office	AR	24
Refugee Resettlement Office	MO	545
Refugee Resettlement Program	AR	26
Refugee Services	MI	508
Refugee Women in Development	DC	251
Rhode Island Dept. of Human Services. State R	RI	799
Rio Grande Defense Comm.	TX	879
Rochester Refugee Services	MN	527
Saint Vincents Services	NY	619
Salvadoran Refugee Comm. (Oscar A. Romero	DC	253
San Antonio Literacy Council	TX	878
San Juan Macias Immigrant Center	CA	104
Sanctuary Covenant of San Francisco	CA	152
Sandigan California	CA	121
Santa Clara County Health Dept. Refugee Heal	CA	163
Sarrlano Chirino Amaya Central Amer. Refuge	CA	85
Saura Center	IL	372
Save the Children. Refugee Child Care Assista	GA	330
Socio-Economic Development Center for Sout	RI	800
Somerville Portuguese Amer. League	MA	481
South Carolina Dept. of Social Services. Refu	SC	803
South Dakota Dept. of Social Services. Refuge	SD	804
South Texas Immigration Council	TX	828
South-East Asia Center	IL	373
Southeast Asian Center	RI	792
Southern Baptist Immigration and Refugee Res	GA	331
Southside Community Mission	NY	620
Sponsors Organized to Assist Refugees	ID	348
Sponsors Organized to Assist Refugees	OR	756
St. Anselm's Immigrant & Refugee Community	CA	52
St. John's Center. Office of Social Ministry	GA	338
St. Paul's United Methodist Church. Refugee Pr	NV	567
Sunyvale Community Services	CA	188
Synapses. Asian Organizing Program	IL	374
Syracuse Interreligious Council. Refugee Assis	NY	692
Tacoma Community House	WA	934
Tennessee Dept. of Human Services. Refugee P	TN	816
Texan Training & Employment Center	TX	868
Texas Dept. of Human Service. Refugee Progra	TX	825
Tolstoy Foundation	AZ	14
Tolstoy Foundation	CA	192
Tolstoy Foundation	MI	498
Tolstoy Foundation	NY	673
Training Program in Human Services for Emigr	NY	674
Traveler and Immigrants Aid	IL	375
Travelers Aid Intl. Institute. Refugee Resource	OH	716
Travelers Aid Society	DC	255
Tressler Lutheran Services. Refugee Services Pr	PA	770
Tucson Ecumenical Council. Central Amer. Tas	AZ	22
U. S. Catholic Conference. Migration & Refug	NY	675
U.S. Catholic Conference. Migration & Refuge	DC	256
U.S. Catholic Conference. Migration & Refuge	CA	154
U.S. Catholic Conference. Migration & Refuge	DC	257
U.S. Catholic Conference. Migration & Refuge	NY	676
U.S. Catholic Conference. Migration & Refuge	TX	848
U.S. Dept. of Health and Human Services. Fam	DC	264
United Cambodian Community	CA	62
United Catholic Social Services. Refugee Reset	NE	562
United Church Board for World Ministries. Ref	NY	678
United Methodist Church. Refugee Concerns C	CA	156
United Methodist Comm. on Relief. Refugee S	NY	679
United Nations High Commissioner for Refuge	DC	274
United Nations. High Commissioner for Refug	NY	680
United Nations. Relief and Works Agency for	NY	681
United Refugee Council	NY	621
U.S. Catholic Conference	IL	388
Utah Dept. of Social Services. Refugee & Alie	UT	885
Valley Religious Task Force on Central Amer.	AZ	15
Vermont Catholic Charities. Refugee Resettlem	VT	890
Vermont State Refugee Coordinator	VT	891
Vietnamese Amer. Assoc. Refugee Center	OK	743
Vietnamese Amer. Civic Assoc.	MA	475
Vietnamese Amer. Cultural Alliance of Colorad	CO	198
Vietnamese Amer. Cultural Organization	NY	682
Vietnamese Assoc. of Illinois	IL	378
Vietnamese Catholic Community	MI	489
Vietnamese Catholic Community in Connectic	CT	214
Vietnamese Community in Virginia	VA	905
Vietnamese Community of Orange County	CA	173
Vietnamese Evangelical Church	MN	525
Vietnamese Lutheran Ministry	WA	927
Vietnamese Mutual Assistance Assoc.	TX	840
Vietnamese Mutual Assistance Assoc. of North	ND	710
Vietnamese Service Center	CA	53
Vietnamese Seventh-Day Adventist Church	OR	757
Virginia Baptist General Board. Div. of Missio	VA	906
Virginia Council of Churches. Refugee Progra	VA	907
Virginia Dept. of Social Services. State Refuge	VA	908
Washington Assoc. of Churches. Immigration	WA	928
Washington Assoc. of Churches. Refugee Rese	WA	932
Washington Bureau of Refugee Assistance	WA	914
West Virginia Dept. of Human Services	WV	937
Wisconsin Div. of Community Services. Refug	WI	946
Woodrow Wilson Intl. Center	DC	278
World Relief	CA	54
World Relief	CA	157
World Relief	CA	187
World Relief	DC	279
World Relief	FL	282
World Relief	GA	333
World Relief	NY	683
World Relief	NC	701
World Relief	TN	817
World Relief	TX	869
World Relief	WA	929
World Relief. Immigration Services	IL	379
Wyoming Dept. of Health & Social Services.	WY	958
Yiu Mienh Assoc. of Oregon	OR	758
YMCA Intl. Services	TX	870
YMCA. Refugee Resettlement Services	IL	380

Youth With a Mission Relief Services   HI   346

Index IV

Clientele

Africa

Cambodian Mutual Assistance Assoc.	OH	720
Catholic Charities. Refugee Service Program	PA	783
Catholic Social Services	OH	729
Cornerstone Ministries	FL	317
Cross Lutheran Church	WI	947
Eritrean Relief Comm.	NY	649
Ethiopian Community Center	DC	236
Ethiopian Community Development Council	VA	895
Ethiopian Community Mutual Assistance Asso	NY	650
Jewish Fed. of Palm Beach County	FL	320
Lutheran Social Services of Iowa	IA	409

Asia (excluding SE Asia)

Adult and Child Guidance Center. Indochinese	CA	159
Afghan Center	CA	190
Afghan Community in Amer.	NY	628
Afghan Refugee Fund	CA	63
Amer. for Intl. Aid	GA	337
Asia Pacific Concerns Comm.	CA	181
Asian Counseling and Referral Service	WA	916
Asian Immigrant Womens Advocates	CA	93
Asian Pacific Amer. Legal Center of Southern	CA	67
Asian Resources	CA	113
Buddhist Council for Refugee Rescue and Reset	CA	133
Catholic Immigration Center	HI	339
Catholic Social Services	MS	540
Catholic Social Services	OH	729
Catholic Social Services. Refugee and Immigra	FL	311
Catholic Social Services. Refugee Resetlement	NE	559
Chinatown Service Center	CA	70
Chinese Amer. Civic Assoc.	MA	459
Chinese Amer. Service League	IL	357
Chinese Newcomer Service Center	CA	135
Fed. of Vietnamese & Allied Veterans	CA	56
Filipinos for Affirmative Action	CA	97
Intl. Buddhist Meditation Assoc.	HI	343
Japanese Amer. Service Comm. of Chicago	IL	361
Japanese Newcomer Service	CA	143
Jewish Family Service	CT	215
Kalihi-Palama Immigrant Service Center	HI	344
Korean Amer. Community Services	IL	363
Korean Amer. Community Services	MD	454
Lao Family Community	UT	887

Mennonite Immigration and Refugee Services	DC	246
Moob Fed. of Amer.	IL	392
Na Loio No Na Kanaka. Lawyers for the Peopl	HI	345
Nevada Dept. of Human Resources. State Refug	NV	563
Organization of Chinese Amer.	DC	248
Philippine Center for Immigrant Rights	NY	669
Synapses. Asian Organizing Program	IL	374
Tacoma Community House	WA	934
Vietnamese Amer. Civic Assoc.	MA	475
Youth With a Mission Relief Services	HI	346

Central Amer./Caribbean/Mexico

AFL/CIO Immigration Project	CA	64
Amer. Civil Liberties Union. South Texas Proj	TX	880
Amer. Friends Service Comm. Florida Undocum	FL	293
Amer. Friends Service Comm. Haitian Women'	NY	636
Amer. Friends Service Comm. Immigration Pro	CA	108
Amer. Immigrant Foundation	CA	164
Anaheim Independencia Center	CA	27
Annunciation House	TX	844
Archdiocese of Chicago. Immigration Services	IL	351
Archdiocese of New York. Office for Immigrant	NY	638
Archdiocese of Portland. Immigration Counseli	OR	752
Arizona Center for Immigrants	AZ	7
Associated Catholic Charities	LA	429
Baptist Assoc. of New Orleans	LA	430
Baptist Conv. of Maryland	MD	447
Bergen County Sanctuary Comm.	NJ	590
Border Assoc. for Refugees from Central Amer.	TX	842
California Southern Baptist Conv. Refugee Res	CA	43
Capuchin Mission Secretariat	MI	491
Caribbean Action Lobby	NY	611
Caritas of Austin	TX	819
CASA	PA	771
Casa de la Esperanza	DC	229
Casa de Proyecto Libertad	TX	855
Casa El Salvador	IL	352
Casa Juan Diego	TX	857
Casa Marianella	TX	820
Catholic Agency for Migration and Refugee Se	KS	411
Catholic Charities	FL	313
Catholic Charities	NE	558
Catholic Charities Refuge & Immigration Ser	MA	458
Catholic Charities. Immigration Counseling C	CA	161
Catholic Charities. Immigration Counseling Se	TX	831

Catholic Charities. Immigration Program	CA	134
Catholic Charities. Immigration Project	CA	94
Catholic Charities. Immigration Project of Im	FL	286
Catholic Charities. Immigration Services	CA	106
Catholic Charities. Resettlement Services	CA	166
Catholic Community Services. Refugee Resettl	FL	295
Catholic Family and Child Services. Family Re	WA	910
Catholic Family Service. Immigration Service	TX	872
Catholic Immigration & Resettlement Office	CA	177
Catholic Immigration Services	FL	296
Catholic Migration Office	NY	605
Catholic Services for Immigrants	TX	874
Catholic Social Service	IL	385
Catholic Social Service of Phoenix	AZ	9
Catholic Social Services. Central Amer. Refuge	TX	827
Catholic Social Services. Refugee Resettlement	CA	179
Catholic Social Services. Resettlement Progra	CA	87
Catholic Social Services. Servicios Para Inmig	TX	871
Center for Central Amer. Refugees	NJ	587
Central Amer. Resource Center	TX	821
Central Amer. Legal Assistance	NY	613
Central Amer. Refugee Center	CA	69
Central Amer. Refugee Center	DC	233
Central Amer. Refugee Center	NY	627
Central Amer. Refugee Center	TX	859
Central Amer. Refugee Program	WA	918
Central Amer. Refugee Project	AZ	10
Central Amer. Refugee Project	CO	200
Central Amer. Resource Center	MN	530
Central Amer. Solidarity and Assistance	MD	455
Central Baptist Church. Sanctuary Group	PA	789
Central Coast Sanctuary	CA	175
Centro Campesino. Projecto de Inmigracion	WA	912
Centro de Ayuda Para Immigrantes	TX	860
Centro Legal	MN	531
Centro Presente	MA	469
Chicago Religious Task Force on Central Amer	IL	356
Christ Church of the Brethren. Sanctuary Com	OH	734
Christian Community Service Agency	FL	297
Christian Community Services	CO	197
Christian Council of Metropolitan Atlanta. Ref	GA	324
City of Berkeley. Public Sanctuary	CA	32
City of Burlington. Office of the Mayor	VT	889
City of Cambridge. Office of the Mayor	MA	470
City of Davis. Office of the Mayor	CA	37
City of East Lansing. Office of the Mayor	MI	497
City of Minneapolis. Office of the Mayor	MN	519
City of Olympia. Office of the Mayor	WA	913
City of Sacramento. Office of the Mayor	CA	116
City of Santa Fe. Office of the Mayor	NM	600
City of Tacoma Park. Office of the Mayor	MD	456
City of West Hollywood. City Council	CA	196
Clinica Msr. Oscar A. Romero	CA	71
Coalition for Haitian Concerns	PA	791
Coalition for Public Sanctuary	OH	735
Coastal Bend Friends Meeting	TX	830
College Hill Presbyterian Church. Sanctuary C	OK	747
Comite de Refugiados Salvadorenos	CA	40
Comite en Defensa de los Immigrantes	CA	110
Commission for the Study of Intl. Migration a	DC	234
Community Friends Meeting. Sanctuary Comm	OH	715
Community Law Center	CA	167
Community Legal Services	CA	36
Concord Friends Meeting Sanctuary	PA	790
Congregation Hakafa. Sanctuary Comm.	IL	384
Conscientious Alliance for Peace	AL	1
Corn-Maya	FL	287
Cornerstone Ministries	FL	317
Corpus Christi Church. Sanctuary Comm.	NY	687
Cross Lutheran Church	WI	947
Cuban Amer. Natl. Council. Refugee Program	FL	299
Detroit Windsor Refugee Coalition	MI	492
Diocesan Migrant & Refugee Services	TX	845
Downtown Legalization Project	CA	72
East Bay Sanctuary Covenant	CA	33
East Side Group	TX	822
Ecumenical Immigration Services	LA	431
Ecumenical Refugee Council	WI	948
El Centro Asylum Project	CA	42
El Concilio. Immigration Project	CA	45
El Paso Legal Assistance Society	TX	846
El Rescate	CA	73
Emmanuel Lutheran Church. Sanctuary Comm.	MO	549
EPIC Immigration Project	WA	911
Faith United Methodist Church. Sanctuary Com	IA	405
Father Moriarty Asylum Program	CA	137
First Lutheran Church	FL	283
First Unitarian Church	CA	183
First Unitarian Church. Sanctuary Comm.	MI	488
Florida Baptist Conv.	FL	290
Florida Dept. of Health and Rehabilitation Ser	FL	315
Florida Rural Legal Services	FL	281
Fort Worth Independent School District. Survi	TX	850
Friendly House	AZ	11
Friends Meeting of Austin. Sanctuary Comm.	TX	823
Good Samaritan Community Center	CA	138
Guatemala Human Rights Commission/USA	DC	240
Haitian Amer. Assoc.	MA	472
Haitian Amer. Community Assoc.	FL	300
Haitian Centers Council	NY	615
Haitian Multi-Service Center	MA	474
Haitian Refugee Center	FL	301
Heart of Texas Legal Services	TX	881
Hispanic Immigration Counseling Program	WA	920
Holy Cross Mission	CA	184
Holy Cross Service Center	FL	288
Hood River Valley Immigration Project	OR	750
Houston Metropolitan Ministries	TX	861
Human Services Assoc.	CA	31
Humboldt Congregations for Sanctuary	CA	28
Humboldt Unitarian-Universalist Fellowship	CA	30
Immigrant Assistance Line	CA	139
Immigrant Legal Resource Center	CA	41
Immigrants' Rights Office	CA	74
Immigration Advocacy Service	NE	561
Immigration Assistance Service	NJ	583

Immigration Counseling Center	TX	862
Immigration Institute	TX	863
Immigration Law Enforcement Monitoring Proj	TX	864
Immigration Law Project	TX	875
Immigration Project	CA	75
Immigration Project	CA	194
Immigration Service of Santa Rosa	CA	189
Immigration Services of Santa Rosa	CA	131
Impact	CA	126
Inland Counties Legal Services	CA	111
Inmigracion Latina Foundation	FL	302
Interfaith Refugee Assistance Project	OK	744
Interfaith Sanctuary Movement	PA	784
Intl. Institute of San Francisco	CA	141
Joint Legal Task Force on Central Amer. Refug	WA	923
Jubilee Partners	GA	334
Kalamazoo Interfaith Sanctuary Project	MI	506
Legal Aid Bureau	MD	453
Legal Aid Society	FL	321
Legal Aid Society. Alien Rights Unit	CA	129
Loyola Univ. School of Law Clinic	LA	433
Lutheran Child and Family Services	IL	365
Lutheran Ministries of Florida	FL	307
Manchester Church of the Brethren. Sanctuary	IN	404
Mennonite Immigration and Refugee Services	DC	246
Mennonite Intl. Refugee Assistance	TX	835
Midwest Coalition in Defense of Immigrants	IL	366
Mission Community Legal Defense	CA	147
Monterey County Sanctuary	CA	103
Multicultural Immigration Center	NY	661
Natl. Assoc. of Evangelicals. Immigration Pro	FL	304
Natl. Coalition for Haitian Refugees	NY	662
Natl. Immigration Project of the Natl. Lawyer	MA	464
Natl. Lawyers Guild. Central Amer. Refugee De	PA	779
Naturalization Project	LA	434
Neil Avenue Mennonite Church. Sanctuary Co	OH	723
New York Circus	NY	664
North Texas Immigration Coalition	TX	836
Northside Sanctuary Coalition	IL	369
O.L.A. Immigration Rights Center	CA	193
O.L.A. Raza	CA	109
Orange County Coalition for Immigrant Rights	CA	171
Orange County Community Consortium	CA	172
Overground Railroad	IL	382
Palo Alto Friends Meeting	CA	107
Partnership for Human Development. Resettle	TX	826
People's Immigration Service	CA	195
People's Law Office for Organized Workers	FL	280
Pioneer Valley Sanctuary Comm., Mt. Toby M	MA	457
Plenty USA	CA	38
Posada Sanctuary	IL	387
Project Deliverance	OH	733
Proyecto Adelante	TX	837
Proyecto Resistencia	IL	371
Refugee Assistance Program	CA	130
Refugee Resettlement Comm.	CA	90
Refugee Resettlement Office	AR	24
Rio Grande Defense Comm.	TX	879
Riverside Church. Sanctuary Comm.	NY	672
Rosenberg Foundation	CA	149
Salvadoran Refugee Comm. (Oscar A. Romero)	DC	253
San Antonio Literacy Council	TX	878
San Francisco Lawyers' Comm. Immigrant & R	CA	150
San Francisco Lawyers' Comm. Political Asylu	CA	151
San Juan Bautista Lutheran Church. Sanctuary	AZ	18
San Juan Macias Immigrant Center	CA	104
Sanctuary Covenant of San Francisco	CA	152
Sandigan California	CA	121
Sarrlano Chirino Amaya Central Amer. Refugee	CA	85
Saura Center	IL	372
Seattle - King County Bar Assoc. Legalization,	WA	924
Sinai Temple. Sanctuary Comm.	MA	484
South and Meso-Amer. Indian Information Cen	CA	34
South Texas Immigration Council	TX	828
South Texas Immigration Council	TX	856
South Texas Immigration Council	TX	873
Southern Arizona Legal Aid	AZ	19
Southern California Interfaith Task Force on C	CA	86
Southern Minnesota Regional Legal Services	MN	517
Southside Community Mission	NY	620
St. John's Center. Office of Social Ministry	GA	338
St. Teresa's Church. Sanctuary Comm.	CA	153
Sunyvale Community Services	CA	188
TECHO Central Amer. Education Center	AZ	20
Temple Beth El. Sanctuary Comm.	WI	944
Temple Emanu-El. Sanctuary Comm.	AZ	21
Temple Israel. Sanctuary Comm.	CA	60
Temple Sinai. Sanctuary Comm.	CA	102
Temple Sinai. Sanctuary Comm.	DC	254
Tennessee Valley Unitarian Church. Sanctuary	TN	808
Texas Rural Legal Aid	TX	843
Texas Rural Legal Aid. Clinica de Inmigracion	TX	841
Tucson Ecumenical Council. Central Amer. Tas	AZ	22
Tucson Ecumenical Council. Legal Assistance	AZ	23
U.S. Catholic Conference. Migration & Refuge	CA	154
U.S. Catholic Conference. Migration & Refuge	TX	848
U.S. Congress. Congressional Border Caucus	DC	258
U.S. Congress. Senate Border Caucus	DC	261
Unitarian Church. Sanctuary Comm.	CT	218
Unitarian Society of Sacramento. Sanctuary Co	CA	122
Unitarian Universalist Church	CA	61
Univ. Church. Sanctuary Project	IL	377
Univ. of California. School of Law. Immigrati	CA	39
Univ. of Florida. Caribbean Migration Progra	FL	284
Univ. Unitarian Church. Sanctuary Comm.	WA	926
Valley Immigrants Rights Center	CA	105
Valley Religious Task Force on Central Amer.	AZ	15
Washington Office on Haiti	DC	277
Wheadon United Methodist Church. Sanctuary	IL	383
Woodrow Wilson Intl. Center	DC	278
World Relief	TX	869

Europe

Amer. Comm. on Italian Migration	NY	632
Amer. Fed. of Jews from Central Europe	NY	635

Amer. Fund for Czechoslovak Refugees	NY	637
Amer. Fund for Slovak Refugees	NJ	596
Amer. Fund for Slovak Refugees	NY	607
Amer. Romanian Comm. for Assistance to Ref	NY	630
Baron de Hirsch Fund	NY	640
Blue Card	NY	641
Bridge Refugee Services	TN	807
Bulgarian Natl. Comm.	NJ	582
Cambridge Organization of Portuguese-Amer.	MA	468
Catholic Social Ministries. Refugee Resettleme	NC	699
Catholic Social Services. Refugee Program	AL	3
Center for Applied Linguistics. Refugee Servic	DC	231
Christian Council of Metropolitan Atlanta. Ref	GA	324
Conference on Jewish Material Claims Agains	NY	646
Diocesan Refugee Coordinator	MI	493
Fed. of Italian-Amer. Societies	NY	606
Fed. of Jewish Agencies of Greater Philadelphi	PA	775
Immigrants Assistance Center	MA	480
Iowa Dept. of Human Services. Bureau of Refug	IA	408
Irish Immigration Reform Movement	NY	629
Jewish Family & Children Services	CA	144
Jewish Family and Children's Service	OH	736
Jewish Family and Children's Services	IN	403
Jewish Family Service	CT	215
Jewish Family Service	FL	314
Jewish Family Service	NY	688
Jewish Family Service	PA	787
Jewish Family Service. Refugee Resettlement P	TX	866
Jewish Family Services	WI	951
Jewish Family Services of Greater Orlando	FL	322
Jewish Philanthropic Fund of 1933	NY	658
Lutheran Social Services of Iowa	IA	409
Mohawk Valley Resource Center for Refugees	NY	693
Mutual Aid Assoc. of the New Polish Immigrat	IL	368
Natl. Slavic Conv.	MD	446
Polish Amer. Immigration and Relief Comm.	NY	670
Polish Amer. Immigration Relief Comm.	IL	370
Polish and Slavic Center. Refugee Assistance	NY	617
Rav Tov. Intl. Jewish Rescue Organization	NY	618
Research Foundation for Jewish Immigration	NY	671
Somerville Portuguese Amer. League	MA	481
Tolstoy Foundation	MI	498
Vermont Catholic Charities. Refugee Resettlem	VT	890
Vietnamese Evangelical Church	MN	525

Middle East

Agudath Israel of Amer.	NY	631
Amer. Arab Anti-Discrimination Comm.	DC	223
Assyrian Universal Alliance	MI	512
Baron de Hirsch Fund	NY	640
Catholic Charities. Refugee Service Program	PA	783
Catholic Social Ministries. Refugee Resettleme	NC	699
Fed. of Jewish Agencies of Greater Philadelphi	PA	775
Hebrew Immigrant Aid Society	NY	651
Human Rights Advocates Intl.	NJ	579
Human Rights Advocates Intl.	NY	652
Jewish Family and Children's Service	OH	736

Jewish Family Service	NJ	575
Jewish Family Service Agency of Central New	NJ	580
Jewish Family Service of Broward County	FL	285
Jewish Family Service of MetroWest	NJ	581
Jewish Family Service. Immigration & Resettl	NM	599
Jewish Family Service. Refugee Resettlement P	TX	866
Jewish Family Service. Resettlement Program	CA	128
Jewish Family Services	FL	318
Jewish Family Services	GA	328
Jewish Family Services	NC	697
Jewish Family Services	UT	884
Jewish Social Services	WI	943
Jewish Voc. Service	OH	713
Natl. Council of Jewish Women. Rescue & Mi	FL	305
New York Assoc. for New Amer.	NY	663
Rav Tov. Intl. Jewish Rescue Organization	NY	618
United Nations. Relief and Works Agency for	NY	681

Oceania

Amer. Friends Service Comm. Immigration Pro	CA	108
Asian Counseling and Referral Service	WA	916
Vietnamese Community in Virginia	VA	905

South America

Annunciation House	TX	844
Archdiocese of New York. Office for Immigrant	NY	638
Cambridge Organization of Portuguese-Amer.	MA	468
Centro Legal	MN	531
Christian Community Service Agency	FL	297
Commission for the Study of Intl. Migration a	DC	234
Hispanic Immigration Counseling Program	WA	920
Human Services Assoc.	CA	31
Immigration Services of Santa Rosa	CA	131
Inmigracion Latina Foundation	FL	302
Somerville Portuguese Amer. League	MA	481
South and Meso-Amer. Indian Information Cen	CA	34
TECHO Central Amer. Education Center	AZ	20
Woodrow Wilson Intl. Center	DC	278

Southeast Asia

Agudath Israel of Amer.	NY	631
Armenian Assembly of Amer.	DC	228
Baron de Hirsch Fund	NY	640
Fed. of Jewish Agencies of Greater Philadelphi	PA	775
Fresno Ecumenical Resettlement Project	CA	46
Hebrew Immigrant Aid Society	NY	651
Hebrew Immigrant Aid Society	PA	776
Jewish Family & Children Services	CA	144
Jewish Family and Child Service	OR	754
Jewish Family and Children's Agency	PA	777

Jewish Family and Children's Service	MA	466
Jewish Family and Children's Service	NJ	571
Jewish Family and Children's Service	OH	736
Jewish Family and Children's Service. Resettle	MN	521
Jewish Family and Children's Services	IN	403
Jewish Family and Children's Services	TX	847
Jewish Family and Community Services	FL	291
Jewish Family Service	AZ	17
Jewish Family Service	FL	314
Jewish Family Service	NJ	574
Jewish Family Service	NJ	575
Jewish Family Service	NY	688
Jewish Family Service	PA	785
Jewish Family Service	PA	787
Jewish Family Service	TN	813
Jewish Family Service	TX	876
Jewish Family Service	VA	904
Jewish Family Service Agency of Central New	NJ	580
Jewish Family Service Assoc.	OH	719
Jewish Family Service of Broward County	FL	285
Jewish Family Service of Delaware Valley	NJ	591
Jewish Family Service of Greater Springfield	MA	483
Jewish Family Service of MetroWest	NJ	581
Jewish Family Service of Somerset County	NJ	588
Jewish Family Service. Immigration & Resettl	NM	599
Jewish Family Service. Refugee Resettlement P	TX	866
Jewish Family Service. Refugee Services	CA	79
Jewish Family Service. Resettlement Program	CA	128
Jewish Family Service. Resettlement Program	FL	306
Jewish Family Services	FL	318
Jewish Family Services	GA	328
Jewish Family Services	ME	440
Jewish Family Services	NC	697
Jewish Family Services	UT	884
Jewish Family Services	WI	951
Jewish Family Services. Refugee Services	IL	362
Jewish Fed. of Palm Beach County	FL	320
Jewish Social Services	TX	852
Jewish Social Services	WI	943
Jewish Social Services Agency	MD	451
Jewish Voc. Service	NJ	577
Jewish Voc. Service	OH	713
Jewish Voc. Service & Community Workshop	MI	515
Natl. Council of Jewish Women. Immigration	MA	487
Natl. Slavic Conv.	MD	446
New York Assoc. for New Amer.	NY	663
Rav Tov. Intl. Jewish Rescue Organization	NY	618
Ukrainian Research Foundation	CO	206

USSR

Agudath Israel of Amer.	NY	631
Armenian Assembly of Amer.	DC	228
Baron de Hirsch Fund	NY	640
Fed. of Jewish Agencies of Greater Philadelphi	PA	775
Fresno Ecumenical Resettlement Project	CA	46

Hebrew Immigrant Aid Society	NY	651
Hebrew Immigrant Aid Society	PA	776
Jewish Family & Children Services	CA	144
Jewish Family and Child Service	OR	754
Jewish Family and Children's Agency	PA	777
Jewish Family and Children's Service	MA	466
Jewish Family and Children's Service	NJ	571
Jewish Family and Children's Service	OH	736
Jewish Family and Children's Service. Resettle	MN	521
Jewish Family and Children's Services	IN	403
Jewish Family and Children's Services	TX	847
Jewish Family and Community Services	FL	291
Jewish Family Service	AZ	17
Jewish Family Service	FL	314
Jewish Family Service	NJ	574
Jewish Family Service	NJ	575
Jewish Family Service	NY	688
Jewish Family Service	PA	785
Jewish Family Service	PA	787
Jewish Family Service	TN	813
Jewish Family Service	TX	876
Jewish Family Service	VA	904
Jewish Family Service Agency of Central New	NJ	580
Jewish Family Service Assoc.	OH	719
Jewish Family Service of Broward County	FL	285
Jewish Family Service of Delaware Valley	NJ	591
Jewish Family Service of Greater Springfield	MA	483
Jewish Family Service of MetroWest	NJ	581
Jewish Family Service of Somerset County	NJ	588
Jewish Family Service. Immigration & Resettl	NM	599
Jewish Family Service. Refugee Resettlement P	TX	866
Jewish Family Service. Refugee Services	CA	79
Jewish Family Service. Resettlement Program	CA	128
Jewish Family Service. Resettlement Program	FL	306
Jewish Family Services	FL	318
Jewish Family Services	GA	328
Jewish Family Services	ME	440
Jewish Family Services	NC	697
Jewish Family Services	UT	884
Jewish Family Services	WI	951
Jewish Family Services. Refugee Services	IL	362
Jewish Fed. of Palm Beach County	FL	320
Jewish Social Services	TX	852
Jewish Social Services	WI	943
Jewish Social Services Agency	MD	451
Jewish Voc. Service	NJ	577
Jewish Voc. Service	OH	713
Jewish Voc. Service & Community Workshop	MI	515
Natl. Council of Jewish Women. Immigration	MA	487
Natl. Slavic Conv.	MD	446
New York Assoc. for New Amer.	NY	663
Rav Tov. Intl. Jewish Rescue Organization	NY	618
Ukrainian Research Foundation	CO	206

World

Access	CA	123
Adelphi Univ. Refugee Assistance Program	NY	626
Adventist Community Services	DC	222
AFL/CIO Immigration Project	CA	64
African Amer. Immigration Service	NY	609
Alabama Baptist State Conv.	AL	4
Alabama Dept. of Human Resources. Refugee R	AL	5
All Culture Friendship Center Refugee & Immi	CA	55
All Culture Friendship Center Refugee & Immi	CA	65
Amer. Baptist Churches. Immigration & Refug	PA	788
Amer. Civic Assoc.	NY	608
Amer. Council for Nationalities Service	NY	633
Amer. Council on Intl. Personnel	NY	634
Amer. Friends Service Comm. Immigration Pro	CA	108
Amer. Immigrant Foundation	CA	164
Amer. Immigration Lawyers Assoc. Pro Bono	FL	294
Amer. Immigration Lawyers Assoc. Texas Cha	OK	737
Amer. Public Welfare Assoc. Task Force on Im	DC	225
Amer. Red Cross. Intl. Services	DC	226
Amer. Refugee Comm.	IL	381
Americanization League	NY	691
Amer. For Immigration Control	DC	227
Amer. for Intl. Aid	GA	337
Amnesty Intl.	CA	66
Amnesty Intl. USA	CA	132
Archdiocese of Chicago. Immigration Services	IL	351
Archdiocese of Detroit. Office of Refugee Reset	MI	490
Archdiocese of New York. Refugee Resettlemen	NY	639
Archdiocese of Portland. Immigration Counseli	OR	752
Arizona Center for Immigrants	AZ	7
Arizona Dept. of Economic Security. Refugee	AZ	8
Arkansas Dept. of Human Services. Refugee Re	AR	25
Asheville Presbytery. Refugee Resettlement Of	NC	702
Asian Pacific Amer. Legal Center of Southern	CA	67
Associated Catholic Charities	LA	429
Associated Catholic Charities. Refugee Employ	MD	441
Balch Institute for Ethnic Studies	PA	772
Baptist Conv. of New Mexico	NM	597
Baptist General Conv. of Oklahoma	OK	738
Bridge Refugee Services	TN	807
Brooklyn Legal Services Corp.	NY	610
California Dept. of Social Services. Office of	CA	114
California Southern Baptist Conv. Refugee Res	CA	43
Cambridge and Somerville Legal Services Immi	MA	467
Catholic Charities	MA	486
Catholic Charities	NE	558
Catholic Charities	NY	684
Catholic Charities Bureau	IN	393
Catholic Charities Bureau. Resettlement Progra	WI	956
Catholic Charities Migration Office	NY	604
Catholic Charities Refugee & Immigration Ser	MA	458
Catholic Charities. Immigration & Refugee Di	CA	68
Catholic Charities. Immigration & Refugee Pro	CA	174
Catholic Charities. Immigration & Refugee Ser	PA	765
Catholic Charities. Immigration Counseling C	CA	161
Catholic Charities. Immigration Counseling Se	TX	831
Catholic Charities. Immigration Program	CA	134
Catholic Charities. Immigration Project	CA	94
Catholic Charities. Immigration Project of Im	FL	286
Catholic Charities. Immigration Services	CA	106
Catholic Charities. Migration & Refugee Servi	MN	528
Catholic Charities. Migration and Refugee Ser	CT	211
Catholic Charities. Migration and Refugee Ser	TX	849
Catholic Charities. Refugee Assistance	IN	396
Catholic Charities. Refugee Assistance Progra	NY	622
Catholic Charities. Refugee Office	IN	394
Catholic Charities. Refugee Program	KS	416
Catholic Charities. Refugee Resettlement Offic	CA	182
Catholic Charities. Refugee Resettlement Offic	FL	289
Catholic Charities. Refugee Resettlement Progr	CA	35
Catholic Charities. Refugee Resettlement Progr	DE	220
Catholic Charities. Refugee Service Center	DC	230
Catholic Charities. Refugee Services	KY	423
Catholic Charities. Resettlement Program	CA	44
Catholic Charities. Resettlement Services	CA	166
Catholic Charities. Resettlement Services	TX	858
Catholic Community Services of Nevada. Immi	NV	564
Catholic Community Services. Migration & Re	LA	424
Catholic Community Services. Office of Migra	NJ	586
Catholic Community Services. Office of Migra	WV	936
Catholic Community Services. Refugee Resettl	FL	295
Catholic Community Services. Resettlement &	CA	125
Catholic Family and Child Service	WA	935
Catholic Family and Child Services. Family Re	WA	910
Catholic Family Center. Refugee Dept.	NY	686
Catholic Family Services. Refugee & Citizensh	TX	818
Catholic Human Development Office. Refugee	MI	502
Catholic Immigration & Resettlement Office	CA	177
Catholic Immigration and Refugee Services	CO	199
Catholic Immigration Services	FL	296
Catholic Migration & Refugee Services	OR	748
Catholic Migration & Refugee Services	VA	893
Catholic Migration and Refugee Office	NY	612
Catholic Migration and Refugee Resettlement	OH	721
Catholic Migration and Refugee Service	NV	566
Catholic Migration and Refugee Service	OK	746
Catholic Migration and Refugee Services	ID	349
Catholic Migration and Refugee Services	NJ	573
Catholic Migration Office	NY	605
Catholic Refugee Services	WA	917
Catholic Refugee Services	WA	933
Catholic Resettlement and Immigration Office	IA	406
Catholic Resettlement Center	IL	353
Catholic Resettlement Services	OR	753
Catholic Services for Immigrants	TX	874
Catholic Social Agency. Migration Services	PA	761
Catholic Social Ministries. Migration & Reset	OK	739
Catholic Social Service	IL	350
Catholic Social Service Bureau. Refugee Resett	KY	420
Catholic Social Service of Phoenix	AZ	9
Catholic Social Service. Refugee Office	NC	696
Catholic Social Service. Refugee Resettlement	FL	309
Catholic Social Service. Refugee Resettlement	CA	115
Catholic Social Service. Resettlement Program	CO	207
Catholic Social Service. Resettlement Program	OH	714
Catholic Social Services	AK	6

Catholic Social Services	FL	316	Diocesan Migrant & Refugee Services	TX	845
Catholic Social Services	IN	398	Diocesan Refugee Resettlement Program	ME	439
Catholic Social Services	KS	413	Diocese of Nashville. Refugee Resettlement Pr	TN	812
Catholic Social Services	LA	427	Diocese of Oregon	OR	751
Catholic Social Services	MI	509	Diocese of Raleigh. Refugee Resettlement Offi	NC	704
Catholic Social Services	MS	540	Diocese of Rhode Island	RI	795
Catholic Social Services	OH	729	Diocese of Richmond. Office of Refugee Resetl	VA	909
Catholic Social Services	OH	731	Diocese of Richmond. Office of Refugee Resett	VA	901
Catholic Social Services	PA	763	Diocese of Springfield. Refugee Resettlement	MA	482
Catholic Social Services	PA	786	Disciples of Christ. Refugee & Immigration M	IN	399
Catholic Social Services	RI	794	District of Columbia Dept. of Human Services.	DC	235
Catholic Social Services	WI	942	Don Bosco Community Center	MO	546
Catholic Social Services	WY	957	Downtown Legalization Project	CA	72
Catholic Social Services Bureau	KY	418	East Central Illinois Refugee Mutual Assistanc	IL	391
Catholic Social Services. Immigration Services	CA	29	Ecumenical Refugee Council	WI	948
Catholic Social Services. Migration & Refugee	PA	773	Ecumenical Refugee Resettlement Services	VA	903
Catholic Social Services. Migration & Refugee	AZ	16	Ecumenical Refugee Services	CO	202
Catholic Social Services. Migration & Refugee	OH	717	Ellis Island Immigration Museum	NY	647
Catholic Social Services. Refugee and Immigra	FL	311	Episcopal Diocese of Minnesota. Refugee Rese	MN	520
Catholic Social Services. Refugee Program	AL	3	Episcopal Diocese of North Carolina. Refugee	NC	705
Catholic Social Services. Refugee Resettlement	CA	179	Episcopal Migration Ministries	NY	648
Catholic Social Services. Refugee Resettlement	GA	323	Episcopal Refugee and Migration Comm.	NH	570
Catholic Social Services. Refugee Resettlement	NM	598	Episcopal Refugee Resettlement Commission	IN	400
Catholic Social Services. Refugee Social Servi	FL	312	Episcopal Social Ministries	MD	442
Catholic Social Services. Resettlement Progra	CA	87	Episcopal Social Service	CT	208
Center for Immigrants Rights	NY	642	Evangelical Crusade of Fishers of Men	NY	614
Center for Immigration Studies	DC	232	Experiment in Intl. Living	VT	888
Center for Migration Studies	NY	689	Faith Lutheran Church	FL	308
Central Amer. Refugee Project	OK	740	First Lutheran Church	FL	283
Central Kentucky Jewish Assoc.	KY	421	First Unitarian Church	CA	183
Centro de Ayuda Para Immigrantes	TX	860	Florida Baptist Conv.	FL	290
Chicago Commission on Human Relations. Re	IL	354	Florida Council of Churches. Refugee Program	FL	310
Chicago Comm. on Immigrant Protection	IL	355	Florida Dept. of Health and Rehabilitation Ser	FL	315
Child and Family Service. Refugee Employmen	HI	340	Florida Rural Legal Services	FL	281
Chinatown Service Center	CA	70	Foreign-Born Information and Referral Networ	MD	448
Christian Community Service Agency	FL	297	Fort Worth Independent School District. Survi	TX	850
Christian Council of Metropolitan Atlanta. Ref	GA	324	Freedom Flight Refugee Center	MI	504
Christian Reformed World Relief Comm.	MI	503	Fresno Ecumenical Resettlement Project	CA	46
Christian Refugee Outreach	VA	894	Friends of the Third World	IN	395
Church of the Brethren. Refugee Resettlement	MD	450	General Conference of Seventh-Day Adventists	DC	238
Church Refugee Center	NY	643	George Washington Univ. Natl. Law Center. I	DC	239
Church World Service. Immigration & Refugee	NY	644	Georgia Baptist Conv. Language Missions Dep	GA	325
Church World Service. Refugee Program	FL	298	Georgia Dept. of Human Resources. Refugee He	GA	326
Coalition for Immigrant and Refugee Rights &	CA	136	Georgia Dept. of Human Resources. Special Pr	GA	327
Colorado Refugee and Immigrant Services Prog	CO	201	Good Samaritan Community Center	CA	138
Columbia Univ. School of Law. Immigration L	NY	645	Greater Boston Legal Services	MA	460
Comm. in Defense of Immigrant Rights	WA	919	Greater Hartford Jewish Fed.	CT	216
Comm. to Defend Immigrant & Refugee Rights	CA	95	Hawaii Dept. of Labor & Industrial Relations.	HI	341
Community Legal Services	CA	36	Hebrew Immigrant Aid Society	NY	651
Community Legal Services	CA	92	Hebrew Immigrant Aid Society	PA	776
Community Legal Services	PA	774	Hebrew Immigrant Aid Society of Baltimore	MD	443
Connecticut Dept. of Human Resources. State	CT	212	Holt Intl. Children's Services	OR	749
Council of Churches. Refugee Resettlement Pro	MO	552	Holy Cross Mission	CA	184
Cultural Survival	MA	471	Hood River Valley Immigration Project	OR	750
Dallas-Fort Worth Refugee Interagency	TX	832	Houston Metropolitan Ministries	TX	861
Datacenter	CA	96	Human Rights Advocates Intl.	NJ	579
Delaware Dept. of Health & Social Services. D	DE	219	Human Rights Advocates Intl.	NY	652
Delaware Dept. of Justice. Service for Foreign	DE	221	Human Rights Internet	MA	473

Idaho Dept. of Health and Welfare. Div. of Fie	ID	347	Intl. Rescue Comm.	CA	142
Illinois Bureau of Naturalization Services	IL	389	Intl. Rescue Comm.	CA	162
Illinois Conference of Churches. Refugee Immi	IL	390	Intl. Rescue Comm.	CA	168
Illinois Conference of Churches. Refugee Rese	IL	358	Intl. Rescue Comm.	CA	185
Immigrant Assistance Line	CA	139	Intl. Rescue Comm.	DC	243
Immigrant Legal Resource Center	CA	41	Intl. Rescue Comm.	FL	303
Immigrant Legal Resource Center	CA	140	Intl. Rescue Comm.	GA	335
Immigrant Students Project of the Natl. Coaliti	MA	461	Intl. Rescue Comm.	NJ	595
Immigrants Assistance Center	MA	480	Intl. Rescue Comm.	NY	656
Immigration Advocacy Service	NE	561	Intl. Rescue Comm.	TX	833
Immigration and Legalization Service	TX	824	Intl. Rescue Comm.	WA	921
Immigration Assistance Service	NJ	583	Intl. Service Center	PA	766
Immigration Counseling Center	TX	862	Intl. Social Service. Amer. Branch	NY	657
Immigration Counseling Migration & Refugee	TX	851	Jesuit Refugee Service	DC	244
Immigration History Society	MN	533	Jewish Family & Children Services	CA	144
Immigration Law Project	TX	875	Jewish Family & Children's Service	AZ	12
Immigration Project	CA	194	Jewish Family and Children's Service	CO	203
Impact	CA	126	Jewish Family and Children's Services	IN	403
Indiana Council of Churches	IN	401	Jewish Family and Community Services	FL	291
Indiana Dept. of Welfare. Policy & Program De	IN	402	Jewish Family and Counseling Service	NJ	572
Inland Counties Legal Services	CA	111	Jewish Family and Voc. Service	KY	422
Inter-Agency Council for Immigrant Services	HI	342	Jewish Family Service	AZ	17
InterAction (Amer. Council for Voluntary Intl.	NY	653	Jewish Family Service	CA	51
Intercultural Action Center	CA	178	Jewish Family Service	CA	99
Intermountain Health Care. Refugee Clinic	UT	883	Jewish Family Service	FL	314
Intl. Catholic Migration Commission	DC	242	Jewish Family Service	LA	436
Intl. Center	NH	569	Jewish Family Service	MN	535
Intl. Center of the Capital Region. Refugee As	NY	602	Jewish Family Service	NY	624
Intl. Community Services	TX	865	Jewish Family Service	OH	712
Intl. Immigrants Foundation	NY	654	Jewish Family Service	PA	785
Intl. Institute	OH	711	Jewish Family Service	RI	797
Intl. Institute of Buffalo	NY	623	Jewish Family Service	TN	813
Intl. Institute of Connecticut	CT	209	Jewish Family Service	WA	922
Intl. Institute of Connecticut	CT	213	Jewish Family Service Agency	NV	565
Intl. Institute of Erie	PA	764	Jewish Family Service of Broward County	FL	285
Intl. Institute of Flint	MI	499	Jewish Family Service of Detroit	MI	514
Intl. Institute of Los Angeles	CA	191	Jewish Family Service of Metro West	NJ	589
Intl. Institute of Los Angeles. Immigrant & Re	CA	76	Jewish Family Service of MetroWest	NJ	581
Intl. Institute of Los Angeles. Refugee Relocat	CA	158	Jewish Family Service of North Middlesex Co	NJ	578
Intl. Institute of Lowell	MA	479	Jewish Family Service of Raritan Valley	NJ	576
Intl. Institute of Metro Detroit	MI	495	Jewish Family Service. Refugee Services	CA	79
Intl. Institute of Metropolitan St. Louis	MO	550	Jewish Family Service. Resettlement Program	FL	306
Intl. Institute of Minnesota	MN	534	Jewish Family Service. Resettlement Program	MD	444
Intl. Institute of New Jersey	NJ	584	Jewish Family Service. Resettlement Services	CT	210
Intl. Institute of Northwest Indiana	IN	397	Jewish Family Services	FL	318
Intl. Institute of Rhose Island	RI	796	Jewish Family Services	GA	328
Intl. Institute of San Francisco	CA	141	Jewish Family Services	NC	697
Intl. Institute of the East Bay	CA	98	Jewish Family Services	TX	834
Intl. Institute of Toledo	OH	732	Jewish Family Services	UT	884
Intl. Institute of Wisconsin	WI	950	Jewish Family Services of Greater Orlando	FL	322
Intl. Ladies Garment Workers Union. Immigrat	CA	77	Jewish Family Services. Refugee Services	IL	362
Intl. Ladies Garment Workers Union. Immigrat	NY	655	Jewish Fed. of Palm Beach County	FL	320
Intl. Ladies Garment Workers Union. Immigrat	IL	359	Jewish Social Services Agency	MD	451
Intl. Refugee Center	IL	360	Jewish Voc. & Career Counseling Service	CA	145
Intl. Rescue Comm.	CA	49	Jewish Voc. Service	NJ	577
Intl. Rescue Comm.	CA	78	Kansas Dept. of Social & Rehabilitation Servi	KS	415
Intl. Rescue Comm.	CA	118	Kentucky Cabinet for Human Resources. Office	KY	419
Intl. Rescue Comm.	CA	127	Khemara Buddhikarma - The Cambodian Buddh	CA	59

Khmer Society of San Antonio. Refugee SOS	TX	877
Korean Amer. Community Services	MD	454
Lao Family Community	CA	91
Lao Family Community	CA	100
Lao Family Community	CA	119
Lao Family Community	CA	169
Lawyers Comm. for Human Rights. Political A	NY	659
Legal Aid of Western Missouri	MO	547
Legal Aid of Western Oklahoma	OK	745
Legal Aid Society	FL	321
Legal Services Center	MA	477
Legal Services Center for Immigrants	IL	364
Legal Services of Northern California	CA	120
Long Island Refugee Resettlement Program	NY	616
Los Angeles County Bar Assoc. Immigration L	CA	80
Louisiana Dept. of Health & Human Resources	LA	432
Louisiana Dept. of Health & Human Services.	LA	425
Lutheran Child & Family Services of Massach	MA	485
Lutheran Child and Family Services	IL	365
Lutheran Children and Family Service	PA	778
Lutheran Church. Synod Board of Social Minis	MO	551
Lutheran Family Service. Refugee Services	OR	755
Lutheran Family Services. Refugee Resettleme	NC	700
Lutheran Immigration & Refugee Services	DC	245
Lutheran Immigration and Refugee Service	NY	660
Lutheran Immigration and Refugee Service	TX	867
Lutheran Ministries of Florida	FL	307
Lutheran Ministries of Florida. Refugee Resett	FL	319
Lutheran Ministries of Georgia	GA	329
Lutheran Refugee and Immigration Services	NJ	592
Lutheran Refugee Resettlement	CO	204
Lutheran Social Ministry of the Southwest. Re	AZ	13
Lutheran Social Services	MN	516
Lutheran Social Services of Kansas and Oklaho	KS	417
Lutheran Social Services of Michigan. Dept. o	MI	510
Lutheran Social Services of Michigan. Refugee	MI	507
Lutheran Social Services of Minnesota. Refuge	MN	522
Lutheran Social Services of North Dakota. Ref	ND	709
Lutheran Social Services of Northeast Florida.	FL	292
Lutheran Social Services of Northern Californi	CA	146
Lutheran Social Services of South Dakota. Ref	SD	805
Lutheran Social Services of Wisconsin & Upp	WI	953
Lutheran Social Services. Immigration & Refu	CA	81
Maine Annual Conference of the United Metho	ME	438
Maine Dept. of Human Services. Bureau of Soc	ME	437
Maryland Dept. of Human Resources. State Re	MD	445
Massachusetts Office for Refugees and Immigr	MA	463
Mecklenburg Presbytery Refugee Resettlement	NC	698
Mennonite Central Comm. Immigration & Ref	PA	760
Mennonite Immigration and Refugee Services	DC	246
Metropolitan Social Services. Refugee Program	TN	814
Miami Presbytery	OH	730
Michigan Dept. of Social Services. Office of R	MI	496
Mid-Cumberland Refugee Assistance Ministry	TN	815
Middlesex County Legal Services Corp.	NJ	585
Midwest Immigrant Rights Center	IL	367
Migration & Refugee Services	SC	802
Migration and Refugee Services Office	NJ	593
Minnesota - Wisconsin Southern Baptist Conv	MN	526
Minnesota Council of Churches. Refugee Prog	MN	537
Minnesota Dept. of Human Services. Refugee	MN	538
Mission Community Legal Defense	CA	147
Mississippi Baptist Conv. Language Missions	MS	542
Missouri Div. of Family Services. Refugee As	MO	544
Montana Assoc. for Refugee Services	MT	554
Montana Dept. of Family Services. Office of R	MT	557
Multicultural Immigration Center	NY	661
Na Loio No Na Kanaka. Lawyers for the Peopl	HI	345
Natl. Assoc. of Evangelicals. Immigration Pro	FL	304
Natl. Center For Immigrants' Rights	CA	82
Natl. Council of Jewish Women. Rescue & Mi	FL	305
Natl. Immigration Project of the Natl. Lawyers	MA	464
Natl. Immigration, Refugee, and Citizenship F	DC	247
Natl. Network for Immigrant & Refugee Right	CA	101
Nationalities Service Center	PA	769
Nationalities Service Center	PA	780
Nationalities Service of Central California	CA	50
Nationalities Services Center	OH	718
Naturalization Project	LA	434
Nebraska Dept. of Social Services. Refugee Af	NE	560
Nevada Dept. of Human Resources. State Refug	NV	563
New Hampshire Office of Refugee Resettlemen	NH	568
New Hope Presbytery	NC	694
New Jersey Dept. of Human Services. State Re	NJ	594
New Mexico Dept. of Human Services. Social	NM	601
New Orleans Legal Assistance Corp.	LA	435
New York Circus	NY	664
New York City. Office of Immigrant Affairs	NY	665
New York Dept. of Social Services. State Refu	NY	603
New York State Assembly. Task Force on New	NY	666
North Carolina Baptist State Conv.	NC	695
North Carolina Dept. of Human Resources. Fa	NC	706
North Carolina Refugee Health Program	NC	707
North Dakota Dept. of Human Services. Refug	ND	708
North Manhattan Coalition for Immigrants' Ri	NY	667
North Texas Immigration Coalition	TX	836
Northern Virginia Family Service. Multicultura	VA	898
O.L.A. Raza	CA	109
Ohio Council of Churches. Refugee Services	OH	724
Ohio Dept. of Human Services. Program Devel	OH	725
Ohio State Conv. of Baptists	OH	726
Oklahoma Dept. of Human Services. Refugee U	OK	742
One Stop Immigration & Educational Center	CA	83
Oregon Dept. of Human Resources. Refugee Pr	OR	759
Partnership for Human Development. Resettle	TX	826
Pennsylvania Dept. of Public Welfare. Office	PA	767
Peylim	NY	668
Philadelphia Refugee Service Center	PA	781
Plattsburg Interfaith Council	NY	685
Presbyterian Synod of Southern California and	CA	84
Presbytery of Long Island	NY	625
Presbytery of Southern Louisiana	LA	426
PRIME Ecumenical Commitment to Refugees	PA	762
Project Deliverance	OH	733
Reformed Church in Amer. Refugee Program	MI	505
Refugee and Immigrant Multi-Service Center	WA	930

Refugee Employment Assistance Project	CA	148
Refugee Employment Center	MI	511
Refugee Policy Group	DC	249
Refugee Resettlement Comm.	CA	90
Refugee Resettlement Office	MO	545
Refugee Resettlement Program	AR	26
Refugee Services	MI	508
Refugee Voices	DC	250
Refugee Women in Development	DC	251
Refugees Intl.	DC	252
Rhode Island Dept. of Human Services. State R	RI	799
Rochester Refugee Services	MN	527
San Francisco Lawyers' Comm. Immigrant & R	CA	150
Santa Clara County Health Dept. Refugee Heal	CA	163
Save the Children. Refugee Child Care Assista	GA	330
Sepulveda Unitarian Universalist Society	CA	180
South Carolina Dept. of Social Services. Refu	SC	803
South Dakota Dept. of Social Services. Refuge	SD	804
South Texas Immigration Council	TX	856
Southern Arizona Legal Aid	AZ	19
Southern Baptist Immigration and Refugee Re	GA	331
Southern Methodist Univ. Law School. Politic	TX	838
Spokane Bar Assoc. Pro Bono Program	WA	931
Sponsors Organized to Assist Refugees	ID	348
Sponsors Organized to Assist Refugees	OR	756
St. Anselm's Immigrant & Refugee Communit	CA	52
St. Paul's United Methodist Church. Refugee P	NV	567
Sunyvale Community Services	CA	188
Syracuse Interreligious Council. Refugee Assis	NY	692
Tacoma Community House	WA	934
Tennessee Dept. of Human Services. Refugee P	TN	816
Texas Dept. of Human Service. Refugee Progra	TX	825
Texas Rural Legal Aid	TX	843
Tolstoy Foundation	AZ	14
Tolstoy Foundation	CA	192
Tolstoy Foundation	MI	498
Tolstoy Foundation	NY	673
Training Program in Human Services for Emig	NY	674
Traveler and Immigrants Aid	IL	375
Travelers Aid Intl. Institute. Refugee Resource	OH	716
Travelers Aid Society	DC	255
Tressler Lutheran Services. Refugee Services P	PA	770
U. S. Catholic Conference. Migration & Refug	NY	675
U.S. Catholic Conference. Migration & Refug	DC	256
U.S. Catholic Conference. Migration & Refug	CA	154
U.S. Catholic Conference. Migration & Refug	DC	257
U.S. Catholic Conference. Migration & Refug	NY	676
U.S. Catholic Conference. Migration & Refug	TX	848
U.S. Congress. Congressional Human Rights	DC	259
U.S. Congress. House Comm. on the Judiciary	DC	260
U.S. Congress. Senate Comm. on the Judiciar	DC	262
U.S. Congress. Senate Human Rights Caucus	DC	263
U.S. Dept. of Health & Human Services. Fami	CA	155
U.S. Dept. of Health & Human Services. Fami	CO	205
U.S. Dept. of Health & Human Services. Fami	GA	332
U.S. Dept. of Health & Human Services. Fami	IL	376
U.S. Dept. of Health & Human Services. Fami	MA	465
U.S. Dept. of Health & Human Services. Fami	MO	548
U.S. Dept. of Health & Human Services. Fami	NY	677
U.S. Dept. of Health & Human Services. Fami	PA	782
U.S. Dept. of Health & Human Services. Fami	TX	839
U.S. Dept. of Health & Human Services. Fami	WA	925
U.S. Dept. of Health and Human Services. Fam	DC	264
U.S. Dept. of Health and Human Services. Pub	MD	452
U.S. Dept. of Justice. Executive Office for Imm	VA	899
U.S. Dept. of Justice. Immigration and Natura	DC	265
U.S. Dept. of Labor. Bureau of Intl. Labor Aff	DC	267
U.S. Dept. of Labor. Foreign Labor Certificati	DC	268
U.S. Dept. of State. Bureau for Refugee Progra	DC	269
U.S. Dept. of State. Bureau of Consular Affair	DC	270
U.S. Dept. of State. Bureau of Human Rights a	DC	271
U.S. Dept. of State. Coordinator for Refugee A	DC	272
Unitarian Church of Arlington	VA	896
United Cambodian Community	CA	62
United Catholic Social Services. Refugee Rese	NE	562
United Church Board for World Ministries. Re	NY	678
United Methodist Church. Refugee Concerns C	CA	156
United Methodist Comm. on Relief. Refugee S	NY	679
United Nations High Commissioner for Refug	DC	274
United Nations. High Commissioner for Refug	NY	680
United Refugee Council	NY	621
U.S. Catholic Conference	IL	388
U.S. Comm. for Refugees	DC	275
Univ. of California. School of Law. Immigrat	CA	39
Utah Dept. of Social Services. Refugee & Alie	UT	885
Utah Immigration Project	UT	886
Valley Immigrants Rights Center	CA	105
Vermont State Refugee Coordinator	VT	891
Vietnamese Amer. Assoc. Refugee Center	OK	743
Vietnamese Amer. Cultural Alliance of Colora	CO	198
Vietnamese Community in Virginia	VA	905
Virginia Baptist General Board. Div. of Missi	VA	906
Virginia Council of Churches. Refugee Progra	VA	907
Virginia Dept. of Social Services. State Refug	VA	908
Washington Assoc. of Churches. Immigration	WA	928
Washington Assoc. of Churches. Refugee Res	WA	932
Washington Bureau of Refugee Assistance	WA	914
Washington Lawyers' Comm. for Civil Rights	DC	276
West Virginia Dept. of Human Services	WV	937
Westside Legal Services	CA	176
Wisconsin Div. of Community Services. Refu	WI	946
World Relief	CA	54
World Relief	CA	157
World Relief	CA	187
World Relief	DC	279
World Relief	FL	282
World Relief	GA	333
World Relief	NY	683
World Relief	NC	701
World Relief	TN	817
World Relief	TX	853
World Relief	TX	869
World Relief	WA	929
World Relief. Immigration Services	IL	379
Wyoming Dept. of Health & Social Services.	WY	958
YMCA Intl. Services	TX	870

YMCA. Refugee Resettlement Services   IL   380

Index V

Religious Affiliation

Baptist

Alabama Baptist State Conv.	AL	4
Amer. Baptist Churches. Immigration & Refug	PA	788
Baptist Assoc. of New Orleans	LA	430
Baptist Conv. of Maryland	MD	447
Baptist Conv. of New Mexico	NM	597
Baptist General Conv. of Oklahoma	OK	738
Baptist State Conv.	MI	513
California Southern Baptist Conv. Refugee Res	CA	43
Central Baptist Church. Sanctuary Group	PA	789
Florida Baptist Conv.	FL	290
Georgia Baptist Conv. Language Missions Dep	GA	325
Hmong Natural Assoc. of North Carolina	NC	703
Minnesota - Wisconsin Southern Baptist Conv	MN	526
Mississippi Baptist Conv. Language Missions	MS	542
North Carolina Baptist State Conv.	NC	695
Ohio State Conv. of Baptists	OH	726
Refugee Resettlement Program	AR	26
Southern Baptist Immigration and Refugee Res	GA	331
Virginia Baptist General Board. Div. of Missio	VA	906

Brethren

Christ Church of the Brethren. Sanctuary Com	OH	734
Church of the Brethren. Refugee Resettlement	MD	450
Manchester Church of the Brethren. Sanctuary	IN	404

Buddhist

Buddhist Council for Refugee Rescue and Reset	CA	133
Intl. Buddhist Meditation Assoc.	HI	343
Khmer Buddhist Society of New England	RI	798
Minnesota Cambodian Buddhist Society	MN	536
New Lao Friendship Club of Oklahoma	OK	741
Oshkosh Lao Hmong Assoc.	WI	954

Catholic

Amer. Comm. on Italian Migration	NY	632
Archdiocese of Chicago. Immigration Services	IL	351
Archdiocese of Detroit. Office of Refugee Rese	MI	490
Archdiocese of New York. Office for Immigran	NY	638
Archdiocese of New York. Refugee Resettlemen	NY	639
Archdiocese of Portland. Immigration Counseli	OR	752
Associated Catholic Charities	LA	429
Associated Catholic Charities. Refugee Employ	MD	441
Capuchin Mission Secretariat	MI	491
Caritas of Austin	TX	819
Catholic Agency for Migration & Refugee Serv	KS	412
Catholic Agency for Migration and Refugee Se	KS	411
Catholic Charities	FL	313
Catholic Charities	IA	410
Catholic Charities	KS	414
Catholic Charities	MA	486
Catholic Charities	NE	558
Catholic Charities	NY	684
Catholic Charities Bureau	IN	393
Catholic Charities Bureau. Resettlement Progra	WI	956
Catholic Charities Migration Office	NY	604
Catholic Charities Refugee & Immigration Ser	MA	458
Catholic Charities. Immigration & Refugee Di	CA	68
Catholic Charities. Immigration & Refugee Pro	CA	174
Catholic Charities. Immigration & Refugee Ser	PA	765
Catholic Charities. Immigration Counseling C	CA	161
Catholic Charities. Immigration Counseling Se	TX	831
Catholic Charities. Immigration Program	CA	134
Catholic Charities. Immigration Project	CA	94
Catholic Charities. Immigration Project of Im	FL	286
Catholic Charities. Immigration Services	CA	106
Catholic Charities. Migration & Refugee Servi	MN	528
Catholic Charities. Migration and Refugee Ser	CT	211
Catholic Charities. Migration and Refugee Ser	TX	849
Catholic Charities. Refugee Assistance	IN	396
Catholic Charities. Refugee Assistance Progra	NY	622
Catholic Charities. Refugee Office	IN	394
Catholic Charities. Refugee Program	KS	416
Catholic Charities. Refugee Resettlement Offic	CA	182
Catholic Charities. Refugee Resettlement Offic	FL	289
Catholic Charities. Refugee Resettlement Prog	CA	35
Catholic Charities. Refugee Resettlement Prog	DE	220
Catholic Charities. Refugee Resettlement Prog	TN	810
Catholic Charities. Refugee Service Center	DC	230
Catholic Charities. Refugee Service Program	PA	783
Catholic Charities. Refugee Services	KY	423
Catholic Charities. Refugee Social Service Cen	MS	541
Catholic Charities. Resettlement Program	CA	44
Catholic Charities. Resettlement Services	CA	166

Catholic Charities. Resettlement Services	TX	858
Catholic Charities. Unaccompanied Refugee M	MN	529
Catholic Community Services of Nevada. Immi	NV	564
Catholic Community Services of Utah. Refugee	UT	882
Catholic Community Services. Migration & Re	LA	424
Catholic Community Services. Office of Migra	NJ	586
Catholic Community Services. Office of Migra	WV	936
Catholic Community Services. Refugee Resettl	FL	295
Catholic Community Services. Resettlement &	CA	125
Catholic Council for Social Concern	IA	407
Catholic Family and Child Service	WA	935
Catholic Family and Child Services. Family Re	WA	910
Catholic Family Center. Refugee Dept.	NY	686
Catholic Family Service. Immigration Service	TX	872
Catholic Family Services. Refugee & Citizensh	TX	818
Catholic Human Development Office. Refugee	MI	502
Catholic Immigration & Resettlement Office	CA	177
Catholic Immigration and Refugee Services	CO	199
Catholic Immigration Center	HI	339
Catholic Immigration Services	FL	296
Catholic Migration & Refugee Services	OR	748
Catholic Migration & Refugee Services	VA	893
Catholic Migration and Refugee Office	NY	612
Catholic Migration and Refugee Resettlement	OH	721
Catholic Migration and Refugee Service	NV	566
Catholic Migration and Refugee Service	OK	746
Catholic Migration and Refugee Services	ID	349
Catholic Migration Office	NY	605
Catholic Refugee Services	WA	917
Catholic Refugee Services	WA	933
Catholic Resettlement and Immigration Office	IA	406
Catholic Resettlement Center	IL	353
Catholic Resettlement Services	OR	753
Catholic Services for Immigrants	TX	874
Catholic Social Agency. Migration Services	PA	761
Catholic Social Ministries. Migration & Reset	OK	739
Catholic Social Ministries. Refugee Resettleme	NC	699
Catholic Social Service	IL	350
Catholic Social Service	IL	385
Catholic Social Service Bureau. Refugee Resett	KY	420
Catholic Social Service of Phoenix	AZ	9
Catholic Social Service. Refugee Office	NC	696
Catholic Social Service. Refugee Resettlement	FL	309
Catholic Social Service. Refugee Resettlement	CA	115
Catholic Social Service. Resettlement Program	CO	207
Catholic Social Service. Resettlement Program	OH	714
Catholic Social Service. Tha Huong Program	IL	386
Catholic Social Services	AK	6
Catholic Social Services	FL	316
Catholic Social Services	IN	398
Catholic Social Services	KS	413
Catholic Social Services	LA	427
Catholic Social Services	MI	509
Catholic Social Services	MS	540
Catholic Social Services	OH	729
Catholic Social Services	OH	731
Catholic Social Services	PA	763
Catholic Social Services	PA	786
Catholic Social Services	RI	794
Catholic Social Services	TX	829
Catholic Social Services	WI	942
Catholic Social Services	WY	957
Catholic Social Services Bureau	KY	418
Catholic Social Services of Fall River	MA	476
Catholic Social Services. Immigration Services	CA	29
Catholic Social Services. Migration & Refugee	PA	773
Catholic Social Services. Migration & Refugee	AZ	16
Catholic Social Services. Migration & Refugee	OH	717
Catholic Social Services. Refugee and Immigra	FL	311
Catholic Social Services. Refugee Program	AL	3
Catholic Social Services. Refugee Resetlement	NE	559
Catholic Social Services. Refugee Resettlemen	CA	179
Catholic Social Services. Refugee Resettlemen	GA	323
Catholic Social Services. Refugee Resettlemen	NM	598
Catholic Social Services. Refugee Social Servi	FL	312
Catholic Social Services. Resettlement Progra	CA	87
Catholic Social Services. Resettlement Progra	MT	556
Catholic Social Services. Servicios Para Inmig	TX	871
Centro de Ayuda Para Immigrantes	TX	860
Corpus Christi Church. Sanctuary Comm.	NY	687
Diocesan Migrant & Refugee Services	TX	845
Diocesan Refugee Resettlement Program	ME	439
Diocese of Green Bay. Dept. of Refugee, Migra	WI	939
Diocese of Lafayette. Migration & Refugee Ser	LA	428
Diocese of Nashville. Refugee Resettlement Pr	TN	812
Diocese of Raleigh. Refugee Resettlement Offi	NC	704
Diocese of Richmond. Office of Refugee Resetl	VA	909
Diocese of Richmond. Office of Refugee Resett	VA	901
Diocese of Springfield - Cape Girardeau. Resett	MO	553
Diocese of Springfield. Refugee Resettlement	MA	482
Father Moriarty Asylum Program	CA	137
Hmong Catholic Center	MN	532
Holy Cross Service Center	FL	288
Immigration Advocacy Service	NE	561
Immigration and Legalization Service	TX	824
Immigration Assistance Service	NJ	583
Immigration Counseling Migration & Refugee	TX	851
Intl. Catholic Migration Commission	DC	242
Jesuit Refugee Service	DC	244
Migration & Refugee Services	SC	802
Migration and Refugee Services Office	NJ	593
Posada Sanctuary	IL	387
Refugee and Immigrant Multi-Service Center	WA	930
Refugee Resettlement Office	MO	545
Refugee Services	MI	508
Saint Vincents Services	NY	619
Salvadoran Refugee Comm. (Oscar A. Romero)	DC	253
Southside Community Mission	NY	620
St. John's Center. Office of Social Ministry	GA	338
St. Teresa's Church. Sanctuary Comm.	CA	153
U. S. Catholic Conference. Migration & Refug	NY	675
U.S. Catholic Conference. Migration & Refuge	DC	256
U.S. Catholic Conference. Migration & Refuge	CA	154
U.S. Catholic Conference. Migration & Refuge	DC	257
U.S. Catholic Conference. Migration & Refuge	NY	676
U.S. Catholic Conference. Migration & Refuge	TX	848

United Catholic Social Services. Refugee Reset   NE   562
U.S. Catholic Conference   IL   388
Vermont Catholic Charities. Refugee Resettlem   VT   890
Vietnamese Catholic Community   MI   489
Vietnamese Catholic Community in Connectic   CT   214
Washington Office on Haiti   DC   277

Church of Christ

Afghan Center   CA   190
Church World Service. Immigration & Refugee   NY   644
Church World Service. Refugee Program   FL   298
Refugee Assistance Program   CA   130
United Church Board for World Ministries. Ref   NY   678

Disciples of Christ

Disciples of Christ. Refugee & Immigration M   IN   399
Univ. Church. Sanctuary Project   IL   377

Episcopal

Church Refugee Center   NY   643
Diocesan Refugee Coordinator   MI   493
Diocese of Oregon   OR   751
Diocese of Rhode Island   RI   795
Ecumenical Refugee Resettlement Services   VA   903
Episcopal Diocese of Minnesota. Refugee Rese   MN   520
Episcopal Diocese of North Carolina. Refugee   NC   705
Episcopal Migration Ministries   NY   648
Episcopal Refugee and Migration Comm.   NH   570
Episcopal Refugee Resettlement Commission   IN   400
Episcopal Social Ministries   MD   442
Episcopal Social Service   CT   208
Good Samaritan Community Center   CA   138
Holy Cross Mission   CA   184

Jewish

Agudath Israel of Amer.   NY   631
Amer. Fed. of Jews from Central Europe   NY   635
Blue Card   NY   641
Catholic Migration and Refugee Services   NJ   573
Central Kentucky Jewish Assoc.   KY   421
Conference on Jewish Material Claims Against   NY   646
Congregation Hakafa. Sanctuary Comm.   IL   384
Fed. of Jewish Agencies of Greater Philadelphi   PA   775
Greater Hartford Jewish Fed.   CT   216
Hebrew Immigrant Aid Society   NY   651
Hebrew Immigrant Aid Society   PA   776

Hebrew Immigrant Aid Society of Baltimore   MD   443
Jewish Family & Children Services   CA   144
Jewish Family & Children's Service   AZ   12
Jewish Family and Child Service   OR   754
Jewish Family and Children's Agency   PA   777
Jewish Family and Children's Service   CO   203
Jewish Family and Children's Service   MA   466
Jewish Family and Children's Service   NJ   571
Jewish Family and Children's Service   OH   736
Jewish Family and Children's Service. Resettle   MN   521
Jewish Family and Children's Services   IN   403
Jewish Family and Children's Services   TX   847
Jewish Family and Community Services   FL   291
Jewish Family and Counseling Service   NJ   572
Jewish Family and Voc. Service   KY   422
Jewish Family Service   AZ   17
Jewish Family Service   CA   51
Jewish Family Service   CA   99
Jewish Family Service   CT   215
Jewish Family Service   FL   314
Jewish Family Service   LA   436
Jewish Family Service   MN   535
Jewish Family Service   NJ   574
Jewish Family Service   NJ   575
Jewish Family Service   NY   624
Jewish Family Service   NY   688
Jewish Family Service   OH   712
Jewish Family Service   PA   785
Jewish Family Service   PA   787
Jewish Family Service   RI   797
Jewish Family Service   TN   813
Jewish Family Service   TX   876
Jewish Family Service   VA   904
Jewish Family Service   WA   922
Jewish Family Service Agency   NV   565
Jewish Family Service Agency of Central New   NJ   580
Jewish Family Service Assoc.   OH   719
Jewish Family Service of Broward County   FL   285
Jewish Family Service of Delaware Valley   NJ   591
Jewish Family Service of Detroit   MI   514
Jewish Family Service of Greater Springfield   MA   483
Jewish Family Service of Metro West   NJ   589
Jewish Family Service of MetroWest   NJ   581
Jewish Family Service of North Middlesex Cou   NJ   578
Jewish Family Service of Raritan Valley   NJ   576
Jewish Family Service of Somerset County   NJ   588
Jewish Family Service. Immigration & Resettl   NM   599
Jewish Family Service. Refugee Resettlement P   TX   866
Jewish Family Service. Refugee Services   CA   79
Jewish Family Service. Resettlement Program   CA   128
Jewish Family Service. Resettlement Program   FL   306
Jewish Family Service. Resettlement Program   MD   444
Jewish Family Service. Resettlement Services   CT   210
Jewish Family Services   FL   318
Jewish Family Services   GA   328
Jewish Family Services   ME   440
Jewish Family Services   NC   697
Jewish Family Services   UT   884

Jewish Family Services   WI   951
Jewish Family Services of Greater Orlando   FL   322
Jewish Family Services. Refugee Services   IL   362
Jewish Fed. of Palm Beach County   FL   320
Jewish Philanthropic Fund of 1933   NY   658
Jewish Social Services   TX   852
Jewish Social Services   WI   943
Jewish Social Services Agency   MD   451
Jewish Voc. & Career Counseling Service   CA   145
Jewish Voc. Service   NJ   577
Jewish Voc. Service   OH   713
Jewish Voc. Service & Community Workshop   MI   515
Natl. Council of Jewish Women. Immigration   MA   487
Natl. Council of Jewish Women. Rescue & Mi   FL   305
New York Assoc. for New Amer.   NY   663
Peylim   NY   668
Rav Tov. Intl. Jewish Rescue Organization   NY   618
Research Foundation for Jewish Immigration   NY   671
Sinai Temple. Sanctuary Comm.   MA   484
Temple Beth El. Sanctuary Comm.   WI   944
Temple Emanu-El. Sanctuary Comm.   AZ   21
Temple Israel. Sanctuary Comm.   CA   60
Temple Sinai. Sanctuary Comm.   CA   102
Temple Sinai. Sanctuary Comm.   DC   254
United Refugee Council   NY   621

Lutheran

Cross Lutheran Church   WI   947
Emmanuel Lutheran Church. Sanctuary Comm.   MO   549
Faith Lutheran Church   FL   308
First Lutheran Church   FL   283
Hmong Community Service   MD   449
Lutheran Child & Family Services of Massachu   MA   485
Lutheran Child and Family Services   IL   365
Lutheran Children and Family Service   PA   778
Lutheran Church. Synod Board of Social Minis   MO   551
Lutheran Family Service. Refugee Services   OR   755
Lutheran Family Services. Refugee Resettlemen   NC   700
Lutheran Immigration & Refugee Services   DC   245
Lutheran Immigration and Refugee Service   NY   660
Lutheran Immigration and Refugee Service   TX   867
Lutheran Ministries of Florida   FL   307
Lutheran Ministries of Florida. Refugee Resett   FL   319
Lutheran Ministries of Georgia   GA   329
Lutheran Refugee and Immigration Services   NJ   592
Lutheran Refugee Resettlement   CO   204
Lutheran Social Ministry of the Southwest. Re   AZ   13
Lutheran Social Services   MN   516
Lutheran Social Services of Iowa   IA   409
Lutheran Social Services of Kansas and Oklaho   KS   417
Lutheran Social Services of Michigan. Dept. o   MI   510
Lutheran Social Services of Michigan. Refugee   MI   507
Lutheran Social Services of Minnesota. Refuge   MN   522
Lutheran Social Services of Montana   MT   555
Lutheran Social Services of North Dakota. Ref   ND   709

Lutheran Social Services of Northeast Florida.   FL   292
Lutheran Social Services of Northern Californi   CA   146
Lutheran Social Services of South Dakota. Ref   SD   805
Lutheran Social Services of Wisconsin & Uppe   WI   953
Lutheran Social Services. Immigration & Refug   CA   81
Lutheran Social Services. Unaccompanied Min   OH   722
Lutheran Welfare Service   PA   768
Mohawk Valley Resource Center for Refugees   NY   693
Redeemer Lutheran Church. Hmong Farm Proje   OH   727
San Juan Bautista Lutheran Church. Sanctuary   AZ   18
Tressler Lutheran Services. Refugee Services P   PA   770
Vietnamese Lutheran Ministry   WA   927

Mennonite

Interfaith Sanctuary Movement   PA   784
Mennonite Central Comm. Immigration & Ref   PA   760
Mennonite Immigration and Refugee Services   DC   246
Mennonite Intl. Refugee Assistance   TX   835
Neil Avenue Mennonite Church. Sanctuary Co   OH   723

Methodist

Downtown Legalization Project   CA   72
Faith United Methodist Church. Sanctuary Com   IA   405
Maine Annual Conference of the United Metho   ME   438
St. Paul's United Methodist Church. Refugee P   NV   567
Synapses. Asian Organizing Program   IL   374
Tacoma Community House   WA   934
United Methodist Church. Refugee Concerns C   CA   156
United Methodist Comm. on Relief. Refugee S   NY   679
Wheadon United Methodist Church. Sanctuary   IL   383

Presbyterian

College Hill Presbyterian Church. Sanctuary C   OK   747
Indochinese Assistance Center   CA   117
Korean Amer. Community Services   IL   363
Lao Khmu Assoc.   CA   186
Miami Presbytery   OH   730
Presbyterian Synod of Southern California and   CA   84
Presbytery of Long Island   NY   625
Presbytery of Southern Louisiana   LA   426

Quaker

Amer. Friends Service Comm. Florida Undocum   FL   293
Amer. Friends Service Comm. Haitian Women'   NY   636
Amer. Friends Service Comm. Immigration Pro   CA   108
Coastal Bend Friends Meeting   TX   830

Community Friends Meeting. Sanctuary Comm OH 715
Concord Friends Meeting Sanctuary   PA 790
Friends Meeting of Austin. Sanctuary Comm. TX 823
Immigration Law Enforcement Monitoring Pro TX 864
Palo Alto Friends Meeting   CA 107

Seventh Day Adventist

Adventist Community Services   DC 222
General Conference of Seventh-Day Adventists DC 238
Vietnamese Seventh-Day Adventist Church   OR 757

Unitarian

First Unitarian Church   CA 183
First Unitarian Church. Sanctuary Comm.   MI 488
Humboldt Unitarian-Universalist Fellowship   CA 30
Interfaith Refugee Assistance Project   OK 744
Riverside Church. Sanctuary Comm.   NY 672
Sepulveda Unitarian Universalist Society   CA 180
Tennessee Valley Unitarian Church. Sanctuary   TN 808
Unitarian Church of Arlington   VA 896
Unitarian Church. Sanctuary Comm.   CT 218
Unitarian Society of Sacramento. Sanctuary Co   CA 122
Unitarian Universalist Church   CA 61
Univ. Unitarian Church. Sanctuary Comm.   WA 926

Ecumenical

All Culture Friendship Center Refugee & Immi   CA 55
All Culture Friendship Center Refugee & Immi   CA 65
Amer. for Intl. Aid   GA 337
Asheville Presbytery. Refugee Resettlement Of   NC 702
Assoc. of Vietnamese in Nashville   TN 811
Bethany Christian Services. Refugee Foster Ca   MI 501
Border Assoc. for Refugees from Central Amer   TX 842
Bridge Refugee Services   TN 807
Cambodian Assoc. of Memphis   TN 809
Cambodian Assoc. of Mobile   AL 2
Cambodian Assoc. of Virginia   VA 902
Casa de la Esperanza   DC 229
Casa Juan Diego   TX 857
Casa Marianella   TX 820
Center for Central Amer. Refugees   NJ 587
Central Amer. Refugee Program   WA 918
Central Amer. Refugee Project   OK 740
Central Amer. Solidarity and Assistance   MD 455
Central Coast Sanctuary   CA 175
Chicago Religious Task Force on Central Ame   IL 356
Christian Community Service Agency   FL 297
Christian Community Services   CO 197
Christian Council of Metropolitan Atlanta. Re   GA 324
Christian Reformed World Relief Comm.   MI 503
Christian Refugee Outreach   VA 894
Clinica Msr. Oscar A. Romero   CA 71
Cornerstone Ministries   FL 317
Council of Churches. Refugee Resettlement Pro   MO 552
East Bay Sanctuary Covenant   CA 33
East Central Illinois Refugee Mutual Assistanc IL 391
Ecumenical Immigration Services   LA 431
Ecumenical Refugee Council   WI 948
Ecumenical Refugee Services   CO 202
Florida Council of Churches. Refugee Program   FL 310
Freedom Flight Refugee Center   MI 504
Fresno Ecumenical Resettlement Project   CA 46
Hmong Mutual Assistance Assoc.   WI 955
Hmong-Amer. Planning & Development Cente   TX 854
Houston Metropolitan Ministries   TX 861
Humboldt Congregations for Sanctuary   CA 28
Illinois Conference of Churches. Refugee Imm   IL 390
Illinois Conference of Churches. Refugee Rese   IL 358
Indiana Council of Churches   IN 401
Inmigracion Latina Foundation   FL 302
Jubilee Partners   GA 334
Kalamazoo Interfaith Sanctuary Project   MI 506
Khemara Buddhikarma - The Cambodian Buddhi   CA 59
Korean Amer. Community Services   MD 454
Lao Consultant Firm   VA 892
Lao Family Community   CA 119
Mecklenburg Presbytery Refugee Resettlement   NC 698
Mid-Cumberland Refugee Assistance Ministry   TN 815
Minnesota Council of Churches. Refugee Progr   MN 537
Monterey County Sanctuary   CA 103
Natl. Assoc. of Evangelicals. Immigration Pro   FL 304
New Hope Presbytery   NC 694
New York Circus   NY 664
Ohio Council of Churches. Refugee Services   OH 724
Orange County Community Consortium   CA 172
Overground Railroad   IL 382
Pioneer Valley Sanctuary Comm., Mt. Toby M   MA 457
Plattsburg Interfaith Council   NY 685
Plenty USA   CA 38
PRIME Ecumenical Commitment to Refugees   PA 762
Project Deliverance   OH 733
Rochester Refugee Services   MN 527
Sanctuary Covenant of San Francisco   CA 152
Southern California Interfaith Task Force on C   CA 86
Sponsors Organized to Assist Refugees   OR 756
St. Anselm's Immigrant & Refugee Community   CA 52
Syracuse Interreligious Council. Refugee Assis NY 692
Tucson Ecumenical Council. Central Amer. Tas   AZ 22
Tucson Ecumenical Council. Legal Assistance   AZ 23
Valley Religious Task Force on Central Amer.   AZ 15
Vietnamese Community in Virginia   VA 905
Vietnamese Evangelical Church   MN 525
Virginia Council of Churches. Refugee Progra   VA 907
Washington Assoc. of Churches. Immigration   WA 928
Washington Assoc. of Churches. Refugee Rese   WA 932
World Relief   CA 157
World Relief   DC 279

World Relief   FL   282
World Relief   GA   333
World Relief   NC   701
World Relief   TN   817
Youth With a Mission Relief Services   HI   346

Index VI

Board of Immigration Appeals

Access	CA	123
African Amer. Immigration Service	NY	609
Agudath Israel of Amer.	NY	631
Amer. Civic Assoc.	NY	608
Amer. Comm. on Italian Migration	NY	632
Amer. Friends Service Comm. Florida Undocu	FL	293
Amer. Fund for Czechoslovak Refugees	NY	637
Amer. Immigration Lawyers Assoc.	DC	224
Amer. Immigration Lawyers Assoc. Pro Bono	FL	294
Amer. Romanian Comm. for Assistance to Re	NY	630
Archdiocese of Chicago. Immigration Service	IL	351
Archdiocese of Detroit. Office of Refugee Res	MI	490
Archdiocese of New York. Office for Immigran	NY	638
Archdiocese of New York. Refugee Resettleme	NY	639
Archdiocese of Portland. Immigration Counse	OR	752
Asian Legal Services Outreach	CA	112
Asian Pacific Amer. Legal Center of Southern	CA	67
Associated Catholic Charities	LA	429
Assyrian Universal Alliance	MI	512
Baptist Assoc. of New Orleans	LA	430
Brooklyn Legal Services Corp.	NY	610
Cambodian Assoc. of Mobile	AL	2
Cambridge and Somerville Legal Services Imm	MA	467
Capuchin Mission Secretariat	MI	491
Catholic Agency for Migration and Refugee S	KS	411
Catholic Charities Migration Office	NY	604
Catholic Charities Refugee & Immigration Se	MA	458
Catholic Charities. Immigration & Refugee Pr	CA	174
Catholic Charities. Immigration & Refugee Se	PA	765
Catholic Charities. Immigration Counseling C	CA	161
Catholic Charities. Immigration Counseling S	TX	831
Catholic Charities. Immigration Program	CA	134
Catholic Charities. Migration and Refugee Se	CT	211
Catholic Charities. Migration and Refugee Se	TX	849
Catholic Charities. Refugee Assistance	IN	396
Catholic Charities. Refugee Assistance Progra	NY	622
Catholic Charities. Refugee Office	IN	394
Catholic Charities. Resettlement Program	CA	44
Catholic Charities. Resettlement Services	TX	858
Catholic Community Services of Nevada. Imm	NV	564
Catholic Community Services. Office of Migr	NJ	586
Catholic Community Services. Resettlement &	CA	125
Catholic Council for Social Concern	IA	407
Catholic Family and Child Services. Family R	WA	910
Catholic Family Service. Immigration Service	TX	872
Catholic Family Services. Refugee & Citizens	TX	818
Catholic Immigration & Resettlement Office	CA	177
Catholic Immigration and Refugee Services	CO	199
Catholic Immigration Center	HI	339
Catholic Immigration Services	FL	296
Catholic Migration & Refugee Services	OR	748
Catholic Migration and Refugee Office	NY	612
Catholic Migration and Refugee Service	OK	746
Catholic Migration and Refugee Services	NJ	573
Catholic Migration Office	NY	605
Catholic Services for Immigrants	TX	874
Catholic Social Agency. Migration Services	PA	761
Catholic Social Service	IL	350
Catholic Social Service	IL	385
Catholic Social Service of Phoenix	AZ	9
Catholic Social Service. Resettlement Program	OH	714
Catholic Social Services	OH	731
Catholic Social Services	PA	786
Catholic Social Services	RI	794
Catholic Social Services	WY	957
Catholic Social Services Bureau	KY	418
Catholic Social Services. Migration & Refuge	PA	773
Catholic Social Services. Migration & Refuge	OH	717
Catholic Social Services. Refugee and Immigr	FL	311
Catholic Social Services. Refugee Resettlemen	GA	323
Catholic Social Services. Refugee Resettlemen	NM	598
Catholic Social Services. Refugee Social Serv	FL	312
Catholic Social Services. Resettlement Progra	MT	556
Catholic Social Services. Servicios Para Inmi	TX	871
Center for Immigrants Rights	NY	642
Central Amer. Refugee Center	DC	233
Central Amer. Refugee Project	AZ	10
Centro Presente	MA	469
Chinese Amer. Civic Assoc.	MA	459
Christian Reformed World Relief Comm.	MI	503
Church World Service. Immigration & Refuge	NY	644
Church World Service. Refugee Program	FL	298
Community Legal Services	CA	36
Community Legal Services	CA	92
Community Legal Services	PA	774
Cornerstone Ministries	FL	317
Delaware Dept. of Justice. Service for Foreign	DE	221
Diocesan Refugee Coordinator	MI	493
Don Bosco Community Center	MO	546
Ecumenical Immigration Services	LA	431
Ecumenical Refugee Council	WI	948
El Centro Asylum Project	CA	42
El Paso Legal Assistance Society	TX	846
Episcopal Migration Ministries	NY	648

Florida Council of Churches. Refugee Program	FL	310
Friendly House	AZ	11
George Washington Univ. Natl. Law Center. I	DC	239
Georgia Dept. of Human Resources. Special Pr	GA	327
Haitian Refugee Center	FL	301
Hebrew Immigrant Aid Society	NY	651
Hebrew Immigrant Aid Society	PA	776
Hispanic Immigration Counseling Program	WA	920
Human Rights Advocates Intl.	NJ	579
Human Rights Advocates Intl.	NY	652
Illinois Conference of Churches. Refugee Imm	IL	390
Immigrant Legal Resource Center	CA	41
Immigrant Legal Resource Center	CA	140
Immigrants' Rights Office	CA	74
Immigration Assistance Service	NJ	583
Immigration Counseling Center	TX	862
Immigration Counseling Migration & Refugee	TX	851
Immigration Project	CA	75
Immigration Service of Santa Rosa	CA	189
Immigration Services of Santa Rosa	CA	131
Impact	CA	126
Inland Counties Legal Services	CA	111
Inmigracion Latina Foundation	FL	302
Intercultural Action Center	CA	178
Interfaith Refugee Assistance Project	OK	744
Intl. Buddhist Meditation Assoc.	HI	343
Intl. Center	NH	569
Intl. Center of the Capital Region. Refugee As	NY	602
Intl. Community Services	TX	865
Intl. Institute	OH	711
Intl. Institute of Buffalo	NY	623
Intl. Institute of Connecticut	CT	209
Intl. Institute of Connecticut	CT	213
Intl. Institute of Erie	PA	764
Intl. Institute of Flint	MI	499
Intl. Institute of Los Angeles	CA	191
Intl. Institute of Los Angeles. Immigrant & Re	CA	76
Intl. Institute of Los Angeles. Refugee Relocat	CA	158
Intl. Institute of Lowell	MA	479
Intl. Institute of Metro Detroit	MI	495
Intl. Institute of Metropolitan St. Louis	MO	550
Intl. Institute of Minnesota	MN	534
Intl. Institute of New Jersey	NJ	584
Intl. Institute of Northwest Indiana	IN	397
Intl. Institute of Rhose Island	RI	796
Intl. Institute of San Francisco	CA	141
Intl. Institute of the East Bay	CA	98
Intl. Institute of Toledo	OH	732
Intl. Institute of Wisconsin	WI	950
Intl. Ladies Garment Workers Union. Immigrat	NY	655
Intl. Refugee Center	IL	360
Intl. Rescue Comm.	CA	49
Intl. Rescue Comm.	CA	78
Intl. Rescue Comm.	CA	118
Intl. Rescue Comm.	CA	127
Intl. Rescue Comm.	CA	142
Intl. Rescue Comm.	CA	185
Intl. Rescue Comm.	NY	656
Japanese Newcomer Service	CA	143
Jewish Family and Children's Service	MA	466
Jewish Family Service	AZ	17
Jewish Family Service	LA	436
Jewish Family Service	RI	797
Jewish Family Service Agency	NV	565
Jewish Family Service of Metro West	NJ	589
Jewish Family Service of MetroWest	NJ	581
Jewish Family Service. Resettlement Program	FL	306
Jewish Family Services of Greater Orlando	FL	322
Jewish Family Services. Refugee Services	IL	362
Jewish Social Services Agency	MD	451
Jewish Voc. Service	NJ	577
Lao Family Community	CA	91
Lao Family Community	UT	887
Legal Aid Bureau	MD	453
Legal Aid of Western Missouri	MO	547
Legal Aid Society. Alien Rights Unit	CA	129
Legal Services Center	MA	477
Legal Services Center for Immigrants	IL	364
Loyola Univ. School of Law Clinic	LA	433
Lutheran Family Services. Refugee Resettlemen	NC	700
Lutheran Immigration and Refugee Service	NY	660
Lutheran Ministries of Florida	FL	307
Lutheran Refugee and Immigration Services	NJ	592
Lutheran Social Services of Iowa	IA	409
Lutheran Social Services of Minnesota. Refuge	MN	522
Lutheran Social Services of Northeast Florida.	FL	292
Lutheran Social Services of Northern Californi	CA	146
Lutheran Social Services. Immigration & Refug	CA	81
Lutheran Social Services. Unaccompanied Min	OH	722
Mennonite Immigration and Refugee Services	DC	246
Mission Community Legal Defense	CA	147
Montana Assoc. for Refugee Services	MT	554
Multicultural Immigration Center	NY	661
Na Loio No Na Kanaka. Lawyers for the Peopl	HI	345
Natl. Assoc. of Evangelicals. Immigration Pro	FL	304
Natl. Center For Immigrants' Rights	CA	82
Natl. Coalition for Haitian Refugees	NY	662
Natl. Council of Jewish Women. Immigration	MA	487
Natl. Council of Jewish Women. Rescue & Mi	FL	305
Nationalities Service Center	PA	769
Nationalities Service Center	PA	780
Nationalities Service of Central California	CA	50
Nationalities Services Center	OH	718
Nevada Dept. of Human Resources. State Refug	NV	563
New Lao Friendship Club of Oklahoma	OK	741
New Orleans Legal Assistance Corp.	LA	435
New York State Assembly. Task Force on New	NY	666
North Carolina Baptist State Conv.	NC	695
North Carolina Refugee Health Program	NC	707
One Stop Immigration & Educational Center	CA	83
Philadelphia Refugee Service Center	PA	781
Philippine Center for Immigrant Rights	NY	669
Proyecto Resistencia	IL	371
Rav Tov. Intl. Jewish Rescue Organization	NY	618
Refugee and Immigrant Multi-Service Center	WA	930
Refugee Assistance Program	CA	130

San Antonio Literacy Council   TX   878
San Juan Macias Immigrant Center   CA   104
Saura Center   IL   372
South Texas Immigration Council   TX   828
South Texas Immigration Council   TX   873
Southside Community Mission   NY   620
Spokane Bar Assoc. Pro Bono Program   WA   931
St. Anselm's Immigrant & Refugee Communit   CA   52
Texas Rural Legal Aid   TX   843
Texas Rural Legal Aid. Clinica de Inmigracion   TX   841
Tolstoy Foundation   AZ   14
Tolstoy Foundation   NY   673
Traveler and Immigrants Aid   IL   375
Travelers Aid Intl. Institute. Refugee Resource   OH   716
Tucson Ecumenical Council. Legal Assistance   AZ   23
U. S. Catholic Conference. Migration & Refug   NY   675
U.S. Catholic Conference. Migration & Refug   DC   256
U.S. Catholic Conference. Migration & Refug   CA   154
U.S. Catholic Conference. Migration & Refug   DC   257
U.S. Catholic Conference. Migration & Refug   NY   676
U.S. Catholic Conference. Migration & Refug   TX   848
U.S. Dept. of State. Bureau of Human Rights a   DC   271
United Catholic Social Services. Refugee Rese   NE   562
United Refugee Council   NY   621
Univ. of California. School of Law. Immigrat   CA   39
Utah Immigration Project   UT   886
Valley Immigrants Rights Center   CA   105
Vietnamese Amer. Civic Assoc.   MA   475
Washington Assoc. of Churches. Refugee Res   WA   932
World Relief   CA   54
World Relief   CA   157
World Relief   CA   187
World Relief   NY   683
World Relief   WA   929
YMCA Intl. Services   TX   870

Refugee and Immigrant Resource Directory
Suggestions, Corrections and Additions

We welcome suggestions, corrections and information on new groups which should be included in the next edition of *RIRD*. Please type if possible, or print clearly.

Is the following information a new entry? _____   Or a correction? _____

Name of Organization:

_____

Complete Mailing Address:

_____

_____   zip _____

Contact Person: _____   Title: _____

Recognition by the Board of Immigration Appeals?   Yes _____   No _____

Services/Activities Offered:

____ Advocacy   ____ Religion
____ Comm. Educ./Pol. Org.   ____ Research
____ Cultural   ____ Sanctuary
____ Education   ____ Scholarships
____ Health   ____ Social Services
____ Legal   ____ Other _____
____ Library/Info

Number of staff _____   Annual Budget $_____   Year Est.: _____

Description of Program and Services:

_____
_____
_____
_____
_____
_____
_____

Please list your newsletters, journals and other publications:

_____
_____
_____

Suggestions for general improvements in *RIRD*:

_____
_____
_____

Please return this form to: **RIRD**
The Denali Press
Box 021535
Juneau, Alaska USA 99802-1535

We would appreciate publications and literature about your organization.